THE HOLLYWOOD RELIABLES

OTHER TITLES BY JAMES ROBERT PARISH

AS AUTHOR:

*The Fox Girls**
*The Paramount Pretties**
*The RKO Gals**
The Slapstick Queens
Good Dames
*Hollywood's Great Love Teams**
Elvis!
Great Movie Heroes
Great Child Stars
Great Western Stars
Film Directors Guide: Western Europe
Film Actors Guide: Western Europe
The Jeanette MacDonald Story
*The Tough Guys**
*Hollywood Character Actors**

AS CO-AUTHOR:

The Emmy Awards: A Pictorial History
The Cinema of Edward G. Robinson
*The MGM Stock Company: The Golden Era**
The Great Spy Pictures
The George Raft File
*The Glamour Girls**
Liza!
*The Debonairs**
*Hollywood Players: The Forties**
*The Swashbucklers**
*The All-Americans**
Vincent Price Unmasked
The Great Gangster Pictures
The Great Western Pictures
*Hollywood Players: The Thirties**
Film Directors Guide: The U.S.
The Great Science Fiction Pictures
Hollywood on Hollywood
*The Leading Ladies**
*The Hollywood Beauties**
*The Funsters**
*The Forties Gals**

AS EDITOR:

The Great Movie Series
Actors Television Credits: 1950–72
(and Supplement)

AS ASSOCIATE EDITOR:

The American Movies Reference Book
(and Supplement)
TV Movies

*Published by Arlington House

THE HOLLYWOOD RELIABLES

JAMES ROBERT PARISH
WITH GREGORY W. MANK

Research Associates:

John Robert Cocchi
Charles Hoyt
William R. Meyer
Paul R. Palmer
Linda J. Sandahl
Florence Solomon

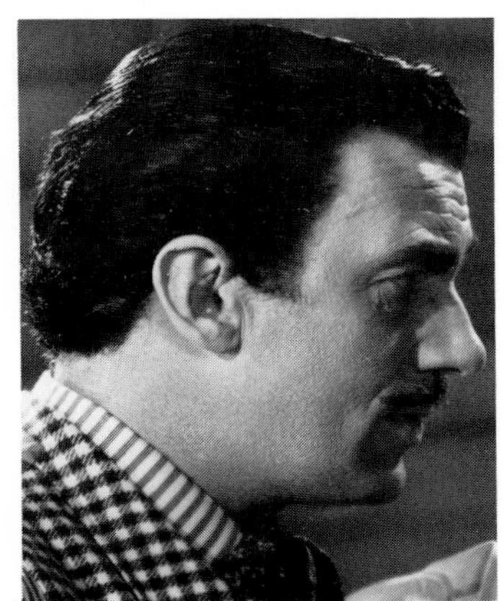

ARLINGTON HOUSE PUBLISHERS
WESTPORT, CONNECTICUT

ACKNOWLEDGMENTS

RESEARCH MATERIAL CONSULTANTS:

Doug McClelland
Jim Meyer

RESEARCH VERIFIER:

Earl Anderson

Bob Board
DeWitt Bodeen
Richard Braff
Kingsley Canham
Robert A. Evans
Morris Everett, Jr.
Film Favorites (Bob Smith, Charles Smith)
Films in Review
Focus on Film
Charles Forsythe
Pierre Guinle
Ken D. Jones
William T. Leonard
David McGillivray
Albert B. Manski
Alvin H. Marill
Mrs. Earl Meisinger
Peter Miglierini
Jeb Perry
Richard Picchiarini
Michael R. Pitts
Screen Facts (Alan G. Barbour)
Tony Slide
Mrs. Peter Smith
Carl Stohn, Jr.
Charles K. Stumpf
T. Allan Taylor
Lou Valentino
Richard Wentzler

And special thanks to Paul Myers, curator of the Theatre Collection at the Lincoln Center Library for the Performing Arts (New York City), and his staff: Monty Arnold, David Bartholomew, Rod Bladel, Donald Fowle, Maxwell Silverman, Dorothy Swerdlove, and Betty Wharton, and Don Madison of Photo Services.

Library of Congress Cataloging in Publication Data

Parish, James Robert.
The Hollywood reliables.

Includes index.
1. Moving picture actors and actresses—United States—Biography. I. Mank, Gregory W., joint author. II. Title.
PN2285.P34 791.43'028'0922 [B] 80-22930
ISBN 0-87000-455-X

Manufactured in the United States of America

CONTENTS

With Love To:

HILTON AND BETTY LEVY

ONE

DANA ANDREWS

6′
168 lbs.
Brown hair
Brown eyes
Capricorn

Not long ago, Dana Andrews told celebrity observer Cleveland Amory:

> The funny thing was that I never wanted to be a star. I wanted to be a good actor. Now I look back at my pictures of the 40s and 50s, and I think I really was pretty good. But I never thought of myself as good-looking or bad-looking, or really any kind of looking. I just thought of myself as an actor.

Some fifteen years earlier, the star had informed movie industry chronicler Lillian Ross:

> In movies, I had been a leading man, and in movies a leading man is usually a man who can do no wrong. I was expected to play pleasantly, to play pleasingly, to play a good man who is always victorious over evil. I've always thought of it as being a boom-boom-boom actor. I'd outshout, outfight, outcharm, out-everything everybody while acting. Meanwhile, the real acting parts were going to the character actors. After all those years in movies, my senses as an actor were dulled.

Dana Andrews is one of those performers who gained a foothold in motion pictures because he was in the right place at the right time. In the early 1940s, however, it did not seem that he would amount to more than a passing fancy. Although his contract was shared by Samuel Goldwyn and 20th Century-Fox, he didn't get the top roles. It was Danny Kaye at the former and Tyrone Power at the latter who received the star assignments. As film magazine editor Allen Eyles would observe in a 1970s interview with Dana, "Despite his acting abilities, Andrews lacked the charisma for front-rank stardom. In many of his films he was secondary to star actresses and—like Joseph Cotten—would not upset their hold on a film's limelight. Indeed, there was about Andrews onscreen a certain hint of weakness allied to stubbornness and, unless this was utilised in a part, he could become a stolid leading man."

But in such films as *The Purple Heart* (1944), *Laura* (1944), and *The Best Years of Our Lives* (1946), Andrews displayed a finely attuned acting sense that catapulted him into the top ranks of leading men. It was a position he was to hold for a decade, until the decline of the studio system and his growing problems with alcoholism caused him to reassess the direction of his career. He turned to television work for media exposure and to real estate for financial security, but it was theatrical assignments that renewed his confidence in his abilities and sustained him over the following decades. Above all, he has displayed over the years that if given an acting part he can be relied upon to turn in a first-rate performance.

Carver Dana Andrews was born on Friday, New Year's Day, 1909 in Collins, Mississippi, the third of thirteen[1] children of the Reverend Charles Forrest and Annis (Speed) Andrews. Dana was named after three clergymen: a Doctor Carver, a Doctor Dana, and, of course, his father. He was born on his grandfather's plantation, but did not remain there long. By the time he graduated from Huntsville High School

[1]Five of the Andrews children were dead by the early 1960s.

in 1926, the Andrews family had moved from Collins to Waelder, to San Antonio, to Rockdale, to Uvalde, and finally, to Huntsville, Texas. Dana's father was a rigid disciplinarian of the old school, a Baptist minister who did not believe children should engage in frivolous pastimes such as dancing.

All of the Andrews children (including Dana's younger brother William, later to gain acting fame as Steve Forrest and not long ago starring in the "S.W.A.T." teleseries) graduated from high school with honors. It was natural that Dana should attend college. He entered Sam Houston State Teachers College in Huntsville in 1926. Although his father still held a tight rein on him, Dana managed to develop non-academic interests in dramatics, debating, and football. Sam Houston State may have been the birthplace of Dana's serious interest in acting. He made his debut in *Lady Windemere's Fan* in 1927 at the Sam Houston Theatre.[2]

While working in a movie theatre after class, Dana had ample opportunity to study the technique of the great silent film stars.[3] He came to a conclusion which has assuredly been the foundation of many a star's career. As far as he was concerned, there was very little those highly paid and praised actors did onscreen that he could not do. Meanwhile more practical problems were at hand. The owner of the theatre could not afford the new equipment required to project the sight and sound of the new talking films like *The Jazz Singer* (1927) and *Lights of New York* (1928). The young Hollywood hopeful persuaded the boss to invest in several huge speakers, a turntable and some records. When hooked up, the overall effect was enough to temporarily satisfy audiences dazzled by any kind of noise in a cinema besides the crunch of popcorn.

There is some debate as to whether Dana graduated from or dropped out of college. Some sources say he majored in business administration, but left in 1929. Others assert that he graduated with a degree in psychology and English. Andrews himself never has been a very public person and is reluctant to discuss his personal life in interviews. But, from the close-knit nature of the Andrews family and the stubbornness of Charles Forrest Andrews, it might be guessed that Dana would have been pressured to complete his higher education. Also, in later years, Dana would speakly highly of the power of education.

In any event, after college, Dana contemplated making the most of his rich baritone voice by becoming a lawyer or a singer. Press releases insist that he had something of a following in Texas nightclubs, but he *did* go to work as an accountant in Houston and then later worked in a similar capacity for a large stationery firm in Austin. As Andrews would recollect, "At that point, I decided definitely to try to be an actor. I threw a large party for my friends in Austin, which left me penniless, and then I packed my bags and hitchhiked west to Van Nuys, a suburb of Los Angeles, where my father was pastor of the Baptist Church."[4] To support himself, while living with his family, Andrews at first was a bus driver for the Van Nuys High School, later becoming a gas station attendant.

When not working at the gas station, Dana made the rounds of the studios, only to meet with rejection.[5] To gain more acting experience, he enrolled in the Van Nuys Night School drama class, where he played a sixty-year-old man in a production of Bayard Veiller's *The Thirteenth Chair.* One of the more productive results of this engagement was meeting fellow performer Janet Murray, who had the year before received her degree in journalism at Northwestern University. On Saturday, December 31, 1932 they would wed. Says Andrews, "She was an inspiration to me in the days that followed; unlike everybody in my family, who refused to recognize acting as a legitimate occupation, she consistently encouraged me. She liked my baritone voice and urged me to become a singing actor, like Lawrence Tibbett. I began to study singing seriously, taking lessons with a local teacher who had sung in the

[2]In high school he had appeared in *The Microbe of Love, Nothing But the Truth,* and a Shakespearean drama; other college productions included *The Rivals, Honor Bright,* and *The Sam Houston Drama.*

[3]Andrews was first an usher, then later graduated to managing two neighboring cinemas owned by the same businessman.

[4]In the course of his trek to California, Dana learned a lesson that he would recount often over the years. On the outskirts of El Paso he was picked up by a man who claimed to be a Hollywood writer. Dana thought that by hitchhiking he would save himself hundreds of miles of wear and tear on his feet. The driver gave Dana ten dollars for a ring and lent a sympathetic ear to the young man's grand talk of stardom. Each time they stopped to gas up the car or to have a meal, the writer paid the check. But just as abruptly as Dana was given hospitality by the man, he was ejected from the car. His "chauffeur" explained, in professorial tones, "This will be a lesson to you. You've let me pay all the checks all the way here and that's sponging. In this world you have to stand on your own two legs."

Dana found himself on his feet, on the side of the road in Deming, New Mexico, three hundred miles from Hollywood. When he eventually reached the cinema capital of the world he looked for the man who taught him the lesson, but they never met again.

[5]His gas station employers were Stanley Twomey and John Wardlaw. They were impressed with their worker's determination and offered Dana a business deal. Twomey and Wardlaw agreed to advance Dana fifty dollars weekly for singing lessons and living expenses until he obtained a film studio contract. After Dana signed his movie contract with a film studio, he would pay the duo twenty-five percent of his salary for the following five years. As it turned out, Dana paid Twomey and Wardlaw anywhere (depending on which report one believes) from $7,000 to $20,000 on their original outlay once he became a contractee of Sam Goldwyn.

original company of *The Desert Song*. Janet and I were very happy."

In 1933 the Andrews' son, David, was born (he would die of a brain tumor three decades later). Then in 1935 Janet contracted pneumonia and died. While still working at the gas station, Andrews recalls, "I worked on my music like a maniac, ran two miles every day to build up my diaphragm, and learned operatic roles in French, German, and Italian."

It was at this point that a professional turning point occurred. Dana auditioned for agent John Columbo, the brother of singer Russ Columbo. Dana would remember, "He told me I had a fair voice but couldn't make any money as a singer. Second-rate actors, he said, could earn more than first-rate singers. He suggested that I get some acting training, and I went to the Pasadena Playhouse and, there, after years of blundering around, I began to learn to be an actor."

The first professional playbill to carry the name Dana Andrews was printed in July 1936. Dana played Menelaus in the Pasadena Playhouse staging of *Antony and Cleopatra.*[6] He was one of the soldiers doomed to die in Sidney Howard's *Paths of Glory* and then played a juvenile in Aurania Rouverol's *Money.* "The part wasn't good, but I was much worse than the part. I didn't have the remotest idea how to play a straight part—one that wasn't full of emotional crises."

It was in 1938, while appearing in a small role in Zöe Akins' play *O Evening Star,* that he won a screen test at Samuel Goldwyn's studio. In December of that year, he signed a $150-a-week contract with the Goldwyn lot.[7] Deciding that Andrews required more seasoning, and ordering him to wear a dental brace to correct his teeth, Goldwyn had his new contractee remain with the Playhouse group. During the next year there, Dana played twenty-four roles at the Pasadena theatre, including that of George Washington in Maxwell Anderson's *Valley Forge.*

In 1939, Dana Andrews, widower and father of David, was amassing a series of fine stage acting credits and becoming comfortably well known along the way. He had been romancing fellow actress Mary Todd at the Pasadena Playhouse. She was a promising performer whom cinema historian and novelist DeWitt Bodeen recently compared to Marion Davies. Deciding the time was ripe to wed again, Dana requested a meeting with Samuel Goldwyn for the mogul's approval. Much to his surprise, Goldwyn answered, "I'll have to think about it." Soon thereafter the studio was thrown into chaos by a blazing fire. In the melee of smoke, flames, waving arms, and screaming, Goldwyn spotted Dana. In his accented voice he shouted across the confusion, "It's all right, my boy. You get married any time you want to." Dana and Mary were married on Friday, November 17, 1939.

After the smoke cleared, Dana appeared briefly in his first film for Goldwyn—William Wyler's rather stylized tale of land disputes, *The Westerner,* released by RKO in 1940. Gary Cooper and Walter Brennan (as Judge Roy Bean) were the stars of this expansive sagebrush outing. Dana spoke his first twelve words into a movie microphone for RKO, playing the role of Bart Cobble. But this was not to be the public's first celluloid glimpse of the future star. While the studio was slowly assembling *The Westerner,* Goldwyn embarked on an economy wave and sold half of Dana's contract to 20th Century-Fox who put him to better use.[8] Andrews was to be paid by whichever studio was using his services. During inactive periods, both companies were to each pay half of his salary.

Fox immediately cast him for the small part of Sergeant Dunn in *Lucky Cisco Kid* (1940), one of its series films starring Cesar Romero. Then he was given co-starring billing in Fox's *Sailor's Lady* (1940) and United Artists' *Kit Carson* (1940), both of which starred Jon Hall and were released before the high-class *The Westerner. Sailor's Lady,* despite the comedy relief of Joan Davis, was only a "mildly farcical escapade" *(New York Times).* It starred Nancy Kelly as a young woman who pretends to have a baby to see if sailor Jon Hall will wed her. As Scrappy Wilson, Dana performed a function he was to learn all too well in the following years—that of playing second-

[6]Some sources list Dana's debut at the Playhouse as being made in *Cymbeline* in 1935.

[7]Dana recalls being taken into see the head casting director of MGM. The agent who took Andrews in said, "I've got another Clark Gable for you." The casting man said, "Why don't you go back to the bicycle shop" (an expression meaning to go back from whence one had come). After examining Dana for forty-five minutes, the casting director waved his hand and exclaimed, "Oh, I could get you work, but it wouldn't mean anything."

Some time later Dana received a note from an agent who had come to Los Angeles from New York. Although he had no California-based clients, Andrews signed with him thinking it might just work to his benefit. A very short time later he was taken in to see Samuel Goldwyn. It developed that Dana's agent was an old pal of the mogul's chief helper. A screen test was arranged and Goldwyn signed the "newcomer."

[8]Years later, while being interviewed in New York City by Cleveland Amory, Dana would recall the following about the release of *The Westerner:* "Probably my biggest 'sheer chance' thing happened right down there on 44th Street. I had just made my first movie, *The Westerner,* starring Gary Cooper. Down there, they put up a huge sign. . . . *The Westerner,* it said, starring Gary Cooper and *Dana Andrews.* I had exactly four lines (left) in the picture. Nobody had ever heard of me. But the publicity department had done that for all the billboards. They thought Dana was a girl's name, and was the girl in the picture, and that it looked more exciting to have Cooper and a girl. . . . If I'd used my first name, Carver, maybe I'd never have made it."

fiddle to a mediocre leading man. He and Hall followed suit in producer Edward Small's *Kit Carson.*

John Ford's adaptation of Erskine Caldwell's *Tobacco Road* (1941), which had been turned into a successful play by Jack Kirkland, did not do much for the career of Ford or, at first, Dana, who played the sympathetic role of Dr. Tim. (Hollywood insisted upon glamorizing *Tobacco Road* nearly out of recognition—for example, casting beautiful Gene Tierney as the hair-lipped Ellie May Lester.) Although the screen *Tobacco Road* may have been "an amusing but pointless film" *(New York Times),* for the first time oncamera Dana's acting warmth showed through, pointing up his potential.

With Cesar Romero and Johnny Sheffield in *Lucky Cisco Kid* (1940).

With Renie Riano, Ward Bond, Lynn Bari, (rear) Jon Hall and William Farnum in *Kit Carson* (1940).

With Eugene Pallette, Paul E. Burns, John Carradine, and Joe Sawyer in *Swamp Water* (1941).

Twentieth Century-Fox had contracted with French refugee director Jean Renoir for several films. As his first project Renoir selected a Dudley Nichols script called *The Man Who Came Back* (changed to *Swamp Water,* 1941) to make into his first American film. Initially producer Irving Pichel cast Linda Darnell in the role of Julie, the daughter of an innocent man (Walter Brennan) hiding from the law in the mire of Georgia's Okefenokee swamp.. Renoir vetoed the use of contractee Darnell and cast another stable player, Anne Baxter, in the demanding part. Perhaps Renoir had seen Dana in *Tobacco Road* or just recognized the actor's aptitude for the part of the boy who clears Julie's dad of murder charges. One thing was sure: Dana's naturally Southern voice and quiet movements were just the right ingredients to bring real dimension to the role of Ben Regan. As a press release stated, "He was fortunate in having a part that showed his versatility. He was gentle and kind and courted the girl he loved with a want of confidence that was sober reality. His face was animated as he accused John Carradine [as Jesse Wick] of murder. His fine voice and delivery helped bring this scene into prominence." The studio release concluded: "Dana Andrews will be a star one of these fine days."

Later Dana would say, "I'm sentimental about my first good part as the Georgia farm boy in *Swamp Water.*" Despite the fine cast and top-notch director, *Swamp Water* opened in September 1941 to unanimously bad reviews. The *New York Times* described the performances as "dangerously close to silly." Noted critic Otis Ferguson said that the film was "so bad it's terrific." The majority concluded that Jean Renoir, a master craftsman on his own home ground, had a good deal to learn about making films in America. Despite the nabobs of negativism, *Swamp Water* was pushed out into distribution along with Fox's Alice Faye/Betty Grable/Carmen Miranda musicals and other entertainments and was thus mildly successful in this country.[9]

Before America became engulfed in World War II, 20th Century-Fox had a full complement of male performers,[10] sufficient to make the going rough for Dana whose quiet resiliency had been not yet fully tapped onscreen. The fact, however, that two stu-

[9]In 1952, one of Renoir's countrymen, Jean Negulesco, remade the film for 20th Century-Fox with Jeffrey Hunter and Jean Peters in the Andrews-Baxter roles, and with Walter Brennan repeating his part. Despite the addition of Technicolor, Negulesco with *Lure of the Wilderness* only created a workmanlike copy of the original atmospheric film.

[10]Among the Fox males were Don Ameche, Jack Benny, Milton Berle, John Carradine, Laird Cregar, Alan Curtis, Henry Fonda, Jean Gabin, Richard Greene, Jack Haley, Dean Jagger, John Loder, Robert Lowery, George Montgomery, Lloyd Nolan, Michael Ted North, Jack Oakie, Pat O'Brien, John Payne, Tyrone Power, George Reeves, Cesar Romero, George Sanders, Randolph Scott, John Sutton, Shepperd Strudwick, and Sidney Toler.

dios owned his contract made him more desirable and when demanding Henry Fonda refused to play the lead in a Western about a notorious outlaw, *Belle Star* (1941) (he had made *The Return of Frank James* at Fox just the year before), Darryl Zanuck ordered a realignment of the cast. Zanuck's favorite, Gene Tierney, would continue in the title role, while Randolph Scott would be switched from the Army major who hunts the lawbreakers to Sam Starr, the man who courts and weds Belle. The film, in color and directed by Irving Cummings, was only a mediocre effort, but the scene in which Belle invites both Sam Starr and Major Thomas Crail (Dana) to dinner was considered notable. The casting change may have been lucky for the film and even more so for Andrews because in the spoiler's role he received another good notice. The *New York Herald-Tribune* reported, "Dana Andrews in the unpleasant role of the Yankee major is equally good."

It next was Goldwyn's turn to make use of Dana, one of his five male contractees (Dana, Walter Brennan, Gary Cooper, Jon Hall, and David Niven). Howard Hawks directed the rambunctious comedy *Ball of Fire* (1941) in which burlesque performer Sugarpuss O'Shea (Barbara Stanwyck) teaches a group of oddball professors, including Bertram Potts (Gary Cooper), something of contemporary American slang. Mixed up in the zany, Damon Runyonesque proceedings are several hoodlums, one of whom was small-time crook Joe Lilac (Dana). While the feature was in production, Goldwyn publicists noted for the press that Dana was not cut from the mean Cagney/Bogart/Robinson mold, but had a freshly evil look about him. At the film's premiere, Dana had an opportunity to socialize with a prominent California hood, Benjamin "Bugsy" Siegel, who probably offered the boy from Mississippi some practical tips on the art of gangsterism.

With Frederick Giermann and Virginia Gilmore in *Berlin Correspondent* (1942).

As Bill Shepperd, the reporter in Fox's programmer *Berlin Correspondent* (1942), Dana retained his moustache from *Ball of Fire.* This time he was the star, but the film was "too pretentious for its own good" *(New York Times)* and did little for the careers of either Dana or Virginia Gilmore (also under a split Goldwyn/Fox deal). *Crash Dive* (1943) was 20th Century-Fox's last opportunity to put Tyrone Power onscreen for the duration, for the studio's leading male star had enlisted in the Marines. Archie Mayo turned out a workmanlike Technicolor product, but it was yet another service story. As the second lead to Tyrone, Andrews lost the girl (Anne Baxter) but the picture won an Oscar for special effects—certainly not including the tired love triangle the script promulgated.

If any film marked the upswing of Dana's screen career it was *The Ox-Bow Incident* (1943). Aggressive director "Wild Bill" Wellman had to fight Darryl Zanuck heartily to produce this depressing story of a lynching based on the Walter Van Tilburg Clark novel. Wellman and Zanuck had battled for years, and once Wellman even threw a brick through the boss's window. They made up long enough to film this classic, sombre Western, but Wellman had to agree to direct several other less stellar projects in return for the "favor."

The story is set in Nevada of 1885, at a time when lynchings were a widespread offspring of law and order. By 1943, the time of production, there were only three recorded lynchings that year, as opposed to the peak season of 1892 when 231 were recorded. This was not the first major Hollywood feature to deal with lynching. MGM's *Fury* (1936) and Warner Bros.' *They Won't Forget* (1937) had treated the same subject.

In Lamar Trotti's scenario for *The Ox-Bow Incident,* three men journeying home are accused of murdering a rancher from whom in reality they have just purchased cattle. Donald Martin (Dana), a Mexican (Anthony Quinn), and a senile old man (Francis Ford —John's brother) become victims of an aggressive mob, led by a vengeful Major Tetley (Frank Con-

With Paul E. Burns and Henry Fonda in *The Ox-Bow Incident* (1943).

roy). Ultimately the men are hanged, and after their innocence is established, the major, having disgraced himself and having earned the further hatred of his son, commits suicide. Before the hangings, Martin is allowed to write a letter to his wife, which is read at the conclusion of the moving film by Gil Carter (Henry Fonda), a wanderer who tries to stop the lynchings. The film ends with Carter and his side-kick (Henry "Harry" Morgan) riding out of town, disgusted by the act of inhumanity they have witnessed.

Although Dana was not given star billing, there is no question but that his performance is a standout in this marvelous but very downbeat film. Bosley Crowther *(New York Times)* credits Dana with being an important party to the film's triumph: "A heart-rending performance by Dana Andrews as the stunned and helpless leader of the doomed trio does much to make the picture a profoundly distressing tragedy." Otis L. Guernsey, Jr. of the *New York Herald-Tribune* agreed that the film was distressing, as he reported: "It is a depressing arrival in days that are depressing enough already."

Years later Dana would say of his performance in this production, "My most satisfying [acting] experience was in the role of Martin in *The Ox Bow Incident.* . . . It gave me a chance to try to do something I'd always wondered whether I could manage—playing a character who was sensitive without making him seem weak."

On a happier note, Andrews' daughter Kathy was born during the shooting of *The Ox-Bow Incident* and when the actor came to work after being up all night waiting for reports on the delivery, Wellman rearranged the shooting schedule. He allowed Dana to perform a sleeping scene out of sequence. It was certainly one of the most realistic bits in the film, for when Wellman told him to go to sleep, he did so without hesitation.

While Hollywood was being depleted of its male players by the war Dana remained busy on the soundstages. Reportedly a back injury was the cause of his being designated 4-F. Samuel Goldwyn and director Lewis Milestone cast him as Kolya, a peace-loving but courageous villager, in the controversial *The North Star* (1943). With a script by Lillian Hellman, the feature was originally a paean to the battle-weary Russian people. (After World War II when the Cold War was in effect the picture would be re-edited into *Armored Attack,* with much of the pro-Soviet propaganda deleted.)

In its time, *Life* magazine called *The North Star* "the movie of the year" and *Time* referred to it as a "cinemaMilestone." The advertising for the picture was panoramic, worthy of the Goldwyn tradition. One ad stated, "See the world's greatest horsemen riding to avenge their women and children!" To a certain extent, that is what the movie was about.

Andrews was only one of the fine performers in the large cast that included Farley Granger, Anne Baxter, Walter Huston, Ann Harding, Walter Brennan, Jane Withers, and the German everyone loved to hate, Erich von Stroheim. The studio emphasized the romance between Granger and Baxter, but did not forget to allow Stroheim's Teutonic Dr. Otto von Harden to die at the finale, to the infinite pleasure of the audience.

Now that Samuel Goldwyn had young Farley Granger and Broadway importee Danny Kaye under contract, Dana Andrews was no longer a focal prop-

With Danny Kaye and Dinah Shore in *Up in Arms* (1944).

erty of the producer. However, he was serviceable and was employed in *Up in Arms* (1944), Kaye's first feature. Although it was a musical, Dana did not sing in this service comedy which co-starred Dinah Shore. One reason was that Dana had never told his studios of his singing ability. "I didn't tell Darryl Zanuck or Sam Goldwyn," he later explained, "because you're dead in Hollywood if you're a singer. Nobody will accept you as an actor. About the time I'd hit Hollywood, they'd stopped making musicals. I'm no fool. I just kept my mouth shut." (There was some chatter in fan magazines about Dana desiring to play a role in one of the smash hit musicals of the time, *Oklahoma!*) The only association Dana wanted with music was the relationship of a listener to a record player or radio. His main musical delights were listening to the Philadelphia Symphony Orchestra, preferably performing Rachmaninoff's second piano concerto, and admiring the tones of idolized pop singer Frank Sinatra.

As Captain Harvey Ross, Andrews led his men in facing the trumped-up trial of the American group accused of being war criminals in *The Purple Heart* (1944) at 20th Century-Fox.[11] Before a court of paid-off witnesses and Axis journalists, the airmen (including Richard Conte, Farley Granger, Sam Levene, and Donald Barry) fight to have their case heard justly. Their voices are strong but no one chooses to hear. One by one, the Japanese psychologically and physically torture the group, but confessions are not forthcoming. The men are doomed anyway, and as they walk down the prison hall to their death, patriotic music swells and the film ends in spiritual if not physical triumph. Although in this Lewis Milestone-directed feature Dana's name was still featured after the title, he turned in a resolute, star performance. Bosley Crowther lauded in the *New York Times,* "Dana Andrews is magnificently congruous as the leader of the bomber crew."

The year 1944 was proving to be the season of Dana's ascendancy to fame; it was also the year of the birth of his third child, Stephen. Fox continued to extract yeoman service from hard-working Dana. He was next presented in *Wing and a Prayer* (1944), directed by Henry Hathaway for 20th Century-Fox release. The film was distinguishable for two reasons. First, it was a production in which, as the *New York Times* noted, "personal heroics are practically non-existent." The James Cady scenario emphasized the collective positive nature of the Allied armed services and the need for a united front against the enemy. Everyone was seen as an integral, if small, part of a very important whole. The second distinction afforded *Wing and a Prayer* was that it marked the end of Dana's debt to his gas station owner benefactors, Stanley Twomey and John Wardlaw. From then on, Dana's salary belonged only to himself and to the government.

When Dana learned that Fox was planning to film *Laura,* based on Vera Caspary's sophisticated murder novel, he requested that he be considered for a key role. With so many of the studio's regular leading men away at war, Dana's bid was granted and he joined a cast consisting of Gene Tierney (in the title role), Vincent Price (as society sycophant Shelby Carpenter), Judith Anderson (as upper-crust, devious, craven Ann Treadwell), and a refugee from Broadway who had last made films in the 1920s, urbane Clifton Webb (as acidy art connoisseur Waldo Lydecker). Andrews was cast as Mark McPherson, the police officer who pieces together the scraps of Laura's life after her apparent murder. (At one stage in the pre-production planning, it was determined that Andrews would co-star with Jennifer Jones, in the title role, and heavy-set Laird Cregar, as Waldo Lydecker.)

[11]Andrews was in Philadelphia with a gaggle of stars and studio officials to promote *Woodrow Wilson* (1944), a major 20th Century-Fox production. At a big affair for the film, each actor was introduced by master of ceremonies Georgie Jessel. The applause for the performers was more than polite, but when Dana was introduced, the audience went wild. Darryl Zanuck and Spyros Skouras later confessed to Andrews that this public reception was what convinced them that he would be a big star. Unknown to the studio executives or Andrews was that many of the women in the audience were in Philadelphia for a meeting of wives of Air Force pilots and the previous week they had seen Dana's *The Purple Heart* and had identified with him and the film.

Rouben Mamoulian (replacing a too busy Lewis Milestone) was set to direct *Laura,* with Otto Preminger producing. Shooting began on April 26, 1944, but by mid-May Mamoulian had left the production. The cultivated director claimed that he resigned to avoid risking harm to new producer Preminger's budding career. Mamoulian was frank enough to admit that he was not particularly interested in the subject matter—particularly as it had been diluted for the screen.

Much confusion arose after Mamoulian's departure, since Preminger had not been allowed on the set during the initial shooting. There was talk of Darryl Zanuck replacing Dana with John Hodiak, who had been a hit in Fox's *Lifeboat* (1944). After the initial storm, *Laura* was continued on a sound basis. Preminger now likes to think his see-sawing career really began with this major picture.

The plotline[12] of the film is relatively simple, but it is detailed in such an adult fashion that it is not only satisfying but engrossing. (Preminger in the course of production had many arguments with studio boss Zanuck because while this was essentially a police story, there was no police station in the scenario). Preminger's theories on how the feature should be interpreted for viewers proved viable and received critical endorsement. Howard Barnes *(New York Herald-Tribune)* enthused, "Under Otto Preminger's acidly accurate direction the new film at the Roxy is as much a comedy of manners as it is a grim melodrama." Barnes also applauded our hero: "Dana Andrews is as good as Clifton Webb." (Also not to be overlooked is David Raksin's fine, haunting music score.)

Alton Cook of the *New York World-Telegram* provided Andrews with perhaps the best review the actor has garnered to date: "In a brief career, Dana Andrews has consistently outdone each of his successive performances. . . . The smoldering force with which he plays the detective leaves one pretty sure that the chain of topping himself will be broken with this picture—unless he turns out to be just about the finest actor of our time."

Autocratic Otto Preminger would later claim that Dana had been cast in *Laura* because "he was available." And available he was, due to his back injury, so Fox employed him in three of its 1945 releases, all of which convinced any doubters that he was a star leading man.

Fox had prospered in 1933 with *State Fair,* based on the Phil Strong novel and starring Will Rogers, Janet Gaynor, and Lew Ayres. Twelve years later the studio was inspired—thanks to the success of the Americana musical *Oklahoma!* on Broadway—to make *State Fair* into a musical. The *Oklahoma!* composing team of Richard Rodgers and Oscar Ham-

[12]In the story, a body, with the face mutilated by a shotgun blast, is discovered outside the apartment of Laura Hunt and the police assume that she was the victim. Detective Mark McPherson visits critic Waldo Lydecker who was a friend of Laura, but the art reviewer is unhelpful. Next McPherson talks with Anne Treadwell, Laura's rich aunt, who admits that she has been indulging in an affair with Shelby Carpenter, who was Laura's fiancé. Later Mark learns that Waldo and Laura were more than just close friends and that he had discouraged many other men from wedding her; in fact, when Laura decided to wed Shelby, Lydecker advised her that Shelby had been having an affair with model Diane Redfern. At this juncture Laura confronts Mark at her apartment, telling him that she had been at her country home and that the victim must be Diane Redfern. Later Mark arrests Laura but tells her that he believes her to be innocent. Further detection reveals that Waldo is the culprit, he having hid his shotgun in a grandfather's clock in Laura's apartment after shooting the girl he thought to be his idolized Laura. McPherson comes upon Waldo just as he is about to shoot the real Laura, but instead the lawman kills him with his police revolver.

With Kevin O'Shea and William Eythe in *Wing and a Prayer* (1944).

With Jeanne Crain in *State Fair* (1945).

merstein II was hired to bring its special magic to the screen, and that the two did with their score for this one-hundred-minute Technicolor songfest. With a scenario by Hammerstein II, the homey delights of an Iowa state fair came to life as Abel and Melissa Frake (Charles Winninger, Fay Bainter) contend, respectively, for top prize in the hog and preserves competitions. Interspered with the frivolity and wonder of the fair are the romances of the Frake children. Wayne (Dick Haymes) succumbs to the charms of band vocalist Emily (Vivian Blaine), only to be later disillusioned by the worldly gal, while lilting Margy (Jeanne Crain) comes under the spell of cynical yet thoughtful *Des Moines Register* reporter Pat Gilbert (Andrews) who is seeking a big-time job on a Chicago newspaper.[13]

The score for *State Fair* included "That's for Me," "It Might As Well Be Spring," "Our State Fair," "Isn't It Kinda Fun?" and the bouncy "It's a Grand Night for Singing." This production number called for Dana's character to join in a chorus or two of the song. Even though in the final release print it seemed as if Andrews were vocalizing, he was not. "I let them hire another singer to dub me," Dana later admitted. "They paid him $150 for it. I could have saved the studio some money and sung the tune a lot better. But I kept my mouth shut. I [still] don't like what happens to singers in Hollywood."

A much more meaningful role for Dana than that of the pensive newshawk in *State Fair* was his role in his third film for director Lewis Milestone, *A Walk in the Sun* (1945).[14] This was an independently produced feature but it so impressed Darryl Zanuck at Fox that he had 20th Century-Fox release it. The film was based on a story by Harry Joe Brown about a valiant battalion of G.I.s in the Italian theatre of war. Milestone and scenarist Robert Rossen had pondered how to adapt the original story into meaningful screenfare. "We racked our brains," said Milestone, "and then it occurred to me that in war you apprehend things more vividly through the ear than the eye."

Milestone recalled the military troubadors from his childhood in Russia and took appropriate bits from Brown's narrative and had Earl Robinson and Millard Lampell produce nine fine ballads, four of which were used. (It should be pointed out this is the origin of the special ballad being created for a film, as opposed to the widely accepted "first" being Tex Ritter's song for *High Noon* in 1952.)

A Walk in the Sun is about man's reaction to war. The emphasis is on bits and pieces of existence, much in the way of Milestone's *All Quiet on the Western Front* (1930). Rather than depict the horrors as they were portrayed in *The North Star* and *The Purple Heart*, *A Walk in the Sun* makes one feel the apathy and confusion of a diverse group of Americans[15] who do not belong in uniform. As one soldier says of their trek through battle-torn Italy, "We've got a grandstand seat, only we can't see nothing. That's the trouble with war, you can't see nothing! You have to find them by ear." Such a film was probably right for the time. World War II had just concluded and people wanted to return to normalcy, minus ration cards, scrap metal drives, and internment

[13] Louanne Hogan performed the vocals for Miss Crain; Vivian Blaine and Dick Haymes provided their own distinctive vocalizing.

[14]Besides Andrews, the cast included Richard Conte, John Ireland, Sterling Holloway, Lloyd Bridges, Steve Brodie, Huntz Hall, Richard Benedict, and Herbert Rudley.

[15]In Allen Eyles' 1976 *Focus on Film* interview with Andrews, the star assesses his relationship with director Lewis Milestone. "Mr. Milestone, early in my career, directed me in a picture called *The North Star*. We became very good friends. But I think it was more the fact that I was under contract to 20th Century-Fox that I got the second one, *The Purple Heart*, which was—according to Mr. [Spyros] Skouras, who was the head of distribution at the time—the picture which made me a star. . . . I do know that Mr. Milestone had something to do with casting me in *A Walk in the Sun* because it was an independent picture and he cast that himself. Twentieth Century-Fox financed the finishing of the picture and got the distribution. However, the choice had been made for the story and the casting, so they didn't really have any control over it other than to release it. . . . It was a very good part and certainly good for me, and I think *A Walk in the Sun* became one of the most often exhibited pictures on television."

camps for Japanese-Americans and conscientious objectors. It was time to lower fists and take off the gloves.

A Walk in the Sun was particularly important for Dana, for it was his official feature as "star." Some reviewers were ecstatic about Milestone's latest war declaration. Bosley Crowther *(New York Times)* must have concurred with a Fox ad which called *A Walk in the Sun:* "The picture that captures the heart of our time—for all time!" As with *The Ox-Bow Incident,* Dana's role as Sergeant Tyne encouraged Crowther to praise Andrews in the *Times* review. "Most impressive is Dana Andrews who makes of Tyne an intelligent, acute, and sensitive leader of the pathetically confused but stubborn group."

Apparently the movie-going public did not want any more of World War II in any form. At first the film flopped financially in domestic release, and then Fox sold it to a minor British distributor. It was retitled *Salerno Beachhead* and sent out on a double-bill in England in 1951 (with Fox's *The Sullivans,* retitled *The Fighting Sullivans*). *A Walk in the Sun* was then reviewed with enthusiasm by the British critics, with many film judges claiming it was the best war film since *All Quiet on the Western Front.* If only Zanuck had had more faith in *A Walk in the Sun* or Dana, the film might have become equally acclaimed in the United States.

Fallen Angel (1945), directed by Otto Preminger for 20th Century-Fox, was released about the same time as *A Walk in the Sun.*[16] Andrews again worked with a director who understood how to bring the actor's boyish sense to the screen and color it with a wry bitterness which was distinctly Andrews. In *Fallen Angel* Dana played Eric Stanton, a wanderer who arrives in Walton and comes into contact with June Mills (Alice Faye in a rare dramatic role), the shy daughter of the late mayor. Meanwhile he meets earthy waitress Stella (Linda Darnell) and falls under her erotic spell. He conspires to wed June for her money, divorce her, and then take off with Stella. But after the marriage to June, the floozie Stella is killed, and only after Eric becomes a fugitive does he discover that local police inspector Mark Judd (Charles Bickford) is the actual killer. Eventually Eric is instrumental in turning Judd over to the authorities and he returns to June whom he now loves sincerely.

While *Fallen Angel* is not a vividly memorable melodrama, it is a thoughtful low-keyed thriller which benefits from sturdy performances, especially from Andrews, Bickford, and Anne Revere (as Faye's solemn "I-told-you-so" sister). As *Time* magazine suggested, "If you go for whodunits, a hard-boiled one with fancy trimmings, you can go for this; you'll get your money's worth." As for Dana, once again his solemn, sober, quietly ambiguous screen persona served to enhance his performance, giving a sincerity and appropriately non-glamorous approach to the characterization.

In a loan-out to producer Walter Wanger at Universal, Dana co-starred with Susan Hayward in the

[16]Regarding *Fallen Angel,* Andrews would claim, "I didn't want to do [it]. I didn't like the character, a kind of a bum ambling around the country, and to me it was quite unbelievable that John Carradine would get up and have a seance in front of a village and tell what the secrets of the village were. . . . It was completely unbelievable because they wouldn't come to the meeting. Mr. Preminger more or less forced me into this picture which sort of put Alice Faye out of business."

With Olin Howland and John Carradine in *Fallen Angel* (1945).

color Western *Canyon Passage* (1946). It was not the type of film or role that would enhance his career, but by now most of the screen stalwarts of the pre-World War II days (Clark Gable, James Stewart, Henry Fonda, Tyrone Power, for example) were back from military duty and resuming their box-office positions. Films such as *Canyon Passage* began to type Dana as the hero of middle-budget action films. Below Gable in strength, but above, say, a Dennis O'Keefe or a James Craig, Andrews was always good, sometimes great, and had enough of a following to merit the roles and publicity he received. The most notable element of the Jacques Tourneur-directed Western was a bloody fistfight between Dana and the film's villain, Ward Bond.

After this spell of solid but decidely unclassic films, Dana received another professional break when he was cast as Fred Derry, one of three returning war veterans in Samuel Goldwyn's *The Best Years of Our Lives* (1946). Although two of the leads, Dana and Fredric March, had not fought in the recent war, Goldwyn felt that they could properly empathize with the characters. (The third returning G.I. was real-life amputee Harold Russell who did not have designs on an acting career and only accepted the role to demonstrate to others maimed in battle that they could lead full post-war lives in society.) It was the first time Dana had been reunited professionally with director William Wyler since *The Westerner.*[17]

With Gene Roth (left) and Susan Hayward in *Canyon Passage* (1946).

RKO's *The Best Years of Our Lives* won an Academy Award as Best Picture of 1946, and even the skeptical James Agee delineated in *The Nation,* "It shows what can be done in the [film] factory by people of adequate talent when they get, or manage to make for themselves, the chance." Almost everybody recognized the sincerity and truth inherent in *The Best Years of Our Lives.* Although the film has not worn well in some eyes, it reflects the American scene when the return to tranquillity after years of sacrifice was not as easy as it seemed.

Summing up Dana's contribution to this landmark drama, Archer Winsten wrote in the *New York Post,* "Caught in a role at once glamorous and trite, [he] does his actor's job, as always, with integrity and intelligence." As the film divides into the stories of the return of the three divergent soldiers, one can most easily emphathize with the plight of Dana's Fred Derry, who comes home to discover that his grasping, attractive wife (Virginia Mayo) has been two-timing him and is continuing to do so. In one of the picture's most memorable scenes, Dana has just received a post-war "Dear John" note from his wife. In something of a daze he treks out to a deserted airfield near the small, typically American town. Former bomber pilot Andrews surveys one junked plane, hanging encapsulized in the hollow silence of obsolete equipment. He climbs inside the plane to meditate. The war has once again come home to the former pilot, and psychological battles replace the simpler bombing raids.

Despite Fredric March and Myrna Loy being top-billed in *The Best Years of Our Lives,* it was Dana who offered the top performance.[18] As the hurt but ultimately stoic war veteran, he typified the returning warrior more than banker March or amputee Russell. But each of the trio picked up the pieces and went on living, and that was what the story was all about.

From there Dana went to another film with a fresh

[17]In the 1976 interview with Eyles, Andrews would recall, "Mr. Wyler didn't want me for *The Best Years of Our Lives.* Since I'd played in *The Westerner* Mr. Wyler hadn't seen me in anything, but in the meantime I'd done a lot of pictures. *The Best Years of Our Lives* was in 1946 and I had worked for him in 1939. When we worked the first day, we were in the scene where Fredric March, the boy with the paraplegic arms and I were coming into Boon City. It was up high and I climbed down a ladder and he said 'Dana, come here! What happened to you? You're a very good actor!' I laughed and said, 'Willie, thank you very much but I've made twenty pictures since I first saw you. Why, if I hadn't improved somewhat, I'd be a pretty stupid actor." In his mind, it was practically yesterday—he'd been in England all during the war with the Eighth Air Force."

[18]Ironically, while March (as Best Actor) and Russell (as Best Supporting Actor) won Oscars that year, Dana was not even nominated. His underplayed performance was taken for granted.

outlook on American society, 20th Century-Fox's *Boomerang* (1947). It was part of the post-war cycle of neo-realistic films, almost a novelty for soundstage-glamor Hollywood. The black-and-white drama was filmed entirely in Stamford, Connecticut. Most of the shooting took place after midnight to avoid huge crowds of onlookers. Despite the tactic, hundreds of people lined the streets to witness Dana, Lee J. Cobb, Arthur Kennedy, Sam Levene, and recruited locals act in the feature. Kazan had to use 350,000-watt bulbs to approximate daylight and the effect is startlingly real. As a Fox press release grandly described, "Kazan . . . used the technique he made famous in *A Tree Grows in Brooklyn* [1945], characterizing real events with real people, the homes they live in, the neighbors they chat with over the backyard fence." In this semi-documentary, Dana added his special blend of authenticity.

Based on a "Reader's Digest" article by Anthony Abbott [Fulton Oursler], the script was fashioned by Richard Murphy and produced by that bastion of Hollywood neo-realism Louis de Rochemont. With so much talent involved, *Boomerang* should have been even better than the good film it was. Kazan himself admits as much. "I could have done better with a lot of it, especially with Dana Andrews who is the only one who looks like an actor to me."

Boomerang concerns the murder of a priest by a psychotic and the following trial of an innocent party (Arthur Kennedy). Prosecutor Henry L. Harvey (Dana) discovers that Kennedy is telling the truth about his innocence and goes to bat for the decorated war veteran, despite political opposition. Eventually the man is exonerated but the guilty party remains free. Instead Dana's law enforcer uncovers political corruption (in Ed Begley's character), and thus we have a more realistic approach to law and order than had been the case in prior Hollywood exercises. The film was released in February 1947 and was favorably reviewed. The *New York Times* reported, "Dana Andrews does another sensitive job." James Agee *(The Nation)* agreed that the film was "notable for Dana Andrews' best performance to date."[19]

In 1947 Dana's split contract at Goldwyn/RKO and 20th Century-Fox was still in effect. By this

[19]It was tentatively set that Dana would be loaned by Fox to Warner Bros. to join with Virginia Mayo in *The Unsuspected* (1947); but when that feature was produced, it would be Joan Caulfield and Hurd Hatfield in the leads.

With Fredric March and Teresa Wright in *The Best Years of Our Lives* (1946).

time he was popular offscreen as well as on. The respected actor, then thirty-seven years old, was voted the "most cooperative star" in Hollywood by the Women's Press Club in 1947. According to the fan magazines of the day, the impeccably dressed Dana only carried a money clip and draft card to avoid bulges in his pockets. He enjoyed classical and pop music and read one book a month, usually with a glass of beer at his side. Curious and competitive, Dana conducted a chess game by mail with actor James Gleason, and lit up when guests discussed his favorite topic, politics. He especially enjoyed doing so with his best friend Lewis Milestone.

More knowing acquaintances of Dana *knew* that his life was *not* the beautiful picture painted by the fan journals. Although he was earning approximately $200,000 a year, he could not manage to save much of his income. As Andrews recently confirmed in a *National Enquirer* interview, "I got caught up in the fast life of Hollywood. . . . The most important thing to me at the time was living like a star was supposed to live. . . . I never worried about where the money went—I was too busy making movies and enjoying life to care about good solid investments. . . . I needed a sharp tax lawyer like the one I have now—but I didn't know it. One year my take-home pay after taxes was only $22,000."

More damaging than his penchant for living high, wide, and handsome was his addiction to alcohol. When drunk, Dana was decidedly not his usually solid, dependable self. For example, while driving one day, Dana was almost pushed off the thoroughfare by a road hog. Incensed, he followed closely behind his quarry; then at the right moment he forced the other car against the curb. Blocking the "game" in police fashion with his car, Dana charged out and collared the man, only to discover it was a friend. Also, when under the influence of drink—which was becoming increasingly frequent—his habit of being late on the set intensified. He was dubbed "the late Andrews," but by the end of the 1940s his drinking caused him to miss some entire days of shooting. At RKO for *Night Song* (1947), Dana was absent from the set at least once because of an all-night imbibing bout the night before. One morning director John Cromwell received a telegram simply stating that the actor would not appear that day, but would be ready the next.

Dana was back the next day, but *Night Song* did little for his already stagnating career. In the film he

With Merle Oberon in *Night Song* (1947).

plays a blind pianist who develops a relationship with a wealthy woman (Merle Oberon). At first, the role might seem like a natural for Dana, with the opportunity to present an embittered man victimized by life. However the script—whose writers, according to one critic, "were frightened by a cornfield"—is simply too soapy for any onscreen participant to emerge with a clean image. One movie magazine of the 1940s reported that Dana had a recurring dream that he was onstage, before a huge audience, and could not remember his lines. Whether this dream was symbolic of an intoxicated actor or one who would rather forget bad material such as *Night Song* was debatable.

It frequently happened that whenever Dana's career was in need of a boost, producer/director Otto Preminger came to the rescue. Such was the case with *Daisy Kenyon* (1947), one of the 20th Century-Fox features Henry Fonda detested making but the public generally adored. Potentially as sudsy as *Night Song,* the film was instead a sophisticated version of the eternal triangle, with Joan Crawford the title lady in question, Fonda her eventual husband, and Dana a wayward married man with covetous eyes for Daisy. Andrews' portrayal of the "heel with a heart of silver" (not gold) helped instill an adult tone to this quiet study of the male/female conflict.

Preparing for a "Lux Radio Theatre" broadcast of *Daisy Kenyon* (CBS, April 5, 1948).

With Joan Crawford in *Daisy Kenyon* (1947).

With Gene Tierney and Edna Best in *The Iron Curtain* (1948).

The year 1947 was also the beginning of the anti-Communist drive in Hollywood. Obviously Dana's contract owners, Goldwyn and 20th Century-Fox, were concerned lest their very liberal Dana be tagged as a Red suspect. Thus it was no accident that at this time there appeared an article in a national magazine by Dana's brother Bill (later Steve Forrest) detailing the wonders of his famous relative. "He has just the right amount of liberalism—he's a full-fledged American without going overboard for any 'isms.' He's intensely interested in world problems; he's a thinker, particularly on politics and world affairs."

Of course, Hollywood was anxious to prove its freedom from undue Russian influence, and the studio produced a series of strong anti-Communist features between 1948 and 1953. Perhaps the first, and arguably the best film in this mold, was William Wellman's *The Iron Curtain* (1948), released by 20th Century-Fox and starring Dana, Gene Tierney, and June Havoc. The title referred to Communist propaganda in general. The script was highly touted as having originated from the true personal story of Igor Gouzenko, a Russian code clerk hunted by the Communists because, once based in Canada, he decides to reveal his knowledge about the Red spy network. Scripted by Milton Krims, the writer of the early anti-Nazi film *Confessions of a Nazi Spy* (1939), *The Iron Curtain* is the least rhetorical of the anti-Communist productions because it reveals a tangible enemy pursuing a courageous man with whom the viewer can sympathize. As Igor Gouzenko, Dana was provided with a fine character and a solid story, and he made the most of each. He was in top form as he was allowed to be the stalwart victim again, but this time a victim with a believably courageous stance against oppressive forces.

It was at this time that Dana had an encounter with Communists. It began with a phone call from an old friend, Bob Shirley. In New York at the time, Dana simply thought that the man was seeking some free tickets to shows from Andrews' Manhattan friends. After all, Dana and Shirley had not met since 1931 when they were roommates at a YMCA in Texas. Dana was suitably impressed when he learned that Shirley was now an aide of Senator Connolly of Texas, and he was asked to do his best in the ticket department for the Senator, Secretary of State James Byrnes, and Russian leader Andrei Gromyko. After arranging matters, Dana and Shirley traveled some distance to pick up the dignitaries. Their car blew a tire, so the two had to amble down a highway hoping to hitch a ride. As fate would have it, they were befriended by a worried man driving a limousine who did not seem to speak English. Eventually the two learned that the man was a Ukranian driver, attached to the Russian embassy, who had been robbed in a delicatessen the day prior, and was now fearful of all Americans.

Back on less dangerous turf, Dana began earning romantic leads at Fox, the best of them being in Henry King's gentle *Deep Waters* (1948) with Jean Peters. Based on Ruth Moore's novel *Spoonhandle,* the story revolves around the daily life of a Maine fishing village and the efforts of social worker Ann Freeman (Peters) to find a suitable home for a little boy (Dean Stockwell). One critic referred to Dana's performance as "magnificent." While this was a bit strong, he certainly was effective as Hod Stillwell, a fisherman who teaches the youth respect for his fellow human beings.

Since Dana's image was being softened to a degree, it was natural that studio publicists should place more emphasis on his home life. In the late 1940s the Andrews family was the subject of several magazine layouts. Articles on the life of Dana and wife Mary, along with children David (by his first marriage), Katharine, Stephen, and Susan (born on January 29, 1948), gave actor Andrews a proper homebody image, which not only offset the screen tough guy but also the heavy drinker who occasionally warranted some bad publicity.

Most of Dana's features in the late 1940s and early 1950s constituted a depressing descent from the heights of *The Ox-Bow Incident* and *The Best Years of Our Lives. No Minor Vices* (1949) was directed by Lewis Milestone but only served to offer up Dana, Lilli Palmer, and Louis Jourdan in a too precious *ménage à trois* situation.[20] Unlike his co-stars, Dana had not yet learned to temper his heavy-handed approach with a lightness of delivery. Along with Maureen O'Hara, Dana was shipped to England to film *The Forbidden Street* (a.k.a. *Britannia Mews*). The setting was London in the 1870s, but director Jean Negulesco hardly made adequate use of the English ambiance. Dana, appearing at his most handsome, had a dual role in the dreary tale. He was first an impoverished painter, embittered by lack of food, who romances upper class Miss O'Hara. Later he was the lazy barrister who weds the aristocratic miss. For the former part, Dana's voice was dubbed by a British player to more closely approximate the diction of the Mews slum.

Dana's next film is rarely screened today. *Sword in the Desert* (1949), with a Robert Buckner script, concerned the refugee problem in post-war Palestine and was withdrawn soon after its initial release because of accusations of bias. Dana had to compete with Universal contractees Stephen McNally and Jeff Chandler for footage in this plodding actioner.

By this time Dana was restless and upset, watching his career dip. He had thoughts of forming his own production company, but the concept did not come to fruition at that time.

His three features for Goldwyn during the 1950–52 period, each directed by Mark Robson, were commercial disappointments. Robson himself has stated, "That was one of the worst periods of my career. I didn't care at all for the films I made with Goldwyn. They were awful."

My Foolish Heart (1949), a poor adaptation of J. D. Salinger's "Uncle Wiggily in Connecticut," teamed Dana with Susan Hayward in a sloppy tearjerker.[21] *Edge of Doom* (1950) was one of Goldwyn's bigger flops, casting Dana as Father Roth, a priest who rehabilitates crook Farley Granger. Goldwyn's latest contractee Joan Evans provided the very mild romantic distraction in the seamy piece. *I Want You* (1951) was Goldwyn's hopeful answer to *The Best Years of Our Lives,* set during the Korean War period. Playing an overaged warrior, Dana joins the army to be able to answer the question, "What were you doing, Daddy, when the world was shaking?" Dorothy McGuire and Farley Granger were Dana's compatriots in this overblown piece of pseudo-Americana.

Along the way, underrated Otto Preminger did his usual rescue job on Dana's sinking career. Twentieth Century-Fox's release of *Where the Sidewalk Ends* (1950) features one of Dana's best, most hard-bitten performances. He is brutal police detective Mark Dixon who accidentally kills a man while questioning him. The Ben Hecht script provides a narrative of Dixon's relentless attempts to shield himself, while delving into the law officer's devotion to duty. It seems that his father had been a criminal, and the

[20]MGM released this picture which Milestone would admit ". . . was a little comedy . . . that we tossed together for Enterprise because they wanted to keep the gates open." Enterprise Studio was defunct by the time the picture was released. The plot had Dana as a psychoanalytical-oriented pediatrician, with Louis Jourdan as a painter and Lilli Palmer as Dana's wife. She sees through Jourdan, but finds charm in his unconventional artist's approach. Each character has a stream-of-consciousness soliloquy to offer. The *New York Times* labeled the movie "cubist humor, spoofing á la Gertrude Stein." Adding insult to injury, Dana had helped to back the film.

[21]The extremely popular theme song by Ned Washington-Victor Young was Oscar-nominated and did a good deal to bolster the popularity of the feature. The reviews were mixed for the film, as well as for the players. Bosley Crowther in the *New York Times* was of the opinion that Dana ". . . is very attractive as a suitor, very charming in a sentimental way, but we fear he is not quite consistent with the man he is meant to be." It was ironic that Andrews, having his share of alcohlic problems offcamera, should be the plotline impetus for driving Susan Hayward's character to despair and drink.

earnest son has long been trying to make amends for that blotch on the family record. Co-starring the elusive, radiant Gene Tierney, this was the fifth and the last time the team would be matched on the soundstages.

Dana was slated to star in *The Gaunt Woman* at RKO, but it never materialized. In 1951 he continued in two unprestigious action films, *The Frogmen* and *Sealed Cargo.* Both were solid entries, but neither was resilient enough to attract much attention or merit wide publicity. In the better of the two, *The Frogmen,* Richard Widmark was top-billed over Dana, with Andrews cast as Flannigan, a chief petty officer of an underwater demolition squad. Otis L. Guernsey, Jr. of the *New York Herald-Tribune* praised the feature for stirring up "plenty of excitement" and commented on the impressive underwater photography. But professionally Dana was losing ground.

The Frogmen was Dana's last film at 20th Century-Fox where Gregory Peck, Tyrone Power, Victor Mature, Richard Widmark, and Clifton Webb were the top leading men. The aforementioned *I Want You* was his swansong at Goldwyn. Dana was insistent upon ending his dual studio contracts and reportedly paid Goldwyn $100,000 to be released from his agreement. In 1952, after a decade of double service to the two studios, Dana was a free agent in a declining film market.

Following the lead of other maturing stars, Dana now decided to establish his own producing unit, Lawrence Productions, to cover film, radio, and television. He was active in the first two media, but refused to become involved with competing television until the late 1950s, by which time he needed work of any sort. On radio, Dana was heard on CBS's "Suspense" in an episode entitled *One Man Crime Wave,* tracking down a homicidal killer.

In 1952 many motion picture stars were also highly paid radio actors. Humphrey Bogart, Lauren Bacall, Irene Dunne, Fred MacMurray, Adolphe Menjou, and Ronald Colman were all doing radio drama, often for as much as $75,000 a performance. Dana joined the well-to-do fold by signing a ten-year pact with the Ziv Company for a transcribed radio series called "I Was a Communist for the F.B.I." Based on the real life exploits of one Matt Cvetic, the thirty-minute weekly dramas were

With Louis Jourdan and Lilli Palmer in *No Minor Vices* (1948).

Posing with Stephen McNally and Marta Toren in *Sword in the Desert* (1949).

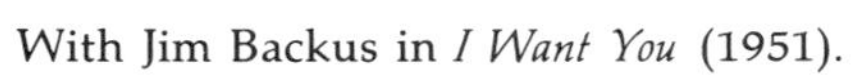

With Jim Backus in *I Want You* (1951).

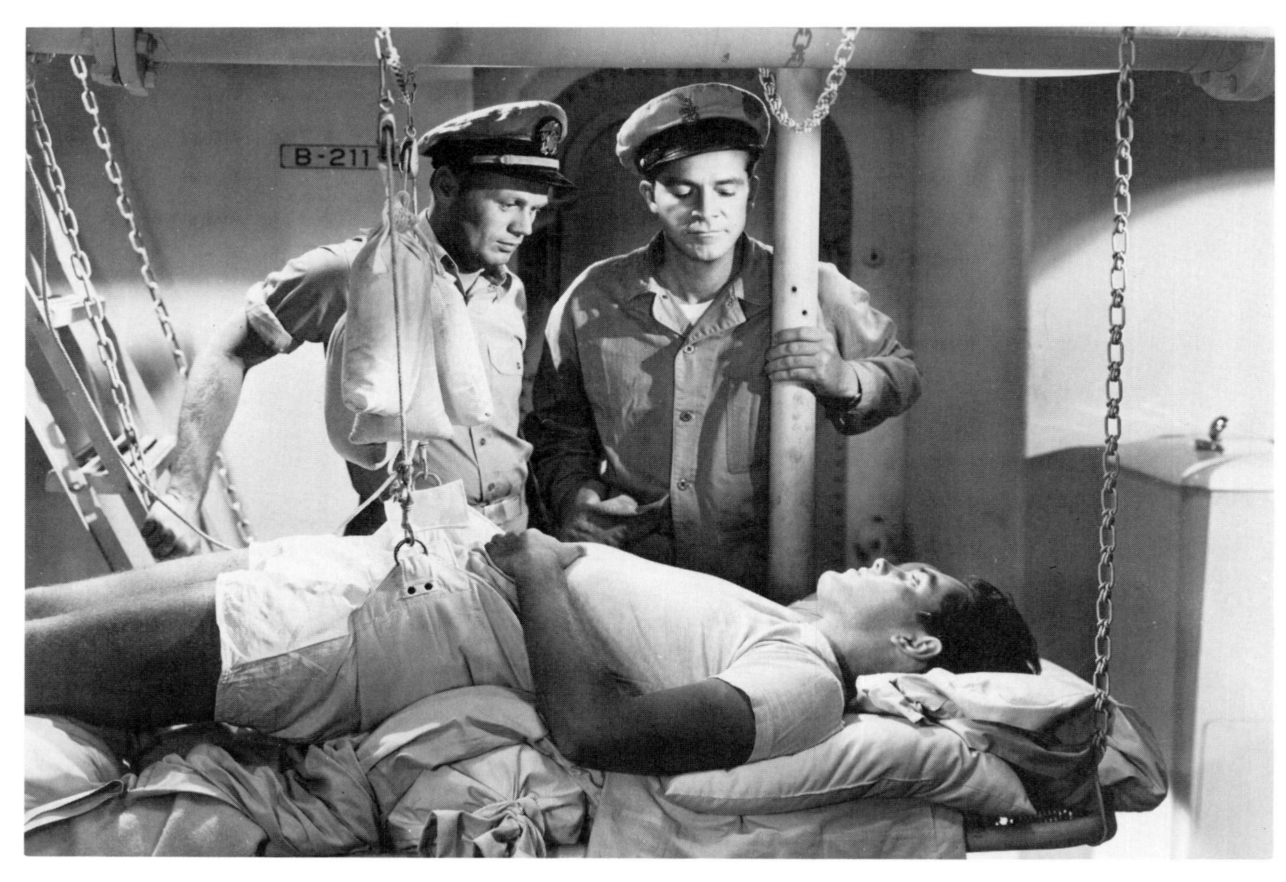

With Richard Widmark and Jeffrey Hunter in *The Frogmen* (1951).

adapted[22] from accounts appearing in the *Saturday Evening Post,* and a book and film on the subject.

Dana's last assignment before a two-year hiatus from cinema work was Columbia's forgettable *Assignment—Paris* (1952). As reporter Jimmy Race, Dana's job was to prove the existence of a Communist plot to subvert Western Europe. By this time, Dana's experience as code clerk Gouzenko (in *The Iron Curtain*) and as Matt Cvetic (in his radio series) made him one of the leading portrayers of the Cold War espionage game in its various facets. Two things must have been memorable about the film to its star. The first was that the picture was shot in Paris. Second, and more humorous, a botched interview while on location revealed very definitely that by the 1950s film was *not* an international language.

Art Buchwald recounts the incident, which resulted from a French interviewer asking questions in the wrong order to an unsuspecting actor who could not speak a word of French but who had memorized his answers phonetically.

Q: How long have you been making films, Mr. Andrews?
A: *Assignment in Paris,* starring Marta Toren and myself.
Q: What are you doing in France now?
A: I have four.
Q: Do you have any children?
A: Yes, Samuel Goldwyn and Darryl Zanuck.
Q: Who are your favorite actresses?
A: Sam Goldwyn and Darryl Zanuck.
Q: And your favorite producers?
A: Myrna Loy and Irene Dunne.
Q: What movie did you like best of the ones you've appeared in?
A: The *Tour D'Argent,* Maxim's and the *Folies Bergere.*

Unlike the above interview, *Assignment—Paris* was received with apathy. The only controversy or point of complaint in the Robert Parrish-directed fodder derived from the film's sloppy characterization of a newspaper office.

For a while it seemed that Dana's career might pick up new momentum. Cast as the captain in RKO's version of George Bernard Shaw's *Androcles and the Lion* (1952), he co-starred with Harpo Marx

[22]A description of some of the episodes follows: *I Walk Alone:* Matt tries to tip the F.B.I. that three real agents have been placed in sensitive positions with American atomic research. *Panic Plan:* the Communists plot to spread rumors about a town's water supply to cause panic. *The Little Red Schoolhouse:* Matt is assigned to lecture on Communism through subversive contacts while in danger of being exposed by a visiting Communist official. *No Visitors:* a traitor is discovered in Matt Cvetic's cell block. At first he thinks the jig is up, but it is another who is scheduled for execution. Matt tries tq inform the F.B.I. and save the man's life.

With Carla Balenda, Onslow Stevens, and Claude Rains in *Sealed Cargo* (1951).

in the title role, supported by Jean Simmons, Rex Harrison, and Robert Newton. However, after production had begun, mercurial studio boss Howard Hughes recast the film and started filming anew. In the new version, Alan Young became Androcles, Victor Mature took Dana's place, and Maurice Evans substituted as Caesar in place of Harrison.

With that chance gone, Dana decided to strike out in another direction—the theatre. He had learned to act on the stage at the Pasadena Playhouse, but he had not appeared in a play since the late 1930s. Now that he had more than ample spare time, Dana accepted a bid from a New England straw hat circuit to co-star with his wife Mary in *The Glass Menagerie;* he played Tom, Mary was Laura, Aline MacMahon was Amanda, and the gentleman caller was Walter Matthau. Critics were divided as to the movie star's suitability for the stage. Vernon Rice of the *New York Post* offered the expected criticism, "Andrews needs what only constant work in the theatre can give him —vocal variety, body movement, interperative powers, poise and ease." However, William Hawkins *(New York World Telegram-Sun)* took the opposite view. "He has composure for the narrator's passages, and plenty of vigorous fire for the stronger personal scenes. Vocally he has plenty of variety, and the natural magnetism that has made him a film star is every bit as much in register in the theatre."

Despite the generally favorable response to his stock fling, no other viable stage offers were forthcoming and Dana had to rely on his radio chores for sustenance.

In 1954 Dana was "cursed" with another film role, cast as Dick Carver, a plantation overseer in Paramount's lethargic *Elephant Walk.* Shot on location in Ceylon by director William Dieterle, the feature was a nightmare both professionally and personally to the newly free-lancing actor. Once more Dana was the other man. Here he was the alternate love interest for Elizabeth Taylor who has become disenchanted with her spouse, Peter Finch.

Accommodations during the shooting were somewhat less than tolerable. Dana described them in this way: "At the hotel we were met by barefoot bellhops who moved around like the place was on fire. The waiters are all called 'boy,' no matter what their age, and they in turn call all white people 'Master.' I tried to get my room-boy to use my name, but he didn't dig me, and continued calling me Master. . . . The first morning I was awakened by hundred of crows squawking outside my window. In Ceylon everything starts at daybreak. Sleep being impossi-

With David Farrar in *Duel in the Jungle* (1954).

ble, I got up and had breakfast sent to my room, but a crow almost beat me to it. Coming out of the shower I found one of those birds taking off with a slice of papaya almost as big as itself. You don't dare leave any bright objects such as jewelry lying around. Those crows are certain to sneak through the window and steal them. . . . I wouldn't recommend Ceylon unless you want your nervous system shattered."

A nervous collapse is exactly what Vivien Leigh experienced during the early weeks of filming *Elephant Walk.* Although the studio economized by retaining the long shots in which Miss Leigh appeared, the close-ups and other scenes were refilmed or freshly shot with her replacement, Elizabeth Taylor.

For all the trouble, the Technicolor *Elephant Walk* was less than a success although Dana earned some respectable notices. James Agee noted, "Dana Andrews responds with his strongest performance in several years."

His last 1954 film was by no means a masterpiece, but it did reflect the modest virtues of a solid B-plus film. *Three Hours to Kill,* a seventy-seven-minute color Western, has Dana as a stagecoach driver falsely accused of killing his fiancée's brother in a fight. Again the victim, he returns to town to prove his innocence and win the girl, Donna Reed. He only appeared in Universal's 1955 color Western, *Smoke Signal,* because Charlton Heston's acting fee was too steep. The story involves an Indian massacre for which Dana, as a scout, is indirectly responsible, according to a zealous army officer (William Talman). His other film that year was Mervyn LeRoy's tired version of one of the West's first women doctors, played by dedicated Greer Garson. As the love interest in *Strange Lady in Town,* shot in Cinema Scope and color, Dana is definitely second-fiddle to redheaded Miss Garson, and perhaps ranks third in interest, behind her surly outlaw brother, Cameron Mitchell.[23]

Trying to make a semi-triumphant return to the theatre, Dana was hired to play in *Harbor Lights,* a new Broadway-bound drama that was to co-star his former 20th Century-Fox leading lady Linda Darnell. For unspecified reasons, which may well be obvious given Dana's personal habits, he was replaced by Robert Alda. (At any rate, the show was a Broadway casualty.) And Dana also flopped in court. He was arrested in California for drunken driving. He pleaded not guilty but was fined $250.

Ironically, one of Dana's more interesting pictures of the decade was Fritz Lang's *While the City Sleeps*

[23]During the location filming in Arizona, Mervyn LeRoy had to cope with both Dana's drinking bouts and Greer Garson's appendicitis (when she would not consent to have operated on until shooting finished).

(1956), which contains a fine drunk scene between the actor and Ida Lupino. It was one of director Lang's favorite bits in the film, and he fought successfully to retain it, particularly the part in which an intoxicated Dana puzzles over the contents of a little color slide held by Lupino. An interesting footnote to this fair suspense film is that Dana's son David played the piano in the barroom scene.

That same year Dana again joined with director Fritz Lang and producer Bert E. Friedlob for *Beyond a Reasonable Doubt* (1956). It was a Hitchcockian exercise about a writer (Andrews) who has himself falsely convicted of murder, in order to challenge the validity of the death penalty. The man (Sidney Blackmer) who could substantiate Dana's innocence dies. The rather contrived plot concludes with the revelation of the writer's true guilt, while his overly loyal fiancée (Joan Fontaine) registers disbelief. The RKO production received such low-key release that it made little dent on the diminished film market.

As originally conceived, *Spring Reunion* (1957) would have teamed Dana with Judy Garland. It was ex-Paramount dynamo Betty Hutton however who played the female part of a couple who meet at a high school reunion after many years and try to pick up the pieces. High-strung Miss Hutton often brought chaos to any sense of order on the set and the resultant drama barely impressed staunch filmgoers.[24]

[24]Of *Spring Reunion,* A. H. Weiler noted in the *New York Times,* "Dana Andrews, the ex-football star aimlessly drifting from job to job, who finally discovers a kindred soul in his school chum, turns in a low-voltage portrayal that is marked by sincerity, if not passion."

Despite his faltering career in motion pictures, Dana was still adverse to television, at least the commercial variety. He did admit, "I'm interested in pay TV. It would eliminate the bookkeepers and pitchmen and give the actor a chance."

Meanwhile, riding on the residue of his 1940s' fame, Dana's agent managed to maneuver his client into pictures, albeit low grade ones. He journeyed to England in 1957 to co-star with Peggy Cummins in *Curse of the Demon* (a.k.a. *Night of the Demon*), and he returned to the United States to join fading Linda Darnell in *Zero Hour!,* the first of Dana's trilogy of air disaster pictures.[25] This modest Paramount production, complete with all the requisite genre clichés, was based on a Canadian teleplay by Arthur Hailey. *The Fearmakers* (1958), dealing with high pressure opinion formers, was no great shakes, nor was the Allan Dwan-directed *Enchanted Island* (1958), derived from Herman Melville's *Typee.* It was shot cheaply at RKO, but when that studio folded its distribution arm it was acquired by Warner Bros. Neither Dana nor ex-MGM operetta star Jane Powell fared well in the tepid happenings. As Dana admitted at this juncture, "They want top box office names for blockbusters, and I'm not in that category."

On Thursday, March 20, 1958, Dana made an impressive video debut in a "Playhouse 90" drama entitled *The Right Hand Man.* Instead of the rough aggressive character he usually portrayed, he acted the part of an executive in a talent agency in danger of being unseated by a determined younger man (Leslie Nielsen).

[25]Paramount's *Airplane* (1980), a spoof of airplane disaster epics in general, is a takeoff of *Zero Hour!* in particular.

With Greer Garson in *Strange Lady in Town* (1955).

With John Litel, Stacy Harris, Whit Bissell, and Nestor Paiva in *Comanche* (1956).

With John Barrymore, Jr., and producer Bert E. Friedlob on the set of *While the City Sleeps* (1956).

With Jane Powell in *Enchanted Island* (1958).

This role was largely considered responsible for the decision to allow Dana to replace Henry Fonda in Broadway's successful two-actor drama-comedy *Two for the Seesaw* with Anne Bancroft. On Wednesday, July 9, 1958, Dana finally made his Broadway bow. At the age of forty-nine, under the direction of Arthur Penn, the movie star made a solid start at a theatrical career.[26] Critics were generally impressed by the continuing production and with its new star. According to Whitney Bolton of the *New York Morning Telegraph,* Dana "comes out swinging and ends up the same way, master of his role, smooth, wise, and in balance." Richard Watts, Jr. *(New York Post)* was more guarded in his praise: "Dana Andrews, who has succeeded Henry Fonda in the part, is giving a skillful and attractive performance, although I think he is less ingratiating than Mr. Fonda was. By making the Nebraskan seem of sterner stuff, Mr. Andrews loses some of the disarming quality of his predecessor's portrayal."

By this juncture Dana felt professionally secure enough to move his family to New York, which pleased him. Always realizing the value of education, he claimed that Eastern schools were generally superior to their Western counterparts and that they turned out a better quality or more interested student. "Out there," he said, "most of the kids don't even go to college."

Dana remained with *Two for the Seesaw* until June 29, 1959 when he left to supervise the filming of *11 O'Clock Road* for his independent company. It was a project that never reached the screen. On the Hollywood scene, Dana had difficulty in finding screen roles. "I was in one of the best plays on Broadway for a year, and when I came back to Hollywood, people asked me where I'd been," he complained. While he was reaffirming his professional capabilities, Dana wisely decided to enroll at UCLA where he spent many months studying real estate in night school. Having recalled his past extravagances ("In 1947 I owned three boats—a twenty-two-foot sloop, a fifty-five-foot cutter, and an eighty-foot ketch that set me back $80,000"), Dana decided to embark on real estate investments. ("In 1960 I borrowed $50,000 on our $150,000 home and bought a forty-four-unit apartment building for $300,000. I refurbished it, filled it with tenants and sold it [later] for $450,000.") Still later he would buy, renovate, and resell some half-dozen other apartment dwellings, making a nice profit on most of the deals. After that he purchased a 5.6 acre tract near Disneyland, constructed a 132-unit apartment building on it and sold the site for $2.5 million.

Finally he did land a part in a semi-major release, Warner Bros.' *The Crowded Sky* (1960), an aerial disaster drama, with a cast that included Rhonda Fleming, Efrem Zimbalist, Jr., Troy Donahue, and Patsy Kelly. "Dana Andrews handles his role in his affably levelheaded fashion," reported *Variety.* The sky drama was geared for quick playoff engagements and as such served its purpose.

To augment the lesser acting roles, Dana began pre-production planning for a property entitled *The Build-Up Boys,* a novel about the jungle of Madison Avenue written by an executive under a pseudonym. Since the right roles were not coming his way,

With Eleanor Parker in *Madison Avenue* (1962).

[26]In *The Player: A Profile of an Art* (1962) by Lillian and Helen Ross, Dana discusses the impact of appearing in *Two for the Seesaw:* "I didn't miss a single performance—not even one time when I had a temperature of a hundred and three. You can grow on the stage. After a year of playing the lead, I had just begun to understand it, to understand what the author meant me to be. When I started out in the play, I was overemotional. Because I was playing the part of a self-pitying man, I had a tendency to whine. My wife pointed that out to me, and I found that if a man feels sorry for himself, he doesn't have to whine to show it. I stopped whining at once. It's not difficult for me to hide emotion, since I've always hidden it in my personal life. What is difficult is to convey feeling in a quiet and reserved way. Coming to Broadway after twenty years in Hollywood appealed to me. When I came to Broadway, I was looking for a kind of revitalization. I found it."

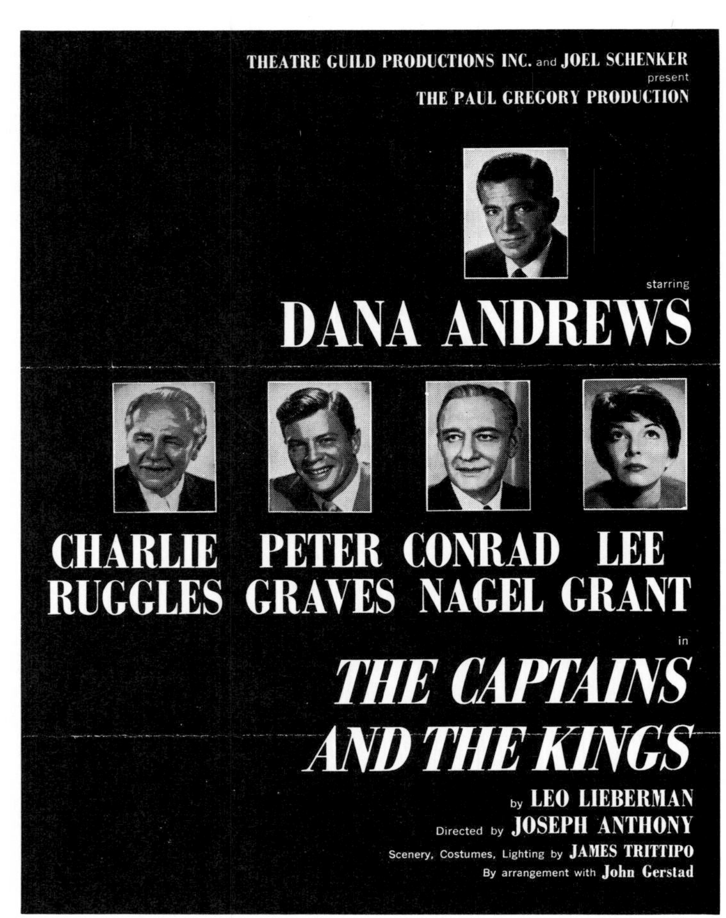

(left) With Marilyn Erskine in *The Boy Who Wasn't Wanted* episode (June 5, 1962) on ABC-TV's "Alcoa Premier" series.

(right) Advertisement for *The Captains and the Kings* during the Philadelphia tryout (1961).

Dana assumed the lead in the film, but he had problems casting the important female part. Suzy Parker and Joan Collins, two 20th Century-Fox contractees, rejected parts in the film and this irked Andrews. "I can't figure out the thinking of so many players these days. Too many of them have inflated egos, think they're already unique and top stars and turn down roles that co-star them just because they aren't in every scene in the picture. . . . Their psychology is all wrong—some of the best roles from a dramatic standpoint aren't the longest ones by any means. I know that in my own case some of my best performances were the shortest in terms of scenes and reels in which I appeared."

The film, called *Madison Avenue* (1962), was no cause for celebration. According to Howard Thompson *(New York Times)*, "*Madison Avenue* is the best advertisement for farming in years." Eleanor Parker, Jeanne Crain, and Eddie Albert rounded out the "starring" parts.

Despite his various business enterprises, Dana still enjoyed stage work and joined the cast of *The Captain and the Kings* which made its bow at the Playhouse Theatre in New York on Tuesday, January 2, 1962. The maritime drama was no descendant of *The Caine Mutiny Court-Martial* and quickly folded.[27] Later in the year Dana made several responsible performances on television, including an episode of "Checkmate," narrating *Emergency Ward,* and a segment of "Dupont Show of the Month." He then returned to the "Dupont" show for *Mutiny* (as a psychotic commander), and was on "Dick Powell Theatre" in *Crazy Sunday*

In 1963 Dana became president of the Screen Actors Guild and immediately made some statements on the movie industry, and television as well. "When you act in television, you know you do not

[27]In this drama of Navy progress and Navy politics by Leon Lieberman, Dana was cast as Richard Kohner, a Naval captain involved with the launching of the first nuclear-powered submarine. Others in the cast were Peter Graves, Conrad Nagel, Charlie Ruggles, Lee Grant, and Gavin MacLeod. During the out-of-town tryout in Philadelphia, Dana received good reviews. Critic Jerry Gaghan noted that Andrews offers ". . . a forceful and compelling characterization and the actor suggests the bridling and play of his own emotion beneath the relentless facade he presents. Reviewer Henry T. Murdock observed that Dana was " . . . utterly convincing". When the show bowed in New York, Howard Taubman *(New York Times)* decided Dana was ". . . stiff-lipped and courageous as the prophetic Kohner"

really mean much to your audience. Television is a built-in mediocrity because it is not drama. It is just an adjunct of the advertising business." One can imagine his need to act if he had been forced to accept a half-dozen television roles by the time he made this caustic statement. Yet the film industry did not escape Dana's critical eye. Like many other studio-bred stars, he did not like the increasingly risqué tendencies of the new Hollywood features. He thought that they caused undue pressure for actors. After taking over the presidency of SAG (until 1965), Dana appeared in only two TV roles before 1970—an episode of "Ben Casey" and one on "Bob Hope Chrysler Theater."

By the mid-1960s Dana's business sense had sharpened to the point where he became his own business manager. "It took me twenty years to realize that no one can handle you but you. Whether it's a business manager or a lawyer, you have to make the decisions; they won't take the risks for you." Dana began taking his own chances. He told the *New York Daily News* in 1965, "I had to keep telling those studio bankers to quit tampering with my hair and let me look my age. The romantic phase is now over; my roles are good, meaty ones, the kind I like at this time in life."

In 1965 Dana's middle-aged face was seen repeatedly on the big screen. He had a variety of parts, and although many of them were little more than bits, Andrews was just happy to be acting. The drinking had taken its toll on his face. Along with the wrinkles of fifty-six years of aging, Dana's countenance sagged with the weight of decades of heavy drinking. The look of desperation which had attracted audiences decades earlier usually had its foundation in the actor's sad eyes. But now the gloom was of a more permanent sort. The air of depression which now controlled an already solemn face took shape on his long, thin mouth, which drooped downward when relaxed. These features could often go undetected to the apathetic eye in many of Andrews' pictures in the 1960s. But some, like *Crack in the World* (1965), filmed in England, where the character is burdened by tragedy, provided a virtual showcase for his own personal sorrow.[28]

The most consequential film appearance by Dana in 1965—he was in six releases that year—was in

[28]Andrews' mental outlook was not helped by the death of his son David on February 15, 1964. Andrews, age thirty, was a San Francisco radio announcer. He died of a cerebral hemorrhage. He was survived by his widow, as well as his parents, brother, and sister.

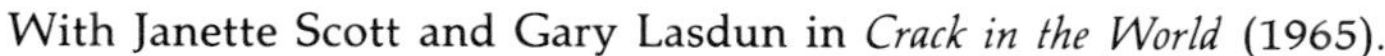
With Janette Scott and Gary Lasdun in *Crack in the World* (1965).

With James MacArthur and Henry Fonda in *Battle of the Bulge* (1965).

Otto Preminger's *In Harm's Way.* The Paramount release provided Dana with a somewhat pivotal (but definitely not starring) role as an admiral opposed to the entry of the United States into World War II. This John Wayne-Kirk Douglas epic received tremendous publicity, and even though Dana was just one of the brass in the 167-minute thriller, it boosted his industry status. In *The Satan Bug,* about the search for a deadly vial of poison, he was a stereotyped worried official, while in the misguided *The Loved One,* he was a lunatic general. *Crack in the World,* a modest antecedent of the super-budgeted disaster picture of the 1970s, showed that Andrews still had the ability to do excellent acting. *Brainstorm,* produced and directed by William "Cannon" Conrad, is not nearly up to the former film. Judith Crist *(New York Herald-Tribune)* labeled it "a plodding potboiler, designed for the illiterate unable to cope with a paperback thriller." As for Dana—cast as the tycoon ultimately killed by his wife's (Anne Francis) lover (Jeffrey Hunter)—Andrews etches a serious version of the paranoid general of *The Loved One.* Reported Miss Crist, "[He] makes the mean mogul about as mean as moguls get." Dana was yet another army officer in the dismal *Battle of the Bulge.* Wrapping up the year was the cheapie *Town Tamer,* one of A. C. Lyles' parcel of inexpensive Westerns mounted at Paramount with has-been performers.

Fortunately Dana's career in the theatre was more successful, even if unspectacular. Since the mid-1960s, he has made a decent living as the star of stock company productions of many established plays and some new ones. Combining this with a large income from his business dealings, the Andrews family has maintained a comfortable income.

In 1965 he made a fifteen-week tour with Susan Oliver in the Leonard Spigelgass comedy *A Remedy for Winter.* Later came Neil Simon's *Plaza Suite* and *The Odd Couple,* the latter with Eddie Bracken, in 1967. At first thought, one strains to imagine Andrews in the role of Oscar, the persistent slob who rooms with overly neat Felix. Dana starred in another established hit, *Paint Your Wagon,* at the Meadowbrook Dinner Theatre in 1969, but then he took on a new drama in 1971 entitled *Is Anyone Listening?* Written by novelist Joseph Hayes, the show premiered on February 4 at the Florida State University Theatre in Tallahassee, Florida. According to *Variety, Is Anyone Listening?* "asks an embarrassing question." Dana portrayed a lawyer who is blackmailed due to an affair with a teenage girl. In 1972 he reteamed with wife Mary Todd for a fine run of the hit play *The Marriage-Go-Round,* which the couple repeated the next year.[29] Also in 1973 Dana and Mary toured in England as well as played an engagement of *Our*

[29]While playing Minneapolis' Friars Dinner Theatre in *The Marriage-Go-Round,* Dana was preparing to give a curtain speech following the opening night performance, when he was surprised by television host Ralph Edwards, who along with Dana's co-star, Mary Todd Andrews, conspired to make him the subject of a January 1973 episode of "This Is Your Life." Among the guests on the program were the Andrews' children, Harold Russell, former actor and then Chairman of the President's Committee on Employment of the Handicapped, and actor John Gavin, who succeeded Dana as president of the Screen Actors Guild.

Town in Surrey, England. It is a tribute to Dana, formerly a major star, to be so cooperative and competent in productions which surely represent a major step down from the old Hollywood days. In 1975 he and Mary played in *The Gang's All Here,* yet another Broadway rehash.

At the end of the 1960s there was a period when Dana's film roles reached near abysmal standards. He must have seriously contemplated retiring to the lucrative businesses he had established on the side. He was the president of Malabar Properties, Inc. and the director of the Apartment Association of Los Angeles County, in connection with his ownership of a hotel in Renor, California. (The hotel is expected to net the actor some $50,000 in revenue annually for life.) In addition, his real estate enterprises have been building and building. "The last year I was in real estate full-time," the actor revealed, "I made more than I ever made in pictures."

That is hardly surprising. He jumped from one mediocre European-made thriller to another. Perhaps the nadir was *The Frozen Dead* (1967), assembled in England with Dana as a mad Teutonic scientist who has deep-freezed a dozen Nazi officers in his English manse. A little more logical was *Hot Rods to Hell* (1967), originally made by MGM as a telefeature but instead shipped to lower-case theatres. It reunited Dana once again with ex-Fox lovely Jeanne Crain in a poorly executed account of a family terrorized by a gang of road hooligans. The once prestigious John Brahm directed this minor entry.

After a cameo as Brigadier General Walter Naylor in *The Devil's Brigade* (1968) starring William Holden and Cliff Robertson, Dana decided to try his luck in a TV soap opera. He explained to Bob Williams of the *New York Post,* "Let's say I'm not doing it for the money. A year ago I cleaned up $250,000 in real estate. But I'm an actor and I found I wanted to act and this show gave me the opportunity. I'm very happy. Most of my friends, all very good actors, are just not working, just not getting into pictures anymore." The continuing daytime serial was called *Bright Promise* and ran on NBC-TV during the 1969–70 season.

Dana was hopeful, at first, that the show might be something more than the run-of-the-mill sudser.

(left) With Jane Russell in *Johnny Reno* (1966).

(right) With co-regular Gail Kobe on the NBC-TV soap opera *Bright Promise* (1970).

With Transportation Secretary John Volpe in Washington D.C. (April 1972), campaign against Drunken Driving.

With Ralph Edwards and Mary Todd Andrews on a Minneapolis stage for the January 1973 episode of "This Is Your Life" devoted to Dana Andrews.

On November 23, 1969, the *New York Daily News* reported that Dana "is personally high on it because it is dealing with contemporary subjects relevant to present-day society." When *Variety* reviewed the new entry, it judged it "promising" and acknowledged that Dana's name still had audience appeal. By April 16, 1970 the *New York Post* indicated that the bubble had burst and that Dana was not sorry to see either the show or his role come to an end, for it had failed to maintain its goal of relevancy.

Prior to his soap opera assignment, Dana had appeared in the October 2, 1969 episode of Brian Keith's "Family Affair" CBS-TV series. Dana played a friend of Keith's trying to get back into the business world after a prison term for attempted bribery. The actor looked every bit of his sixty years. Dana's more recent TV appearances have been a cameo role in the telefeature *The Failing of Raymond* (1971) starring Jane Wyman and Dean Stockwell, playing in a segment of the "Night Gallery" series in December 1971, and performing in two more made-for-TV movies, *Shadow in the Street* and *The First 36 Hours of Dr. Durant* in 1975.

Perhaps the most dramatic television appearance made by Dana occurred in 1972 when he made a TV commercial. "I'm Dana Andrews," he said facing camera front, "and I'm an alcoholic. I don't drink anymore but I used to all the time." The commercial aired across the country and Dana assisted the Alcohol Safety Counter Measure Program to bring drunks out into the open. Certainly his wife, Mary, was in favor of publicizing Dana's drinking problem, for on several occasions she almost divorced him because of it. But others were not as sure about Dana's frank admission to the public. "Some of my friends said I shouldn't say publicly anything about a drinking problem, but I'm willing to take the chance that my problem has been much like those of thousands of others, and speaking out about it won't hurt my career."

As Morgan in *Take a Hard Ride* (1975).

With Robert De Niro in *The Last Tycoon* (1976).

Self-realization was a major step toward his recovery. "My wife and I used to say, we'll just have one . . . make it a double . . . 'stead of buying a pint, buy a quart. . . . Us Hollywood alkies used to meet at Bob Young's house. One famous actor wouldn't come, saying everybody'd say he was an alkie. 'Everybody says it now but you,' we told him."

Dana now admits: "My life didn't start to turn around until I beat the bottle. I had a problem and I conquered it—but by then I'd spent most of my money on high living and bad investments." He also realized, "I've got fifteen, maybe twenty years left, and I'm going to live out the twilight my own way. Going to move slowly, doing what I feel like, living it day by day." But he still respects craftsmanship in his profession: "Gone are the days when the unschooled and uneducated can survive in our business. An actor must be literate to understand his role, and flexibility skilled to interpret and project before an audience."

Whatever the role, large or small, Dana is a pro. He played Scott Freeman, the pilot of a small plane which crashes into a 747 passenger craft, in *Airport '75* (1974), and the next year he was seen in *Take a Hard Ride* (1975), a Western filmed in the Canary Islands with Jim Brown and Lee Van Cleef in the leads. Dana had a cameo as the cattle ranch boss who is soon dispatched by a fatal heart attack. More recently, Dana had a featured role in the picture version of F. Scott Fitzgerald's *The Last Tycoon* (1976), playing a film director replaced on a star's (Jeanne Moreau) latest Hollywood picture. The Elia Kazan-directed feature failed to emerge as the important production everyone intended. *Good Guys Wear Black* (1978) highlighted the acrobatics of karate expert Chuck Norris in a tale of CIA-backed American assassins assigned to rescue government agents behind enemy lines in Vietnam. Linda Gross, writing in the *Los Angeles Times,* championed, "Dana Andrews gives a poignant performance as an alcoholic career diplomat who can no longer control his better impulses." In *Born Again* (1978), based on lawyer Charles Colson's autobiography dealing with his spiritual rebirth after the chaos of Watergate, Andrews was cast as the legal client who leads Colson (Dead Jones) to Christ. He was a replacement for actor Arthur Kennedy. Others in the cast of this critically lambasted but hinterland-approved feature were Anne Francis, Jay Robinson, and George Brent. Andrews' most recent feature film appearance was in the Cliff Robertson-directed *The Pilot* (1980), in which Robertson stars as an alcohol-prone pilot.

More important to Andrews' professional wellbeing has been his continued appearances in other media. During the bi-cenntennial year of 1976, Dana (Thomas Jefferson) joined with Howard Duff

NEXT AT Beef 'n' Boards
DANA ANDREWS & MARY TODD
SEPTEMBER 22nd THRU OCTOBER 31st

THE HIT BROADWAY COMEDY
by Muriel Resnick
"ANY WEDNESDAY"

Advertisement for the Cincinnati appearance of husband and wife in 1976.

With Dean Jones in *Born Again* (1978).

(Alexander Hamilton) and Monte Markham (Aaron Burr) in Norman Corwin's *Together Tonight! Jefferson, Hamilton and Burr,* which dealt with the American political scene in 1799. After touring the country with this production, Andrews was seen the following summer in *Come Back, Little Sheba,* co-starred with Rosemary Murphy. During the two-week August engagement at the Unicorn Theatre at Stockbridge, Dana performed as the alcohol-drenched Doc, a chiropractor who had once dreamed of becoming a doctor. There was naturally much speculation in the press that Dana had been given the role because of his own battle with drink.[30] Whatever the reason for the casting, Andrews gave a well-delineated performance. (When Paramount had filmed the William Inge drama in 1952, Dana had been offered the lead role opposite Shirley Booth, but he felt he was too young to play the middle-aged Doc and Burt Lancaster took the part.)

In the early part of 1978 Dana was on tour with *Any Wednesday,* playing dinner theatres. A previous commitment to the American Film Institute cut short the engagement at the West End Dinner Theatre of the Stars in Virginia. He was one of the guest hosts (including Rouben Mamoulian and Loretta Young) aboard the *Pacific Princess* for a seven day cruise to Mexico, during which time classic films were unspooled and celebrity discussion panels held. Dana's *Laura* and *The Best Years of Our Lives* were shown, as well as footage Andrews shot in 1950 when he and his brother, Steve Forrest, took a South American sailing trek.

On television neither Dana (in the small role as Shanley) nor star Carroll O'Connor (as Frank Skeffington) nor the rest of the ensemble (Patrick O'Neal, Burgess Meredith, Mariette Hartley, Arthur Franz, et al.) fared very well in the "Hallmark Hall of Fame" rendition of *The Last Hurrah* (NBC-TV, (November 16, 1977). Too many people remembered the fine 1956 novel and the well-produced 1958 feature film version with Spencer Tracy. On September 23, 1978, he was among the guest stars on the short-lived ABC-TV series "American Girls." In the May 3, 4, 6, 1979 ABC-TV mini-series "Ike," which offered Robert Duvall as General Eisenhower and Lee Remick as his driver and confidante Kay Summersby, Dana portrayed General George Marshall.

Today Dana Andrews limits himself to about one film a year and admits that he prefers the theatre to Hollywood filmmaking. The California entertainment industry scene is no longer fun for Dana. "Everything has gone to television. You couldn't get a television producer to put anything serious on the air because people have an attention span of two minutes. They're ruining the whole entertainment business." Actually, according to Andrews, he does not have to work. "I learned one thing from the experience of making and losing a fortune during my career in the movies. And that was how to save something for a rainy day." Says Dana, "I have one hotel that brings me in $200,000 a year."

With Rosemary Murphy in *Come Back, Little Sheba* at the Berkshire Theater in Stockbridge, Massachusetts (August 1977).

[30]In an interview with James K. Harris *(Berkshire Courier),* Andrews talked of his alcoholism problem. "It took twenty-five years for me to become an alcoholic. People just need to know that it's a dangerous drug, and to use it accordingly. . . . I didn't drink in the studio, unless it was Christmas eve or something like that. But I did get a reputation among some of the producers as getting pretty drunk at parties. . . . I now understand that alcoholism isn't psychological, it's biological, it's physical. I spent a fortune on psychiatrists. I ended up with the president of the American Psychiatric Association asking me, 'I'm darned if I know why you want to drown yourself, Dana. Why do you think you drink?' 'Just to have fun, I guess.' 'That's about as good a reason as I can give you,' he answered."

FILMOGRAPHY

LUCKY CISCO KID
(20th Century-Fox, 1940) 68 min.

Associate Producer: John Stone
Director: H. Bruce Humberstone
Based on the character created by O. Henry
Screen Story: Julian Johnson
Screenplay: Robert Ellis, Helen Logan
Camera: Lucien Andriot
Editor: Fred Allen

Cesar Romero *(Cisco Kid);* Mary Beth Hughes *(Lola);* Dana Andrews *(Sergeant Dunn);* Evelyn Venable *(Mrs. Lawrence);* Chris-Pin Martin *(Gordito);* Willard Robertson *(Judge McQuade);* Joe Sawyer *(Stevens);* John Sheffield *(Tommy Lawrence);* William Royle *(Sheriff);* Francis Ford *(Court Clerk);* Bob Hoffman, Boyd Morgan *(Soldiers);* Dick Rich *(Stagecoach Driver);* Harry Strang *(Corporal);* Gloria Roy *(Dancehall Girl);* Adrian Morris, Jimmie Dundee, William Pagan *(Stagecoach Passengers);* Frank Lackteen *(Bandit);* Spencer Charters *(Hotel Guest).*

SAILOR'S LADY
(20th Century-Fox, 1940) 66 min.

Producer: Sol M. Wurtzel
Director: Allan Dwan
Story: Lieutenant Commander Frank "Spig" Wead
Screenplay: Frederick Hazlitt Brennan
Additional Dialogue: Lou Breslow, Owen Francis
Camera: Ernest Palmer
Editor: Fred Allen

Nancy Kelly *(Sally Gilroy);* Jon Hall *(Danny Malone);* Joan Davis *(Myrtle);* Dana Andrews *(Scrappy Wilson);* Mary Nash *(Miss Purvis);* Larry "Buster" Crabbe *(Rodney);* Katherine [Kay] Aldridge *(Georgine);* Harry Shannon *(Father McGann);* Wally Vernon *(Goofer);* Bruce Hampton *(Skipper);* Charles D. Brown *(Captain Roscoe);* Selmer Jackson *(Executive Officer);* Edgar Dearing *(Chief Master-at-Arms);* Edmund McDonald *(Barnacle);* William B. Davidson *(Judge Hinsdale);* Kane Richmond *(Division Officer);* Ward Bond *(Marine);* Pierre Watkin *(Arizona Captain);* Harry Strang *(Messenger);* Edward Keane *(Captain's Aide);* Charles Trowbridge *(Aide);* Emmett Vogan *(Medical Officer);* William Conselman, Jr., Charles Tannen, Murray Alper, John Kellogg *(Sailors);* Irving Bacon *(Storekeeper);* Peggy Ryan *(Ellen, the High School Girl);* Gaylord [Steve] Pendleton *(Sailor #111);* Cyril Ring *(Lieutenant Commander of Arizona);* Barbara Pepper *(Maude);* Bernadene Hayes *(Babe);* Ruth Clifford *(Maid);* James Flavin *(Motorcycle Cop);* Billy Wayne *(Sail Maker);* Eddie Acuff *(Guide);* Ruth Warren *(Mother);* Donald Barry *(Paymaster);* Marie Blake, Gladys Blake, Frances Morris *(Beauty Operators).*

KIT CARSON
(United Artists, 1940) 97 min.

Producer: Edward Small
Director: George B. Seitz
Screenplay: George Bruce
Art Director: John DuCasse Schulze
Music: Edward Ward
Special Effects: Jack Cosgrove, Howard A. Anderson
Camera: John Mescall, Robert Pittack
Editors: Fred Feitshans, Jr., William Claxton

Jon Hall *(Kit Carson);* Lynn Bari *(Dolores Murphy);* Dana Andrews *(John C. Fremont);* Harold Huber *(Lopez);* Ward Bond *(Ape);* Renie Riano *(Genevieve Pilchard);* Clayton Moore *(Paul Terry);* Rowena Cook *(Alice Terry);* Raymond Hatton *(Jim Bridger);* Harry Strang *(Sergeant Clanahan);* C. Henry Gordon *(General Castro);* Lew Merrill *(General Vallejo);* Stanley Andrews *(Larkin);* Edwin Maxwell *(John Sutter);* Peter Lynn *(James King);* Charley Stevens *(Ruiz);* William Farnum *(Don Miguel Murphy);* Iron Eyes Cody *(Indian).*

THE WESTERNER
(United Artists, 1940) 99 min.

Producer: Samuel Goldwyn
Director: William Wyler
Story: Stuart N. Lake
Screenplay: Jo Swerling, Niven Busch
Art Director: James Basevi
Set Decorator: Julia Heron
Music: Dmitri Tiomkin
Costumes: Irene Saltern
Assistant Director: Walter Mayo
Sound: Fred Lau
Camera: Gregg Toland
Assistant Camera: Archie Stout
Editor: Daniel Mandell

Gary Cooper *(Cole Hardin);* Walter Brennan *(Judge Roy Bean);* Doris Davenport *(Jane-Ellen Mathews);* Fred Stone *(Caliphet Mathews);* Paul Hurst *(Chickenfoot);* Chill Wills *(Southeast);* Charles Halton *(Mort Borrow);* Forrest Tucker *(Wade Harper);* Tom Tyler *(King Evans);* Arthur Aylesworth *(Mr. Dixon);* Lupita Tovar *(Teresita);* Julian Rivero *(Juan Gomez);* Lilian Bond *(Lily Langtry);* Dana Andrews *(Bart Cobble);* Roger Gray *(Eph Stringer);* Jack Pennick *(Bantry);* Trevor Bardette *(Shad Wilkins);* Bill Steele *(Tex Cole);* Blackjack Ward *(Buck Harrigan);* Jim Corey *(Lee Webb);* Buck Moulton *(Charles Evans);* Ted Wells *(Joe Lawrence);* Joe De La Cruz *(Mex);* Frank Cordell *(Man);* Philip Connor *(John Yancy);* Art Mix *(Seth Tucker);* Buck Connor *(Abraham Wilson);* Speed Hanson *(Walt McGary);* Miriam Sherwin *(Martha);* Connie Leon *(Langtry's Maid);* Charles Coleman *(Langtry's Manager);* Heinie Conklin *(Man at Window);* Lucien Littlefield *(Stranger);* Stanley Andrews *(Sheriff);* Hank Bell *(Deputy).*

TOBACCO ROAD
(20th Century-Fox, 1941) 84 min.

Producer: Darryl F. Zanuck
Associate Producers: Jack Kirkland, Harry Oshrin
Director: John Ford
Based on the play by Kirkland and the novel by Erskine Caldwell
Screenplay: Nunnally Johnson
Art Directors: Richard Day, James Basevi
Set Decorator: Thomas Little
Music: David Buttolph
Sound Effects Editor: Robert Parrish
Camera: Arthur C. Miller
Editor: Barbara McLean

Charley Grapewin *(Jeeter Lester);* Marjorie Rambeau *(Sister Bessie);* Gene Tierney *(Ellie May Lester);* William Tracy *(Dude Lester);* Elizabeth Patterson *(Ada Lester);* Dana Andrews *(Dr. Tim);* Slim Summerville *(Henry Peabody);* Ward Bond *(Lov Bensey);* Grant Mitchell *(George Payne);* Zeffie Tilbury *(Grandma Lester);* Russell Simpson *(Sheriff);* Spencer Charters *(Employee);* Irving Bacon *(Teller);* Jack Pennick *(Deputy Sheriff);* Dorothy Adams *(Payne's Secretary);* Francis Ford *(Vagabond);* George Chandler *(Clerk);* Harry Tyler *(Auto Dealer);* John Skins Miller *(Garage Attendant);* Mae Marsh *(Bit).*

BELLE STARR
(20th Century-Fox, 1941) C-87 min.

Producer: Darryl F. Zanuck
Associate Producer: Kenneth Macgowan
Director: Irving Cummings
Story: Niven Busch and Cameron Rogers
Screenplay: Lamar Trotti
Technicolor Consultant: Natalie Kalmus
Music: Alfred Newman
Art Directors: Richard Day, Nathan Juran
Set Decorator: Thomas Little
Camera: Ernest Palmer, Ray Rennahan
Editor: Robert Simpson

Randolph Scott *(Sam Starr);* Gene Tierney [*Belle Shirley (Belle Starr)*]; Dana Andrews *(Major Thomas Crail);* John Shepperd [*later Shepperd Strudwick*] *(Ed Shirley);* Elizabeth Patterson *(Sarah);* Chill Wills *(Blue Duck);* Louise Beavers *(Mammy Lou);* Olin Howland *(Jasper Tench);* Paul Burns *(Confederate Sergeant);* Joe Sawyer *(John Cole);* Joseph Downing *(Jim Cole);* Charles Trowbridge *(Colonel Bright);* Howard Hickman *(Colonel Thornton);* James Flavin *(Union Sergeant);* Charles Middleton *(Carpetbagger);* Hugh Chapman *(Tench, Jr.);* Stymie Beard *(Young Jake);* Adrian Morris *(Fat Union Orderly);* Dolores Hurlic *(Black Girl);* Clarence Muse *(Black Man in Bar);* Clinton Rosemond *(Black Man);* George Melford *(Preacher);* Mae Marsh *(Preacher's Wife);* Herbert Ashley *(Jailer);* Davison Clark *(Bartender);* Dick Rich, Franklyn Farnum

(Barflies); George Reed *(Old Jake);* Kermit Maynard *(Union Officer);* Cecil Weston *(Mother);* Mary Currier *(Dressmaker).*

SWAMP WATER
(20th Century-Fox, 1941) 90 min.
(British release title:
THE MAN WHO CAME BACK)

PRODUCER:	Irving Pichel
ASSOCIATE PRODUCER:	Len Hammond
DIRECTOR:	Jean Renoir
STORY:	Vereen Bell
SCREENPLAY:	Dudley Nichols
CAMERA:	Peverell Marley
EDITOR:	Walter Thompson

Walter Brennan *(Tom Keefer);* Walter Huston *(Thursday Regan);* Anne Baxter *(Julie);* Dana Andrews *(Ben);* Virginia Gilmore *(Mabel McKenzie);* John Carradine *(Jesse Wick);* Mary Howard *(Hannah);* Eugene Pallette *(Jeb McKane);* Ward Bond *(Tim Dorson);* Guinn "Big Boy" Williams *(Bud Dorson);* Russell Simpson *(Marty McCord);* Joe Sawyer *(Hardy Ragan);* Paul Burns *(Tulle McKenzie);* Matt Willis *(Miles Tonkey);* Dave Morris *(Barber);* Frank Austin *(Fred Ulm);* Edward Clark *(Dekle);* Red Larkin *(Clem Hooper);* Charles Miller *(Fiskus);* Mae Marsh *(Mrs. McCord);* Sherman Sanders *(Caller).*

BALL OF FIRE
(RKO, 1941) 111 min.

PRODUCER:	Samuel Goldwyn
DIRECTOR:	Howard Hawks
BASED ON THE STORY "FROM A TO Z" BY THOMAS MONROE AND BILLY WILDER	
SCREENPLAY: Charles Brackett and Wilder	
MUSIC:	Alfred Newman
SONG:	Gene Krupa and Roy Eldridge
ART DIRECTOR:	Perry Ferguson
SET DECORATOR:	Julia Heron
SOUND:	Thomas T. Moulton
CAMERA:	Gregg Toland
EDITOR:	Daniel Mandell

Gary Cooper *(Professor Bertram Potts);* Barbara Stanwyck *(Sugarpuss O'Shea);* Oscar Homolka *(Professor Gurkakoff);* Henry Travers *(Professor Jerome);* S. Z. Sakall *(Professor Magenbruch);* Tully Marshall *(Professor Robinson);* Leonid Kinskey *(Professor Quintana);* Richard Haydn *(Professor Oddly);* Aubrey Mather *(Professor Peagram);* Allen Jenkins *(Garbage Man);* Dana Andrews *(Joe Lilac);* Dan Duryea *(Duke Pastrami);* Ralph Peters *(Asthma Anderson);* Kathleen Howard *(Miss Bragg);* Mary Field *(Miss Totten);* Charles Lane *(Larson);* Elisha Cook, Jr. *(Waiter);* Alan Rhein *(Horseface);* Charles Arnt *(McNeary);* Eddie Foster *(Pinstripe);* Aldrich Bowker *(Justice of the Peace);* Pat West *(Bum);* Kenneth Howell *(College Boy);* Tim Ryan *(Motor Cop);* Will Lee *(Benny the Creep);* Gene Krupa and His Orchestra *(Themselves);* Otto Hoffman *(Stage Doorman);* Pat Flaherty, George Sherwood *(Deputies);* June Horne, Ethelreda Leopold *(Nursemaids in Park);* Jack Perry *(Fighting Bum);* Gerald Pierce *(Delivery Boy);* Geraldine Fissette *(Hula Dancer);* Ken Christy, Dick Rush *(Cops at Motor Court);* Edward Clark *(Proprietor at Motor Court);* Del Lawrence *(Irish Gardener).*

BERLIN CORRESPONDENT
(20th Century-Fox, 1942) 70 min.

PRODUCER:	Bryan Foy
DIRECTOR:	Eugene Forde
SCREENPLAY:	Steve Fisher, Jack Andrews
ART DIRECTORS:	Richard Day, Lewis Creber
MUSIC DIRECTOR:	Emil Newman
CAMERA:	Virgil Miller
EDITOR:	Fred Allen

Virginia Gilmore *(Karen Hauen);* Dana Andrews *(Bill Shepperd);* Mona Maris *(Maxine);* Martin Kosleck *(Captain Carl Von Rue);* Sig Rumann *(Dr. Dietrich);* Kurt Katch *(Weiner);* Erwin Kalser *(Mr. Hauen);* Torben Meyer *(Manager);* William Edmunds *(Gruber);* Hans Schumm *(Gunther);* Leonard Mudie *(English Prisoner);* Hans von Morhart *(Actor);* Curt Furberg *(Doctor);* Henry Rowland *(Pilot);* Christian Rub *(Prisoner);* William Vaughn, Louis Arco, Arno Frey *(Censors);* John Bleifer, Egon Brecher *(Prisoners);* Otto Reichow, Harold F. "Dutch" Schlickenmayer *(Guards);* Wolfgang Zilzer *(Patient);* Tom Seidel *(Radio Man);* Frederick Giermann, Rudolf Myzet *(Waiters);* Lionel Royce *(High Official);* Emmett Vogan *(Announcer).*

CRASH DIVE
(20th Century-Fox, 1943) C-105 min.

PRODUCER:	Milton Sperling
DIRECTOR:	Archie Mayo
STORY:	W. R. Burnett
SCREENPLAY:	Jo Swerling
TECHNICAL ADVISOR:	M. K. Kirkpatrick, Commander, U.S.N.
ART DIRECTORS:	Richard Day, Wiard B. Ihnen
SET DECORATORS:	Thomas Little, Paul Fox
MUSIC:	David Buttolph
MUSIC DIRECTOR:	Emil Newman
ASSISTANT DIRECTOR:	John Johnston
SOUND:	Roger Heman
SPECIAL CAMERA EFFECTS:	Fred Sersen
CAMERA:	Leon Shamroy
EDITOR:	Walter Thompson, Ray Curtiss

Tyrone Power *(Lieutenant Ward Stewart);* Anne Baxter *(Jean Hewlitt);* Dana Andrews *(Lieutenant Commander Dewey Connors);* James Gleason *(McDonnell);* Dame May Whitty *(Grandmother);* Henry "Harry" Morgan *(Brownie);* Ben Carter *(Oliver Cromwell Jones);* Frank Conroy *(Captain Bryson);* Minor Watson *(Admiral Bob Stewart);* Kathleen Howard *(Miss Bromley);* Charles Tannen *(Hammond);* Florence Lake *(Doris);* John Archer *(Curly);* Frank Dawson *(Henry, the Butler);* George Holmes *(Crew Member);* Paul Stanton, James Eagles *(Officers);* Betty McKinney, Ruth Jordan, Dorothy Brent, Sally Harper, Ruth Thomas, Sue Jolley *(Schoolgirls);* Chester Gan *(Lee Wong, the Waiter);* Bruce Wong *(Waiter);* Edward Earle, James Metcalf *(Men);* Otto Reichow *(German Signalman);* Lionel Royce *(Captain of Q Boat);* Cecil Weston *(Woman);* Peter Leeds *(Shore Police);* Trudy Marshall *(Telephone Operator).*

THE OX-BOW INCIDENT
(20th Century-Fox, 1943) 75 min.
(British release title STRANGE INCIDENT)

PRODUCER:	Lamar Trotti
DIRECTOR:	William Wellman
BASED ON THE NOVEL BY WALTER VAN TILBURY CLARK	
SCREENPLAY:	Trotti
ART DIRECTORS:	Richard Day, James Basevi
SET DECORATORS:	Thomas Little, Frank Hughes
MUSIC:	Cyril J. Mockridge
ASSISTANT DIRECTOR:	Ad Schaumer
SOUND:	Alfred Bruzlin, Roger Heman
CAMERA:	Arthur Miller
EDITOR:	Allen McNeil

Henry Fonda *(Gil Carter);* Dana Andrews *(Donald Martin);* Mary Beth Hughes *(Rose Mapen);* Anthony Quinn *(Mexican);* William Eythe *(Gerald);* Henry "Harry" Morgan *(Art Croft);* Jane Darwell *(Ma Grier);* Matt Briggs *(Judge Daniel Tyler);* Harry Davenport *(Arthur Davies);* Marc Lawrence *(Farnley);* Victor Kilian *(Darby);* Paul Hurst *(Monty Smith);* Chris-Pin Martin *(Poncho);* Michael Ted North *(Joyce);* George Meeker *(Mr. Swanson);* Almira Sessions *(Mrs. Swanson);* Dick Rich *(Deputy Butch Mapes);* Francis Ford *(Old Man);* Stanley Andrews *(Bartlett);* George Lloyd *(Moore);* Paul Burns *(Winder);* Rondo Hatton *(Hart);* Billy Benedict *(Greene);* Tom London *(Deputy);* Ed Richard, Tex Cooper, Clint Sharp, Larry Dods, Tex Driscoll, Donald House, Ben Watson, Walter Robbins *(Posse);* Leigh Whipper *(Sparks).*

THE NORTH STAR
(RKO, 1943) 106 min.
(Reissue title: ARMORED ATTACK, 82 min.)

ASSOCIATE PRODUCER:	William Cameron Menzies
DIRECTOR:	Lewis Milestone
SCREENPLAY:	Lillian Hellman
SONGS: Aaron Copland and Ira Gershwin	
MUSIC:	Copland
CHOREOGRAPHY:	David Lichine
ART DIRECTORS:	Perry Ferguson, McClure Capps
SET DECORATOR:	Howard Bristol
ASSISTANT DIRECTOR:	Sam Nelson
SOUND:	Fred Lau
SPECIAL EFFECTS:	R. O. Binger, Clarence Slifer
CAMERA:	James Wong Howe
EDITOR:	Daniel Mandell

Anne Baxter *(Marina);* Farley Granger *(Damian);* Jane Withers *(Clavdia);* Eric Roberts *(Grisha);* Dana Andrews *(Kolya);* Walter Brennan *(Karp);* Dean Jagger *(Rodion);* Ann Harding *(Sophia);* Carl Benton Reid *(Boris);* Ann Carter *(Olga);* Esther Dale *(Anna);* Ruth Nelson *(Nadya);* Paul Guilfoyle *(Iakin);* Erich von Stroheim *(Dr. Otto von Harden);* Martin Kosleck *(Dr. Max Richter);* Tonio Selwart *(German Captain);* Peter Pohlenz *(First Lieutenant);* Gene O'Donnell *(Russian Gunner);* Frank Wilcox *(Petrov);* Charles Bates *(Petya);* Robert Lowery *(Russian Pilot);* George Lynn *(German Pilot);* Minna Phillips *(Old Lady in Wagon);* Bill Walker, Clarence Straight *(Young Men in Wagons);* Jack Perrin *(Farmer);* John Bagni *(Guard at Desk);* Lynne Winthrop *(Guerrilla Girl);* Patricia Parks *(Sonya);* Ferdinand Schumann-Heink *(Doctor's Assistant);* Lane Chandler, Harry Strang *(Guerrillas);* Inna Gest, Marie Vlaskin, Tamara Laub, Clair Freeman, William Sabbot, Jack Valskin, George Kole, Tommy Hall, Eric Braunsteiner *(Specialty Dancers).*

UP IN ARMS
(RKO, 1944) C-106 min.

PRODUCER: Samuel Goldwyn
ASSOCIATE PRODUCER: Don Hartman
DIRECTOR: Elliott Nugent
BASED ON THE PLAY *The Nervous Wreck* BY OWEN DAVIS
SCREENPLAY: Hartman, Allen Boretz
ART DIRECTORS: Perry Ferguson, Stewart Chaney, McClure Capps
SET DECORATOR: Howard Bristol
MUSIC ARRANGER: Ray Heindorf
MUSIC DIRECTOR: Louis Forbes
SONGS: Harold Arlen and Ted Koehler; Sylvia Fine and Max Liebman
ASSISTANT DIRECTOR: Louis Germonprez
SOUND: Fred Lau
SPECIAL CAMERA EFFECTS: Clarence Slifer, R. O. Binger
CAMERA: Ray Rennahan
EDITOR: Daniel Mandell

Danny Kaye *(Danny Weems);* Dinah Shore *(Virginia);* Dana Andrews *(Joe);* Constance Dowling *(Mary Morgan);* Louis Calhern *(Colonel Ashley);* George Mathews *(Blackie);* Benny Baker *(Butterball);* Elisha Cook, Jr. *(Info Jones);* Lyle Talbot *(Sergeant Gelsey);* Walter Catlett *(Major Brock);* George Meeker, Richard Powers [*Tom Keene*] *(Ashley's Aides);* Charles Arnt *(Mr. Higginbotham);* Margaret Dumont *(Mrs. Willoughby);* Tom Dugan *(Pitchman);* Sig Arno *(Waiter).*

THE PURPLE HEART
(20th Century-Fox, 1944) 99 min.

PRODUCER: Darryl F. Zanuck
DIRECTOR: Lewis Milestone
STORY: Melville Crossman [Zanuck]
SCREENPLAY: Jerry Cady
ART DIRECTORS: James Basevi, Lewis Creber
SET DECORATORS: Thomas Little, Walter M. Scott
ASSISTANT DIRECTOR: Artie Jacobson
SOUND: Alfred Bruzlin
SPECIAL CAMERA EFFECTS: Fred Sersen
CAMERA: Arthur Miller
EDITOR: Douglas Biggs

Dana Andrews *(Captain Harvey Ross);* Richard Conte *(Lieutenant Canelli);* Farley Granger *(Sergeant Clinton);* Kevin O'Shea *(Potoski);* Donald Barry *(Lieutenant Vincent);* Trudy Marshall *(Mrs. Ross);* Sam Levene *(Lieutenant Greenbaum);* Charles Russell *(Lieutenant Bayforth);* John Craven *(Sergeant Stoner);* Tala Birell *(Johanna);* Richard Loo *(Mitsubi);* Peter Chong *(Toyama);* Gregory Gaye *(Voshensky);* Torben Meyer *(Kappel);* Kurt Katch *(Kruger);* Martin Garralaga *(Siva);* Erwin Kalser *(Schleswig);* Igor Dolgoruki *(Boris Evenik);* Alex Papana *(Ludovescu);* H. T. Tsiang *(Ling);* Key Chang *(Admiral Yamagichi);* Allen Jung *(Sakai);* Wing Foo *(Police Captain);* Paul Fung *(Court Clerk);* Joseph Kim *(Procurator);* Luke Chan *(Court Stenographer);* Beal Wong *(Toma Nogato);* Marshall Thompson *(Morrison);* Lee Tung-Foo *(Third Judge);* Spencer Chan, Leon Lontoc, Roque Espiritu, Harold Fong, Bruce Wong, Johnny Dong *(Naval Aides);* James Leong, Eddie Lee, King Kong, Pete Katchenaro, Angel Cruz *(Army Aides);* Philip Ahn *(Saburo Goto);* Clarence Lung *(Japanese Lieutenant).*

WING AND A PRAYER
(20th Century-Fox, 1944) 97 min.

PRODUCERS: William A. Bacher, Walter Morosco
DIRECTOR: Henry Hathaway
SCREENPLAY: Jerome Cady
ART DIRECTORS: Lyle Wheeler, Lewis Creber
SET DECORATORS: Thomas Little, Fred J. Rode
MUSIC DIRECTOR: Emil Newman
MUSIC: Hugo Friedhofer
ASSISTANT DIRECTOR: Henry Weinberger
SOUND: Alfred Bruzlin
SPECIAL CAMERA EFFECTS: Fred Sersen
CAMERA: Glen MacWilliams
EDITOR: Watson Webb

Don Ameche *(Bingo Harper);* Dana Andrews *(Moulton);* William Eythe *(Oscar Scott);* Charles Bickford *(Captain Waddell);* Sir Cedric Hardwicke *(Admiral);* Kevin O'Shea *(Cookie Cunningham);* Richard Jaeckel *(Beezy Bessemer);* Henry "Harry" Morgan *(Malcolm Brainard);* Richard Crane *(Ensign Gus Chisholm);* Glenn Langan *(Executive Officer);* Renny McEvoy *(Ensign Cliff Hale);* Bob Bailey *(Paducah Holloway);* Reed Hadley *(Commander O'Donnell);* George Mathews *(Dooley);* B. S. Pulley *(Flat Top);* Dave Willock *(Hans Jacobson);* Murray Alper *(Benny O'Neill);* Charles Lang *(Ensign Chuck White);* Irving Bacon *(Scissors);* John Miles *(Ensign "Lovebug" Markham);* Joseph Haworth *(Murphy);* Charles B. Smith *(Alfalfa);* Ray Teal *(Executive Officer);* Charles Trowbridge *(Medical Officer);* John Kelly *(Lew);* Larry Thompson *(Sam Cooper);* Billy Lechner *(Anti-Aircraft Gunner);* Jerry Shane *(Foley);* Robert Condon, Frank Ferry, William Manning, Mel Schubert, Blake Edwards, Mike Kilian *(Pilots);* Carl Knowles, *(Marine Orderly);* John Kellogg *(Assistant Air Officer);* Eddie Acuff, Billy Lechner, Eddie Friedman, Frank Marlowe, Irving Bacon *(Sailors);* Terry Ray, Chet Brandenburg, Jimmy Dodd, Robin Short, Jay Ward *(Mail Orderlies);* Raymond Roe *(Gunner);* Edward Van Sloan, Charles Waldron, Frederic Worlock, Frank McLure, Selmer Jackson, Jack Mower, Crane Whitley, Pierre Watkin, Van Antwerp *(Admirals);* Stanley Andrews *(Marine General).*

LAURA
(20th Century-Fox, 1944) 88 min.

PRODUCER/DIRECTOR: Otto Preminger
BASED ON THE NOVEL BY VERA CASPARY
SCREENPLAY: Jay Dratler, Samuel Hoffenstein, Betty Reinhardt
ART DIRECTORS: Lyle Wheeler, Leland Fuller
SET DECORATORS: Thomas Little, Paul S. Fox
MUSIC: David Raksin
MUSIC DIRECTOR: Emil Newman
ASSISTANT DIRECTOR: Tom Dudley
SOUND: E. C. Ward
SPECIAL CAMERA EFFECTS: Fred Sersen
CAMERA: Joseph La Shelle
EDITOR: Louis Loeffler.

Gene Tierney *(Laura Hunt);* Dana Andrews *(Mark McPherson);* Clifton Webb *(Waldo Lydecker);* Vincent Price *(Shelby Carpenter);* Judith Anderson *(Ann Treadwell);* Dorothy Adams *(Bessie Clary);* James Flavin *(McAvity);* Clyde Fillmore *(Bullitt);* Ralph Dunn *(Fred Callahan);* Grant Mitchell *(Corey);* Kathleen Howard *(Louise);* Harold Schlickenmayer, Harry Strang, Lane Chandler *(Detectives);* Frank La Rue *(Hairdresser);* Aileen Pringle, Dorothy Christy, Cyril Ring, Forbes Murray, Jean Fenwick, Kay Linaker *(Bits);* Cara Williams, Kay Connors, Frances Gladwin *(Girls);* Buster Miles *(Office Boy);* Jane Nigh *(Secretary);* John Dexter *(Jacoby).*

STATE FAIR
(20th Century-Fox, 1945) C-100 min.
(TV title: IT HAPPENED ONE SUMMER)

PRODUCER: William Perlberg
DIRECTOR: Walter Lang
BASED ON THE NOVEL BY PHIL STONG
ADAPTORS: Sonya Levien, Paul Green
SCREENPLAY: Oscar Hammerstein II
SONGS: Richard Rodgers and Hammerstein II
MUSIC DIRECTORS: Alfred Newman, Charles Henderson
ORCHESTRATOR: Edward Powell
ART DIRECTORS: Lyle Wheeler, Lewis Creber
SET DECORATORS: Thomas Little, Al Orenbach
TECHNICOLOR CONSULTANTS: Natalie Kalmus, Richard Mueller
ASSISTANT DIRECTOR: Gaston Glass
SOUND: Bernard Freericks, Roger Heman
SPECIAL CAMERA EFFECTS: Fred Sersen

CAMERA: Leon Shamroy
EDITOR: J. Watson Webb

Jeanne Crain *(Margy Frake)*; Dana Andrews *(Pat Gilbert)*; Dick Haymes *(Wayne Frake)*; Vivian Blaine *(Emily)*; Charles Winninger *(Abel Frake)*; Fay Bainter *(Melissa Frake)*; Donald Meek *(Hippenstahl)*; Frank McHugh *(McGee)*; Percy Kilbride *(Miller)*; Henry "Harry" Morgan *(Barker)*; Jane Nigh *(Eleanor)*; William Marshall *(Marty)*; Phil Brown *(Harry Ware)*; Paul Burns *(Hank)*; Josephine Whittell *(Mrs. Metcalfe)*; Paul Harvey *(Simpson)*; Emory Parnell *(Senator)*; Tom Fadden *(Eph)*; William Frambes *(Pappy)*; Coleen Gray *(Girl)*; Steve Olson *(Another Barker)*; Neal Hart, Walter Baldwin *(Farmers)*; Margo Woode, Jo-Carroll Dennison *(Girls)*; Francis Ford *(Mr. Martin, Whirlwind's Owner)*; Harry Depp *(Secretary to Judge)*; Will Wright *(Judge)*; Earle S. Dewey, Wheaton Chambers *(Assistant Judges)*; Almira Sessions, Virginia Brissac *(Farmers' Wives)*; Minerva Urecal *(Woman)*; Frank Mayo *(Man)*.

A WALK IN THE SUN
(20th Century-Fox, 1945) 117 min.
(British release title: SALERNO BEACHHEAD)

PRODUCER/DIRECTOR: Lewis Milestone
STORY: Harry Joe Brown
SCREENPLAY: Robert Rossen
ART DIRECTOR: Max Bertisch
MUSIC: Frederic Efrem Rich
SONGS: Millard Lampell and Earl Robinson
TECHNICAL ADVISOR: Colonel Thomas D. Drake
CAMERA: Russell Harlan
EDITOR: Duncan Mansfield

Dana Andrews *(Sergeant Tyne)*; Richard Conte *(Rivera)*; John Ireland *(Windy)*; George Tyne *(Friedman)*; Lloyd Bridges *(Sergeant Ward)*; Sterling Holloway *(McWilliams)*; Herbert Rudley *(Sergeant Porter)*; Norman Lloyd *(Archimbeau)*; Steve Brodie *(Judson)*; Huntz Hall *(Carraway)*; James Cardwell *(Sergeant Hoskins)*; Chris Drake *(Rankin)*; Richard Benedict *(Tranella)*; George Offerman, Jr. *(Tinker)*; Danny Desmond *(Trasker)*; Victor Cutler *(Cousins)*; Anthony Dante *(Giorgio)*; Harry Cline *(Corporal Kramer)*; Jay Norris *(James)*; Al Hammer *(Johnson)*; Don Summers *(Dugan)*; Malcolm O'Guinn *(Phelps)*; Grant Maiben *(Smith)*; John Kellogg *(Riddle)*; Dick Daniels *(Long)*.

FALLEN ANGEL
(20th Century-Fox, 1945) 98 min.

PRODUCER/DIRECTOR: Otto Preminger
BASED ON THE NOVEL BY MARTY HOLLAND
SCREENPLAY: Harry Kleiner
MUSIC: David Raksin
MUSIC DIRECTOR: Emil Newman
SONGS: Raksin and Kermit Goell
ART DIRECTORS: Lyle Wheeler, Leland Fuller
SET DECORATORS: Thomas Little, Helen Hansard
ASSISTANT DIRECTOR: Tom Dudley
SOUND: Bernard Freericks, Harry M. Leonard
SPECIAL CAMERA EFFECTS: Fred Sersen
CAMERA: Joseph LaShelle
EDITOR: Harry Reynolds

Alice Faye *(June Mills)*; Dana Andrews *(Eric Stanton)*; Linda Darnell *(Stella)*; Charles Bickford *(Mark Judd)*; Anne Revere *(Clara Mills)*; Bruce Cabot *(Dave Atkins)*; John Carradine *(Professor Madley)*; Percy Kilbride *(Pop)*; Olin Howlin *(Joe Ellis)*; Mira McKinney *(Mrs. Judd)*; Garry Owen *(Waiter)*; Leila McIntyre *(Bank Clerk)*; Martha Wentworth *(Hotel Maid)*; Horace Murphy *(Police Chief)*; Dorothy Adams *(Woman Neighbor)*; Chick Collins *(Bus Driver)*; Harry Strang *(Cop)*; Broderick O'Farrell *(Bit)*; Max Wagner *(Bartender)*; J. Farrell MacDonald *(Bank Guard)*; Betty Boyd *(Another Bank Clerk)*.

CANYON PASSAGE
(Universal, 1946) C-90 min.

PRODUCER: Walter Wanger
ASSOCIATE PRODUCER: Alexander Golitzen
DIRECTOR: Jacques Tourneur
BASED ON THE NOVEL BY ERNEST HAYCOX
SCREENPLAY: Ernest Pascal
TECHNICOLOR CONSULTANTS: Natalie Kalmus, William Ritsche
ART DIRECTORS: John B. Goodman, Richard H. Riedel
SET DECORATORS: Russell A. Gausman, Leigh Smith
MUSIC DIRECTOR: Frank Skinner
ASSISTANT DIRECTOR: Fred Frank
SOUND: Bernard B. Brown
SPECIAL CAMERA: D. S. Horsley
CAMERA: Edward Cronjager;
EDITOR: Milton Carruth

Dana Andrews *(Logan Stuart)*; Brian Donlevy *(George Camrose)*; Susan Hayward *(Lucy Overmire)*; Patricia Roc *(Caroline Dance Marsh)*; Hoagy Carmichael *(Hi Linnet)*; Ward Bond *(Honey Bragg)*; Andy Devine *(Ben Dance)*; Stanley Ridges *(Jonas Overmire)*; Lloyd Bridges *(Johnny Steele)*; Fay Holden *(Mrs. Overmire)*; Victor Cutler *(Vane Blazier)*; Tad Devine *(Asa Dance)*; Denny Devine *(Bushrod Dance)*; Onslow Stevens *(Lestrade)*; Rose Hobart *(Marta Lestrade)*; Dorothy Peterson *(Mrs. Dance)*; Halliwell Hobbes *(Clenchfield)*; James Cardwell *(Gray Bartlett)*; Ray Teal *(Neil Howison)*; Virginia Patton *(Liza Stone)*; Francis McDonald *(Cobb)*; Erville Alderson *(Judge)*; Ralph Peters *(Stutchell)*; Jack Rockwell *(Teamster)*; Joseph P. Mack, Gene Stutenroth, Karl Hackett, Jack Clifford, Daral Hudson, Dick Alexander *(Miners)*; Wallace Scott *(MacIvar)*; Chief Yowlachie *(Indian Spokesman)*; Will Kaufman *(Man Player)*; Sherry Hall *(Clerk)*; Rex Lease *(Second Man Player)*; Janet Ann Gallow, Ann Burr *(Girls)*.

THE BEST YEARS OF OUR LIVES
(RKO, 1946) 172 min.

PRODUCER: Samuel Goldwyn
DIRECTOR: William Wyler
BASED ON THE NOVEL *GLORY FOR ME* BY MACKINLAY KANTOR
SCREENPLAY: Robert E. Sherwood
ART DIRECTORS: Perry Ferguson, George Jenkins
SET DECORATOR: Julia Heron
MUSIC: Hugo Friedhofer
SONG: Sidney Arodin and Hoagy Carmichael
MUSIC DIRECTOR: Emil Newman
ASSISTANT DIRECTOR: Joseph Boyle
SOUND: Richard De Weese
CAMERA: Gregg Toland
EDITOR: Daniel Mandell

Myrna Loy *(Milly Stephenson)*; Fredric March *(Al Stephenson)*; Dana Andrews *(Fred Derry)*; Teresa Wright *(Peggy Stephenson)*; Virginia Mayo *(Marie Derry)*; Cathy O'Donnell *(Wilma Cameron)*; Hoagy Carmichael *(Butch Engle)*; Harold Russell *(Homer Parrish)*; Gladys George *(Hortense Derry)*; Roman Bohnen *(Pat Derry)*; Ray Collins *(Mr. Milton)*; Minna Gombell *(Mrs. Parrish)*; Walter Baldwin *(Mr. Parrish)*; Steve Cochran *(Cliff)*; Dorothy Adams *(Mrs. Cameron)*; Don Beddoe *(Mr. Cameron)*; Ray Teal *(Mr. Mollett)*; Howard Chamberlain *(Thorpe)*; Marlene Aames *(Luella Parrish)*; Erskine Sanford *(Bullard)*; Dean White *(Novak)*; Norman Phillips *(Merkle)*; Teddy Infuhr *(Dexter)*; Ralph Sanford *(Mr. Gibbons)*; Bert Conway *(ATC Sergeant)*; Blake Edwards *(Corporal)*; Jack Rice *(Desk Clerk)*; Harry Cheshire *(Minister)*; Ben Erway *(Latham)*; Claire DuBrey *(Mrs. Talburt)*; Ruth Sanderson *(Miss Garrett)*; Donald Kerr *(Steve, the Bartender)*.

BOOMERANG
(20th Century-Fox, 1947) 88 min.

EXECUTIVE PRODUCER: Darryl F. Zanuck
PRODUCER: Louis de Rochemont
DIRECTOR: Elia Kazan
BASED ON THE MAGAZINE ARTICLE BY ANTHONY ABBOTT [FULTON OURSLER]
SCREENPLAY: Richard Murphy
ART DIRECTORS: Richard Day, Chester Gore
SET DECORATORS: Thomas Little, Phil D'Esco
MUSIC: David Buttolph
MUSIC DIRECTOR: Alfred Newman
ORCHESTRATOR: Edward Powell
ASSISTANT DIRECTOR: Tom Dudley
SOUND: W. D. Flick, Roger Heman
CAMERA: Norbert Brodine
EDITOR: Harmon Jones

Dana Andrews *(Henry L. Harvey)*; Jane Wyatt *(Mrs. Harvey)*; Lee J. Cobb *(Chief Robinson)*; Cara Williams *(Irene Nelson)*; Arthur Kennedy *(John Waldron)*; Sam Levene *(Woods)*; Taylor Holmes *(Wade)*; Robert Keith *(McCreery)*; Ed Begley *(Harris)*; Philip Coolidge *(Crossman)*; Lewis Leverett *(Whitney)*; Barry Kelley *(Sergeant Dugan)*; Richard Garrick *(Mr. Rogers)*; Karl Malden *(Lieutenant White)*; Ben Lackland *(James)*; Helen Carew *(Annie)*; Wyrley Birch *(Father Lambert)*; Johnny Stearns *(Reverend Gardiner)*; Dudley Sadler *(Dr. Rainsford)*; Walter Greaza *(Mayor Swayze)*; Helen Hatch *(Miss Manion)*; Guy Thomajan *(Cartucci)*;

Joe Kazan *(Mr. Lukash);* Ida McGuire *(Miss Roberts);* Lester Lonergan *(Cary);* Clay Clement *(Judge Tate);* E. G. Ballantine *(McDonald);* William Challee *(Stone);* Edgar Stehli *(Coroner);* Jimmy Dobson *(Bill, the Reporter);* Leona Roberts *(Mrs. Crossman);* Lawrence Paquin *(Sheriff);* John Hamilton, Pat Dillon, Sam Rosen, Frank Overton, Mickey Cochran, Brian Keith, Harry Landers, Michael Knox *(Men);* Harry Kaddison *(Maloney).*

NIGHT SONG

(RKO, 1947) 101 min.

EXECUTIVE PRODUCER: Jack J. Gross
PRODUCER: Harriet Parsons
DIRECTOR: John Cromwell
STORY: Dick Irving Hyland
SCREENPLAY: Frank Fenton, Hyland
ADAPTOR: DeWitt Bodeen
ART DIRECTORS: Albert S. D'Agostino, Jack Okey
SET DECORATORS: Darrell Silvera, Joseph Kish
MUSIC: Leith Stevens
MUSIC DIRECTOR: C. Bakaleinikoff
SONG: Hoagy Carmichael, Fred Spielman, and Janice Torre
ASSISTANT DIRECTOR: Maxwell Henry
SOUND: John Tribby, Clem Portman
SPECIAL EFFECTS: Russell A. Cully
CAMERA: Lucien Ballard
EDITOR: Harry Marker

Dana Andrews *(Dan);* Merle Oberon *(Cathy);* Ethel Barrymore *(Miss Willey);* Hoagy Carmichael *(Chick);* Arthur Rubinstein *(Himself);* Eugene Ormandy *(Himself);* Jacqueline White *(Connie);* Donald Curtis *(George);* Walter Reed *(Jimmy);* Jane Jones *(Mamie);* Whit Bissell *(Ward Oates);* Lennie Bremen *(Headwaiter at Chez Mamie);* Jack Gargan *(Waiter);* Vic Romito, Charles Cirillo *(Sailors);* Luis Alberni *(Flower Vendor);* Ervin Richardson *(Artist);* Hector Sarno *(Proprietor);* George Chandler *(Bartender).*

DAISY KENYON

(20th Century-Fox, 1947) 99 min.

PRODUCER/DIRECTOR: Otto Preminger
BASED ON THE NOVEL BY ELIZABETH JANEWAY
SCREENPLAY: David Hertz
ART DIRECTORS: Lyle Wheeler, George Davis
SET DECORATORS: Thomas Little, Walter W. Scott
MUSIC: David Raksin
MUSIC DIRECTOR: Alfred Newman
ASSISTANT DIRECTOR: Tom Dudley
SOUND: Eugene Grossman, Roger Heman
SPECIAL EFFECTS: Fred Sersen
CAMERA: Leon Shamroy
EDITOR: Louis Loeffler

Joan Crawford *(Daisy Kenyon);* Dana Andrews *(Dan O'Mara);* Henry Fonda *(Peter);* Ruth Warrick *(Lucile O'Mara);* Martha Stewart *(Mary Angelus);* Peggy Ann Garner *(Rosamund O'Mara);* Connie Marshall *(Marie O'Mara);* Nicholas Joy *(Coverly);* Art Baker *(Lucile's Attorney);* Robert Karnes *(Attorney);* John Davidson *(Mervyn);* Victoria Horne *(Marsha);* Charles Meredith *(Judge);* Roy Roberts *(Dan's Attorney);* Griff Barnett *(Thompson);* Tito Vuolo *(Dino);* Marion Marshall *(Telephone Operator);* Ann Staunton *(Secretary);* George E. Stone *(Waiter);* John Garfield *(Man in Restaurant);* Norman Leavitt *(Cab Driver);* Monya Andre, Mauritz Hugo *(The Ameses);* Roger Neury, Don Avalier *(Hotel Captains).*

THE IRON CURTAIN

(20th Century-Fox, 1948) 87 min.
(a.k.a. BEHIND THE IRON CURTAIN)

PRODUCER: Sol C. Siegel
DIRECTOR: William Wellman
BASED ON THE PERSONAL STORY OF IGOR GOUZENKO
SCREENPLAY: Milton Krims
ART DIRECTORS: Lyle Wheeler, Mark-Lee Kirk
SET DECORATOR: Thomas Little
MUSIC: Dmitri Shoshtakovich, Serge Prokofieff, Aram Khachaturian, Nicholas Miaskovsky
MUSIC DIRECTOR: Alfred Newman
COSTUMES: Bonnie Cashin
ASSISTANT DIRECTOR: William Eckhardt
MAKEUP: Ben Nye, Dick Smith
SOUND: Bernard Freericks, Harry M. Leonard
SPECIAL EFFECTS: Fred Sersen
CAMERA: Charles G. Clarke
EDITOR: Louis Loeffler

Dana Andrews *(Igor Gouzenko);* Gene Tierney *(Anna Gouzenko);* June Havoc *(Karanova);* Berry Kroeger *(Grubb);* Edna Best *(Mrs. Foster);* Stefan Schnabel *(Ranev);* Nicholas Joy *(Dr. Norman);* Eduard Franz *(Major Kulin);* Frederic Tozere *(Colonel Trigorin);* Noel Cravat *(Bushkin);* Christopher Robin Olsen *(Andrei);* Peter Whitney *(Winikov);* Leslie Barrie *(Editor);* Mauritz Hugo *(Leonard Leetz);* John Shay *(Sergeyev);* Victor Wood *(Captain Class);* Anne Curson *(Helen Tweedy);* Helena Dare *(Mrs. Kulin);* Eula Morgan *(Mrs. Trigorin);* Reed Hadley *(Commentator);* John Ridgely *(Policeman Murphy);* Michael J. Dugan *(Man);* John Davidson *(Secretary);* Joe Whitehead *(William Hollis);* Michael J. Dugan *(Policeman).*

DEEP WATERS

(20th Century-Fox, 1948) 85 mins.

PRODUCER: Samuel C. Engel
DIRECTOR: Henry King
BASED ON THE NOVEL *SPOONHANDLE* BY RUTH MOORE
SCREENPLAY: Richard Murphy
ART DIRECTORS: Lyle Wheeler, George W. Davis
SET DECORATOR: Thomas Little
MUSIC: Cyril J. Mockridge
ORCHESTRATOR: Maurice De Packh
MUSIC DIRECTOR: Lionel Newman
ASSISTANT DIRECTOR: Joseph Behm
MAKEUP: Ben Nye, Harry Maret
WARDROBE DIRECTOR: Charles Le Maire
SOUND: Bernard Freericks, Roger Heman
SPECIAL EFFECTS: Fred Sersen
CAMERA: Joseph La Shelle
EDITOR: Barbara McLean

Dana Andrews *(Hod Stillwell);* Jean Peters *(Ann Freeman);* Cesar Romero *(Joe Sangor);* Dean Stockwell *(Danny Mitchell);* Anne Revere *(Mary McKay);* Ed Begley *(Josh Hovey);* Raymond Greenleaf *(Judge Tate);* Leona Powers *(Mrs. Freeman);* Mae Marsh *(Molly Thatcher);* Will Geer *(Nick Driver);* Bruno Wick *(Druggist);* Cliff Clark *(Harris);* Harry Tyler *(Hopkins);* Harry Malcolm Cooke *(Bus Station Operator);* Eleanor Moore *(Secretary).*

NO MINOR VICES

(Enterprise/MGM, 1948) 96 min.

PRODUCER/DIRECTOR: Lewis Milestone
SCREENPLAY: Arnold Manoff
PRODUCTION DESIGNER: Nicholai Remisoff
SET DECORATOR: Edward G. Boyle
MUSIC/MUSIC DIRECTOR: Franz Waxman
ASSISTANT DIRECTOR: Nate Watt
MAKEUP: Gus Norim
COSTUMES: Marian Herwood
SOUND: Frank McWhorter
CAMERA: George Barnes
EDITOR: Robert Parrish

Dana Andrews *(Dr. Perry Aswell);* Lilli Palmer *(April Aswell);* Louis Jourdan *(Octavio Quaglini);* Jane Wyatt *(Miss Darlington);* Norman Lloyd *(Dr. Sturdevant);* Frank Kreig *(Cab Driver);* Beau Bridges *(Bertram);* Ann Doran *(Mrs. Farraday);* Jerry Mullins *(Boy);* Inna Gest *(Mrs. Fleishgelt);* Roy Roberts *(Mr. Felton);* Fay Baker *(Mrs. Felton);* Sharon McManus *(Gloria Felton);* Kay Williams *(Receptionist);* Bobby Hyatt *(Genius);* Joy Rogers, Eileen Coghlin *(Nurses);* Frank Conlan *(Window Cleaner).*

THE FORBIDDEN STREET

(20th Century-Fox, 1949) 91 min.

PRODUCER: William Perlberg
DIRECTOR: Jean Negulesco
BASED ON THE NOVEL *BRITANNIA MEWS* BY MARGERY SHARP
SCREENPLAY: Ring Lardner, Jr.
ASSISTANT DIRECTOR: Guy Hamilton
ART DIRECTOR: Andrew Andrejew
MUSIC: Malcolm Arnold
MUSIC DIRECTOR: Muir Mathieson
SOUND: Buster Ambier
SOUND EDITOR: Ben Hopkins
CAMERA: George Perinal
EDITOR: Richard Best

Maureen O'Hara *(Adelaide Culver);* Dana Andrews *(Gilbert Lauderhale/Henry Lambert);* Dame Sybil Thorndike *(Mrs. Mounsey);* June Allen *(Adelaide as a Child);* Anthony Tancred *(Treff Culver);* Anthony Lamb *(Treff as a Child);* Wilfrid Hyde-White *(Mr.*

Culver); Fay Compton *(Mrs. Culver);* Anne Butchart *(Alice Mambro);* Suzanne Gibbs *(Alice as a Child);* Diane Hart *(The Blazer);* Heather Latham *(Blazer as a Child);* Herbert Walton *(The Old 'Un);* A. E. Matthews *(Mr. Bly);* Mary Martlew *(Milly Lauderdale);* Gwen Whitby *(Miss Bryant);* Scott Harold *(Benson);* Neil North *(Jimmy Hambro).*

SWORD IN THE DESERT
(Universal, 1949) 100 min.

PRODUCER: Robert Buckner
DIRECTOR: George Sherman
SCREENPLAY: Buckner
ART DIRECTORS: Bernard Herzbrun, Alexander Golitzen
SET DECORATOR: Al Fields
MUSIC: Frank Skinner
ASSISTANT DIRECTOR: Frank Shaw
MAKEUP: Emile LaVigne
SOUND: Glen Anderson
SPECIAL EFFECTS: Nick Carmona
CAMERA: Irving Glassberg
EDITOR: Otto Ludwig

Dana Andrews *(Mike Dillon);* Marta Toren *(Sabra);* Stephen McNally *(David Vogel);* Jeff Chandler *(Kurta);* Philip Friend *(Lieutenant Ellerton);* Hugh French *(Major Sorrell);* Liam Redmond *(McCarthy);* Lowell Gilmore *(Major Stephens);* Stanley Logan *(Colonel Bruce Evans);* Hayden Rorke *(Captain Beaumont);* George Tyne *(Dov);* Peter Coe *(Tarn);* Paul Marion *(Jeno);* Marten Lamont *(Captain Fletcher);* David Wolfe *(Gershon);* Campbell Copelin *(Sergeant Chapel);* Art Foster *(Sergeant Rummins);* Gilchrist Stuart *(Radio Operator);* Emil Rameau *(Old Man);* Jack Webb *(Hoffman);* Jerry Paris *(Levitan);* Shepherd Menken, Joseph Turkel, Sam Resnick, Russ Kaplan *(Haganah Soldiers);* Dennis Dengate *(Driver);* Martin Garralaga *(Ahmed the Great);* James Craven *(Brigadier General Vincent);* Robin Hughes *(Soldier);* George Dockstader *(British Soldier).*

MY FOOLISH HEART
(RKO, 1949) 98 min.

PRODUCER: Samuel Goldwyn
DIRECTOR: Mark Robson
BASED ON THE STORY "UNCLE WIGGILY IN CONNECTICUT" BY J. D. SALINGER
SCREENPLAY: Julius J. and Philip G. Epstein
ART DIRECTOR: Richard Day
SET DECORATOR: Julia Heron
MUSIC: Victor Young
ORCHESTRATORS: Leo Shuken, Sidney Cutner
MUSIC DIRECTOR: Emil Newman
SONG: Young and Ned Washington
ASSISTANT DIRECTOR: Ivan Volkman
COSTUMES: Mary Wills, Edith Head
SOUND: Fred Lau
SPECIAL EFFECTS: John Fulton
CAMERA: Lee Garmes
EDITOR: Daniel Mandell.

Dana Andrews *(Walt Dreiser);* Susan Hayward *(Eloise Winters);* Kent Smith *(Lew Wengler);* Lois Wheeler *(Mary Jane);* Jessie Royce Landis *(Martha Winters);* Robert Keith *(Henry Winters);* Gigi Perreau *(Ramona);* Karin Booth *(Miriam Ball);* Todd Karns *(Her Escort);* Philip Pine *(Sergeant Lucey);* Martha Mears *(Nightclub Singer);* Edna Holland *(Dean Whiting);* Marietta Canty *(Grace);* Barbara Woodell *(Red Cross Receptionist);* Regina Wallace *(Mrs. Crandall);* Jerry Paris *(Usher);* Marcel de la Brosse *(Waiter);* Phyllis Coates *(Girl on Phone);* Ed Peil, Sr. *(Conductor);* Billy Lord, Tom Gibson, Bob Strong, Kay Marlowe, Sam Ash *(Spectators).*

WHERE THE SIDEWALK ENDS
(20th Century-Fox, 1950) 95 min.

PRODUCER/DIRECTOR: Otto Preminger
BASED ON A NOVEL BY WILLIAM L. STUART AND THE STORY "NIGHT CRY" BY FRANK P. ROSENBERG
SCREENPLAY: Ben Hecht
ADAPTORS: Victor Trivas, Rosenberg, Robert E. Kent
ART DIRECTORS: Lyle R. Wheeler, J. Russell Spencer
SET DECORATORS: Thomas Little, Walter M. Scott
MUSIC: Cyril J. Mockridge
MUSIC DIRECTOR: Lionel Newman
ORCHESTRATOR: Edward Powell
WARDROBE DESIGNERS: Charles Le Maire, Oleg Cassini (for Gene Tierney)
SPECIAL EFFECTS: Fred Sersen
CAMERA: Joseph La Shelle
EDITOR: Louis Loeffler

Dana Andrews *(Mark Dixon);* Gene Tierney *(Morgan Taylor);* Gary Merrill *(Tommy Scalise);* Bert Freed *(Paul Klein);* Tom Tully *(Jiggs Taylor);* Karl Malden *(Lieutenant Thomas);* Ruth Donnelly *(Martha);* Craig Stevens *(Ken Paine);* Robert Simon *(Inspector Nicholas Foley);* Harry von Zell *(Ted Morrison);* Don Appell *(Willie Bender);* Neville Brand *(Steve);* Grace Mills *(Mrs. Tribaum);* Lou Krugman *(Mike Williams);* David McMahon *(Harrington);* David Wolfe *(Sid Kramer);* Steve Roberts *(Gilruth);* Phil Tully *(Tod Benson);* Ian MacDonald *(Casey);* John Close *(Hanson);* John McGuire *(Gertessen);* Lou Nova *(Ernie);* Oleg Cassini *(Oleg, the Fashion Designer);* Louise Lorimer *(Mrs. Jackson);* Lester Sharpe *(Friedman);* Chili Williams *(Teddy);* Robert Foulk *(Fenney);* Eda Reiss Merin *(Shirley Klein);* Mack Williams *(Jerry Morris);* Duke Watson *(Cab Driver);* Clancy Cooper *(Lieutenant Arnaldo);* Bob Evans *(Sweatshirt);* Joseph Granby *(Fat Man);* Harry Brooks, Anthony George *(Thugs);* Wanda Smith, Shirley Tegge *(Models);* Fred Graham *(Man);* Charles J. Flynn *(Schwartz);* Larry Thompson *(Riley);* Ralph Peters *(Counterman);* Robert B. Williams *(Detective);* Bob Patten *(Medical Examiner);* John Marshall, Clarence Straight *(Detectives);* Peggy O'Connor *(Model).*

EDGE OF DOOM
(RKO, 1950) 99 min.

PRODUCER: Samuel Goldwyn
DIRECTOR: Mark Robson
BASED ON THE NOVEL BY LEO BRADY
SCREENPLAY: Philip Yordan
ART DIRECTOR: Richard Day
MUSIC DIRECTOR: Emil Newman
CAMERA: Harry Stradling
EDITOR: Daniel Mandell

Dana Andrews *(Father Roth);* Farley Granger *(Martin Lynn);* Joan Evans *(Rita Conroy);* Robert Keith *(Mandel);* Paul Stewart *(Craig);* Adele Jergens *(Irene);* Mala Powers *(Julie);* Harold Vermilyea *(Father Kirkman);* John Ridgely, Douglas Fowley *(Detectives);* Mabel Paige *(Mrs. Pearson);* Howland Chamberlin *(Mr. Murray);* Houseley Stevenson, Sr. *(Mr. Swanson);* Jean Innes *(Mrs. Lally);* Ellen Corby *(Mrs. Moore);* Ray Teal *(Ned Moore);* Mary Field *(Mary Jane Glennon);* Virginia Brissac *(Mrs. Dennis);* Frances Morris *(Mrs. Lynn).*

THE FROGMEN
(20th Century-Fox, 1951) 96 min.

PRODUCER: Samuel G. Engel
DIRECTOR: Lloyd Bacon
STORY: Oscar Millard
SCREENPLAY: John Tucker Battle
ART DIRECTORS: Lyle Wheeler, Albert Hogsett
MUSIC DIRECTOR: Lionel Newman
CAMERA: Norbert Brodine
EDITOR: William Reynolds

Richard Widmark *(Lieutenant Commander John Lawrence);* Dana Andrews *(Flannigan);* Gary Merrill *(Lieutenant Commander Pete Vincent);* Jeffrey Hunter *(Creighton);* Warren Stevens *(Hodges);* Robert Wagner *(Lieutenant J. C. Franklin);* Harvey Lembeck *(Canarsie);* Robert Rockwell *(Lieutenant Doyle);* Henry Slate *(Sleepy);* Robert Adler *(Chief Ryan);* Bob Patten *(Lieutenant Klinger);* Harry Flowers *(Kinsella);* William Bishop *(Ferrino);* Fay Roope *(Admiral Dakers);* William M. Neil *(Commander Miles);* James Gregory *(Chief Petty Officer Lane);* Russell Hardie *(Captain Radford);* Parley Baer *(Dr. Ullman);* Peter Leeds *(Pharmacist's Mate);* Richard Allan, Frank Donahue, Jack Warden *(Crew Members);* Rollin Moriyama *(Coxswain);* Frank Iwanga, Edward Sojin, Jr. *(Japanese Sentries);* Sydney Smith *(General Coleson);* Ray Hykě *(Repair Man).*

SEALED CARGO
(RKO, 1951) 89 min.

PRODUCER: William Duff
DIRECTOR: Alfred Werker
BASED ON THE NOVEL *The Gaunt Woman* BY EDMUND GILLIGAN
SCREENPLAY: Dale Van Every, Oliver H. P. Garrett, Roy Huggins

ART DIRECTOR: Albert S. D'Agostino
MUSIC DIRECTOR: C. Bakaleinikoff
CAMERA: George E. Diskant
EDITOR: Ralph Dawson

Dana Andrews *(Pat Bannon);* Carla Balenda *(Margaret McLean);* Claude Rains *(Skalder);* Philip Dorn *(Conrad);* Onslow Stevens *(McLean);* Skip Homeier *(Steve);* Eric Feldary *(Holger);* J. M. Kerrigan *(Skipper Ben);* Arthur Shields *(Dolan);* Morgan Farley *(Caleb);* Dave Thursby *(Ambrose);* Henry Rowland *(Anderson);* Charles A. Browne *(Smitty);* Don Dillaway *(Owen);* Al Hill *(Tom);* Lee MacGregor *(Lieutenant Cameron);* William Andrews *(Holtz);* Richard Norris *(Second Mate);* Kathaleen Ellis, Karen Norris, Harry Mancke *(Villagers);* Whit Bissell *(Shuster);* Hay Morley *(Wharf Official);* Bert Kennedy *(Old Seaman);* Larry Johns *(Mark);* Bruce Cameron, Ned Roberts *(Nazi Machinegunners);* Art Dupuis *(Bit);* Dick Crockett, Bob Morgan, Wes Hopper *(Nazis);* Bob Smitts *(German Sailor).*

I WANT YOU
(RKO, 1951) 102 min.

PRODUCER: Samuel Goldwyn
DIRECTOR: Mark Robson
BASED ON STORIES BY EDWARD NEWHOUSE
SCREENPLAY: Irwin Shaw
MUSIC: Leigh Harline
ART DIRECTOR: Richard Day
CAMERA: Harry Stradling
EDITOR: Daniel Mandell

Dana Andrews *(Martin Greer);* Dorothy McGuire *(Nancy Greer);* Farley Granger *(Jack Greer);* Peggy Dow *(Carrie Turner);* Robert Keith *(Thomas Greer);* Mildred Dunnock *(Sarah Greer);* Ray Collins *(Judge Turner);* Martin Milner *(George Kress, Jr.);* Jim Backus *(Harvey Landrum);* Marjorie Crossland *(Mrs. Turner);* Walter Baldwin *(George Kress, Sr.);* Walter Sande *(Ned Iverson);* Peggy Maley *(Gladys);* Jerrilyn Flannery *(Anne Greer);* Erik Nielsen *(Tony Greer);* Ann Robin *(Gloria);* Carol Savage *(Caroline Krupka);* James Adamson *(Train Porter);* Harry Lauter *(Art Stacey);* Robert Johnson *(Porter);* David McMahon *(Taxi Driver);* Melodi Lowell *(Girl);* Frank Sully *(Bartender);* Jimmy Ogg *(Soldier);* Jean Andren *(Secretary);* Charles Marsh *(Mr. Jones);* Don Hayden *(Another Candidate);* Dee Carroll *(Woman);* Lee Turnbull *(Fat Boy);* Ralph Brooks *(Albert);* Roland Morris *(Sergeant);* Al Murphy *(Man).*

ASSIGNMENT—PARIS
(Columbia, 1952) 85 min.

PRODUCERS: Samuel Marx and Jerry Bresler
DIRECTOR: Robert Parrish
BASED ON THE BOOK *Trial by Terror* BY PAUL GALLICO
SCREENPLAY: William Bowers
ADAPTORS: Walter Boretz, Jack Palmer White
ART DIRECTOR: John Meehan
MUSIC DIRECTOR: Morris Stoloff
MUSIC: George Dunning
CAMERA: Burnett Guffey, Ray Corey
EDITOR: Charles Nelson

Dana Andrews *(Jimmy Race);* Marta Toren *(Jeanne);* George Sanders *(Nick Strang);* Audrey Totter *(Sandy Tate);* Sandro Giglio *(Grischa);* Donald Randolph *(Anton Borvitch);* Herbert Berghof *(Andreas Ordy);* Ben Astar *(Vajos);* Willis Bouchey *(Biddle);* Earl Lee *(Dan Pelham);* Maurice Doner *(Victor);* Leon Askin *(Franz);* Paul Hoffman *(Kedor);* Jay Adler *(Henry);* Peter Votrian *(Jan);* Georgianna Wulff *(Gogo);* Don Gibson *(Male Phone Operator);* Mari Blanchard *(Wanda Marlowe);* Joe Forte *(Barker);* Hanne Axman *(Secretary);* Paul Javor *(Laslo Boros);* Victor Sutherland *(Larry);* Andre Simeon *(Waiter);* Fay Roope *(American Ambassador);* Harold Stiller *(American Sergeant);* Vito Scotti *(Italian Reporter);* Gene Gary *(Man Receptionist);* Ken Terrell *(Military Aide).*

ELEPHANT WALK
(Paramount, 1954) C-103 min.

PRODUCER: Irving Asher
DIRECTOR: William Dieterle
BASED ON THE NOVEL BY ROBERT STANDISH
SCREENPLAY: John Lee Mahin
ART DIRECTORS: Hal Pereira, Joseph MacMillan Johnson
CHOREOGRAPHY: Ram Gopal
MUSIC: Franz Waxman
TECHNICOLOR CONSULTANT: Richard Mueller
ASSISTANT DIRECTOR: Francisco Day
CAMERA: Loyal Griggs
EDITOR: George Tomasini

Elizabeth Taylor *(Ruth Wiley);* Dana Andrews *(Dick Carver);* Peter Finch *(John Wiley);* Abraham Sofaer *(Appuhamy);* Noel Drayton *(Atkinson the Planter);* Abner Biberman *(Dr. Pereira);* Rosalind Ivan *(Mrs. Lakin);* Barry Bernard *(Strawson the Planter);* Philip Tonge *(Ralph the Planter);* Edward Ashley *(Gregory the Planter);* Leo Britt *(Chisholm the Planter);* Mylee Haulani *(Rayna);* Jack Raine *(Norbert the Planter);* Victor Millan *(Koru the Servant);* Norma Varden *(Mrs. Beezeley);* Carlos Rivero *(Car Servant);* Delmar Costello *(Native Patient);* Satini Pualioa *(Foreman);* Vivien Leigh *(Ruth Wiley—Ceylon Long Shots);* Madhyma Lanka Mandala Dancers *(Themselves).*

DUEL IN THE JUNGLE
(Warner Bros., 1954) C-102 min.

PRODUCERS: Martin Hellman, Tony Owen
DIRECTOR: George Marshall
SCREENPLAY: Sam Marx, T. J. Morrison
ART DIRECTOR: Terence Verity
MUSIC: Mischa Spoliansky
SONG: Spoliansky and Norman Newell
MUSIC DIRECTOR: Louis Levy
DIALOGUE DIRECTOR: David Farrar
TECHNICAL ADVISOR: Cris Jammins
SOUND: Harold V. King
CAMERA: Edwin Hiller
EDITOR: E. B. Jarvis

Dana Andrews *(Scott Walters);* Jeanne Crain *(Marian Taylor);* David Farrar *(Perry and Arthur Henderson);* Patrick Barr *(Superintendent Roberts);* George Coulouris *(Captain Malburn);* Charles Goldner *(Martel);* Wilfrid Hyde-White *(Pitt);* Mary Merrall *(Mrs. Henderson);* Heather Thatcher *(Lady on the Nigeria);* Michael Mataka *(Vincent);* Paul Carpenter *(Clerk);* and Mary Mackenzie *(Secretary);* and Bee Duffell, Alec Finter, Patrick Parnell, Bill Shine, Robert Sansom, Delphi Lawrence, Simone Silva.

THREE HOURS TO KILL
(Columbia, 1954) C-77 min.

PRODUCER: Harry Joe Brown
ASSISTANT PRODUCER: David Breen
DIRECTOR: Alfred Werker
STORY: Alex Gottlieb
SCREENPLAY: Richard Alan Simmons, Roy Huggins
ART DIRECTOR: George Brooks
MUSIC: Paul Sawtell
ASSISTANT DIRECTOR: Sam Nelson
CAMERA: Charles Lawton, Jr.

Dana Andrews *(Jim Guthrie);* Donna Reed *(Laurie Mastin);* Dianne Foster *(Chris Plumber);* Stephen Elliott *(Ben East);* Richard Coogan *(Niles Hendricks);* Laurence Hugo *(Marty Lasswell);* James Westerfield *(Sam Minor);* Richard Webb *(Carter Mastin);* Carolyn Jones *(Polly);* Charlotte Fletcher *(Betty);* Whit Bissell *(Deke);* Felipe Turich *(Esteban);* Arthur Fox *(Little Carter);* Francis McDonald *(Vince);* Frank Hagney *(Cass);* Paul E. Burns *(Albert);* Julian Rivero *(Dominguez);* Robert A. Paquin *(Storekeeper);* Elsie Baker *(Woman);* Reed Howes, Ada Adams *(Bits);* Edward Earle *(Rancher);* Buddy Roosevelt *(Drunk);* Hank Mann *(Man).*

SMOKE SIGNAL
(Universal, 1955) C-88 min.

PRODUCER: Howard Christie
DIRECTOR: Jerry Hopper
STORY/SCREENPLAY: George F. Slavin, George W. George
ART DIRECTORS: Alexander Golitzen, Richard H. Riedel
MUSIC DIRECTOR: Joseph Gershenson
ASSISTANT DIRECTORS: Joseph E. Kenny, Gordon McLean
COSTUMES: Bill Thomas
CAMERA: Clifford Stine
EDITORS: Milton Carruth, Eddie Broussard

Dana Andrews *(Brett Halliday);* Piper Laurie *(Laura Evans);* Rex Reason *(Lieutenant Ford);* William Talman *(Captain Harper);* Gordon Jones *(Rogers);* Milburn Stone *(Miles);* Douglas Spencer *(Garode);* William Schallert *(Livingston);* Bill Phipps *(Porter);* Bob Wilkie *(Daly);* Pat Hogan *(Delche);* Peter Coe *(Ute Prisoner).*

STRANGE LADY IN TOWN
(Warner Bros., 1955) C-117 min.

Producer/Director: Mervyn LeRoy
Story/Screenplay: Frank Butler
Art Director: Gabriel Scognamillo
Assistant Directors: Russ Saunders, William Kissel
Music Director: Dmitri Tiomkin
Song: Tiomkin and Ned Washington
Choreography: Peggy Carroll
Costumes: Emile Santiago
Camera: Harold Rosson
Editor: Folmar Blangsted

Greer Garson *(Julia Garth);* Dana Andrews *(Rork O'Brien);* Cameron Mitchell *(David Garth);* Lois Smith *(Spurs);* Walter Hampden *(Father Gabriel Mendoza);* Gregory Walcott *(Scanlon);* Douglas Kennedy *(Slade Wickstrom);* Pedro Gonzalez-Gonzalez *(Trooper Martinez-Martinez);* Frank De Kova *(Anse Hatlo);* Jose Torvay *(Bartolo Diaz);* Bob Wilke *(Karg);* Russell Johnson *(Shadduck);* Joan Camden *(Norah Muldoon);* Jack Williams *(Ribstock);* Anthony Numkena [*Earl Holliman*] *(Tomasito Diaz);* Joey Costarello *(Alfredo);* Nick Adams *(Billy the Kid);* Bob Foulk *(Joe);* Adele Jergens *(Belle Brown);* Jose Gonzalez-Gonzalez *(Jose);* Jose Lopez *(Pueblo Indian);* Louise Lorimer *(Mrs. Wallace);* Ralph Moody *(General Wallace);* Helen Spring *(Mrs. Harker);* Joe Hamilton *(Mr. Harker);* George Wallace *(Curley);* Marshall Bradford *(Sheriff);* Antonio Triana, Luisa Triana *(Flamenco Dancers).*

COMANCHE
(United Artists, 1956) C-87 min.

Producer: Carl Krueger
Associate Producer: Henry Spitz
Director: George Sherman
Screenplay: Carl Krueger
Music Director: Herschel Burke Gilbert
Camera: Jorge Stahl, Jr.
Editor: Charles L. Kimball

Dana Andrews *(Reed);* Kent Smith *(Quanah Parker);* Linda Cristal *(Margarita);* Nestor Paiva *(Puffer);* Henry Brandon *(Black Cloud);* John Litel *(General Nelson A. Miles);* Reed Sherman *(French);* Stacy Harris *(Downey);* Lowell Gilmore *(Ward);* Mike Mazurki *(Flat Mouth).*

WHILE THE CITY SLEEPS
(RKO, 1956) 100 min.

Producer: Bert E. Friedlob
Director: Fritz Lang
Based on the novel *The Bloody Spur* by Charles Einstein
Screenplay: Casey Robinson
Art Director: Carroll Clark
Set Decorator: Jack Mills
Costumes: Norma
Music: Herschel Burke Gilbert
Assistant Director: Ronnie Rondell
Camera: Ernest Laszlo
Editor: Gene Fowler, Jr.

Dana Andrews *(Edward Mobley);* Rhonda Fleming *(Dorothy Kyne);* Sally Forrest *(Nancy Liggett);* Thomas Mitchell *(Griffith);* Vincent Price *(Walter Kyne, Jr.);* Howard Duff *(Lieutenant Kaufman);* Ida Lupino *(Mildred);* George Sanders *(Mark Loving);* James Craig *(Harry Kritzer);* John Barrymore, Jr. *(Robert Manners);* Vladimir Sokoloff *(George Palsky);* Robert Warwick *(Amos Kyne);* Ralph Peters *(Meade);* Larry Blake *(Police Sergeant);* Edward Hinton *(O'Leary);* Mae Marsh *(Mrs. Manners);* Sandy White *(Judith Fenton);* Celia Lovsky *(Miss Dodd);* Pitt Herbert *(Bartender);* Andrew Lupino *(Bit);* David Andrews *(Bar Pianist).*

BEYOND A REASONABLE DOUBT
(RKO, 1956) 80 min.

Producer: Bert E. Friedlob
Director: Fritz Lang
Story/Screenplay: Douglas Morrow
Art Director: Carroll Clark
Set Decorator: Darrell Silvera
Music: Herschel Burke Gilbert
Song: Gilbert and Alfred Perry
Assistant Director: Maxwell Henry
Camera: William Snyder
Editor: Gene Fowler, Jr.

Dana Andrews *(Tom Garrett);* Joan Fontaine *(Susan Spencer);* Sidney Blackmer *(Austin Spencer);* Philip Bourneuf *(District Attorney Roy Thompson);* Shepperd Strudwick *(Jonathan Wilson);* Arthur Franz *(Bob Hale);* Edward Binns *(Lieutenant Kennedy);* Barbara Nichols *(Dolly Moore);* Robin Raymond *(Terry LaRue);* William Leicester [*Lester*] *(Charles Miller);* Dan Seymour *(Greco);* Rusty Lane *(Judge);* Joyce Taylor *(Joan Williams);* Carleton Young *(Alan Kirk);* Trudy Wroe *(Hatcheck Girl);* Joe Kirk *(Clerk);* Charles Evans *(Governor);* Dorothy Ford *(Blonde);* Joey Ray *(Eddie);* Larry Barton *(Customer);* Frank Mitchell *(Waiter at Burlesque House);* Billy Reed *(M.C.);* Carl Sklover *(Cab Driver);* Phil Barnes *(Policeman);* Baynes Barron *(John Higgens, the Fingerprint Man);* Jeffrey Sayre *(Jury Foreman);* Hal Taggert *(Court Clerk);* Bob Whitney *(Bailiff);* Wendell Niles *(Announcer);* Franklyn Farnum *(Spectator at Electrocution).*

SPRING REUNION
(United Artists, 1957) 79 min.

Producer: Jerry Bresler
Director: Robert Pirosh
Based on a story by Robert Alan Authur
Screenplay: Pirosh, Elick Moll
Music: Herbert Spencer, Earle Ugen
Song: Johnny Mercer and Harry Warren
Choreography: Sylvia Lewis
Assistant Director: John Burch
Camera: Harold Lipsteen

Dana Andrews *(Fred Davis);* Betty Hutton *(Maggie Brewster);* Jean Hagen *(Barna Forrest);* Sara Burner *(Paula Kratz);* Robert Simon *(Harry Brewster);* Laura LaPlante *(May Brewster);* Gordon Jones *(Jack Frazer);* James Gleason *(Mr. Collyer);* Irene Ryan *(Miss Stapleton);* Richard Shannon *(Nick);* Ken Curtis *(Al);* Herbert Anderson *(Edward);* Richard Benedict *(Jim);* Vivi Janiss *(Grace);* Florence Sundstrom *(Mary);* Shirley Mitchell *(Receptionist);* Richard Deacon *(Sidney);* Mimi Doyle *(Alice);* Sid Tomack *(Caterer);* George Chandler *(Zimmie);* Dorothy Neumann *(Roseanne);* Barbara Drew *(Verna);* Don Haggerty *(Pete);* Leon Tyler *(Teenager in Car).*

ZERO HOUR!
(Paramount, 1957) 81 min.

Producer: John C. Champion
Director: Hall Bartlett
Based on the teleplay by Arthur Hailey
Screenplay: Hailey, Bartlett
Assistant Director: Lee Lukather
Music: Ted Dale
Camera: John F. Warren
Editor: John C. Fuller

Dana Andrews *(Ted Stryker);* Linda Darnell *(Ellen Stryker);* Sterling Hayden *(Treleaven);* Elroy "Crazylegs" Hirsch *(Captain Wilson);* Geoffrey Toone *(Dr. Baird);* Jerry Paris *(Tony Decker);* Peggy King *(Stewardess);* Carole Eden *(Mrs. Wilson);* Charles Quinlivan *(Burdick);* Raymond Ferrell *(Joey Stryker);* David Thursby *(Whitmond);* Russell Thorsen *(Flight Dispatcher);* Richard Keith *(Station Manager);* Steve London *(Co-Pilot Stewart);* Willis Bouchey *(RCAF Doctor).*

CURSE OF THE DEMON
(Columbia, 1957) 95 min.
(a.k.a. NIGHT OF THE DEMON)

Producer: Hal E. Chester
Director: Jacques Tourneur
Based on the story "Casting the Runes" by Montague R. James
Screenplay: Charles Bennett, Chester
Production Designer: Ken Adam
Assistant Art Director: Peter Glazier
Music: Clifton Parker
Music Director: Muir Mathieson
Sound: Arthur Bradburn
Special Effects: George Blackwell, Wally Veevers
Camera: Ted Scaife
Editor: Michael Gordon.

Dana Andrews *(John Holden);* Peggy Cummins *(Joanna Harrington);* Niall MacGinnis *(Dr. Karswell);* Maurice Denham *(Professor Harrington);* Athene Seyler *(Mrs. Karswell);* Lian Redmond *(Mark O'Brien);* Reginald Beckwith *(Mr. Meek);* Ewan Roberts *(Lloyd Williamson);* Peter Elliot *(Kumar);* Rosamund Greenwood *(Mrs. Meek);* Brian Wilde *(Rand Hobart);* Richard Leech *(Inspector Mottram);* Lloyd Lamble *(Detective Simmons);* Lynn Tracy *(Air Hostess);* Janet Barrow *(Mrs. Hobart);* John Salew *(Librarian);* Charles Lloyd-Pack *(Chemist);* Peter Hobbes *(Superintendent).*

THE FEARMAKERS
(United Artists, 1958) 83 min.

Producer: Martin H. Lancer
Associate Producer: Leon Chooluck

DIRECTOR: Jacques Tourneur
BASED ON THE NOVEL BY DARWIN L. TEILHET
SCREENPLAY: Elliott West, Chris Appley
ART DIRECTOR: Serge Krizman
MUSIC: Irving Gertz
SOUND: John Kean
CAMERA: Sam Leavitt
EDITOR: J. R. Whittredge

Dana Andrews *(Alan Eaton);* Dick Foran *(Jim McGinnis);* Mel Torme *(Barney Bond);* Marilee Earle *(Lorraine Dennis);* Veda Ann Borg *(Vivian Loder);* Kelly Thordsen *(Harold Loder);* Robert Fortier *(Colonel Buchane);* Roy Gordon *(Senator Walder);* Joel Marston *(Rodney Hillyer).*

ENCHANTED ISLAND
(Warner Bros., 1958) C-94 min.

PRODUCER: Benedict Bogeaus
DIRECTOR: Allan Dwan
BASED ON THE NOVEL *Typee* BY HERMAN MELVILLE
SCREENPLAY: James Leicester, Harold Jacob Smith
MUSIC: Raul LaVista
SONG: Robert Allen
ART DIRECTOR: Hal Wilson Cox
ASSISTANT DIRECTOR: Nacio Real
WARDROBE: Georgette
MAKEUP: Burris Grimwood
SOUND: Weldon Coe
SPECIAL CAMERA EFFECTS: Albert M. Simpson
SPECIAL EFFECTS: Lee Zavitz
CAMERA: George Stahl
EDITOR: Leicester

Dana Andrews *(Abner Bedford);* Jane Powell *(Fayaway);* Don Dubbins *(Tom);* Arthur Shields *(Jimmy Dooley);* Ted DeCorsia *(Captain Vangs);* Friedrich Ledebur *(Chief Mehevi);* Augustin Fernandez *(Kory Kory);* Francisco Reiguera *(Medicine Man);* Les Hellman *(First Mate Moore).*

THE CROWDED SKY
(Warner Bros., 1960) C-105 min.

PRODUCER: Michael Garrison
DIRECTOR: Joseph Pevney
BASED ON THE NOVEL BY HANK SEARLS
SCREENPLAY: Charles Schnee
MAKEUP: Gordon Bau
MUSIC: Leonard Rosenman
ASSISTANT DIRECTOR: Chuck Hansen
COSTUMES: Howard Shoup
TECHNICAL ADVISOR: Paul Mantz
ART DIRECTOR: Eddie Imazu
SET DECORATOR: William L. Kuehl
SOUND: M. A. Merrick
CAMERA: Harry Stradling, Jr.
EDITOR: Tom McAdoo

Dana Andrews *(Dick Barnett);* Rhonda Fleming *(Cheryl Heath);* Efrem Zimbalist, Jr. *(Dale Heath);* John Kerr *(Mike Rule);* Anne Francis *(Kitty Foster);* Keenan Wynn *(Nick Highland);* Troy Donahue *(McVey);* Patsy Kelly *(Gertrude Ross);* Joe Mantell *(Louie Capelli);* Donald May *(Norm Coster);* Louis Quinn *(Norm Coster);* Mary Patton *(Pat Benedict);* Warren Parker *(Dr. Ed Benedict);* Edward Kemmer *(Caesar);* Jean Willes *(Gloria Panawek);* Tom Gilson *(Rob Fermi);* Hollis Irving *(Beatrice Wiley);* Paul Genge *(Samuel N. Poole);* Saundra Edwards *(Didi);* Nan Leslie *(Bev);* Frieda Inescourt *(Mrs. Mitchell);* Karen Green *(Anne);* Ken Currie *(Dick, Jr.);* Dave Alpert *(Mel);* Ed Prentiss *(J.B.);* Mary Benoit *(Nurse);* Theodore Eccles *(Dick, Jr. at Age Four);* Jimmy Martin *(Dick, Jr. at Age Seven);* S. John Launer *(Police Captain);* Jane Crowley *(Mrs. Z.);* John Garrett *(Lieutenant Commander).*

MADISON AVENUE
(20th Century-Fox, 1962) 94 min.

PRODUCER/DIRECTOR: Bruce Humberstone
BASED ON THE NOVEL *The Build-Up Boys* BY JEREMY KIRK
SCREENPLAY: Norman Corwin
MUSIC/MUSIC DIRECTOR: Harry Sukman
SONG: Harry Harris
ORCHESTRATORS: Leo Shuken, Jack Hayes
ART DIRECTORS: Duncan Cramer, Leland Fuller
SET DECORATORS: Walter M. Scott, John Sturtevant
MAKEUP: Ben Nye
SOUND: Donald McKay, Warren B. Delaplain
CAMERA: Charles G. Clarke
EDITOR: Betty Steinberg

Dana Andrews *(Clint Lorimer);* Eleanor Parker *(Anne Tremaine);* Jeanne Crain *(Peggy Shannon);* Eddie Albert *(Harvey Ames);* Howard St. John *(T. C. Jocelyn);* Henry Daniell *(Stipe);* Kathleen Freeman *(Miss Haley);* David White *(Brock);* Betti Andrews *(Miss Katie Olsen);* Jack Orrison *(Mayor of Bellefield);* Yvonne Peattie *(Miss Mulloy);* Arlene Hunter *(Miss Horn);* Doris Fesette *(Blonde);* Grady Sutton *(Dilbock);* Leon Alton *(Maitre d').*

CRACK IN THE WORLD
(Paramount, 1965) C-96 min.

PRODUCERS: Bernard Glasser, Lester A. Sansom
DIRECTOR: Andrew Marton
STORY: Jon Manchip White
SCREENPLAY: White, Julian Harvey
ART DIRECTOR: Eugene Lourie
MUSIC: John Douglas
COSTUMES: Laure De Zarate
SOUND: Kurt Hernfeld
SPECIAL EFFECTS: Alec Weldon
CAMERA: Manuel Berenguer
EDITOR: Derek Parsons

Dana Andrews *(Dr. Stephen Sorensen);* Janette Scott *(Mrs. Maggie Sorensen);* Kieron Moore *(Ted Rampion);* Alexander Knox *(Sir Charles Eggerston);* Peter Damon *(Masefield);* Gary Lasdun *(Markov);* Mike Steen *(Steele);* Todd Martin *(Simpson);* Jim Gillen *(Rand).*

THE SATAN BUG
(United Artists, 1965) C-113 min.

PRODUCER/DIRECTOR: John Sturges
BASED ON THE NOVEL BY IAN STUART [ALISTAIR MACLEAN]
SCREENPLAY: James Clavell, Edward Anhalt
ASSISTANT DIRECTOR: Jack Reddish
ART DIRECTOR: Herman Blumenthal
SET DECORATOR: Chuck Vassar
MUSIC/MUSIC DIRECTOR: Jerry Goldsmith
SOUND: Harold Lewis
SPECIAL EFFECTS: Paul Pollard
CAMERA: Robert Surtees
EDITOR: Ferris Webster

George Maharis *(Lee Barrett);* Richard Basehart *(Dr. Hoffman);* Anne Francis *(Ann);* Dana Andrews *(General);* Edward Asner *(Veretti);* Frank Sutton *(Donald);* John Larkin *(Michaelson);* Richard Bull *(Cavanaugh);* Martin Blaine *(Martin);* John Anderson *(Reagan);* Russ Bender *(Mason);* Simon Oakland *(Tesserly);* Hari Rhodes *(Johnson);* John Clare *(Raskin);* Henry Beckman *(Dr. Baxter);* Harold Gould *(Dr. Ostrer);* James Hong *(Dr. Yang).*

IN HARM'S WAY
(Paramount, 1965) 167 min.

PRODUCER/DIRECTOR: Otto Preminger
BASED ON THE NOVEL BY JAMES BASSETT
SCREENPLAY: Wendell Mayes
ASSISTANT DIRECTORS: Daniel McCauley, Howard Joslin, Michael Daves
PRODUCTION DESIGNER: Lyle Wheeler
ASSOCIATE ART DIRECTOR: Al Roelofs
SET DECORATORS: Morris Hoffman, Richard Mansfield
MUSIC: Jerry Goldsmith
TITLES: Saul Bass
SOUND: Harold Lewis, Charles Grenzbach
SPECIAL EFFECTS: Farciot Edouart
CAMERA: Loyal Griggs
SECOND UNIT CAMERA: Philip Lathrop
EDITORS: George Tomasini, Hugh S. Fowler

John Wayne *(Captain Rockwell Torrey);* Kirk Douglas *(Commander Paul Eddington);* Patricia Neal *(Maggie);* Tom Tryon *(Lieutenant William McConnel);* Paula Prentiss *(Bev McConnell);* Brandon de Wilde *(Jeremiah Torrey);* Jill Haworth *(Annalee);* Dana Andrews *(Admiral Broderick);* Stanley Holloway *(Clayton Canfil);* Burgess Meredith *(Commander Egan Powell);* Franchot Tone *(Cincpac I Admiral);* Henry Fonda *(Cincpac II Admiral);* Patrick O'Neal *(Commander Neal Owynn);* Carroll O'Connor *(Lieutenant Commander Burke);* Slim Pickens *(C.P.O. Culpepper);* James Mitchum *(Ensign Griggs);* George Kennedy *(Colonel Gregory);* Bruce Cabot *(Quartermaster Quoddy);* Barbara Bouchet *(Liz Eddington);* Tod Andrews *(Captain Tuthill);* Larry Hagman *(Lieutenant Cline);* Stewart Moss *(Ensign Balch);* Richard Le Pore *(Lieutenant Tom Agar);* Chet Stratton *(Ship's Doctor);* Soo Young *(Tearful Woman);* Dort Clark *(Boston);* Phil Mattingly *(PT-Boat Skipper);* Hugh O'Brian *(Air Force Major).*

BRAINSTORM
(Warner Bros., 1965) 110 min.

PRODUCER/DIRECTOR: William Conrad
STORY: Larry Marcus
SCREENPLAY: Mann Rubin
ART DIRECTOR: Robert Smith
SET DECORATOR: Hoyle Barrett
MUSIC: George Duning
SOUND: M. A. Merrick
CAMERA: Sam Leavitt
EDITOR: William Ziegler

Jeffrey Hunter *(James Grayam);* Anne Francis *(Lorrie Benson);* Dana Andrews *(Cort Benson);* Viveca Lindfors *(Dr. Elizabeth Larstedt);* Stacy Harris *(Josh Reynolds);* Kathie Browne *(Angie DeWitt);* Phillip Pine *(Dr. Ames);* Michael Pate *(Dr. Mills);* Joan Swift *(Clara);* George Pelling *(Butler);* Victoria Meyerink *(Julie);* Strother Martin *(Clyde);* Steven Roberts *(Judge);* Pat Cardi *(Bobby);* Robert McQueeney *(Sergeant Dawes);* Pamelyn Ferdin *(Little Girl in Lobby);* Barbara Dodd, George Neise, Wendy Russell, James O'Hara, Eleaina Martone *(Party Guests);* James Seay *(Judge at Scavenger Hunt);* Lloyd Kino *(Mr. Komato);* Suzanne Benoit *(Nurse);* Steve Ihnat *(Interne);* Victor Rodman, Roberto Contreras, John Mitchum *(Inmates);* Richard Kiel *(Giant Inmate);* William Quinn *(Psychiatrist);* Will Duffy, Don Chaffin *(Orderlies).*

TOWN TAMER
(Paramount, 1965) C-89 min.

PRODUCER: A. C. Lyles
DIRECTOR: Lesley Selander
BASED ON THE NOVEL BY FRANK GRUBER
SCREENPLAY: Gruber
ASSISTANT DIRECTOR: Howard Roessel
ART DIRECTORS: Hal Pereira, Al Roelofs
SET DECORATOR: Claude Carpenter
MUSIC: Jimmie Haskell
SONG: Haskell and By Dunham
SOUND: Hugo Grenzbach
CAMERA: W. Wallace Kelley
EDITOR: George Gittens

Dana Andrews *(Tom Rosser);* Terry Moore *(Susan Tavenner);* Bruce Cabot *(Riley Condor);* Lyle Bettger *(Lee Ring);* Lon Chaney, Jr. *(Leach);* Barton MacLane *(James Fennimore Fell);* Richard Arlen *(Dr. Kent);* DeForest Kelley *(Guy Tavenner);* Richard Jaeckel *(Honsinger);* Coleen Gray *(Carol Rosser);* Pat O'Brien *(Judge Murcott);* Philip Carey *(Slim Akins);* Sonny Tufts *(Carmichael);* Roger Torrey *(Flon);* James Brown *(Davis);* Richard Webb *(Kevin);* Jeanne Cagney *(Mary);* Don Barry, Robert Ivers *(Texans);* Bob Steele *(Ken, a Vigilante).*

THE LOVED ONE
(MGM, 1965) 119 min.

EXECUTIVE PRODUCER: Martin Ransohoff
PRODUCERS: John Calley, Haskell Wexler
ASSOCIATE PRODUCER: Neil Hartley
DIRECTOR: Tony Richardson
BASED ON THE NOVEL BY EVELYN WAUGH
SCREENPLAY: Terry Southern, Christopher Isherwood
PRODUCTION DESIGNER/COSTUMES: Rouben Terarutunian
SET DECORATOR: Jim Payne
MAKE-UP SUPERVISOR: Emil La Vigne
MUSIC/MUSIC DIRECTOR: John Addison
SOUND: Stan Fiferman
SPECIAL EFFECTS: G. G. Gaspar
CAMERA: Wexler
SUPERVISING EDITOR: Anthony Gibbs
EDITORS: Hal Ashby, Brian Smedley-Aston

Robert Morse *(Dennis Barlow);* Jonathan Winters *(Wilbur Glenworthy/Harry Glenworthy);* Anjanette Comer *(Aimee Thanatogenos);* Rod Steiger *(Mr. Joyboy);* Dana Andrews *(General Brinkman);* Milton Berle *(Mr. Kenton);* James Coburn *(Immigration Officer);* John Gielgud *(Sir Francis Hinsley);* Tab Hunter *(Guide);* Margaret Leighton *(Mrs. Kenton);* Liberace *(Mr. Starker);* Roddy McDowall *(D.J., Jr.);* Robert Morley *(Sir Ambrose Abercrombie);* Lionel Stander *(Guru Brahmin);* Ayllene Gibbons *(Joyboy's Mother);* Bernie Kopell *(Assistant to the Guru Brahmin);* Asa Maynor *(Secretary to D.J., Jr.);* Alan Napier *(English Club Official).*

BATTLE OF THE BULGE
(Warner Bros., 1965) C-167 min.

PRODUCERS: Milton Sperling, Philip Yordan
DIRECTOR: Ken Annakin
SCREENPLAY: Yordan, Sperling, John Melson
ASSISTANT DIRECTORS: Jose Lopez Rodero, Martin Sacristan, Luis Garcia
ART DIRECTOR: Eugene Lourié
MUSIC/MUSIC DIRECTOR: Benjamin Frankel
SONG: Frankel and Kurt Wiehle
COSTUMES: Laure De Zarate
SOUND: Kurt Herrnfeld, Alban Streeter
TECHNICAL ADVISORS: General Meinrad von Lauchert, Colonel Sherman Joffe, Major Edward King
SPECIAL EFFECTS: Alex Weldon
CAMERA: Jack Hildyard
SECOND UNIT CAMERA: John Cabrera
AERIAL CAMERA: Jack Willoughby
EDITOR: Derek Parsons

Henry Fonda *(Lieutenant Colonel Kiley);* Robert Shaw *(Colonel Hessler);* Robert Ryan *(General Grey);* Dana Andrews *(Colonel Pritchard);* George Montgomery *(Sergeant Duquesne);* Ty Hardin *(Schumacher);* Pier Angeli *(Louise);* Barbara Werle *(Elena);* Charles Bronson *(Major Wolenski);* Werner Peters *(General Kohler);* Hans Christian Blech *(Conrad);* James MacArthur *(Lieutenant Weaver);* Telly Savalas *(Guffy);* Steve Rowland, Karl Alberty *(Bits).*

JOHNNY RENO
(Paramount, 1966) C-83 min.

PRODUCER: A. C. Lyles
DIRECTOR: R. G. Springsteen
STORY/SCREENPLAY: Steve Fisher
ASSISTANT DIRECTOR: Jim Rosenberger
ART DIRECTORS: Hal Pereira, Malcolm Brown
SET DECORATORS: Robert Benton, Jerry Welch
MUSIC: Jimmie Haskell
SONG: Haskell and By Dunham
SOUND: Harold Lewis, John H. Wilkinson
CAMERA: Hal Stine
EDITOR: Bernard Matis

Dana Andrews *(Johnny Reno);* Jane Russell *(Nona Williams);* Lon Chaney, Jr. *(Sheriff Hodges);* John Agar *(Ed Tomkins);* Lyle Bettger *(Jess Yates);* Tom Drake *(Joe Connors);* Richard Arlen *(Ned Duggan);* Robert Lowery *(Jake Reed);* Tracy Olsen *(Maria Yates);* Paul Daniel *(Chief Little Bear);* Dale Van Sickel *(Ab Connors);* Reg Parton (Bartender); Rodd Redwing *(Indian);* Charles Horvath *(Wooster);* Chuck Hicks *(Bellows);* Edmund Cobb *(Townsman).*

BERLINO, APPUNTAMENTO PER LE SPIE
(SPY IN YOUR EYE)
(American International, 1966)
C-88 min.

PRODUCERS: Fulvio Lucisano, Luciano Marcuzzo
DIRECTOR: Vittoria Sala
SCREENPLAY: Romano Ferraro, Adriano Baracco, Adriano Bolzoni
ASSISTANT DIRECTOR: Stefano Rolla
MUSIC: Riz Ortolani
CAMERA: Fausto Zuccoli
EDITOR: Robert and Renato Cinquini

Brett Halsey *(Bert Morris);* Pier Angeli *(Paula Krauss);* Dana Andrews *(Colonel Lancaster);* Gaston Moschin *(Boris);* and: Tania Beryl, Mario Valdemarin, Aldo de Francesco, Marco Origlielmi, Alessandro Sperli, Tino Bianchi, Renato Baldini, Luciana Angiolillo.

SUPERCOLPO DA 7 MILIARDI
(THE TEN MILLION DOLLAR GRAB)
(Italian, 1966) C-105 min.

DIRECTOR/STORY/SCREENPLAY: Bitte Albertini
MUSIC: Nico Fidence
CAMERA: Emilio Varriane
EDITOR: Jolanda Benvenuti

Brad Harris *(Robert Colman);* Elina De Witt *(Gaby);* Dana Andrews *(George Kimmins);* and: Franco Andrei, Nando Pozzi, Gilberto Galimberti, Marisa Traversi, Arrigo Peri, Antonio Corevi, Giuseppe Leghissa, Danilo Turk.

I DIAMANTI CHE NESSUNO VOLEVA RUBARE
(THE DIAMONDS NOBODY WANTED TO STEAL/NO DIAMONDS FOR URSULA)
(Italian, 1966) C-85 min.

Director:	Gino Mangini
Story:	Sergio Pisani
Screenplay:	Pisani, Hannes Schmidhauser, Fiorella Ricciardello, Mangini
Music:	Carlo Rustichelli
Camera:	Angelo Filippini

Jeanne Valerie *(Ursula);* Salvo Randone *(Spiros);* Dana Andrews *(Maurizio);* John Elliot *(Giorgio);* Kathy Baron *(Maurizio's Wife);* Aldo Giuffre *(Fangio);* Mario Brega *(Samson);* and: Dan Harrison, Roger Beaumont, Giovanni Petrucci-Aimo, Lili Mantovani.

HOT RODS TO HELL
(MGM, 1967) C-92 min.

Producer:	Sam Katzman
Director:	John Brahm
Story:	Alex Gaby
Screenplay:	Robert E. Kent
Music:	Fred Karger
Camera:	Lloyd Ahern
Editor:	Ben Lewis

Dana Andrews *(Tom Phillips);* Jeanne Crain *(Peg Phillips);* Mimsy Farmer *(Gloria);* Laurie Mock *(Tina Phillips);* Paul Bertoya *(Duke);* Gene Kirkwood *(Ernie);* Tim Stafford *(Jamie Phillips);* Hortense Petra *(Wife at Picnic);* William Mims *(Man at Picnic);* Paul Genge *(Policeman);* Peter Oliphant *(Little Boy);* Harry Hickox *(Bill Phillips);* Charles P. Thompson *(Charlie);* Jim Hennagan *(Youth);* Mickey Rooney, Jr. *(Combo Leader).*

THE FROZEN DEAD
(Warner Bros.-Seven Arts, 1967) C-95 min.

Executive Producer:	Robert Goldstein
Producer/Director/Screenplay:	Herbert J. Leder
Art Director:	Scott MacGregor
Camera:	David Bolton
Editor:	Tom Simpson

Dana Andrews *(Dr. Norberg);* Anna Palk *(Jean);* Philip Gilbert *(Dr. Ted Roberts);* Karel Stepanek *(General Lubeck);* Kathleen Breck *(Elsa);* Alan Tilvern *(Karl Essen);* Tom Chatto *(Police Inspector Witt);* Basil Henson *(Captain Tirpitz);* Oliver MacGreevy *(Joseph).*

IL COBRA (COBRA)
(American International, 1968) C-93 min.

Producer:	Fulvio Lucisano
Director:	Mario Sequi
Story:	Adriano Bolzoni
Screenplay:	Cumersindo Mollo
Assistant Director:	Stefano Rolla
Music:	Jose Antonio Abril
Camera:	Enrique Toran

Dana Andrews *(Chief Kelly);* Peter Martell *(Mike Rand);* Anita Ekberg *(Lou);* Elisa Montes *(Corinne);* Jesus Puente *(Stiarkos);* Peter Dane *(Hullinger);* Luciana Vincenzi *(Ulla);* George Histman *(Crane);* Omar Zolficar *(Sadek);* Giovanni Petrucci *(King);* Chang'e *(Li Fang);* Ehsane Sadek *(Gamal).*

THE DEVIL'S BRIGADE
(United Artists, 1968) C-131 min.

Producer:	David L. Wolper;
Associate Producers:	Theodore Strauss, Julian Ludwig
Director:	Andrew V. McLaglen
Based on the book by Robert H. Anderson and Colonel George Walton	
Screenplay:	William Roberts
Music/Music Director:	Alex North
Orchestrator:	Henry Brant
Stunt Coordinator:	Hal Needham
Titles:	Don Record
Makeup:	Donald W. Robertson
Assistant Directors:	Terry Morse, Jr., Newt Arnold, Dennis Donnelly
Art Director:	Al Sweeney, Jr.
Set Decorator:	Morris Hoffman
Sound:	Al Overton, Clem Portman
Special Effects:	Logan Frazee
Camera:	William H. Clothier
Editor:	William Cartwright

William Holden *(Lieutenant Colonel Robert T. Frederick);* Cliff Robertson *(Major Alan Crown);* Vince Edwards *(Major Cliff Bricker);* Michael Rennie *(Lieutenant General Mark Clark);* Dana Andrews *(Brigadier General Walter Naylor);* Gretchen Wyler *(A Lady of Joy);* Andrew Prine *(Private Theodore Ransom);* Claude Akins *(Rocky Rockman);* Carroll O'Connor *(Major General Hunter);* Richard Jaeckel *(Omar Greco);* Jack Watson *(Corporal Wilfred Peacock);* Paul Hornung *(Lumberjack);* Gene Fullmer *(Bartender);* Jeremy Slate *(Patrick O'Neill);* Richard Dawson *(Hugh MacDonald);* Tom Stern *(Captain Cardwell);* Tom Troupe *(Al Manella);* Luke Askew *(Hubert Hixon);* Bill Fletcher *(Bronc Guthrie);* Harry Carey, Jr. *(Captain Rose);* Norman Alden *(M.P. Lieutenant);* James Craig *(American Officer);* Patric Knowles *(Admiral Lord Louis Mountbatten).*

THE FAILING OF RAYMOND
(ABC-TV, 1971) C-90 min.

Producer:	George Eckstein
Director:	Boris Sagal
Teleplay:	Adrian Spies
Music:	Pat Williams
Camera:	Ben Colman
Editor:	John Kaufman, Jr.

Jane Wyman *(Mary Bloomquist);* Dean Stockwell *(Raymond);* Dana Andrews *(Allan MacDonald);* Paul Henreid *(Dr. Abel);* Murray Hamilton *(Sergeant Manzak);* Tim O'Connor *(Cliff Roeder);* Priscilla Pointer *(History Teacher);* Mary Jackson *(Latin Teacher);* Arienne Marden *(Librarian);* Catherine Louise Sagal *(Girl Patient);* Robert Karnes *(City Editor);* Ray Ballard *(Store Owner).*

INNOCENT BYSTANDERS
(Paramount, 1972) C-111 min.

Producer:	George H. Brown
Director:	Peter Collinson
Based on the novel by James Munro [Mitchell]	
Screenplay:	Mitchell
Assistant Director:	Clive Reed
Art Director:	Maurice Carter
Music:	John Keating
Song:	Hurricane Smith
Sound:	Bill Daniels, Gordon K. McCallum
Special Effects:	Pat Moore
Camera:	Brian Probyn
Editor:	Alan Pattilo

Stanley Baker *(John Craig);* Geraldine Chaplin *(Miriam Loman);* Dana Andrews *(Blake);* Donald Pleasence *(Loomis);* Sue Lloyd *(Joanna Benson);* Vladek Sheybal *(Aaron Kaplan);* Darren Nesbitt *(Royce);* Warren Mitchell *(Omar);* Ferdy Mayne *(Marcus Kaplan);* John Collin *(Asimov);* Frank Maher *(Daniel).*

AIRPORT '75
(Universal, 1974) C-107 min.

Executive Producer:	Jennings Lang
Producer:	William Frye
Director:	Jack Smight
Inspired by the film *Airport* which was based on the novel by Arthur Hailey	
Screenplay:	Don Ingalls
Second Unit Director:	James Gavin
Assistant Director:	Alan Crosland, Jr.
Art Director:	George C. Webb
Set Decorator:	Mickey S. Michaels
Music:	John Cacavas
Songs:	Helen Reddy and R. Burton
Costumes:	Edith Head
Technical Advisor:	Captain Donald McBain
Stunt Coordinator:	Joe Canutt
Sound:	Melvin M. Metcalfe, Sr., Robert Hoyt
Special Effects:	Ben McMahon
Camera:	Philip Lathrop
Second Unit Camera:	Rex Metz
Washington Camera:	Richard Kratina
Editor:	J. Terry Williams

Charlton Heston *(Alan Murdock);* Karen Black *(Nancy);* George Kennedy *(Joe Patroni);* Helen Reddy *(Sister Ruth);* Efrem Zimbalist, Jr. *(Captain Stacy);* Susan Clark *(Mrs. Patroni);* Linda Blair *(Janice Abbott);* Dana Andrews *(Scott Freeman);* Roy Thinnes *(Urias);* Sid Caesar *(Barney);* Myrna Loy *(Mrs. Devaney);* Ed Nelson *(Major John Alexander);* Nancy Olson *(Mrs. Abbott);* Larry Storch *(Purcell);* Martha Scott *(Sister Beatrice);* Jerry Stiller *(Sam);* Norman Fell *(Bill);* Conrad Janis *(Arnie);* Beverly Garland *(Mrs. Freeman);* Augusta Summerland [*Linda Harrison*] *(Winnie);* Guy Stockwell *(Colonel Moss);* Erik Estrada *(Julio);* Kip Niven *(Lieutenant Thatcher);* Charles White *(Fat Man);* Brian Morrison *(Joe Patroni, Jr.);* Amy Farrell *(Amy);* Irene Tsu *(Carol);* Ken Sansom *(Gary);* Alan

Fudge *(Danton);* Christopher Norris *(Bette);* Austin Stoker *(Air Force Sergeant);* Gene Dynarski *(Friend);* John Lupton *(Oringer);* Laurette Spang *(Arline);* Gloria Swanson *(Herself).*

SHADOW IN THE STREET
(NBC-TV, 1975) C-78 min.

PRODUCERS: John D. F. Black, Richard D. Donner
DIRECTOR: Donner
TELEPLAY: Black
MUSIC: Charles Bernstein
CAMERA: Gayne Rescher
EDITOR: David Rawlins

Tony Lo Bianco *(Pete Mackey);* Sheree North *(Gina Pulaski);* Dana Andrews *(Len Raeburn);* Ed Lauter *(Siggy Taylor);* Jesse Welles *(Debby);* Bill Henderson *(Leroy);* Dick Balduzzi *(Bense);* Richard Keith *(Steemson);* Sherwood Price *(Gardner);* Jack O'Leary *(Hazlett);* Lieux Dressler *(Lila);* Lee deBroux *(Lee);* John Sylvester *(Cavelli).*

THE FIRST 36 HOURS OF DR. DURANT
(ABC-TV, 1975) C-78 min.

EXECUTIVE PRODUCER: Stirling Silliphant
PRODUCER: James H. Brown
DIRECTOR: Alexander Singer
TELEPLAY: Silliphant
MUSIC: Leonard Roseman
ART DIRECTORS: Ross Bellah, Robert Purcell
CAMERA: Gerald Perry Finnerman
EDITOR: Jack Kampschroer

Scott Hylands *(Dr. Chris Durant);* Lawrence Pressman *(Dr. Konrad Zane);* Katherine Helmond *(Nurse Katherine Gunther);* Karen Carlson *(Nurse Olive Olin);* Renne Jarrett *(Dr. Lynn Peterson);* Alex Henteloff *(Dr. Alex Keefer);* Michael Conrad *(Graham);* Peter Donat *(Dr. Bryce);* David Doyle *(Dr. Atkinson);* James Naughton *(Dr. Baxter);* Dennis Patrick *(Mr. Wesco);* Joyce Jameson *(Mrs. Craham);* Janet Brandt *(Surgical Secretary);* Davis Robert *(Dr. Dorsett);* and special cameo appearance by Dana Andrews *(Dr. Hutchins).*

TAKE A HARD RIDE
(20th Century-Fox, 1975) C-103 min.

PRODUCER: Harry Bernsen
CO-PRODUCER: Leon Chooluck
DIRECTOR: Anthony M. Dawson [Antonio Margheriti]
SCREENPLAY: Eric Bercovici, Jerry Ludwig
MUSIC: Jerry Goldsmith
ART DIRECTOR: Julio Molina
ASSISTANT DIRECTORS: Scott Maitland, Pepe Lopez Rodero
SECOND UNIT DIRECTOR: Hal Needham
WARDROBE SUPERVISOR: Agustin Jimenez
STUNT COORDINATORS: Needham, Juan Majan
SOUND: Edit-International, Ltd.
SPECIAL EFFECTS: Luciano D'Achille, Antonio Molina
CAMERA: Riccardo Pallotini
SECOND UNIT CAMERA: Raul Perez-Cubero
EDITORS: Stanford C. Allen, Dennis Mosher

Jim Brown *(Pike);* Lee Van Cleef *(Kiefer);* Fred Williamson *(Tyree);* Catherine Spaak *(Catherine);* Jim Kelly *(Kashtok);* Barry Sullivan *(Kane);* Harry Carey, Jr. *(Dumper);* Robert Donner *(Skave);* Charles McGregor *(Cloyd);* Leonard Smith *(Cangey);* Ronald Howard *(Halsey);* Ricardo Palacios *(Calvera);* Robin Levitt *(Chico);* Buddy Joe Hooker *(Angel);* Dana Andrews *(Morgan).*

THE LAST TYCOON
(Paramount, 1976) C-122 min.

PRODUCER: Sam Spiegel
DIRECTOR: Elia Kazan
BASED ON THE UNFINISHED NOVEL BY F. SCOTT FITZGERALD
SCREENPLAY: Harold Pinter
MUSIC: Maurice Jarre
PRODUCTION DESIGNER: Gene Callahan
ART DIRECTOR: Jack Collis
SET DECORATORS: Bill Smith, Jerry Wunderlich
COSTUMES/WARDROBE: Anna Hill Johnstone, Anthea Sylbert, Thalia Phillips, Richard Bruno
ASSISTANT DIRECTOR: Danny McCauley
SOUND: Dick Vorisek, Larry Jost
CAMERA: Victor Kemper
EDITOR: Richard Marks

Robert DeNiro *(Monroe Stahr);* Tony Curtis *(Rodriguez);* Robert Mitchum *(Pat Brady);* Jeanne Moreau *(Didi);* Jack Nicholson *(Brimmer);* Donald Pleasence *(Boxley);* Ingrid Boulting *(Kathleen Moore);* Ray Milland *(Fleishacker);* Dana Andrews *(Red Ridingwood);* Theresa Russell *(Cecilia Brady);* Peter Strauss *(Wylie);* Tige Andrews *(Popolos);* Morgan Farley *(Marcus);* John Carradine *(Guide);* Jeff Corey *(Doctor);* Angelica Huston *(Edna);* Don Brodie *(Assistant);* Seymour Cassell *(Seal Trainer);* Leslie Curtis *(Mrs. Rodriguez);* Lloyd Kino *(Butler);* Peggy Feury *(Hairdresser);* Betsy Jones-Moreland *(Lady Writer).*

GOOD GUYS WEAR BLACK
(Mar Vista, 1978) C-96 min.

EXECUTIVE PRODUCER: Michael Leone
PRODUCER: Allan F. Bodoh
DIRECTOR: Ted Post
STORY: Joseph Fraley
SCREENPLAY: Bruce Cohn, Mark Medoff
ART DIRECTOR: B. B. Neel
SET DECORATOR: Robinson Royce
ASSISTANT DIRECTORS: Gene Maru, John Patterson, Bob Shue
MAKEUP: Bob Dawn
SPECIAL EFFECTS: Bob Dawson
CAMERA: Bob Steadman
SECOND UNIT CAMERA: Tom Harvey, Danny O'Reilly, Wendy Shoemaker, Jose P. Bencome
EDITORS: William Moore, Millie Moore

Chuck Norris *(John T. Booker);* Anne Archer *(Margaret);* Lloyd Haynes *(Murray);* James Franciscus *(Conrad Morgan);* Dana Andrews *(Edgar J. Narolds);* Jim Backus *(Hotel Doorman);* Matsuo Uda *(Shoeshine Man);* Virginia Wing *(Mrs. Mhin Van Thieu);* Viola Harris *(Airline Ticket Agent);* Jacki Robins *(Fat Lady);* Pat Johnson *(CIA Agent);* Warren Smit *(Morgan's Chauffeur);* Dick Shoemaker *(Newscaster);* Aaron Norris *(Al);* Don Pike *(Hank);* James Bacon *(Senator);* Kathy McCullen *(Kelly);* David Starwalt *(Steagle);* Stack Pierce *(Holly Washington);* Michael Payne *(Mitch).*

BORN AGAIN
(Avco Embassy, 1978) C-110 min.

EXECUTIVE PRODUCER: Robert L. Munger
ASSOCIATE PRODUCER: Paul Temple
PRODUCER: Frank Capra, Jr.
DIRECTOR: Irving Rapper
BASED ON THE AUTOBIOGRAPHY OF CHARLES COLSON
SCREENPLAY: Walter Bloch
MUSIC: Les Baxter
ASSISTANT DIRECTOR: Bob Bender
PRODUCTION DESIGNER: William J. Kenney
SET DECORATOR: Mark Poll
SOUND: Bert Hallberg
CAMERA: Harry Stradling, Jr.
EDITOR: Axel Hubert

Dean Jones *(Charles Colson);* Anne Francis *(Patty Colson);* Jay Robinson *(David Shapiro);* Dana Andrews *(Thomas L. Phillips);* Raymond St. Jacques *(Jimmy Newsom);* George Brent *(Judge Gerhard Gesell);* Senator Harold Hughes *(Himself);* Harry Spillman *(President Nixon);* Christopher Conrad *(Chris Colson);* Stuart Lee *(Wendell Colson);* Alicia Fleer *(Emily Colson);* William Zuckert *(E. Howard Hunt);* Brigid O'Brien *(News Reporter);* and: Richard Caine, Scott Walker, Robert Broyles, Byron Morrow, William Benedict.

THE PILOT
(New Line, 1979)

PRODUCER: C. Gregory Earls
DIRECTOR: Cliff Robertson
BASED ON THE NOVEL BY ROBERT P. DAVIS
SCREENPLAY: Davis, Robertson
PRODUCTION DESIGNER: Davis
SET DECORATOR: Bonnie De Rahm
COSTUMES: Jody Mecurio
ASSISTANT DIRECTOR: James Bigham
SOUND: Bruce Shearin
CAMERA: Walter Lassaly
EDITOR: Fima Noveck

With: Cliff Robertson, Frank Converse, Diane Baker, Gordon MacRae, Dana Andrews, Milo O'Shea, Ed Binns.

TWO

WALLACE BEERY

6′ 1″
240 pounds
Brown hair
Brown eyes
Aries

Former child star Margaret O'Brien matured in one of the most bizarre of climates—the MGM studios, where the great stars of Hollywood paraded before the cameras and collected their awesome paychecks. Today Margaret is often queried about the many idols she met and/or worked with during her tear-dispensing tenure at Culver City. She has nice things to say about them all except Wallace Beery, her co-star in *Bad Bascomb* (1946). She explains, "He pinched my bottom once because he thought I was stealing a scene—and once he even stole my lunch!"

So goes the notorious reputation of gruff Wallace Beery, summed up in David Niven's *Bring on the Empty Horses* (1975) as "the ex-female impersonator Wallace Beery whose lovable 'Aw shucks, ma'am' on-screen personality was in direct contrast with his belligerent, rude, egotistical side which made him easily the most unpopular actor at Metro-Goldwyn-Mayer."

Indeed, since Beery's demise in 1949, he has been inscribed in Hollywood history as a virtual monster, labeled as everything from a sexual sadist to a stingy tipper. So severe were the unattractive aspects of Beery's personality that Howard Strickling, Metro's publicity chief, once went to Louis B. Mayer to ask permission "to give good old Wally the harpoon." Even Mayer the mogul, never the most couth of the cinema's potentates, found Beery's personal and professional habits so displeasing that he finally constructed a special contract for the star. It insured the actor's presence on the lot for as *little* time as absolutely necessary.

While waves of similar antipathy have splashed on Wallace Beery's name, nothing can erode the fact that he was one of the most colorful actors in Hollywood. Indeed, before he settled into his repetitious stock slob characterizations, he was one of the most versatile performers ever to act in films. Yet Wally was rapid to dismiss the question of his own talent, saying: "Like my dear friend Marie Dressler, my mug has been my fortune." He truly possessed and displayed genuine virtuosity before laziness and ill temper launched him into a lengthy swan song of overly familiar (if constantly profitable) plots and performances.

Beery's early life reads like a screenplay from one of his latter day motion pictures. He was born on Wednesday, April Fool's Day, 1885. He was the youngest son of policeman Noah Webster Beery, who stubbornly survived the dangers of the brutal 12th and Paseo district of Kansas City, Missouri.

The oldest boy was William, the middle son was Noah, Jr.,[1] and Wally was the "baby." He had to endure the last of the hand-me-down clothes as the family battled poverty.

Mrs. Beery tried ardently to keep her boys in line, with contrary results. William finished high school, but Noah quit academics before the seventh grade, and Wally never reached that level of educational training. At the age of fourteen he was still in the third grade. His little classmates found the gawky lad in the back of the room to be most amusing and soon bestowed on him the nickname of "Jumbo" which he despised. As he would recall, "I managed to race through the third grade—in eight years—before my hatred of everything connected with school got the best of the promises I'd made to my mother."

In lieu of the schoolroom, Wally began sneaking into the boxcars of departing St. Louis trains, hobnobbing in hobo jungles and panhandling until he was expected home. When his parents learned of his extracurricular activities, he took off with the intention of running away forever. After two months, a very homesick and hungry Wally returned to "the soundest thrashing a kid ever received." But his parents did provide the prodigal with a new suit and a promise that he could look for "decent" work instead of returning to the humiliating schoolroom.

Wally earned paychecks in a variety of jobs: engine wiper, blast furnace feeder, railroad laborer, etc. Meanwhile, his loyal brothers were on the lookout for positions for him. Will, having just been promoted to the position of concessions manager of the Ringling Brothers Circus, thought that Wally might find a future under the folds of the Big Top. Wally rushed to join the show as soon as he received word from Will, and for three seasons his task was "manicuring the elephants." Wally worked with the pachyderms, doing everything from teaching them tricks to keeping them calm during storms to running behind them with a broom or shovel. Wally eventually left his $3.50-a-week-plus-board post with Ringling Brothers to join the Forepaugh-Sells Circus, again working with the elephants. Indeed, Beery enjoyed this early vocation. In fact, he would tell the press in 1934, at the peak of his fame, "I wish that sometime I could do a picture with an elephant. There is no animal in the world so lovable. If I had time to take care of it, I'd have one for a pet."

While this work agreed emotionally with Wally, the money was consistently poor and he was forced to fill in the off-season months by working with his

At age five, with his father, mother, Noah (center) and William C. II (right).

[1]Noah was born January 17, 1884. He got his start in the New York theatre selling items at a concession stand. Allegedly a producer heard his hawking and suggested he try out for chorus work. His vibrant voice soon stood him well as a singer, and he sang for a season with the "Electric Park" in Kansas City and later played a week's engagement at Hammerstein's Roof Garden in New York City. He soon forsook singing to sign with William A. Brady, a producer of stage melodrama.

Noah (later known to filmgoers as Noah Beery, Sr.) came to Hollywood to save himself financially; his son Noah, Jr. (the future film and TV performer) had been very ill and an $8,000 medical bill had to be paid. Noah came to Hollywood and sold his extra suit for funds before landing a bit in Cecil B. DeMille's *Joan the Woman* (1917). Realizing that film work offered much more money than stage acting, Noah persisted in the new medium. He landed a role in Mae Murray's *The Mormon Maid* (1917) and was signed to a Paramount contract. Over the next decade, he played some fine screen scoundrels, notably the unspeakable sergeant of Ronald Colman's *Beau Geste* (1926) and the brutal reformatory school guard in *The Godless Girl* (1928).

With the coming of talkies, Noah left Paramount and worked very much in the shadow of his brother. Most of his films were B products. By the 1940s Wally was looking out for him, guaranteeing him roles in pictures like *Barbary Coast Gent* (1944). Noah returned to Broadway in *Up in Central Park*. He took a two-week vacation on March 21, 1946 from the musical and came West to visit Wally in Beverly Hills. On April 1, 1946, on Wally's birthday, Noah was at his brother's home when he died of a heart attack in his brother's arms. Noah, Wally, and Carol Ann (Wally's daughter) were all scheduled that evening to do a radio broadcast. Wally and Carol Ann went on and completed the broadcast.

Like Wally, Noah had little to do with Hollywood society, preferring to live in a lonely section of the San Fernando Valley. However, unlike Wally, he took himself and his work sometimes too seriously. As he said of any actor who undertakes a villainous role, "If he puts his heart into his work, he can't throw off his characterization promptly and at will . . . They linger hours, sometimes days, in the mind."

dad who had gone into business in Leavenworth, Kansas. Thus when Noah contacted Wally and informed him of the $25 he was making as a chorus boy in New York shows, Wally headed for Broadway. He began making casting rounds with Noah, both unlikely candidates for the slim-hipped, tenor-toned legions who glittered in Broadway musicals. "Chorus men wore tights and frills and carried pink wands with ribbons on them, and made thorough asses of themselves," recalled Wally. "I didn't like it, but it was the place to start. I had a good voice and hoped to sing my way into a handsome hero's part." The brothers' close relationship became even stronger during their Broadway period, with one looking out for the other as much as for himself.

Husky and quite good-looking, Wally soon landed a spot in the musical *A Japanese Nightingale,* which opened on Thursday, November 19, 1903 at Daly's Theatre and ran for forty-six performances. After it closed, Wally moved over to the Majestic Theatre, joining the company of Victor Herbert's *Babes in Toyland* which had opened in October of that year. In this operetta, Wally's enthusiasm soon became evident and the producers quickly gave him a comedy bit to play. When the production closed in the spring of 1904, Wally studied "eccentric dancing" in New York and worked in summer stock in Kansas City with the Woodard Stock Company. He then returned to Broadway, winning spots in the chorus of *The Prince of Pilsen* (New York Theatre: April 3, 1905, forty performances) and *The Student King* (Garden Theatre: December 25, 1906, forty performances). Though Wally worked relatively steadily, reports of his contemporaries indicate that he was *not* Broadway's most agile sprite. Edward Everett Horton remembered dancing in the chorus on one occasion with Wally and recalled the only advantage of the adventure, "Keeping out of his way greatly improved my agility."

In August 1907 Wally opened in a small role in *The Yankee Tourist,* a play starring Raymond Hitchcock and his wife, Flora Zabelle. Shortly thereafter, Hitchcock was arrested for infringing on the morals of a fifteen-year-old girl. Though released on bail, he mysteriously vanished on the morning of October 30, 1907. That day was a Wednesday, with a 2:15 matinee scheduled. As the crowd filed into the Astor Theatre, the management panicked. In desperation they yanked Wally from his humble post, squeezed him into Hitchcock's costumes, and sent him on stage in the lead. In later years Wally would roar how his "overnight success" joyously went to his head. "A punk kid from Kansas City, son of a $80-a-month cop, had made good. Hot diggety dog! I bought me a brown derby and a yellow cane and buff spats, and stood on the corner of 42nd and Broadway with my ears cocked waiting for people to say, 'That's Wallace Beery, the new star of *The Yankee Tourist.*' If anybody said it, he whispered. . . . if anything, he said, 'That's the guy that's playing Hitchcock's part. Let's don't go to that show!' "

Wally had sent for his mother to come witness his triumph as "Copeland Schuyler" and was even considering scrounging up $500 for a facelift when, after eight performances, the bubble burst. Hitchcock returned as magically as he had vanished, announced "I am going to play," and Beery was returned to his bit role. Still, the producers were sufficiently impressed with his emergency fill-in. They starred Wally in the touring company that weaved about the country for two years after the play concluded its 103-performance Manhattan run.

Thereafter Beery remained busy on the road, playing in traveling productions of such plays as *The Prince of Pilsen* and *The Balkan Princess.* When the latter folded in Chicago, Wally was stranded and without prospects. However, he had been spotted in one of his last performances by "Henry McRae Webster, director general of the Essanay Film Company. . . . I don't know what he thought and I am perfectly willing not to know. It might hurt my vanity."

In actuality, Webster was impressed by Beery's stage presence and showmanship. He had a feeling that the actor could be a distinct asset to his Chicago-based film company, where Francis X. Bushman, Beverly Bayne, and Charlie Chaplin were the headliners. At $75 weekly, Wally signed as a director and performer, making his debut as "Mr. Strong" in *His Athletic Wife* (1913). A string of one-reelers with Miss Bayne and a bevy of comedies based on George Ade fables led to a film series that won Beery his first screen notoriety. It was the role of Sweedie, the gangly maid (!) who, due to Beery's humorous size and mugging face, convulsed picture-goers. In episodes such as *Sweedie Learns to Swim* (1914) and *Sweedie and Her Dog* (1914), Wally appeared to be having a fun-filled romp. Actually, however, he was unhappy and self-conscious about appearing in these raucous one-reelers. Yet he recognized that the job offered compensations that greatly appealed to him after years of touring. "For one thing, I could live in one place and I could have my evenings free."

In the 1915 knee-slapper *Sweedie Goes to College,* Wally enjoyed working with a seventeen-year-old ingenue whom he later described as "a darned sweet kid, modest as could be and pretty." This angelic teenager proved to be Gloria Swanson. Soon Wally was in love with her. He wanted to wed the novice, and she gave him ample reason for optimism, but before the wedding march could start, Webster

As the Swedish maid in the 1914 short subject series.

transferred Wally to the company's Niles Studios in northern California near San Jose. His partner there was "Bronco Billy" Anderson. "Bronco Billy directed the first company," Wally would recall, "and I directed those who were left over, including Vic Potel, Lloyd Bacon, Ethel Clayton, and Ben Turpin."

After several unhappy months, Beery went south to Carl Laemmle's Universal lot and worked in the capacity of producer, director, and actor on such films as *The Janitor* (1916) and *Bombs and Banknotes* (1916). Then came "a real break for me"—Mack Sennett signed him to a $125 weekly contract as a featured comedian with his Keystone Company. To celebrate this good fortune, Beery sent for Gloria Swanson. After reinforcing her happiness by negotiating a contract for herself with the Sennett Studio, Gloria married Wally on Sunday, February 20, 1916. While they set up housekeeping in a bungalow across from the Sennett lot, the couple sometimes acted together onscreen. One good example of their tandem work is the often-revived *Teddy at the Throttle* (1917), a two-reeler in which black-caped, top-hatted Wally ties Gloria to a railroad track, where she is saved by Teddy—an early cinema wonder dog.

Domestic bliss between the thirty-one-year-old Wally and eighteen-year-old Gloria soon evaporated in the Beery household. Beery thought that his bride would become domesticated and want to start a family, but Gloria was already enjoying a rapid rise to popularity in films, in contrast to her husband's career rut. Soon the couple began having tiffs that often spilled over into public view. On one occasion he bought her a robin's egg blue car to match a similarly colored outfit she had obtained. To surprise her, he drove it to the Ambassador Hotel where she was gossiping with some chums. When she exited and saw her gift, she cooed and twittered about the roadster, languished in the back seat, curtly motioned her husband into the front, and purred, "Home, James." To the shocked delight of Gloria's pals, Wally lurched around, bodily yanked his dainty wife out of the back seat into the front, and bellowed, "Don't ever give me that 'Home, James' stuff!"

Indeed, Wally's expansive temper was a sight to behold. Further gossip relates how Gloria was frightened by the surly domination of her mate who weekly collected not only his own $125 paycheck but her $75 paycheck as well. By June 1, 1917 the couple had separated, and on December 13, 1918 Wally won a final divorce from Gloria on grounds of desertion. Newspapers delighted over a letter to Wally from Gloria in which she advised her spouse, "I don't want you to cry. Please don't coax me." Wally dismissed the union in these words: "She wanted the fancy life—to put on airs and all that. Me, I like huntin' and fishin' and the simple life." However, Wally's experiences with the woman who would become one of the 1920s' great cinema legends hurt him deeply. He once admitted in the 1940s that his love affair with Gloria was "the real romance of my life." Few things riled him more than being asked by interviewers to discuss his marital misadventures with Swanson.

While Wally's marriage was floundering, so was his career. Keystone did not renew his contract, and for a time he just "relaxed," preferring to fish rather than try to resurrect his drowsing career. He did play

With Gloria Swanson in 1915.

in the fifteen-chapter spy thriller of serial *Patria* (1917) with Irene Castle and Milton Sills, and then villainized America's sweetheart, Mary Pickford, in *The Little American* (1917) and *Johanna Enlists* (1918). By now Beery was becoming known as an effective screen scoundrel.

Beery credited two events with saving him from film obscurity. One was the war. "If Woodrow Wilson had kept us out of it, I'd probably be back training elephants right now. But the United States did declare war, Hollywood heard about it, and I got back on my feet. To show my gratitude, I have voted the straight Democratic ticket ever since." The other force he credited with rescuing his career was Gloria, who, prior to the divorce, was dating top producer Marshall "Mickey" Neilan. Neilan was casting a war picture *The Unpardonable Sin,* a melodrama which reeked of hatred for the German people. One night, as Wally would relate later, Neilan was telling Gloria that he was having difficulty casting the role of the dastardly chief villain, a Teutonic beast who tries to rape Blanche Sweet. Gloria laughingly suggested her estranged husband. Neilan saw that her mirth contained the germ of a good idea and he did cast Wally in the picture. "That was the turn," smiled Wally later. "I put into the part all the hatred against the world that had been piling up inside me for a year. I must have been mean enough to suit, for after that

I walked right into picture after picture." Though the war concluded before the spring 1919 release of *The Unpardonable Sin,* audience reaction to Beery was powerful and he was again on the rise in Hollywood.[2]

On a new wave of popularity, Wally began averaging six releases a year for a variety of studios. Usually he was typecast as a black-hearted louse. In Paramount's *Behind the Door* (1919) he was a despicable German submarine commander, and the actor later boasted, "Millions of patriots cheered when Hobart Bosworth skinned me alive." He played the role of Magua, the evil Indian of *The Last of the Mohicans* (1920), and in Metro's *The Four Horsemen of the Apocalypse* (1921) "with Rudolph Valentino, I was at my artistic worst when I laughed and ate an apple as I watched my men shoot down 150 defenseless Belgian women and children." His performance as Lieutenant Colonel von Richthoffen was enthusiastically praised by critics and hissed at by audiences. Beery's name became popular with top producers.

One person who became impressed by Beery's cinema possibilities was Douglas Fairbanks, Sr., the enormously popular hero of the swashbuckling silents. Fairbanks was preparing to star in *Robin Hood* (1922) and felt that Beery's picturesque countenance would be at home in the rowdy adventure. When Beery was summoned for an interview, he felt that he should play the wicked usurper John, but Fairbanks had enough faith in Wally's ability that he cast him as the gallant Richard the Lion-Hearted.[3] It was evident that Wally was becoming a respected name in films by his salary for this motion picture —the then-lofty weekly amount of $800.

Robin Hood was a huge success when it was released in the fall of 1922, winning *Photoplay*'s Gold Medal

[2]In a 1934 interview Wally claimed that as a favor to pal Lon Chaney he appeared in a silent horror film as "a creature that was nine-tenths ape. . . . I agreed to do it, with the understanding that no one was to know I had degraded my profession for a friend and $10,000."

[3]Beery would play Richard the Lion-Hearted again, in a 1923 film of the same title, based on Sir Walter Scott's *The Talisman.*

With Mary Pickford in *Johanna Enlists* (1918).

With Raymond Hatton (3rd from left), Anna Q. Nilsson, and Wallace Reid in *The Love Burglar* (1919).

With Tully Marshall in *The Life Line* (1919).

In *The Northern Trail* (1921).

With Noble Johnson and Raymond Hatton in *Adventure* (1925).

Award for Best Picture. Wally won praise and later called the film the greatest movie ever made. He was also impressed with Fairbanks: "After the preview, Doug came to me and said, 'Wally, you're great! In the scenes you play with me, nobody will look at me. They'll all have their eyes on you. I'm delighted with the job you did.' That shows Douglas Fairbanks' character as well as anything I've ever heard. He was delighted to think an actor had stolen scenes from him—the star!"

Another event had occurred during the filming of *Robin Hood* that placed the film in a special category for Wally. Since the debacle of his marriage to Gloria Swanson, Wally had shied away from cinema nightlife, preferring to hunt and fish. But during the filming of the banquet scene for Robin Hood, a large-eyed blonde extra caught his attention—Mary Arieta Gillman, known as "Rita," who had come from Astoria, Oregon to make a name in the movies. She brought out the playfulness in Wally. During a break in the filming, he broke open a loaf of bread, formed a dough ball, and chucked it at the lovely girl. "It hit her just under the left ear," he would fondly recall. He began teasing her throughout the remainder of the production, and she greeted his prophetic taunts that he would someday wed her, with derisive hoots.

Rita chose to wed another suitor while Wally continued his career.[4] But by the time Wally villainized Milton Sills in Associated First National's *The Sea Hawk* (1924), Rita's marriage was on the rocks and she was an extra in the production. Wally resumed the courtship and shortly after the summer release of this epic[5] (which became the biggest money-maker of the movie year), Wally wed Rita in the home of director Frank Lloyd on Monday, August 4, 1924. Like Wally's first wife, she was thirteen years his junior; unlike his first wife, she abandoned her acting aspirations to supervise the Beery household.

As Beery entered the mid-1920s his career continued to prosper. After solid roles in such popular and heralded features as First National's *So Big* (1924), a Colleen Moore epic, and Metro-Goldwyn's sprawling *The Great Divide* (1925), he signed a contract with Paramount Pictures. Though occasionally lent out (for example, to First National in 1925 for his role[6] of Professor Challenger in *The Lost World,* in which he captures a raging brontosaurus), he spent most of the next five years at the Paramount lot. "I played all sorts of heavy parts and had just about decided that I couldn't be anything but a rogue on the screen no matter how bad I wanted to be good. Then a break of luck came out of a clear sky, and with Ray Hatton I enjoyed playing in a long series of comedy pictures."

Indeed, six months after the release of Paramount's Western epic *The Pony Express* (1925), Beery and Hatton were clowning it up in *Behind the Front* (1926), directed by comedy expert Edward Sutherland. When the film clicked at the box office, Paramount rapidly teamed Beery and Hatton in a string of military misadventures much as Warner Bros. would do a decade later with James Cagney and Pat O'Brien in a more serious vein. *We're in the Navy Now* (1926) and *Now We're in the Air* (1927) continued the duo's military antics. (The latter project so impressed Wally that he bought his own plane and became an enthusiastic pilot.) The successful pair cut similar capers in such vehicles as *Fireman, Save My Child* (1927), *Wife Savers* (1928), and *Partners in Crime* (1928). The team of Beery and Hatton broke up before their playing became overly predictable, and Wally kept busy at the studio playing ne'er-do-wells in such Paramount products as *Stairs of Sand* (1929).

It was now 1929. "Everything seemed to be going great," Wally related years later. "I was getting $4,500 a week. I had proved I could play almost anything—despicable Huns, noble kings, and comedy soldiers and sailors." But Beery's career was in a shakier condition than he realized. The ending of his comedies with Hatton was a form of cinema euthanasia; the films were beginning to tire audiences rather than amuse them, and Hatton would never fully recover professionally from the setback that those films ultimately provided him. Paramount, in converting its facilities to sound production, decided to economize, and it did not renew the contracts of seven once top-drawing artists: Bebe Daniels, Richard Dix, Emil Jannings, Adolphe Menjou, Pola Negri, Florence Vidor, and Wallace Beery. Wally's first all-talking picture, *Chinatown Nights,* directed by William A. Wellman and co-starring Florence Vidor, Warner Oland, and Jack Oakie, did not convince the studio that his gravely voice would take well to the new medium. After a benign role in a Booth Tarkington-based *River of Romance* (1929), Wallace left the Paramount lot. George Bancroft replaced him in burly, roguish leading characterizations that he might have played there.

It seemed that nobody was professionally interested in Beery thereafter, and the stock market crash of 1929 made his woes complete. He recalled: "$750,000 of stocks that I had bought outright went

[4]The *New York Times* reported, "Wallace Beery rises to every moment in his interesting part of the man who can be bribed to do almost anything."

[5]The *New York Times* championed, "The laurels of the picture . . . fall to Mr. Beery, who is convincing and pugnacious. . . . One would almost think that he was looking for a pet dog when he runs out to capture his brontosaurus."

[6]When Universal Pictures producer Irving Thalberg replaced Erich von Stroheim as director of *Merry-Go-Round* (1923), Beery lost his role as the sadistic Shani Huber. When production began again under Rupert Julian's direction, George Siegmann inherited the villainous assignment of the evil concessionaire.

With Sterling Holloway and Ford Sterling in *Casey at the Bat* (1927).

With Raymond Hatton in a pose from *Now We're in the Air* (1927).

down to almost nothing, and in two bank failures I lost $165,000 in cash. All I owned was my home—and that burned down." Shortly afterward his plane crashed, killing two passengers and his mechanic, and another bank crash wiped out his reserves. For a year Beery faced unemployment and financial ruin, but he revealed a stoical approach to the entire mess. " 'It's probably for the best,' I told my wife. 'When you haven't any money, you can't make a fool of yourself.' "

Seemingly, the last place in Hollywood where Wallace Beery could have hoped to rebuild his collapsed career was at the Metro-Goldwyn-Mayer Studios, Culver City's Olympus of the most glorified stars of the cinema. Louis B. Mayer and Irving Thalberg populated their Washington Avenue constellations with such glamorous international idols as John Gilbert, Ramon Novarro, Norma Shearer, Joan Crawford, and Greta Garbo. Yet, though the studio selected glamor as a talisman, talent also appealed strongly to the studio brass, and this union of talent and pulchritude cemented MGM's reputation as the number one studio of the world.

In early 1930 Thalberg was enthused about a Frances Marion script concerning prison life, inspired by topical riots at Auburn Prison. The dominant role, Butch the hardened convict, was slated for the talents of Lon Chaney, Sr., long a major Metro star. He had just completed his sound debut in a remake of *The Unholy Three* (1930). Chaney, however, was ill with a malignant throat cancer which finally killed him on August 26, 1930. In a gamble, Thalberg, at the urging of Beery's agent, Phil Berg, contracted Beery, aware of the actor's talent as well as his persona non grata status within the film colony. Wally admired the script, signed on, and with Chester Morris and Robert Montgomery as co-stars and George Hill as director he gave a performance that once again resurrected his career—this time never to expire.

The Big House, released in the summer of 1930, had mammoth popular appeal and was a triumph in the eyes of the critics, all of whom hailed Wally's splendid portrayal of Butch. The latter is the character who whiles away his imprisonment by bragging of his murders, pounding his cup in the commissary, organizing cockroach races, and planning one of the most exciting prison breaks ever recorded in motion pictures. The *New York Evening Post* reported, "In the acting of *The Big House,* it is Wallace Beery who runs

With Marie Dressler in *Min and Bill* (1931).

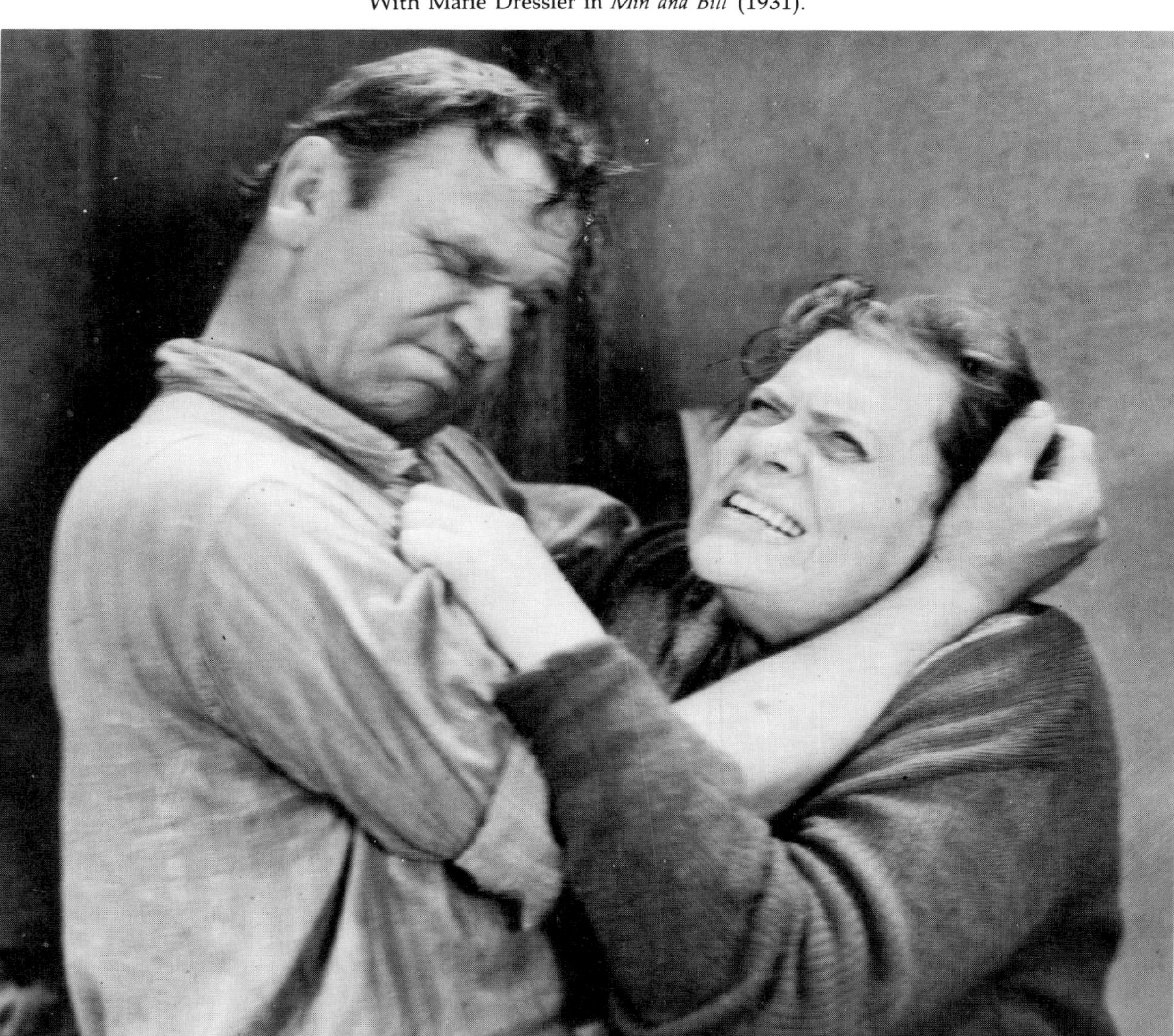

With Paul Hurst, John Miljan, and Louis Natheaux in *The Secret Six* (1931).

off with the glory. . . . Beery, in his brawling, bullying way, epitomizes the underworld; he is the incarnation of a convict, and it is his motives and behavior in bringing about the desperate prison break which throw an interesting light on criminal psychology." Suddenly Wally was a major film attraction again. He joined George Arliss *(The Green Goddess* and *Disraeli),* Maurice Chevalier *(The Love Parade* and *The Big Pond),* Ronald Colman *(Bulldog Drummond* and *Condemned),* and Lawrence Tibbett *(The Rogue Song)* as a candidate for the Best Actor Oscar of 1929–30. Although Arliss won the Oscar, it was Beery who maneuvered a long-term MGM contract.

Wally's popularity swelled immediately, and before 1930 was over he had scored in several touted Metro releases. In *Way for a Sailor* (1930) he co-starred with John Gilbert, the latter the most tragic casualty of the conversion to sound. Gilbert gagged when he saw the name of Beery topping his (and double the size) on the marquee of the Los Angeles Pantages Theatre. *Billy the Kid* (1930) cast Wally as Pat Garrett and was filmed in Metro's "Realife" seventy millimeter widescreen process, making it all the easier for audiences to observe how he stole the picture from Johnny Mack Brown's title character. *A Lady's Morals* (1930) offered him the picturesque role of P. T. Barnum, playing in tandem to Grace Moore's Jenny Lind. However, it was *Min and Bill* (1930) that fully capped his stardom as he aided Marie Dressler in raising Dorothy Jordan. (Miss Dressler won an Oscar for her zesty performance.) Though Beery and Marie only appeared in two more features, *Tugboat Annie* and *Dinner at Eight*—both 1933 releases—they are still hailed today as one of the great "pairs" of the cinema.

In a matter of six months Wally had become a major Hollywood star and the recipient of critical tributes, international fan mail, and $7,500 per week. He accepted this new popularity in idiotically unpredictable Hollywood one day at a time, but on his own terms. As he would later drawl throughout his reign of popularity, "It can be here today and gone tomorrow."

The year 1931 was one of the more colorful seasons in the annals of Hollywood, and one of the several popular genres that expanded that year was the gangster cycle. Warner Bros. had released *Little Caesar* with Edward G. Robinson in late 1930, followed by James Cagney's *The Public Enemy* in 1931. Fox offered *Hush Money* (1931) with Joan Bennett and *Quick Millions* (1931) with Spencer Tracy, while Metro released its own vice opus, *The Secret Six.* As Louis "Slaughterhouse" Scorpio, a bootlegging ganglord, Beery top-billed Lewis Stone, Johnny Mack Brown, Ralph Bellamy, and two newcomers who would respectively win high places on Beery's good-bad lists: Clark Gable and Jean Harlow. While Gable, as a flirtatious reporter, impressed Wally with his let's-get-on-with-it professionalism and lack of ego, Jean, as Wally's moll, displayed an insecurity that required retakes and enraged the star. In addition, Harlow's status as an "overnight sensation" due to her playing in *Hell's Angels* (1931) bothered the actor who had been through so many hard times. Her breezy personality and love of gossip was in direct contrast to Wally's gruff, introverted social style. The cast was shocked repeatedly by the Olympian insults Wally hurled at the shapely blonde. In later years, when she was a top MGM attraction herself, Jean freely returned his remarks and was once quoted as referring to Wally as "a mean old son of a bitch whose grave I'd love to piss on."

After the popular reception of *The Secret Six,* MGM supplied Beery with the role that would win him an Oscar and provide him with a characterization that he could repeat perennially without boring his public.[7] The movie was *The Champ* (1931), based on a Frances Marion story, in which he was teamed with young Jackie Cooper, who had been Oscar-nominated for his performance in *Skippy* (1930). The powerful, amusing story of a boozy ex-boxer who battles his way back to a championship to fulfill his son's faith was ideal Depression fare, acted with sufficient schmaltz and perfectly handled by director King Vidor.

Years later, in discussing this picture for the National Educational Television series "The Men Who Made the Movies," Vidor recalled of Wally: "I remember a little incident with Wally Beery. When I talked to him about playing it, he said, 'If I have to do any fighting, I can't do it.' I said, 'All right, we'll get doubles. I'd like to have you do the film.' One day at lunch when we were getting ready to do the prizefight scene, I noticed him with a couple of pretty girls, extra girls, having lunch, and I was having lunch with the assistant director, and I said, 'Go over and get the girls' names—I have an idea.' We took them off the set where they were working, put them in the front row of the prizefight audience, and then when I called for the doubles to do the fighting Wally said, 'What do you mean doubles? I want to do it. I don't like doubles doing it for me.' So he got up in the ring and did some tough fighting because these two pretty girls he'd had lunch with were sitting there. He was a wonderful character."

Jackie Cooper fails to remember Wally as a "wonderful character." The tyke's beautifully controlled grief at the end, as Wally dies of a heart attack after recouping the boy's admiration, assured audiences that the two performers truly loved one another. The studio's publicity department quoted Jackie as calling Wally Beery the most wonderful man in the world. In actuality, Jackie did at one point feel this, but when the ten-year-old tried to show his love after one tender scene by impulsively hugging his co-star, Wally brusquely disentangled himself from the boy and ordered the shattered Jackie to control his emotions. Today Cooper hesitates to talk of Beery, with whom he would co-star in five features, because he does not want "to put him down," but he recently did tell the *New York Daily News* that "Beery was a sad man," frightened of becoming close to a little boy who was not his own. Wally still wanted children very much, and Cooper feels that "that had a lot to do with his unhappiness—plus, I think, the fact that he started out in this business as a female impersonator. This also might have haunted him." None of these complex feelings were evident in *The Champ. The Nation* enthused that "Jackie Cooper and Wallace Beery are at their best," and during the picture's exceptionally popular long run at Grauman's Chinese Theatre, Vidor and his friend Charles Chaplin would often stand across Hollywood Boulevard and watch the packed house weep its way out of the theatre.

Wally's final 1931 release was *Hell Divers,* in which he co-starred with MGM's sensation Clark Gable, fresh from films with Garbo, Shearer, and Joan Crawford.[8] Predictably big box-office, the naval aviation yarn featured a realistic brawl between the two stars and an exciting climax in which Wally rescues Clark but dies in a crash landing. After completing the production, Wally told a reporter, "I like playing with Clark Gable. Folks seem surprised that we see quite a lot of each other outside the studio. . . . He's a regular outdoors man and we're interested in the same things, guns and flying and stuff like that. He's no faintin' Romeo, the way they try to make him out."

[7]MGM had wanted Beery to star in *Trader Horn* (1931) the W. S. Van Dyke II production that had been shot on location in Africa as well as on the MGM backlot. But the comfort-loving Beery would have none of it, and his part went to Harry Carey.

[8]Beery joined with some three dozen stars (including Maurice Chevalier, Gary Cooper, Fay Wray, Loretta Young, Buster Keaton, Norma Shearer, Barbara Stanwyck, Irene Dunne, Jack Oakie, Warner Baxter, Joe E. Brown, Wheeler and Woolsey) for a twenty-minute short subject, *The Stolen Jools* (a.k.a. *The Slippery Pearls*), produced by the Hollywood Masquers Club as a fund-raising item. It was a jovial spoof of whodunits.

Rapidly regaining solvency, Wally did nothing with his paychecks to insure acceptance in the film colony. He hosted no lavish parties and attended few functions. By now he had purchased a new plane and a cabin at June Lake near Yosemite, and he spent most of his time between films off on hunting jaunts. In December 1931, Rita's mother's half-sister, Juanita Priester, died, leaving three children: nine-year-old George, four-year-old William, and nine-month-old Carol Ann. Wally's marriage to Rita had been childless, so he planned to adopt all three children. As it turned out, the two boys would be raised by their grandmother, and only Carol Ann was reared by Wally and Rita. The girl became the delight of her proud father, and the one subject he liked discussing with the press.

On November 13, 1930, *Grand Hotel,* a play based on Vicki Baum's *Menschen im Hotel,* opened at Broadway's National Theatre to great acclaim, enjoying a 444-performance run. During a New York vacation, Wally and Rita saw the show. Upon leaving the theatre, Wally expressed an unfavorable opinion about the character of Preysing, a lascivious tycoon who seduces the stenographer Flaemmchen and kills the dashing Baron von Gaigern. "He doesn't murder women," said Wally to Rita in the lobby, "but he's lower than anybody I've ever played." Shortly after his return to Hollywood, Thalberg notified Beery of his next project. The film was *Grand Hotel,* and he would play the role of Preysing.

Any other actor would have been honored to join the company. Garbo was to play Grusinskaya, the fading ballerina, John Barrymore won the role of the baron (originally intended for the declining John Gilbert); Joan Crawford had the part of Flaemmchen, the bitter stenographer; Lionel Barrymore was the dying Kringelein; Lewis Stone was the scar-faced doctor; and Jean Hersholt was the porter with a wife in labor. But these awesome stars did not impress Beery in the least. On the contrary, he feared that the set would be the sort of temperamental prize ring he so detested. In addition, he disliked his role. "I hate the lousy part I'm playing in *Grand Hotel.* I told 'em I didn't want to do it. I shot my mouth off to everyone in power on the lot and it didn't do a hell of a bit of good!" So adamant was Wally about not doing the film that when the cast met on January 9, 1932 under the direction of Ed-

With Judge Samuel Baake of Los Angeles, wife Areta, and their newly adopted daughter, Carol Ann (March 1932).

With Joan Crawford in *Grand Hotel* (1932).

mund Goulding, Beery stayed away from the set on a two-day strike.

Wally was finally coerced to appear on the sound stage, but he did not immediately find things any better than he had anticipated. On his first day there, he forced himself to grumble a hello to John Barrymore, who, in turn, replied only with a scornful cocked eyebrow. This particular antipathy dissolved on the eighth day of shooting when Barrymore shocked Beery by slapping him on the knee and roaring so all could hear, "Not that I'm falling in love with you or anything, but I'd like to make a statement. You're the best actor on this set!"

In actuality, a very minimal amount of temperament blazed on the *Grand Hotel* set. Much of this was due to Goulding who cleverly structured the filming so that the stars worked separately as much as possible. Beery would recall later that he scarcely saw Garbo during the production, as she worked on a closed set; even though she appears in the lobby scene in which he is arrested, her footage was shot at a different time and edited into the film. The film was completed in forty-eight days and earned Goulding the nickname of "The Lion Tamer."

Metro publicists hailed the fact that the stars all played so well together, but they glossed over one incident that was typical Wallace Beery. Many of Wally's scenes were in tandem with Joan Crawford. When *Grand Hotel* was shot, her favorite habit was having an assistant on the set whose task was to set up a phonograph and play moody concertos which placed Joan "in the mood" for her more dramatic scenes. This situation infuriated Beery. As they rehearsed the climax of their joint scenes, Wally decided that he had had enough. One day he asked Joan—with the most serious face he could manage—if she would mind if he had some music played to get him into the proper mood before the cameras rolled. Joan agreed with empathy. "So I raised my hand, giving the signal, and in marched two big guys, in blue uniforms, covered with gold braid, one banging a bass drum and the other playing 'Marching Through Georgia' on a piccolo. Joan wouldn't speak to me, except professionally, for a week!"

When *Grand Hotel* premiered in the spring of 1932, it was a sensational box-office and critical hit. The reviewers were laudatory about all the principals and at least one newspaper, the *Des Moines Register,* gave Beery the prize for best performance. Certainly his performance is a strong one and skillfully varied, showing Preysing as a happy family man delighted to reach his family by long distance, as an arrogant businessman desperately lying at a crucial bargaining session, as a pathetic lover trying to make love gingerly to the sleepy Crawford (telling her "Be nice to me"), and finally as a petrified and guilt-stricken murderer near hysterics as he begs his abused former employee Lionel Barrymore not to tell the police that he killed the Baron. Beery offered a tremendously effective blend of human ingredients to his sharp portrayal.

Despite his personal success in the venture, Wally had no warm feeling for *Grand Hotel,* and the Hollywood premiere at Grauman's Chinese Theatre did not help matters. Sid Grauman, a notorious practical joker, promised the packed theatre that the elusive Garbo had agreed to make a personal appearance onstage after the film presentation. The delighted house waited after the picture to see the most idolized creature of the movies—and out came Wally, bedecked in a long blonde wig and ludicrous dress, a willing accomplice to Grauman's latest farce. The star-packed audience unleashed a hideous groan and stomped to the doors, leaving the humiliated Wally onstage with the challenge of making a graceful exit. Also, Wally had agreed to the request of Garbo's manager that he loan the star his cabin retreat so that she could enjoy a secluded vacation. He never got over the shock of discovering that the prima donna "left it with the bed not made and the dishes dirty!"

After *Grand Hotel,* Wally indulged himself in a long break from filmmaking, enjoying a spree of flying and hunting. He summed up his Hollywood life style in a 1932 interview with *Motion Picture* magazine, "Evenings we sit around and Rita sews and I do a lot of reading about aeronautics and things like that. . . . I never go to parties. Haven't been to one for fifteen years. Fifteen years ago, or more, Viola Dana gave some sort of bust and I went to that and I've never been to one since."

His only other 1932 release was *Flesh,* a very offbeat drama in which Wally played Polikai, a German wrestler, scorched by a bitchy wife (Karen Morley—in a role refused by comeback-seeking Coleen Moore). Many feel director John Ford drew out Beery's best acting. Though the film won the star some great reviews and allowed him to display a definite sex appeal not often realized (or expected) in his screen work, the picture was not box-office and Metro dismissed it as an "artistic" experiment.

MGM was by now most delighted with Wally's work. Not only had he reached the top ten box-office draw list of 1932 (he was number seven), but he was also nominated for an Oscar for *The Champ.*[9]

[9]MGM would rework *The Champ* into a Red Skelton picture, *The Clown* (1953), and again later release the property as *The Champ* (1978), a Franco Zeffirelli vehicle for Jon Voight.

At the 1931–32 Oscar dinner, Beery found himself in competition with Fredric March *(Dr. Jekyll and Mr. Hyde)* and Alfred Lunt *(The Guardsman).* Louis B. Mayer was confident that Beery would win and was aghast when Fredric March's name was announced. Mayer and his minions marched backstage to check out the matter and learned that Wally had lost by one vote. Mayer influenced the Academy that one vote was so minimal a win that a second Oscar should be bestowed. Thus for the first time in the brief history to date of the Academy Awards, a tie was announced. Lionel Barrymore, the previous year's winner for *A Free Soul,* presented the Oscar to Wally who appeared to be quite proud.

Starting with Louis B. Mayer (who at this juncture, while Thalberg was away on a European trip, took over control of Beery's career) and working his way down, Wally appeared to take delight in bullying, insulting, and aggravating everybody who passed his professional path. With his status so enviable, Mayer offered Beery a new contract—a fifty-two-page deluxe tome filled with the small print and technicalities that most stars love to peruse. Beery took the contract, curtly ripped it in two before Mayer's ashen face, yanked a piece of memo paper from the mogul's desk, and scrawled, "I Wally Beery will star exclusively in Metro-Goldwyn-Mayer pictures five days a week for a period of forty weeks this year at $7500 a week; quitting time is 5:30 P.M. punctually! Wally Beery." This was enough for Mayer and Beery went on with his Metro paces, stalking the sound stages like a surly bear. He insisted on an afternoon nap every day, despite the structure of the day's shooting. He would take no part in the set-side parties and tomfooleries and almost never agreed to spend a portion of his working day with an interviewer or reporter. Perhaps the habit that most annoyed his co-stars was his penchant for altering dialogue and ad-libbing while the cameras were rolling, leaving his co-player literally speechless as he or she searched for the proper cue.

Some years later makeup artist Jack Young joined Metro, and he recently spoke of Beery to a *National Enquirer* reporter. "There was nothing likeable about the man," laments Young, offering the theory: "Beery once confided he had a rough time getting to the top and a lot of people hurt him. He made sure they and everyone else never forgot it or that he was on top at the box office."

On April 15, 1933, Beery was enormously proud when he became a Lieutenant Commander of the U.S. Naval Reserves. He arrived at Long Beach Airport in his own Bellanca monoplane and took the formal oath of allegiance. In addition to his new post and his great love of hunting, Beery was becoming increasingly close to his young daughter Carol Ann, and all these personal touches made him less and less patient with whatever delays Metro held in store for him.

Wally's initial 1933 release was *Tugboat Annie,* rematching him with Marie Dressler in the title role. Mervyn LeRoy directed and the stars again were the source of irresitible fun, their barnacled relationship summed up in Marie's line, "He's never struck me—except in self-defense!" By this time, the Dressler-Beery pairing was drawing more attention than ever on the lot, since Marie was the most popular star of the studio among her co-workers, while Wally was rapidly becoming the most despised. Wally remarked shortly afterward, "Marie Dressler and I get along fine. My only complaint against her is that she's everybody's mother. With property men, electricians, carpenters, actors, she's just like an old hen with chicks. If you cough, she's off like a streak to her dressing room to get some old-fashioned remedy to cure it. She's made me eat a barrel of sulphur and molasses!"

In his next project, Wally joined not only Marie, but John and Lionel Barrymore, Billie Burke, Edmund Lowe, Lee Tracy, Karen Morley, Phillips Holmes—and Jean Harlow—for *Dinner at Eight* (1933), delightfully directed by George Cukor, and adapted from the play by George S. Kaufman and Edna Ferber. The all-star opus stands up far better than *Grand Hotel* and was shot in exactly half the time—an incredible twenty-four days.

The stars of *Dinner at Eight* all enjoyed great roles, with John Barrymore as a drunken has-been matinee idol, brother Lionel as a dying shipping magnate, Dressler as a gone-to-seed stage star, Lowe as a philandering doctor, Burke as the fluttery society matron wife of Lionel Barrymore, and Tracy as a fast-talking theatrical agent, etc. But audiences reacted most joyously in 1933 and still do now to the gargantuan squabbles of Wally as blowhard tycoon Dan Packard and Jean Harlow as Kitty, his cuckolding "poisonous little rattlesnake" of a wife. Neither performer needed any warmups to verbally lacerate one another. Director Cukor allowed their mutual animosity to boil and to create the most memorable display of matrimonial war of the 1930s' cinema.

HARLOW: You're not gonna step on my face to get where ya' wanna go, ya' big windbag!

BEERY: Listen, you little piece of scum, you! I've got a good notion to drop you right back where I picked you up—in the checkroom of the Hottentot Club—or wherever the dirty joint was!

HARLOW: Oh-no-you-won't.

BEERY: And then you can go back to that sweet-smelling family of yours—back of the railroad tracks in Passaic! And get this—if that sniveling, money-grubbing, whining old mother of yours comes fooling around my offices anymore, I'm going to give orders to have her thrown down those sixty flights of stairs, so help me!

The finale of *Dinner at Eight* sees Harlow, who has been "putting it over" on Wally with Lowe, save Lionel Barrymore's business from her husband's dirty clutches. The film was a great success. The *New York Times* reported: "Mr. Beery fits into the role of Dan Packard as though it were written especially for him, and Miss Harlow makes the most of the part of Kitty. . . . A grand evening of entertainment." Wally enjoyed only a few moments of screen time with Marie Dressler, and *Dinner at Eight* would be their last film together, for the beloved actress died of cancer on July 28, 1934.

After completing *Dinner at Eight,* Metro loaned Beery to United Artists for *The Bowery* (1933), which teamed him again with Jackie Cooper, as well as with on-the-rise leading man George Raft. The Gay Nineties' atmosphere was splendidly suggested in the direction of Raoul Walsh.

Then followed Beery's greatest performance, as Pancho Villa in Metro's sprawling adventure *Viva Villa!* (1934).[10] All the braggadocio, savagery, and heart of Villa shone through Beery's performance, and if facts were tampered with in the film's plotline, the picture was all the better for it.

MGM intended *Viva Villa!* to be its lavish project of the year, and producer David O. Selznick envisioned a film of epic proportions, but fate battled them each step of the way. Mayer spitefully assigned cameraman Hal Rosson to travel with the company to Mexico for location shooting, certain that it would destroy Rosson's newlywed bliss with Jean Harlow, whom he had married without Mayer's customary consent. Rosson protested violently, and Mayer irritably replaced him with James Wong Howe. In late 1933 director Howard Hawks traveled to Mexico with a cast which included Beery, Leo Carrillo (as Villa's loyal lieutenant Drego), Joseph Schildkraut (as the evil General Pascal), and hundreds of others, including Lee Tracy as the American reporter Johnny Sykes.

The production company arrived in Mexico at a time when seasonal holidays were clashing with political upheaval. Mistrust met the studio workers, aggravated by opinions that Beery's casting as Villa was an insult to the Mexican people and that the studio was exploiting the Mexican extras by paying them only fifty cents daily instead of the dollar minimum. This turmoil came to an ugly climax on a Sunday morning when Tracy, who was drunk, awoke to a parade of Mexican troops passing in the

[10]Years before, in the 1917 serial *Patria,* Beery had played Pancho Villa on screen for the first time.

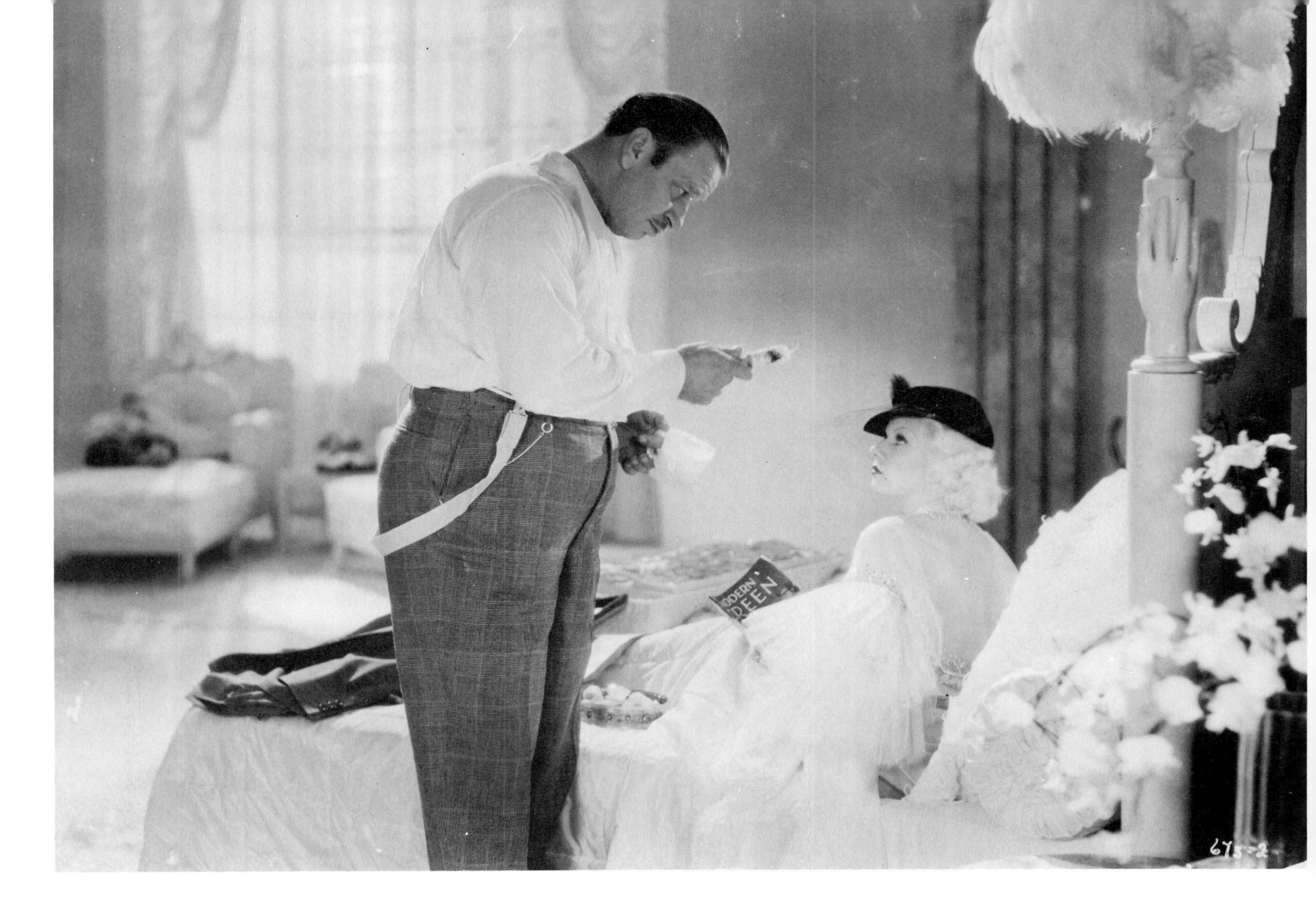

With Jean Harlow in *Dinner at Eight* (1933).

street below his hotel balcony. One account has it that Tracy wandered onto the balcony clad only in a blanket that slid off and that he expressed his opinion of the racket below by urinating on the Mexican flag and its bearers. Police arrived and arrested him. He was released the same day and went to a bullfight. Meanwhile, the incident gained notoriety and the Mexican government was demanding that Tracy be fired or else they would ban the distribution of all MGM films.

Louis B. Mayer not only withdrew Tracy from the production but cancelled his MGM contract. Stuart Erwin was hastily substituted as the reporter and the role had to be rewritten. (This pleased Beery. Rumors insisted that he was intimidated by Tracy's scene-stealing and did nothing to come to his costar's aid in the fracas.)

But trouble was just beginning for *Viva Villa!* Wally's wife, Rita, was ill and he kept his plane in readiness to fly to her side should an emergency develop. When location shooting was completed, an airplane crash destroyed the entire footage and the company had to start all over again. Hawks argued with the front office over Beery's interpretation of Villa and was replaced by Jack Conway. Mexico continued to be uncooperative. Nevertheless, *Viva Villa!* limped to completion on January 12, 1934. MGM had surmounted every obstacle that blocked the production.

The results were outstanding. *Viva Villa!* was a rousing adventure film, spotlighted by Beery's high-level portrayal which mixed humor, ignorance, nobility, and a most effective note of blood-thirstiness. Indeed, for a 1930s' epic, *Viva Villa!* contains a number of unusually sadistic scenes, particularly Pancho's whipping of the aristocratic Teresa (Fay Wray), and the famous execution of General Pascal. Villa has him killed not by a firing squad but by having him tied near an anthill, with honey poured over him, leaving him as dinner for the ants. Beery is unforgettable as he orders, "Put it [the honey] on his ears, his eyes, his nose, his mouth. Put it everyplace on him—everyplace!"

For all the gore, Beery managed to make Pancho a sympathetic personality simply by having the character lack comprehension of the seriousness of the atrocities he commits. He totally believes he is a hero, as displayed in the final scene where a dying Pancho, expiring from an assassin's bullet, asks reporter Johnny Sykes to create his "last words":

ERWIN: Pancho Villa spoke for the last time. He said . . . he said . . .
BEERY: Hurry, Johnny . . . Johnny. What were my last words?
ERWIN: "Goodbye, my Mexico," said Pancho Villa. "Forgive me for my crimes. Remember, if I sinned against you, it was because I loved you too much."
BEERY: Forgive me? Johnny . . . what I done wrong?

When released in the spring of 1934, *Viva Villa!* was an enormous hit, cheered by the public as well as the critics. Beery received some of the best laurels of his career. *Literary Digest* insisted, "It is acted quite brilliantly in the title role by Wallace Beery." Many expected he would be Oscar-nominated, but he was not. However, he was the recipient of the Best Actor Prize at the Venice Festival for his robust Pancho.

Beery's income was making him a wealthy man again. As he observed in a 1934 interview, "I believe the reason I've survived so long is that I've never taken myself very seriously. I have a good 'rebound.' I've always taken things as they've come, made the best of them, and never wasted any time wailing over spilt milk or lost opportunities. . . . No matter what happens, I can never be poorer than I have been—so why worry? It's the downs that place a premium on the ups. Life's like a screen drama; it needs sharp contrasts to make it interesting and enjoyable."

MGM followed up by casting Beery as another notorious character—this one fictional: Robert Louis Stevenson's Long John Silver in *Treasure Island* (1934). Victor Fleming directed, Jackie Cooper was young Jim Hawkins, and such character names as Lionel Barrymore (Billy Bones), Lewis Stone (Captain Smollett), Nigel Bruce (Squire Trelawney), and Otto Kruger (Dr. Livesey) maneuvered through their rich roles. They gave rich competition to Beery who had a formidable peg leg on which he hobbled with gleeful ease and a parrot on his shoulder, both delicious aids for his accustomed scene-stealing.

After a trip to Europe to indulge his recuperating Rita, Wally was loaned to 20th Century to again play P. T. Barnum in *The Mighty Barnum* (1934). Adolphe Menjou co-starred, with Virginia Bruce this time as Jenny Lind. Walter Lang's direction faithfully captured the circus atmosphere. Revealing in such meaty roles, Wally experienced his most popular career year in 1934. Exhibitor polls placed him number three among the box-office favorites.

Metro kept Beery running through his paces. In *West Point of the Air* (1935) he was "Big Mike," a military tower of strength. Robert Young played his son, "Little Mike," and the cast included a new MGM contractee, Robert Taylor. Wally offered the newcomer the advice: "You're too handsome. Better go huntin' and fishin' with me, so folks won't think you're a sissy!" Taylor took him up on his offer. *O'Shaughnessy's Boy* (1935) again teamed him with Jackie Cooper. This reworking of *The Champ* cast Wally in the picaresque character of a one-armed

With Jackie Cooper and Nigel Bruce in *Treasure Island* (1934).

With Adolphe Menjou in *The Mighty Barnum* (1934).

With Ben Hendricks, Jr. (center), Charles Ludwig (midget), and Willard Robertson in *O'Shaughnessy's Boy* (1935).

lion-tamer. When the scene was shot in which the arm was "lost," Wally actually took on a tiger while sharp shooters took aim out of camera range in case the tiger overacted. Wally's work with Jackie was becoming increasingly unsubtle, and he lamented that when Jackie "is in a scene, you might as well be over at the commissary eating lunch, for all the good you do in advancing the story, for audiences won't take their eyes off of him!"

Ah, Wilderness! (1935) top-billed Wally over Lionel Barrymore, with Beery as the alcoholic Uncle Sid in this adaptation of the Eugene O'Neill play. His scenes with straitlaced love Aline MacMahon were better executed than was his time oncamera with Barrymore, wherein both men indulged in an orgy of favorite mannerisms. Metro even managed to incorporate Wally (as well as Gable, Shearer, Marion Davies, and Lionel Barrymore) into a one-reel short, *Jackie Cooper's Christmas.* Also that year, Wally guested on a particularly impressive radio broadcast, *Napoleon's Barber,* in which he played with John Barrymore and Lola Lane on the "Shell Chateau" program.

Wally's biggest success in that great movie year[11] was in Irving Thalberg's blockbuster *China Seas,* a melodrama of delicious clichés delivered by Gable, Harlow, Lewis Stone, and Rosalind Russell. It is great fun as pirate Wally plots to snare 250,000 pounds of gold from Gable's ship, has a bacchanalian drinking bout with Harlow's "China Doll," sadistically tortures a spartan Gable, and, after losing an epically mounted battle, takes poison with the tag line to Harlow, "Lovin' you is the only decent thing I ever did in my life—and even that was a mistake!" "As for the principals, none of the three has ever been better," wrote the *New York American.* The film, proudly promoted as an ocean-going *Grand Hotel,* was an immense crowd-pleaser. Director Tay Garnett recalls that the cast[12] had a great deal of fun

[11]Beery almost climaxed 1935 as Captain Bligh in the studio's Oscar-winning *Mutiny on the Bounty.* Thalberg originally wanted him, but decided he was too "American." It was of course Charles Laughton who ultimately portrayed the infamous sea captain.

[12]Beery's daughter Carol Ann had a small bit in the film.

accomplishing the picture-making, though there were again some problems in the private working relationship between Wally and Jean. The provocative and delightful Harlow, whose "China Doll" won her a *Time* magazine cover story, was at her peak, and for the first time in her three films with Wally she topped him in the billing. When the "Blonde Bombshell" turned twenty-four on March 3, 1935, the cast and crew hosted a surprise birthday party for the very popular girl. Wally was the only cast principal not to attend. He claimed he had a stomach ache. (When Jean tragically died of uremic poisoning on June 7, 1937, Beery was one of the few co-stars of the actress not to offer the press a sympathy statement.)[13]

Wally's 1935 film output placed him number eight in the exhibitors' polls. After being lent to 20th Century-Fox for the Cuban jungle thriller *A Message to Garcia* (1936) with Barbara Stanwyck and John Boles, Beery began a personal appearance theatre tour in Boston. Illustrative of his drawing power was his stipend for the engagement. He received his usual $7500 weekly Metro paycheck plus fifty percent over the house's average take.

Still all was not well with Beery's standing at Metro. Louis B. Mayer was finding it embarrassing and difficult to handle Wally's agitation of directors, co-stars, and interviewers. There were more and more incidents resembling the star's treatment of an English fan magazine representative in the mid-1930s. A British poll had placed Wally in the number one spot in screen popularity, and the magazine dispatched a publicity squad all the way to Culver City with a trophy. Unfortunately, they arrived just as Wally was beginning his nap. When informed of the arrival of his visitors, he drawled, "Aw, now ain't that nice"—his favorite expression—but he drove the front office to despair as he refused to terminate his nap to accept the award. "Thank 'em again," instructed Wally. "Take 'em in the studio cafe and buy 'em some of that there good old Louis B. Mayer chicken soup, and put the check on me." As it turned out, the English visitors waited outside the studio set door until 5:30 when Wally punctually left, stuck the trophy in his hands, and snapped

[13]MGM had planned to reteam Beery and Harlow, along with Robert Taylor in *Spring Tide,* based on the play by J. B. Priestly and George Billam, but Harlow's death cancelled the project.

With Rudy Vallee and Noah Beery in New York (February 1935).

The MGM star of the mid-Thirties.

Advertisement for *Good Old Soak* (1937).

some quick pictures as the star smiled a perfunctory thanks and then proceeded to his car.

In the midst of these problems, on September 14, 1936, Irving Thalberg died of pneumonia. Wally understandably felt that he owed a large share of his current success to the brilliant producer and attended the funeral services at Synagogue B'nai B'rith. Yet, with characteristic aloofness, he did not join the parade of limousines that made their way to the interment at Forest Lawn Cemetery. Instead, he rushed to his plane and flew over the mausoleum, tossing three bunches of red roses from the plane's cabin. However, Wally's rather touching gesture almost backfired. One clump of fauna came within thirty yards of hitting widow Norma Shearer on the head as she emerged from her limousine.

With Thalberg dead, Beery's management again fell within the domain of Mayer. A metamorphosis then developed in the star's screen output. Urged by Howard Strickling, studio publicity head, to fire Wally due to his nasty idiosyncrasies, Mayer declined. He stated that Beery was "one of us," but he did recognize that the problem was severe enough to require special attention. Mayer decided that Beery would rarely work again in the lot's major projects or co-star with the studio's biggest attractions. Instead, he would be given mainly minor vehicles where, as the only major star, he was free to ad-lib, chomp scenery, and complain to his heart's content. Two such examples followed: *Old Hutch* (1936), in which he was a bum forced to become respectable to claim a stash of money, and *Good Old Soak* (1937), where he played a town sop who redeems himself out of love for son Eric Linden.

After lurching through these programmers, Wally was lent to Darryl F. Zanuck's increasingly prestigious 20th Century-Fox lot where he co-starred with the studio's top-paid name, Warner Baxter, in the costume adventure yarn *Slave Ship* (1937).[14] Accompanying Wally from Culver City's Metro base to Fox's Westwood lot was MGM contractee Mickey Rooney, whose popularity would soar that year when he began the famed *Andy Hardy* series back at his home studio.

Slave Ship made an effort to revive the lovable ne'er-do-well vs. mischievous boy relationship that Beery had had with the now maturing Jackie Cooper. However, Rooney was not only a natural scene stealer like Cooper but an ambitious one as well. Director Tay Garnett was unable to completely refine the obviously brutal battle the pair waged in their tandem scenes.

As Garnett recalls in his book *Light Your Torches and Pull Up Your Tights* (1973), the situation began to get a little rough: "In our script Rooney—the Mick—was cast as the cabin boy. In one sequence he slipped ashore, hoisted himself onto the first available barstool, and ordered a drink. At that point Beery—the first mate—swaggered into the bar, slapped the kid around, then lifted him by his lapels and promised him a cracked head if he ever again went into a saloon. The action was intended to clue the audience to Beery's 'heart of gold' under all those layers of flab.

"Instead of faking the slaps, Beery whacked the kid hard. I yelled, 'Cut!' Mickey slipped off the set and ran to a darkened corner of the stage. When I caught up with him, a thin trickle of blood was sliding down his chin, and he was trying manfully to suppress tears of rage. I promised Mickey it wouldn't happen again.

"It didn't. While the cameraman was lighting the next set-up, I called Beery aside and said, 'Look, Wally, every guy on this set and UP IN THOSE CATWALKS loves that kid. You're awfully good in this part, and I'd hate to lose you because somebody had parted your hair with a sun arc.' "

The film was completed without further problem, but it was Beery's last loan-out from MGM. His studio was so upset by the gossip his surliness inspired that they kept him under wraps in Culver City.

Back at the home lot, Beery began a long string of films that required little of him, being built around his "Aw, shucks" screen persona, and shot briskly and usually without name co-stars. His other 1937 release was the sepia-toned *The Bad Man of Brimstone,* with Wally mugging away as gunslinger Trigger Bill. Brother Noah Beery, whose career in the talkies had slumped badly, had a small role, and Dennis O'-Keefe landed his first major screen assignment as Beery's rival—who turns out in the final reel to be Wally's long lost son. Beery was even more ill-tempered on this film than on most others. Midway through filming he accidentally fired a gun into his leg, and he had to play most of the later scenes on his posterior.

Much better was *Port of Seven Seas* (1938), loosely based on Marcel Pagnol's trilogy of plays dealing with *Maius, Fanny,* and *Cesar.* MGM had initially purchased the screen rights as a vehicle for double-Oscar winner Luise Rainer, but Maureen O'Sullivan took over as the heroine and the emphasis rested on Beery's Cesar and Frank Morgan's Panisse. Consid-

[14]At one point, 20th Century-Fox planned to have Beery star in *Nancy Steele Is Missing* (1937). Allegedly Wally told that studio's mogul Darryl F. Zanuck, he refused to do the picture because he would not make a film with a director (Otto Preminger), whose name he could not pronounce. Victor McLaglen took the assignment of the ex-convict who pretends June Lang is a once-kidnapped child. As it turned out, George Marshall directed the eighty-five minute thriller.

ering the dilution from the French originals (and the trio of Gallic films based on the properties), it was an excellent picture. Director James Whale coaxed a creative and splendid performance from Beery. Sadly, it was the actor's last really notable screen role. Wally ended 1938 with *Stablemates,* which was a reworking once more of *The Champ,* this time set on a racetrack with Beery as a has-been veterinarian father of Mickey Rooney.

The year 1939 also saw Beery through three releases. In *Stand Up and Fight,* the MGM front office actually co-starred Wally with one of their top draws, Robert Taylor. However, Taylor was a hunting crony of Beery so things went smoothly in this Western, where Taylor saves the basically worthless neck of slave-running Wally. *Sergeant Madden* was the cause of another Beery blow-up. The director was Josef von Sternberg, in decline since severing his association with Marlene Dietrich. Von Sternberg had come to Metro to direct Hedy Lamarr in *I Take This Woman.* This project was delayed and he begrudgingly accepted the Beery film to brusquely honor his contract. Painstaking Josef was shocked at the casual attitude of free-wheeling Wally, and a clash broke out when Beery refused to rehearse. When the story of a policeman (Beery) who has to arrest his son was finally completed—after much front office mediation—von Sternberg bitterly disowned it. Beery was more in his element in *Thunder Afloat,* a simplistic navy story in which he played a boorish tugboat skipper who thumbs his nose at navy procedures.[15] It was a good parallel to his actual disrespect for the rules of professionalism at Metro-Goldwyn-Mayer studios.

Apparently Beery's sourness was infiltrating his home life. Shortly after the Beerys moved into a sprawling while colonial mansion at 816 North Al-

[15]Before Virginia Grey was given the female lead in the picture, Barbara Stanwyck had been sought. Others tested were Lana Turner and Laraine Day.

With Frank Morgan in *Port of Seven Seas* (1938).

pine Drive on the corner of Sunset Boulevard in Beverly Hills, Rita shocked her husband by asking for a divorce. Beery was quiet about the split, but Rita was delighted to inform newsmen in Reno, "We just got along happily for fifteen years—and now we don't. . . . I have an agreement on property, custody, and everything else, despite what he may say. He has his public and I shall make no statement that might cause him embarrassment or hurt his career. After all, it is to my advantage to protect him." On May 1, 1939, Rita won her divorce on the standard grounds of extreme mental cruelty, winning a settlement that included a home, a duplex apartment, and $100,000 in cash. Though mystery clouded the divorce initially, Wally at one point growled, "She fell in love with some gigolo, so I'm letting her have him!" Rita shed light on her decision six days later when she wed oil tycoon Albert Jesson Foyt, whom she had met on her first European junket with Wally. The actor was flabbergasted, and he labeled Rita's marriage (by the same Reno judge who had granted her divorce) "the greatest shock of my life." Though Rita won custody of Carol Ann initially, Wally's cherished daughter returned to her father a few months after her mother's marriage, and he became her legal guardian.

Beery might have been a fat, fifty-four-year-old grouch, but he was Wallace Beery, and his now single status brought many females circling around him. Some of the interested parties were celebrities. Mae Murray, the "Merry Widow" of the silent screen who had long suffered on Mayer's private and powerful blacklist, became a regular companion at the Hollywood Brown Derby where he kept a table reserved three days weekly for lunch. Wally enjoyed her beauty but realized that the ex-princess was searching desperately for an escape from severe money problems. Once Mae began circulating the story that she was going to wed the star, Beery never again escorted the fluttery "has-been." The noted

In *Stablemates* (1938).

With Robert Taylor and director W. S. Van Dyke II on the set of *Stand Up and Fight* (1939).

With Virginia Grey and Clem Bevans in *Thunder Afloat* (1939).

socialite Cobina Wright, Sr. also made a stab for Beery's wedding band, but destroyed her chances when she turned Beery's home into a salon for her party-loving society friends. Beery gagged on such goings-on and Cobina departed the scene. While Wally was seen occasionally with a "name," columnists noted that "Wally preferred the company of nice young girls—usually girls who were not in the business." What Wally perceived in this category of companion would become more publicized at the close of his life.

Since 1936, when Beery's career emphasis moved from the profitably creative to the profitably predictable, he had dropped out of the top ten box-office attraction listing, though remaining a big favorite with less sophisticated and demanding audiences.[16] However, in 1940 Beery was number eight in the popularity polls. The films were certainly no better, but the packaging seemed more appropriate for Beery's overaged overweight bad boy specialty act. In *The Man from Dakota* (1940), Beery was teamed with John Howard, both as Union soldiers on the run from Confederates, heading to General Grant with the help of a lovely Mexican. The latter was Dolores Del Rio, whose appearance in this minor Western demonstrated how desperate she was for screen exposure after a two-year cinema absence. In *20 Mule Team* (1940), he co-starred with Leo Carrillo, his lieutenant from *Viva Villa!*, and tough-talking Marjorie Rambeau, whose performance led Metro to believe that they had found a new Dressler.[17] Tragically Miss Rambeau was permanently crippled in an automobile accident in which she was almost killed. It was in his next film, *Wyoming* (1940), again with Carrillo and with favorite Metro ingenue Ann Rutherford, that the studio discovered its "new Dressler"—Marjorie Main.

The drawling, big-boned Miss Main had been turning in delightful characterizations of harridans for years, being particularly memorable as Humphrey Bogart's ma in *Dead End* (1937). The press applauded her chemistry with Beery—"I've been waiting all these years to see her whack Beery in the seat of the pants with a shovel," wrote Wanda Hale in the *New York Daily News*—and Louis B. Mayer quickly signed her to a seven-year contract, primarily to supply Wally with a formidable distaff sparring partner. It was not a job that obliging Marjorie particularly relished. As she would tell *Films in Review* in 1966, "Working with Wally wasn't always easy. He'd never rehearse his lines or 'bits of business,' but he'd want me to rehearse mine. I've always been extremely conscientious in my work and his behavior sometimes unnerved me." Carrillo, who had learned to cope with Wally on a private and professional level, advised her, "You'll never get the same cue twice. Just look at him, and listen to him, and when he stops talking, say your line." This method usually worked, but the flustered Marjorie was frequently thrown by Wally's oncamera ramblings. Then he would curse the delays her "blown lines" had "caused."

There were three 1941 Beery releases. *The Bad Man* co-starred him with Lionel Barrymore, now permanently confined to a wheelchair, and Ronald Reagan, on loan-out from Warner Bros. *Barnacle Bill* again starred the trio of Wally, Main, and Carrillo, with Wally trying to elude the matrimonial designs of Marjorie. Miss Main again found acting with Wally and Leo an exasperating experience, and told the press that MGM should pay her "one salary for the actin', the other for workin' with those two. I deserve it every time I come out alive!" *The Bugle Sounds* was yet another pairing of Beery and Main, this go-round set on an Army post with George Bancroft cast as a Fifth Columnist saboteur.

If anything, Beery was becoming an increasingly aggravating employee. Now that he had little contact with the top talent on the lot, he seemed to take pleasure in abusing the "little people." Cliff Collins, a Hollywood shoeshine man of some thirty-years experience, recently recalled: "I used to think that Wallace Beery was the tightest man in Hollywood." (Wally would pay Collins a dollar to wash his car, then try to win the money back by shooting dice.) Similar calumny was constantly being spread, and Mayer again reassessed the star's worth. The mogul cringed whenever some visiting V.I.P. witnessed Wally spitting on the manicured lawn or heard him belch in the studio commissary. "Get Beery in and get him out!" became Mayer's motto, and to better implement this, a new contract was designed. It required Wally to appear on the lot only thirteen weeks a year, at $15,000 a week. Though this meant a cut in per annum pay, Wally accepted the terms during his latter years with Metro. He did not require the extra money, and the arrangement meant more free time to accomplish the things he really enjoyed doing away from the movie glamor factory.

[16]One role Beery tested for but was not given was the title role in MGM's color production, *The Wizard of Oz* (1939), a part that was considered for the likes of W. C. Fields but eventually went to studio contractee Frank Morgan.

[17]Anne Baxter, on loan from 20th Century-Fox, played the ingenue in *20 Mule Team* and has her own recollections of Beery: "I was paired with Noah Beery Jr., who had been given his part by his uncle as a wedding present. The senior Beery did not seem to notice me. He was too busy keeping an eye on Marjorie Rambeau, who tried to steal his big moments. But after our first scene together, he ran over to director Dick Thorpe to complain that I was overacting."

With fiancée Mrs. Loreen Robinson in Los Angeles (March 1941).

With Hobart Cavanaugh, Marjorie Main, Joe Whitehead (bartender), Joe Yule, and Louis Mason in *Jackass Mail* (1942).

With Marilyn Maxwell and Fay Bainter in *Salute to the Marines* (1943).

With Frances Rafferty in *Barbary Coast Gent* (1944).

Hence Wally labored through the World War II years in such fare as the Westerns *Jackass Mail* (1942) and *Barbary Coast Gent* (1944) and two war stories, *Salute to the Marines* (1943) and *Rationing* (1944).[18] The critics continued to lament his acting predictability while the public adored it. The star brought an attitude to his work that while not laudatory was realistic. He once estimated that he had earned Metro approximately $50,000,000. He owed the company nothing, and since the fans seemed never to tire of his good-natured slobs, Wally gave them just what they expected. When starting production on a new film, Wally developed a ritual. He would throw dirt on his face and hat, mash the hat down on his head, turn to the director, and state, "I'm ready. My makeup is on."

Meanwhile, away from picture-making, Wally embraced other interests. He was deeply proud of his post as a U.S. Naval Commander in the Navy Reserves. When not busy devoting his spare time to this activity, he continued his hunting and fishing. He bought a beautiful ranch near Jackson Hole, Wyoming. There he quickly won the accolade of catching the lake's biggest fish on record.

If the aging process did not convince Wally that life was temporal, the death of his brother Noah on April 1, 1946 did. Yet Wally refused to slow his pace, even though he began to develop heart trouble. During his last years, the old hell-raiser appeared to be definitely mellowing. On one occasion, three high-schoolers, on vacation in Hollywood, purchased a movie star map and dashed about to stars' homes, harvesting autographs. When they arrived at Beery's doorstep, the man uncharacteristically answered himself, jovially signed the books, and, when learning that the youths were from his home town of Kansas City, Missouri, boomed "Why, that makes us practically relatives!" He invited them in, and he and Carol Ann insisted they stay for dinner. Beery seemed more himself when, after the newspapers learned of the story, he begged them not to run it lest his Alpine Drive mansion be swamped with hungry fans.

He told an interviewer that his love of hunting, still very strong, had slightly changed over the years. He could no longer kill deer. "I take one look at their beautiful big brown baby eyes, and I just shoot them with my camera," he smiled. At times he even made a shy effort to explain himself. Once he told of how proud he was to see his name in gold letters as vice president of a Beverly Hills bank. "But the bank went bust and I lost three and a half million dollars for that there prestige. After that I never let anyone sucker me, not even for a nickel." Even more from the heart was his observation of the movie industry: "This profession of mine has more ups and downs than any other profession on earth, and I've always noticed that the people who go to the top and stay at the top are the people who were kicked around as kids. People who had too easy a time of it seldom last."

After a screen absence of over a year, Beery returned to MGM to star with Marjorie Main and super tyke Margaret O'Brien in the Western *Bad Bascomb,* where he was not on his best behavior with little Maggie. It was his only 1946 release. *The Mighty McGurk,* another *The Champ* format with Wally saving orphan Dean Stockwell from nasty Edward Arnold, was his only 1947 film. Even Beery was weary of the rehashed celluloid stories from which he earned his paycheck. He also became vocal about his onscreen recurring pairing with hearty Marjorie Main. "My idea of a good picture would be to team me with Billie Burke. I always go out with pretty ladies—in fact, beautiful girls. I can get inspired more if they'd give me a good pretty actress to work with."

Just how inspired beautiful girls made Wally became obvious on Friday, February 13, 1948 when thirty-two-year-old Gloria Schumm, a statuesque honey-blonde, accused Wally of being the father of her week-old son. Mrs. Schumm, who had remarried her spouse Hans "to give the child a name," began an expansive campaign to win medical and legal expenses and support for the baby. Posing for the press with the bawling infant, she said that she was a close pal of Wally's Carol Ann, and that she had frequently stayed over at Beery's Wyoming ranch as "a friend of the family."

Wally was an hour away from having just settled a court battle with his ex-wife Rita over Carol Ann's $100,000 trust fund when Gloria filed her lawsuit. The initial response of the sixty-two-year-old was, "I am flattered." The public found the charge hilarious, but as Gloria pressed her charges, Wally began to fidget. He admitted that he had known the lady since 1933 and that he had recently seen to it that she obtained walk-ons in some of his recent films under the name of Gloria Whitney. "But she's only a casual acquaintance," he said. "Why she wants to do such a thing to me I can't figure out."

Wally allowed his attorney, Martin Gang, to di-

[18]Beery maintained a steady assignment of radio performances. He was a frequent guest on "Lux Radio Theatre" from the mid-1930s onward: *The Plutocrat* (1936) with Cecelia Parker; *Viva Villa!* (1938) with Noah Beery and Ellen Drew; *The Champ* (1939) with Josephine Hutchinson; *Stablemates* (1941) with Mickey Rooney and Fay Wray; *The Champ* (1942) with Josephine Hutchinson, Noah Beery, and Bobbie Larson; *The Bugle Sounds* (1943) with Marjorie Rambeau and Noah Beery; *Salute to the Marines* (1943) with Fay Bainter and Noah Beery.

rect the course of action as Gloria pressed her suit. Lawyer Gang assured the press that "Mr. Beery denies every allegation contained in this action and will take appropriate steps to prove his innocence of these unjustified charges." In actuality, Beery knew he was in a tight situation. In typical fashion, he quickly added a statement to his will that swore he had fathered no children.

Looking puffy and old, Beery appeared in three more features. *Alias a Gentleman* (1948) was a B melodrama with Beery in a familiar role as an ex-convict trying to go straight. *A Date with Judy,* released later that year, starred a surprisingly scrubbed-up Wally in a well-mounted Technicolor musical, in which he as the paterfamilias was flanked by Jane Powell and Elizabeth Taylor and learned to dance by the coaching of Carmen Miranda. The class feature revealed that Wally had a lot of personality left, but his heart condition was becoming increasingly serious. His health was not helped by his next picture *Big Jack* (1949)[19] in which he portrayed the title role of Big Jack Horner and worked for the seventh time with Marjorie Main. As usual, their working relationship was volatile, and Beery roared to a reporter, "She has blown her lines thirteen times on this one take. If I have to make another picture with her, I'll have a heart attack!"

[19]When the film was released, the *New York Times* reported, "It is hardly likely that this standard characterization will go down as the crowning achievement of his long career. . . . To put it awkwardly, *Big Jack*—bad movie." After that movie, Beery had been scheduled to be loaned to United Artists for *Johnny Holiday* (1949). He was replaced by William Bendix.

With fiancée Miss Lucille Bannister aboard the Queen Mary (August 1947).

It was a prophetic statement. On Friday, April 15, 1949, Wally was reading in the living room of his Alpine Drive mansion. At about 10 P.M. a heart attack struck the star. He slumped to the floor and shortly thereafter was dead. He was sixty-four.

Beery's death claimed front page headlines across the nation, due not only to his enormous popularity, but also to the paternity suit that Gloria Schumm continued to wage. (A week before his death, Gloria rejected Beery's offer of a $20,000 settlement.) While journalists cranked out rather specious tributes ("He was soft-spoken and unexcitable in private life"), the remarks of Gloria's attorney, Carly Warner, interrupted the honorary prose. "It is possible that the child can come into the estate unless Beery specifically disinherited him in his will."

Eighteen-year-old Carol Ann, Wally's brother Will, and ex-wife Rita decided to honor Beery's career by providing one of the most lavish funerals Hollywood would ever witness. On Tuesday, April 19, 1949, the cinema's great and not-so-great filed past Beery's body, bedecked in his beloved Navy uniform. The Reverend Ross Shaffer eulogized the star thusly, "Perhaps Wally's most outstanding characteristics to those who knew him best were his childlikeness, his enthusiasm, and his great warmth." The pallbearers who bore the casket to the interment at Forest Lawn Memorial Park included Edward J. Mannix and Louis B. Mayer himself, and honorary pallbearers included Bing Crosby, Clark Gable, Robert Taylor, Spencer Tracy, Leo Carrillo, George Murphy, Frank Capra, Jesse Lasky, Mervyn LeRoy, Joseph Schenck, Nicholas Schenck, Mack Sennett, Sam Wood, Darryl F. Zanuck, and Jack Dempsey.

Beery had long taken a strong interest in his will. He once commented that his estate was all to go to Carol Ann. "I ain't got no other heirs, so she'll get whatever I have." But upon his demise, his estate, valued at $2,220,150, was divided into three parts, going to Carol Ann, brother Will, and nephew Noah, Jr. Then Rita Beery Foyt re-appeared on the scene. Her marriage to the oil tycoon had failed miserably. She had moved back to Hollywood, keeping close to her ex-spouse in a house at 602 North Alpine Drive. She had attempted an acting career in 1944's *Dark Waters* with Merle Oberon, but no further offers came. After Wally's death, Rita demanded a share (one-half) of the estate. She claimed that Beery had fooled her about his true financial worth at the time

With Richard Conte and Marjorie Main in *Big Jack* (1949).

of their 1939 divorce, and that she had run the household in the 1930s on a paltry $25 weekly. Her campaign was aided when William Beery died several months after Wally, and the court indeed granted her $400,000—half of what was left of the stipend after taxes and administrative expenses were settled. It took three years for the monies to be properly doled, during which time little Johann Schumn. grew to be such a miniature Wallace Beery that Gloria eventually received a $25,000 settlement in 1952.

The Beery surname continues before the public via Noah Beery, Jr. Since appearing in bits in Noah, Sr. films such as *The Mark of Zorro* and *Penrod and Sam,* Noah, Jr. has appeared in over one hundred features and serials, and has been a regular on many teleseries, including James Garner's "The Rockford Files." He spends much of his time with his family on a remote Mojave Desert ranch, displaying the same love for escaping the Hollywood system that characterized his father and uncle.

Though many of his traits were hardly admirable, Wallace Beery was light years ahead of his colleagues in one admirable area—he never took himself too seriously. With his unabashed burps, unstifled yawns, and assorted gaucheries, Beery lumbered through a Golden Age Culver City. As giant a rebel in life as he was an actor in the motion pictures, Beery said it all when he once took time to grumble of his stardom: "Keep them guessing. As long as they spell the name right, that's okay by me. I'd rather go huntin' and fishin' and fly my big plane about the country than sit there balancin' a cup of tea, and have some sob sister simperin' over me. Like, 'Mr. Beery, do you really fly that big plane?' 'Mr. Beery, what was it like when you were married to Gloria Swanson?' 'Mr. Beery, is Carol Ann secretly your real child instead of being adopted?' Aw shucks—I can't sit still for that sissy stuff. Nope, I don't give no interviews. As long as the people keep coming in to see my pictures—nobody can complain."

FILMOGRAPHY

PATRIA
(International Film Service, 1917) 15 chapters

Chapters: (1) Last of the Fighting Channings, (2) The Treasure, (3) Winged Millions, (4) Double Crossed, (5) The Island God Forgot, (6) Alias Nemesis, (7) Red Dawn, (8) Red Night, (9) Cat's Paw and Scapegoat, (10) War in the Dooryard, (11) Sunset Falls, (12) Peace on the Border or Peace Which Passeth All Understanding, (13) Wings of Death, (14) Border Peril, (15) For the Flag.

DIRECTORS: The Whartons, Jacques Jaccard
SCREENPLAY: Joseph Vance

Irene Castle *(Patria)*; Milton Sills *(Donald Parr)*; Wallace Beery *(Pancho Villa)*; and: Warner Oland, Floyd Buckley, Marie Walcamp, George Maharoni, Allen Murnane, Dorothy Green.

THE LITTLE AMERICAN
(Paramount, 1917) 6 reels

DIRECTOR: Cecil B. DeMille
STORY-SCREENPLAY: Jeannie MacPherson, DeMille

Mary Pickford *(Angela Moore)*; Jack Holt *(Karl von Austreim)*; Raymond Hatton *(Count Julues de Deatin)*; Hobart Bosworth *(German Colonel)*; James Neill *(Senator John Moore)*; Ben Alexander *(Bobby Moore)*; Walter Long *(German Captain)*; Guy Oliver *(Frederick von Austreim)*; Lillian Leighton *(Angela's Great Aunt)*; DeWitt Jennings *(English Barrister)*; Edythe Chapman *(Von Austreim's American Wife)*; and: Wallace Beery, Ramon Novarro, Sam Wood.

JOHANNA ENLISTS
(Paramount, 1918) 5 reels

DIRECTOR: William Desmond Taylor
BASED ON THE STORY "THE MOBILIZING OF JOHANNA"
SCREENPLAY: Frances Marion

Mary Pickford *(Johanna Renssaller)*; Fred Huntley *("Paw" Renssaller)*; Monte Blue *(Private Vibbard)*; Anna Schaefer *("Maw" Renssaller)*; Douglas MacLean *(Captain Van Renssaller)*; Emory Johnson *(Lieutenant Le Roy)*; John Steppling *(Major Wappington)*; Wallace Beery *(Colonel Fanner)*; Wesley Barry *(Johanna's Brother)*; June and Jean Prentis *(Johanna's Twin Sisters)*.

THE UNPARDONABLE SIN
(Equity, 1919) 8 reels

PRODUCER: Harry Garson
DIRECTOR: Marshall Neilan
STORY: Rupert Hughes

With: Blanche Sweet, Edwin Stevens, Wallace Beery, Mary Alden, Matt Moore, Wesley Barry, Bobby Connolly, Bull Montana.

THE LOVE BURGLAR
(Paramount, 1919) 5 reels

DIRECTOR: James Cruze
BASED ON THE PLAY *One of Us* BY JACK LAIT
SCREENPLAY: Walter Woods

Wallace Reid *(David Strong)*; Anna Q. Nilsson *(Jean Gray)*; Raymond Hatton *(Smith)*; Wallace Beery *(Coast-to-Coast Taylor)*; Wilton Taylor *(Miller)*; Edward Burns *(Arthur Strong)*; Alice Taffe *(Elsie Strong)*; Richard Wayne *(Rosswell)* Henry Woodward *(Dave Dorgan)*; Loyola O'Connor *(Mrs. Strong)*.

THE LIFE LINE
(Paramount, 1919) 5 reels

DIRECTOR: Maurice Tourneur
BASED ON THE PLAY *The Romany Rye* BY GEORGE R. SIMMS
ADAPTOR-SCREENPLAY: Charles S. Whittaker

Jack Holt *(Jack Hearne)*; Lew J. Cody *(Philip Royston)*; Pauline Stark *(Ruth Heckett)*; Seena Owen *(Lura the Gypsy Fortune Teller)*; Tully Marshall *(Joe Heckett)*; Wallace Beery *(Gypsy Thief)*.

SOLDIERS OF FORTUNE
(Realart, 1919) 7 reels

DIRECTOR: Allan Dwan
BASED ON THE STORY BY RICHARD HARDING DAVIS AND THE PLAY BY AUGUSTUS THOMAS
SCREENPLAY: Dwan

Norman Kerry *(Robert Clay)*; Pauline Stark *(Hope Langham)*; Anna Q. Nilsson *(Alice Langham)*; Wallace Beery *(Mendoza)*; Wilfred Lucas *(President Alvarez)*; and: Melbourne McDowell, Ward Crane, Phil McCullough, Fred Kohler, Ogden Crane, Frank Wally.

BEHIND THE DOOR
(Paramount, 1919) 7 reels

PRODUCER: Thomas H. Ince
DIRECTOR: Irvin Willat
BASED ON THE NOVEL BY GOUVENER MORRIS
SCREENPLAY: Luther Reed

Hobart Bosworth *(Oscar Krug)*; Jane Novak *(Alice Morse)*; Wallace Beery *(Lieutenant Brandt)*; James Gordon *(Bill Tavish)*; Dick Wain *(McQuestion)*; J. P. Lockney *(Matthew Morse)*; Gibson Gowland *(Gideon Blank)*; Otto Hoffman *(Mark Arnold)*.

VICTORY
(Paramount, 1920) 8 reels

DIRECTOR: Maurice Tourneur
BASED ON THE NOVEL BY JOSEPH CONRAD
SCREENPLAY: Stephen Fox

Jack Holt *(Axel Heyst)*; Seena Owen *(Alma)*; Lon Chaney *(Ricardo)*; Wallace Beery *(Sohomberg)*; Ben Deeley *(Mr. Jones)*; Laura Winston *(Mrs. Sohomberg)*; Bull Montana *(Pedro)*; George Nicholls *(Captain Davison)*.

THE VIRGIN STAMBOUL
(Universal, 1920) 7,500

DIRECTOR: Tod Browning
STORY: H. H. Van Loan
SCREENPLAY: Browning

Priscilla Dean *(Sari)*; Wheeler Oakman *(Captain Carlise Pemberton)*; Wallace Beery *(Achmed Hamid)*; Edward Burns *(Hector Baron)*; Eugenie Forde *(Sari's Mother)*; E. D. Warren *(Yusef Bey)*; Nigel de Brulier *(Kaptain Kassan)*; Ethel Ritchie *(Resha)*.

THE MOLLYCODDLE
(United Artists, 1920) 6 reels

PRODUCER: Douglas Fairbanks
DIRECTOR: Victor Fleming
STORY: Harold McGrath
SCREENPLAY: Fairbanks, Tom Geraghty
CAMERA: William C. McGann

Douglas Fairbanks *(Richard Marshall)*; Wallace Beery *(Henry Von Holkar)*; Ruth Renick *(Virginia Hale)*; Charles Stevens *(Yellow Horse the Bad Indian)*; Betty Boulton *(Mollie Waren)*; George Stewart *(Ole Olsen)*; Albert MacQuarrie *(Driver of the Desert Yacht)*; Paul Burns *(Samuel Levinski)*; Morris Hughes *(Patrick O'Flannigan)*; Adele Farrington *(Mrs. Warren)*; Lewis Hippe *(First Mate)*.

THE ROUND UP
(Paramount, 1920) 6,419 ′

DIRECTOR: George Melford
BASED ON THE PLAY BY EDMUND DAY
ADAPTOR: Tom Forman

Roscoe "Fatty" Arbuckle *(Slim Hector the Sheriff)*; Tom Forman *(Jack Payson)*; Irving Cummings *(Dick Lane)*; Mabel Juliane Scott *(Echo Allen)*; Jean Acker *(Polly Hope)*; Guy Oliver *(Uncle Jim)*; Lucien Littlefield *(Porenthesis the Cowboy)*; Fred Huntley *("Sagebrush" Charlie)*; Wallace Beery *(Buck McKee)*; Jane Wolffe *(Aunt Josephine)*;

George Kuwa *(Chinese Boy);* Edward Sutherland *(Bud Lane).*

THE LAST OF THE MOHICANS
(Associated Productions, 1920) 6 reels

DIRECTORS: Maurice Tourneur, Clarence Brown
BASED ON THE NOVEL BY JAMES FENIMORE COOPER
SCREENPLAY: Robert A. Dillon
CAMERA: Philip R. Dubois, Charles E. Van Engre

Wallace Beery *(Magua);* Barbara Bedford *(Cora Munro);* Albert Roscoe *(Uncas);* Lillian Hall *(Alice Munro);* George Hackathorne *(Captain Randolph);* Nelson McDowell *(David Gamut);* Henry Woodward *(Major Heyward);* Harry Lorraine *(Hawkeye);* Theodore Lorch *(Chingachgook);* Jack MacDonald *(Tamenund);* Sidney Deane *(General Webb);* James Gordon *(Colonel Munro).*

EIGHT-THIRTEEN
(Robertson-Cole, 1920) 5 reels

DIRECTOR: Scott Sidney
BASED ON THE NOVEL BY MAURICE LEBLANC
SCREENPLAY: Darling

Wedgewood Nowell *(Arsene Lupin/Le Normand/Prince Sernine);* Wallace Beery *(Major Parbury/Ribiera);* Kathryn Adams *(Dolores Castleback);* J. P. Lockney *(Formerie);* Frederick Vroom *(Prefect of Police);* William V. Mong *(Chapman);* Ralph Lewis *(Castleback);* Colin Kenny *(Baupre/Leduc);* Vera Stedman *(Suzanne);* Laura La Plante *(Genevieve).*

THE ROOKIES RETURN
(Paramount, 1921) 4,123´

DIRECTOR: Thomas H. Ince
STORY/SCREENPLAY: Archer McMackin
CAMERA: Bert Cann

Douglas MacLean *(James Stewart Lee);* Doris May *(Alicia);* Frank Currier *(Dad);* Kathleen Key *(Gloria);* Frank Clark *(Tubbs);* Wallace Beery *(Francois Dupont);* Elinor Hancock *(Mrs. Radcliffe);* William Courtwright *(Gregg);* Leo White *(Henri);* Aggie Herring *(Mrs. Perkins).*

PATSY
(Truart Film Corporation, 1921) 5,300´

DIRECTOR: John McDermott
BASED ON THE PLAY BY ER LAWSHE
SCREENPLAY: McDermott

ZaSu Pitts *(Patsy);* John MacFarlane *(Pops);* Tom Gallery *(Bob Brooks);* Marjorie Daw *(Margaret Vincent);* Fannie Midgley *(Mrs. Vincent);* Wallace Beery *(Gustave Ludermann);* Harry Todd *(Tramp);* Milla Davenport *(Matron);* Henry Fortson *(Bones).*

A TALE OF TWO WORLDS
(Goldwyn, 1921) 5,649´

PRODUCER: Samuel Goldwyn
DIRECTOR: Frank Lloyd
STORY: Gouverneur Morris
SCREENPLAY: J. E. Nash
ASSISTANT DIRECTOR: Harry Weil
CAMERA: Norbert Brodine

J. Frank Glendon *(Newcombe);* Leatrice Joy *(Sui Sen);* Wallace Beery *(Ling Jo);* E. A. Warren *(Ah Wing);* Margaret McWade *(Attendant);* Togo Yamamoto *(One Eye);* Jack Abbe *(The Worm);* Louie Cheung *(Chinaman);* Chow Young *(Slave Girl);* Etta Lee *(Ah Fah);* Ah Wing *(Servant Spy);* Goro Kino *(Windlass Man);* Arthur Soames *(Dr. Newcombe);* Edythe Chapman *(Mrs. Newcombe);* Dwight Crittenden *(Mrs. Carmichael);* Irene Rich *(Mrs. Carmichael).*

THE FOUR HORSEMEN OF THE APOCALYPSE
(Metro, 1921) 11 reels

DIRECTOR: Rex Ingram
BASED ON THE NOVEL BY VICENTE BLASCO-IBANEZ
TRANSLATION: Charlotte Brewster Jordan
ADAPTOR: June Mathis
ASSISTANT DIRECTOR: Walter Mayo
ART TITLES: Jack W. Robson
ART DIRECTORS: Joseph Calder, Amos Myers
MUSIC: Louis F. Gottschalk
CAMERA: John F. Seitz, Starret Ford, Walter Mayo
EDITOR: Grant Whytock

Rudolph Valentino *(Julio Desnoyers);* Alice Terry *(Marguerite Laurier);* Pomeroy Cannon *(Madariaga the Centaur);* Josef Swickard *(Marcelo Desnoyers);* Brinsley Shaw *(Celendonio);* Alan Hale *(Karl von Hartrott);* Bridgetta Clark *(Dona Luisa);* Mabel Van Buren *(Elena);* Nigel De Brulier *(Tchernoff);* Bowditch Turner *(Argensola);* John Sainpolis *(Laurier);* Mark Fenton *(Senator Lacour);* Virginia Warwick *(Chichi);* Derek Ghent *(Rene Lacour);* Stuart Holmes *(Captain von Hartrott);* Jean Hersholt *(Professor von Hartrott);* Henry Klaus *(Henrich von Hartrott);* Edward Connelly *(Lodgekeeper);* Georgia Woodthorpe *(Lodgekeeper's Wife);* Kathleen Key *(Georgette);* Wallace Beery *(Lieutenant Colonel von Richthoffen);* Curt Rehfeld *(Major Blumhardt);* Claire De Lorez *(Mademoiselle Lucette, the Model);* Bull Montana *(French Butler);* Arthur Hoyt *(Lieutenant Schnitz);* Noble Johnson *(Conquest).*

THE GOLDEN SNARE
(Associated First National, 1921) 5,900´

DIRECTOR: David M. Hartford
BASED ON THE NOVEL BY JAMES OLIVER CURWOOD
SCREENPLAY: Curwood, Hartford
CAMERA: Walter Griffin

Lewis Stone *(Sergeant Philip Raine);* Wallace Beery *(Bram Johnson);* Melbourne MacDowell *("Doug" Johnson);* Ruth Renick *(Celie);* Wellington Playter *("Black" Dawson);* DeWitt Jennings *("Fighting" Fitzgerald);* Francis McDonald *(Pierre Thoreau);* Little Esther Scott *(Baby).*

THE LAST TRAIL
(Fox, 1921) 6,355´

PRESENTER: William Fox
DIRECTOR: Emmett J. Flynn
BASED ON THE NOVEL BY ZANE GREY
SCREENPLAY: Jules Furthman, Paul Schofield
CAMERA: Lucien Andriot

Maurice B. Flynn *(The Stranger);* Eva Novak *(Winifred Samson);* Wallace Beery *(Willian Kirk);* Rosemary Theby *(Chiquita);* Charles K. French *(Sheriff Nelson);* Harry Springler *(Campbell);* Harry Dunkinson *(Kenworth Samson).*

THE MAN FROM HELL'S RIVER
(Western Pictures Exploitation Company, 1922) 5 reels

PRODUCER/DIRECTOR, Irving Cummings
BASED ON THE STORY "GOD OF HER PEOPLE" BY JAMES OLIVER CURWOOD
SCREENPLAY: Cummings
CAMERA: Abe Fried

Irving Cummings *(Pierre de Barre);* Eva Novak *(Mabella);* Wallace Beery *(Gaspard the Wolf);* Frank Whitson *(Sergeant McKenna);* Robert Klein *(Lopente);* William Herford *(The Padre);* Rin-Tin-Tin *(The Dog).*

THE ROSARY
(Associated First National, 1922) 7,045´

PRODUCERS: William N. Selig, Sam E. Rork
DIRECTOR: Jerome Storm
BASED ON THE PLAY BY EDWARD E. ROSE
SCREENPLAY: Bernard McConville
TECHNICAL DIRECTOR: Gabe Pollock
CAMERA: Edwin Linden

Lewis S. Stone *(Father Brian Kelly);* Jane Novak *(Vera Mather);* Wallace Beery *(Kenwood Wright);* Robert Gordon *(Bruce Wilton);* Eugenie Besserer *(Widow Kathleen Wilton);* Dore Davidson *(Isaac Abrahamson);* Pomeroy Cannon *(Donald MacTavish);* Bert Woodruff *(Captain Caleb Mather);* Mildred June *(Alice Wilton);* Harold Goodwin *(Skeeters Martin).*

WILD HONEY
(Universal, 1922) 6,422´

PRESENTER: Carl Laemmle
DIRECTOR: Wesley Ruggles

BASED ON THE STORIES
BY CYNTHIA STOCKLEY
SCREENPLAY: Lucien Hubbard
CAMERA: Harry Thorpe

Priscilla Dean *(Lady Vivienne);* Noah Beery *(Henry Porthen);* Lloyd Whitlock *(Freddy Sutherland);* Raymond Blathwayt *(Sir Hugh);* Percy Challenger *(Ebenezer Leamish);* Helen Raymond *(Joan Rudd);* Landers Stevens *(Wolf Montague);* Robert Ellis *(Kerry Burgess);* Wallace Beery *(Buck Roper);* Carl Stockdale *(Liverpool Blondie);* Christian Frank *(Repington);* Harry De Roy *(Koos).*

I AM THE LAW
(Affiliated Distributors, 1922) 6,800 ′

PRESENTER: C. C. Burr
DIRECTOR: Edwin Carewe
BASED ON THE STORY
"THE POETIC JUSTICE OF UKO SAN"
BY JAMES OLIVER CURWOOD
SCREENPLAY: Raymond L. Schrock
CAMERA: Robert B. Kurrle

Alice Lake *(Joan Cameron);* Kenneth Harlan *(Robert Fitzgerald);* Rosemary Theby *(Mrs. Georges Mardeaux);* Gaston Glass *(Tom Fitzgerald);* Noah Beery *(Sergeant Georges Mardeaux);* Wallace Beery *(Fu Chang).*

HURRICANE'S GAL
(Associated First National, 1922) 7,844 ′

PRESENTER/DIRECTOR: Allen Holubar
STORY: Harvey Gates
ADAPTOR: Holubar
TITLES: Max Abramson
ASSISTANT DIRECTOR: Harold S. Bucquet
NAVAL TECHNICAL ADVISOR:
Lieutenant Thomas Berrian, U.S.N.
CAMERA: Byron Haskin, William McGann
EDITOR: Frank Lawrence

Dorothy Phillips *(Lola);* Robert Ellis *(Steele O'Connor);* Wallace Beery *(Chris Borg);* James O. Barrows *(Cap'n Danny);* Gertrude Astor *(Phyllis Fairfield);* William Fong *(Sing);* Jack Donovan *(Lieutenant Grant);* Frances Raymond *(Mrs. Fairfield).*

TROUBLE
(Associated First National, 1922) 4,912 ′

PRESENTER: Sol Lesser
PRODUCER: Jack Coogan, Sr.
DIRECTOR: Albert Austin
TITLES: Max Abramson
CAMERA: Glen MacWilliams, Robert Martin
EDITOR: Irene Morra

Jackie Coogan *(Danny, the Kid);* Wallace Beery *(Ed Lee, the Plumber);* Gloria Hope *(Mrs. Lee);* Queenie *(The Dog).*

ROBIN HOOD
(United Artists, 1922) 10,680

PRODUCER: Douglas Fairbanks
DIRECTOR: Allan Dwan
STORY: Elton Thomas [Fairbanks]
SCREENPLAY EDITOR: Lotta Woods
ART DIRECTORS: William Buckland, Irvin J. Martin, Edward M. Langley
RESEARCH DIRECTOR: Arthur Woods
LITERARY CONSULTANT: Edward Knoblock
TECHNICAL DIRECTOR: Robert Fairbanks
COSTUMES: Mitchell Leisen
CAMERA: Paul Eagler
FILM ASSEMBLY: William Nolan

Douglas Fairbanks [*The Earl of Huntingdon (Robin Hood)*]; Wallace Beery *(Richard the Lion-Hearted);* Sam De Grasse *(Prince John);* Enid Bennett *(Lady Marian Fitzwalter);* Paul Dickey *(Sir Guy of Gisbourne);* William Lowery *(The High Sheriff of Nottingham);* Roy Coulson *(The King's Jester);* Billie Bennett *(Lady Marian's Serving Woman);* Merrill McCormick, Wilson Benge *(Henchmen to Prince John);* Willard Louis *(Friar Tuck);* Alan Hale *(Little John);* Lloyd Talman *(Alan-a-Dale);* Maine Geary *(Will Scarlett),* Rita Gillman *(Extra).*

THE SAGEBRUSH TRAIL
(Western Pictures Exploitation Company, 1922) 4,471 ′

PRESENTER: Hugh B. Evans, Jr.
DIRECTOR: Robert T. Thornby
STORY/SCREENPLAY: H. H. Van Loan

Roy Stewart *(Larry Reid, Sheriff of Silvertown);* Marjorie Daw *(Mary Gray);* Johnny Walker *(Neil, Her Brother);* Wallace Beery *(Jose Fugaro).*

ONLY A SHOP GIRL
(C. B. C. Film Sales, 1922) 6,400 ′

PRODUCER: Harry Cohn
DIRECTOR: Edward J. Le Saint
BASED ON THE PLAY
BY CHARLES E. BLANEY
SCREENPLAY: Le Saint

Estelle Taylor *(Mame Mulvey);* Mae Busch *(Josie Jerome);* Wallace Beery *(Jim Brennan);* William Scott *(Danny Mulvey);* James Morrison *(Charles Black);* Josephine Adair *(Angelina Jerome);* Willard Louis *(James Watkins);* Claire Du Brey *(Mrs. Watkins);* Tully Marshall *(Manager of Watkins' Store).*

THE FLAME OF LIFE
(Universal, 1923) 5,780 ′

PRESENTER: Carl Laemmle
DIRECTOR: Hobart Henley
BASED ON THE PLAY
That Lass O'Lowrie's
BY FRANCES HODGSON BURNETT
SCREENPLAY: Elliott J. Clawson
CAMERA: Virgil Miller

Priscilla Dean *(Joan Lowrie);* Robert Ellis *(Fergus Derrick);* Kathryn McGuire *(Alice Barholm);* Wallace Beery *(Dan Lowrie);* Fred Kohler *(Spring);* Beatrice Burnham *(Liz);* Emmett King *(Barholm);* Frankie Lee *(Jud);* Grace De Garro *(Mag);* Dorothy Hagan *(Baroness);* Evelyn McCoy *(Fauntleroy).*

STORMSWEPT
(Film Booking Offices of America, 1923) 5,000 ′

PRODUCER/DIRECTOR: Robert Thornby
STORY: H. H. Van Loan
SCREENPLAY: Winifred Dunn
CAMERA: Ben Reynolds

Wallace Beery *(William McCabe);* Noah Beery *(Shark Moran);* Virginia Browne Faire *(Ann Reynolds);* Arline Pretty *(Helda McCabe);* Jack Carlyle *(Snape).*

THREE AGES
(Metro, 1923) 5,251 ′

PRODUCER: Joseph M. Schenck
DIRECTORS: Buster Keaton, Eddie Cline
STORY/TITLES: Clyde Bruckman, Joseph Mitchell, Jean Havez
ART DIRECTOR: Fred Gabourie
CAMERA: William McGann, Elgin Lessley

Buster Keaton *(The Hero);* Margaret Leahy *(The Girl);* Wallace Beery *(The Villain);* Joe Roberts *(The Father);* Horace Morgan *(The Emperor);* Lillian Lawrence *(The Mother).*

BAVU
(Universal, 1923) 6,986 ′

DIRECTOR: Stuart Paton
BASED ON THE PLAY
BY EARL CARROLL
SCREENPLAY: Raymond L. Schrock, Albert Kenyon
CAMERA: Allen Davey

Wallace Beery *(Felix Bavu);* Estelle Taylor *(Princes Annia);* Forrest Stanley *(Mischa Vleck);* Sylvia Breamer *(Olga Stropik);* Josef Swickard *(Prince Markoff);* Nick De Ruiz *(Kuroff);* Martha Mattox *(Piplette);* Harry Carter *(Shadow);* Jack Rollens *(Michael Revno).*

DRIFTING
(Universal, 1923) 7,394 ′

PRESENTER: Carl Laemmle
DIRECTOR: Tod Browning
BASED ON THE PLAY
BY JOHN COLTON
AND DAISY H. ANDREWS
SCREENPLAY: Browning, A. P. Younger
TITLES: Gardner Bradford
CAMERA: William Fildew
EDITOR: Errol Taggart

Priscilla Dean *(Cassie Cook/Lucille Preston);* Matt Moore *(Captain Arthur Jarvis);* Wallace Beery *(Jules Repin);* J. Farrell MacDonald *(Murphy);* Rose Dione *(Madame Polly Voo);* Edna Tichenor *(Molly Norton);* William V. Mong *(Dr. Li);* Anna May Wong *(Rose Li);* Bruce Guerin *(Billy Hepburn);* Marie De Albert *(Mrs. Hepburn);* William Moran *(Mr. Hepburn);* Frank Lanning *(Chang Wang).*

ASHES OF VENGEANCE
(Associated First National, 1923) 9,893 ′

PRESENTER/PRODUCER: Joseph M. Schenck
DIRECTOR: Frank Lloyd
BASED ON THE NOVEL BY
H. B. SOMERVILLE
ADAPTOR: Lloyd
CAMERA: Tony Gaudio

Norma Talmadge *(Yolande de Breux)*; Conway Tearle *(Rupert de Vrieac)*; Wallace Beery *(Duc de Tours)*; Josephine Crowell *(Catherine de Medicis)*; Betty Francisco *(Margot de Vancoire)*; Claire McDowell *(Margot's Aunt)*; Courtenay Foote *(Comte de la Roche)*; Howard Truesdell *(Vicomte de Briege)*; Jeanne Carpenter *(Anne—Yolande's Invalid Sister)*; Forrest Robinson *(Father Paul)*; James Cooley *(Paul)*; Boyd Irwin *(Duc de Guise)*; Winter Hall *(Bishop)*; William Clifford *(Andre)*; Murdock MacQuarrie *(Carlotte)*; Hector V. Sarno *(Gallon)*; Earl Schenck *(Blais)*; Lucy Beaumont *(Charlotte)*; Frank Leigh *(Lupi)*; Carmen Phillips *(Marie)*; Andre de Beranger *(Charles IX)*.

THE ETERNAL STRUGGLE
(Metro, 1923) 7,374 ′

PRESENTER/PRODUCER: Louis B. Mayer
DIRECTOR: Reginald Barker
BASED ON THE NOVEL *The Law-Bringers*
BY G. B. LANCASTER
SCREENPLAY: Monte M. Katterjohn
ADAPTOR: J. G. Hawks
CAMERA: Percy Hilburn
EDITOR: Robert J. Kern

Renee Adoree *(Andree Grange)*; Earle Williams *(Sergeant Neil Tempest)*; Barbara La Marr *(Camille Lenoir)*; Pat O'Malley *(Bucky O'Hara)*; Wallace Beery *(Barode Dukane)*; Josef Swickard *(Pierre Grange)*; Pat Harmon *(Oily Kirby)*; Anders Randolf *(Captain Jack Scott)*; Edwin J. Brady *(Jean Cardeau)*; Robert Anderson *(Olaf Olafson)*; George Kuwa *(Wo Long)*.

RICHARD THE LION-HEARTED
(Allied Producers and Distributors, 1923) 7,298 ′

PRODUCERS: Frank E. Woods, Thompson Buchanan, Elmer Harris, Clark W. Thomas
DIRECTOR: Chet Withey
BASED ON THE NOVEL *The Talisman*
BY SIR WALTER SCOTT
SCREENPLAY: Frank E. Woods
HISTORICAL RESEARCH: Arthur Woods
MUSIC SYNOPSIS: James C. Bradford
CAMERA: Joseph Walker

Wallace Beery *(King Richard the Lion-Hearted)*; Charles Gerrard *(Sultan Saladin)*; Kathleen Clifford *(Queen Berangaria)*; Marguerite De La Motte *(Lady Edith Plantagenet)*; John Bowers *(Sir Kenneth—Knight of the Leopard)*; Clarence Geldert *(Sir Conrade de Montserrat)*; Wilbur Higby *(Sir Thomas Devaux)*; Tully Marshall *(The Bishop of Tyre)*.

THE SPANISH DANCER
(Paramount, 1923) 8,434 ′

PRESENTER: Adolph Zukor
PRODUCER/DIRECTOR: Herbert Brenon
BASED ON THE NOVEL *Don Cesar de Bazan*
BY ADOLPHE PHILIPPE DENNERY
AND PHILIPPE FRANÇOIS PINEL
ADAPTORS: June Mathis, Beulah Marie Dix
CAMERA: James Wong Howe

Pola Negri *(Maritana, a Gypsy Dancer)*; Antonio Moreno *(Don Cesar de Bazan)*; Wallace Beery *(King Philip IV)*; Kathlyn Williams *(Queen Isabel of Bourbon)*; Gareth Hughes *(Lazarillo, a Prisoner)*; Adolphe Menjou *(Don Salluste, a Courtier)*; Edward Kipling *(Marquis de Rotundo)*; Anne Shirley *(Don Balthazar Carlos)*; Charles A. Stevenson *(Cardinal's Ambassador)*; Robert Agnew *(Juan, the Thief)*.

THE DRUMS OF JEOPARDY
(Truart Film Corporation, 1923) 6,529 ′

PRESENTER: M. H. Hoffman
SUPERVISOR: Roland G. Edwards
DIRECTOR: Edward Dillon
BASED ON THE NOVEL
BY HAROLD MACGRATH
ADAPTOR: Arthur Hoerl
TITLES: Alfred A. Cohn, A. Carle Palm
ART DIRECTOR: Horace Jackson
CAMERA: James Diamond
EDITORS: Cohn, Palm.

Elaine Hammerstein *(Dorothy Burrows)*; Jack Mulhall *(Jerome Hawksley)*; Wallace Beery *(Gregor Karlov)*; David Torrence *(Cutty)*; Maude George *(Olga Andrevich)*; Eric Mayne *(Banker Burrows)*; Forrest Seabury *(Stefani)*.

THE WHITE TIGER
(Universal, 1923) 7,177 ′

DIRECTOR/STORY: Tod Browning
SCREENPLAY: Browning, Charles Kenyon
CAMERA: William Fildew

Priscilla Dean *(Sylvia Donovan)*; Matt Moore *(Dick Longworth)*; Raymond Griffith *(Roy Donovan)*; Wallace Beery [*Count Donelli (Hawkes)*].

UNSEEN HANDS
(Associated Exhibitors, 1924) 5,382 ′

PRODUCER: Walker Coleman Graves, Jr.
DIRECTOR: Jacques Jaccard
SCREENPLAY: Graves

Wallace Beery *(Jean Scholast)*; Joseph J. Dowling *(Georges Le Quintrec)*; Fontaine La Rue *(Madame Le Quintrec)*; Jack Rollins *(Armand Le Quintrec)*; Cleo Madison *(Matoaka)*; Jim Corey *(Wapita)*; Jamie Gray *(Nola)*.

THE SEA HAWK
(Associated First National, 1924) 12,045 ′

DIRECTOR: Frank Lloyd
BASED ON THE NOVEL
BY RAFAEL SABATINI
SCREENPLAY: J. G. Hawks
TITLES: Walter Anthony
ART DIRECTOR: Stephen Goosson
SHIPS DESIGNED AND EXECUTED BY FRED GABOURIE
DIRECTOR OF RESEARCH: William J. Reiter
COSTUMES: Walter J. Israel
THEME SONG: Modest Altschuler and John LeRoy Johnson
CAMERA: Norbert F. Brodine
EDITOR: Fred Gabourie

Milton Sills [*Sir Oliver Tressilian (Sakr-el-Bahr, the Sea Hawk)*]; Enid Bennett *(Rosamund Godolphin)*; Lloyd Hughes *(Master Lionel Tressilian)*; Wallace MacDonald *(Master Peter Godolphin)*; Marc MacDermott *(Sir John Killigrew)*; Wallace Beery *(Jasper Leigh, a Freebooter)*; Frank Currier *(Asad-el Din, Basha of Algiers)*; Medea Radzina *(Fenzileh, His Wife)*; William Collier, Jr. *(Marzak, His Son)*; Lionel Belmore *(Justice Baine)*; Fred De Silva *(Ali, Asad's Lieutenant)*; Hector V. Sarno *(Tsamanni, Asad's Personal Aide)*; Albert Prisco *(Yusuf, a Moorish Leader)*; George E. Romain *(Spanish Commander)*; Robert Bolder *(Ayoub, Fenzileh's Servant)*; Al Jennings *(Captain of Asad's Guards)*; Claire Du Brey *(The Siren)*; Edward Davis *(Chief Justice of England)*; Theodore Lorch *(Turkish Merchant)*; Rita Gillman *(Bit)*.

THE SIGNAL TOWER
(Universal, 1924) 6,714 ′

PRESENTER: Carl Laemmle
DIRECTOR: Clarence Brown
BASED ON THE STORY
BY WADSWORTH CAMP
SCREENPLAY: James O. Spearing
CAMERA: Ben Reynolds

Virginia Valli *(Sally Tolliver)*; Rockliffe Fellowes *(Dave Tolliver)*; Frankie Darro *(Sonny Tolliver)*; Wallace Beery *(Joe Standish)*; James O. Barrows *(Old Bill)*; J. Farrell MacDonald *(Pete)*; Dot Farley *(Gertie)*; Clarence Brown *(Switch Man)*; Jitney *(The Dog)*.

ANOTHER MAN'S WIFE
(Producers Distributing Corporation, 1924) 5,015 ′

DIRECTOR: Bruce Mitchell
SCREENPLAY: Mitchell, Elliott Clawson
CAMERA: Steve Norton

James Kirkwood *(John Brand)*; Lila Lee *(Helen Brand)*; Wallace Beery *(Captain Wolf)*; Matt Moore *(Phillip Cochran)*; Zena Keefe *(Dancer)*; Chester Conklin *(Rumrunner)*.

THE RED LILY
(Metro-Goldwyn, 1924) 6,975 ′

DIRECTOR/STORY: Fred Niblo
SCREENPLAY: Bess Meredyth

Art Director: Ben Carré
Assistant Director: Doran Cox
Camera: Victor Milner
Editor: Lloyd Nosler

Enid Bennett *(Marise La Noue);* Ramon Novarro *(Jean Leonnec);* Wallace Beery *(Bobo);* Frank Currier *(Hugo Leonnec);* Rosemary Theby *(Nana);* Mitchell Lewis *(D'Agut);* Emily Fitzroy *(Mama Bouchard);* George Periolat *(Papa Bouchard);* Milla Davenport *(Madame Poussot);* Dick Sutherland *(The Toad);* Gibson Gowland *(Le Turc);* George Nichols *(Concierge).*

DYNAMITE SMITH
(Pathé, 1924) 6,400′

Director: Ralph Ince
Story/Screenplay: C. Gardner Sullivan
Camera: Henry Sharp

Charles Ray *(Gladstone Smith);* Jacqueline Logan *(Kitty Gray);* Bessie Love *(Violet);* Wallace Beery *("Slugger" Rourke);* Lydia Knott *(Aunt Mehitabel);* S. D. Wilcox *(Marshal);* Russell Powell *(Colin MacClintock);* Adelbert Knott *(Dad Gray).*

MADONNA OF THE STREETS
(First National, 1924) 7,507′

Presenter/Director: Edwin Carewe
Based on the novel *The Ragged Messenger* by William Babington Maxwell
Adaptor: Frank Griffin
Titles: Frederic Hatton, Fanny Hatton
Art Director: John D. Schulze
Assistant Director: Wallace Fox
Camera: Robert Kurrle

Nazimova *(Mary Carlson/Mary Ainsleigh);* Milton Sills *(Reverend John Morton);* Claude Gillingwater *(Lord Patrington);* Courtenay Foote *(Dr. Colbeck);* Wallace Beery *(Bill Smythe);* Anders Randolf *("Bull" Morgan);* John T. Murray *("Slippery" Eddie Foster);* Vivien Oakland *(Lady Sarah Joyce);* Harold Goodwin *(Walter Bowman);* Rosa Gore *(Mrs. Elyard);* Maybeth Carr *(Judy Smythe);* Herbert Prior *(Nathan Norris).*

SO BIG
(First National, 1924) 8,562′

Supervisor: Earl Hudson
Director: Charles Brabin
Based on the novel by Edna Ferber
Screenplay: Adelaide Heilbron
Adaptor: Earl Hudson
Art Director: Milton Menasco
Camera: T. D. McCord
Editor: Arthur Tavares

Colleen Moore *(Selina Peake);* Joseph De Grasse *(Simeon Peake);* John Bowers *(Pervus DeJong);* Ben Lyon *(Dirk DeJong);* Wallace Beery *(Klass Poole);* Gladys Brockwell *(Maartje Poole);* Jean Hersholt *(Aug Hempel);* Charlotte Merriam *(Julie Hempel);* Dot Farley *(Widow Paarlenburg);* Ford Sterling *(Jacob Hoogenduck);* Frankie Darro *(Dirk DeJong as a Boy);* Henry Herbert *(William Storm);* Dorothy Brock *(Dirk DeJong as a Baby);* Rosemary Theby *(Paula Storm);* Phyllis Haver *(Dallas O'Meara).*

LET WOMEN ALONE
(Producers Distributing Corporation, 1925) 5,620′

Producer: Frank Woods
Director: Paul Powell
Based on the story "On the Shelf" by Viola Brothers Shore
Adaptor: Woods
Technical Director: H. S. Wilcox
Camera: Joseph Walker

Pat O'Malley *(Tom Benham);* Wanda Hawley *(Beth Wylie);* Wallace Beery *(Cap Bullwinkle);* Ethel Wales *(Ma Benham);* J. Farrell MacDonald *(Commodore John Gordon);* Harris Gordon *(Jim Wylie);* Betty Jane Snowdon *(Jean Wylie);* Lee Willard *(Alec Morrison);* Marjorie Morton *(Isabel Morrison).*

COMING THROUGH
(Paramount, 1925) 6,522′

Presenters: Adolph Zukor, Jesse L. Lasky
Director: Edward Sutherland
Based on the novel *Bed Rock* by Jack Bethea
Screenplay: Paul Schofield
Camera: Faxon M. Dean

Thomas Meighan *(Tom Blackford);* Lila Lee *(Alice Rand);* John Miltern *(John Rand);* Wallace Beery *(Joe Lawler);* Lawrence Wheat *(Munds);* Frank Campeau *(Shackleton);* Gus Weinberg *(Dr. Rawls);* Alice Knowland *(Mrs. Rawls).*

THE DEVIL'S CARGO
(Paramount, 1925) 7,980′

Presenters: Adolph Zukor, Jesse L. Lasky
Director: Victor Fleming
Story: Charles E. Whittaker
Screenplay: A. P. Younger
Camera: C. Edgar Schoenbaum

Wallace Beery *(Ben);* Pauline Starke *(Faro Sampson);* Claire Adams *(Martha Joyce);* William Collier, Jr. *(John Joyce);* Raymond Hatton *(Mate);* George Cooper *(Jerry Dugan);* Dale Fuller *(Millie);* Spec O'Donnell *(Jimmy);* Emmett C. King *(Square Deal Sampson);* John Webb Dillon *(Farwell);* Louis King *(Briggs).*

THE GREAT DIVIDE
(Metro-Goldwyn, 1925) 7,811′

Presenter: Louis B. Mayer
Supervisor: Irving Thalberg
Director: Reginald Barker
Based on the play by William Vaughn Moody
Adaptor: Benjamin Glazer
Continuity: Waldemar Young
Assistant Director: Harry Schneck
Costumes: Sophie Wachner
Art Director: Cedric Gibbons
Camera: Percy Hilburn
Editor: Robert Kern

Alice Terry *(Ruth Jordan);* Conway Tearle *(Stephen Ghent);* Wallace Beery *(Dutch);* Huntley Gordon *(Philip Jordan);* Allan Forrest *(Dr. Winthrop Newbury);* George Cooper *(Shorty);* ZaSu Pitts *(Polly Jordan);* William Orlamond *(Lon).*

THE NIGHT CLUB
(Paramount, 1925) 5,732′

Presenters: Adolph Zukor, Jesse L. Lasky
Directors: Frank Urson, Paul Iribe
Based on the play by William C. De Mille and Cecil B. De Mille
Screenplay: Keene Thompson
Adaptor: Walter Woods
Camera: Peverell Marley

Raymond Griffith *(Robert White);* Vera Reynolds *(Grace Henderson);* Wallace Beery *(Diablo);* Louise Fazenda *(Carmen).*

ADVENTURE
(Paramount, 1925) 6,602′

Presenters: Adolph Zukor, Jesse L. Lasky
Director: Victor Fleming
Based on the novel by Jack London
Screenplay: A. P. Younger, L. G. Rigby
Camera: C. Edgar Schoenbaum

Tom Moore *(David Sheldon);* Pauline Starke *(Joan Lackland);* Wallace Beery *(Morgan);* Raymond Hatton *(Raff);* Walter McGrail *(Tudor);* Duke Kahanamoku *(Noah Noa);* James Spencer *(Adam);* Noble Johnson *(Googomy).*

THE LOST WORLD
(First National, 1925) 9,700′

By arrangement with Watteson R. Rothacker
Supervisor: Earl Hudson
Director: Harry O. Hoyt
Based on the novel by Arthur Conan Doyle
Adaptor/Screenplay: Marion Fairfax
Technical Director: Willis H. O'Brien
Chief Technician: Fred W. Jackman
Architecture: Milton Menasco
Camera: Arthur Edeson
Editor: Fairfax

Bessie Love *(Paula White);* Lloyd Hughes *(Ed Malone);* Lewis Stone *(Sir John Roxton);* Wallace Beery *(Professor Challenger);* Arthur Hoyt *(Professor Summerlee);* Margaret McWade *(Mrs. Challenger);* Finch Smiles *(Austin—Challenger's Butler);* Jules Cowles *(Zambo);* Bull Montana *(Apeman);* George

Bunny *(Colin McArdle)*; Charles Wellesley *(Major Hilbbard)*; Alma Bennett *(Gladys Hungerford)*; Jocko *(The Monkey)*; Gilbert Roland *(Bit)*; Nelson McDowell *(Lawyer)*.

IN THE NAME OF LOVE
(Paramount, 1925) 5,862´

PRESENTERS: Adolph Zukor, Jesse L. Lasky
DIRECTOR: Howard Higgin
BASED ON THE NOVEL *The Lady of Lyons* BY EDWARD BULWER-LYTTON
SCREENPLAY: Sada Cowan
CAMERA: C. Edgar Schoenbaum

Ricardo Cortez *(Raoul Melnotte)*; Greta Nissen *(Marie Dufrayne)*; Wallace Beery *(Monsieur Glavis)*; Raymond Hatton *(Marquis de Beausant)*; Lillian Leighton *(Mother Dufrayne)*; Edythe Chapman *(Mother Melnotte)*; Richard Arlen *(Dumas Dufrayne)*.

RUGGED WATER
(Paramount, 1925) 6,015´

PRESENTERS: Adolph Zukor, Jesse L. Lasky
DIRECTOR: Irvin Willat
BASED ON THE NOVEL BY JOSEPH CROSBY LINCOLN
SCREENPLAY: James Shelley Hamilton
CAMERA: Alfred Gilks

Lois Wilson *(Norma Bartlett)*; Wallace Beery *(Captain Bartlett)*; Warner Baxter *(Calvin Homer)*; Phyllis Haver *(Myra Fuller)*; Dot Farley *(Mrs. Fuller)*; J. P. Lockney *(Superintendent Lockney)*; James Mason *(Wally Oakes)*; Willard Cooley *(Sam Bearse)*; Walter Ackerman *(Cook)*; Knute Erickson *(Jarvis)*; Thomas Delmar *(Gammon)*; Jack Byron *(Orrin Hendricks)*; Walter Rodgers *(Bloomer)*; Warren Rodgers *(Josh Phinney)*.

THE PONY EXPRESS
(Paramount, 1925) 9,949´

PRESENTERS: Adolph Zukor, Jesse L. Lasky
DIRECTOR: James Cruze
BASED ON THE NOVEL BY HENRY JAMES FORMAN AND WALTER WOODS
SCREEN STORY: Forman, Woods
SCREENPLAY: Woods
MUSIC: Hugo Riesenfeld
ASSISTANT DIRECTOR: Harold Schwartz
CAMERA: Karl Brown

Betty Compson *(Molly Jones)*; Ricardo Cortez *(Jack Weston)*; Ernest Torrence *("Ascension" Jones)*; Wallace Beery *("Rhode Island" Red)*; George Bancroft *(Jack Slade)*; Frank Lackteen *(Charlie Bent)*; John Fox, Jr. *(Billy Cody)*; William Turner *(William Russell)*; Al Hart *(Senator Glen)*; Charles Gerson *(Sam Clemens)*; Rose Tapley *(Aunt)*; Vondell Darr *(Baby)*; Hank Bell *(Townsman)*; Toby Wing *(Girl)*; Ernie Adams *(Bit)*.

THE WANDERER
(Paramount, 1926) 8,173´

PRESENTERS: Adolph Zukor, Jesse L. Lasky
DIRECTOR: Raoul Walsh
BASED ON THE PLAY BY MAURICE V. SAMUELS
SCREENPLAY: James T. O'Donohoe
CAMERA: Victor Milner

Greta Nissen *(Tisha)*; William Collier, Jr. *(Jether)*; Ernest Torrence *(Tola)*; Wallace Beery *(Pharis)*; Tyrone Power Sr. *(Jesse)*; Kathryn Hill *(Naomi)*; Kathlyn Williams *(Huldah)*; George Regas *(Gaal)*; Holmes Herbert *(Prophet)*; Snitz Edwards *(Jeweler)*.

BEHIND THE FRONT
(Paramount, 1926) 5,555´

PRESENTERS: Adolph Zukor, Jesse L. Lasky
DIRECTOR: Edward Sutherland
BASED ON THE STORY "THE SPOILS OF WAR" BY HUGH WILEY
SCREENPLAY: Ethel Doherty
ADAPTOR: Monte Brice
CAMERA: Charles Boyle

Wallace Beery *(Riff Swanson)*; Raymond Hatton *(Shorty McGee)*; Mary Brian *(Betty Barlett-Cooper)*; Richard Arlen *(Percy Brown)*; Hayden Stevenson *(Captain Bartlett-Cooper)*; Chester Conklin *(Scottie)*; Tom Kennedy *(Sergeant)*; Frances Raymond *(Mrs. Bartlett-Cooper)*; Melbourne MacDowell *(Mr. Bartlett-Cooper)*; Jerry Mandy *(Limburger Soldier)*; Charles Sullivan *(Soldier)*; Gertrude Astor *(French Barmaid)*.

OLD IRONSIDES
(Paramount, 1926) 7,910´

PRESENTERS: Adolph Zukor, Jesse L. Lasky
SUPERVISOR: B. P. Schulberg
DIRECTOR: James Cruze
STORY: Laurence Stallings
ADAPTORS: Harry Carr, Walter Woods
SCREENPLAY: Dorothy Arzner, Woods, Carr
TITLES: Rupert Hughes
ASSISTANT DIRECTOR: Harold Schwartz
SPECIAL EFFECTS: Roy Pomeroy
CAMERA: Alfred Gilks, Charles Boyle

Esther Ralston *(Esther)*; Wallace Beery *(Bos'n)*; George Bancroft *(Gunner)*; Charles Farrell *(The Commodore)*; Johnny Walker *(Lieutenant Stephen Decatur)*; George Godfrey *(Cook)*; Guy Oliver *(First Mate)*; Eddie Fetherston *(Lieutenant Somers)*; Effie Ellsler *(Esther's Mother)*; William Conklin *(Esther's Father)*; Fred Kohler *(Second Mate)*; Charles Hill Mailes *(Commodore Prebe)*; Nick De Ruiz *(Bashaw)*; Mitchell Lewis *(Pirate Chief)*; Frank Jonasson, Frank Bonner, Duke Kahanamoku *(Pirate Captains)*; Boris Karloff *(Saracen Guard)*.

VOLCANO
(Paramount, 1926) 5,462´

PRESENTERS: Adolph Zukor, Jesse L. Lasky
DIRECTOR: William K. Howard
BASED ON THE PLAY *Martinique* BY LAURENCE EYRE
SCREENPLAY: Bernard McConville
CAMERA: Lucien Andriot

Bebe Daniels *(Zabette de Chauvalons)*; Ricardo Cortez *(Stephane Sequineau)*; Wallace Beery *(Quembo)*; Arthur Edmund Carewe *(Maurice Sequineau)*; Dale Fuller *(Cedrien)*; Eulalie Jensen *(Madame de Chauvalons)*; Brandon Hurst *(Andre de Chauvalons)*; Marjorie Gay *(Marie de Chauvalons)*; Robert Perry *(Pere Benedict)*; Snitz Edwards *(Auctioneer)*; Emily Barrye *(Azaline)*; Bowditch Turner *(Cafe Manager)*; Edith Yorke *(Mother Superior)*; Mathilde Comont *(Madame Timbuctoo)*.

WE'RE IN THE NAVY NOW
(Paramount, 1926) 5,519´

PRESENTERS: Adolph Zukor, Jesse L. Lasky
ASSOCIATE PRODUCER: B. P. Schulberg
DIRECTOR: Edward Sutherland
STORY: Monte Brice
SCREENPLAY: John McDermott
TITLES: George Marion, Jr.
CAMERA: Charles Boyle

Wallace Beery *(Knockout Hansen)*; Raymond Hatton *(Stinky Smith)*; Chester Conklin *(Captain Smithers)*; Tom Kennedy *(Percival Scruggs)*; Donald Keith *(Radio Officer)*; Lorraine Eason *(Madelyn Phillips)*; Joseph W. Girard *(U.S. Admiral)*; Max Asher *(Admiral Puckerlip)*.

CASEY AT THE BAT
(Paramount, 1927) 6,040´

PRESENTERS: Adolph Zukor, Jesse L. Lasky
PRODUCER: Hector Turnbull
DIRECTOR: Monte Brice
BASED ON THE POEM BY ERNEST THAYER
SCREEN STORY: Turnbull
SCREENPLAY: Jules Furthman
TITLES: Sam Hellman, Grant Clarke
ADAPTORS: Reginald Morris, Monte Brice
CAMERA: Barney McGill

Wallace Beery *(Casey)*; Ford Sterling *(O'Dowd)*; ZaSu Pitts *(Camille)*; Sterling Holloway *(Putnam)*; Spec O'Donnell *(Spec)*; Iris Stuart [*Trixie (Floradora Girl)*]; Sidney Jarvis *(McGraw)*; Lotus Thompson, Rosalind Byrne, Anne Sheridan, Doris Hill, Sally Blane *(Other Floradora Girls)*.

FIREMAN, SAVE MY CHILD
(Paramount, 1927) 5,399´

PRESENTERS: Adolph Zukor, Jesse L. Lasky

ASSOCIATE PRODUCER: B. P. Schulberg
DIRECTOR: Edward Sutherland
STORY/SCREENPLAY: Monte Brice, Tom J. Geraghty
CAMERA: H. Kinley Martin

Wallace Beery *(Elmer)*; Raymond Hatton *(Sam)*; Josephine Dunn *(Dora Dumston)*; Tom Kennedy *(Captain Kennedy)*; Walter Goss *(Walter)*; Joseph Girard *(Chief Dumston)*.

NOW WE'RE IN THE AIR
(Paramount, 1927) 5,798 ′

PRESENTERS: Adolph Zukor, Jesse L. Lasky
DIRECTOR: Frank Strayer
STORY: Monte Brice, Keene Thompson
SCREENPLAY: Tom J. Geraghty
TITLES: George Marion, Jr.
CAMERA: Harry Perry

Wallace Beery *(Wally)*; Raymond Hatton *(Ray)*; Russell Simpson *(Lord Abercrombie McTavish)*; Louise Brooks *(Grisette Chelaine)*; Emile Chautard *(Monsieur Chelaine)*; Malcolm Waite *(Professor Saenger)*; Duke Martin *(Top Sergeant)*.

WIFE SAVERS
(Paramount, 1928) 5,434 ′

PRESENTERS: Adolph Zukor, Jesse L. Lasky
PRODUCER: James Cruze
ASSOCIATE PRODUCER: B. P. Schulberg
DIRECTOR: Ralph Cedar
BASED ON THE PLAY *Louie the Fourteenth* BY PAUL FRANK WILHELM, JULIUS WILHELM, AND ARTHUR WIMPERIS
SCREENPLAY: Tom J. Geraghty, Grover Jones
TITLES: George Marion, Jr.;
CAMERA: Alfred Gilks, H. Kinley Martin
EDITOR: George Nichols, Jr.

Wallace Beery *(Louis Hozenozzle)*; Raymond Hatton *(Rodney Ramsbottom)*; ZaSu Pitts *(Germaine)*; Sally Blane *(Colette)*; Tom Kennedy *(General Lavoris)*; Ford Sterling *(Tavern Keeper)*; George Y. Harvey *(Major)*; August Tollaire *(Mayor)*.

PARTNERS IN CRIME
(Paramount, 1928) 6,600 ′

PRESENTERS: Adolph Zukor, Jesse L. Lasky
DIRECTOR: Frank Strayer
STORY/SCREENPLAY: Grover Jones, Gilbert Pratt
TITLES: George Marion, Jr.
CAMERA: William Marshall
EDITOR: William Shea

Wallace Beery *(Mike Doolan, the Detective)*; Raymond Hatton *("Scoop" McGee, the Reporter/"Knife" Reagan)*; Mary Brian *(Marie Burke, the Cigarette Girl)*; William Powell *(Smith)*; Jack Luden *(Richard Deming, the Assistant District Attorney)*; Arthur Housman *(Barton)*; Albert Roccardi *(Kanelli, the Restaurant Owner)*; Joseph W. Girard *(Chief of Police)*; George Irving *(B. R. Cornwall)*; Bruce Gordon *(Dodo)*; Jack Richardson *(Jake)*.

THE BIG KILLING
(Paramount, 1928) 5,930 ′

PRESENTERS: Adolph Zukor, Jesse L. Lasky
PRODUCER: F. Richard Jones
ASSOCIATE PRODUCER: B. P. Schulberg
DIRECTOR: F. Richard Jones
STORY: Grover Jones
SCREENPLAY: Gilbert Pratt
TITLES: Herman J. Mankiewicz
CAMERA: Alfred Gilks
EDITORS: B. F. Zeidman, William Shea

Wallace Beery *(Powder-Horn Pete)*; Raymond Hatton *(Dead-Eye Dan)*; Anders Randolph *(Old Man Beagle)*; Mary Brian *(Beagle's Daughter)*; Gardner James *(Jim Hicks)*; Lane Chandler *(George Hicks)*; Paul McAllister *(Old Man Hicks)*; James Mason, Ralph Yearsley, Ethan Laidlaw, Leo Willis, Buck Moulton, Robert Kortman *(Beagle's Sons)*; Walter James *(Sheriff)*; Roscoe Ward *(Barker)*.

BEGGARS OF LIFE
(Paramount, 1928) 7,560 ′

PRESENTERS: Adolph Zukor, Jesse L. Lasky
SUPERVISOR: Benjamin Glazer
DIRECTOR: William A. Wellman
BASED ON THE NOVEL BY JIM TULLY
SCREENPLAY: Glazer, Tully
TITLES: Julian Johnson
CAMERA: Henry Gerrard
EDITOR: Allyson Shaffer

Wallace Beery *(Oklahoma Red)*; Louise Brooks *(Nancy)*; Richard Arlen *(Jim)*; Edgar Blue Washington *(Mose)*; H. A. Morgan *(Skinny)*; Andy Clark *(Skelly)*; Mike Donlin *(Bill)*; Roscoe Karns *(Hopper)*; Robert Perry *(Arkansas Snake)*; Johnnie Morris *(Rubin)*; George Kotsonaros *(Baldy)*; Jacques Chapin *(Ukie)*; Robert Brower *(Blind Sims)*; Frank Brownlee *(Farmer)*.

CHINATOWN NIGHTS
(Paramount, 1929) 7,481 ′

ASSOCIATE PRODUCER: David O. Selznick
DIRECTOR: William A. Wellman
BASED ON THE STORY "TONG WAR" BY SAMUEL ORNITZ
ADAPTOR: Oliver H. P. Garrett
SCREENPLAY: Ben Grauman Kohn
DIALOGUE: William B. Jutte
TITLES: Julian Johnson
TECHNICAL DIRECTOR: Tom Gubbins
CAMERA: Henry Gerrard
EDITOR: Allyson Shaffer

Wallace Beery *(Chuck Riley)*; Florence Vidor *(Joan Fry)*; Warner Oland *(Boston Charley)*; Jack McHugh *(The Shadow)*; Jack Oakie *(Reporter)*; Tetsu Komai *(Woo Chung)*; Frank Chew *(Gambler)*; Mrs. Wong Wing *(Maid)*; Pete Morrison *(Bartender)*; Freeman Wood *(Gerald)*.

STAIRS OF SAND
(Paramount, 1929) 5,020 ′

DIRECTOR: Otto Brower
BASED ON THE NOVEL BY ZANE GREY
ADAPTORS: Agnes Brand Leahy, Sam Mintz, J. Walter Ruben
TITLES: Ben Grauman Kohn
CAMERA: Rex Wimpy
EDITOR: Frances Marsh

Wallace Beery *(Guerd Larey)*; Jean Arthur *(Ruth Hutt)*; Phillips Holmes *(Adam Wansfell)*; Fred Kohler *(Boss Stone)*; Chester Conklin *(Tim)*; Guy Oliver *(Sheriff Collishaw)*; Lillian Worth *(Babe)*; Frank Rice *(Stage Driver)*; Clarence Sherwood *(Waiter)*;

RIVER OF ROMANCE
(Paramount, 1929) 7,009 ′

DIRECTOR: Richard Wallace
BASED ON THE PLAY *Magnolia* BY BOOTH TARKINGTON
ADAPTORS: Dan Totheroh, John V. A. Weaver
SCREENPLAY: Ethel Doherty
TITLES: Joseph Mankiewicz
SONG: Leo Robin and Sam Coslow
SOUND: Harry M. Lindgren
CAMERA: Victor Milner
EDITOR: Allyson Shaffer

Charles "Buddy" Rogers *(Tom Rumford-/Colonel Blake)*; Mary Brian *(Lucy Jeffers)*; June Collyer *(Elvira Jeffers)*; Henry B. Walthall *(General Jeff Rumford)*; Wallace Beery *(General Orlando Jackson)*; Fred Kohler *(Captain Blackie)*; Natalie Kingston *(Mexico)*; Walter McGrail *(Major Patterson)*; Anderson Lawler *(Joe Patterson)*; Mrs. George Fawcett *(Madame Rumford)*; George Reed *(Rumbo)*.

THE BIG HOUSE
(MGM, 1930) 80 min.

DIRECTOR: George Hill
STORY/SCREENPLAY/DIALOGUE: Frances Marion
ADDITIONAL DIALOGUE: Joe Farnham, Martin Flavin
ART DIRECTOR: Cedric Gibbons
SOUND: Robert Shirley, Douglas Shearer
CAMERA: Harold Wenstrom
EDITOR: Blanche Sewell

Chester Morris *(John Morgan)*; Wallace Beery *(Butch Schmidt)*; Lewis Stone *(Warden James Adams)*; Robert Montgomery *(Kent Marlowe)*; Leila Hyams *(Anne Marlowe)*; George F. Marion *(Pop Riker)*; J. C. Nugent

(Mr. Marlowe); Karl Dane *(Olsen)*; De Witt Jennings *(Captain Wallace)*; Matthew Betz *(Gopher)*; Claire McDowell *(Mrs. Marlowe)*; Robert Emmet O'Connor *(Donlin)*; Tom Wilson *(Sandy, the Guard)*; Eddie Foyer *(Dopey)*; Roscoe Ates *(Putnam)*; Fletcher Norton *(Oliver)*; Adolph Seidel *(Prison Barber)*; Eddie Lambert, Michael Vavitch *(Bits)*.

WAY FOR A SAILOR
(MGM, 1930) 88 min.

DIRECTOR: Sam Wood
BASED ON THE NOVEL BY ALBERT RICHARD WETJEN
SCREENPLAY: Laurence Stallings, W. L. River
ADDITIONAL DIALOGUE: Charles MacArthur, Al Boasberg
ART DIRECTOR: Cedric Gibbons
WARDROBE: Vivian Beer
SOUND: Robert Shirley, Douglas Shearer
CAMERA: Percy Hilburn
EDITOR: Frank Sullivan

John Gilbert *(Jack)*; Wallace Beery *(Tripod)*; Jim Tully *(Ginger)*; Leila Hyams *(Joan)*; Polly Moran *(Polly)*; Doris Lloyd *(Flossy)*.

BILLY THE KID
(MGM, 1930) 98 min.
(TV title: THE HIGHWAYMAN RIDES)

DIRECTOR: King Vidor
BASED ON THE NOVEL *The Saga of Billy the Kid* BY WALTER NOBLE BURNS
CONTINUITY: Wanda Tuchock
DIALOGUE: Laurence Stallings
ADDITIONAL DIALOGUE: Charles MacArthur
WARDROBE: David Cox
ART DIRECTOR: Cedric Gibbons
SOUND: Paul Neal, Douglas Shearer
CAMERA: Gordon Avil
EDITOR: Hugh Wynn

John Mack Brown *(Billy the Kid)*; Wallace Beery *(Pat Garrett)*; Kay Johnson *(Claire)*; Wyndham Standing *(Tunston)*; Karl Dane *(Swenson)*; Russell Simpson *(McSween)*; Blanche Frederici *(Mrs. McSween)*; Roscoe Ates *(Old Stuff)*; Warner Richmond *(Ballinger)*; James Marcus *(Donovan)*; Nelson McDowell *(Hatfield)*; Jack Carlyle *(Brewer)*; John Beck *(Butterworth)*; Chris-Pin Martin *(Santiago)*; Marguerita Padula *(Nicky Whoosiz)*; Aggie Herring *(Mrs. Hatfield)*.

A LADY'S MORALS
(MGM, 1930) 87 min.
(a.k.a. THE SOUL KISS)

DIRECTOR: Sidney Franklin
STORY: Dorothy Farnum
SCREENPLAY: Hans Kraly, Claudine West
DIALOGUE: John Meehan, Arthur Richman
SONGS: Clifford Grey and Oskar Straus; Arthur Freed; Herbert Stothart and Harry M. Woods; Carrie Jacob Bond; Howard Johnson and Stothart
CHOREOGRAPHY: Sammy Lee
ART DIRECTOR: Cedric Gibbons
GOWNS: Adrian
SOUND: K. Brock, Douglas Shearer
CAMERA: George Barnes
EDITOR: Margaret Booth

Grace Moore *(Jenny Lind)*; Reginald Denny *(Paul Brandt)*; Wallace Beery *(P. T. Barnum)*; Gus Shy *(Olaf)*; Jobyna Howland *(Josephine)*; Gilbert Emery *(Broughm)*; George F. Marion *(Innkeeper)*; Paul Porcasi *(Maretti)*; Giovanni Martino *(Zerga)*; Bodil Rosing *(Innkeeper's Wife)*; Joan Standing *(Louise)*; Mavis Villiers *(Selma)*; Judith Vosselli *(Rosatti)*.

MIN AND BILL
(MGM, 1930) 66 min.

DIRECTOR: George Hill
BASED ON THE NOVEL *Dark Star* BY LORNA MOON
SCREENPLAY: Frances Marion, Marion Jackson
WARDROBE: Rene Hubert
ART DIRECTOR: Cedric Gibbons
SOUND: Douglas Shearer
CAMERA: Harold Wenstrom
EDITOR: Basil Wrangell

Marie Dressler *(Min)*; Wallace Beery *(Bill)*; Dorothy Jordan *(Nancy)*; Marjorie Rambeau *(Bella)*; Donald Dillaway *(Dick)*; De Witt Jennings *(Groot)*; Russell Hopton *(Alec)*; Frank McGlynn *(Mr. Southard)*; Greta Gould *(Mrs. Southard)*; Jack Pennick *(Merchant Seaman)*; Hank Bell *(Sailor)*; Henry Roquemore *(Bella's Stateroom Lover)*; Miss Vanessi *(Woman)*.

THE SECRET SIX
(MGM, 1931) 83 min.

DIRECTOR: George Hill
STORY/SCREENPLAY: Frances Marion
SOUND: Robert Shirley
CAMERA: Harold Wenstrom
EDITOR: Blanche Sewell

Wallace Beery *(Louis Scorpio)*; Lewis Stone *(Newton)*; John Mack Brown *(Hank Rogers)*; Jean Harlow *(Anne Courtland)*; Marjorie Rambeau *(Peaches)*; Paul Hurst *(Nick Mizoski, the Gouger)*; Clark Gable *(Carl Luckner)*; Ralph Bellamy *(Johnny Franks)*; John Miljan *(Smiling Joe Colimo)*; De Witt Jennings *(Chief Donlin)*; Murray Kinnell *(Dummy Metz)*; Fletcher Norton *(Jimmy Delano)*; Louis Natheaux *(Eddie)*; Frank McGlynn *(Judge)*; Theodor Von Eltz *(District Attorney)*; Tom London *(Hood)*.

THE CHAMP
(MGM, 1931) 87 min.

PRODUCER/DIRECTOR: King Vidor
STORY: Frances Marion
DIALOGUE: Leonard Praskins
ADDITIONAL DIALOGUE: Wanda Tuchock
ART DIRECTOR: Cedric Gibbons
SOUND: Douglas Shearer
CAMERA: Gordon Avil
EDITOR: Hugh Wynn

Wallace Beery *(Andy Purcell)*; Jackie Cooper *(Dink Purcell)*; Irene Rich *(Linda Carlton)*; Jesse Scott *(Johnah)*; Rosco Ates *(Sponge)*; Hale Hamilton *(Tony Carlton)*; Edward Brophy *(Tim)*; Marcia Mae Jones *(Mary Lou Carlton)*; Lee Phelps *(Bartender)*; Frank Hagney *(Manuel Caroza)*.

HELL DIVERS
(MGM, 1931) 100 min.

PRODUCER-DIRECTOR: George Hill
STORY: Lieutenant Commander Frank Wead
SCREENPLAY: Harvey Gates, Malcolm Stuart Boylan
CAMERA: Harold Wenstrom
EDITOR: Blanche Sewell

Wallace Beery *(Windy)*; Clark Gable *(Steve)*; Conrad Nagel *(Duke)*; Dorothy Jordan *(Ann)*; Marjorie Rambeau *(Mame Kelsey)*; Marie Prevost *(Lulu)*; Cliff Edwards *(Baldy)*; John Miljan *(Griffin)*; Landers Stevens *(Admiral)*; Reed Howes *(Lieutenant Fisher)*; Alan Roscoe *(Captain)*; Frank Conroy *(Chaplain)*; Robert Young *(Young Officer)*; Jack Pennick *(Trainee)*; John Kelly *(Sailor)*; Virginia Bruce *(Girl)*.

GRAND HOTEL
(MGM, 1932) 115 min.

DIRECTOR: Edmund Goulding
BASED ON THE PLAY *Menschen im Hotel* BY VICKI BAUM
AMERICAN VERSION: William A. Drake
GOWNS: Adrian
ASSISTANT DIRECTOR: Charles Dorian
ART DIRECTOR: Cedric Gibbons
SOUND: Douglas Shearer
CAMERA: William Daniels
EDITOR: Blanche Sewell

Greta Garbo *(Grusinskaya)*; John Barrymore *(Baron Felix von Geigern)*; Joan Crawford *(Flaemmchen)*; Wallace Beery *(Preysing)*; Lionel Barrymore *(Otto Kringelein)*; Lewis Stone *(Dr. Otternschlag)*; Jean Hersholt *(Senf)*; Robert McWade *(Meierheim)*; Purnell B. Pratt *(Zinnowitz)*; Ferdinand Gottschalk *(Pimenov)*; Rafaela Ottiano *(Suzette)*; Morgan Wallace *(Chauffeur)*; Tully Marshall *(Gerstenkorn)*; Frank Conroy *(Rohna)*; Murray Kinnell *(Schweimann)*; Edwin Maxwell *(Dr. Waitz)*; Mary Carlisle *(Honeymooner)*; John Davidson *(Hotel Manager)*; Rolfe Sedan, Herbert Evans *(Clerks)*; Sam McDaniel *(Bartender)*; Lee Phelps *(Man in Lobby)*.

FLESH
(MGM, 1932) 95 min.

DIRECTOR: John Ford
STORY: Edmund Goulding
SCREENPLAY: Leonard Praskins, Edgar Allan Woolf
DIALOGUE: Moss Hart
CAMERA: Arthur Edeson
EDITOR: William S. Gray

Wallace Beery *(Polikai);* Karen Morley *(Lora Nash);* Ricardo Cortez *(Nicky Grant);* Jean Hersholt *(Mr. Herman);* John Miljan *(Joe Willard);* Vincent Barnett *(Waiter);* Herman Bing *(Pepi);* Edward Brophy *(Dolan);* Greta Meyer *(Mrs. Herman).*

TUGBOAT ANNIE
(MGM, 1933) 88 min.

ASSOCIATE PRODUCER: Henry Rapf
DIRECTOR: Mervyn LeRoy
BASED ON THE STORIES BY NORMAN REILLY RAINE
ADAPTORS: Zelda Sears, Eve Greene
ART DIRECTOR: Merrill Pye
SET DECORATOR: Edwin B. Willis
CAMERA: Gregg Toland
EDITOR: Blanche Sewell

Marie Dressler *(Annie Brennan);* Wallace Beery *(Terry Brennan);* Robert Young *(Alec Brennan);* Maureen O'Sullivan *(Pat Severn);* Willard Robertson *(Red Severn);* Tammany Young *(Shif'less);* Frankie Darro *(Alec as a Boy);* Jack Pennick *(Pete);* Paul Hurst *(Sam);* Oscar Apfel *(Reynolds);* Robert McWade *(Mayor of Secoma);* Robert Barrat *(First Mate);* Vince Barnett *(Cabby);* Robert E. Homans *(Old Salt);* Guy Usher *(Auctioneer);* Willie Fung *(Chow, the Cook);* Hal Price *(Mate);* Christian Rub *(Sailor);* Major Sam Harris *(Onlooker).*

DINNER AT EIGHT
(MGM, 1933) 113 min.

PRODUCER: David O. Selznick
DIRECTOR: George Cukor
BASED ON THE PLAY BY GEORGE S. KAUFMAN AND EDNA FERBER
ADAPTORS: Frances Marion, Donald Ogden Stewart, Herman J. Mankiewicz
GOWNS: Adrian
ART DIRECTOR: Cedric Gibbons
SOUND: Douglas Shearer
CAMERA: William Daniels
EDITOR: Ben Lewis

Marie Dressler *(Carlotta Vance);* John Barrymore *(Larry Renault);* Wallace Beery *(Dan Packard);* Jean Harlow *(Kitty Packard);* Lionel Barrymore *(Oliver Jordan);* Lee Tracy *(Max Kane);* Edmund Lowe *(Dr. Wayne Talbot);* Billie Burke *(Millicent Jordan);* Madge Evans *(Paula Jordan);* Jean Hersholt *(Jo Stengel);* Karen Morley *(Lucy Talbot);* Louise Closser Hale *(Hattie Loomis);* Phillips Holmes *(Ernest De Graff);* May Robson *(Mrs. Wendel, the Cook);* Grant Mitchell *(Ed Loomis);* Phoebe Foster *(Miss Alden);* Elizabeth Patterson *(Miss Copeland);* Hilda Vaughn *(Tina—Kitty's Maid);* Harry Beresford *(Fosdick);* Edwin Maxwell *(Fitch, the Hotel Manager);* John Davidson *(Mr. Hatfield, the Assistant Manager);* Herman Bing *(Waiter);* Anna Duncan *(Dora, the Maid);* George Baxter *(Gustave, the Butler);* Edward Woods *(Eddie).*

THE BOWERY
(United Artists, 1933) 90 min.

PRODUCER: Darryl F. Zanuck
ASSOCIATE PRODUCERS: William Goetz, Raymond Griffith
DIRECTOR: Raoul Walsh
BASED ON THE NOVEL CHUCK CONNORS BY MICHAEL L. SIMMONS AND BESSIE ROTH SOLOMON
SCREENPLAY: Howard Estabrook, James Gleason
MUSIC DIRECTOR: Alfred Newman
ART DIRECTOR: Richard Day
CAMERA: Barney McGill
EDITOR: Allen McNeil

Wallace Beery *(Chuck Connors);* George Raft *(Steve Brodie);* Jackie Cooper *(Swipes McGurk);* Fay Wray *(Lucy Calhoun);* Pert Kelton *(Trixie Odbray);* George Walsh *(John L. Sullivan);* Oscar Apfel *(Mr. Herman);* Harold Huber *(Slick);* Fletcher Norton *(Googy Cochran);* John Kelly *(Lumpy Hogan);* Lillian Harmer *(Carrie Nation);* Ferdinand Munier *(Honest Mike, the Bartender);* Herman Bing *(Mr. Rummel);* Tammany Young *(Himself);* Esther Muir *(The Tart);* John Bleifer *(Mumbo, the Mute);* Pueblo Jim Flynn, Al McCoy, Joe Glick, Phil Bloom, Joe Herrick, Jack Herrick, Sailor Vincent, Kid Broad *(Pugs);* Heinie Conklin *(Drunk /Fight Spectator);* Andrew Tombes *(Shill);* Irving Bacon *(Hick with Tailors);* Harry Semels *(Artist);* Phil Tead *(Tout);* Harvey Parry *(Double for George Raft);* Charles Lane *(Doctor).*

VIVA VILLA!
(MGM, 1934) 115 min.

PRODUCER: David O. Selznick
DIRECTOR: Jack Conway
SUGGESTED BY THE BOOK BY EDGCUMB PINCHON AND O. B. STADE
SCREENPLAY: Ben Hecht
ASSISTANT DIRECTORS: Art Rosson, Johnny Walters
MUSIC CONSULTANT: Juan Aguilar
ART DIRECTOR: Harry Oliver
INTERIOR DECORATOR: Edwin B. Willis
COSTUMES: Dolly Tree
MUSIC: Herbert Stothart
TECHNICAL ADVISORS: Carlos Novarro, Matias Santoyo
SOUND: Douglas Shearer
CAMERA: James Wong Howe, Charles G. Clarke
EDITOR: Robert J. Kern

Wallace Beery *(Pancho Villa);* Fay Wray *(Teresa Sykes);* Leo Carrillo *(Diego);* Donald Cook *(Don Felipe);* Stuart Erwin *(Johnny Sykes);* George E. Stone *(Chavito);* Joseph Schildkraut *(Pascal);* Henry B. Walthall *(Madero);* Katherine DeMille *(Rosita);* David Durand *(Bugle Boy);* Phillip Cooper *(Villa as a Boy);* Frank Puglia *(Father);* Charles Stevens, Steve Clemento, Pedro Regas, John Merkel *(Pascal's Aides);* Harry Cording *(Major Domo);* Francis McDonald *(Villa's Man);* Clarence Hummel Wilson *(Jail Official);* Nigel De Brulier *(Political Judge);* Sam Godfrey *(Prosecuting Attorney);* Julian Rivero *(Telegraph Operator);* Dan Dix *(Drunkard);* Mischa Auer *(Military Attache);* Belle Mitchell *(Spanish Wife);* Francis X. Bushman, Jr., *(Calloway);* William Von Brincken *(German Reporter);* Michael Visaroff *(Russian Reporter);* Andre Cheron *(French Reporter);* Chris-Pin Martin, Nick De Ruiz *(Peons);* Arthur Thalasso *(Butcher).*

TREASURE ISLAND
(MGM, 1934) 105 min.

PRODUCER: Hunt Stromberg
DIRECTOR: Victor Fleming
BASED ON THE NOVEL BY ROBERT LOUIS STEVENSON
SCREENPLAY: John Lee Mahin
ART DIRECTORS: Cedric Gibbons, Merrill Pye, Edwin B. Willis
MUSIC: Herbert Stothart
ADVISER: Dwight Franklin
SOUND: Douglas Shearer
CAMERA: Ray June, Cyde DeVinn, Harold Rosson
EDITOR: Blanche Sewell

Wallace Beery *(Long John Silver);* Jackie Cooper *(Jim Hawkins);* Lionel Barrymore *(Billy Bones);* Otto Kruger *(Dr. Livesey);* Lewis Stone *(Captain Smollett);* Nigel Bruce *(Squire Trelawney);* Charles "Chic" Sale *(Ben Gunn);* William V. Mong *(Pew);* Charles McNaughton *(Black Dog);* Dorothy Peterson *(Mrs. Hawkins);* Douglass Dumbrille, Edmund Breese, Olin Howland, Charles Irwin, Edward Pawley, Richard Powell, James Burnke, John Anderson, Charles Bennett *(Pirates).*

THE MIGHTY BARNUM
(United Artists, 1934) 87 min.

PRODUCER: Darryl F. Zanuck
DIRECTOR: Walter Lang
STORY: Gene Fowler, Bess Meredyth
MUSIC: Alfred Newman
CAMERA: Peverell Marley
EDITORS: Allen McNeill, Bobby McLean

Wallace Beery *(P. T. Barnum);* Janet Beecher *(Mrs. Barnum);* Adolphe Menjou *(Bailey Walsh);* Rochelle Hudson *(Ellen);* John Hyams *(J. P. Skiff);* Virginia Bruce *(Jenny Lind);* Lucille La Verne *(Joyce Heth);* George Brasno *(Tom Thumb);* Olive Brasno *(Lavinia);* Davison Clark *(Horace Greeley);* George MacQuarrie *(Daniel Webster);* Tex

Madsen *(Cardiff Giant);* Herman Bing *(Man with Frog);* Ian Wolfe *(Swedish Consul);* Sam Adams, Sam Godfrey, Milton Wallace *(Collectors);* May Boley *(Mme. Zorro);* Franklyn Ardell *(Sam);* Tammany Young *(Tod);* Brenda Fowler, Theresa Maxwell Conovor, Ethel Wales *(Matrons);* Captain E. H. Calvert *(House Detective);* Charles Judels *(Maitre d');* Frank McGlynn, Sr. *(Barnum's Butler);* Christian Rub *(Ole, the Masseur);* Frank Morgan *(Joe);* Greta Meyer *(Jenny Lind's Maid);* Gertrude Astor, Maude Ogle, Alice Lake, Naomi Childers *(Women in Museum);* John Lester Johnson *(Black Attendant);* Billy McClain *(Barnum's Footman);* Matt Gillman *(Wallace Beery's Stand-In);* Gale Mogul *(Adolphe Menjou's Stand-In);* Isabel Sheridan *(Virginia Bruce's Stand-In);* Emily Baldwin *(Rochelle Hudson's Stand-In);* Peggy Dale *(Janet Beecher's Stand-In).*

WEST POINT OF THE AIR
(MGM, 1935) 88 min.

PRODUCER: Monta Bell
DIRECTOR: Richard Rosson
STORY: John Monk Saunders
SCREENPLAY: Frank Wead, Arthur J. Beckhard
ART DIRECTORS: Cedric Gibbons, H. R. Campbell
WARDROBE: Dolly Tree
MUSIC: Charles Maxwell
CAMERA: Clyde DeVinna
AERIAL CAMERA: Charles Marshall, Elmer Dyer
EDITOR: Frank Sullivan

Wallace Beery *(Big Mike);* Robert Young *(Little Mike);* Maureen O'Sullivan *(Skip Carter);* Russell Hardie *(Phil Carter);* Lewis Stone *(General Carter);* James Gleason *(Joe Bags);* Rosalind Russell *(Dare);* Henry Wadsworth *(Pettis);* Robert Livingston *(Pippinger);* Robert Taylor *(Jaskarelli);* Frank Conroy *(Captain Cannon);* G. Pat Collins *(Lieutenant Kelly);* Ronnie Cosbey *(Little Mike as a Boy);* Bobbie Caldwell *(Phil as a Boy);* Marilyn Spinner *(Skip as a Girl);* Richard Tucker *(Club Manager).*

O'SHAUGHNESSY'S BOY
(MGM, 1935) 88 min.

PRODUCER: Philip Goldstone
DIRECTOR: Richard Boleslawsky
STORY: Harvey Gates, Malcolm Stuart Boylan
SCREENPLAY: Leonard Praskins, Wanda Tuchock, Otis Garrett
ART DIRECTORS: Cedric Gibbons, Stan Rogers
SET DECORATOR: Edwin B. Willis
MUSIC: William Axt
CAMERA: James Wong Howe
EDITOR: Frank Sullivan

Wallace Beery *(Windy);* Jackie Cooper *(Stubby);* George "Spanky" McFarland *(Stubby as a Child);* Henry Stephenson *(Valkenburg);* Sara Haden *(Martha);* Leona Maricle *(Cora);* Willard Robertson *(Hastings);* Clarence Muse *(Jeff);* Ben Hendricks *(Franz);* Wade Boteler *(Callahan);* Jack Daley *(Mack);* Oscar Apfel *(Lawyer);* Wally Albright, Jr. *(Child);* Hooper Atchley *(Secretary);* Alf James *(Farmer);* Al Williams, Ernie Alexander *(Acrobats);* Mable Waldman *(Fat Lady);* Charles Ludwig *(Midget);* Frank LaMont *(Human Skeleton);* Jack Baxley, Nick Copeland *(Barkers);* Lee Shumway *(Detective).*

CHINA SEAS
(MGM, 1935) 89 min.

PRODUCER: Albert Lewin
DIRECTOR: Tay Garnett
BASED ON THE NOVEL BY CROSBIE GARSTIN
SCREENPLAY: Jules Furthman, James Kevin McGuinness
SONG: Arthur Freed and Nacio Herb Brown
ART DIRECTOR: Cedric Gibbons, James Havens, David Townsend
SET DECORATOR: Edwin B. Willis
GOWNS: Adrian
CAMERA: Ray June
EDITOR: William Levanway

Clark Gable *(Captain Alan Gaskell);* Jean Harlow [*China Doll (Dolly Portland)*]; Wallace Beery *(Jamesy MacArdle);* Lewis Stone *(Tom Davids);* Rosalind Russell *(Sybil Barclay);* Dudley Digges *(Dawson);* C. Aubrey Smith *(Sir Guy Wilmerding);* Robert Benchley *(Charlie McCaleb);* William Henry *(Rockwell);* Live Demaigret *(Mrs. Volberg);* Lilian Bond *(Mrs. Timmons);* Edward Brophy *(Wilbur Timmons);* Soo Yong *(Yu-Lan);* Carol Ann Beery *(Carol Ann);* Akim Tamiroff *(Romanoff);* Ivan Lebedeff *(Ngah);* Hattie McDaniel *(Isabel McCarthy);* Donald Meek *(Chess Player);* Emily Fitzroy *(Lady);* Pat Flaherty *(Second Officer Kingston);* Forrester Harvey *(Steward);* Tom Gubbins *(Ship's Officer);* Charles Irwin *(Bertie the Purser);* Willie Fung *(Cabin Boy);* Ferdinand Munier *(Police Superintendent);* Chester Gan *(Rickshaw Boy);* John Ince *(Pilot).*

AH, WILDERNESS!
(MGM, 1935) 101 min.

PRODUCER: Hunt Stromberg
DIRECTOR: Clarence Brown
BASED ON THE PLAY BY EUGENE O'NEILL
SCREENPLAY: Albert Hackett, Frances Goodrich
MUSIC: Herbert Stothart
ART DIRECTOR: Cedric Gibbons, William A. Horning
WARDROBE: Dolly Tree
CAMERA: Clyde DeVinna
EDITOR: Frank Hull

Wallace Beery *(Sid Miller);* Lionel Barrymore *(Nat Miller);* Aline MacMahon *(Lily);* Eric Linden *(Richard);* Cecilia Parker *(Muriel);* Mickey Rooney *(Tommy);* Spring Byington *(Essie Miller);* Charley Grapewin *(Mr. McComber);* Frank Albertson *(Arthur);* Edward Nugent *(Wint Selby);* Bonita Granville *(Mildred);* Helen Flint *(Belle);* Helen Freeman *(Miss Hawley).*

A MESSAGE TO GARCIA
(20th Century-Fox, 1936) 90 min.

PRODUCER: Darryl F. Zanuck
ASSOCIATE PRODUCER: Raymond Griffith
DIRECTOR: George Marshall
SUGGESTED BY THE ESSAY BY ELBERT HUBBARD AND THE BOOK BY LIEUTENANT ANDREW S. ROWAN
SCREENPLAY: W. P. Lipscomb, Gene Fowler
MUSIC DIRECTOR: Louis Silvers
ART DIRECTORS: William Darling, Rudolph Sternad
SET DECORATOR: Thomas Little
TECHNICAL DIRECTOR: Francois B. DeWaldes
ASSISTANT DIRECTOR: Booth McCracken
CAMERA: Rudolph Maté
EDITOR: Herbert Levy

Wallace Beery *(Sergeant Dory);* John Boles *(Lieutenant Andrew Rowan);* Barbara Stanwyck *(Raphaelita Mederos);* Herbert Mundin *(Henry Piper);* Martin Garralaga *(Rodriguez);* Juan Torena *(Luis Mederos);* Alan Hale *(Dr. Krug);* Enrique Acosta *(General Garcia);* Jose Luis Tortosa *(Pasquale Castova);* Mona Barrie *(Spanish Spy);* Warren Hymer *(Sailor);* Andre Cuyas, Juan Duval *(Sentries);* Count Stefenelli *(Raphaelita's Father);* Pedro Vinas *(Servant);* Rosita Harlan *(Girl);* Fred Goday *(Citizen);* Octavio Giraud *(Spanish Commandant);* Fredrik Vogeding *(German Stoker);* Patrick Moriarty *(Irish Stoker);* Augustin Guzman *(Sentry);* Iris Adrian *(Bit);* Dell Henderson *(President McKinley);* John Carradine *(Voice of President McKinley);* Manuel Paris *(Lieutenant);* George Irving *(Colonel Wagner);* Davison Clark *(Admiral).*

OLD HUTCH
(MGM, 1936) 79 min.

PRODUCER: Harold Rapf
DIRECTOR: J. Walter Ruben
BASED ON THE STORY "OLD HUTCH LIVES UP TO IT" BY GARRET SMITH
SCREENPLAY: George Kelly
MUSIC: Dr. William Axt
ART DIRECTORS: Cedric Gibbons, Stan Rogers
SET DECORATOR: Edwin B. Willis
CAMERA: Clyde DeVinna
EDITOR: Frank Sullivan

Wallace Beery *(Hutch);* Cecilia Parker *(Irene);* Eric Linden *(Dave);* Elizabeth Patterson *(Mrs. Hutch);* Robert McWade *(Jolly);* Donald Meek *(Gunnison);* James Burke *(Teller);* Caroline Anne Perkins *(Sally);* Julia Ellen Perkins *(Florrie);* Delmar Watson *(Allie);* Harry Watson *(Freddie);* Virginia Grey *(Girl);* Scotty Beckett *(Roy);* Frank Reicher *(District Attorney);* Norman Willis *(Surveyor);* Wilbur Mack *(Judge);* Frank Jenks *(Crook);* Zeffie Tilbury *(Elderly*

Woman); George Chandler *(Cigar Store Clerk).*

GOOD OLD SOAK
(MGM, 1937) 76 min.

PRODUCER:	Harry Rapf
DIRECTOR:	J. Walter Ruben
STORY:	Don Marquis
SCREENPLAY:	A. E. Thomas
MUSIC:	Edward Ward
CHOREOGRAPHY:	Val Raset
SONGS:	Walter Donaldson, Bob Wright, and Chet Forrest
CAMERA:	Clyde DeVinna
EDITOR:	Frank Sullivan

Wallace Beery *(Clem Holly);* Janet Beecher *(Mathildae Holly);* Ted Healy *(Al Simmons);* Una Merkel *(Nellie);* Betty Furness *(Lucy);* Eric Linden *(Clemmy);* Judith Barrett *(Inez);* George Sidney *(Kennedy);* James Bush *(Tom);* Oscar O'Shea *(Jake);* Granville Bates *(Sam);* Bert Roach *(Mike);* Robert McWade *(Webster Parsons);* Margaret Hamilton *(Minnie);* Donald Briggs *(Fred);* Libby Taylor *(Maid);* Torben Meyer *(Headwaiter);* Guy Rennie *(Master of Ceremonies);* Almeda Fowler *(Clemmy's Secretary);* Louis Mason *(Watchman);* Frank Darien *(Jasper).*

SLAVE SHIP
(20th Century-Fox, 1937) 92 min.

PRODUCER:	Darryl F. Zanuck
ASSOCIATE PRODUCER:	Nunnally Johnson
DIRECTOR:	Tay Garnett
STORY:	William Faulkner
SCREENPLAY:	Sam Hellman, Lamar Trotti, Gladys Lehman
ART DIRECTOR:	Hans Peters
MUSIC:	Alfred Newman
CAMERA:	Ernest Palmer
EDITOR:	Lloyd Nosler

Warner Baxter *(Jim Lovett);* Wallace Beery *(Jack Thompson);* Elizabeth Allan *(Nancy Marlowe);* Mickey Rooney *(Swifty);* George Sanders *(Lefty);* Jane Darwell *(Mrs. Marlowe);* Joseph Schildkraut *(Danelo);* Miles Mander *(Corey);* Arthur Hohl *(Grimes);* Minna Gombell *(Mabel);* Billy Bevan *(Atkins);* Douglas Scott *(Boy);* Francis Ford *(Scraps);* Jane Jones *(Ma Belcher);* J. P. McGowan *(Helmsman);* Chester Gan, Bobby Dunn, Jack Low, John Bleifer, Sven Borg *(Crew Members);* De Witt Jennings *(Snodgrass);* Dewey Robinson *(Bartender);* Stymie Beard *(Black Boy on Pier);* J. Farrell MacDonald *(Blacksmith);* Eddie Dunn *(Ostler);* Lon Chaney, Jr., Russ Clark *(Laborers);* Herbert Heywood *(Sea Captain);* Holmes Herbert *(Judge);* Landers Stevens *(Owner);* Winter Hall *(Minister);* Anita Brown *(Slave Woman);* Dewey Robinson, Tom Kennedy *(Bartenders).*

THE BAD MAN OF BRIMSTONE
(MGM, 1937) 90 min.*

PRODUCER:	Harry Rapf
DIRECTOR:	J. Walter Ruben
STORY:	Ruben, Maurice Rapf
SCREENPLAY:	Cyril Hume, Richard Maibaum
ART DIRECTORS:	Cedric Gibbons, James Havens
SET DECORATOR:	Edwin B. Willis
COSTUMES:	Dolly Tree
MUSIC:	Dr. William Axt
SOUND:	Douglas Shearer
CAMERA:	Clyde DeVinna
EDITOR:	Frank Sullivan

Wallace Beery *(Trigger Bill);* Virginia Bruce *(Loretta Douglas);* Dennis O'Keefe *(Jeff Barton);* Joseph Calleia *(Portygee Ben);* Guy Kibbee *(Eight Ball Harrigan);* Bruce Cabot *(Blackjack McCreedy);* Cliff Edwards *(Buzz McCreedy);* Guinn "Big Boy" Williams *(Vulch McCreedy);* Arthur Hohl *(Doc Laramie);* Robert Gleckler *(Skunk Rogers);* Raymond Hatton *(Cal Turner);* Noah Beery *(Ambrose Crocker);* Scotty Beckett *(Sammy Grant);* Charley Grapewin *(Sheriff Barney Lane);* John Wray *(Mr. Grant);* John Qualen *(Loco);* Robert Barrat *(Hank Summers);* Lewis Stone *(Jackson Douglas);* Virginia Brissac *(Mrs. Grant);* Jules Cowles *(Saddlenose Sawtelle);* Stanley Andrews *(Clergyman);* Spencer Charters *(Rufus Odlum);* Eddy Waller *(Cassius Bundy).*
*In sepia.

PORT OF SEVEN SEAS
(MGM, 1938) 81 min.

PRODUCER:	Henry Henigson
DIRECTOR:	James Whale
BASED ON THE PLAY *Fanny* BY MARCEL PAGNOL	
SCREENPLAY:	Preston Sturges
CAMERA:	Karl Freund
EDITOR:	Frederick Y. Smith

Wallace Beery *(Cesar);* Maureen O'Sullivan *(Madelon);* Frank Morgan *(Panisse);* John Beal *(Marius);* Jessie Ralph *(Honorine);* Cora Witherspoon *(Claudine);* Etienne Girardot *(Brun);* E. Alyn Warren *(Captain Escartefigue);* Robert Spindola *(Boy);* Doris Lloyd *(Customer);* Jack Latham *(Man);* Paul Panzer *(Postman);* Jerry Colonna *(Arab Rug Dealer);* Fred Malatesta *(Bird Seller);* George Humbert *(Organ Grinder);* Moy Ming *(Chinese Peddler).*

STABLEMATES
(MGM, 1938) 89 min.

PRODUCER:	Harry Rapf
DIRECTOR:	Sam Wood
STORY:	William Thiele, Reginald Owen
SCREENPLAY:	Leonard Praskins, Richard Maibaum
MUSIC:	Edward Ward
ART DIRECTORS:	Cedric Gibbons, Urie McCleary
SET DECORATOR:	Edwin B. Willis
SOUND:	Douglas Shearer
CAMERA:	John Seitz
EDITOR:	W. Dan Hayes

Wallace Beery *(Tom Terry);* Mickey Rooney *(Mickey);* Margaret Hamilton *(Beulah Flanders);* Marjorie Gateson *(Mrs. Shepherd);* Minor Watson *(Barney Donovan);* Arthur Hohl *(Mr. Gale);* Oscar O'Shea *(Pete Whalen);* Frank Hagney *(Pool Room Owner);* Cliff Nazarro *(Himself);* Johnnie Morris *(Dwarfish Ex-Jockey);* James Morton *(Bartender);* Pat West, Kenneth Nolan *(Railbirds);* Sam McDaniel *(Black Bookie);* Charles Dunbar *(Stable Hand);* Scoop Martin *(Groom);* Stanley Andrews *(Track Steward);* Spencer Charters *(Choir Master).*

STAND UP AND FIGHT
(MGM, 1939) 105 min.

PRODUCER:	Mervyn LeRoy
ASSOCIATE PRODUCER:	J. Walter Ruben
DIRECTOR:	W. S. Van Dyke, II
STORY:	Forbes Parkhill
SCREENPLAY:	James M. Cain, Jane Murfin, Harvey Furgusson
ART DIRECTORS:	Cedric Gibbons, Urie McCleary
SET DECORATORS:	Edwin B. Willis
WOMEN'S COSTUMES:	Dolly Tree
MEN'S COSTUMES:	Valles
MUSIC:	Dr. William Axt
SOUND:	Douglas Shearer
CAMERA:	Leonard Smith
EDITOR:	Frank Sullivan

Robert Taylor *(Blake Cantrell);* Wallace Beery *(Captain Starkey);* Florence Rice *(Susan Griffith);* Helen Broderick *(Amanda Griffith);* Charles Bickford *(Arnold);* Barton MacLane *(Crowder);* Charley Grapewin *(Old Puff);* John Qualen *(Davey);* Clinton Rosemond *(Enoch);* Jonathan Hale *(Colonel Webb);* Claudia Morgan *(Carolyn Talbot);* Robert Gleckler *(Sheriff Barney);* Cy Kendall *(Foreman Ross);* Paul Everton *(Allan);* Selmer Jackson *(Whittingham Talbot);* Minor Watson *(Marshal Cole);* Frank Darien *(Daniels);* William Tannen *(Lewis);* Edward Hearn *(Joe);* Edward Keane *(Donnelly);* Robert Middlemass *(Starkrider);* John Dilson *(Auctioneer);* Ben Welden *(Foreman);* Louise Springer *(Violet);* Eddy Waller *(Conductor);* Victor Potel *(Coach Driver);* Harry Allen *(Engineer);* Walter Soderling *(Passenger);* Syd Saylor *(Stooge);* Clem Bevans *(Bum);* James Kilgannon *(Fireman);* George Ovey *(Conductor);* Al Ferguson, Sam Ash *(Teamsters);* Trevor Bardette *(Mob Leader);* Claire McDowell *(Woman).*

SERGEANT MADDEN
(1939) 82 min.

PRODUCER:	J. Walter Ruben
DIRECTOR:	Josef von Sternberg
BASED ON THE STORY "A GUN IN HIS HAND" BY WILLIAM A. ULLMAN	
SCREENPLAY:	Wells Root
ART DIRECTORS:	Cedric Gibbons, Randall Duell
SET DECORATOR:	Edwin B. Willis
TECHNICAL ADVISOR:	Val O'Toole

MUSIC:	Dr. William Axt
SOUND:	Douglas Shearer
MONTAGE EFFECTS:	Peter Ballbusch
CAMERA:	John F. Seitz

Wallace Beery *(Shaun Madden);* Tom Brown *(Al Boylan, Jr.);* Alan Curtis *(Dennis Madden);* Laraine Day *(Eileen Daly);* Fay Holden *(Mary Madden);* Marc Lawrence *(Piggy Ceders);* Marion Martin *(Charlotte);* Donald Douglas *(Al Boylan, Sr.);* Dickie Jones *(Dennis Madden as a Boy);* Drew Roddy *(Al Boylan, Jr. as a Boy);* Donald Haines *(Milton);* David Gorcey *(Punchy);* Ben Welden *(Stemmy);* John Kelly *(Nero);* Charles Trowbridge *(Commissioner);* Horace McMahon *(Philadelphia);* Etta McDaniel *(Dove);* Ivan "Dusty" Miller *(Frawley);* Neil Fitzgerald *(Casey);* Mary Field *(Woman);* Esther Dale *(Mrs. McGillivray);* Reed Hadley *(Lawyer);* Wade Boteler *(Niles);* Harold Minjir *(Couturier);* James Flavin, Lee Phelps, Harry Strang *(Cops);* Jack Pennick, Charles Sullivan *(Prisoners);* E. Alyn Warren *(Judge);* Milton Kibbee *(Foreman);* Claire Rochelle *(Phone Operator);* Clayton Moore *(Interne);* Dale Van Sickel *(Rookie/Alan Curtis' Double);* John Webb Dillon *(Court Attendant);* Barbara Bedford *(Nurse);* Bess Flowers, Nell Craig *(Reception Nurses).*

THUNDER AFLOAT
(MGM, 1939) 94 min.

PRODUCER:	J. Walter Ruben
DIRECTOR:	George B. Seitz
STORY:	Ralph Wheelwright, Harvey Haislip
SCREENPLAY:	Wells Root, Haislip
ART DIRECTORS:	Cedric Gibbons, Urie McCleary
SET DECORATOR:	Edwin B. Willis
WOMEN'S COSTUMES:	Dolly Tree
MEN'S COSTUMES:	Valles
MUSIC:	Edward Ward, David Snell
SOUND:	Douglas Shearer
CAMERA:	John Seitz
EDITOR:	Frank E. Hull

Wallace Beery *(John Thorson);* Chester Morris *(Rocky Blake);* Virginia Grey *(Susan Thorson);* Douglass Dumbrille *(District Commander);* Carl Esmond *(U-Boat Captain);* Clem Bevans *("Cap" Finch);* John Qualen *(Milt);* Regis Toomey *(Ives);* Charles Lane *(Captain Sabin);* Phillip Terry *(Lieutenant West);* Addison Richards *(Admiral Ross);* Wade Boteler *(Recruiting Officer);* Harry Strang *(Sailor);* Frank Faylen *(Petty Officer);* Leon Ames *(Recruiting Officer);* Leigh De Lacy *(Mrs. Gill);* Don Castle *(Radio Operator);* Roger Moore *(Orderly);* Howard Hickman *(Surgeon);* Milton Kibbee, Philip Morris *(Fishermen);* Walter Thiele *(Young German Sailor);* Bud Fine *(Survivor);* Claire McDowell *(Nurse);* Wolfram Von Bock *(German Officer);* Larry McGrath *(Radio Operator);* Charles Johnson *(Signal Man).*

THE MAN FROM DAKOTA
(MGM, 1940) 75 min.

PRODUCER:	Edward Chodorov
DIRECTOR:	Leslie Fenton
BASED ON THE NOVEL *Arouse and Beware* by MACKINLAY KANTOR	
SCREENPLAY:	Laurence Stallings
ART DIRECTORS:	Cedric Gibbons, Malcolm Brown
SET DECORATOR:	Edwin B. Willis
MEN'S COSTUMES:	Gile Steele
WARDROBE:	Dolly Tree
MAKEUP:	Jack Dawn
CAMERA:	Ray June
EDITOR:	Conrad A. Nervig

Wallace Beery *(Sergeant Barstow);* John Howard *(Oliver Clark);* Dolores Del Rio [Eugenia *(Jenny)*]; Donald Meek *(Mr. Vestry);* Robert Barrat *(Parson Summers);* Addison Richards *(Provost Marshal);* Frederick Burton *(Campbellite);* William Haade *(Union Soldier);* John Wray *(Mr. Carpenter);* Gregory Gaye *(Colonel Borodin);* Frank Hagney *(Guard);* William Royle *(Supervisor);* Ted Oliver, Buddy Roosevelt *(Officers);* Hugh Sothern *(General);* Edward Hearn *(Captain);* John Butler *(Voss);* Tom Fadden *(Driver);* Francis Ford *(Horseman).*

20 MULE TEAM
(MGM, 1940) 84 min.

PRODUCER:	J. Walter Ruben
DIRECTOR:	Richard Thorpe
STORY:	Robert C. Dusoe, Owen Atkinson
SCREENPLAY:	Cyril Hume, E. E. Paramore, Richard Maibaum
CAMERA:	Clyde DeVinna
EDITOR:	Frank Sullivan

Wallace Beery *(Bill Bragg);* Leo Carrillo *(Piute Pete);* Marjorie Rambeau *(Josie Johnson);* Anne Baxter *(Jean Johnson);* Douglas Fowley *(Stag Roper);* Noah Beery, Jr. *(Mitch);* Berton Churchill *(Jackass Brown);* Arthur Hohl *(Salters);* Clem Bevans *(Chuckawalla);* Eddy Waller *(Horsecollar);* Charles Halton *(Adams);* Minor Watson *(Marshal);* Oscar O'Shea *(Conductor);* Ivan Miller *(Alden);* Lew Kelly, John Beck, Henry Sylvester *(Men);* Katherine Kenworthy *(Woman);* Sam Appel *(Proprietor);* Lloyd Ingraham *(Stockholder).*

WYOMING
(MGM, 1940) 89 min.

PRODUCER:	Milton Bren
DIRECTOR:	Richard Thorpe
STORY:	Jack Jevne
SCREENPLAY:	Jevne, Hugo Butler
CAMERA:	Clyde DeVinna
EDITOR:	Robert J. Kern

Wallace Beery *(Reb Harkness);* Leo Carrillo *(Pete);* Ann Rutherford *(Lucy Kincaid);* Lee Bowman *(Sergeant Connolly);* Joseph Calleia *(Buckley);* Bobs Watson *(Jimmy Kincaid);* Marjorie Main *(Mehitabel);* Henry Travers *(Sheriff);* Paul Kelly *(General Custer);* Stanley Fields *(Curley);* William Tannen *(Reynolds);* Chill Wills *(Lafe);* Donald MacBride *(Bart);* Clem Bevans *(Pa McKinley);* Russell Simpson *(Bronson);* Addison Richards *(Kincaid);* Dick Alexander *(Gus);* Chief Thundercloud *(Lightfoot);* Francis McDonald *(Dawson);* Glenn Strange *(Bill Smalley);* Art Belasco *(Man);* Howard Mitchell *(Conductor);* Edgar Dearing *(Officer);* Archie Butler, Harley Chambers *(Cavalrymen).*

THE BAD MAN
(MGM, 1941) 70 min.

PRODUCER:	J. Walter Ruben
DIRECTOR:	Richard Thorpe
STORY:	Porter Emerson Browne
SCREENPLAY:	Wells Root
CAMERA:	Clyde DeVinna
EDITOR:	Conrad Nervig

Wallace Beery *(Lopez);* Lionel Barrymore *(Uncle Henry Jones);* Laraine Day *(Lucia Pell);* Ronald Reagan *(Gil Jones);* Henry Travers *(Mr. Hardy);* Tom Conway *(Morgan Pell);* Chill Wills *("Red" Giddings);* Nydia Westman *(Angela Hardy);* Chris-Pin Martin *(Pedro);* Charles Stevens *(Venhustiano);* Artie Ortego *(Policeman);* Daniel Rea *(Peon);* Joe Dominguez *(Policeman).*

BARNACLE BILL
(MGM, 1941) 98 min.

PRODUCER:	Milton Bren
DIRECTOR:	Richard Thorpe
STORY:	Jack Jevne
SCREENPLAY:	Jevne, Hugo Butler
ART DIRECTORS:	Cedric Gibbons, Urie McCleary
SET DECORATOR:	Edwin B. Willis
MUSIC:	Bronislau Kaper
SOUND:	Douglas Shearer
CAMERA:	Clyde DeVinna
EDITOR:	Frank E. Hull

Wallace Beery *("Bill" Johansen);* Marjorie Main *(Marge Cavendish);* Leo Carrillo *(Pico Rodriquez);* Virginia Weidler *(Virginia Johansen);* Barton MacLane *(John Kelly);* Connie Gilchrist *(Mamie);* Sara Haden *(Aunt Letty Breckenridge);* William Edmunds *(Joe Petillo);* Don Terry *(Dixon);* Alec Craig *(MacDonald);* Monte Montague *(Dolan);* Irving Bacon *(Deckhand);* Walter Baldwin, Milton Kibbee, Harry Burns *(Fishermen);* William Forrest *(Naval Officer);* William Gould *(Constable);* Charles Lane *(Auctioneer).*

THE BUGLE SOUNDS
(MGM, 1941) 110 min.

PRODUCER:	J. Walter Ruben
DIRECTOR:	S. Sylvan Simon
STORY:	Lawrence Kimble, Cyril Hume
SCREENPLAY:	Hume
CAMERA:	Clyde DeVinna
EDITOR:	Ben Lewis

Wallace Beery *("Hap" Doan);* Marjorie Main *(Susie);* Lewis Stone *(Colonel Lawton);* George Bancroft *(Russell);* William Lundigan *(Joe Hanson);* Donna Reed *(Sally Hanson);* Henry O'Neill *(Lieutenant Colonel Seton);* Chill Wills *(Dillon);* Roman Bohnen *(Leech);* Jerome Cowan *(Nichols);* Tom Dugan *(Strong);* Guinn "Big Boy" Williams *(Krim);* Ernest Whitman *(Cartaret);* Arthur Space *(Hank);* Lane Chandler, Ed Parker, Ray Teal, Alexander Lockwood *(Sergeants);* Walter Sande *(Headquarters Sergeant);* Stanley Andrews *(Vet);* Reed Hadley *(T. J. A.);* Kane Richmond *(Captain);* Jack Luden, Bradley Page *(Adjutants);* Dorothy Granger *(Girl).*

JACKASS MAIL
(MGM, 1942) 80 min.

Producer:	John W. Considine, Jr.
Director:	Norman Z. McLeod
Story:	C. Gardner Sullivan
Screenplay:	Lawrence Hazard
Art Directors:	Cedirc Gibbons, Leonid Vasian
Set Decorator:	Edwin B. Willis
Gowns:	Howard Shoup
Men's Costumes:	Gile Steele
Music:	David Snell, Earl Brent
Choreography:	Sammy Lee
Camera:	Clyde DeVinna
Editor:	Gene Ruggiero

Wallace Beery *(Marmaduke "Just" Baggott);* Marjorie Main *(Clementine "Tiny" Tucker);* J. Carroll Naish *(O'Sullivan);* Darryl Hickman *(Tommie Gargan);* William Haade *("Red" Gargan);* Hobart Cavanaugh *("Gospel" Jones);* Dick Curtis *(Jim Swade);* Joe Yule *(Barky);* Harry Fleischmann *(Carp);* Louis Mason *(Slim);* George Carleton *(Pastor);* Bobby Larson *(Boy);* Mary Currier *(Mother);* Harry Woods *(Ranch Owner);* Paul "Tiny" Newlan *(Rancher);* Murdock MacQuarrie *(Hickory Jake);* LeRoy Mason *(Vigilante);* Frank Darien *(Postmaster);* Malcolm Waite *(Cocky).*

SALUTE TO THE MARINES
(MGM, 1943) C-101 min.

Producer:	John W. Considine, Jr.
Director:	S. Sylvan Simon
Story:	Robert D. Andrews
Adaptor:	Wells Root
Screenplay:	George Bruce
Art Directors:	Cedric Gibbons, Stanley Rogers, Lynden Sparhawk
Set Decorators:	Edwin B. Willis, Glen Barner
Music:	Lennie Hayton
Assistant Director:	Al Jennings
Technicolor Consultants:	Natalie Kalmus, W. Howard Greene
Sound:	J. Edmondson
Special Effects:	Arnold Gillespie, Warren Newcombe
Camera:	Charles Schoenbaum
Editor:	Frederick Y. Smith

Wallace Beery *(Sergeant Major William Bailey);* Fay Bainter *(Jennie Bailey);* William Lundigan *(Rufus Cleveland);* Marilyn Maxwell *(Helen Bailey);* Reginald Owen *(Mr. Casper);* Keye Luke *("Flashy" Logaz);* Ray Collins *(Colonel Mason);* Donald Curtis *(Randall James);* James Davis *(Saunders);* Mark Daniels *(Myers);* Leonard Strong *(Karitu);* Rose Hobart *(Mrs. Carson);* Fritz Leiber *(Mr. Agno);* Charles Trowbridge *(Mr. Selkirk);* Bobby Blake *(Small Boy);* Noah Beery, Sr. *(Adjutant);* Mary Field *(Mrs. Riggs);* William Bishop *(Corporal Anderson);* Hugh Beaumont, Dave O'Brien *(Sergeants);* Myron Healey *(Gunner);* Tom Yuen *(Filipino);* Chester Gan, Kaem Tong *(Japanese Officers).*

RATIONING
(MGM, 1944) 93 min.

Producer:	Orville O. Dull
Director:	Willis Goldbeck
Screenplay:	William R. Lipman, Grant Garrett, Harry Ruskin
Art Directors:	Cedric Gibbons, Howard Campbell
Set Decorators:	Edwin B. Willis, Glen Barner
Music:	David Snell
Assistant Director:	Al Raboch
Sound:	William R. Edmondson
Camera:	Sidney Wagner
Editor:	Ferris Webster

Wallace Beery *(Ben Barton);* Marjorie Main *(Iris Tuttle);* Donald Meek *(Wilfred Ball);* Dorothy Morris *(Dorothy Tuttle);* Howard Freeman *(Cash Riddle);* Connie Gilchrist *(Mrs. Porter);* Tommy Satten *(Lance Barton);* Gloria Dickson *(Miss McCue);* Henry O'-Neill *(Senator Edward A. White);* Richard Hall *(Teddy);* Charles Halton *(Ezra Weeks);* Morris Ankrum *(Mr. Morgan);* Douglas Fowley *(Dixie Samson);* Chester Clute *(Roberts);* Chill Wills *(Bus Driver);* Al Hill *(Greenie);* Milton Kibbee *(Wright);* Eddy Waller *(Smith);* Anne O'Neal *(Woman);* Ed Kilroy *(Minister);* Robert Emmet O'Connor *(Sheriff McGuinness).*

BARBARY COAST GENT
(MGM, 1944) 87 min.

Producer:	Orville O. Dull
Director:	Roy Del Ruth
Story:	William Lipman, Grant Garrett
Screenplay:	Lipman, Garrett, Harry Ruskin
Art Directors:	Cedric Gibbons, William Ferrari
Set Decorator:	Edwin B. Willis
Assistant Director:	George Rhein
Music:	David Snell
Sound:	James Z. Flaster
Camera:	Charles Salerno
Editor:	Adrienne Fazan

Wallace Beery *(Honest Plush Brannon);* Binnie Barnes *(Lil Damish);* John Carradine *(Duke Cleat);* Bruce Kellogg *(Bradford Bellamy III);* Frances Rafferty *(Portia Adair);* Chill Wills *(Sheriff Hightower);* Noah Beery, Sr. *(Pete Hanibal);* Henry O'Neill *(Colonel Watrous);* Ray Collins *(Johnny Adair);* Morris Ankrum *(Alec Veeder);* Donald Meek *(Bradford Bellamy I);* Addison Richards *(Wade Gamelin);* Harry Hayden *(Elias Porter);* Paul E. Burns *(Tim Shea);* Paul Hurst *(Jake Compton);* Victor Kilian *(Curry Slake);* Cliff Clark *(Jake Coda);* Louise Beavers *(Bedelia);* Robert Emmet O'Connor *(Joe, the Bartender);* Ray Teal *(Bouncer);* Jack Norton, Will Stanton, Harry Rose *(Drunks);* George Lloyd *(Barker);* Ralph Sanford *(Bouncer);* Byron Foulger *(Holcomb, the Assayer);* Tom Dugan *(Engineer);* Alan Bridge *(Businessman);* Lee Phelps *(Shotgun Messenger).*

THIS MAN'S NAVY
(MGM, 1945) 100 min.

Producer:	Samuel Marx
Director:	William A. Wellman
Screen Idea:	Commander Herman E. Halland, U.S.N. (Retired)
Screenplay:	Borden Chase (uncredited: John Twist, Allen Rivkin, Hugh Allen)
Art Directors:	Cedric Gibbons, Howard Campbell
Set Decorators:	Edwin B. Willis, Glen Barner
Assistant Director:	Horace Hough
Music:	Nathaniel Shilkret
Sound:	Lowell Kinsall
Special Effects:	A. Arnold Gillespie, Donald Jahraus
Montage Effects:	Peter Ballbusch
Camera:	Sidney Wagner
Editor:	Irving Warburton

Wallace Beery *(Ned Trumpett);* James Gleason *(Jimmy Shannon);* Tom Drake *(Jess Weaver);* Jan Clayton *(Cathey Cortland);* Selena Royle *(Maude Weaver);* Henry O'Neill *(Lieutenant Commander Graystone);* Paul Cavanagh *(Sir Anthony Tivall);* Noah Beery, Sr. *(Joe Hodum);* George Chandler *(Bert Bland);* Steve Brodie *(Tim Shannon);* Arthur Walsh *(Cadet Rayshek);* Will Fowler *(David);* Donald Curtis *(Operations Officer);* Richard Crockett *(Sparks);* Connie Weiler *(Wave);* Dick Rich *(Shore Patrolman);* John Kellogg *(Junior Pilot);* Blake Edwards *(Flier);* Bruce Kellogg, George Ramsey *(Pilots);* Henry Daniels, Jr. *(Crew Member);* Carlyle Blackwell, Jr., Bob Lowell *(Mechanics).*

BAD BASCOMB
(MGM, 1946) 112 min.

Producer:	Orville O. Dull
Director:	S. Sylvan Simon
Story:	D. A. Loxley
Screenplay:	William Lipman, Grant Garrett
Music:	David Snell
Orchestrator:	Wally Heglin
Assistant Director:	Earl McAvoy
Art Directors:	Cedric Gibbons, Paul Youngblood

Set Decorators:	Edwin B. Willis, Jack Ahern
Sound:	Howard Fellows
Special Effects:	Warren Newcombe
Camera:	Charles Schoenbaum
Editor:	Ben Lewis

Wallace Beery *(Zeb Bascomb);* Margaret O'-Brien *(Emmy);* Marjorie Main *(Abbey Hanks);* J. Carroll Naish *(Bart Yancy);* Frances Rafferty *(Dora);* Marshall Thompson *(Jimmy Holden);* Russell Simpson *(Elijah Walker);* Warner Anderson *(Luther Mason);* Donald Curtis *(John Fulton);* Connie Gilchrist *(Annie Freemont);* Sara Haden *(Tillie Lovejoy);* Renie Riano *(Lucy Lovejoy);* Wally Cassell *(Curley);* Jane Green *(Hanna);* Henry O'Neill *(Governor Winter);* Frank Darien *(Elder McCabe);* Joseph Crehan *(Governor Ames);* Clyde Fillmore *(Governor Clark);* Arthur Space *(Sheriff);* Stanley Andrews *(Colonel Cartright).*

THE MIGHTY McGURK
(MGM, 1946) 87 min.

Producer:	Nat Perrin
Director:	John Waters
Screenplay:	William R. Lipman, Grant Garrett, Harry Clark
Art Directors:	Cedric Gibbons, Hubert Hobson
Set Decorators:	Edwin B. Willis, Alfred E. Spencer
Music:	David Snell
Assistant Director:	Tom Andre
Sound:	Douglas Shearer
Camera:	Charles Schoenbaum
Editor:	Ben Lewis

Wallace Beery *("Slag" Morgan);* Dean Stockwell *(Nipper);* Edward Arnold *(Mike Pfieffer);* Aline MacMahon *(Mamie Steeple);* Cameron Mitchell *(Johnny Burden);* Dorothy Patrick *(Caroline Pfieffer);* Aubrey Mather *(Milbane);* Morris Ankrum *(Towles);* Clinton Sundberg *(Chisholm);* Charles Judels, Torben Meyer *(Brewery Men);* Stuart Holmes *(Sightseer);* Edward Earle *(Martin);* Tom Kennedy *(Man at Punching Machine);* Trevor Tremaine *(Cockney);* Lee Phelps *(Cop);* Joe Yule *(Irish Immigrant);* Jimmy Dundee, Frank Marlowe *(Mugs);* Fred Gilman, Frank Mayo, Lew Smith *(Agents);* Skeets Noyes *(Panhandler).*

ALIAS A GENTLEMAN
(MGM, 1948) 76 min.

Producer:	Nat Perrin
Director:	Harry Beaumont
Story:	Peter Ruric
Screenplay:	William R. Lipman
Art Directors:	Cedric Gibbons, Stan Rogers
Set Decorators:	Edwin B. Willis, Alfred E. Spencer
Music:	David Snell
Assistant Director:	Tom Andre
Makeup:	Jack Dawn
Sound:	Douglas Shearer, Charles J. Burbridge
Camera:	Ray June
Editor:	Ben Lewis

Wallace Beery *(Jim Breedin);* Tom Drake *(Johnny Lorgen);* Dorothy Patrick *(Elaine Carter);* Gladys George *(Madge Parkson);* Leon Ames *(Matt Enley);* Warner Anderson *(Captain Charlie Lopen);* John Qualen *(No End);* Sheldon Leonard *(Harry Bealer);* Trevor Bardette *(Jig Johnson);* Jeff Corey *(Zu);* John Goldsworthy *(Morton);* Marc Krah *(Spats);* Frank McGrath *(Murph);* John A. Butler *(Gimp);* Jack Norton *(Charnell);* Morris Ankrum *(O.K.);* George Chandler *(Curly Britt);* Bud Wolfe *(Driver);* Charles Wagenheim *(Con);* Max Willenz *(Tailor);* Eddie Dunn, Jack Lee *(Men);* Robert Emmet O'Connor *(Doorman);* Bill Hall *(Hendricks);* Lee Phelps *(Maheffy);* Howard Mitchell *(Detective);* Lou Lubin *(Pickpocket);* Paul Maxey *(Man with Wallet).*

A DATE WITH JUDY
(MGM, 1948) C-113 min.

Producer:	Joe Pasternak
Director:	Richard Thorpe
Based on characters created by Alan Leslie	
Screenplay:	Dorothy Cooper, Dorothy Kingsley
Technicolor Consultants:	Natalie Kalmus, Henri Jaffa
Art Directors:	Cedric Gibbons, Paul Groesse
Set Decorators:	Edwin B. Willis, Richard A. Pefferle
Music Director:	Georgie Stoll
Songs:	Jimmy McHugh and Harold Adamson; Don Raye and Gene dePaul; Stella Unger and Alec Templeton
Assistant Director:	Jerome Bergman
Choreography:	Stanley Donen
Costumes:	Helen Rose
Sound:	Douglas Shearer, Norwood A. Fenton
Special Effects:	Warren Newcombe
Camera:	Robert Surtees
Editor:	Harold F. Kress

Wallace Beery *(Melvin R. Foster);* Jane Powell *(Judy Foster);* Elizabeth Taylor *(Carol Foster);* Carmen Miranda *(Rosita Conchellas);* Xavier Cugat *(Cugat);* Robert Stack *(Stephen Andrews);* Selena Royle *(Mrs. Foster);* Scotty Beckett *(Ogden "Oogie" Pringle);* Leon Ames *(Lucien T. Pringle);* George Cleveland *(Gramps);* Lloyd Corrigan *(Pop Scully);* Clinton Sundberg *(Jameson);* Jean McLaren *(Mitzie);* Jerry Hunter *(Randolph Foster);* Buddy Howard *(Jo-Jo Hoffenpepper);* Lillian Yarbo *(Nightingale);* Eula Guy *(Miss Clarke);* Francis Pierlot *(Professor Green);* Rena Lenart *(Olga);* Polly Bailey *(Elderly Woman);* Paul Bradley *(Headwaiter).*

BIG JACK
(MGM, 1949) 85 min.

Producer:	Gottfried Reinhardt
Director:	Richard Thorpe
Story:	Robert Thoeren
Screenplay:	Gene Fowler, Marvin Borowsky, Osso Van Eyss
Art Directors:	Cedric Gibbons, Randall Duell
Set Decorators:	Edwin B. Willis, Hugh Hunt
Music:	Herbert Stothart
Music Director:	Andre Previn
Assistant Director:	Al Jennings
Makeup:	Jack Dawn
Costumes:	Valles
Sound:	Douglas Shearer, John A. Williams
Camera:	Robert Surtees
Editor:	George Boemler

Wallace Beery *(Big Jack Horner);* Richard Conte *(Dr. Alexander Meade);* Marjorie Main *(Flapjack Kate);* Edward Arnold *(Mayor Mahoney);* Vanessa Brown *(Beatrice Mahoney);* Clinton Sundberg *(C. Petronius Smith);* Charles Dingle *(Mathias Taylor);* Clem Bevans *(Saltlick Joe);* Jack Lambert *(Bud Valentine);* Will Wright *(Will Farnsworth);* William "Bill" Phillips *(Toddy);* Syd Saylor *(Pokey);* Vince Barnett *(Tom Speed);* Trevor Bardette *(John Oakes);* Andy Clyde *(Putt Cleghorn);* Edith Evanson *(Widow Simpson);* Tom Fadden *(Sheriff Summers);* Minerva Urecal *(Mrs. Summers);* Ann Doran *(Sarah);* Fred Gilman, Dick Alexander, Cactus Mack, Lane Bradford, Lynn Farr *(Bandits).*

THREE

PAT O'BRIEN

5′ 11″
175 pounds
Brown hair
Blue eyes
Scorpio

For nearly sixty years, Pat O'Brien has offered the public variations of Irish charm, sometimes brash and frenetic; on other occasions, soulful; and, sometimes, just thoughtful. It proved to be a winning commodity for the fast-talking performer, as he weaved his way through careers on the stage, radio, television, and silver screen. O'Brien's congenial personality, away from the limelight, also helped bolster his image in the industry. He was everybody's pal.

In the early 1930s, O'Brien might easily have been dismissed as merely another rival for bombastic Lee Tracy, but O'Brien proved he was a survivor. As part of the growing Warner Bros. stock company, he was teamed with offcamera friend James Cagney in a series of hearty and profitable adventure pictures. Cagney was the superstar in these happy-go-lucky entries, but Pat was ever the professional. It would usually be feisty Cagney who won the heroine, while a dewey-eyed Pat wished them God's speed and much happiness. Yet he was such a likeable player that moviegoers did not relegate him to the "just the other man" category.

Film critics might complain that O'Brien too often played a one-dimensional caricature of himself. However, such diverse entries as *Boy Meets Girl* (1938), *Knute Rockne—All American* (1940), and *The Boy with Green Hair* (1948) demonstrated that he could handle a range of subtle variations in his portrayal of the Gaelic charmer. One astute observer of the O'Brien personae noted that he was a master of reaction, able to register a variety of emotions in any given scene. It is this capacity, along with his well-exploited shamrock blarney, that has made him such an enduring favorite to generations of entertainment seekers.

Pat O'Brien was born on Saturday, November 11, 1899 and christened William Joseph O'Brien. He is pure Irish on both sides of his family. His mother's parents were William and Margaret McGovern, immigrants from Galway, Ireland. They settled in Waukesha, Wisconsin. In his autobiography, *The Wind at My Back* (1964), he described the family in this way: "The frisky McGovern girls were May, Agnes, Katherine and Margaret. The large and active boys were Philip and William. There were others but . . . they died in infancy. . . . There was no money in the McGovern pocket to aid any of the brood to higher education. The McGovern girls went to the Lee House to work at the tables as waitresses. Sara Lee and her husband had the finest eating place in the area and catered to all of the paunch-proof downtown business trade. The girls got their keep: food and lodging and a minimum salary, and tips—

which were meager. Free came the wonderful counsel of Aunt Sara Lee. . . . It was a great blessing to Ma and Dad McGovern to know 'our brood,' the girl contingency at least, was looked after with such darling care."

Pat's paternal grandfather, Patrick O'Brien, was an apprentice architect, a widower, who was killed trying to stop a fight in a saloon. His son William (also called Bill or Tip) O'Brien was then twelve. He lived with relatives for a few years but soon was off to earn his own livelihood, first in Chicago, then in Milwaukee. Pat would recall it this way: "During his daily visits to the Lee House, Bill O'Brien had occasion to meet young men of other lines of work. One was an aspiring young butcher, Charles Sclenger; the other, a salesman of sorts, Charles Taberner, with derby tilted at a fashionable angle. They were giving their undivided attention to Margaret's sisters, Mary and Agnes. It didn't take long for passion to overcome reason, and soon wedding bells clanged over three weddings; rice was flung and mothers wept. Margaret McGovern, in proud crisp white . . . became Mrs. William O'Brien."

Their only son, William Joseph, was later called Pat after his grandfather. Two other boys were born to the O'Brien family, Edward and Robert, but they died in infancy. Pat remembers his childhood in downtown Milwaukee, with its sandlots and street games, and the largely Irish gang of boys with whom he associated. Like most boys his age, he collected baseball cards and cigar bands. In the summer, he recalls, "it was an open air world of wonderful Saturday picnics at West Park! My mother would make up sandwiches of pork and corned beef, pickles, pies, and potato salads, the like of which memory hints I have never tasted since. Picnics were the great summer adventure. We would rise early in the morning laughing and howling, scramble into our clothes, shout and dance, observe the sky and scare off the clouds . . . and make great plans for the rest of the day. . . . We would embark for the park on the trolley for a glorious day of fun, eating, wading, snoozing on the trampled grass, sassing the Keystone helmeted cops; and plan big game hunts among the small animals of the park. . . . Near dusk we poured from the park . . . sunburned, fire scorched . . . and at last the trolley car trip home."

Pat's parents were devout Catholics, and he made them proud when he became an altar boy at nearby Gesu Church, where he attended the local parochial school: "I shall always remember my first day in school as my personal Stations of the Cross. My mother left me there alone like Robinson Crusoe on his island—worse, it seemed like I was being exiled to Siberia, till a very beautiful nun, Sister Mary Norbert, took my small hand and consoled me in the voice of angels—and things became all right again and I could focus on my classmates, on sharp pencils and things called reading and writing."

Pat would later reflect on his religious upbringing: "We were not, in our church, goodie-goodie boys, and the priests and nuns had their hands full with us. And they weren't the holy waxworks, the pious sighers, the films often show them as. . . . They may have had some human failings, and could give you the back of the hand as well as lead you to the remission of mortal sin. . . . They were pioneers in the faith in my childhood, when Catholics were still not accepted in some places. . . . A child's impressions last longest of all memories, and no matter where, later, I was, or how badly things were going, I could always depend on the faith I had learned as a child."

During Pat's childhood, the O'Briens moved uptown to a flat with electric lights—which seemed a great luxury and wonder at the time. Gregarious Pat made friends quickly, and he and his new gang soon began organizing a baseball team, which they called the Bullet Stoppers.

Of the adolescent years (1910–16), Pat recalls: "There were kid gangs in those days, just as there are now, but they didn't have the hoodlum aura that a lot of the younger lawbreakers seem to be immersed in today. . . . Our adolescent feuds never involved anything more than panting, shouting hand-to-hand encounters, standing up in the stance of a famous prize fighter and exchanging fisticuffs."

Pat has fond memories of attending the theatre—from the highest balcony—where he saw such greats as David Warfield, Sir Johnston Forbes-Robertson, Maude Adams, Ethel Barrymore, and Nance O'Neill perform their repertoire of showcase roles. "I was infected and didn't know it," O'Brien would later remark. "Actors' blood boiled in me, but as yet at a simmer." He did participate in school plays and class debates.

In Pat's neighborhood, the dream of every Irish parent was to send his or her offspring to Marquette Academy, but its cost was prohibitive. The only chance for O'Brien to matriculate there was to win one of the few scholarships offered. He wrote "a vast composition" on the history of Ireland and was rewarded with free tuition to the Academy. He entered Marquette with a heightened sense of Irish pride that has remained with him ever since.

In early 1917, Spencer Tracy, who was to become a lifelong friend, also entered Marquette. In 1918 both of them left school to join the navy and to participate in World War I. They were stationed, like other local boys, at the Great Lakes Naval Station. It was a large installation, but not very exciting for two young men reveling in the first flush of patriotism. Most of their excess energy was devoted to playing sports, especially football. In late 1918, after Pat and Tracy were given honorable discharges from the navy, both decided that the next step was to complete high school.

Pat graduated from Marquette Academy and entered Marquette University. Initially he planned to study law, but soon he was smitten with acting and deeply involved with the college theatre group. As he would explain: "The theater had settled into me as a major love. I played my first important dramatic role in the college production of *Charley's Aunt* as the star, in borrowed skirts. I was adorable. . . . I had a secret image—throughout the football, scholastics, fraternities, the theater was always hovering uppermost on my thoughts. How and why was I to become an actor? I didn't know. I knew no one, I was unknown."

In a stroke of luck which took him toward the professional theatre, Pat spent the summer with an aunt and uncle who lived in New York City. He stayed on to look for work on Broadway, and in a display of the brashness of youth and Irish confidence, he found it. He faked a few steps at an audition for dancers for the show *Adrienne* (1923), starring George Bancroft and Vivienne Segal, and won a job as a chorus boy. However, when Pat's dad became ill suddenly and wanted him home, Pat reluctantly returned, dispirited, and re-entered Marquette University.

It wasn't long before his attention was rapidly diverted back to the stage. Making use of his "professional experience," however brief, Pat produced, directed, and starred in the amateur Junior League show in Milwaukee. The production was a big hit and Pat became a star in his hometown.

His father's ailment proved of short duration and Pat resolved to become an actor in earnest. Two problems presented themselves: (1) where to get theatrical training, and (2) how to pay for it. Pat and his pal Spencer Tracy (who had discovered the same vocation) thought of using their serviceman's allowance to enter the best acting school around. This was Sargent's Acting Academy, located in Carnegie Hall. (The organization evolved into the American Academy of Dramatic Arts.)

Thus the two would-be actors descended on New York, finding quickly a small, inexpensive flat to share. Both of them also found work in the famous play of the time, *R.U.R.,* cast as robots. They lived in what Pat termed an "underworld" of struggling actors—a group of young hopefuls working as extras or not at all, existing on nothing tangible. They socialized with one another, talked shop, and traded dreams.

Pat accepted what walk-ons and extra jobs he could find while studying his craft. Then he began the rounds of agents and casting directors. He found employment with a stock company in Plainfield, New Jersey. The play in which he was cast was *Getting Gertie's Garter.*

Following that short, undistinguished engagement came a spell of small parts, lost jobs, replacement parts, stock companies, and stretches of being "at liberty." Among the Broadway shows Pat performed in were *A Man's Man* (October 1925),[1] *You Can't Win* (February, 1926), *Henry, Behave* (August, 1926) with Edward G. Robinson, and *Gertie* (November, 1926), with Constance MacKay. During the run of *Henry, Behave,* Pat became a member of the famed Lambs Club, proposed by John Cumberland and seconded by Edward G. Robinson. The show business club has been a constant source of happiness and moral support for Pat over the decades.

After *Gertie,* Pat again found decent stage work difficult to obtain. He settled for a small part in a stock company based in Asbury Park, New Jersey, reasoning he at least could stay with relatives and save money. The next step, fortunately, was upward. He landed a role in the road company of the popular Broadway play *Broadway.* The touring company was playing the South. After Pat was with the group for several weeks, he was promoted to the Chicago troupe, with the same secondary role—the tough cop, Dan McCorn.[2]

In the Windy City company were performers who were to become close friends with Pat, Wallace Ford and Allen Jenkins. Also in the group was a beautiful young actress named Eloise Taylor, who would eventually be his closest friend of all—his wife. After a successful run, *Broadway* closed in Chicago. To Pat's chagrin he could not find a new job, while Eloise was hired for stock in Worcester, Massachusetts.

[1]Years later veteran actress Josephine Hutchinson would recall Pat's performance in *A Man's Man,* in which he replaced the heavy: "Pat, bless his heart, was no heavy. He used to cry with his upstage eye during the play because he was being so naughty to me! I used to say, 'That's great—but how can you cry with just one eye?' "

[2]During the Chicago run of *Broadway,* Pat would recall, "Mother and Dad came down from Milwaukee to see our show. When I made my entrance in the first act, Mom couldn't contain herself, and she cried for all to hear: 'That's my boy!' Applause. . . . Up till that time, I had never gotten a hand on my entrance."

Then Pat joined a stock company in Baltimore for a season. In the repertory group were Spencer Tracy and Frank McHugh. Pat next was engaged for *The Door Between,* a Broadway-bound venture which opened and closed in Cleveland. It developed that the drama had been plagiarized from another already produced play, and Pat and the rest of cast just managed to squeak out of town ahead of the sheriff.

Meanwhile, Pat's personal life was unsatisfactory. Smitten at first sight, he had repeatedly asked Eloise to marry him, but she was not sure and refused any definite commitment. She had moved from stock in Massachusetts to stock in Duluth, Minnesota, so they could communicate only by letter.

Pat was again out of work in New York. After a while, he secured jobs in several unsuccessful plays, then was hired for a stock troupe in Cleveland. Among the other actors employed there was Lloyd Nolan. Here Helen Hayes, even then the "First Lady of the Theatre," guest-starred in *Coquette* for two weeks, and Pat was thrilled at being cast in the lead opposite her.

Soon Pat and Eloise were back in New York, looking for work together. Despite their poverty, Pat found their situation idyllic—except that Eloise would still not say yes. All too quickly, from his point of view, she obtained work in Chicago. Pat, meanwhile, found and lost a small role. During this period he was living at the Lambs Club where he became well acquainted with such celebrity members as Ring Lardner, Joe Frisco, and Frank Fay. These men would remain friends—as well as conversation pieces—for years to come.

Determined O'Brien continued to haunt the casting offices, and he was rewarded with a small role in a show called *The Nut Farm.* When he first heard the title he quipped, "It must be about actors." The show opened in Cleveland and went on to Chicago for a run of twenty-four weeks. Professionally, everything was taking an upturn and he was elated, but then his luck changed when he was stricken with tonsillitis, which can be very serious for an adult. Pat suffered a hemorrhage that was severe enough for the priest to be called to administer the final rites. Thanks to quick emergency measures, he survived and soon recovered his strength.

Finally Pat landed a good strong lead role in *The Up and Up,* playing a fast-talking bookie named Curley in a cast which included Dorothy Stickney, Sam Levene, and Percy Kilbride. The play tried out in Asbury Park to lukewarm reviews, but business was sufficient to warrant opening the show at the Biltmore Theatre on Broadway (September 8, 1930). After several years of work, Pat was finally discovered by the New York critics. He received personal raves, but the play was unlucky.[3] The juvenile left for a better role, Dorothy Stickney became ill and had to be replaced, and they even had to change theatres in mid-run. *The Up and Up* closed after seventy-two performances.

However, on closing night, O'Brien was presented with a script entitled *Overture* by William Bolitho. An early anti-Communist play that eventually starred Colin Clive and was directed by Marc Connelly, it was another critical hit (opening December 5, 1930), but enjoyed only a short run of forty-one performances. By this point, Pat's professional career had built momentum. A week after *Overture* closed, playwright Philip Barry personally asked for him to appear in his new play *Tomorrow and Tomorrow* with Herbert Marshall and Zita Johann. Pat had become a well-regarded actor, if not a star.

During the first week of rehearsal, Eloise (then back in New York) surprised Pat by informing him that she had decided to become a Catholic. He was deeply moved by her action and was with her at the religious ceremony.

In December 1930, before the Barry play opened (January 13, 1931), Pat received a phone call at the Lambs Club from multimillionaire film producer Howard Hughes. Hughes asked a stunned Pat to go to Hollywood to star in the picture version of *The Front Page.* O'Brien could not decide at first whether to go. However, after talking to star Herbert Marshall and the play's producer, Gilbert Miller, he concluded that it would be wise to do it.

In the meantime, Pat had made his first feature film, Paramount's *Honor Among Lovers,*[4] released in February 1931. It was filmed at the studio's Astoria, Long Island facility and featured a heavily moustached Fredric March and a coy Claudette Colbert. It was a weak melodrama directed by Dorothy Arzner, in which Pat and another screen newcomer named Ginger Rogers had minimal roles.

When Pat arrived with trepidation in Hollywood, he discovered to his dismay that all the personnel at

[3]The critics were enthusiastic about O'Brien's interpretation: "... the measured playing of Pat O'Brien, ... is the sole ornament of the production" *(New York Times).* "This play should give thanks ... to the acting of Pat O'Brien, who has a very remarkable style and economy, and who knows down to ground the art of the cool, level voice and the straight face" *(New York World).* "It is Pat O'Brien, as Curley, the master-mind among the bookmakers who walks away with the evening ... he endows even the most uncertain portions of the script with an undeniable persuasion whenever he is on stage" *(New York Evening Post).*

[4]There was another Pat O'Brien working as an actor in Hollywood in the 1920s and 1930s. The screen credits of this character player are often confused with those of this chapter's subject. In the mid-1930s the "lesser" Pat O'Brien would go to court to sue to keep his name; he won the case and continued onward until his death in the early 1940s.

Hughes' production unit thought that he had played fast-talking newsman Hildy Johnson on Broadway.[5] He had to disillusion them. Nevertheless, the director, Lewis Milestone, had seen O'Brien onstage in *The Up and Up* and was confident that he could handle the part.

The filming of *The Front Page* had just begun when Louis Wolheim, who was to portray the irascible editor Walter Burns, was taken ill and died within a week (on February 18, 1931). He was replaced by Adolphe Menjou. The latter was well-known for his portrayals of smooth men-about-town and the cast was convinced that he would ruin the milieu of the rough-and-ready comedy. Yet it turned out to be a stroke of genius on Milestone's part. He was superb in the role, and in fact he came to prefer that type of part. (The first bit of business on Menjou's first day on the set was a crap game which included Pat, Frank McHugh, other actors, and Adolphe. When Menjou emerged the winner, he was considered one of the boys.)

During the filming of this United Artists release, Myron Selznick, already one of the best known and most useful agents in Hollywood, visited the set and suggested to Pat that he sign with him. However, O'Brien, who was not sure that he was going to remain in Hollywood or that he required an agent, refused the proposal. Another visitor was more heartily welcomed. That was Eloise who had come to Hollywood to wed O'Brien. On Wednesday, January 21, 1931 they were finally married. She found an apartment for them near the Blessed Sacrament Church. (Both felt more secure in the Hollywood jungle residing near the church.)

[5]When Lee Tracy, who had originated the role of Hildy Johnson on Broadway, but was committed elsewhere at the time the feature was made, learned that Pat was to do the role in Hollywood, he gave him his original script with notes and business written in the margins.

With Mary Brian in *The Front Page* (1931).

The Front Page opened to rave reviews and solid box-office business. Pat was discovered again as a "promising newcomer" and the picture was considered a landmark of film technique. In a recent interview with Karyn Kay and Gerald Peary for *The Velvet Light Trap* magazine Pat discussed the unusual methods used: "The shots of Menjou and me around the table were Milestone's innovation [a 360-degree turn of the camera]. He said, 'I'm the director. Don't tell me they can't be done.' The camera was set up in the flies, and it worked."

For *Personal Maid* (1931), starring Nancy Carroll and to be shot at Paramount's Astoria, Long Island studio, Pat (and Eloise) returned to New York. It was not the simple filming of a romantic melodrama everyone anticipated, for Miss Carroll demanded extensive script rewrites. Producer Howard Hughes arranged a suite for the O'Briens at the Ritz Hotel for the duration of the extended shooting. Pat was cast as Peter Shea, the self-made businessman who proposes that Miss Carroll become his mistress. She refuses, remaining true to her sweetheart (Gene Raymond). Reviewing this run-of-the-mill entertainment, *Photoplay* noted, "Mary Boland [as Carroll's rich employer] is grand, but the story just isn't there—which makes it kind of hard on the actors. Pat O'Brien and Gene Raymond help."

The O'Briens returned to California and to a Hollywood they were now beginning to understand and like: "Actually I soon found that a few well-publicized scandals . . . gave the whole industry a bad name it didn't deserve. Making films is very hard work, leaving little time for the leisure of seduction, or the extra energy for rape. The actor or actress has to be up at dawn, get to a studio usually miles from home, and get made up. . . . After ten or twelve nerve-breaking takes a day . . . an actor just wanted to get home from work, have a highball, some dinner, listen to Amos 'n' Andy on the radio, and sleep."

Next Pat was loaned to RKO for *Consolation Marriage* (1931), starring Irene Dunne and featuring Myrna Loy and John Halliday. It remains one of O'Brien's favorite film assignments. On this production, location shots were needed for one scene, so the entire crew was sent, along with the necessary equipment, to San Francisco. Pat and Eloise were enjoying their travels.

Then, without warning, mercurial Howard Hughes dropped Pat's option and allowed his contract to lapse. Somewhat surprised, Pat hustled into

With Cedric Gibbons (second from left), Dolores Del Rio, and Eloise O'Brien (c. 1931).

action. He recalled Myron Selznick's offer to represent him and signed with the agent. The Selznick office operated on a simple motto: "Stars should get as much money as they can, while they can. They don't last long." Selznick's partner, Frank Joyce, accompanied O'Brien to Culver City to meet with executive producer Irving G. Thalberg at Metro-Goldwyn-Mayer. Thalberg was sufficiently impressed to sign Pat to a two-year contract at $1,750 weekly.

O'Brien was enthused about his salary increase. He had been earning only $750 weekly from Hughes. Yet years later he would have nothing but good words for the mysterious, iconoclastic businessman. "Actually, Howard was very kind, a wonderful man. I can honestly say that he was the best boss I ever had in this profession, and I'm going into my fifty-fifth year in show business."

Strangely, MGM preferred loaning out Pat's screen services rather than keeping him employed on the home lot. He did make *Flying High* (1931) there, teamed with Bert Lahr, Charlotte Greenwood, Guy Kibbee, and Hedda Hopper (in her pre-columnist days). The film was derived from the Buddy De Sylva, Lew Brown, Ray Henderson, and John McGowan Broadway musical that had starred Lahr. The wide-eyed actor again played the innocent, screwy inventor onscreen, surrounded by people wanting to steal his latest gimmick. It was an enjoyable but strange picture, whose stage roots could be seen all too clearly. Pat's role as the impoverished hero, Sport Wardell, was definitely subordinate to the madcap antics of Lahr and Miss Greenwood.

With a guarantee of a healthy income, the O'Briens soon rented a Beverly Hills home and invited their respective parents to come out to visit. Pat also purchased a new Ford, which they used for taking weekend jaunts about southern California.

Pat's next four 1932 films on loan-out from MGM were undistinguished. No studio had yet found the right showcase for his talent and personality. The films were: *Hell's House* with Bette Davis, *Final Edition* with Mae Clarke, *Scandal for Sale* with Charles Bickford and Rose Hobart, and *The Strange Case of Clara Deane* with Wynne Gibson and Frances Dee.

Pat then returned to Columbia Pictures—where he had made *Final Edition*—for Frank Capra's *American Madness* (1932). It was a timely tale of the Depression and bank failures. Sicilian-born Capra was already then one of the better known directors and perhaps the most American-oriented. With this picture he was just beginning to hit his stride as a proselytizer of democracy. In *American Madness,* the main role was handled by Walter Huston, with Pat just another member of a large though excellent cast. Before O'Brien had first gone to Columbia he had been warned about Harry Cohn, the head of the studio. Myron Selznick insisted that Pat would find him unbearable, but convivial O'Brien got along sufficiently well with the mogul. He attributes this to a willingness to talk back to Cohn and to ignore his rash of insults. In short, Pat was able to engage in the kind of verbal contests that delighted Cohn.

Pat remained at Columbia for *Hollywood Speaks,* his fifth of eight 1932 releases. It was a rather flimsy variation of *What Price Hollywood* (released a month earlier) or the later *A Star Is Born.* Genevieve Tobin is the glamor-struck movie newcomer, with O'Brien as the all-knowing news reporter who promises to get her a break in pictures. Already Pat was suffering from stereotype casting, so strong an impression had his fast-talking Hildy Johnson made on the filmmaking community. Of his shallow role in *Hollywood Speaks,* the *New York Times* reported, "Mr. O'Brien does satisfactorily in his part, but he is often handicapped by his lines."

Eddie Buzzell, as director, and Columbia Pictures, as employer, were again in charge of O'Brien for his *Virtue* (1932). Carole Lombard starred as a Manhattan tart reformed by wisecracking, candid Jimmy (Pat). At least this time his screen profession, if not his character changed, since he played a New York City cabbie.

About the rather frenzied Hollywood life style of the time, Pat would later observe: "It was all hard to resist, that publicity that we read about ourselves. It was so charming and so flattering to the ego of the actor. . . . It was my home and my church that saved me in Hollywood. . . . When I was in church, I joined the prayers, with a little private one added to the others, 'Let me be as I was. . . .' "

Despite his religious convictions, Pat was never any more sanguine about the unreal film censorship system than anyone else: "We did, in some ways, make heroes of gangsters, but the underdog always got a break among Americans, who hate regulations. . . . Crime never paid under the Hays Office codes. Will Hays, the film czar, had issued twelve Commandments for clean filmmaking. Frank Fay said, 'Just like Hollywood, two more than even God thought the world needed.' "

At about this time Pat and Eloise moved to a house overlooking Malibu Beach, preferring to be nearer to the ocean. He enjoyed the drive along the beach each day, going to and from the studio. And in 1932 the Olympics came to Los Angeles, much to the delight of Pat, the inveterate sport fan. He cheerfully rooted for Ireland in all games, with a few bets on the side.

In early 1932, director John Ford was preparing to film *Air Mail* at Universal, and he requested that Pat O'Brien test for a key role. Pat objected and pro-

Posing with Mae Clarke for *Final Edition* (1932).

With Bette Davis and Junior Durkin in *Hell's House* (1932).

With Wynne Gibson in *The Strange Case of Clara Deane* (1932).

tested to agent Selznick, "An actor has his pride." Selznick retorted, "Don't give me that. This director happens to be one guy that people in this business would be happy just to shake his hand." (It later developed that Irish-born Ford had asked O'Brien to test, just to get his goat.)

During the filming of *Air Mail,* which starred Ralph Bellamy and Gloria Stuart, Ford needled Pat into performing his own stunts, including taking a plane off the ground himself. Pat had never even been in a plane before, and they had to reshoot the sequence several times. Despite the touches of realism, *Air Mail* is not an outstanding picture.

Another loan-out to Columbia was for *Laughter in Hell* (1933), based on a novel by Pat's Irish pal, writer Jim Tully. Tully would become a close friend of the whole O'Brien clan and would later write a tale in which Pat's mother was a main character. *Laughter in Hell* was forced heavy drama, a part of the chain gang film cycle. As Barney Slaney, Pat is a locomotive driver sentenced to life imprisonment for killing his wife and her lover. The *New York Times* branded this a "cheerless piece of work."

Pat's next job was a single at Universal, *Destination Unknown* (1933), directed by Tay Garnett. This picture had many unusual touches, but its fantasy plot was actually a quickie imitation of Garnett's previous *One Way Passage* (1933). Like Lee Tracy who had also been typecast by Hollywood as a rat-a-tat-tat fast-speaking reporter, Pat could not escape the brand. In *The World Gone Mad* (1933), directed by Christy Cabanne and released by the independent company Majestic, O'Brien appeared as Andy Terrell who battles unscrupulous bankers and murdering crooks. The *New York Times,* no champion of this blood-and-guts entry, commended O'Brien for his "well-acted" performance.

Two years after his last MGM film, O'Brien was called back to the home lot for *Bombshell* (1933), a crackling comedy vehicle for Jean Harlow. Thanks to the Jules Furthman-John Lee Mahin snappy dialogue, the ninety-one-minute film never lags, punching home its satire on Hollywood at every instance. For the first time, Pat and his prototype, Lee Tracy, were cast in the same picture. However, it was Tracy who had the more demanding role as Lola Burns' (Harlow) flippant press agent. Pat was relegated to the minimal role of Jim Brogan, the film director who wants to wed gorgeous, smart-mouthed Lola. She refuses him and decides to adopt a baby instead.

There was good reason why Metro did not showcase Pat in *Bombshell.* The company had decided to drop his contract. Just about this time, Hal B. Wallis replaced Darryl F. Zanuck as production head of Warner Bros./First National, and in June 1933 he

With Betty Compson in *Destination Unknown* (1933).

negotiated a three-year contract for O'Brien with agent Selznick. It certainly did not hurt Pat's case that his good pal James Cagney was already ensconsed at the studio as a top attraction, nor that such other Hibernian friends as Allen Jenkins and Frank McHugh were part of the Warner Bros. stock company. Probably no one realized how important this pact would be for Pat's career. He was a good actor and a strong personality,[6] but he had not yet had the string of screen roles necessary to establish him firmly in the public's affections. He was to find them at Warner Bros.

Pat's parents for some time had had an apartment in Hollywood where they would stay on bi-yearly visits. Now that he had a secure berth again, O'Brien and Eloise suggested that they move out west for good. They agreed and he bought them their own small house, the first they had ever owned, near the Blessed Sacrament Church. They also bought Eloise's parents, the McGoverns, a home in the San Bernardino area.

[6]In analyzing his celluloid appeal, O'Brien would tell Karyn Kay and Gerald Peary in 1975: "All [Cagney, Jimmy Gleason, Joan Blondell, Lee Tracy] of us were gifted, I suppose, with a quality of naturalness. What is the secret of good acting? I think Booth said it first, 'Don't act.' That was a brand new experience for film audiences. They'd seen a lot of closeups of the eyes and phony tears. Now they had people from the theater who could really cry, and on cue: Tracy, Stanwyck, Cagney could. I could too."

Not to be different, Pat and Eloise decided to purchase their own residence instead of just renting. They found one to their liking near the ocean in Brentwood. It was in the Spanish style and had a swimming pool.[7] They intended to build a home of their own design on the lot next door, which they also acquired. The latter is the site of their present house, a white-pillared plantation-style mansion which they would name "Tara."

In 1933 Pat spoke at the annual University of Southern California Banquet the night before their big football match with Notre Dame. O'Brien was amused to find Archbishop Cantwell of Southern California speaking in favor of the U.S.C. squad, while Pat spoke for Notre Dame. This was one of the first banquet dates that O'Brien undertook. As with George Jessel it has become a second—or maybe third—career for him.

Family-oriented as Pat was then and now, he occasionally embarked on a "wild" weekend. In his autobiography *Light Your Torches and Pull Up Your Tights* (1973), director Tay Garnett recollects one such ex-

[7]Pat would later reminisce: "Studios had a flavor in those days. At the completion of a picture at Warner Bros., we would stage a cast party at our Brentwood home—have a barbecue and swimming party. We didn't throw the *first* dressed guest into a swimming pool, but we hold the record for the distance flung."

cursion. He, O'Brien, and pals Frank Morgan, Alan Hale, and Louis Calhern took a trip to Mexico. Garnett was due at the studio early on Monday morning. He was determined to start back to Hollywood at Sunday noon—sharp. He writes:

I stopped the car short of the border crossing, got out and leaned over the rear door to deliver a sermon: "Look, you guys. We're going to be questioned at the border by an immigration officer and I don't want any comedy routines or we'll be stuck here all night. I'm going to rehearse each of you, and you'd better be up in your parts. When you're asked if you're an American citizen, Morgan, just nod."

Morgan, in the front seat, nodded.

"Hale, are you an American citizen?"

Hale, in the right rear, focused his eyes with a noble effort and nodded.

"O'Brien, are you an American citizen?"

"That I am."

"Calhern?"

"Indeed I am," said Calhern in his best Bond Street manner.

"Just nod, you guys," I ordered. "No ad-libbing."

At the border the guard was letter perfect in his part. He asked to see my driver's license, then turned to Morgan in the front and asked, "Are you an American citizen?"

Morgan scored with a dignified nod. . . . Hale nodded with a charming smile. Passing over O'Brien as if he were invisible, the officer jerked his thumb toward Calhern.

"That I am," purred that worthy.

O'Brien had been cheated, his part cut cold. You don't upstage Knute Rockne. Leaning out of the car he yelled, "I'M AN ALIEN!"

It was two in the morning before my exasperated business manager arrived from Beverly Hills with identification papers that freed us.

Pat began his Warner Bros. contract well with *Bureau of Missing Persons,* released in September 1933, a month before *Bombshell.* It boasted a cast of veterans, including Hugh Herbert and Pat's chum Allen Jenkins. Pat was reunited with Bette Davis, she as a wrongly accused killer trying to prove her innocence and he as the rugged detective who aids her. While the film verges between morbid humor and stark melodrama, director Roy Del Ruth keeps the plot and weird assortment of characters moving.

O'Brien's following Warner Bros. releases were not great, but better fare than his earlier Columbia efforts. *College Coach* (1933) was William A. Wellman's film featuring an unusual slant on school sports. A strange filmmaking fate seemed to be following Pat, for this was again a lesser picture from a highly rated director. In *College Coach,* he was the tough, almost fanatical Coach Gore who endangers his personal happiness for the sake of the game. Top-featured Dick Powell is one of his students, the lovely Ann Dvorak plays his wife, and John Wayne appears in a small bit.

In this first year of his Warner Bros. tenure, Pat and Eloise went on a cruise to the Hawaiian Islands.

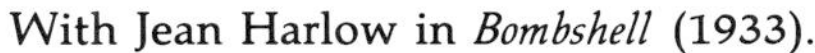
With Jean Harlow in *Bombshell* (1933).

With William Boyd (center) in *Flaming Gold* (1934).

They sailed on the S.S. *Mariposa,* along with fellow passengers Al Jolson and wife Ruby Keeler, the comedy team of Bert Wheeler and Bob Woolsey, Mrs. Frank Borzage, and Mrs. John Ford. The O'Briens were enchanted by the trip and were to repeat it many years later. Another jaunt Pat often enjoyed was traveling back to Manhattan between pictures and visiting the Lambs Club with such cronies as Frank McHugh and Spencer Tracy (still at Fox Pictures). After O'Brien, an enthusiastic joiner, was voted a member of the Players Club in New York, he had another welcome excuse to visit the metropolis.

Bouncy Joan Blondell was an excellent leading lady for O'Brien, seemingly making him more vital oncamera. They were teamed in *I've Got Your Number* (1934), a breezy account of telephone repairmen. *Gambling Lady* (1934) was pure soap opera and a vehicle for Barbara Stanwyck (the gambler's daughter) who marries above her (Joel McCrea). Archie Mayo directed this tale of the fast buck, with Pat reduced to a secondary role. At this point the studio was having Pat audition oncamera in a variety of screen parts to determine what mold he best fit.

For some reason, one of the more frequently used ploys at Warner Bros. was to cast tough, cigar-chewing Pat as the nemesis and protector of studio crooner Dick Powell. Such was the case in *College Coach,* and now again in *20 Million Sweethearts* (1934), a rather jaunty musical that boasted a fine cast (including Ginger Rogers, the Mills Brothers, and Allen Jenkins), and a silly plot, loosely strung together with pleasant numbers. As Rush Blake, O'Brien is the unscrupulous agent trying to cash in on Powell's radio success. The ten-percenter's role was all right —he was always good playing energetic, ambitious promoters—but Pat was not really cut out for musicals. He liked to have more to do.

He had his opportunity in *Here Comes the Navy* (1934), directed by Lloyd Bacon and co-starring Pat with Jimmy Cagney. In his autobiography, *Cagney by Cagney* (1975), the superstar relates of his long time friend: "He's remarkable in more than one way. He has, for instance, more durability than anyone I've ever known. He would arrive on the set in the morning, having been up all night—clear-eyed, knowing all his words—and step cheerfully in front of the camera. At day's end, he'd go home, have dinner, then he and Eloise would go out and would again stay up all night. . . . In those early days, I was always the cautious one. In our more serious moments, I'd say, 'Pat, stop and take stock. Where do we stand? Is this going to give us security for the rest of our lives?' But Pat never listened. He was for the jokes, the laughter, the nightclubs."

Here Comes the Navy was the first of Pat O'Brien's eight screen appearances with Cagney. The film immediately established a format: Pat would be the individual of superior rank, discipline, and wisdom, while Cagney, being just the reverse, would get in all the scrapes, win the prettiest girl, and garner the limelight. In *Cagney* (1973) by Andrew Bergman, the author analyzes, "It made sense: Cagney played shanty Irish. O'Brien seemed to have moved up to the lace curtain class. Cagney was the club fighter and O'Brien the classy, stand-up counter-puncher. O'Brien's wit relied more on irony and side-of-the-mouth cynicism than Cagney's, which exercised the body as well as the brain; a punch in the mouth was never far away. But the two men shared a great natural warmth and rectitude; the friendship so obvious onscreen was carried on off the screen."

A goodly portion of *Here Comes the Navy* was filmed on location aboard the U.S.S. *Arizona* (later sunk at Pearl Harbor), which was then docked at San Diego. One danger-prone scene has chief petty officer Biff Martin (Pat) and gob Chesty O'Connor (Cagney) dangling from a rope attached to a dirigible. As Cagney descended to "rescue" O'Brien, he lost his footing and dislodged Pat from the rope. The latter grabbed onto Cagney and the two slid to the ground (fortunately nearby), but each suffered bad rope burns.

At about this time the O'Briens became the proud parents of their first child, a daughter, named Margaret Mavourneen. Pat wrote, "The joy in the first born can never be adequately put into words. . . . Perhaps the love of a child is the greatest love."

The Personality Kid (1935) remains one of Pat's favorites, despite some mishaps in the making. He was sent to train for the part of a boxer with Jackie Fields, the ex-welterweight champion of the world, and "Mushy" Callaghan, the studio trainer, at Lake Arrowhead in the mountains. Pat was forced to diet unhappily on boiled eggs and toast. He was not fat, but he never photographed slim and the front office wanted him to lose a few pounds for the ring scenes. During the boxing sequences, his sparring partner accidentally hit him in the jaw. Pat was not only knocked unconscious, but he fractured his jaw as well. The scene, incidentally, was a take and would be used in the actual picture. Pat would describe his role of Ritzy McCarty as "a sort of forerunner of Muhammed Ali." Playing a cocky, wisecracking fighter was another well-defined characterization for him.

Flirtation Walk (1934) certainly shows Dick Powell and Ruby Keeler at their campiest. It also saddled O'Brien with one of his strangest cinema roles. As in the past he is Powell's superior, but here he is not only the young man's army boss and guardian angel in the Hawaii segment, but a combination of confidante and duenna. *He* is the one—not girlfriend Keeler—who roots for, cheers, and cries as Powell embarks on a West Point career and learns to become a good officer. The closing bit on the parade field finds misty-eyed O'Brien watching his protégé march by with honors. Thankfully Pat carried off his bizarre acting task with a forthrightness that made it all seem almost forgivable.

I Sell Anything (1934) was another talk-a-mile-a-minute role for him. This characteristic was becoming his Warner Bros. trademark and suited him quite well. The title explains that Pat is a boardwalk huckster.

Having conquered the navy, Pat and James Cagney (he was now in the top ten at the box office) tackled the Marine Flying Corps in *Devil Dogs of the Air* (1935). True to formula, O'Brien was the sympathetic officer who must harness fresh recruit Cagney, the latter anxious to break all the rules before learning discipline the hard way. Along the way it is rambunctious and not square-dealing Pat who wins the affections of waitress Margaret Lindsay. Shot on a $350,000-plus budget in eight weeks, *Devil Dogs of the Air* contains the action, romance, and flip talk that endeared the Warner Bros. product to audiences. Of Pat's co-starring but subordinate role, Richard Watts, Jr. *(New York Herald-Tribune)* offered: "[He] is vigorous and ingratiating."

Had Alice Tisdale Hobart's *Oil for the Lamps of China* (1935) been given a more prestigious instead of efficient screen mounting, it might have launched Pat into the same category as his pal and rival, Cagney. The original novel focused on the ruthlessness of a giant oil corporation practicing dollar diplomacy in the Orient, whereas the ambivalent script condones the policies of the Atlantis Oil Company, even suggesting that it has acted out of nobility. O'Brien was given the focal role of Stephen Chase who, with his wife (marvelously acted by Josephine Hutchinson), spends several years in the interior of China. Pat's character is so engulfed on his saintly mission (enlightening the Chinese heathens) that he becomes a robot pawn for his bosses, ignores his wife, and fires his best friend. For his valiant if misguided efforts the company demotes him; but later (to make a less solemn finale) he is rewarded for his devotion to the organization. Andre Sennwald *(New York Times)* was among those who bestowed high praise on the two co-stars, labeling their interpretations "brilliantly acted" and performed with "touching directness." If

With Margaret Lindsay in *Devil Dogs of the Air* (1935).

With Josephine Hutchinson in *Oil for the Lamps of China* (1935).

this entry had been given special promotion by the studio, it might have propelled Pat into the top ranks.

In Caliente, (1935), a lesser Warner Bros. musical of the period, is memorable for showcasing the beautiful Dolores Del Rio and for the Busby Berkeley-staged "The Lady in Red" number (sung by Wini Shaw and in mock counterpoint by comedienne Judy Canova). As a hyperactive press agent Larry MacArthur, Pat was his staccato self.

Page Miss Glory (1935) was the first of four Marion Davies' post-MGM Warner films which matched her with her favorite (on and off the set) leading man, Dick Powell. Where goes Powell, so goes O'-Brien, and here he was a quick-talking (naturally) con-man lightening the action between the Davies-Powell romantic scenes.

As was her custom, fun-loving Miss Davies invited Pat and Eloise to William Randolph Hearst's lavish estate, San Simeon, after the completion of the film. Pat liked puckish Marion, as indeed did most people. Since his abiding interest has always been studying human nature, he observed the aging Hearst with great curiosity. He found the tycoon "unlovable" but fascinating.

Pat, one of the founders of the Del Mar Race Track, did his own grand entertaining at the sporting place. Unfortunately, unlike co-founder Bing Crosby and others, O'Brien sold his stock in the track before he could make a fortune the way some of the others did.

For *The Irish in Us* (1935), he was teamed with James Cagney again in a cheerful, lively, shamrock-drenched feature. Cagney is a ne'er-do-well boxing promoter, with Pat as his brother, the steadfast cop. The film had a good, hard-working cast speeding up the proceedings: Olivia de Havilland as the girl they both love (but whom Cagney wins), Mary Gordon (as their mother), and such backlot regulars as Allen Jenkins, J. Farrell MacDonald, Frank McHugh, and Edward Gargan. As Irene Thirer *(New York Post)* summed it up, "It's down-to-earth, and mellow and punch-packed."

Obliging O'Brien merely did box-office duty holding together the loose threads of *Stars over Broadway* (1935), his sixth of seven Warner Bros. releases for the year. The modest film was intended to be a vehicle for singers James Melton and Jane Froman, with choreography by Busby Berkeley and Bobby Connolly. Then it was back to the Cagney-O'Brien format, this time in *Ceiling Zero* (1935).[8] Jimmy and Pat were rival pilots in love with the same girl (June Travis), and of course it is Cagney who wins her. It was snappily directed by Howard Hawks who gave experienced attention to the aerial sequences. *Photoplay* magazine reported that Pat and Hawks "kept a direct wire humming from the set to the [race] tracks all during the filming of *Ceiling Zero.* In between scenes they telephoned their bets."

Warner Bros. had produced a substantial silent film version of Sinclair Lewis' *Main Street* (1923) starring Florence Vidor and Monte Blue. Its misguided attempt to remake the project as *I Married a Doctor* (1936) distorted the biting satire of the original book and forced the cast to sink in a marshmallow plotline. The studio reteamed Josephine Hutchinson and O'Brien for this Archie Mayo-directed entry. Both offered sincere performances but could not counter the weak script. The film's indifferent reception helped to seal Miss Hutchinson's fate with the studio (she would soon leave) and to convince the hierarchy that O'Brien, like contractee George Brent, was a serviceable but not high-powered leading man.

In early March 1936, about a month before *I Married a Doctor* was released, Pat joined the ranks of rebellious Bette Davis and James Cagney and went on suspension.[9] He was due on the soundstages on Monday, March 16 to start Busby Berkeley's musical *Stage Struck* supporting Dick Powell and Joan Blondell. Trade sources reported: "One of the significant factors in the situation is that the part is one that was in line for James Cagney when his differences with Warner Bros. came to a head." Having failed to cast either Cagney or O'Brien in the role of producer Fred Harris, the studio turned to smooth Warren William who acquiesced and performed the thankless part. (Ironically, after the picture was completed, William's contract option at Warner Bros. was dropped and Pat's was picked up.) O'Brien did not mind having some free time.

While his working relationship with Warner Bros. was being renegotiated, two other O'Brien studio releases went into distribution. *Public Enemy's Wife* (1936), part of the new gangster film cycle engendered by James Cagney's *G-Men* (1935), was sensationalistic and hopelessly confused. It proved how badly Warner Bros. was wasting co-star Margaret Lindsay, and impressed very few. Pat had come to terms with his employers by the time (August 1936) *China Clipper* was released.[10] This was a workmanlike drama about a stubborn pilot determined to develop

[8]Warner Bros. obligingly revamped some crash scenes scheduled for the film when some airlines objected and offered the use of planes and equipment in exchange for a revamped scenario. The studio agreed.

[9]In 1934 Pat had dropped out of Bette Davis' *Fog over Frisco,* being replaced by Donald Woods. This was due to overlapping of schedules rather than temperament on O'Brien's part.

[10]In 1936, O'Brien earned $108,750; in 1937, his gross income from films was $119,500.

With Edward Gargan, Robert Light, and James Bush in *Ceiling Zero* (1935).

With Josephine Hutchinson in *I Married a Doctor* (1936).

With Donald Crisp and Ann Sheridan in a pose for *The Great O'Malley* (1936).

With John Litel in *Slim* (1937).

transpacific flights. A solid cast included Beverly Roberts (the neglected wife), Ross Alexander and Humphrey Bogart (as fellow pilots), and Henry B. Walthall (the inspired aviation engineer). It is a well-made picture in the classic Warner Bros. style.

It was also in 1936 that Pat and Eloise added a second child to their family, a son christened Patrick Sean. Mrs. Joe E. Brown and Walter Catlett were the godparents.

Next came *The Great O'Malley* (1937), a rather strange film, with definite overtones of the plot of *Les Miserables.* As James Aloysius O'Malley, Pat is a ruthless cop chasing sympathetic criminal Humphrey Bogart who is supporting a crippled daughter (Sybil Jason). The competent cast, including Ann Sheridan and Donald Crisp, seemed a little at sea in the sentimentally written material.

On the other hand, *Slim* (1937) has in it one of Pat's best screen performances. He is a tough, footloose electrical lineman showing the ropes to admiring novice Henry Fonda. This is one of the studio's unmatched "workingman" dramas, and the direction (by Ray Enright) and performances make it memorable. O'Brien rises above his usual competence to capture the basic immaturity of his character, a pitiful but likable individual who successfully avoids any personal involvements. Fonda too is excellent, as is Margaret Lindsay as the nurse who eventually comes between the two male friends. Jane Wyman appears in one of her supporting, dumb-dame parts, of which she had many in her earlier years at Warner Bros. She plays Stuart Erwin's daffy date.

Workmanlike Pat was next assigned to *San Quentin* (1937), cast as a prison warden. He did his best, naturally, but the experiment with yet another type of role was unsuccessful. He required a part with more color than the basically bureaucratic, actionless character he played here. Humphrey Bogart had the plum acting role as a convict whose sister, Ann Sheridan, falls in love with the warden. It is Bogart who eventually sacrifices himself for their happiness. Barton MacLane made his usual stark impression as a rough guard.

Throughout the years, gregarious Pat had acquired some unusual friends. During the making of *San Quentin* he got one of them, known as "Doc" Stone, a job at the studio. Director Lloyd Bacon asked the actor one day, "Any of your crook friends want a job?" Pat said he didn't know why he should be supposed to have crooked friends, but he managed to come up with Doc Stone who had been in and out of jail for fifty years. Doc was hired as technical advisor on the picture and worked in that capacity at Warner Bros. for the remainder of his declining years.

Back in Circulation (1937) was one of the reasons Joan Blondell chose to leave Warner Bros. It was another frenetic newspaper yarn with O'Brien as the high-pressure city editor who cajoles and romances glamorous ace reporter Blondell, with Margaret Lindsay as a murderess headlined in their paper. During the filming of *Submarine D-1* (1937), underwater shots of a diving bell were required. Lloyd Bacon, again Pat's director, decided that realism demanded the actors in the scene (O'Brien, George Brent, and Wayne Morris) to be filmed in a real submarine bell underwater. When they submerged to the bottom and prepared for the take, the equipment in the bell suddenly broke, the gauges went dead, and the bell was mired at the bottom of the blue water. About twenty-five slow minutes passed while repairs were effected. When the shaken actors emerged, George Brent said waspishly about directors in general and this incident in particular, "Realism frequently becomes synonymous with sadism."

Despite the quantity and the poorer quality of Pat's films, he was relatively content with his secure niche in the Warner Bros. gallery. Asked about the typical week at the Burbank studio, he said, "I would be there at nine o'clock. . . . There was a six-day week in those days. We'd even work on Sundays, and in the evenings until eleven or midnight until the picture was finished." He also commented on the comparisons of the various studios: "Columbia we used to call 'The Germ of the Ocean.' MGM was the aristocrats, we were the peasants, although we were getting a chunk of money."

While James Cagney, Edward G. Robinson, Paul Muni, Errol Flynn, John Garfield, George Brent, Claude Rains and Wayne Morris were given a variety of roles, Pat was submerged all too often in program fodder.[11] It seemed that whenever the studio had a one-time top leading lady who was being eased out of the studio through a series of B films,

[11]Among the male leading players in the Warner Bros. stock company, the following weekly salary scale was in effect as of late 1939: James Cagney $12,500, Edward G. Robinson $8,500, Claude Rains $6,000, George Raft $5,500, Errol Flynn $5,000, Pat O'Brien $4,000, George Brent $2,000, Frank McHugh $1,600, Donald Crisp $1,500, John Garfield $1,500, and Humphrey Bogart $1,250.

Although the above players were highly paid, they were not unmindful of the less fortunate walk-ons performing in front of the cameras. It was not too uncommon for Cagney to say to O'Brien, "Paddy, let's blow a few lines so we can get the extras some overtimes."

The camaraderie that pervaded the soundstages and the commissary extended to time away from the studio. If the gang were not going to the horse races, they might be seen down at Long Beach watching the boat competition.

With Sam McDaniel and Kay Francis in *Women Are Like That* (1938).

Pat would be used as her vis-à-vis. Such was the case with Kay Francis' *Women Are Like That* (1938), turned out by Warner Bros.' B production unit. George Brent had rejected the role of the copywriter loved by the boss' daughter (Francis), but O'Brien accepted the assignment. *The Cowboy from Brooklyn* (1938) turned out to be yet another weightless musical with Pat as an agent with the now usual accompanying cast of Dick Powell, Dick Foran, Priscilla Lane, Ann Sheridan, and Ronald Reagan.

However, his next film, *Boy Meets Girl* (1938), was a very good one. It is a pushy but delightful Warner Bros. wisecracker, based on a hit Broadway play. Its title was derived from the time-honored Hollywood formula, "Boy meets girl, boy loses girl, boy gets girl." Pat was again teamed with an antic Jimmy Cagney, and the film boasted an excellent cast: Ralph Bellamy, Frank McHugh, Dick Foran, Ronald Reagan, and Marie Wilson. As two wild screenwriters, O'Brien and Cagney struck sparks with one another, with Pat's more subdued character keeping Cagney's even crazier one believably earthbound.[12]

His next film, *Garden of the Moon* (1938), was a mediocre Busby Berkeley musical. However, the following one, *Angels with Dirty Faces* (1938), was a top-grade picture in all ways. Its main characters are practically immortal: Father Jerry (Pat) and Rocky Sullivan (Cagney)—the two slum kids who went in opposite ways and who clashed fatally in the end. The picture featured unobtrusive but powerful direction from Michael Curtiz and benefited from the presence of Ann Sheridan, Humphrey Bogart, George Bancroft, and the Dead End Kids. O'Brien's priest has one of the most memorable closing lines of any 1930s film: "Okay, boys. Let's go say a prayer for a boy who couldn't run as fast as I could." While Hollywood, the critics, and the public were impressed anew by O'Brien's resourcefulness as an actor, and wondering why no one had thought to cast him as a priest before, it was Cagney who stole the acting honors. He was nominated for his first Academy Award, but lost to MGM's Spencer Tracy *(Boys Town).*

If *Back in Circulation* had angered peppery Joan Blondell, the quickie *Off the Record* (1939) was the final straw. It was another newspaper story made cheaply—with Pat rehashing his *The Front Page*-type newsman once again—and it was all too much for the talented Miss Blondell. She and the studio came to a parting of the ways, but O'Brien remained and performed in *The Kid from Kokomo* (1939), a Dalton Trumbo story intended to foster the career of Wayne Morris. Pat played a crooked boxing promoter.

[12]There were plans for Warner Bros. to purchase John Steinbeck's *Of Mice and Men* for O'Brien and James Cagney, but when the acclaimed novel/play was produced for the screen in 1939 it would be Lon Chaney Jr. and Burgess Meredith who were starred.

With Dick Powell in *The Cowboy from Brooklyn* (1938).

With Penny Singleton, Dick Foran (cowboy), and James Cagney in *Boy Meets Girl* (1938).

With James Cagney in *Angels with Dirty Faces* (1938).

With Joan Blondell and Bobby Jordan in *Off the Record* (1939).

Assemblyline filmmaking has no regard for actors' feelings, but one can only wonder what Pat must have thought of playing James Cagney's role in *Indianapolis Speedway* (1939), an inferior variation of the superior *The Crowd Roars* (1932). He was race driver Joe Greer, with John Payne as his kid brother who insists on entering the dangerous sport, and with Ann "The Oomph Girl" Sheridan and Gale Page as the two understanding women. Frank S. Nugent *(New York Times)* thought it "on the stereotripe side," but he did take the occasion to editorialize about Pat: "What impressed us most about the picture is Pat O'Brien's cigar. Mr. O'Brien is probably the best cigar-mouther in Hollywood today. What a profile is to John Barrymore, an enigmatic smile to Marlene Dietrich, a broad New England 'a' to Katharine Hepburn—that's the beginning of a cigar to Mr. O'B. Held straight out, from the center of the mouth, his cigar is as sober as Rodin's Thinker. Pushed up and angling left of right, it's as jaunty as a sailor with a 48-hour ticket. Drooping, pendent from the lower lip, it's a flag at half-mast. Between thumb and forefinger, count it an offensive weapon more potent than Joe Louis' left cross. We shouldn't be surprised if it won an Academy Award some day for the year's best supporting performance."

In *The Night of Nights* (1939), made on loan to Paramount, Pat plays a tragic clown in full makeup—a role strangely similar to James Stewart's years later in *The Greatest Show on Earth.* During the filming of this Lewis Milestone-directed feature, Pat's father suddenly died at the age of sixty-seven. Pat's mother insisted that his dad would have wanted him to return to work without a break and not to give way to grief. The next morning O'Brien reported to the studio as usual and several scenes were shot. (They are not to be seen in the release print, however, for Milestone found Pat's performance that day unusable.)

Pat was loaned to Walter Wanger for Tay Garnett's *Slightly Honorable* (1939) at United Artists. This was a top-notch, crackling detective story with a boisterous cast including O'Brien, Broderick Crawford, Eve Arden, and Claire Dodd. It possessed extremely fast-paced dialogue at which Pat excelled. One of the few people not to like the entry was its director. The film was recut before its release without Garnett's knowledge.

Returning to Warner Bros., Pat's next project was the plum part of Father Duffy in *The Fighting Sixty-Ninth,* his first release of 1940. It was tailor-made for his talents, and he had met the famous priest years before at the Lambs Club in New York. For some, the expensively mounted production was an over-stuffed patriotic melodrama—the too-familiar plot concerning the exploits of the noted Irish battalion in World War I. The film is saved by the studio stock company cast, including Pat, Cagney, George Brent, Jeffrey Lynn, Alan Hale, Frank McHugh, and Dennis Morgan. The *New York Times'* Frank S. Nugent wrote, "The picture is better if you can manage to forget the plot . . . and think of it instead as the human, amusing, and frequently gripping record of a regiment's marching off to war." Pat was singled out for praise: "Pat O'Brien [gives a] dignified and eloquent portrayal of the famous fighting chaplain whose monument stands in Times Square."

Pat always enjoyed the opportunity of working with Cagney and the boys and considers *The Fighting Sixty-Ninth* one of his best roles. The picture was given an elaborate New York premiere and it received the full-blast publicity treatment. Pat was invited to stop at Washington, D.C. on the way to attend the opening and be a guest at the President's birthday banquet. The O'Briens were thrilled to be able to accept, and Pat was introduced to President Roosevelt. (During the 1940 Presidential campaign, Pat would be among the Hollywood faction—including Cagney, Edward G. Robinson, Rosalind Russell, James Gleason, Jane Wyman, Henry Fonda, George Raft, Betty Grable, and Humphrey Bogart—who supported the Democratic incumbent in his bid for a third term.)

In his next two pictures, Pat found the reason behind Darryl F. Zanuck's famous remark, "Only the first picture of a cycle really succeeds; all the imitators dwindle." *Castle on the Hudson* (1940) was a remake of the powerful *20,000 Years in Sing Sing* (1933) with John Garfield in the old Spencer Tracy role and a fine Warner Bros. cast including Pat, Ann Sheridan, Jerome Cowan, and Burgess Meredith. Though it was popular enough, this prison melodrama did not compare favorably with the original. *'Til We Meet Again* (1940) was another rehash, this time of the classic weeper *One Way Passage* (1933), with George Brent and Merle Oberon as the lovers originally played by William Powell and Kay Francis. Pat played Steve Burke, the tough cop who turns soft-hearted, and Frank McHugh repeated his con artist role from the earlier film. Again, it was far from being of the same quality as the first edition.

Even in today's "anything goes" market, *Torrid Zone* (1940) remains a landmark of spicy dialogue, steamy performances, and pell-mell action. It was the final teaming of Cagney and Pat, and for good measure had Ann Sheridan as the snappy club singer with the shady past. Although filmed on the studio backlot, it almost seemed as if it had been filmed on

With Ann Sheridan and John Garfield in a pose for *Castle on the Hudson* (1940).

With James Cagney in *Torrid Zone* (1940).

a banana plantation in Central America (the story's locale). Once more Pat was Cagney's boss, this time as a two-fisted land owner. No matter how many times it is seen, the verbal sparring of the cast is a joy to hear.

In *Flowing Gold* (1940) Pat performed for a second and final time with John Garfield. Unfortunately, this is a generally boring tale of men in the oil fields; it was well below studio standards, with a meandering script. An electric performance by youngish Garfield and the presence of beautiful Frances Farmer are the film's main attractions.

Warner Bros. had been long considering a film biography of *Knute Rockne—All American,* and in 1940 put it into production. Surprisingly, the studio offered the prime role to Pat. However, when one considers the alternatives among the Warner Bros. stock company, the choice of O'Brien becomes not only sensible but inevitable.[13] When Ronald Reagan learned that Pat had the title role, he asked him to intercede with the front office and help him land the part of George Gipp, the Notre Dame football star. O'Brien was always eager to assist, and he brought Reagan to the special attention of producers Jack L. Warner, Hal B. Wallis, and Robert Fellows. Reagan got the role.

[13]At one point, Warner Bros. wanted Spencer Tracy for the lead; at another juncture, they were "talking" about casting Thomas Mitchell in the role.

Because Rockne's death had been relatively recent (in 1931), a strong degree of authenticity was aimed ror in the film. Pat had to undertake several makeup tests for the approval of the coach's widow, Mrs. Bonnie Rockne. Quite naturally O'Brien considered the telling assignment to be one of his hardest screen parts. Not only did Knute Rochne dominate the entire ninety-eight-minute feature, but O'Brien could not follow his usual procedure for appearing before the klieg lights. In this film it was not a matter of slipping into a business suit, slapping a bit of pancake makeup on his face, and shoving an unlit cigar into his mouth. Here he had undergo a three-hour or more daily makeup session to age him or make him appear more youthful, depending which bit of the chronology they were shooting that day.[14]

In his autobiography, Pat recounts: "Eloise would bring Mavourneen and Sean to pick me up at the end of the day's shooting. . . . [Once] Sean, aged four, was gazing with horror at the assistant makeup man as he peeled the rubber features from my face. It didn't hurt . . . but Sean couldn't stand it. He cried out, his eyes wet, sobbing, 'Please stop tearing my

[14]Years before—in 1931—Universal had filmed *The Spirit of Notre Dame* in which a Knute Rockne-like "coach" was played by J. Farrell MacDonald, with Andy Devine as a George Gipp-like football player named Truck McCall, and Donn Miller, Elmer Layden, Jim Crawley, and Harry Stuhldreher as the Four Horsemen of the gridiron squad.

With John Garfield and Frances Farmer in *Flowing Gold* (1940).

daddy's face! Please!' It took us quite a while to assure him that nothing injurious was happening to his dad."

Technical advisors on the film were Nick Lukats, a former football star at Notre Dame, and the great Jim Thorpe, an all-round athletic champ who had been reduced in Hollywood to playing mostly bit parts. Pat made use of his own school and navy football experience, and no double was employed in the football scenes. Mrs. Rockne helped the star with his characterization throughout the making of the movie, on which she served as general advisor.

Pat's performance in *Knute Rockne—All American* ranks as a landmark of his long career. Within the film, his famous pep talk to the squad "Get out there and win one for the Gipper" remains a highlight of the sentimental narrative.[15]

While the public endorsed the film as popular, patriotic entertainment, movie critics of the day and later film historians scoffed at the plot's endorsement of football as representative of the American way of democratic life. Ted Sennett in *Warner Brothers Presents* asserts: "With Pat O'Brien as Rockne, it was a reverent but stickily sentimental film written by Robert Buckner in the style of a grade school primer. Since the coach's life apparently lacked high drama —there was not much suspense in the development of a backfield shift—the studio decided to make the film an ardent defense of the game of football, rather than a biography of its leading exponent. The screenplay's solemn veneration of the game teeters and sometimes topples over the edge of absurdity. We see little Knute discovering that football is 'the most wonderful game in the world.' We have Notre Dame's Father Callahan (Donald Crisp) telling Rockne that his decision to coach football instead of teaching chemistry is 'helping mankind.' And the climax has Rockne defending the game before a committee investigating scandal in the sport. Football, Rockne asserts, is a safe outlet for the spirit of combat and serves the nation's best interests. 'We're getting soft—inside and out,' he exclaims. Unfortunately, the rest of the film is on this level, reaching the peak of simple-mindedness when Mrs. Rockne (Gale Page) has a grim foreboding of his death in a plane crash. 'It's gotten cold all of a sudden,' she cries, making an anticlimax of the subsequent headline about the crash."

Pat's Warner Bros. contract had expired following the completion of *Flowing Gold,* made after but released before *Knute Rockne—All American,* during the time *Rockne* was being given a big publicity buildup. Jack L. Warner and Pat's long-time agent Myron Selznick were unable to come to terms on a satisfactory renewal proposal. Pat wanted a well-deserved $500 raise in salary per week, but Warner, engaging in capricious bickering, refused. So after eight years, Pat left the Burbank lot.[16] Within two weeks, Selznick had negotiated a two-picture deal for Pat with Columbia Pictures, at a flat $50,000 per film. Happy-go-lucky forty-one-year old O'Brien was unaware that his cinema career was quickly escalating downward.

His two pictures for Harry Cohn's studio were unfortunately poor. *Submarine Zone* (1941) was a silly war story with a foolish secret ray plot device. Even beautiful co-star Constance Bennett (whose career was on the skids) could not help buoy the pedestrian project. *Two Yanks in Trinidad* (1942) was off-the-cuff trivia of two crooks (Pat and Brian Donlevy) who join the army to fight for democracy. Leading lady Janet Blair looked baffled and embarrassed by the shenanigans.

Far less prestigious than his teaming with James Cagney was Pat's screen partnership with George Raft. For their joint vehicle at Universal, that studio decided to remake *Broadway* (1942), this time converting the granddaddy of nightclub-gangster stories into a biographical plot centering around Raft and the colorful Prohibition years. Some two decades after he had last played straight-dealing law enforcer Dan McCorn, Pat was back playing his old stage part. However, it was beefed up to co-lead size, and pretty Janet Blair was borrowed to play the harassed heroine. The jaunty supporting cast included Broderick Crawford, Marjorie Rambeau, S. Z. Sakall, Marie Wilson, and Iris Adrian. Mack Gray, Raft's long-standing bodyguard and confidant, had a small role playing himself. Considering the vintage property William A. Seiter had to work with, the new *Broadway* emerged as an entertaining diversion. On the other hand, *Flight Lieutenant* (1942), made at Columbia, did little to advance the careers of Pat, Glenn Ford, or leading lady Evelyn Keyes.

On a more positive note, in 1941 Pat and Eloise became parents of a second son, Terence Kevin, and O'Brien signed a long-term contract with RKO, then under the aegis of Charles Koerner, a man Pat grew to admire greatly. This seemed a solid career move, for O'Brien had done well under the protective one-studio system. However, RKO put out a different

[15]Ironically, due to a copyright law vagary, the notable scene has been cut from TV prints of *Knute Rockne—All American.* However, Pat has often performed the speech as a showpiece on TV variety shows, and sometimes includes it in his club and college campus act without apparent legal difficulty.

[16]In 1940 when Pat's studio contract came due for renewal, even gentle Eloise exploded when she was asked once too often, "Doesn't your husband ever get the girl [oncamera]?" On one occasion she retorted, "No! And if he doesn't get her pretty soon, people are going to think I won him on a punchboard!"

With Constance Bennett, Francis Pierlot, Frank Sully, Stanley Logan, (rear) John Halliday, Edgar Buchanan, Alan Baxter, and Leslie Denison in *Submarine Zone* (1941).

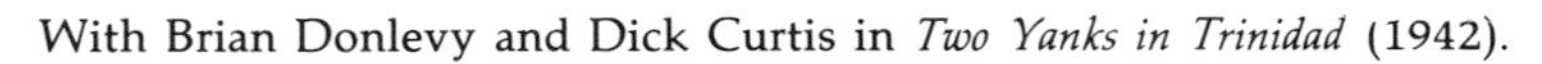

With Brian Donlevy and Dick Curtis in *Two Yanks in Trinidad* (1942).

type of product than Warner Bros. RKO had been a glossier studio, but less flavorful and usually less humorous, and its reputation as a major picture company was faltering in the 1940s. A wartime crack was: "In case of an air raid, go directly to RKO; they haven't had a hit in years." Thus, caught in the midst of generally mediocre products, Pat's career was in danger of taking a permanent nosedive. After all, he was not the type to argue very often with the front office over the choice of roles. He usually took what was assigned to him.

When the U.S. entered World War II in December 1941, Pat considered trying to re-enlist in the navy, but Myron Selznick pointed out that at his age he would probably be ordered behind a desk in the regular armed forces. The agent suggested that he sign up with the U.S.O. instead, and Pat did.

His first picture under the RKO contract was far from inspired. *The Navy Comes Through* (1942) was a wartime quickie that looked almost like a second feature. In it were Jane Wyatt, who became a close friend of the O'Brien family, and George Murphy. Another overused plot surfaced in *Bombardier* (1943). It concerned World War II flight training at the Bombardier School in Albuquerque, New Mexico, where portions of it were filmed on location. Pat played Major Chick Davis, the founder of the school. He enjoyed this project, for he always liked the challenge of portraying real characters. With him in this one were Randolph Scott, Anne Shirley, Eddie Albert, Robert Ryan, and Barton MacLane.

The U.S.O. sent Pat on his first overseas tour in 1942 to the British and Dutch Guianas to entertain the members of the merchant marine stationed

In a publicity pose with George Raft and Janet Blair for *Broadway* (1942).

there. Real cannibals inhabited the area, prompting jovial Pat to send a message to Eloise, "Luckily it was Lent, and they weren't eating anyone." He was cheerful as usual, but found the constant traveling hot, comfortless, and exhausting, with hours of flying in cramped, rickety planes. The trips were filled with days of bad food, with airless tents the only shelter, and, to top it off, a variety of tropical insects. Nevertheless, conscientious Pat was glad to be active in the Allied war effort.

He learned that a simple format of entertainment was best for the small troupe's shows. He told a few jokes, and then the girls would come out to dance, sing, and flash their legs. The marines loved it, especially the live cheesecake.

After his tour to the Guianas, Pat returned to RKO to begin shooting the next project Charles Koerner had lined up for him, *The Iron Major* (1943). It concerned famed Holy Cross, Dartmouth, and Fordham football coach Frank Cavanaugh and was directed by Warner Bros. veteran Ray Enright. This was Pat's sturdiest role at RKO to date and he empathized greatly with the character who was a family man with eleven children. O'Brien was in tune with the rest of the cast, especially Robert Ryan who was cast as Father Tim Donovan. Superficially *The Iron Major* was a reshuffling of the *Knute Rochne—All American* story, but the two characters were really quite different, certainly enough to give Pat another strong, appealing portrait. The timely theme of the picture could be summed up in Frank Cavanaugh's last words, "Always remember these three important things: love of God—love of country—love of family."

Although the movie was a crowd-pleaser, it won no endorsements from the sterner critics. The *New York Times* judged it a "quite bad picture . . . and it does not fail to include the ancient cliché about the boy who gets to the front lines and breaks—breaks, that is, till the major gives him another pep talk." But even the austere *Times* had to admit: "It is a tribute to Pat O'Brien, not to the script, that he manages to make of the coach a character who is sometimes real and credible. Against such handicaps, Mr. O'Brien must be made of iron, indeed."

RKO loaned Pat to Universal for *His Butler's Sister* (1943), a big change of pace for him, and not an entirely welcome one. Under Frank Borzage's direction it was a lively enough romantic comedy, but Deanna Durbin and Franchot Tone were the love interest and Pat's role as the proper servant with a penchant for the race track was decidedly secondary. What saved the saccharine exercise set in pre-war days were Miss Durbin's singing of "In the Spirit of the Moment," an aria from Puccini's "Turnandot," and "When You're Away" and the comedic relief of her array of oddball suitors (Sig Arno, Hans Conried, Frank Jenks, Alan Mowbray, and Akim Tamiroff).

It was obvious that RKO had no real idea of how to further Pat's career. In late 1942 he had made *Marine Raiders,* which the studio did not release until early 1944. It was another formula account of servicemen in training. In the cast were Ruth Hussey, Frank McHugh, Barton MacLane, and Robert Ryan (whom Pat requested as his co-star).

Pat's other release of the year, *Secret Command* (1944), has an interesting genesis. A friend of his approached him with an offer to co-produce an FBI story about corruption on the waterfront. Phil Ryan had acquired the screen rights and agreed to be a partner with O'Brien in a one-shot production venture. Part of the financial package required the picture to be shot and released by Columbia. RKO head Charles Koerner gave Pat permission to go on loan-out. The producing company was called Terneen after O'Brien's children Mavourneen and Terry. Since he could not fit Sean into the title, he named a character after his second son. Pat had a large hand in the casting and signed the well-liked Carole Landis as the female lead, fast-talking Chester Morris as his brother, and Wallace Ford, Barton MacLane, and Ruth Warrick in supporting parts.

Secret Command proved to be a tough, fast-moving story with the still topical theme of combating the Nazis on the homefront (here a West Coast shipyard). While it was very reminiscent of the Pine-Thomas B films turned out by Paramount in the 1940s, it won the endorsement of the critics and the public for its enthusiastic brandishing of the Irish spirit. There was no subtlety to the plot or characterizations. As the *New York Post* perceived, "This is a movie for the action fans, that is, the millions who never hit anyone but like to indulge in viciously vicarious tumblings to the death in the cushioned seats of an air-cooled movie house." It was a pity that vital Pat never tackled another producing assignment.

A great professional loss to Pat and others was the untimely death of Myron Selznick on March 23, 1944 at the age of forty-five. Pat attended the services at Temple Israel in Beverly Hills where William Powell read the eulogy composed by Gene Fowler. Thereafter William Morris became Pat's show business representative.

It was also in early 1944 that the U.S.O. called on O'Brien again. He began another tour, this one far more extensive than the last, with his eventual destination China. In Pat's small group of performers were Jinx Falkenberg, James and Ruth Dodd, Betsy Eaton, and Harry Brown (a musician-pianist). On their way east, they stopped at Bermuda, the Azores, Casablanca, Tripoli, Cairo, Karachi, New Delhi, and finally Chabua, India. There the troupe was briefed about the next leg of the journey. It was to be the most dangerous part of the trip, over the Himalayas, across Burma, and into China. After their briefing, they were each given an oxygen tank and instructions on bailing out in case of an emergency. Pat admits to having been terrified.

The group landed in Kumming, China and immediately gave a performance in a nearby aircraft hanger. Pat met and became friendly with General Chennault. Air-hopping around Allied-held China was confusing at best and often quite dangerous. Pat asked permission for his troupe to entertain at Luchow, the outpost closest to enemy lines. When O'Brien and company arrived, Luchow was an open battlefield. The Japanese were beginning to advance on the post, but the game actors decided to give a show anyway. Pat later said, "I couldn't believe I had gotten myself into an actual battle."

Sometimes O'Brien's troupe had no idea where they were going, as on the occasion when they were transported to an "unknown destination" to present their show at a navy intelligence base. On occasion the performers would hold religious services en route, which might be at a jungle clearing. Though Pat and Harry Brown were the only Catholics in the group, all would attend.

The actor thrived on new experiences and made the most of his globe-hopping during the war. He wrote in later years, "As a boy reading about the 'Seven Wonders of the World,' I never expected a war would make it possible for me to see the Taj Mahal, the Sphinx, the Pyramids, and the Nile, and they were all just as they were in books."

When O'Brien returned to the United States, he and Harry Brown put together a small act and placed themselves on call with the U.S.O. for visits to local camps and hospitals. Eloise also became part of the act in her first performing venture since their marriage. Still later, toward the end of the war, Pat joined the Hollywood Victory Caravan, joining in an all-star variety show which toured the country to raise money for the Navy Relief Fund. Among the celebrities involved were Charles Boyer, Jimmy Cagney, Claudette Colbert, Bing Crosby, Cary Grant, Bob Hope, Frank McHugh, and Laurel and Hardy. Throughout the tour, Pat was bemused to find that the latter duo always received the greatest ovation. The show opened in Washington, D.C. with a White House reception and ended several weeks later in San Francisco where Al Jolson joined the troupe for one performance.

Ever since MGM turned out the classic *The Thin Man* in 1934, other studios had been seeking to copy the format of a wacky murder caper. Even a decade later, RKO was offering a belated entry, *Having Wonderful Crime* (1945). It cast George Murphy and Carole Landis as an adventure-loving married couple who drag their pal into murder cases, hoping that they can prove themselves as amateur sleuths. "The intent is comedy, an intent too seldom realized," carped Eileen Creelman *(New York Sun)*. "This picture may safely be forgotten as a pitiful but harmless offense," ordained Bosley Crowther *(New York Times)*. But once again, as had become tradition with his middling films, Pat received sterling notices. Alton Cook *(New York World-Telegram)* headlined his brief review, "Pat O'Brien Handles Deadly Dialogue Valiantly," and wrote: "When Pat O'Brien appears in a picture, his followers can come away full of respect for one thing, at least. You can't question his courage. His new picture . . . makes it clear that he has nerve enough to tackle any kind of a script. The picture allots him one of the feeblest collections of jokes ever assembled, but he valiantly strides through the scenes, smirking and smiling as gaily as if he had material that was very funny. No matter how confused the murder mystery part of the picture becomes, Pat keeps right on with the pretense that these raucous doings could hold the attention of a man of sense."

Man Alive (1945) was no celebration, but it had more substance than his prior release. He played Speed, a man presumed dead, who pretends to be a ghost to scare away his wife's suitor. Adolphe Menjou (his *The Front Page* co-star), Ellen Drew, and Rudy Vallee shared the antics. *Man Alive* had been made in 1943 but then been temporarily shelved during RKO's reorganization period.

One role that Pat was born to play was that of the idealistic drunk Johnny Nolan, the ill-fated father in 20th Century-Fox's *A Tree Grows in Brooklyn* (1945). However the sympathetic role went to James Dunn, a Fox star of the early 1930s who was making a film comeback. The job won Dunn an Academy Award as Best Supporting Actor of the Year.

O'Brien says of his film work at this time, "I loved that RKO lot as did most everyone who worked there. . . . It exuded more friendliness and warm camaraderie than any other studio in which I ever worked." But the company was struck by misfortune when on February 2, 1946 studio head Charles Koerner died of leukemia. As Pat sadly recalls, "He was endowed with more warmth, charm, and generosity than anyone who had ever headed a studio during my time. . . . When he died, so did RKO." N. Peter Rathvon succeeded Koerner as chief executive of RKO for a year, followed in February 1947 by the appointment of Dore Schary as executive vice-president in charge of production.

With Desi Arnaz in *The Navy Comes Through* (1942).

With Gloria Holden in *Having Wonderful Crime* (1945).

With Audrey Long in *Perilous Holiday* (1946).

Pat's first release of 1946 was Columbia's *Perilous Holiday* in which he plays a traveler who encounters a gang of counterfeiters in Mexico. His co-players were Ruth Warrick and Alan Hale. More suspenseful was his RKO entry, *Crack-Up* (1946), directed by Irving Reis. Pat seemed more his old Warner Bros. self as a fast-talking art expert who suffers a bout of amnesia and must solve a homicide and a swindle. Abetting him in this caper were Wallace Ford (as Police Lieutenant Cochrane) and a line-up of intriguing suspects: Ray Collins, Herbert Marshall, Erskine Sanford, and Claire Trevor.

With World War II finally over, Pat was happy to settle back into his domestic life, with his family, home, and job. Eloise was expecting another child in June 1946. Late in her pregnancy she slipped and fell and had to be rushed to St. John's Hospital in Santa Monica for an emergency delivery via Caesarean section. Both mother and daughter survived. Pat says that this youngest child, christened Kathleen Brigid, was "spoiled rotten by her brothers and sisters, to say nothing of her mother and dad." Pat's friend, Mayor William O'Dwyer of New York, was her godfather.

In late 1946, Pat was asked to undertake a command performance for the King and Queen of England. Also requested to appear were Ray Milland, Mr. and Mrs. Reginald Gardner, Dorothy Malone, and Katina Paxinou. Toots Shor gave them a going-away party at his Manhattan restaurant. Bob Hope, William Powell, James Barton, Mark Hellinger, Gene Fowler, and Jackie Gleason were among those attending.

After arriving in London, Pat caused a mild furor by refusing to be presented to the royalty unless Eloise was too. This was against centuries of protocol, but Pat's Irish was up, and finally the monarchs' staff agreed. When Pat shook hands with the Queen, a publicity photograph was taken showing the event clearly. He had a few hundred copies made and sent them to friends at home.

After a few days in England, the O'Briens went to Ireland. They traveled around the island, meeting various friends such as actress Maureen O'Hara and being introduced to Kathleen Kennedy (the sister of the President, later killed in a plane crash) and the Brooklyn-born president of Ireland, Eamon De Valera. They visited Killarney and Blarney Castle, where Pat kissed the Blarney Stone. The O'Briens then returned to London and later flew on to Switzerland, and thereafter to Rome where Cardinal Spellman had arranged an audience for them with the Pope. Both O'Briens were very nervous, but their interview was calm and pleasant. Pius XII had visited the United States and California before he became Pope, and he spoke English fluently.

After sightseeing in Rome, Pat and Eloise journeyed to Paris where they met Maurice Chevalier who acted as their host. The boulevardier took them one day to a dubbing studio where a French soundtrack was being put to *Angels with Dirty Faces.* Pat said of this experience, "You have not lived until you have heard Bogart, Cagney, and O'Brien converse in sharp underworld French!"

On their return to the States, Pat went to Pennsylvania to be presented with an Honorary Doctor of Literature degree from St. Francis College. Cardinal Spellman received the identical honor at the same ceremony.

Rancor has never been a visible part of Pat's personality, but he displayed a degree of it regarding his next RKO film, *Riff-Raff* (1947). When he was handed Martin Rackin's script, he was so impressed by its slickness that he suggested his studio place the young writer under contract. They did. Pat would state pointedly in his autobiography, "Marty is now one of the top executives at Paramount Studios. Strange I don't hear from him any more." *Riff-Raff* was set in Panama with Pat protecting an old friend from crooks. Its well-meaning cast included Anne Jeffreys, Walter Slezak, and Jerome Cowan.

Pat's old friend and sometime partner Phil Ryan purchased *Fighting Father Dunne* (1948) as a vehicle for Pat. It concerned the turn-of-the-century St. Louis priest who worked devotedly with underprivileged newsboys. Pat was impressed with the talents of Darryl Hickman, who played one of the troubled youths, and his part was right for him. However, the film (co-scripted by Martin Rackin) was deeply unoriginal. It emerged as a second-rate *Boys Town,* and RKO was not MGM, nor was Pat a Spencer Tracy. The *New York Times* complained that the performances were too "deliberately calculated" and that the black-and-white feature was nothing more than a "misguided inspirational salute."

As he would also demonstrate during his later MGM reign, executive producer and administrator Dore Schary was extremely message-conscious in his filmmaking. One of his pet projects was *The Boy with Green Hair* (1948), an allegorical study of the effect of war on children and the need for worldwide peace. Dean Stockwell had the title role, with Barbara Hale as the earnest school teacher, Robert Ryan as the police psychiatrist, and Pat, in his first character role, as the white-haired gramps. The color feature had been filmed in late 1947, but when Howard Hughes purchased the studio in mid-1948, he had the picture re-edited to remove a good deal of the

With George Raft and Roland Winters in *A Dangerous Profession* (1949).

leftist slant instilled by director Joseph Losey and the scripters. A new ad campaign ("Please don't tell why his hair turned green!") did nothing to enhance the project with prospective filmgoers who wanted entertainment, not messages. The *New York Times* adjudged the venture "a bright notion gone wrong" and kindly admitted that Pat's subordinate characterization was "softly sentimental."

Pat's next release was very low-keyed. *A Dangerous Profession* (1949) concerned the world of bail bondsmen. It rematched him with George Raft and offered lovely Ella Raines as the woman in trouble. Ted Tetzlaff, who had helmed two previous O'Brien RKO films, directed this minor effort.

By the time *A Dangerous Profession* went into release in December 1949, Pat's RKO contract had expired. Studio head Howard Hughes was more concerned with promoting the physical attributes of Jane Russell and Faith Domergue, and if he needed a string of leading men, he preferred the muscular Robert Mitchum type. He most definitely was not interested in maintaining veterans like Pat on his payroll.

O'Brien did not immediately feel the pinch of his precarious position, for there were two freelance jobs. The first was at United Artists. *Johnny One-Eye* (1950) was an amiable if minor Damon Runyon story about a good-natured crook (Pat) on the lam. The other was 20th Century-Fox's *The Fireball* (1950). The latter starred Mickey Rooney as the dynamic orphaned youth who becomes engulfed in the roller skating world. Pat was cast by director-pal Tay Garnett as kindly Father O'Hara, and Marilyn Monroe had a bit in the drama.

Slowly it was dawning on Pat that his screen career was grinding to a halt, but he could not (or refused to) understand why. "I was not a political figure, either right or left, I wasn't a sex maniac, dope user, dog molester, nudist, enemy agent, flag or barn burner, epileptic, leper or vampire. . . . But I was out."

In this distressing period, fifty-one-year-old Pat turned to his family and religion for support. He also was aided by friends. Pal Spencer Tracy agreed to do *The People Against O'Hara* (1951), even though it was not a very promising project, because it offered a role —that of police detective Vincent Ricks—that was suitable for Pat. (Metro's Dore Schary was against hiring Pat until Tracy demanded it.) *Criminal Lawyer* (1951) with Jane Wyatt and *Okinawa* (1952) with Cameron Mitchell were both made at Columbia for the declining double-bill film market. They did nothing to stem the downward trend of Pat's career.

Pat turned to television as an alternate career and means of support. He debuted on CBS-TV's "Video Theatre" on Monday, February 26, 1951 in the episode *The Irish Drifter* and soon became a regular on the various anthology shows.[17] The William Morris office booked him into the Desert Inn in Las Vegas and he was surprised to find himself enjoying the club work very much.

There were a few film roles along the way. He played minor support, as an alcoholic doctor, to Vera Ralston and Joan Leslie in the overly expansive Republic Western *Jubilee Trail* (1954). Then he joined animal trainer Clyde Beatty in *King of Fear* (1954) and was teamed with Dennis O'Keefe in *Inside Detroit* (1955), yet another entry in the gangland exposé cycle.

Ironically, in 1955, Pat was chosen to be one of the actors representing Hollywood at the Uruguay Film Festival in Montevideo. At least Pat and Eloise received a trip, a good way to celebrate their twenty-fourth wedding anniversary. Tony Di Santis, who operated a tent theatre in Evergreen Park, Illinois, asked Pat to play Hildy Johnson, his old part, in a production of *The Front Page* there. Though Di Santis could offer him only a drastically reduced salary, he was still glad to accept. Since that engagement, Pat has been happily busy with live theatre. It was not long before he persuaded Eloise to return to acting so that they could travel and work together. The couple disliked being away from home and family, but as the actor explained: "I had work. I thought of the hundreds of talented men and women in Holly-

[17]Though not inactive, Pat felt the urge to really act. One day in 1953, Pat reported to a TV studio for what he thought was a routine part in a pilot starring Fay Wray. To his complete astonishment, it turned out to be "This Is Your Life," starring Pat O'Brien. On the show appeared old friends Allen Jenkins, Wallace Ford, and James Gleason, his *The Front Page* leading lady Mary Brian, Eloise and their four children, and Sister Mary Norbert, his first grade teacher. Pat was stunned.

With Mavourneen, Terry, Eloise, Brigid, and Sean at home in 1948.

With Jane Wyatt in *Criminal Lawyer* (1951).

wood who just rust away, waiting, waiting, for a call that never comes. They stand in front of Schwabs, testing free toothpicks; sit at home in some shabby room, looking at their youth on television's ancient movies. Some end life suddenly; some exist, but no longer live."

It was in 1956 that Pat's mother died at the age of ninety-two. She had been bedridden for several years. Pat remarked: "[I] only thanked the Lord for the privilege of being able to take care of Mom those last years of her life. I never missed a day seeing her right up until the fearful parting hour of her death. She led a full and wonderful life."

In the mid-1950s the work routine for Pat was basically, six weeks of stock in Chicago, nightclub and toastmaster engagements, and assorted TV outings. In his club act he would combine nostalgia and Americanism, often performing "Yankee Doodle Dandy" as a soft-shoe routine, and reciting the "Win one for the Gipper" speech from *Knute Rockne —All American.* It was not a stellar follow-up career to his film career, but as he said: "I survived and worked—and survival and work for an actor is all."

Pat jumped at the chance to star in an English-made film, even if it was modestly budgeted. *Kill Me Tomorrow* (1957) was a regressive assignment for the once-big star. He played a reporter solving a murder-and-smuggling case. Also in the Terence Fisher-directed entry were Lois Maxwell and George Coulouris.[18]

[18]The London-based *Today's Cinema* reported, "The figure of a hard-bitten, tippling, newspaperman is familiar enough, but Pat O'Brien injects his likeable methods as usual. The double murders take place fairly early in the story, and the situations, logical in sequence, mount with complications and twists that never lose their clarity."

Back in the United States, Pat made a Broadway return in an inauspicious play version of Nathaniel West's novel *Miss Lonelyhearts.* The Howard Teichmann adaptation was branded "ineffectual" by the *New York Post* and only lasted a few performances after its October 3, 1957 opening at the Music Box Theatre. Similar to his program features at RKO in the 1940s, O'Brien's performance was rated the highlight of the offering. "Things came to life with a wham the minute Pat O'Brien walked on at the Music Box last evening. He rode a role that fitted him, and what's becoming to Mr. O'Brien is something tough, fast, funny, pithy, violent, and reasonably realistic" *(New York World-Telegram and Sun).* "A *Front Page* alumnus, Pat plays a hard-talking, lecherous and liquorish feature editor, and he acts him with great charm and easy skill" *(New York Daily News).* "Mr. O'Brien retains all of his old-time stage authority, and it's good to see him again" *(New York Post).* "He gave the part that wonderful fast-talking Irish-American delivery for which he owns the copyright" *(New York Journal American).*

Others in the cast included Fritz Weaver (as the newsman assigned to the lonelyhearts column), Ruth Warrick (as O'Brien's suffering spouse), Pippa Scott (as Weaver's girl), and Irene Dailey (as the high-living book reviewer). The Nathaniel West novel had been filmed in 1933 as *Advice to the Lovelorn,* with Paul Harvey in Pat's role. In the 1958 filming of *Lonelyhearts,* Robert Ryan would play O'Brien's part.

Much more rewarding were Pat's next film assignments in Hollywood. John Ford recruited an authentic Irish team for *The Last Hurrah* (1958). Spencer Tracy starred as the old-line party boss mayor, with a cast that included Pat, Donald Crisp, James Gleason, Edward Brophy, Wallace Ford, and Frank McHugh. This political narrative is a near classic, featuring top ensemble playing. Each character is superb.

Pat recently commented about director Ford and the making of *The Last Hurrah:* "He never talked the part you were playing. He'd tell you what he wanted, like Capra. 'I hope you can get it,' he'd say, with that patch over his eye and chewing that hankerchief. When you failed, he'd say, 'That's not what I wanted. Try to get what I wanted.' 'Well, okay, Pappy, let's take another whack at it.' And he'd answer, 'Well, you're to take another whack at it, and it better be all right.' When it was finally good, he'd go over and hug you. 'Why the hell didn't you get it in the first place?' "

In *Some Like It Hot* (1959) Pat hit exactly the right note in the Billy Wilder joyous 1920s' farce. He was Mulligan, the ramrod-straight cop chasing archetypical gangster Spats Colombo, played by ex-star George Raft. The well-regarded comedy starred Jack Lemmon, Tony Curtis, Marilyn Monroe, and Joe E. Brown. On stage, Pat joined with Allen Jenkins in a Harold J. Kennedy-directed revival of *The Front Page.*

In 1960, John Ford directed the stage play *What Price Glory?* as a benefit for the Purple Heart Organization, of which he was president. In the stellar cast were John Wayne, Gregory Peck, Frank McHugh, Robert Armstrong, Ed Begley, Oliver Hardy, and Henry O'Neill. Pat and Ward Bond played the two leading characters, Quirt and Flagg, while Maureen O'Hara undertook the only female role. The show toured throughout southern California, opening in Hollywood, and going on to Long Beach, San Jose, San Francisco, and then back down the coast to Los Angeles. All the proceeds went to charity.[19]

Also in 1960, an eventful year, Pat filmed thirty-six episodes of the teleseries "Harrigan and Son," about a family law firm. The show debuted on Friday, October 14, 1960 over the CBS-TV network. Roger Perry played Pat's son. Viewers can still remember the program's opening credits unrolling over a back view of the beautiful office secretary (Georgine D'Arcy) walking down the hall, her hip-length blonde braid swinging. For the closing credits, Pat and Perry sang the famous Geroge M. Cohan song, "H-A-Double-R-I-G-A-N Spells Harrigan," which doubtless inspired the series' title. Pat loved being the star of a television show. He called the program "human, amusing, yet earnest." And indeed it was, a most superior program, but, recalls Pat, "the Ivy League suited gods of Madison Avenue thought otherwise. It was replaced by a chimpanzee show, half ape, half human."

Pat and Eloise continued with their stage ventures. They went on a tour to Australia in 1963, but their contract stipulated that they could return to the States for two weeks in June. During that month Brigid would graduate from Marymount College in California, and son Terry would receive a degree from the Diplomatic School of Georgetown Univer-

[19]In the early 1960s, Pat played in San Francisco at the Alcazar Theatre in a rather dull play titled *Strike a Match,* teamed with Eva Gabor and Richard Egan. In 1967, for the Civic Light Opera Association, he would perform in San Francisco and Los Angeles as Cap'n Andy in a revival of *Show Boat* which lasted for fifteen weeks. Jacqueline McKeever was Magnolia, Charles Fredericks was Ravenal, and Gale Sherwood was Julie. The role seemed too strenuous for O'Brien at his age, and he did not match such other stage and film Cap'n Andys as Charles Winninger, Guy Kibbee, Joe E. Brown, and Gene Lockhart.

With Ed Brophy, Spencer Tracy, William Leslie, and Ricardo Cortez in *The Last Hurrah* (1958).

With Roger Perry in the ABC-TV series "Harrigan and Son" (1960).

sity in Washington, D.C. Their oldest daughter Mavourneen had married a Scandinavian, David Garton, and Sean O'Brien, Pat and Eloise's oldest son, had become a master sergeant in the army, serving four tours in Vietnam and being hospitalized for injuries suffered in Cambodia. He would marry a French girl named Monique and now has three children. Sean's first son was Pat's first grandchild and was named Patrick, Jr. Terence would receive another degree in 1972, this time from Loyola Law School. Brigid has more recently become an actress and frequently works with her parents on tours.

Six years after his last theatrical film release, Pat accepted the eleventh-billed role of Judge Marcott in *Town Tamer* (1965), a low-budget Western shot at Paramount. It was part of A. C. Lyles' quickie series featuring one-time film names. This entry boasted Dana Andrews, Terry Moore, Bruce Cabot, Lon Chaney, Jr., Richard Arlen, Sonny Tufts, and James Cagney's sister, Jeanne. Pat's next theatrical film release was a cameo bit in *The Phynx* (1970), an embarrassingly shoddy bit of nostalgia and camp which featured a rock group (known as The Phynx) and brief glimpses of such once-familiar faces as Ruby Keeler, Marilyn Maxwell, Cass Daley, Patsy Kelly, Andy Devine, Dorothy Lamour, Huntz Hall, and Pat.

Occasionally Pat's TV assignments in the 1960s would be worthy of his veteran status. He had the lead in the ABC-TV telefeature *The Over-the-Hill Gang* (1969), playing Captain Oren Hayes, a retired Texas Ranger who unites three old pals (Walter Brennan, Chill Wills, and Edgar Buchanan) in a battle against corruption in the town of Boulder, Nevada. Among their foes are Sheriff Jack Elam, Judge Andy Devine, and crooked mayor Edward Andrews. Others in the cast were Gypsy Rose Lee and Rick Nelson. It was a delightful spoof and engendered a sequel, *The Over-the-Hill Gang Rides Again* (1970), which unfortunately did not have Pat in the cast.

The 1970s would find Pat guest-starring in such telefeatures as *Welcome Home, Johnny Bristol* (1972) starring Martin Landau and *The Adventures of Nick Carter* (1972) featuring Robert Conrad, Shelley Winters, and Broderick Crawford. Pat was cast as a colorful character named Hallelujah Harry. He also had cameo assignments on such series as "Tenafly" and "The Bold Ones" in 1973. However, it was for his role as the country doctor on the ABC-TV daytime special *The Other Woman* (December 4, 1973) that he received his greatest praise in recent years. Katherine Helmond starred as a lonely woman in a midwestern town who is pregnant and hopes to keep her child. *Variety* labeled Pat's performance "first-rate," and the American Academy of Television Arts and Sciences agreed. In May 1974, Pat won his only major acting award,[20] an Emmy. His rival was Macdonald Carey, star of the daytime dramatic series "Days of Our Lives." "I finally won a big one!" Pat jubilantly told the press. "My heart is still pounding from it. I'm really thrilled."

On Thursday, July 24, 1975, while preparing for a performance with Eloise in *Skip and Go Naked* at the Drury Lane Theatre, Pat suddenly collapsed and was immediately hospitalized. Some confusion about his condition existed, and it was reported to be either heart trouble or simply complete exhaustion. He was listed in critical condition for a week while at the Illinois Research Hospital. Only later was it revealed that heart surgery had been performed. Friend Dennis Morgan stepped in to substitute for Pat onstage, to be later replaced by Eddie Bracken. When Pat was released from the hospital after four weeks, the O'Briens returned to Los Angeles and planned a Hawaiian vacation. However, on September 14, Pat was again stricken and was hospitalized. He remained incapacitated for about ten days, the official diagnosis being an "ulcer condition." Since his release he has eased back into a performing schedule with a variety of benefits, testimonials, and roasts.

On Saturday, November 8, 1975, Pat was given the "Duty, Honor, and Country" Award at the annual military ball of the West Point Society of Los Angeles. For the first time O'Brien was seen in public using the aid of a cane, but the *Hollywood Reporter* stated that he "wowed them" with his acceptance speech. Pat mentioned that he and Eloise wept when the flag passed them at the annual West Point graduation exercises. "Now when it goes by, my heart pounds an extra beat because I've got a pacemaker. If you're worried about my cane, I'm still nursing my wounds from Gettysburg." At the same ceremony, he was presented with a commendation from Mayor Bradley of Los Angeles. *Variety* termed the evening "A Schmaltzy Hail and Name Dropsy."

[20]In 1972 the American Academy of Dramatic Arts presented Pat with its Alumni Achievement Award.

In early 1976 Pat was back on the social scene, dining with Eloise at Mme. Wu's Garden in Santa Monica. "Everyone's here but Anna May Wong," he insisted. That February he was signed as special guest star for the ABC-TV telefeature "D.A.'s Investigator," shooting at the old Warner Bros. home lot in Burbank. In the mid-1970s, he could be seen on TV in an episode of "Tenafly" (1974), a two-part "World of Disney" entry entitled *The Sky's the Limit* (1975), and in the 1976 ABC-TV movie *Kiss Me, Kill Me,* he joined Stella Stevens, Robert Vaughn, and Michael Anderson, Jr. for seventy-eight minutes of chasing the psychopathic killer of a young schoolteacher. Pat was on hand in a cameo as a morgue attendant.

In recent years, Pat has played stock for ten weeks every summer, usually co-starring with Eloise, at the Drury Lane Theatre in Chicago. Among their vehicles have been *Daddy Dear Daddy* and *Paris Is Out.* In the latter play, Pat and Eloise toured the country, opening in Dallas in early 1975. On their anniversary that January 21, they appeared on the "Merv Griffin Show" for a nostalgic TV talk show evening with old friends, including former Governor Ronald Reagan.[21]

On Wednesday, June 11, 1975 Pat was honored by the Westwood Al Malaikah Shrine Club for his "Talents and Humanitarianism." Art Linkletter was

[21]In describing her affection for Pat to the press, Eloise has said, "Pat and I have four children and six grandchildren. And from the beginning, we both have been happiest whenever the family is all together. . . . Pat will never accept a job which would mean working at Christmas time. His family is more important than his career. There's no sacrifice too great for the people he loves. . . . He's always been around to help the kids with their problems and always available for advice. His children matter to him. That's what makes him a good father. . . . But I don't want people to think that Pat doesn't have time for people other than his family. There have been hundreds of times when he's helped people he didn't have to."

In *Town Tamer* (1965).

the Master of Ceremonies. At the testimonial dinner were Lloyd Nolan, Jane Wyatt, Mary Brian, Jane Wyman, Ruth Hussey, Ann Doran, Henry Fonda, Jack Albertson, Red Buttons, Mervyn LeRoy, Maureen Reagan (Ronald and Jane Wyman Reagan's daughter), Margaret Lindsay, Mrs. Spencer Tracy,[22] Hunty Hall, and Dennis Murphy (son of George). All of the guests spoke. Pat's sentimental but humorous replies won cheers and a standing ovation. Messages were read from Bob Hope and Jack Haley. Ronald Reagan and Jimmy Cagney[23] sent taped greetings.

While daughter Brigid was appearing in Los Angeles in the Masquers' Club version of *Light Up the Sky* in the spring of 1976, Pat and Eloise were preparing a return to Chicago's Drury Lane Theatre South to do *Skip and Go Naked* which had been retitled *Hotline to Heaven.* It was also a year of awards and tributes for Pat. He and Eloise were guests at the White House dinner honoring Prime Minister Cosgrave of Ireland, he was a guest at the Hollywood Women's Press Club Golden Apple Awards luncheon (along with Barbara Stanwyck, he garnered the most publicity), he was named as the 1976 recipient of the May Mann Award given to an entertainer who has served the cause of humanity, and he was the second performer (Bob Hope was given the honor in 1946) to receive the American Legion's highest honor, the Distinguished Service Medal.

In July of 1976, Pat was in front of the cameras, co-starring in *Billy Jack Goes to Washington,* a remake of *Mr. Smith Goes to Washington* (1939). The new *Billy Jack* picture, the fourth in producer-director-scripter-star Tom Laughlin's series, found Pat cast as the Vice President, the Senate head role originally played by Harry Carey. (Interestingly, at the time of production, Laughlin was living in the Brentwood mansion Pat had built for his clan; proving how the times had changed.) Because of O'Brien's stage contracts, for some scenes in the Senate, a double—Mike Lally—was used to sit in for Pat. The expensive *Billy Jack* finished production in the fall of 1976 and, while Pat returned to *Hotline to Heaven,* Laughlin was undergoing financial problems which seemingly doomed the future of the picture. The movie, in a 155-minute version, would be previewed at the National Theatre in West Los Angeles in April 1977. *Variety* reported that the picture "compensates for its artlessness and lack of subtlety with an angry, energetic attack on governmental corruption." The trade paper termed veteran performers O'Brien, E. G. Marshall, and Sam Wanamaker as "excellent." But after a few test engagements in August 1977 in Ohio, the feature disappeared from sight, not even resurfacing—as yet—on television.

Apparently undaunted by age, Pat continued onward into 1977. He would appear on TV talk shows, such as "Over Easy" with Hugh Downs, continue tours of *Hot Line to Heaven,* do a Los Angeles-to-Melbourne, Australia live telephone interview to add a touch of authenticity to St. Patrick's Day celebrations Down Under, receive the "Man of the Year" Award from the Notre Dame Club in San Diego, join Cary Grant, Henry Fonda, Karl Malden, and Joan Blondell in a Westwood Shriners salute to producer-director Mervyn LeRoy, and be the guest of honor at the first annual Screen Extras Guild dinner and dance held at the Sheraton Universal Hotel in Universal City on October 15. While daughter Brigid took on her first big screen role, as a reporter in Frank Capra, Jr.'s production of *Born Again,* Pat and Eloise toured in *Paris Is Out.* When director Steve Paul began filming *Memories,* a feature film written by Ted Allen, Pat joined Deborah Raffin, Kurt Vonnegut,

With wife Eloise on tour in Dallas (February 1975).

[22]Pat joined with Robert Wagner, George Raft, Joan Bennett, Stanley Kramer, and Adela Rogers St. Johns in an ABC-TV "Wide World Special" (May 8, 1976) devoted to the career of Spencer Tracy.

[23]When James Cagney was the subject of the American Film Institute's Life Achievement Award in Los Angeles on March 13, 1974, O'Brien was unable to attend the festivities but his wife Eloise and son Terry were present.

With Myrna Loy and Burt Reynolds in *The End* (1978).

Jr., and Susannah York for the New York City lensing in late 1977. The Sam Shaw production has yet to reach the screen.

More fortuitous was Pat's participation in Burt Reynolds' black comedy *The End,* made in 1977 and released in mid-1978. There was tremendous promotion concerning the re-teaming of O'Brien and Myrna Loy as Reynolds' parents, with all sources noting it was the first pairing of the veteran stars since *Consolation Marriage* for RKO in 1931. O'Brien would admit to Gene Lees for *American Film* magazine. "It was a complete revelation. I had known the man [Reynolds], but never knew he was endowed with such great directorial ability. . . . It was his idea for me to play the part the way I did. I came on the set, and he said, 'Pat, what would you think of playing this fellow deaf?' 'Yeah, that's good,' I said. 'It'll make for a different kind of characterization, it will inject a type of humor that won't be offensive, it will be fun for everyone.' So I ended up playing the part that way. . . . I marveled every day, watching him not only with Myrna Loy and me but with all the other people. He had so many different types of personalities to direct. He had the young people, the middle-aged, and then the old codgers like myself. I've never had an experience quite like it." As with most every Burt Reynold feature released in the mid-1970s, *The End* garnered its share of public endorsement, despite the critical reservations. It proved to be a good credit for O'Brien, providing him with ample opportunity to discuss his latest role on assorted video and audio talk programs.

In June 1978 Pat was in Shannon, Ireland to receive the John F. Kennedy Memorial Medal, the only performer to be so honored in the decade since the Award was founded. O'Brien was performing at the Country Dinner Playhouse in Columbus, Ohio in mid-July when he was hospitalized to replace a depleted battery in his pacemaker. By August he and Eloise were back performing in *The Second Time Around.* When the Masquers' Club gave a dinner honoring Shirley Temple in late 1978, Pat joined the dais for the tribute.

As a change of pace, Pat assumed the duties of host for the "Delta Queen" riverboat Hollywood Heyday cruise on the Mississippi River in February 1979. It provided a fine post-celebration for the O'Briens forty-eighth wedding anniversary. When the Friars Club toasted George Jessel in May, Pat was among the notables attending. Then, when not appearing on a television talk show to reminisce about the "good old days" of Hollywood, he and Eloise

Pat O'Brien, supporting cast 'knock out' Derby audience

DUDLEY SAUNDERS
Times critic

Irish-American actor Pat O'Brien, who used to trade screen-punches with the likes of Jimmy Cagney and other tough guys of the 1930-40s, knocked out his opening-night audience last night in "The Second Time Around" at Derby Dinner Playhouse.

They gave O'Brien, his wife Eloise and a bright supporting cast a standing ovation at show's end. They gave O'Brien a second standing ovation after he bowled them over with a series of Irish jokes after the curtain call.

Other film stars from earlier generations have received enthusiastic welcomes at Derby, but none compare with the royal welcome O'Brien got.

His timing is sharp. He can clown one minute and turn crisply subtle next. His voice can sting with sarcasm or drip with honeyed Irish blarney. He is very funny and thoroughly likable. Even if you hadn't seen any of his films in years, you'd immediately recognize the voice.

Henry Denker's "The Second Time Around" is a good vehicle for the O'Briens. O'Brien is delightful. Mrs. O'Brien is charming.

The O'Briens have that something

By MARY PHYLLIS RIEDLEY
Louisville Times Staff Writer

There's something about the Irish. Charm. A sense of fun. A sense of humor. They can make you cry and then, quicker than you can say Rosie O'Grady, they have you laughing again.

Pat O'Brien and his wife Eloise have that something in super abundance. The opening night audience at Derby Dinner Theatre was so taken with the O'Briens' low-key, professional performance in "Second Time Around" it gave them the most spontaneous standing ovation we have yet seen at the dinner theater.

O'Briens are big hit in play

Pat O'Brien, another living showbiz legend (now in his 59th year) charmed me along with a packed opening night crowd last week at the Derby Dinner Playhouse in Clarksville.

I thoroughly enjoyed the performance. It was such a smooth, polished, easy-going performance that I felt at times that he was not playing a part at all, just being Pat O'Brien at ease in his own living room. I may go again.

–John Stein

PAT O'BRIEN

By CHAS. R. BRODERICK

Like vintage wine, Pat O'Brien seems to get better with age. This is especially evident during his current appearance with his wife, Eloise, in Derby Dinner Playhouse's current comedy, "Second Time Around."

O'Brien, who has starred in over 110 motion pictures and a myriad television and theatre and performances, displays a magnificent sense of timing and pace in his role as grandfatherly Samuel Jonas. Gruff and grumbly, but thoroughly likeable.

His wife Eloise, clearly an excellent actress in her own right, plays Laura Curtis, an elderly widow he falls in love with.

But despite a fine supporting cast, O'Brien is such a towering personality, even in a low key role, that he absolutely dominates nearly every scene. At the same time, he retains the Irish warmth and jollity that has been his acting trademark for almost 60 years.

The premiere night audience took the O'Briens to its heart and enthusiastically applauded in bursts of camaraderie.

O'Brien departed from the regular format at the conclusion of the performance by telling a series of Irish jokes in his own inimitable style and absolutely brought down the house with laughter.

That session alone was worth the price of admission.

By GREGG SWEM
Courier-Journal Critic

A director could cast Pat O'Brien in just about any role.

He could play a policeman, a doctor or a priest. It could be a melodrama, a comedy or a serious play. It wouldn't matter. People would flock to see him.

However, it's hard to imagine a more receptive audience that the one that turned out Tuesday night at Derby Dinner Playhouse.

O'Brien and his wife of many years, Eloise, are starring in the comedy "Second Time Around."

The audience perked up the minute O'Brien walked on stage. The actor was quick to please, pulling out all the stops on his Irish charm.

But O'Brien isn't the only one who can bring an audience to its feet. His wife has her share of charisma. They're an attractive couple.

CONTEMPORARY-KORMAN

All Equity Bookings
Ben Pearson

Stage star, 1979-style.

would return to their theatre work. When the couple played Louisville, Kentucky in *The Second Time Around* in late summer 1979, the critics were full of compliments. "Like vintage wine, Pat O'Brien seems to get better with age. . . . He displays a magnificent sense of timing and pace in his role as grandfatherly Samuel Jonas. Gruff and grumbly, but thoroughly likeable. . . . Despite a fine supporting cast, O'Brien is such a towering personality, even in a low-key role, that he absolutely dominates nearly every scene. At the same time, he retains the Irish warmth and jollity that has been his acting trademark for almost sixty years. . . . O'Brien departed from the regular format at the conclusion of the performance by telling a series of Irish jokes in his own inimitable style and absolutely brought down the house with laughter" (Charles R. Broderick). "His timing is sharp. He can clown one minute and turn crisply subtle the next. His voice can sting with sarcasm or drip with honeyed Irish blarney. He is very funny and thoroughly likable. Even if you hadn't seen any of his films in years, you'd immediately recognize the voice" *(Louisville Times).*

Starting off 1980, on January 18th, Pat received the Carbon Mike Award of the Pacific Pioneer Broadcasters at a luncheon held in Studio City. To keep active professionally, he joined the regulars of TV's comedy series "Happy Days" for the *Roaring Twenties* segment, playing Tom Bosley's grand uncle, and later in the year, joined with Gary Coleman in the NBC-TV movie, *Scout's Honor,* cast as Mr. Caboose, the town's hobby shop owner.

Now Hibernian pals Spencer Tracy, James Gleason, Donald Crisp, Allen Jenkins, and Wallace Ford are dead, while James Cagney and Frank McHugh are in retirement, but Pat insists that he is an "ageless leprechaun" and will not retire. "I tried retiring about [nine] years ago, but my retirement lasted only three months. I was going nuts. I told myself then that I'll never retire again."

FILMOGRAPHY

HONOR AMONG LOVERS
(Paramount, 1931) 75 min.

DIRECTOR:	Dorothy Arzner
STORY/SCREENPLAY:	Austin Parker
DIALOGUE:	Parker, Gertrude Purcell
SOUND:	C. A. Tuthill
CAMERA:	George Folsey
EDITOR:	Helene Turner

Claudette Colbert *(Julia Traynor);* Fredric March *(Jerry Stafford);* Monroe Owsley *(Philip Craig);* Charlie Ruggles *(Monty Dunn);* Ginger Rogers *(Doris Blake);* Avonne Taylor *(Maybelle);* Pat O'Brien *(Conroy);* Janet McLeary *(Margaret);* John Kearney *(Inspector);* Ralph Morgan *(Riggs);* Jules Epailly *(Louis);* Leonard Carey *(Butler).*

THE FRONT PAGE
(United Artists, 1931) 101 min.

PRODUCER:	Howard Hughes
DIRECTOR:	Lewis Milestone
BASED ON THE PLAY BY BEN HECHT AND CHARLES MACARTHUR	
SCREENPLAY:	Bartlett V Cormack
DIALOGUE:	Cormack, Charles Lederer
ART DIRECTOR:	Richard Day
ASSISTANT DIRECTOR:	Nate Watt
SOUND:	Frank Grenzbach
CAMERA:	Glen MacWilliams
EDITOR:	Duncan Mansfield

Adolphe Menjou *(Walter Burns);* Pat O'Brien *(Hildy Johnson);* Mary Brian *(Peggy Grant);* Edward Everett Horton *(Bensinger);* Walter Catlett *(Murphy);* George E. Stone *(Earl Williams);* Mae Clarke *(Molly);* Slim Summerville *(Pincus);* Frank McHugh *(McCue);* Matt Moore *(Kruger);* Clarence H. Wilson *(Sheriff Hartman);* Phil Tead *(Wilson);* Fred Howard *(Schwartz);* Eugene Strong *(Endicott);* Spencer Charters *(Woodenshoe);* Maurice Black *(Diamond Louie);* Effie Ellsler *(Mrs. Grant);* James Gordon *(The Mayor);* Lewis Milestone, Herman J. Mankiewicz *(Bits);* Dick Alexander *(Jacobi);* James Donlan *(Reporter);* Dorothea Wolbert *(Jenny).*

PERSONAL MAID
(Paramount, 1931) 70 min.

DIRECTOR:	Monta Bell
BASED ON THE NOVEL BY GRACE PERKINS	
SCREENPLAY:	Adelaide Heilbron
SOUND:	C. A. Tuthill
CAMERA:	Karl Freund
EDITOR:	Arthur Ellis

Nancy Carroll *(Nora Ryan);* Pat O'Brien *(Peter Shea);* Gene Raymond *(Dick Gary);* Hugh O'Connell *(Kipp);* Mary Boland *(Mrs. Otis Gary);* George Fawcett *(Gary Gary);* Ernest Lawford *(Barrows);* Charlotte Wynters *(Gwen Gary);* Jessie Busley *(Ma Ryan);* Donald Meek *(Pa Ryan);* Clara Langsaner *(Mrs. Wurtz);* Terry Carroll *(Anna Ryan).*

CONSOLATION MARRIAGE
(RKO, 1931) 82 min.

PRODUCER:	William Le Baron
ASSOCIATE PRODUCER:	Myles Connolly
DIRECTOR:	Paul Sloane
STORY:	Bill Cunningham
SCREENPLAY:	Humphrey Pearson
MUSIC DIRECTOR:	Max Steiner
SONG:	Connolly and Steiner
SOUND:	John Tribby
CAMERA:	J. Roy Hunt
EDITOR:	Archie Marshek

Irene Dunne *(Mary);* Pat O'Brien *(Steve "Rollo" Porter);* Myrna Loy *(Elaine);* John Halliday *(Jeff);* Matt Moore *(Colonel);* Lester Vail *(Aubrey);* Wilson Benge *(Butler).*

FLYING HIGH
(MGM, 1931) 80 min.

DIRECTOR:	Charles F. Riesner
BASED ON THE STAGE MUSICAL BY BUDDY DESYLVA, LEW BROWN, RAY HENDERSON, AND JOHN MCGOWAN	
SCREENPLAY:	A. P. Younger, Charles F. Reisner
DIALOGUE:	Younger, Robert E. Hopkins
SONGS:	Dorothy Fields, Jimmy McHugh
CAMERA:	Merritt B. Gerstad
EDITOR:	William S. Gray

Bert Lahr *(Rusty Krause);* Charlotte Greenwood *(Pansy Botts);* Pat O'Brien *(Sport Wardell);* Kathryn Crawford *(Eileen);* Charles Winninger *(Dr. Brown);* Hedda Hopper *(Mrs. Smith);* Guy Kibbee *(Mr. Smith);* Herbert Braggioti *(Gordon).*

HELL'S HOUSE
(Capitol Film Exchange, 1932) 72 min.

PRODUCER:	Benjamin F. Zeidman
DIRECTOR/STORY:	Howard Higgin
SCREENPLAY:	Paul Gangelin, B. Harrison Orkow
CAMERA:	Allen S. Siegel
EDITOR:	Edward Schroeder

Junior Durkin *(Jimmy Mason);* Pat O'Brien *(Kelly);* Bette Davis *(Peggy Gardner);* Junior Coghlan *(Shorty);* Charley Grapewin *(Uncle Henry);* Emma Dunn *(Aunt Emma);* Morgan Wallace *(Frank Gebhardt);* Hooper Atchley *(Captain of the Guards);* Wallis Clark *(Judge Robinson);* James Marcus *(Superintendent Thompson);* Mary Alden *(Mrs. Lucy Mason).*

FINAL EDITION
(Columbia, 1932) 66 min.

DIRECTOR:	Howard Higgin
STORY:	Roy Chanslor
SCREENPLAY:	Dorothy Howell
SOUND:	Edward Bernds
CAMERA:	Benjamin Kline
EDITOR:	Jack Dennis

Pat O'Brien *(Sam Bradshaw);* Mae Clarke *(Anne Woodman);* Mary Doran *(Patsy King);* Bradley Page *(Sid Malvern);* Morgan Wallace *(Neil Selby);* James Donlan *(Freddie);* Phil Tead *(Dan Cameron);* Wallis Clark *(Jim Conroy);* Bertha Mann *(Mrs. Conroy).*

SCANDAL FOR SALE
(Universal, 1932) 75 min.

DIRECTOR:	Russell Mack
BASED ON THE STORY "HOT NEWS" BY EMILE GAUVREAU	
SCREENPLAY:	Ralph Graves, Robert Keith
DIALOGUE:	Graves
CAMERA:	Karl Freund

Charles Bickford *(Jerry Strong);* Rose Hobart *(Claire Strong);* Pat O'Brien *(Waddell);* Claudia Dell *(Dorothy Pepper);* J. Farrell MacDonald *(Treadway);* Harry Beresford *(Brownie);* Berton Churchill *(Bynnweather);* Glenda Farrell *(Stella);* Mary Jane Graham *(Mildred Strong);* Buster Phelps *(Bobby Strong);* Paul Nicholson *(Detective);* James Farley *(Police Lieutenant);* Mitchell Harris *(Carrington);* Heinrich [Hans] von Twardofski *(Affner the Aviator);* Tully Marshall *(Simpkins);* Lew Kelly, Jack Richardson *(Compositors);* Angie Norton *(Nurse).*

THE STRANGE CASE OF CLARA DEANE
(Paramount, 1932) 78 min.

DIRECTORS:	Louis Gasnier, Max Marcin
BASED ON THE PLAY BY ARTHUR M. BRILANT	
SCREENPLAY:	Marcin
CAMERA:	Henry Sharp

Wynne Gibson *(Clara Deane);* Pat O'Brien *(Frank Deane);* Frances Dee *(Nancy);* Dudley Digges *(Detective Garrison);* George Barbier *(Ware);* Russell Gleason *(Norman);* Florence Britton *(Miriam);* Lee Kohlmar *(Herzman);* Arthur Pierson *(Lew Severen);* Clara Blandick *(Mrs. Lyons);* Cora Sue Collins *(Nancy as a Child).*

AMERICAN MADNESS
(Columbia, 1932) 76 min.

DIRECTOR:	Frank Capra
STORY/SCREENPLAY:	Robert Riskin

SOUND: E. L. Bernds
CAMERA: Joseph Walker
EDITOR: Maurice Wright

Walter Huston *(Thomas Dickson);* Pat O'Brien *(Matt Brown);* Kay Johnson *(Mrs. Dickson);* Constance Cummings *(Helen);* Gavin Gordon *(Cyril Cluett);* Robert Ellis *(Dude Finlay);* Jeanne Sorel *(Cluett's Secretary);* Walter Walker *(Schultz);* Berton Churchill *(O'Brien);* Arthur Hoyt *(Ives);* Edward Martindale *(Ames);* Edwin Maxwell *(Clark);* Robert Emmet O'Connor *(Inspector);* Anderson Lawler *(Charlie);* Pat O'Malley *(Pat).*

HOLLYWOOD SPEAKS
(Columbia, 1932) 72 min.

DIRECTOR: Eddie Buzzell
STORY: Norman Krasna
SCREENPLAY: Krasna, Jo Swerling
SOUND: Edward Bernds
CAMERA: Ted Tetzlaff
EDITOR: Gene Havlick

Genevieve Tobin *(Gertrude Smith);* Pat O'Brien *(Jimmie Reed);* Lucien Prival *(Frederick Landau);* Ralf Harolde *(Carp);* Rita LaRoy *(Millie Coreen);* Leni Stengel *(Mrs. Landau);* Anderson Lawlor *(Joe Hammond).*

VIRTUE
(Columbia, 1932) 87 min.

DIRECTOR: Eddie Buzzell
STORY: Ethel Hill
SCREENPLAY: Robert Riskin
SOUND: Edward Bernds
ASSISTANT DIRECTOR: Sam Nelson
CAMERA: Joseph Walker

Carole Lombard *(Mae);* Pat O'Brien *(Jimmy);* Mayo Methot *(Lil);* Jack LaRue *(Toots);* Shirley Bond *(Gert);* Ed LeSaint *(Magistrate).*

AIR MAIL
(Universal, 1932) 83 min.

PRODUCER: Carl Laemmle, Jr.
DIRECTOR: John Ford
SCREENPLAY: Dale Van Every, Frank Wead
AVIATION INSTRUCTRESS: Florence Lowe Barnes
SPECIAL EFFECTS: John P. Fulton
CAMERA: Karl Freund
EDITOR: Harry W. Lieb

Ralph Bellamy *(Mike Miller);* Gloria Stuart *(Ruth Barnes);* Pat O'Brien *(Duke Talbot);* Slim Summerville *(Slim McCune);* Lilian Bond *(Irene Wilkins);* Russell Hopton *(George "Dizzy" Wilkins);* Leslie Fenton [*Tony Dressel (Larry Thomas)*]; Frank Albertson *(Tommy Bogan);* Hans Furberg *(Heinie Kramer);* Tom Carrigan *(Sleepy Collins);* William Daly *(Tex Lane);* David Landau *(Pop the Radio Operator);* Charles de la Montte, Lieutenant Pat Davis *(Passenger Plane Pilots);* Lew Kelly *(Drunken Passenger);* Louise Mackintosh *(Passenger's Wife);* Francis Ford *(Bostonian Passenger);* Beth Milton *(Stewardess);* Frank Beal, James Donlan, Katherine Perry *(Passengers);* Jim Thorpe *(Indian);* Enrico Caruso, Jr., Billy Thorpe, Alene Carroll *(Bits);* Jimmy James, Paul Mantz, Elmer Dyer *(Stunt Pilots);* Ward Bond *(Joe Barnes, the Pilot);* Chief John Big Tree *(Another Indian);* George Irving *(Jack Montgomery, the Official);* Wade Boteler *(Doc Andrews);* Harry Tenbrook *(Mechanic);* Edmund Burns *(Captain Jones).*

LAUGHTER IN HELL
(Universal, 1933) 70 mins.

DIRECTOR: Edward L. Cahn
BASED ON THE NOVEL BY JIM TULLY
SCREENPLAY: Tom Reed
DIALOGUE: Russell Hopton
CAMERA: John Stumar.

Pat O'Brien *(Barney Slaney);* Berton Churchill *(Mike Slaney);* Gloria Stuart *(Lorraine);* Merna Kennedy *(Marybelle Evans);* Tom Conlon *(Barney Slaney as a Boy);* Tom Brown *(Barton);* Lew Kelly *(Mileaway);* Arthur Vinton *(Grover Perkins);* Mickey Bennett *(Grover Perkins as a Boy);* Clarence Muse *(Jackson);* Douglass Dumbrille *(Ed Perkins);* Dick Winslow *(Ed Perkins as a Boy);* Noel Madison *(Brownfield);* Tom Ricketts *(Judge);* William H. Turner *(I. N. Tree).*

DESTINATION UNKNOWN
(Universal, 1933) 65 min

DIRECTOR: Tay Garnett
STORY/SCREENPLAY: Tom Buckingham
SOUND: Gilbert Kurlland
CAMERA: Edward Snyder
EDITOR: Milton Carruth

Pat O'Brien *(Matt Brennan);* Ralph Bellamy *(Stowaway);* Alan Hale *(Lundstrom);* Russell Hopton *(Georgie);* Tom Brown *(Johnny);* Betty Compson *(Ruby Smith);* Noel Madison *(Maxie);* Stanley Fields *(Gattallo);* Rollo Lloyd *(Dr. Fram);* Willard Robertson *(Joe Shano);* Charles Middleton *(Turk);* Richard Alexander *(Alex);* Forrester Harvey *(Ring);* George Regas *(Tauru).*

THE WORLD GONE MAD
(Majestic, 1933) 80 min.
(a.k.a. PUBLIC BE DAMNED)

PRODUCER: Phil Goldstone
DIRECTOR: Christy Cabanne
SCREEN STORY: Edward T. Lowe
ART DIRECTOR: Daniel Hall
SOUND: Dean Daily
CAMERA: Ira Morgan
EDITOR: Otis Garrett

Pat O'Brien *(Andy Terrell);* Evelyn Brent *(Carlotta Lamont);* Neil Hamilton *(Lionel Houston);* Mary Brian *(Diane Cromwell);* Louis Calhern *(Chris Bruno);* J. Carroll Naish *(Ramon Salvadore);* Buster Phelps *(Ralph Henderson);* Richard Tucker *(Graham Gaines);* John St. Polis *(Grover Cromwell);* Geneva Mitchell *(Evelyn Henderson);* Wallis Clark *(District Attorney Avery Henderson);* Max Davidson *(Cohen);* Huntley Gordon *(Osborne);* Joseph Girard *(Nicholas);* Lloyd Ingraham *(Baird);* Inez Courtney *(Susan Bibens).*

BUREAU OF MISSING PERSONS
(Warner Bros., 1933) 75 min.

PRODUCER: Henry Blanke
DIRECTOR: Roy Del Ruth
BASED ON THE BOOK *Missing Men* BY JOHN H. AYERS AND CAROL BIRD
SCREENPLAY: Robert Presnell
ART DIRECTOR: Robert Haas
CAMERA: Barney McGill
EDITOR: James Gibbon

Bette Davis *(Norma Phillips);* Lewis Stone *(Captain Webb);* Pat O'Brien *(Butch Saunders);* Glenda Farrell *(Belle);* Allen Jenkins *(Joe Musik);* Ruth Donnelly *(Pete);* Hugh Herbert *(Slade);* Alan Dinehart *(Therme Roberts);* Marjorie Gateson *(Mrs. Paul);* Tad Alexander *(Caesar Paul);* Noel Francis *(Alice);* Wallis Clark *(Mr. Paul);* Adrian Morris *(Irish Conlin);* Clay Clement *(Kingman);* Henry Kolker *(Mr. Arno).*

BOMBSHELL
(MGM, 1933) 91 min.
(a.k.a. BLONDE BOMBSHELL)

ASSOCIATE PRODUCER: Hunt Stromberg
DIRECTOR: Victor Fleming
BASED ON THE PLAY BY CAROLINE FRANCKE AND MACK CRANE
SCREENPLAY: Jules Furthman, John Lee Mahin
ART DIRECTOR: Merrill Pye
SET DECORATOR: Edwin B. Willis
GOWNS: Adrian
CAMERA: Chester Lyons, Harold G. Rosson
EDITOR: Margaret Booth

Jean Harlow *(Lola Burns);* Lee Tracy *(Space Hanlon);* Frank Morgan *(Pop Burns);* Franchot Tone *(Gifford Middleton);* Pat O'Brien *(Jim Brogan);* Una Merkel *(Miss Mac);* Ted Healy *(Junior Burns);* Ivan Lebedeff *(Marquis di Binelli);* Isabel Jewell *(Junior's Girl);* Louise Beavers *(Loretta);* Leonard Carey *(Winters);* Mary Forbes *(Mrs. Middleton);* C. Aubrey Smith *(Mr. Middleton);* June Brewster *(Alice Cole).*

COLLEGE COACH
(Warner Bros., 1933) 75 min.

DIRECTOR: William A. Wellman
STORY/SCREENPLAY: Niven Busch, Manuel Seff
ART DIRECTOR: Jack Okey
CAMERA: Arthur Todd
EDITOR: Thomas Pratt

Dick Powell *(Phil Sargent);* Ann Dvorak *(Claire Gore);* Pat O'Brien *(Coach Gore);* Arthur Byron *(Dr. Phillip Sargent);* Lyle Talbot *(Buck Weaver);* Hugh Herbert *(J. Marvin Barnett);* Arthur Hohl *(Seymour Young);* Guinn "Big Boy" Williams *(Matthews);* Nat Pendleton *(Petrowski);* Donald Meek *(Spencer Trask);* Berton Churchill *(Otis);* Harry Beresford *(Professor);* John Wayne, Ward Bond *(Bits);* Joe Sawyer *(Holcomb);* Philip Reed *(Westerman).*

I'VE GOT YOUR NUMBER
(Warner Bros., 1934) 68 min.

DIRECTOR: Ray Enright
STORY: William Rankin
SCREENPLAY: Warren Duff, Sidney Sutherland
CAMERA: Arthur Todd
EDITOR: Clarence Kolster

Joan Blondell *(Marie);* Pat O'Brien *(Terry);* Allen Jenkins *(John);* Glenda Farrell *(Bonnie);* Eugene Pallette *(Flood);* Hobart Cavanaugh *(Happy Dooley);* Henry O'Neill *(Schuyler);* Gordon Westcott *(Nicky);* Henry Kolker *(Robert Kirkland);* Charles Wilson *(Welch);* Renee Whitney *(Loretta Kennedy);* Robert Ellis *(Turk);* Tom Costello *(Ed);* Selmer Jackson *(Joe);* Douglas Cosgrove *(Turner);* Wallis Clark *(Madison);* Cliff Saum *(Operator);* Rita LaRoy, Rickey Newell, Lorraine Marshall *(Girls);* Louise Beavers *(Crystal);* Lucille Ford *(Sarah);* Milton Kibbee *(Dispatcher).*

GAMBLING LADY
(Warner Bros., 1934) 66 min.

DIRECTOR: Archie Mayo
STORY: Doris Malloy
SCREENPLAY: Ralph Block, Malloy
ART DIRECTOR: Anton Grot
COSTUMES: Orry-Kelly
CAMERA: George Barnes
EDITOR: Harold McLernon

Barbara Stanwyck *(Lady Lee);* Joel McCrea *(Garry Madison);* Pat O'Brien *(Charlie Lang);* C. Aubrey Smith *(Peter Madison);* Claire Dodd *(Shiela Aiken);* Phillip Reed *(Steve);* Philip Faversham *(Don);* Robert Barrat *(Mike Lee);* Arthur Vinton *(Fallin);* Ferdinand Gottschalk *(Cornelius);* Robert Elliott *(Graves);* Arthur Treacher *(Pryor);* Margaret Morris *(Operator);* Willie Fung *(Ching);* Stanley Mack *(Secretary);* Renee Whitney *(Baby Doll);* Reverend Neal Dodd *(Minister);* Brooks Benedict *(Lou);* Leonard Carey *(Butler);* Frank Thornton *(Man Servant);* Edward Keane *(Duke);* Jay Eaton *(Clerk);* Charles C. Wilson, Guy Usher, James Burke *(Detectives);* Milton Kibbee, Eddie Shubert, Ralph Brooks *(Reporters);* Maurice Brierre *(Croupier);* Albert Conti *(French Lawyer);* Charles Fallen *(Attendant);* Huey White *(Bodyguard);* Laura Treadwell *(Guest);* Willard Robertson *(District Attorney);* Howard Hickman *(Judge);* Isabel Lammal *(French Maid);* Edward Le Saint *(Sheila's Attorney);* Bob Montgomery *(Crooked Gambler);* Louis Natheaux *(Dope).*

20 MILLION SWEETHEARTS
(First National, 1934) 89 min.

DIRECTOR: Ray Enright
STORY: Paul Finder Moss, Jerry Wald
SCREENPLAY: Warren Duff, Harry Sauber
MUSIC DIRECTOR: Leo F. Forbstein
SONGS: Harry Warren and Al Dubin
CAMERA: Sid Hickox
EDITOR: Clarence Kolster

Dick Powell *(Buddy Clayton);* Pat O'Brien *(Rush Blake);* Ginger Rogers *(Peggy Cornell);* Four Mills Brothers, Ted Fio Rito and His Band, The Radio Rogues *(Themselves);* Allen Jenkins *(Pete);* Grant Mitchell *(Chester A. Sharpe);* Joseph Cawthorn *(Herbert Brockman);* Leo F. Forbstein *(Conductor);* Bill Ray *(Announcer);* Marjorie Briggs, Dorothy Hill, Betty Noyes *(Debutantes);* Grace Hayle *(Martha Brockman);* Muzzy Marcellino *(Himself);* Bob Perry *(Cafe Manager);* Nora Cecil *(Lady in Bed);* Charles Sullivan *(Cabby);* Milton Kibbee *(Pete's Announcer);* Charles Lane *(Reporter);* Sam McDaniel *(Deacon the Waiter);* William Davidson *(Woodcliff Inn Manager);* George Humbert *(Headwaiter);* Eddie Kane, Gordon "Bill" Elliott *(Boys in Perry's);* Joan Wheeler *(Marge);* Henry O'Neill *(Lemuel Tappan);* Johnny Arthur *(Secretary).*

HERE COMES THE NAVY
(Warner Bros., 1934) 86 min.

DIRECTOR: Lloyd Bacon
STORY: Ben Markson
SCREENPLAY: Markson, Earl Baldwin
ART DIRECTOR: Esdras Hartley
MUSIC DIRECTOR: Leo F. Forbstein
SONG: Irving Kahal and Sammy Fain
MAKEUP: Perc Westmore
TECHNICAL ADVISOR: Commander Herbert A. Jones
CAMERA: Arthur Edeson
EDITOR: George Amy

James Cagney *(Chesty O'Connor);* Pat O'Brien *(Biff Martin);* Gloria Stuart *(Dorothy Martin);* Frank McHugh *(Droopy);* Dorothy Tree *(Gladys);* Robert Barrat *(Commander Denny);* Willard Robertson *(Lieutenant Commander);* Guinn "Big Boy" Williams *(Floor Manager);* Maude Eburne *(Droopy's Ma);* Martha Merrill, Lorena Layson *(Girls);* Ida Darling *(Aunt);* Henry Otho *(Riveter);* Pauline True *(Hatcheck Girl);* Sam McDaniel *(Porter);* Frank La Rue *(Foreman);* Joseph Crehan *(Recruiting Officer);* James Burtis *(C.P.O.);* Leo White *(Professor);* Niles Welch *(Officer);* Fred "Snowflake" Toone *(Sailor);* Eddie Shubert *(Skipper);* George Irving *(Admiral);* Gordon "Bill" Elliott *(Officer);* Eddie Acuff *(Marine Orderly).*

THE PERSONALITY KID
(Warner Bros., 1934) 67 min.

DIRECTOR: Alan Crosland
BASED ON THE STORY "ONE MAN WOMAN" BY GENE TOWNE AND C. GRAHAM BAKER
SCREENPLAY: F. Hugh Herbert, Erwin Gelsey, David Boehm
CAMERA: William Rees
EDITOR: Terry Morse

Pat O'Brien *(Ritzy McCarty);* Glenda Farrell *(Joan McCarty);* Claire Dodd *(Patricia Merrill);* Henry O'Neill *(Jay Stephens);* Robert Gleckler *(Gavin);* Thomas E. Jackson *(Bill Rankin);* Arthur Vinton *(McPhail);* G. Pat Collins *(Ed);* Clarence Muse *(Shamrock);* Jack Perry *(Sailor White);* Harry Seymour *(Referee);* Mary Russell *(Waitress);* Mushy Callahan *(Biff Sullivan);* Paul Power *(Freddie);* Clay Clement *(Duncan King);* Marvin Shechter *(Kearney);* Phil Regan *(Murray the Sports Writer);* Billy Arnold *(Sam—Sullivan's Manager);* Howard Russell *(Doctor);* Margaret Morris *(Secretary);* Landers Stevens *(Executive);* Jack Kennedy *(Proprietor);* Sailor Vincent *(Spike);* George Cooper *(Tiny);* Bess Flowers *(Nurse);* Howard Hickman *(Doctor);* Al Hill *(Al);* Heinie Conklin *(Drinker);* Renee Whitney *(Party Guest).*

FLIRTATION WALK
(First National, 1934) 97 min.

PRODUCER: Robert Lord
DIRECTOR: Frank Borzage
SCREENPLAY: Delmer Daves, Lou Edelman
ART DIRECTOR: Jack Okey
MUSIC DIRECTOR: Leo F. Forbstein
SONGS: Mort Dixon and Allie Wrubel
CHOREOGRAPHY: Bobby Connolly
COSTUMES: Orry-Kelly
CAMERA: Sol Polito, George Barnes
EDITOR: William Holmes

Dick Powell *(Dick "Canary" Dorcy);* Ruby Keeler *(Kit Fitts);* Pat O'Brien *(Sergeant Scrapper Thornhill);* Ross Alexander *(Oskie);* John Arledge *(Spike);* John Eldredge *(Lieutenant Robert Biddle);* Henry O'Neill *(General Jack Fitts);* Guinn "Big Boy" Williams *(Sleepy);* Frederick Burton *(General Paul Landacre);* John Darrow *(Case);* Glen Boles *(Eight Ball);* University of Southern California and Army Polo Teams *(Polo Players);* Lieutenant Joe Cummins *(Cadet);* Gertrude Keeler *(Dancer);* Colonel Tim Lonergan *(General);* Tyrone Power *(Cadet).*

I SELL ANYTHING
(First National, 1934) 70 min.

DIRECTOR: Robert Florey
STORY: Albert J. Cohen, Robert T. Shannon
SCREENPLAY: Brown Holmes, Sidney Sutherland
CAMERA: Sid Hickox
EDITOR: Terry Morse

Pat O'Brien *("Spot Cash" Cutler);* Ann Dvorak *(Barbara);* Claire Dodd *(Millicent Clark);* Roscoe Karns *(Monk);* Russell Hopton *(Smiley);* Hobart Cavanaugh, Harry Tyler, Gus Shy *(Stooges);* Ferdinand Gottschalk *(Baruche);* Clay Clement *(Van Gruen);* Robert Barrat *(Morgerson);* Leonard Carey *(Pert-*

wee); Dave Calles *(Half-Witted Customer);* Milton Kibbee *(Spectator);* Sherry Hall *(Porter);* Pudgy White *(Taxi Driver);* Eddie Shubert *(Truck Driver);* John Elliott *(Lawyer);* Herman King *(Dutch Man);* Arthur Hoyt *(Pedestrian).*

DEVIL DOGS OF THE AIR

(Warner Bros., 1935) 86 min.

PRODUCER: Lou Edelman
DIRECTOR: Lloyd Bacon
BASED ON THE STORY "AIR DEVILS" BY JOHN MONK SAUNDERS
SCREENPLAY: Malcolm Boylan, Earl Baldwin
ART DIRECTOR: Arthur J. Kooken
MUSIC DIRECTOR: Leo F. Forbstein
ASSISTANT DIRECTOR: Eric Stacey
MAKEUP: Perc Westmore
COSTUMES: Orry-Kelly
TECHNICAL ADVISOR: Major Ralph J. Mitchell
CAMERA: Arthur Edeson
EDITOR: William Clemens

James Cagney *(Tommy O'Toole);* Pat O'Brien *(Lieutenant William Brannigan);* Margaret Lindsay *(Betty Roberts);* Frank McHugh *(Crash Kelly);* Helen Lowell *(Ma Roberts);* John Arledge *(Mac);* Robert Barrat *(Commandant);* Russell Hicks *(Captain);* William B. Davidson *(Adjutant);* Ward Bond *(Senior Instructor);* Samuel S. Hinds *(Fleet Commander);* Harry Seymour, Bill Beggs, Newton House, Ralph Nye *(Officers);* Selmer Jackson *(Medical Officer);* Dennis O'Keefe *(Student);* Gordon "Bill" Elliott *(Instructor);* Don Turner, Dick French, Charles Sherlock *(Other Students);* Carlyle Blackwell, Jr. *(Messenger);* Martha Merrill *(Girl);* Olive Jones *(Mrs. Brown);* Joseph Crehan *(Communications Officer).*

OIL FOR THE LAMPS OF CHINA

(Warner Bros., 1935) 110 min.

PRODUCER: Robert Lord
DIRECTOR: Mervyn LeRoy
BASED ON THE NOVEL BY ALICE TISDALE HOBART
SCREENPLAY: Laird Doyle
CAMERA: Tony Gaudio
EDITOR: William Clemens

Pat O'Brien *(Stephen Chase);* Josephine Hutchinson *(Hester Chase);* Jean Muir *(Alice Wellman);* John Eldredge *(Don Wellman);* Lyle Talbot *(Jim);* Arthur Byron *(Ross);* Henry O'Neill *(Mr. Hartford);* Donald Crisp *(MacCargar);* Tetsu Komai *(Ho);* William B. Davidson *(Swaley);* Ronnie Cosbey *(Bunsy);* Joe Crehan *(Clements);* Christian Rub *(Dr. Jorgen);* Willie Fung *(Kim);* George Meeker *(Kendall);* Edward McWade *(Dan);* Keye Luke *(Young Chinese);* Willard Robertson *(Speaker);* Miki Morita *(Japanese Tailor);* Teru Shimada *(Japanese Proprietor);* Samuel S. Hinds *(George);* Florence Fair *(Miss Cunningham, the Secretary);* Bess Flowers, Lotus Liu *(Secretaries);* Cyril Ring *(Graves);* George Irving *(Bit).*

IN CALIENTE

(First National, 1935) 84 min.

DIRECTOR: Lloyd Bacon
STORY: Ralph Block, Warren Duff
SCREENPLAY: Jerry Wald, Julius J. Epstein
SONGS: Mort Dixon and Allie Wrubel; Al Dubin and Harry Warren
MUSICAL NUMBERS STAGED BY BUSBY BERKELEY
CAMERA: Sol Polito, George Barnes
EDITOR: Jimmy Gibbons

Dolores Del Rio *(Rita Gomez);* Pat O'Brien *(Larry MacArthur);* Leo Carrillo *(Jose Gomez);* Glenda Farrell *(Clara);* Edward Everett Horton *(Harold Brandon);* Phil Regan *(Pat Casey);* Winifred Shaw *(Singer—"Lady in Red");* Dorothy Dare *(Baby Blonde);* Harry Holman *(Biggs);* Herman Bing *(Mexican Florist);* William B. Davidson *(Man);* Luis Alberni *(Magistrate);* George Humbert *(Mexican Photographer);* Soledad Jimenez *(Maid);* Olive Jones *(Singer);* Judy, Anne, Zeke, and Pete Canova, Sally and Tony DeMarco *(Specialty Numbers);* John Hyams *(Bob the Reporter);* Florence Fair *(Miss G.—Larry's Secretary);* James Donlan *(Swanson);* Chris-Pin Martin, C. I. Dafau, Carlos Salazer, L. R. Felix *(Mexican Quartet);* Harry Holman *(Man at Table in "Lady in Red" Number).*

PAGE MISS GLORY

(Warner Bros., 1935) 93 min.

DIRECTOR: Mervyn LeRoy
STORY: Joseph Schrank, Philip Dunning
SCREENPLAY: Delmer Daves, Robert Lord
SONG: Harry Warren and Al Dubin
MUSIC DIRECTOR: Leo F. Forbstein
CAMERA: George Folsey
EDITOR: William Clemens

Marion Davies [*Loretta Dalrymple (Dawn Glory)*]; Dick Powell *(Bingo Nelson);* Pat O'Brien *(Dan Click Wiley);* Mary Astor *(Gladys Russell);* Frank McHugh *(Ed Olson);* Lyle Talbot *(Slattery of The Express);* Patsy Kelly *(Betty);* Allen Jenkins *(Petey);* Barton MacLane *(Blackie);* Berton Churchill *(Mr. Yates, the Assistant Hotel Manager);* Hobart Cavanaugh *(Joe Bonner);* Joseph Cawthorn *(Frieschutz);* Al Shean *(Hamburgher);* Helen Lowell *(Mother);* Lionel Stander *(Nick Papadopolis, the Greek Baggage Clerk);* Mary Treen *(Beauty Operator);* Gavin Gordon *(Metz);* Edward Cooper *(Doorman);* John Quillan, Ernie Alexander *(Bellboys);* Emmett Vogan *(Hotel Clerk);* Claudia Coleman *(Elaine);* Charles Irwin *(Staff Announcer);* Jack Norton, Jack Mulhall, Gordon "Bill" Elliott *(Reporters);* Huntley Gordon *(Radio Official);* Rudy Cameron, Edward Keane *(Advertising Men);* Irving Bacon *(Waiter);* Franklyn Farnum *(Dance Extra);* Edward Hearn *(Detective);* Phil Tead *(Announcer);* Charles R. Moore *(Porter);* Pat West *(Cabby).*

THE IRISH IN US

(Warner Bros., 1935) 84 min.

PRODUCER: Samuel Bischoff
DIRECTOR: Lloyd Bacon
STORY: Frank Orsatti
SCREENPLAY: Earl Baldwin
COSTUMES: Orry-Kelly
ASSISTANT DIRECTOR: Jack Sullivan
ART DIRECTOR: Esdras Hartley
MUSIC DIRECTOR: Leo F. Forbstein
CAMERA: George Barnes
EDITOR: James Gibbons

James Cagney *(Danny O'Hara);* Pat O'Brien *(Pat O'Hara);* Olivia de Havilland *(Lucille Jackson);* Frank McHugh *(Mike O'Hara);* Allen Jenkins *(Car-Barn McCarthy);* Mary Gordon *(Mrs. O'Hara);* J. Farrell MacDonald *(Captain Jackson);* Thomas Jackson *(Doc Mullins);* Harvey Parry *(Joe Delancy);* Mabel Colcord *(Neighbor);* Bess Flowers *(Lady in Ring);* Edward Keane *(Doctor);* Jack McHugh *(Messenger Boy);* Mushy Callahan *(Referee);* Sailor Vincent *(Chick);* Harry Seymour *(Announcer);* Edward Gargan, Huntley Gordon, Emmett Vogan, Will Stanton *(Men);* Lucille Collins *(Girl).*

STARS OVER BROADWAY

(Warner Bros., 1935) 90 min.

PRODUCER: Sam Bischoff
DIRECTOR: William Keighley
STORY: Mildred Cram
SCREENPLAY: Jerry Wald, Julius J. Epstein
SONGS: Al Dubin and Harry Warren; Carson J. Robison
CHOREOGRAPHY: Busby Berkeley, Bobby Connolly
CAMERA: George Barnes
EDITOR: Bert L'Orle

Pat O'Brien *(Al McGillevray);* James Melton *(Jan King);* Jane Froman *(Joan Garrett);* Frank McHugh *(Bugs Cramer);* Marie Wilson *(Molly);* Frank Fay *(Announcer at Amateur Program);* William Ricciardi *(Minotti);* Craig Reynolds *(Announcer);* E. E. Clive *(Butler);* Maurice Black *(Jim Flugel);* Eddy Conrad *(Freddie);* Emmett Vogan *(Archie McNeish);* George Chandler *(Charlie);* Paul Porcasi *(Luigi);* Gordon "Bill" Elliott *(Young Man);* Frank Moran *(Champ);* Ferdinand Munier, Bob Montgomery, Pat West, Larry McGrath, Sam Ash *(Men);* Mr. Marlowe *(Milkman);* Sarah Edwards *(Woman);* Esther Howard *(Amateur Singer);* Moran Family *(Entertainers);* Lillian Worth *(Buxom Singer).*

CEILING ZERO

(First National, 1935) 95 min.

PRODUCER: Harry Joe Brown
DIRECTOR: Howard Hawks
BASED ON THE PLAY BY FRANK WEAD
SCREENPLAY: Wead
ART DIRECTOR: John Hughes
MUSIC DIRECTOR: Leo F. Forbstein
ASSISTANT DIRECTOR: Les Selander
COSTUMES: Orry-Kelly
MAKEUP: Perc Westmore

CAMERA:	Arthur Edeson
EDITOR:	William Holmes

James Cagney *(Dizzy Davis);* Pat O'Brien *(Jake Lee);* June Travis *(Tommy Thomas);* Stuart Erwin *(Texas Clark);* Henry Wadsworth *(Tay Lawson);* Isabel Jewell *(Lou Clark);* Barton MacLane *(Al Stone);* Martha Tibbets [*Mary Lee (Mary Miller)*]; Craig Reynolds *(Joe Allen);* James Bush *(Buzz Gordon);* Robert Light *(Lee Bogan);* Addison Richards *(Fred Adams);* Carlyle Moore, Jr. *(Eddie Payson);* Dick Purcell *(Smiley Johnson);* Gordon "Bill" Elliott *(Transportation Agent);* Pat West *(Baldy Wright);* Edward Gargan *(Doc Wilson);* Garry Owen *(Mike Owens);* Mathilde Comont *(Mama Gini);* Carol Hughes *(Birdie);* Jimmy Aye, Howard Allen, Mike Lally, Harold Miller *(Pilots);* Louise Seidel, Helen Erickson *(Hostesses);* Frank Tomick, Paul Mantz *(Stunt Fliers);* Margaret Perry *(Girl);* Jayne Manners *(Tall Girl);* Jerry Jerome *(Mechanic).*

I MARRIED A DOCTOR

(First National, 1936) 83 min.

PRODUCER:	Harry Joe Brown
DIRECTOR:	Archie Mayo
BASED ON THE NOVEL *Main Street* BY SINCLAIR LEWIS AND THE PLAY BY HARRIET FORD AND HARVEY O'HIGGINS	
ADAPTOR:	Casey Robinson
ART DIRECTOR:	Carl Weyl
MUSIC DIRECTOR:	Leo F. Forbstein
CAMERA:	Byron Haskin
EDITOR:	Owen Marks

Pat O'Brien *(Dr. William P. Kennicott);* Josephine Hutchinson *(Carol "Carrie" Kennicott);* Ross Alexander *(Eric Valborg);* Guy Kibbee *(Sam Clark);* Louise Fazenda *(Bes Sorenson);* Robert Barrat *(Nels Valborg);* Willard Robertson *(Guy Pollock);* Alma Lloyd *(Vern Winters);* Grace Stafford *(Vera Sherwin);* Ray Mayer *(Miles Bjorstam);* Margaret Irving *(Maude Dyer);* Olin Howland *(Dave Dyer);* Hedwiga Reicher *(Bessie Valborg);* Harry Hayden *(Professor George Edwin Mott);* Sam Wren *(Chester Dashaway);* Gaby Fay *(Ella Stowbody);* Frank Rhodes *(Ezra Stowbody);* Edythe Elliott *(Mrs. Clark);* Janet Young *(Dolly Perry);* Thomas Pogue *(Reverend Champ Perry);* Dora Clemant *(Mrs. Jackson Elder);* John T. Murray *(Nat Hicks);* Raymond Brown *(Grocer);* Ralph Remley *(Oleson);* George Hayes *(Agent);* Leo White *(Dance Extra);* Milton Kibbee *(Station Agent).*

PUBLIC ENEMY'S WIFE

(Warner Bros., 1936) 65 min.
(British release title: G-MAN'S WIFE)

DIRECTOR:	Nick Grinde
STORY:	P. J. Wolfson
SCREENPLAY:	Abem Finkel, Harold Buckley
CAMERA:	Erenst Haller
EDITOR:	Thomas Pratt

Pat O'Brien *(Lee Laird);* Margaret Lindsay [*Judith Maroc (Roberts)*]; Robert Armstrong *(Gene Ferguson);* Cesar Romero *(Maroc);* Dick Foran *(Thomas Duncan McKay);* Joseph King *(Wilcox);* Dick Purcell *(Louie);* Addison Richards *(Warden William);* Paul Graetz *(Mr. Schultz);* Selmer Jackson *(Duffield);* Hal K. Dawson *(Daugherty);* Alan Bridge *(Swartzman);* Mary Green, Isabel Withers *(Operators);* Kathrin Clare Ward *(Matron);* Bernice Pilot *(Miranda the Black Maid);* Don Downen *(Bellhop);* Ted Oliver, Jack Mower, Ed Hart, Emmett Vogan *(G-Men);* Ralph Dunn *(Cop);* Harry Harvey, William Wayne, Bert Kennedy *(Mail Clerks);* Harry Hayden *(Justice of the Peace);* Stuart Holmes *(Telephone Repair Chief);* Milton Kibbee *(Charlie the Repair Man).*

CHINA CLIPPER

(First National, 1936) 85 min.

SUPERVISOR:	Sam Bischoff
ASSOCIATE PRODUCER:	Louis F. Edelman
DIRECTOR:	Ray Enright
STORY/SCREENPLAY:	Frank Wead
ART DIRECTOR:	Max Parker
TECHNICAL ADVISOR:	William I. Van Dusen
DIALOGUE DIRECTOR:	Gene Lewis
ASSISTANT DIRECTOR:	Lee Katz
GOWNS:	Orry-Kelly
MUSIC:	Bernhard Kaun, W. Franke Harling
SOUND:	Everett A. Brown
SPECIAL EFFECTS:	Fred Jackman, Willard Van Enger, H. F. Koenekamp
AERIAL CAMERA:	Elmer G. Dyer, Keenekamp
CAMERA:	Arthur Edeson
EDITOR:	Owen Marks

Pat O'Brien *(Dave Logan);* Beverly Roberts *(Jean Logan);* Ross Alexander *(Tom Collins);* Humphrey Bogart *("Hap" Stuart);* Marie Wilson *(Sunny Avery);* Henry B. Walthall *(Dad Brunn);* Joseph Crehan *(Horn);* Joseph King *(Pierson);* Ruth Robinson *(Mama Brunn);* Carlyle Moore, Jr. *(Clipper Radio Operator);* Wayne Morris *(Clipper Engineer);* Dennis Moore, Lyle Moraine *(Clipper Co-Pilots);* Alexander Cross *(Bill Andrews);* Shirley Lloyd *(Horn's Secretary);* Kenneth Harlan *(Inspector);* Pierre Watkin *(Secretary of State);* Marjorie Weaver, Anne Nagel *(Secretaries);* Emmett Vogan, Hal K. Dawson, Edwin Stanley, Harland Tucker, John Marston *(Airplane Designers);* Frank Faylen, Joseph Cunningham *(Weathermen);* Walter Miller *(Instructor);* Milton Kibbee *(Mechanic);* Irving Bacon *(Sam the Janitor);* Gordon "Bill" Elliott, William Wright *(Pilots);* Milburn Stone, Owen King *(Radio Operators);* Ralph Dunn *(Plane Announcer at Miami Airport);* Philip Morris *(Plane Announcer at Alameda Airport);* Demetrius Emanuel *(Cuban Radio Announcer);* John Spacey *(Australian Broadcaster).*

THE GREAT O'MALLEY

(Warner Bros., 1937) 71 min.

ASSOCIATE PRODUCER:	Harry Joe Brown
DIRECTOR:	William Dieterle
BASED ON THE STORY "THE MAKING OF O'MALLEY" BY GERALD BEAUMONT	
SCREENPLAY:	Milton Krims, Tom Reed
MUSIC:	Heinz Roemheld
MUSIC DIRECTOR:	Leo F. Forbstein
GOWNS:	Milo Anderson
ART DIRECTOR:	Hugh Reticker
ASSISTANT DIRECTOR:	Frank Shaw
DIALOGUE DIRECTOR:	Irving Rapper
SOUND:	Francis J. Scheid
SPECIAL EFFECTS:	James Gibbons, Fred Jackman, Jr., H. F. Koenekamp
CAMERA:	Ernest Haller
EDITOR:	Warren Low

Pat O'Brien *(James Aloysius O'Malley);* Sybil Jason *(Barbara Phillips);* Humphrey Bogart *(John Phillips);* Ann Sheridan *(Judy Nolan);* Frieda Inescort *(Mrs. Phillips);* Donald Crisp *(Captain Cromwell);* Henry O'Neill *(Defense Attorney);* Craig Reynolds *(Motorist);* Hobart Cavanaugh *(Pinky Holden);* Gordon Hart *(Doctor);* Mary Gordon *(Mrs. O'Malley);* Mabel Colcord *(Mrs. Flaherty);* Frank Sheridan *(Father Patrick);* Lillian Harmer *(Miss Taylor);* Delmar Watson *(Tubby);* Frank Reicher *(Dr. Larson);* Bob Perry *(Man Getting Shine);* Charles Wilson *(Cop);* Max Wagner *(Bus Driver);* Jack Mower, Arthur Millett *(Detectives).*

SLIM

(Warner Bros., 1937) 80 min.

PRODUCER:	Hal B. Wallis
ASSOCIATE PRODUCER:	Sam Bischoff
DIRECTOR:	Ray Enright
BASED ON THE NOVEL BY WILLIAM WISTER HAINES	
SCREENPLAY:	Haines
DIALOGUE DIRECTOR:	Gene Lewis
ART DIRECTOR:	Ted Smith
MUSIC DIRECTOR:	Leo F. Forbstein
SPECIAL CAMERA EFFECTS:	Byron Haskin
CAMERA:	Sid Hickox
EDITOR:	Owen Marks

Pat O'Brien *(Red Blayd);* Henry Fonda *(Slim);* Margaret Lindsay *(Cally);* Stuart Erwin *(Stumpy);* J. Farrell MacDonald *(Pop);* Dick Purcell *(Tom);* Joe Sawyer *(Wilcox);* John Litel *(Wyatt Ranstead);* Harland Tucker *(Lafe Garretson);* Carlyle Moore, Jr. *(Al);* Henry Otho *(Mitch);* Max Wagner *(Griff);* Craig Reynolds, Alonzo Price *(Gamblers);* Jane Wyman *(Stumpy's Girl);* Joseph King *(Steve);* James Robbins *(Joe Braithewaite);* Dick Wessel *(Ed);* Ben Hendricks *(Kelly);* Maidel Turner *(Mrs. Johnson);* Walter Miller *(Sam).*

SAN QUENTIN

(Warner Bros., 1937) 70 min.

ASSOCIATE PRODUCER:	Samuel Bischoff
DIRECTOR:	Lloyd Bacon
STORY:	Robert Tasker, John Bright
SCREENPLAY:	Peter Milne, Humphrey Cobb

Music: Heinz Roemheld, Charles Maxwell, David Raksin
Orchestrators: Joseph Nussbaum, Ray Heindorf
Song: Harry Warren and Al Dubin
Assistant Director: Dick Mayberry
Art Director: Esdras Hartley
Gowns: Howard Shoup
Technical Advisor: Doc Stone
Sound: Everett A. Brown
Special Effects: James Gibbons, H. F. Koenekamp
Camera: Sid Hickox
Editor: William Holmes

Pat O'Brien *(Captain Stephen Jameson);* Humphrey Bogart *(Red Kennedy);* Ann Sheridan *(May Kennedy);* Barton MacLane *(Lieutenant Druggins);* Joe Sawyer *("Sailor Boy" Harrison);* James Robbins *(Mickey Callahan);* Veda Ann Borg *(Helen);* Joseph King *(Warden Taylor);* Gordon Oliver *(Lieutenant);* Emmett Vogan *(Captain);* Garry Owen *(Dopey);* Marc Lawrence *(Venetti);* Max Wagner *(Prison Runner);* William Pawley, George Lloyd, Frank Faylen, Al Hill *(Convicts);* Raymond Hatton *(Pawnbroker);* Hal Neiman *(Convict #38216);* William Williams *(Convict Conklin);* Glen Cavender *(Convict Hastings);* Lane Chandler *(Guard);* Dennis Moore *(Convict Simpson);* Ralph Dunn *(Head Guard);* Ralph Byrd *(Cop on Phone);* John Ince *(Old Convict);* Bob Wilke *(Young Convict in Riot);* Frank Fanning *(Cop in Radio Car);* Jack Mower, Claire White *(Couple in Car).*

BACK IN CIRCULATION
(Warner Bros., 1937) 82 min.

Producer: Hal B. Wallis
Associate Producer: Sam Bischoff
Director: Ray Enright
Story: Adela Rogers St. John
Screenplay: Warren Duff
Art Director: Hugh Reticker
Music Director: Leo F. Forbstein
Dialogue Director: Jo Graham
Camera: Arthur Todd
Editor: Clarence Kolster

Pat O'Brien *(Bill Morgan);* Joan Blondell *(Timothea Blake);* Margaret Lindsay *(Arlene Wade);* John Litel *(Dr. Forde);* Eddie Acuff *(Murphy);* Regis Toomey *(Buck);* George E. Stone *(I. R. Daniels);* Craig Reynolds *(Si Rothwell);* Ben Welden *(Sam Sherman);* Walter Byron *(Carleton Whitney);* Granville Bates *(Dr. Evans);* Herbert Rawlinson *(Stephen A. Saunders);* Raymond Brown *(Bottsford);* Anderson Lawler *(Dutch Jason);* Frank Faylen *(James Maxwell);* Bill Hopper *(Pete Edington);* Milton Kibbee *(Pink Thomas);* Edward Price *(Sid Roark);* Howard Hickman *(Judge);* Veda Ann Borg *(Gertrude);* Ellen Clancy [*Janet Shaw (Alice)*]; Willard Parker *(Ben);* John Harron *(George);* Bernice Pilot *(Dorinda);* Gordon Hart *(Mr. Hanley);* Spencer Charters *(Sheriff);* Loia Cheaney *(Enid);* Robert Darrell *(Assistant Dispatcher);* Emmett Vogan *(Chief Dispatcher);* Eddy Chandler *(Chief Operator);* Tom Brower *(Foreman);* Spec O'Donnell, Jack Bart *(Newsboys);* Stuart Holmes *(Barman);* Patsy "Babe" Kane *(Switchboard Operator);* Edward Gargon *(Cop).*

SUBMARINE D-1
(Warner Bros., 1937) 98 min.

Director: Lloyd Bacon
Story: Frank Wead
Screenplay: Wead, Warren Duff, Lawrence Kimble
Music Director: Leo F. Forbstein
Camera: Arthur Edeson
Editor: William Holmes

Pat O'Brien *(Butch Rogers);* George Brent *(Lieutenant Commander Matthews);* Wayne Morris *(Sock McGillis);* Doris Weston *(Ann Callam);* Frank McHugh *(Lucky);* Henry O'Neill *(Admiral Thomas);* Dennie Moore *(Arabella);* Veda Ann Borg *(Dolly);* Regis Toomey *(Tom Callam);* John Ridgely *(Lieutenant Junior Grade);* Owen King *(Lieutenant Senior Grade);* Wally Maher *(Listener);* Jerry Fletcher *(Lieutenant Mason);* Dick Wessel, Ralph Dunn, Jeffrey Sayre, Don DeFore, Dick French, Allan Kenward, Sol Gorss, Don Turner, John Shea, Mike Lally, Billy Vincent, Eric Pettit, Gordon Clifford *(Sailors);* Don Briggs *(Instructor);* Eddie Fetherston *(Bluejacket);* Pat Flaherty *(Disagreeable Sailor);* Walter Miller *(Salvage Officer);* Lee Phelps *(Marine Orderly);* John Elliott, Jim Farley *(Fathers);* Allan Cavan *(Skipper);* Walter Clyde *(Orderly);* Loia Cheaney, Fern Barry *(Wives).*

WOMEN ARE LIKE THAT
(Warner Bros., 1938) 78 min.

Director: Stanley Logan
Story: Albert Z. Carr
Adaptor: Horace Jackson
Gowns: Orry-Kelly
Music Director: Leo F. Forbstein
Art Director: Max Parker
Sound: Stanley Jones
Camera: Sid Hickox
Editor: Thomas Richards

Kay Francis *(Claire Landin);* Pat O'Brien *(Bill Landin);* Ralph Forbes *(Martin Brush);* Melville Cooper *(Mainwaring);* Thurston Hall *(Claudius King);* Grant Mitchell *(Mr. Snell);* Gordon Oliver *(Howard Johns);* John Eldredge *(Charles Braden);* Herbert Rawlinson *(Avery Flickner);* Hugh O'Connell *(George Dunlap);* Georgia Caine *(Mrs. Amelia Brush);* Joyce Compton *(Miss Hall);* Sarah Edwards *(Mrs. Snell);* Josephine Whittell *(Miss Douglas);* Loia Cheaney *(Miss Perkins);* Edward Broadley *(Holliwell);* Sam McDaniel *(Porter).*

THE COWBOY FROM BROOKLYN
(Warner Bros., 1938) 77 min.

Producer: Hal B. Wallis
Associate Producer: Lou Edelman
Director: Lloyd Bacon
Based on the play *Howdy, Stranger* by Robert Sloan and Louis Peletier, Jr.
Screenplay: Earl Baldwin
Art Director: Esdras Hartley
Music Director: Leo F. Forbstein
Songs: Richard Whiting, Johnny Mercer, and Harry Warren
Camera: Arthur Edeson
Editor: James Gibbons

Dick Powell *(Elly Jordan);* Pat O'Brien *(Roy Chadwick);* Priscilla Lane *(Jane Hardy);* Dick Foran *(Sam Thorne);* Ann Sheridan *(Maxine Chadwick);* Johnnie Davis *(Jeff Hardy);* Ronald Reagan *(Pat Dunn);* Emma Dunn *(Ma Hardy);* Granville Bates *(Pop Hardy);* James Stephenson *(Professor Landis);* Hobart Cavanaugh *(Mr. Jordan);* Elisabeth Risdon *(Mrs. Jordan);* Dennie Moore *(Abby Pitts);* Rosella Towne *(Panthea);* May Boley *(Mrs. Kirkenheim);* Harry Barris *(Louie);* Candy Candido *(Spec);* Donald Briggs (Star *Reporter*); Jeffrey Lynn (Chronicle *Reporter*); John Ridgely (Beacon *Reporter);* William B. Davidson *(Mr. Alvey);* Mary Field *(Myrtle Semple);* Monte Vandergrift, Eddy Chandler *(Brakemen);* Cliff Saum *(Conductor);* Sam Hayes *(News Commentator);* Jack Wise, Eddie Graham *(Reporters);* Dorothy Vaughan *(Fat Woman);* Jack Moore *(Timekeeper);* Ben Hendricks *(Judge);* Emmett Vogan *(Loudspeaker Announcer).*

BOY MEETS GIRL
(Warner Bros., 1938) 80 min.

Producer: George Abbott
Director: Lloyd Bacon
Based on the play by Bella and Samuel Spewack
Screenplay: The Spewacks
Music Director: Leo F. Forbstein
Song: Jack Scholl and M. K. Jerome
Art Director: Esdras Hartley
Costumes: Milo Anderson
Makeup: Perc Westmore
Sound: Dolph Thomas
Camera: Sol Polito
Editor: William Holmes

James Cagney *(Robert Law);* Pat O'Brien *(J. Carlyle Benson);* Marie Wilson *(Susie);* Ralph Bellamy *(E. Elliott Friday);* Dick Foran *(Larry Toms);* Frank McHugh *(Rosetti);* Bruce Lester *(Rodney Bevan);* Penny Singleton *(Peggy);* Dennie Moore *(Miss Cruz);* Ronald Reagan *(Announcer);* James Stephenson *(Major Thompson);* Bert Hanlon *(Green);* Harry Seymour *(Slade);* Pierre Watkin *(B. K.);* John Ridgely *(Cutter);* George Hickman *(Office Boy);* Carole Landis *(Commissary Cashier);* Curt Bois *(Dance Director);* Dorothy Vaughan, Jan Holm, Rosella Towne, Loia Cheaney *(Nurses);* Paul Clark *(Happy);* Peggy Moran *(New York Operator);* Nanette Lafayette *(Paris Operator);* Janet Shaw *(Los Angeles Operator).*

GARDEN OF THE MOON
(Warner Bros., 1938) 94 min.

Director: Busby Berkeley
Story: H. Bedford-Jones, Barton Browne

SCREENPLAY: Jerry Wald, Richard Macauley
SONGS: Johnny Mercer, Al Dubin, and Harry Warren; V. Rose, Larry Stock, and J. Cavanaugh
MUSIC DIRECTOR: Leo F. Forbstein
CAMERA: Tony Gaudio
EDITOR: George Amy

Pat O'Brien *(John Quinn);* John Payne *(Don Vincente);* Margaret Lindsay *(Toni Blake);* Jimmy Fidler *(Himself);* Johnnie Davis *("Slappy" Harris);* Melville Cooper *(Maurice);* Isabel Jeans *(Mrs. Lornay);* Mabel Todd *(Mary Stanton);* Penny Singleton *(Miss Calder);* Dick Purcell *(Ric Fulton);* Curt Bois *(Maharajah of Sind);* Ray Mayer, Jerry Colonna, Joe Venuti *(Band Members);* Granville Bates *(Angus MacGillicuddy);* Edward McWade *(Duncan MacGillicuddy);* Larry Williams *(Trent);* Bob Sherwood *(Fidler's Announcer);* Nat Carr *(Joe);* Jack Richardson, Jack Mower *(Waiters);* Rosella Towne *(Secretary);* Harry Seymour *(Sammy);* Don DeFore *(Buck Delaney the Cowboy);* Mira McKinney *(Woman);* John Ridgely *(Control Man);* John Heistand *(Announcer);* Selmer Jackson *(Doctor);* Eddie Marr *(Thug);* Sonny Chorre *(Leaping Dear the Indian).*

ANGELS WITH DIRTY FACES
(Warner Bros., 1938) 97 min.

PRODUCER: Sam Bischoff
DIRECTOR: Michael Curtiz
STORY: Rowland Brown
SCREENPLAY: John Wexley, Warren Duff
ART DIRECTOR: Robert Haas
ASSISTANT DIRECTOR: Sherry Shourds
TECHNICAL ADVISOR: Father J. J. Devlin
MUSIC: Max Steiner
ORCHESTRATOR: Hugo Friedhofer
SONG: Fred Fisher and Maurice Spitalny
COSTUMES: Orry-Kelly
DIALOGUE DIRECTOR: Jo Graham
MAKEUP: Perc Westmore
SOUND: Everett A. Brown
CAMERA: Sol Polito
EDITOR: Owen Marks

James Cagney *(Rocky Sullivan);* Pat O'Brien *(Father Jerry Connelly);* Humphrey Bogart *(James Frazier);* Ann Sheridan *(Laury Ferguson);* George Bancroft *(Mac Keefer);* Billy Halop *(Soapy);* Bobby Jordan *(Swing);* Leo Gorcey *(Bim);* Bernard Punsley *(Hunky);* Gabriel Dell *(Patsy);* Huntz Hall *(Crab);* Frankie Burke *(Rocky as a Boy);* William Tracy *(Jerry as a Boy);* Marilyn Knowlden *(Laury as a Girl);* Joe Downing *(Steve);* Adrian Morris *(Blackie);* Oscar O'Shea *(Guard Kennedy);* Edward Pawley *(Guard Edwards);* William Pawley *(Bugs the Gunman);* Charles Sullivan, Theodore Rand *(Gunmen);* John Hamilton *(Police Captain);* Earl Dwire *(Priest);* The St. Brendan's Church Choir *(Themselves);* William Worthington *(Warden);* James Farley *(Railroad Yard Watchman);* Pat O'Malley, Jack C. Smith *(Railroad Guards);* Roger McGee, Vince Lombardi, Sonny Bupp *(Boys);* Chuck Stubbs *(Red);* Eddie Syracuse *(Maggione Boy);* George Sorel *(Headwaiter);* Harry Hayden *(Pharmacist);* Dick Rich, Steven Darrell, Joe Devlin *(Gangsters);* Donald Kerr, Jack Goodrich, Al Lloyd, Jeffrey Sayre, Charles Marsh, Alexander Lockwood, Earl Gunn, Carlyle Moore, Jr. *(Reporters);* Vera Lewis *(Soapy's Mother);* Frank Coghlan, Jr., David Durand *(Boys in Poolroom);* Mary Gordon *(Mrs. Patrick McGee);* Charles Trowbridge *(Norton J. White, the Press Editor);* William Crowell *(Whimpering Convict);* Poppy Wilde *(Girl at Gaming Table);* Jack Perrin *(Guard in Death Row).*

OFF THE RECORD
(Warner Bros., 1939) 62 min.

DIRECTOR: James Flood
STORY: Saul Elkins, Sally Sandlin
SCREENPLAY: Niven Busch, Lawrence Kimble, Earl Baldwin
CAMERA: Charles Rosher
EDITOR: Thomas Richards

Pat O'Brien *(Thomas "Breezy" Elliott);* Joan Blondell *(Jane Morgan);* Bobby Jordan *(Mickey Fallon);* Alan Baxter *(Joe Fallon);* William Davidson *(Scotty);* Morgan Conway *(Lou Baronette);* Clay Clement *(Jaeggars);* Selmer Jackson *(Detective Mendall);* Addison Richards *(Brand);* Pierre Watkin *(Barton);* Joe King *(Brown);* Douglas Wood *(J. W.);* Armand Kaliz *(Chatteau);* Sarah Padden *(Mrs. Fallon);* Howard Hickman *(Doctor);* Mary Gordon *(Mrs. Finnegan);* Lottie Williams *(Woman);* Tommy Bupp *(Boy);* Frank Coghlan, Jr. *(Copyboy);* Dick Rich, Galan Galt *(Railroad Cops);* Barbara Pepper *(Flossie, the Telephone Operator);* Isabel Withers, Betty Mack, Maris Wrixon, Lia Rhodas, Fern Barry, Caroline Clare, Alice Connors *(Telephone Operators);* Pat Flaherty *(Bartender).*

THE KID FROM KOKOMO
(Warner Bros., 1939) 95 min.

DIRECTOR: Lewis Seiler
STORY: Dalton Trumbo
SCREENPLAY: Jerry Wald, Richard Macaulay
CAMERA: Sid Hickox
EDITOR: Jack Killifer

Pat O'Brien *(Bill Murphy);* Wayne Morris *(Homer Baston);* Joan Blondell *(Doris Harvey);* Jane Wyman *(Miss Bronson);* May Robson *(Ma "Maggie" Martin);* Maxie Rosenbloom *(Curly Bender);* Ed Brophy *(Eddie Black);* Stanley Fields *("Muscles");* Sidney Toler *(Judge Bronson);* Winifred Harris *(Mrs. Bronson);* Morgan Conway *(Louie);* John Ridgely *(Sam);* Frank Mayo *(Durb);* Ward Bond *(Riewicke);* Clem Bevans *(Jim);* Olin Howland *(Stan);* Paul Burst, Tom Wilson, Frank Hagney, Bob Perry *(Old Men);* Herbert Evans *(Bronson's Butler);* Loia Cheaney *(Bronson's Maid);* Robert Homans *(Old Cop);* Ned Crawford *(Young Cop);* Emmett Vogan *(Fight Announcer).*

INDIANAPOLIS SPEEDWAY
(Warner Bros., 1939) 85 min.
(British release title: DEVIL ON WHEELS)

ASSOCIATE PRODUCER: Max Seigel
DIRECTOR: Lloyd Bacon
ORIGINAL SCREEN IDEA: Howard and William Hawks
SCREENPLAY: Sig Herzig, Wally Klein
CAMERA: Sid Hickox
EDITOR: William Holmes

Pat O'Brien *(Joe Greer);* John Payne *(Eddie Greer);* Ann Sheridan *(Frankie Merrick);* Gale Page *(Lee Mason);* Frank McHugh *(Spud Connors);* Grace Stafford *(Mrs. Martha Connors);* Granville Bates *(Mr. Greer);* Regis Toomey *(Wilbur Shaw);* John Ridgely *(Ted Horn);* John Harron *(Red);* William Davidson *(Duncan Martin);* Ed McWade *(Tom Dugan);* Irving Bacon *(Fred Haskill);* Tommy Bupp *(Haskill's Son);* Robert Middlemass *(Edward Hart);* Charles Halton *(Mayor);* Sam Hayes, John Conte, Wendell Niles, Reid Kilpatrick *(Announcers);* Patsy O'Byrne *(Vinegary Female);* Creighton Hale *(Official);* Ed Parker *(Man);* Evelyn Mulhall *(Mrs. Martin);* George Renavent *(Headwaiter);* Billy Wayne *(Stubby);* Monroe Lee *(Baby).*

THE NIGHT OF NIGHTS
(Paramount, 1939) 86 min.

PRODUCER: George Arthur
DIRECTOR: Lewis Milestone
SCREENPLAY: Donald Ogden Stewart
CAMERA: Leo Tover
EDITOR: Doane Harrison

Pat O'Brien *(Dan O'Farrell);* Olympe Bradna *(Marie-Alyce O'Farrell/Alyce Martelle);* Roland Young *(Barry Keith-Trimble);* Reginald Gardiner *(J. Neville Prime);* George E. Stone *(Sammy Kane);* Murray Alper *(Muggins the Chauffeur);* Frank Shannon *(Frank, the Bartender);* Doodles Weaver *(Flower Delivery Man);* Russ Powell *(Pop the Doorman);* D'Arcy Corrigan, Pat O'Malley *(Actors);* Wyndham Standing *(Naval Commander);* Charles Miller *(Wilton);* Frank Melton *(Newcomb the Author);* Aileen Pringle *(Perfume/Dress Saleslady);* Oscar O'Shea *(Mr. Conway);* Theodor von Eltz *(John—Man with Silk Hat);* Laura Treadwell *(Abigail Keith-Trimble);* Mary Gordon *(Pencil Woman);* Richard Denning *(Call Boy);* Larry Steers *(Wellwisher);* Ethan Laidlaw *(Roustabout in Play).*

SLIGHTLY HONORABLE
(United Artists, 1939) 85 min.

EXECUTIVE PRODUCER: Walter Wanger
PRODUCER/DIRECTOR: Tay Garnett
BASED ON THE STORY SEND ANOTHER COFFIN BY E. G. PRESNELL
SCREENPLAY: John Hunter, Lay, Robert Allman, Ken Englund

ART DIRECTOR: Alexander Golitzen
MUSIC: Werner Janssen
SONG: George R. Brown and Jule Styne
CAMERA: Merritt Gerstad
EDITOR: Otho Lovering

Pat O'Brien *(John Webb);* Broderick Crawford *(Russell Sampson);* Edward Arnold *(Vincent Cushing);* Ruth Terry *(Ann Seymour);* Bernard Nedell *(Pete Godena);* Alan Dinehart *(District Attorney Joyce);* Claire Dodd *(Alma Brehmer);* Douglass Dumbrille *(George Taylor);* John Sheehan *(Mike Deley);* Addison Richards *(Inspector Melvyn Fromm);* Cliff Clark *(Captain Graves);* Eve Arden *(Miss Ater);* Phyllis Brooks *(Serilla Cushing);* Ernest Truex *(P. Hemingway Collins);* Douglas Fowley *(Charles Madder);* Janet Beecher *(Mrs. Cushing);* Evelyn Keyes *(Miss Vlissenger);* Willie Best *(Art the Elevator Operator);* Eddy Chandler *(O'Leary, the Cop);* Bud Jamison *(Humboldt the Cop);* Robert Middlemass *(Senator Barry);* Frank Dae *(President of Senate);* George Magrill, Tay Garnett *(Reporters);* Charles K. French *(Pallbearer);* Art Baker *(Radio Announcer);* Howard Hickman *(Senator Sam Scott);* Wheaton Chambers *(Guest);* Babe Kane *(Switchboard Operator);* Jack Greene, Dick Rush *(Detectives);* Vic Potel *(Proprietor);* Zack Williams *(Black Preacher).*

THE FIGHTING 69TH
(Warner Bros., 1940) 89 min.

EXECUTIVE PRODUCER: Jack L. Warner
PRODUCER: Hal B. Wallis
DIRECTOR: William Keighley
SCREENPLAY: Norman Reilly Raine, Fred Niblo, Jr., Dean Franklin
ART DIRECTOR: Ted Smith
ASSISTANT DIRECTOR: Frank Heath
TECHNICAL ADVISORS: Captain John T. Prout, Mark White
MUSIC: Adolph Deutsch
ORCHESTRATOR: Hugo Friedhofer
MUSIC DIRECTOR: Leo F. Forbstein
MAKEUP: Perc Westmore
SOUND: Charles Lang
SPECIAL EFFECTS: Byron Haskin, Rex Wimpy
CAMERA: Tony Gaudio
EDITOR: Owen Marks

James Cagney *(Jerry Plunkett);* Pat O'Brien *(Father Duffy);* George Brent *(Wild Bill Donovan);* Jeffrey Lynn *(Joyce Kilmer);* Alan Hale *(Sergeant Big Mike Wynn);* Frank McHugh *("Crepe Hanger" Burke);* Dennis Morgan *(Lieutenant Ames);* Dick Foran *(Lieutenant Long John Wynn);* William Lundigan *(Timmy Wynn);* Guinn "Big Boy" Williams *(Paddy Dolan);* Henry O'Neill *(Colonel);* John Litel *(Captain Mangan);* Sammy Cohen *(Mike Murphy);* Harvey Stephens *(Major Anderson);* George Reeves *(Jack O'Keefe);* Tom Dugan *(Private McManus);* Bill Hopper *(Private Turner);* Herbert Anderson *(Casey);* Frank Wilcox *(Lieutenant Norman);* J. Anthony Hughes *(Healey);* Frank Mayo *(Captain Bootz);* George Kilgen *(Ryan);* John Harron *(Carroll);* Richard Clayton *(Tierney);* Edward Dew *(Regan);* Joseph Crehan *(Doctor);* James Flavin *(Supply Sergeant);* Frank Coghlan, Jr. *(Jimmy);* George O'Hanlon *(Eddie);* Edgar Edwards *(Engineering Officer);* Ralph Dunn *(Medical Captain);* Jacques Lory *(Waiter);* Jack Boyle, Jr. *(Chuck).*

CASTLE ON THE HUDSON
(Warner Bros., 1940) 77 min.
(British release title: YEARS WITHOUT DAYS)

ASSOCIATE PRODUCER: Samuel Bischoff
DIRECTOR: Anatole Litvak
BASED ON THE BOOK *20,000 Years in Sing Sing* BY WARDEN LEWIS E. LAWES
SCREENPLAY: Seton I. Miller, Brown Holmes, Courteney Terrett
CAMERA: Arthur Edeson
EDITOR: Thomas Richards

John Garfield *(Tommy Gordon);* Ann Sheridan *(Kay Manners);* Pat O'Brien *(Warden Walter Long);* Burgess Meredith *(Steven Rockford);* Jerome Cowan *(Ed Crowley);* Henry O'Neill *(District Attorney);* Guinn "Big Boy" Williams *(Mike Cagle);* John Litel *(Prison Chaplain);* Edward Pawley *(Black Jack);* Grant Mitchell *(Dr. Ames);* Margot Stevenson *(Ann Rockford);* Willard Robertson *(Ragan);* Robert Homans *(Clyde Burton);* Nedda Harrigan *(Mrs. Long);* Wade Boteler *(Mac, the Principal Keeper);* Billy Wayne *(Pete);* Joseph Downing, Sol Gorss *(Gangsters);* Barbara Pepper *(Goldie);* Robert Strange *(Joe Harris);* Charles Sherlock, Mike Lally, Jack Mower, Frank Mayo, Pat O'Malley, Walter Miller *(Guards);* Pat Flaherty *(Stretcher Attendant);* Ed Kane *(Club Manager);* Claude Wisberg, Michael Conroy *(Newsboys);* Frank Faylen *(Guard Who Is Slugged);* Nat Carr, William Telaank, Bill Hopper *(Reporters);* Lee Phelps *(Guard in Visitors' Room);* James Flavin *(Guard on Death Row).*

'TIL WE MEET AGAIN
(Warner Bros., 1940) 99 min.

PRODUCERS: Jack L. Warner, Hal B. Wallis
ASSOCIATE PRODUCER: David Lewis
DIRECTOR: Edmund Goulding
STORY: Robert Lord
SCREENPLAY: Warren Duff
GOWNS: Orry-Kelly
ORCHESTRATOR: Ray Heindorf
MUSIC DIRECTOR: Leo F. Forbstein
SOUND: E. A. Brown
SPECIAL EFFECTS: Byron Hasken
CAMERA: Tony Gaudio
EDITOR: Ralph Dawson

Merle Oberon *(Joan Ames);* George Brent *(Dan Hardesty);* Pat O'Brien *(Steve Burke);* Geraldine Fitzgerald *(Bonnie Coburn);* Binnie Barnes *(Countess de Vaubert);* Frank McHugh *(Achilles Peddicord);* Eric Blore *(Sir Harold Landamuir);* George Reeves *(Jimmy Coburn);* Henry O'Neill *(Dr. Cameron);* Frank Wilcox *(Assistant Purser);* Doris Lloyd *(Louise the Maid);* John Ridgely *(Junior Officer);* Marjorie Gateson *(Mrs. Hestor);* Regis Toomey *(Freddy);* William Halligan *(Barman);* Victor Kilian *(McGillis);* Wade Boteler *(Stoddard);* Charles Sherlock *(Master-at-Arms);* Frank Orth *(Bartender);* Maris Wrixon, Jane Gilbert, Mary Anderson *(Girls);* Frank Mayo, William Hopper *(Men);* Jeffrey Sayre, Jack Mower *(Stewards);* Lynn Merrick *(Daughter of Fussy Woman);* Grace Hayle *(Fussy Woman Passenger);* William Gould *(Chief of Police);* Robert Elliott, Edwin Parker *(Detectives);* Walter Miller *(American Bartender);* Frank Puglia, George Regas *(Mexican Bartenders).*

TORRID ZONE
(Warner Bros., 1940) 88 min.

PRODUCER: Mark Hellinger
DIRECTOR: William Keighley
SCREENPLAY: Richard Macaulay, Jerry Wald
ART DIRECTOR: Ted Smith
SET DECORATOR: Edward Thorne
MUSIC: Adolph Deutsch
MUSIC DIRECTOR: Leo F. Forbstein
SONG: M. K. Jerome and Jack Scholl
COSTUMES: Howard Shoup
TECHNICAL ADVISOR: John Mari
MAKEUP: Perc Westmore
SOUND: Oliver S. Garretson
SPECIAL EFFECTS: Byron Haskin, H. F. Koenekamp
CAMERA: James Wong Howe
EDITOR: Jack Killifer

James Cagney *(Nick Butler);* Pat O'Brien *(Steve Case);* Ann Sheridan *(Lee Donley);* Andy Devine *(Wally Davis);* Helen Vinson *(Gloria Anderson);* George Tobias *(Rosario);* Jerome Cowan *(Bob Anderson);* George Reeves *(Sancho);* Victor Kilian *(Carlos);* Frank Puglia *(Rodriguez);* John Ridgely *(Gardiner);* Grady Sutton *(Sam, the Secretary);* George Humbert *(Hotel Manager);* Paul Porcasi *(Garcia the Hotel Bar Proprietor);* Frank Yaconelli *(Lopez);* Paul Hurst *(Daniels);* Jack Mower *(Schaeffer);* Frank Mayo *(McNamara);* Dick Botiller *(Hernandez);* Elvira Sanchez *(Rita);* Paul Renay *(Jose);* Rafael Corio *(Man);* George Regas *(Sergeant);* Trevor Bardette, Ernesto Piedra *(Policeman);* Don Orlando *(Employee);* Manuel Lopez *(Chico);* Joe Dominguez *(Manuel);* Joe Molinas *(Native);* Tony Paton *(Charley).*

FLOWING GOLD
(Warner Bros., 1940) 82 min.

ASSOCIATE PRODUCER: William Jacobs
DIRECTOR: Alfred E. Green
suggested by a story by Rex Beach
SCREENPLAY: Kenneth Gamet
CAMERA: Sid Hickox
EDITOR: James Gibbons

John Garfield *(Johnny Blake);* Pat O'Brien *(Hap O'Connor);* Frances Farmer *(Linda Chalmers);* Raymond Walburn *(Wildcat Chalmers);* Cliff Edwards *(Hotrocks);* Tom

Kennedy *(Petunia);* Granville Bates *(Charles Hammond);* Jody Gilbert *(Tillie);* Edward Pawley *(Collins);* John Alexander *(Sheriff);* Jack Mower *(Deputy);* Frank Mayo *(Mike Branigan);* William Marshall *(Joe);* Sol Gorss *(Duke);* Virginia Sale *(Nurse);* G. Pat Collins, William Haade, Dutch Hendrian *(Workmen);* Harry Strang *(Detective);* Eddie Acuff *(Orchestra Leader);* Monica Bannister *(Girl);* Lee Shumway *(Guard).*

KNUTE ROCKNE—ALL AMERICAN
(Warner Bros., 1940) 98 min.

PRODUCERS: Jack L. Warner, Hal B. Wallis
ASSOCIATE PRODUCER: Robert Fellows
DIRECTOR: Lloyd Bacon
BASED ON THE PRIVATE PAPERS OF MRS. KNUTE ROCKNE
SCREENPLAY: Robert Buckner
ART DIRECTOR: Robert Haas
GOWNS: Milo Anderson
MAKEUP: Perc Westmore
MUSIC DIRECTOR: Leo F. Forbstein
ORCHESTRATOR: Ray Heindorf
SPECIAL EFFECTS: Byron Haskin, Ray Wimpy
SOUND: Charles Lang
CAMERA: Tony Gaudio
EDITOR: Ralph Dawson

Pat O'Brien *(Knute Rockne);* Gale Page *(Bonnie Rockne);* Ronald Reagan *(George Gipp);* Donald Crisp *(Father Callahan);* Albert Bassermann *(Father Nieuwland);* John Litel *(Chairman of Committee of Educators);* Henry O'Neill *(Doctor);* Owen Davis, Jr. *(Gus Dormis);* John Qualen *(Lars Knutson Rockne);* Dorothy Tree *(Martha Rockne);* John Sheffield *(Knute Rockne as a Boy);* Mick Lukate *(Harry Stueldreher);* Kane Richmond *(Elmer Layden);* William Marshall *(Don Miller);* William Byrne *(James Crowley);* John Ridgeley *(Reporter);* Dutch Hendrian *(Hunk Anderson);* Gaylord [*Steve*] Pendleton *(Player);* Richard Clayton *(Student);* Howard Jones, Glenn "Pop" Warner, Alonzo Stagg, Bill Spaulding *(Themselves);* Robert O. Davis [*Rudolph Anders*] Egon Brecher, Fred Vogeding *(Elders);* William Haade, Eddy Chandler, Pat Flaherty *(Workers);* Creighton Hale *(Secretary);* David Bruce, Bill Hopper, Frank Mayo *(Reporters);* Frank Coghlan, Jr. *(Messenger);* Harry Hayden *(Professor);* Bill Sheffield *(Knute Rockne at Age Four);* Peter B. Good *(Bill Rockne at Age Two);* Bunky Fleischman *(Bill Rockne at Age Five);* David Dickson *(Bill Rockne at Age Ten);* Jack Grant, Jr. *(Bill Rockne at Age Fourteen);* David Mado *(Knute Rockne at Age Seven);* Billy Dawson *(Knute Rockne at Age Twelve);* Bill Gratton *(Jackie Rockne at Age Four);* Patricia Hayes *(Jeanne Rockne at Age Ten).*

SUBMARINE ZONE
(Columbia, 1940) 74 min.
(a.k.a. ESCAPE TO GLORY)

PRODUCER: Sam Bischoff
DIRECTOR: John Brahm
STORY: Sidney Biddell, Fredric Frank
SCREENPLAY: P. J. Wolfson
CAMERA: Franz Planer
EDITOR: Al Clark

Pat O'Brien *(Mike Farrough);* Constance Bennett *(Christine Blaine);* John Halliday *(John Morgan);* Melville Cooper *(Penney);* Alan Baxter *(Larry Perrin);* Edgar Buchanan *(Charles Atterbee);* Marjorie Gateson *(Mrs. Winslow);* Francis Pierlot *(Professor Mudge);* Jessie Busley *(Mrs. Mudge);* Stanley Logan *(Captain Hollister);* Frank Sully *(Tommy Malone);* Erwin Kalser *(Dr. Sehrens);* Don Beddoe *(Chief Engineer);* Leslie Denison *(First Mate);* Bruce Bennett *(Lieutenant);* Bert Kennedy *(Stand-In for Pat O'Brien);* Kay Smith *(Stand-In for Constance Bennett);* Olaf Hytten *(Agent);* Frank Baker, Arthur Mulliner *(Detectives);* Jimmie Kilgannon *(Sailor);* Arno Frey *(Submarine Gunner).*

TWO YANKS IN TRINIDAD
(Columbia, 1942) 88 min.

PRODUCER: Samuel Bischoff
DIRECTOR: Gregory Ratoff
STORY: Sy Bartlett
SCREENPLAY: Bartlett, Richard Carroll, Harry Segall
ADDITIONAL DIALOGUE: Jack Henley
CAMERA: Philip Tannura
EDITOR: Viola Lawrence

Pat O'Brien *(Tim Reardon);* Brian Donlevy *(Vince Barrows);* Janet Blair *(Patricia Dare);* Roger Clark *(James W. Buckingham III);* Donald MacBride *(Sergeant Valentine);* John Emery *(Chicago Hagen);* Frank Jenks *(Joe Scavenger);* Frank Sully *(Mike Paradise);* Veda Ann Borg *(Bubbles);* Clyde Fillmore *(Colonel Powers);* Dick Curtis *(Sea Captain);* Sig Arno *(Maitre d');* Dewey Robinson *(Tony);* George Allen, John Daheim, Dave Harper, Duke Taylor, Earl Bunn, William "Bing" Conley *(Seamen);* Al Hill, Bud Geary *(Bartenders);* Ralph Peters *(Sentry);* William Billy Newell *(Taxi Driver);* Julius Tannen *(Doctor).*

BROADWAY
(Universal, 1942) 91 min.

PRODUCER: Bruce Manning
ASSOCIATE PRODUCER: Frank Shaw
DIRECTOR: William A. Seiter
BASED ON THE PLAY BY PHILLIP DUNNING AND GEORGE ABBOTT
SCREENPLAY: Felix Jackson, John Bright
ART DIRECTOR: Jack Otterson
MUSIC DIRECTOR: Charles Previn
COSTUMES: Vera West
ASSISTANT DIRECTOR: Seward Webb
SONGS: Joe Young, Sam Lewis, and Harry Akst; Ben Bernie, Kenneth Casey, and Maceo Pinkard; Noble Sissle and Eubie Blake; Shelton Brooks; Gus Kahn and Walter Donaldson; B. G. DeSylva, Lew Brown, and Ray Henderson
CHOREOGRAPHY: John Mattison
CAMERA: George Barnes

George Raft *(George);* Pat O'Brien *(Dan McCorn);* Janet Blair *(Billie);* Broderick Crawford *(Steve Crandall);* Marjorie Rambeau *(Lil);* Anne Gwynne *(Pearl);* S. Z. Sakall *(Nick);* Edward S. Brophy *(Porky);* Marie Wilson *(Grace);* Gus Schilling *(Joe);* Ralf Harolde *(Dolph);* Arthur Shields *(Pete Dailey);* Iris Adrian *(Maisie);* Elaine Morey *(Ruby);* Dorothy Moore *(Ann);* Nestor Paiva *(Rinati);* Abner Biberman *(Trado);* Damian O'Flynn *(Scar Edwards);* Mack Gray *(Himself);* Jennifer Holt *(T.W.A. Hostess);* Benny Rubin, Anthony Warde, Charles Jordan, Sammy Stein, Larry McGrath, Charles Sullivan, Tony Paton, Jimmy O'Gatty, Lee Moore *(Gangsters);* Tom Kennedy *(Kerry the Cop);* Joe Cunningham, Arthur Loft, Lee Phelps *(Detectives);* Harry Seymour *(Piano Tuner);* Jimmy Conlin *(Newsman);* A. Kenneth Stevens *(Himself);* Pat Gleason, Frank Ferguson *(Reporters).*

FLIGHT LIEUTENANT
(Columbia, 1942) 80 min.

PRODUCER: B. P. Schulberg
DIRECTOR: Sidney Salkow
STORY: Richard Carroll, Betty Hopkins
SCREENPLAY: Michael Blankfort
ART DIRECTOR: Lionel Banks
MUSIC: Werner R. Heymann
MUSIC DIRECTOR: Morris Stoloff
CAMERA: Franz F. Planer
EDITOR: Charles Nelson

Pat O'Brien *(Sam Doyle);* Glenn Ford *(Danny Doyle);* Evelyn Keyes *(Susie Thompson);* Jonathan Hale *(Sanford);* Minor Watson *(Major Thompson);* Frank Puglia *(Father Carlos);* Edward Pawley *(Larsen);* Gregory Gaye *(Becker);* Clancy Cooper *(Scanlon);* Trevor Bardette *(Carey);* Marcel Dalio *(Foulet);* John Gallaudet *(Jackson);* Larry Parks *(Sandy Roth);* Lloyd Bridges *(Bill Robbins);* Hugh Beaumont *(John McGinnis);* Douglas Croft *(Danny Doyle as a Boy);* Ralph Simone *(Bartender);* Ferdinand Munier *(Photographer);* Robert Frazer *(Captain Hall);* William Forrest *(Captain);* George Neise *(Radio Operator);* Craufurd Kent *(Company Official);* Sidney Kibrick *(Pudgy).*

THE NAVY COMES THROUGH
(RKO, 1942) 81 min.

PRODUCER: Islim Auster
DIRECTOR: A. Edward Sutherland
BASED ON THE STORY "Pay to Learn" BY BORDEN CHASE
SCREENPLAY: Roy Chanslor, Aeneas MacKenzie
ADAPTORS: Earl Baldwin, John Twist
MUSIC DIRECTOR: C. Bakaleinikoff

Art Directors: Albert S. D'Agostino, Carroll Clark
Special Effects: Vernon L. Walker
Camera: Nicholas Musuraca
Editor: Samuel E. Beetley

Pat O'Brien *(Mallory);* George Murphy *(Sands);* Jane Wyatt *(Myra);* Jackie Cooper *(Babe);* Carl Esmond *(Kroner);* Max Baer *(Barringer);* Desi Arnaz *(Tarriba);* Ray Collins *(Captain McCail);* Lee Bonnell *(Kovac);* Frank Jenks *(Sampter);* John Maguire *(Bayliss);* Frank Fenton *(Hodum);* Joey Ray *(Dennis);* Cyril Ring *(First Officer);* Edgar Dearing *(C.P.O.);* Monte Montague *(Third Mate);* Mary Young *(Mrs. Duttson);* Joe Cunningham *(Mr. Duttson);* Ralph Dunn *(Cop);* Helmut Dantine *(Young German Seaman);* George Melford *(Chief Engineer);* George Blagoi *(Captain of German Submarine).*

BOMBARDIER
(RKO, 1943) 99 min.

Producer: Robert Fellows
Director: Richard Wallace
Story: John Twist, Martin Rackin
Screenplay: Twist
Assistant Director: Edward Killy
Song: M. K. Jerome and Jack Scholl
Music: Roy Webb
Music Director: C. Bakaleinikoff
Art Directors: Albert S. D'Agostino, Al Herman
Set Decorators: Darrell Silvera, Claude Carpenter
Montage: Bailey Fesler
Sound: James G. Stewart
Special Effects: Vernon L. Walker
Camera: Nicholas Musuraca
Editor: Robert Wise

Pat O'Brien *(Major Chick Davis);* Randolph Scott *(Captain Buck Oliver);* Anne Shirley *(Burt Hughes);* Eddie Albert *(Tom Hughes);* Walter Reed *(Jim Carter);* Robert Ryan *(Joe Connor);* Barton MacLane *(Sergeant Dixon);* Richard Martin *(Chito Rafferty);* Russell Wade *(Paul Harris);* James Newill *(Captain Rand);* Bruce Edwards *(Lieutenant Ellis);* John Miljan *(Chaplain Craig);* Harold Landon *(Pete Jordan);* Margie Stewart *(Mamie);* Bud Geary *(Sergeant);* Kirby Grant, Eddie Dew *(Pilots);* Joan Barclay, Marty Faust *(Bits);* John James *(Lieutenant);* Hugh Beaumont *(Soldier);* Lee Shumway, Ed Peil, Robert Middlemass *(Officers).*

THE IRON MAJOR
(RKO, 1943) 85 min.

Producer: Robert Fellows
Director: Ray Enright
Story: Florence M. Cavanaugh
Screenplay: Aben Kandel, Warren Duff
Football Technical Advisors: William "Hiker" Joy, Ernest E. LaBlanche
Assistant Director: Edward Killy
Music: Roy Webb
Music Director: C. Bakaleinikoff
Art Directors: Albert S. D'Agostino, Carroll Clark
Set Decorators: Darrell Silvera, Al Fields
Sound: Terry Kellum, James G. Stewart
Camera: Robert De Grasse
Editors: Robert Wise, Philip Martin, Jr.

Pat O'Brien *(Frank Cavanaugh);* Ruth Warrick *(Florence "Mike" Ayres Cavanaugh);* Robert Ryan *(Father Tim Donovan);* Leon Ames *(Robert Stewart);* Russell Wade *(Private Manning);* Bruce Edwards *(Lieutenant Jones);* Richard Martin *(Davis Cavanaugh);* Robert Bice *(Coach);* Virginia Brissac *(Mrs. Ayres);* Robert Anderson, Mike Lally, Lee Phelps, Craig Flanagan, Michael Road *(Bits);* Bud Geary *(Sergeant);* Frank Puglia *(Nurse);* Pierre Watkin *(Colonel White);* Billy Roy *(Bob as a Boy);* Robert Winkler *(Frank as a Boy);* Barbara Hale *(Sarah Cavanaugh);* Joel Davis *(Davie as a Boy);* Dean Benton *(William Cavanaugh);* Myron Healey *(Paul Cavanaugh);* Kirk Alyn *(John Cavanaugh);* Victor Kilian *(Francis Cavanaugh);* Margaret Landry *(Sis Cavanaugh);* Ian Wolfe *(Professor Runnymead);* Joseph Crehan *(Judge);* John Miljan *(Oregon Coach);* Brooks Benedict, Brandon Beach *(Alumni);* Roland Dupree, Michael Miller, Bobby Larson, Richard Dillon *(Boys);* Dorothy Vaughan *(Ma Cavanaugh);* Frank Shannon *(Pa Cavanaugh);* Paul McVey *(Athletic Coach).*

HIS BUTLER'S SISTER
(Universal, 1943) 93 min.

Producer: Felix Jackson
Associate Producer: Frank Shaw
Director: Frank Borzage
Screenplay: Samuel Hoffenstein, Betty Reinhardt
Art Directors: John Goodman, Martin Obzina
Set Decorator: Russell A. Gausman, T. F. Offenbecker
Music: Hans J. Salter
Songs: Bernie Grossman and Walter Jurmann; Sam Lerner, Victor Herbert and Henry M. Blossom
Music Arranger: Max Rabinowich
Assistant Director: Lou Borzage
Sound: B. Brown, E. Wetzel
Special Camera: John P. Fulton
Camera: Woody Bredell
Editor: Ted J. Kent

Deanna Durbin *(Ann Carter);* Franchot Tone *(Charles Gerard);* Pat O'Brien *(Martin Murphy);* Akim Tamiroff *(Popoff);* Alan Mowbray *(Jenkins);* Walter Catlett *(Kalb);* Elsa Janssen *(Severing);* Evelyn Ankers *(Elizabeth Campbell);* Frank Jenks *(Emmett);* Sig Arno *(Moreno);* Hans Conried *(Reeves);* Florences Bates *(Lady Cloughberry);* Roscoe Karns *(Fields);* Russell Hicks *(Sanderson);* Andrew Tombes *(Brophy);* Stephanie Bachelor *(Dot Stanley);* Marion Pierce *(Margaret Howard);* Iris Adrian, Robin Raymond *(Sunshine Twins);* Leo Mostovoy *(Headwaiter);* Halliwell Hobbes *(Wildebrandt);* Joe King *(Conductor);* Alice Draper *(Spinster);* Virginia Gardner *(Blonde).*

MARINE RAIDERS
(RKO, 1944) 91 min.

Producer: Robert Fellows
Director: Harold Schuster
Story: Martin Rackin, Warren Duff
Screenplay: Duff
Art Directors: Albert S. D'Agostino, Walter E. Keller
Set Decorators: Darrell Silvera, Harley Miller
Music: Roy Webb
Music Director: C. Bakaleinikoff
Assistant Director: Edward Killy
Sound: James S. Thomson
Special Effects: Vernon Walker
Camera: Nicholas Musuraca
Editor: Philip Martin, Jr.

Pat O'Brien *(Major Steve Lockhard);* Robert Ryan *(Captain Dan Craig);* Ruth Hussey *(Ellen Foster);* Frank McHugh *(Sergeant Louis Leary);* Barton MacLane *(Sergeant Maguire);* Richard Martin *(Jimmy);* Edmund Glover *(Miller);* Russell Wade *(Tony Hewitt);* Robert Andersen *(Lieutenant Sherwood);* Michael St. Angel *(Lieutenant Sherwood);* Martha Vickers *(Sally);* Harry Brown *(Cook);* Sammy Stein *(Sergeant);* William Forrest *(Colonel Carter);* Mike Kilian *(Shoe Gag Soldier);* Audrey Manners *(Aussie WAAF);* Harry Clay *(Wounded Marine);* Eddie Woods *(Officer on Ship);* Blake Edwards *(Marine);* John Elliott *(Admiral);* Barry Macollum *(Innkeeper).*

SECRET COMMAND
(Columbia, 1944) 82 min.

Producer: Phil L. Ryan
Director: A. Edward Sutherland
Based on the story "The Saboteurs" by John and Ward Hawkins
Screenplay: Roy Chanslor
Art Directors: Lionel Banks, Edward Jewell
Set Decorator: Robert Priestley
Assistant Director: Rex Bailey
Music: Paul Sawtell
Music Director: Morris Stoloff
Sound: Ed Bernds
Process Camera: David Allen, Ray Cory
Special Effects: Robert Wright
Montages: Aaron Nipley
Camera: Franz F. Planer
Editor: Viola Lawrence

Pat O'Brien *(Sam Gallagher);* Carole Landis *(Jill McCann);* Chester Morris *(Jeff Gallagher);* Ruth Warrick *(Lee Damaron);* Barton MacLane *(Red Kelly);* Tom Tully *(Brownell);* Wallace Ford *(Miller);* Howard Freeman *(Max Lessing);* Erik Rolf *(Ben Royall);* Matt McHugh *(Curly);* Frank Sully *(Shawn);* Frank Fenton *(Simms);* Charles D.

Brown *(James Thane);* Carol Nugent *(Joan);* Richard Lane *(Paul).*

HAVING WONDERFUL CRIME
(RKO, 1945) 70 min.

Producer: Robert Fellows
Associate Producer: Theron Warth
Director: A. Edward Sutherland
Story: Craig Rice
Screenplay: Howard J. Green, Stewart Sterling, Parke Levy
Art Directors: Albert S. D'Agostino, Al Herman
Set Decorators: Darrell Silvera, Claude Carpenter
Music: Leigh Harline
Music Director: C. Bakaleinikoff
Assistant Director: Clem Beauchamp
Sound: Jean Speak
Special Effects: Vernon L. Walker
Camera: Frank Redman
Editor: Gene Milford

Pat O'Brien *(Michael J. Malone);* George Murphy *(Jake Justus);* Carole Landis *(Helen);* Lenore Aubert *(Gilda);* George Zucco *(King);* Anje Berens *(Phyllis);* Richard Martin *(Lance);* Charles D. Brown *(Winslow);* William "Wee Willie" Davis *(Zacharias);* Blanche King *(Elizabeth Lenhart);* Josephine Whittel *(Myra);* Edward Fielding *(Dr. Newcomb);* Jimmy Jordan *(Usher);* Frank Mayo *(Cop);* Virginia Belmont, Harry Clay, Tom Burton, Lee Trent, Elaine Riley, Margie Stewart, Nancy Marlow, Chili Williams *(Guests);* Alex Pollard *(Waiter);* Cyril Ring *(Hotel Clerk);* Don Barclay *(Bartender);* Lorraine Clark, Kerry Vaughn, Evalene Bankston, Sheryle Starr, Mary Starr, Marlyn Gladstone, Ellen Hall, Virginia Cruzon, Shelby Payne, Mary Jane Dolan, Shirley Johnson, Karen Haven *(Bathing Beauties);* Emory Parnell *(Sergeant);* Larry Wheat *(Butler).*

MAN ALIVE
(RKO, 1945) 70 min.

Producer: Robert Fellows
Associate Producer: Theron Warth
Director: Ray Enright
Story: Jerry Cady, John Tucker Battle
Screenplay: Edwin Harvey Blum
Music: Leigh Harline
Music Director: C. Bakaleinikoff
Orchestrator: Gil Grau
Art Directors: Albert S. D'Agostino, Al Herman
Set Decorators: Darrell Silvera, Victor Gangelin
Assistant Director: James Casey
Sound: Francis M. Sarver
Special Effects: Vernon L. Walker
Camera: Frank Redman
Editor: Marvin Coil

Pat O'Brien *(Speed);* Adolphe Menjou *(Kismet);* Ellen Drew *(Connie);* Rudy Vallee *(Gordon Tolliver);* Fortunio Bonanova *(Professor Zorada);* Joseph Crehan *(Doc Whitney);* Jonathan Hale *(Osborne);* Minna Gombell *(Aunt Sophie);* Jason Robards *(Fletcher);* Jack Norton *(Willie the Wino);* Donn Gift *(Messenger Boy);* Myrna Dell *(Sister);* Carl Alfalfa Switzer *(Ignatius);* Gertrude Short *(Frowsy Dame);* Robert Clarke *(Cabby);* Robert Homans *(Uncle Barney).*

PERILOUS HOLIDAY
(Columbia, 1946) 89 min.

Producer: Phil L. Ryan
Director: Edward H. Griffith
Story: Robert Carson
Screenplay: Roy Chanslor
Art Directors: Stephen Goosson, Rudolph Sternad
Set Decorator: Frank Tuttle
Songs: Allan Roberts and Doris Fisher
Assistant Director: Milton Feldman
Sound: Jack Haynes
Special Effects: Ray Cory
Camera: Charles Lawton
Editor: Viola Lawrence

Pat O'Brien *(Patrick Nevil);* Ruth Warrick *(Agnes Stuart);* Alan Hale *(Dr. Lilley);* Edgar Buchanan *(George Richards);* Audrey Long *(Audrey Latham);* Willard Robertson *(Graeme);* Minna Gombell *(Mrs. Latham);* Martin Garralaga *(Manuel Perez);* Jay Novello *(Luigi);* Al Hill *(Benny Lockner);* Pedro Regas *(Pedro);* Eddie LeBaron and His Continental Orchestra *(Themselves);* Nacho Galindo *(Proprietor);* Manuel Paris *(Waiter);* Ralph Navarro *(Maitre d');* Joe Dominguez *(Police Car Driver);* Don Avalier *(Police Lieutenant);* Chris-Pin Martin *(Servant);* David Cota *(Shoeshine Boy);* Delmar Costello *(Pageboy);* Jack Del Rio *(Bartender).*

CRACK-UP
(RKO, 1946) 93 min.

Producer: Jack J. Gross
Director: Irving Reis
Suggested by the story "Madman's Holiday" by Fredric Brown
Screenplay: John Paxton, Ben Bagal, Ray Spencer
Art Directors: Albert S. D'Agostino, Jack Okey
Music: Leigh Harline
Music Director: C. Balcallinikoff
Special Effects: Russell A. Cully
Camera: Robert de Grasse
Editor: Frederic Knudston

Pat O'Brien *(George Steele);* Claire Trevor *(Terry);* Herbert Marshall *(Traybin);* Ray Collins *(Dr. Lowell);* Wallace Ford *(Police Lieutenant Cochrane);* Dean Horens *(Reynolds);* Damian O'Flynn *(Stevenson);* Erskine Sanford *(Barton);* Mary Ware *(Mary).*

RIFF RAFF
(RKO, 1947) 80 min.

Executive Producer: Jack L. Gross
Producer: Nat Holt
Director: Ted Tetzlaff
Screenplay: Martin Rackin
Art Directors: Albert S. D'Agostino, Walter E. Keller
Set Decorators: Darrell Silvera, Michael Orenbach
Assistant Director: Maxwell Henry
Music: Roy Webb
Music Director: C. Bakaleinikoff
Sound: John Tribby, Terry Kellum
Special Effects: Russell A. Cully
Camera: George E. Diskant
Editor: Philip Martin

Pat O'Brien *(Dan);* Walter Slezak *(Molinar);* Anne Jeffreys *(Maxine);* Percy Kilbride *(Pop);* Jerome Cowan *(Walter Gredson);* George Givot *(Rues);* Jason Robards *(Dominguez);* Marc Krah *(Hasso);* Bonnie Blair *(Girl at Airport);* Drew Miller *(Pilot);* Julian Rivero *(Passenger Agent);* Bob O'Connor *(Taxi Driver);* Tom Noonan *(Drunk);* Betty Hill, Virginia Owen *(Singers);* Carmen Lopez *(Hula Dancer);* Lou Lubin *(Rabbit);* Eduardo Noriega *(Felice);* Eddie Borden *(Man).*

FIGHTING FATHER DUNNE
(RKO, 1948) 93 min.

Executive Producer: Jack J. Gross
Producer: Phil L. Ryan
Director: Ted Tetzlaff
Story: William Rankin
Screenplay: Martin Rackin, Frank Davis
Dialogue Director: Eugene Busch
Art Directors: Albert S. D'Agostino, Walter E. Keller
Set Decorators: Darrell Silvera, Adolph Kurt
Music: Roy Webb
Music Director: C. Bakaleinikoff
Assistant Director: John Pommer
Costumes: Adele Balkan
Makeup: Webb Phillips
Sound: Frank Sarver, Terry Kellum
Special Effects: Russell A. Cully
Camera: George E. Diskant
Editor: Fredric Knudtson

Pat O'Brien *(Father Dunne);* Darryl Hickman *(Matt Davis);* Charles Kemper *(Emmett Mulvey);* Una O'Connor *(Miss O'Rourke);* Arthur Shields *(Mr. O'Donnell);* Harry Shannon *(John Lee);* Joe Sawyer *(Steve Davis);* Anna Q. Nilsson *(Mrs. Knudson);* Donn Gift *(Jimmy);* Myrna Dell *(Paula);* Ruth Donnelly *(Kate Mulvey);* Jim Nolan *(Danny Briggs);* Billy Cummings *(Tony);* Billy Gray *(Chip);* Eric Roberts *(Monk);* Gene Collins *(Lefty);* Lester Matthews *(Archbishop);* Griff Barnett *(Governor);* Jason Robards *(Sonin);* Rudy Wissler *(Soloist);* Don Haggerty *(Blake);* Ricky Berger *(Boy);* Paul Dunn *(Harry);* Buddy Roosevelt *(Pedestrian);* Raymond Burr *(Prosecuting Attorney);* Emmett Vogan *(Defense Attorney);* Ellen Corby *(Colpeck's Secretary);* Frank Ferguson *(Colpeck);* Phillip Morris *(Prison Guard);* Harry Hayden *(Mr. Dunfee);* Robert Clarke, Robert Bray *(Priests);* Ralph Dunn, Chuck Flynn *(Workmen).*

THE BOY WITH GREEN HAIR
(RKO, 1948) C-82 min.

EXECUTIVE PRODUCER: Dore Schary
PRODUCER: Stephen Ames
DIRECTOR: Joseph Losey
BASED ON THE STORY BY BETSY BEATON
SCREENPLAY: Ben Barzman, Alfred Lewis Levitt
ART DIRECTORS: Albert S. D'Agostino, Ralph Berger
SET DECORATORS: Darrell Silvera, William Stevens
MUSIC: Leigh Harline
ORCHESTRATOR: Gil Grau
MUSIC DIRECTOR: C. Bakaleinikoff
ASSISTANT DIRECTOR: James Lane
MAKEUP: Gordon Bau
COSTUMES: Adele Balkan
TECHNICOLOR CONSULTANTS: Natalie Kalmus, Morgan Padelford
SOUND: Earl Wolcott, Clem Portman
CAMERA: George Barnes
EDITOR: Frank Doyle

Pat O'Brien *(Gramp);* Robert Ryan *(Dr. Evans);* Barbara Hale *(Miss Brand);* Dean Stockwell *(Peter);* Richard Lyon *(Michael);* Walter Catlett *("The King");* Samuel S. Hinds *(Dr. Knudson);* Regis Toomey *(Mr. Davis);* Charles Meredith *(Mr. Piper);* David Clarke *(Barber);* Billy Sheffield *(Red);* John Calkins *(Danny);* Teddy Infuhr *(Timmy);* Dwayne Hickman *(Joey);* Eilene Janssen *(Peggy);* Curtis Jackson *(Classmate);* Charles Arnt *(Mr. Hammond);* Don Pietro *(Newsboy);* Billy White, Rusty Tamblyn, Baron White, Spear Martin *(Boys);* Dayle Robertson *(Cop);* Anna Q. Nilsson, Lynn Whitney *(Townswomen);* Eula Guy *(Mrs. Fisher).*

A DANGEROUS PROFESSION
(RKO, 1949) 79 min.

EXECUTIVE PRODUCER: Sid Rogell
PRODUCER: Robert Sparks
DIRECTOR: Ted Tetzlaff
SCREENPLAY: Martin Rackin, Warren Duff
ART DIRECTORS: Albert S. D'Agostino, Al Herman
SET DECORATORS: Darrell Silvera, Harley Miller
MUSIC: Frederick Hollander
MUSIC DIRECTOR: C. Bakaleinikoff
CHOREOGRAPHY: Michael Woulfe
ASSISTANT DIRECTOR: James Casey
MAKEUP: Irving Berns
SOUND: Earl Mounce, Clem Portman
CAMERA: Robert de Grasse
EDITOR: Frederic Knudtson

George Raft *(Vince Kane);* Ella Raines *(Lucy Brackett);* Pat O'Brien *(Joe Farley);* Bill Williams *(Claude Brackett);* Jim Backus *(Nick Ferrone);* Roland Winters *(McKay);* Betty Underwood *(Elaine);* Robert Gist *(Collins);* David Wolfe *(Matthew Dawson);* Mack Gray *(Fred, the Taxi Driver);* Charmiene Harker *(Helen);* Lynne Roberts *(Miss Wilson);* Steven Flagg *(Roberts);* Jonathan Hale *(Lennert);* Gloria Gabriel *(Kane's Secretary);* Dick Dickinson *(Thin Man);* Don Dillaway *(Young Man Drunk);* Ralph Volke *(Man);* Jacqueline Hammette *(Girl in Mink Coat);* Mike Lally *(Cop);* Burk Symon *(Herman);* Phyllis Kennedy *(Maid in Kane's Apartment);* Frances Morris *(Mrs. Farley);* Harry Brown *(Room Clerk);* Frank Shannon *(Barman).*

JOHNNY ONE-EYE
(United Artists, 1950) 78 min.

PRODUCER: Benedict Bogeaus
DIRECTOR: Robert Florey
BASED ON THE STORY BY DAMON RUNYON
SCREENPLAY: Richard Landau
MUSIC DIRECTOR: Louis Forbes
CAMERA: Lucien Andriot
EDITOR: Frank Sullivan

Pat O'Brien *(Martin Martin);* Wayne Morris *(Dane Cory);* Dolores Moran *(Lily White);* Gayle Reed *(Elsie);* Lawrence Cregar *(Ambrose);* Jack Overman *(Lippy);* Raymond Largay *(Lawbooks);* Donald Woods *(Vet);* Harry Bronson *(Freddy).*

THE FIREBALL
(20th Century-Fox, 1950) 84 min.

PRODUCER: Bert Friedlob
DIRECTOR: Tay Garnett
STORY/SCREENPLAY: Garnett, Horace McCoy
ART DIRECTOR: Van Nest Polglase
MUSIC: Victor Young
CAMERA: Lester White
EDITOR: Frank Sullivan

Mickey Rooney *(Johnny Casar);* Pat O'Brien *(Father O'Hara);* Beverly Tyler *(Mary Reeves);* Glenn Corbett *(Mack Miller);* Marilyn Monroe *(Polly);* James Brown *(Allen);* Ralph Dumke *(Bruno);* Bert Begley *(Shilling);* Milburn Stone *(Jeff Davis);* Sam Flint *(Dr. Barton);* John Hedloe *(Ullman).*

THE PEOPLE AGAINST O'HARA
(MGM, 1951) 102 min.

PRODUCER: William H. Wright
DIRECTOR: John Sturges
BASED ON THE NOVEL BY ELEAZAR LIPSKY
SCREENPLAY: John Monks, Jr.
ART DIRECTORS: Cedric Gibbons, James Basevi
SET DECORATORS: Edwin B. Willis, Jacques Mapes
MUSIC: Carmen Dragon
SOUND: Douglas Shearer
SPECIAL EFFECTS: A. Arnold Gillespie, Warren Newcombe
CAMERA: John Alton
EDITOR: Gene Ruggiero

Spencer Tracy *(James Curtayne);* Pat O'Brien *(Vincent Ricks);* Diana Lynn *(Ginny Curtayne);* John Hodiak *(Louis Barra);* Eduardo Ciannelli *("Knuckles" Lanzetta);* James Arness *(Johnny O'Hara);* Yvette Duguay *(Mrs. Lanzetta);* Jay C. Flippen *(Sven Norson);* William Campbell *(Frank Korvac);* Richard Anderson *(Jeff Chapman);* Henry O'Neill *(Judge Keating);* Arthur Shields *(Mr. O'Hara);* Louise Lorimer *(Mrs. O'Hara);* Ann Doran *(Betty Clark);* Emile Meyer *(Captain Tom Mulvaney);* Regis Toomey *(Fred Colton);* Paul Bryar *(Detective Howie Pendleton);* Peter Mamakos *(James Korvac);* Frank Ferguson *(Al);* Don Dillaway *(Monty);* Lee Phelps *(Emmett Kimbaugh);* Lawrence Tolan *(Vincent Korvac);* Jack Lee *(Court Clerk);* Tony Barr *("Little" Wolfie);* Jan Kayne, Virginia Hewitt *(Girls);* Mae Clarke *(Receptionist);* Dan Foster *(Assistant District Attorney);* Charles Bronson *(Angelo Korvac);* Celia Lovsky *(Mrs. Korvac);* Bill Fletcher *(Pete Korvac);* Richard Bartlett *(Tony Korvac);* Tiny Kelly *(Leigh Keighley);* Bud Wolfe *(Fingerprint Technician);* Frank Sully, Ernest Morelli *(Fishmongers);* Jeff Richards *(Ambulance Driver);* William Schallert *(Interne).*

CRIMINAL LAWYER
(Columbia, 1951) 74 min.

PRODUCER: Rudolph C. Flothow
DIRECTOR: Seymour Friedman
STORY/SCREENPLAY: Harold R. Greene
ART DIRECTOR: Harold MacArthur
SET DECORATOR: Frank Tuttle
MUSIC DIRECTOR: Mischa Bakaleinikoff
CAMERA: Philip Tannura
EDITOR: Charles Nelson

Pat O'Brien *(James Reagan);* Jane Wyatt *(Maggie Powell);* Carl Benton Reid *(Tucker Bourne);* Mary Castle *(Gloria Lydendecker);* Robert Shayne *(Clark Sommers);* Mike Mazurki *(Moose Hendricks);* Jerome Cowan *(Walter Medford);* Marvin Kaplan *(Sam Kutler);* Douglas Fowley *(Harry Cheney);* Mickey Knox *(Vincent Cheney);* Louis Jean Heydt *(Frank Burnett);* Harlan Warde *(Byron Claymore);* Wallis Clark *(Melville Webber);* Mary Alan Hokanson *(Mrs. Johnson);* Lewis Martin *(Judge Selders);* Charles Lane *(Frederick Waterman);* Guy Beach *(Edward Cranston);* Grandon Rhodes *(Judge Larrabee);* Darryl Hickman *(Bill Webber);* Amanda Blake *(Receptionist);* Joey Ray *(Attendant);* Pat O'Malley *(Bailiff).*

OKINAWA
(Columbia, 1952) 67 min.

PRODUCER: Wallace MacDonald
DIRECTOR: Leigh Jason
STORY: Arthur Ross
SCREENPLAY: Jameson Brewer, Ross
ADDITIONAL DIALOGUE: Leonard Stern
ART DIRECTOR: George Brooks
MUSIC DIRECTOR: Mischa Bakaleinikoff
CAMERA: Henry Freulich
EDITOR: Jerome Thomas

Pat O'Brien *(Lieutenant Commander Hale);* Cameron Mitchell *(Grip);* Richard Denning *(Lieutenant Phillips);* Rhys Williams *(Roberg);* James Dobson *(Emerson);* Richard Benedict *(Delagado);* Rudy Robles *(Felix);* Don Gibson *(Lieutenant Sanders);* George Cooper *(Yeoman);* Alan Dreeben *(Chief Pharmacist's Mate);* Norman Budd *(Smith);* Alvy Moore *(Quartermaster).*

JUBILEE TRAIL
(Republic, 1954) C-103 min.

Producer: Herbert J. Yates
Associate Producer/Director: Joseph Kane
Based on the novel by Gwen Bristow
Screenplay: Bruce Manning
Music/Music Director: Victor Young
Songs: Young and Sidney Clare
Choreography: Bob Mark
Technical Advisor: D. R. O. Hatswell
Assistant Director: A. J. Vitarelli
Costumes: Adele Palmer
Art Director: Frank Arrigo
Set Decorators: John McCarthy, Jr., George Milo
Sound: Earl Crain, Sr., Howard Wilson
Camera: Jack Marta
Editor: Richard L. Van Enger

Vera Ralston [*Florinda Grove (Julie Latour)*]; Joan Leslie *(Garnet Hale);* Forrest Tucker *(John Ives);* John Russell *(Oliver Hale);* Ray Middleton *(Charles Hale);* Pat O'Brien *(Ernest "Texas" Conway);* Buddy Baer *(Nicholai Gregorovitch Karakozeff);* Jim Davis *(Silky);* Barton MacLane *(Deacon Bartlett);* Richard Webb *(Captain Brown);* James Millican *(Rinardi);* Nina Varela *(Doña Manuela);* Martin Garralaga *(Don Rafael Velasco);* Charles Stevens *(Pablo—a Peon);* Nacho Galinda *(Rico, the Bartender);* William Haade *(Jake the Sailor);* Don Beddoe *(Mr. Maury, the Hotel Manager);* Sayre Dearing, John Halloran *(Turner's Men);* Marshall Reed *(Detective);* Claire Carleton *(Estelle the Madame);* Frank Puglia *(Don Orosco);* Glenn Strange *(Tom Branders);* Emmett Lynn *(Drunk Man with Little Hat);* Pilar Del Rey *(Carmelita Velasco);* Raymond Johnson *(Corporal);* Robert "Buzz" Henry, Ted Smile *(Velasco's Sons).*

RING OF FEAR
(Warner Bros., 1954) C-93 min.

Producer: Robert M. Fellow
Director: James Edward Grant
Screenplay: Paul Fix, Philip MacDonald, Grant
Music: Emil Newman, Arthur Lange
Assistant Director: Melvin A. Dellar
Camera: Edwin DuPar
Editor: Fred MacDowell

Clyde Beatty *(Himself);* Pat O'Brien *(Frank Wallace);* Mickey Spillane *(Himself);* Sean McClory *(Dublin O'Malley);* Marian Carr *(Valerie St. Denis);* John Bromfield *(Armand St. Denis);* Pedro Gonzalez-Gonzalez *(Gonzalez);* Emmett Lynn *(Twitchy);* Jack Stang *(Paul Martin);* Kenneth Tobey *(Shreveport);* Kathy Cline *(Suzette);* Clyde Beatty Circus *(Themselves).*

INSIDE DETROIT
(Columbia, 1955) 82 min.

Producer: Sam Katzman
Director: Fred F. Sears
Screenplay: Robert E. Kent, James B. Gordon
Art Director: Paul Palmentola
Music Director: Mischa Bakaleinikoff
Assistant Director: Gene Anderson, Jr.
Camera: Henry Freulich
Editor: Gene Havlick

Dennis O'Keefe *(Blair Vickers);* Pat O'Brien *(Gus Linden);* Tina Carver *(Joni Calvin);* Margaret Field *(Barbara Linden);* Mark Damon *(Gregg Linden);* Larry Blake *(Max Harkness);* Ken Christy *(Ben Macauley);* Joseph Turkel *(Pete Link);* Paul Bryar *(Sam Foran);* Robert E. Griffin *(Hoagy Mitchell);* Guy Kingsford *(Jenkins);* Dick Rich *(Toby Gordon);* Norman Leavitt *(Preacher);* Katherine Warren *(Ethel Linden).*

KILL ME TOMORROW
(Renown, 1957) 80 min.

Producer: Francis Searle
Director: Terence Fisher
Screenplay: Robert Falconer, Manning O'Brien
Music: Temple Abady
Camera: Geoffrey Faithfull
Editor: Ann Chetwidden

Pat O'Brien *(Bart Crosbie);* Lois Maxwell *(Jill Brook);* George Coulouris *(Heinz Webber);* Wensley Pithey *(Inspector Lane);* Freddie Mills *(Waxy);* Ronald Adam *(Brook);* Robert Brown *(Steve);* Richard Pascoe *(Dr. Fisher);* April Olrich *(Bella Braganza);* Tommy Steele *(Himself).*

THE LAST HURRAH
(Columbia, 1958) 121 min.

Producer/Director: John Ford
Based on the novel by Edwin O'Connor
Screenplay: Frank Nugent
Art Director: Robert Peterson
Set Decorator: William Kiernan
Assistant Directors: Wingate Smith, Sam Nelson
Sound: Harry Mills
Camera: Charles Lawton, Jr.
Editor: Jack Murray

Spencer Tracy *(Frank Skeffington);* Jeffrey Hunter *(Adam Caulfield);* Dianne Foster *(Maeve Caulfield);* Pat O'Brien *(John Gorman);* Basil Rathbone *(Norman Cass, Sr.);* Donald Crisp *(Cardinal);* James Gleason *(Cuke Gillen);* Edward Brophy *(Ditto Boland);* John Carradine *(Amos Force);* Willis Bouchey *(Roger Sugrue);* Basil Ruysdael *(Bishop Gardner);* Ricardo Cortez *(Sam Weinberg);* Wallace Ford *(Hennessey);* Frank McHugh *(Festus Garvey);* Carleton Young *(Mr. Winslow);* Frank Albertson *(Jack Mangan);* Bob Sweeney *(Degnan);* William Leslie *(Dan Herlihy);* Anna Lee *(Gert);* Ken Curtis *(Monsignor Killian);* Jane Darwell *(Delia);* O. Z. Whitehead *(Norman Cass, Jr.);* Charles Fitzsimons *(Kevin McCluskey);* Helen Westcott *(Mrs. McCluskey);* Mimi Doyle *(Mamie Burns);* Dan Borzage *(Pete);* Charlie Sullivan *(Chauffeur);* Frank Sully *(Fire Captain);* William Forrest *(Doctor);* Edward Featherstone, Frank Marlowe, Jack Henderson *(Men);* Bill Henry, Harry Lauter *(Young Politicians);* Jack Pennick *(Riley);* Debbie Cooney *(McClusky Daughter);* Edward "Skipper" McNally *(Ward Heeler);* Julius Tannen *(Mr. Kowalsky);* Robert Levin *(Jules Kowalsky);* Richard Deacon *(Club Secretary);* Anna Stein *(Bit).*

SOME LIKE IT HOT
(United Artists, 1959) 120 min.

Producer/Director: Billy Wilder
Suggested by a story by R. Thoren and M. Logan
Screenplay: Wilder, I. A. L. Diamond
Miss Monroe's Gowns: Orry-Kelly
Music: Adolph Deutsch
Songs' Supervisor: Matty Malneck
Art Director: Ted Haworth
Set Decorator: Edward G. Boyle
Wardrobe: Bert Henrickson
Makeup: Emile LaVigne
Assistant Director: Sam Boyle
Sound: Fred Lau
Camera: Charles Lang, Jr.
Editor: Arthur Schmidt

Marilyn Monroe *(Sugar Kane);* Tony Curtis [*Joe (Josephine)*]; Jack Lemmon [*Jerry (Daphne)*]; George Raft *(Spats Colombo);* Pat O'Brien *(Mulligan);* Nehemiah Persoff *(Little Bonaparte);* Joe E. Brown *(Osgood Fielding III);* Joan Shawlee *(Sue);* Billy Gray *(Poliakoff);* George E. Stone *(Toothpick Charlie);* Dave Barry *(Beinstock);* Mike Mazurki, Harry Wilson *(Spats' Henchmen);* Beverly Wills *(Dolores);* Barbara Drew *(Nellie);* Edward G. Robinson, Jr. *(Johnny Paradise).*

TOWN TAMER
(Paramount, 1965) C-89 min.

Producer: A. C. Lyles
Director: Lesley Selander
Based on the novel by Frank Gruber
Screenplay: Gruber
Art Directors: Hal Pereira, Al Roelofs
Set Decorator: Claude Carpenter
Music/Song: Jimmie Haskell
Sound: Hugo Grenzbach
Camera: W. Wallace Kelley
Editor: George Gittens

Dana Andrews *(Tom Rosser);* Terry Moore *(Susan Tavenner);* Bruce Cabot *(Riley Condor);* Lyle Bettger *(Lee Ring);* Lon Chaney, Jr. *(Leach);* Barton MacLane *(James Fennimore*

Fell); Richard Arlen *(Dr. Kent);* DeForest Kelley *(Guy Tavenner);* Richard Jaeckel *(Honsinger);* Coleen Gray *(Carol Rosser);* Pat O'Brien *(Judge Marcott);* Philip Carey *(Slim Akins);* Sonny Tufts *(Carmichael);* Roger Torrey *(Flon);* James Brown *(Davis);* Richard Webb *(Kevin);* Jeanne Cagney *(Mary);* Don Barry, Robert Ivers *(Texans);* Bob Steele *(Vigilante).*

THE OVER-THE-HILL GANG
(ABC-TV, 1969) C-73 min.

PRODUCERS: Danny Thomas and Aaron Spelling
DIRECTOR: Jean Yarbrough
TELEPLAY: Jameson Brewer
ART DIRECTOR: Paul Sylos, Jr.
MUSIC: Hugo Friedhofer
CAMERA: Henry Cronjager
EDITOR: Joe Gluck

Pat O'Brien *(Captain Oren Hayes);* Walter Brennan *(Nash Crawford);* Chill Wills *(Gentleman George);* Edgar Buchanan *(Jason Finch);* Edward Andrews *(Mayor Lundy);* Jack Elam *(Sheriff Clyde Barnes);* Andy Devine *(Judge Amos Polk);* Gypsy Rose Lee *(Cassie);* Rick Nelson *(Jeff);* Kris Harmon Nelson *(Hannah);* William Smith *(Amos).*

THE PHYNX
(Warner Bros., 1970) C-91 min.

PRODUCER: Bob Booker
DIRECTOR: Lee H. Katzin
STORY: Booker
SCREENPLAY: Stan Cornyn
ASSISTANT DIRECTOR: Les Sheldon
PRODUCTION DESIGNER: Stan Jolley
MUSIC: Mike Stoller
SONGS: Stoller and Jerry Leiber
SOUND: John Kean
CAMERA: Michel Hugo
EDITOR: Danny Cohn

A. Michael Miller, Ray Chippeway, Dennis Larden, Lonny Stevens *(The Phynx);* Lou Antonio *(Corrigan);* Mike Kellin *(Bogey);* Michael Ansara *(Colonel Rostinov);* George Tobias *(Markvitch);* Joan Blondell *(Ruby);* Martha Raye *(Foxy);* Larry Hankin *(Philbaby);* Teddy Eccles *(Wee Johnny Urlso);* Ultra Violet *(Herself);* Pat McCormack *(Father O'Hoolihan);* Joseph Gazal *(Yakov);* Bob Williams *(Number One);* Barbara Noonan *(Bogey's Secretary);* Rich Little *(Voice in Box);* Sue Bernard, Ann Morrell, Sherry Mills *(Girls);* Patty Andrews, Busby Berkeley, Xavier Cugat, Fritz Feld, John Hart, Ruby Keeler, Joe E. Louis, Marilyn Maxwell, Maureen O'Sullivan, Harold "Oddjob" Sakata, Ed Sullivan, Rona Barrett, James Brown, Cass Daley, Leo Gorcey, Louis Hayward, Patsy Kelly, Guy Lombardo, Butterfly McQueen, Richard Pryor, Colonel Harland Sanders, Rudy Vallee, Johnny Weissmuller, Edgar Bergen, Dick Clark, Andy Devine, Huntz Hall, George Jessel, Dorothy Lamour, Trini Lopez, Pat O'Brien, Jay Silverheels, Clint Walker *(Themselves);* Sally Struthers *(No. 1 Fan).*

WELCOME HOME, JOHNNY BRISTOL
(CBS-TV, 1972) C-100 min.

PRODUCER: Arthur Joel Katz
DIRECTOR: George McGowan
TELEPLAY: Stanley R. Greenberg
MUSIC: Lalo Schifrin
CAMERA: Robert L. Morrison
EDITOR: Carroll Sax

Martin Landau *(Captain Johnny Bristol);* Jane Alexander *(Anne Palmer);* Brock Peters *(Dr. Berdall);* Martin Sheen *(Graytak);* Pat O'Brien *(Sergeant McGill);* Forrest Tucker *(Harry McMartin);* Mona Freeman *(Margaret Bristol);* Jane Elliott *(Virginia);* Claudia Bryar *(Mrs. Tyson);* John Hoyt *(Minister);* Simon Scott *(Colonel Anderson);* Mark Roberts *(Mr. Bristol);* James McEachin *(Loughton);* Alan Bergman *(Suster);* Richard Evans *(Franks).*

THE ADVENTURES OF NICK CARTER
(ABC-TV, 1972) C-72 min.

EXECUTIVE PRODUCER: Richard Irving
PRODUCER: Stan Kallis
DIRECTOR: Paul Krasny
TELEPLAY: Ken Pettus
MUSIC: John Andrew Tartaglia
ART DIRECTOR: Henry Bumstead
SET DECORATOR: James Payne
COSTUMES: Burton Miller
CAMERA: Alric Edens
EDITOR: Robert F. Shugrue

Robert Conrad *(Nick Carter);* Shelley Winters *(Bess Tucker);* Broderick Crawford *(Otis Duncan);* Neville Brand *(Captain Dan Keller);* Pernell Roberts *(Neal Duncan);* Pat O'Brien *(Hallelujah Harry);* Sean Garrison *(Lloyd Deems);* Laraine Stephens *(Joyce Jordan);* Dean Stockwell *(Freddy Duncan);* Brooke Bundy *(Roxy O'Rourke);* Sorrell Booke *(Dr. Zimmerman);* Joseph R. Maross *(Archer);* Ned Glass *(Maxie);* Paul Mantee *(O'Hara);* Jaye P. Morgan *(Plush House Singer);* Arlene Martel *(Flo);* Byron Morrow *(Sam Bates).*

KISS ME, KILL ME
(ABC-TV, 1976) C-78 min.

EXECUTIVE PRODUCER: Stanley Kalis
DIRECTOR: Michael O'Herlihy
TELEPLAY: Robert E. Thompson
MUSIC: Richard Markowitz
ART DIRECTORS: Ross Bellah, Robert Peterson
CAMERA: Meredith Nicholson
EDITOR: Arthur D. Hilton

Stella Stevens *(Stella Stafford);* Michael Anderson, Jr. *(Dan Hodges);* Dabney Coleman *(Captain Hogan);* Claude Akins *(Harry Grant);* Bruce Boxleitner *(Douglas Lane);* Alan Fudge *(Lieutenant Dugget);* Bruce Glover *(Hovak);* Morgan Paull *(Deukmajian);* Tisha Sterling *(Maureen);* Charles Weldon *(Hicks);* Pat O'Brien *(Jimmy the Morgue Attendant);* Robert Vaughn *(Fuller).*

BILLY JACK GOES TO WASHINGTON
(Taylor-Laughlin, 1977) C-155 min.

EXECUTIVE PRODUCER: Delores Taylor
PRODUCER: Frank Capra, Jr.
DIRECTOR: T. C. Frank (Tom Laughlin);
BASED ON THE SCREENPLAY *Mr. Smith Goes to Washington* BY SIDNEY BUCHMAN AND THE STORY BY LEWIS R. FOSTER
SCREENPLAY: Frank and Teresa Cristina (Laughlin, Taylor)
MUSIC: Elmer Bernstein
ART DIRECTOR: Hilyard Brown
CAMERA: Jack Merta

Tom Laughlin *(Billy Jack);* Delores Taylor *(Jean Roberts);* E. G. Marshall *(Senator Joseph Paine);* Teresa Laughlin *(Staff Worker);* Sam Wanamaker *(Bailey);* Lucie Arnaz *(Saunders McArthur);* Dick Gautier *(Governor Hubert Hopper);* Pat O'Brien *(Vice President).*

THE END
(United Artists, 1978) C-100 min.

EXECUTIVE PRODUCER: Hank Moonjean
PRODUCER: Lawrence Gordon
DIRECTOR: Burt Reynolds
SCREENPLAY: Jerry Belson
MUSIC: Paul Williams
ORCHESTRATOR: Harry Betts
COSTUMES/WARDROBE: Norman Salling, Gene Deardorff, Violet Cane
ASSISTANT DIRECTOR: Kurt Baker
STUNT COORDINATOR: Hal Needham
PRODUCTION DESIGNER: Jan Scott
SET DECORATOR: John Franco, Jr.
CHOREOGRAPHY: Lisa Mordente
MAKEUP: Tom Ellingwood
SOUND: Richard Portman, Jack Solomon
CAMERA: Bobby Byrne
EDITOR: Donn Cambern

Burt Reynolds *(Sonny Lawson);* Dom DeLuise *(Maron Borunki);* Sally Field *(Mary Ellen);* Strother Martin *(Dr. Kling);* David Steinberg *(Marty Lieberman);* Joanne Woodward *(Jessica);* Norman Fell *(Dr. Krugman);* Myrna Loy *(Maureen Lawson);* Kristy McNichol *(Julie Lawson);* Pat O'Brien *(Ben Lawson);* Robby Benson *(Priest);* Carl Reiner *(Dr. Maneet);* James Best *(Pacemaker Patient);* Jock Mahoney *(Old Man);* Peter Gonzales *(Latin Lover);* Connie Fleming *(Girl Dancer);* Ken Johnson *(Whistling Lunatic);* Janice Carroll *(Ballet Teacher);* Louise Letourneau *(Receptionist);* Bill Ewing *(Hearse Driver);* Robert Rothwell *(Limousine Driver).*

FOUR

WALTER PIDGEON

6′ 3″
195 pounds
Black hair
Blue eyes
Libra

Walter Pidgeon's virile, Olympian professionalism has been such a winning asset for so many stellar films that it seems almost tragic that he devoted his golden MGM years to being a straight man for Miss Greer Garson.

Towering and handsome, he has been a busy actor for over fifty years, changing his professional status several times as he weathered the many seasons of Hollywood. Throughout, he never openly fretted about the ups and downs of his career. Now past eighty, the rascally, delightfully unpretentious actor retains a strong dedication to his acting craft.

Pidgeon was the type of actor who fit perfectly in the sprawling, grandiose studio system that characterized the great days of Metro-Goldwyn-Mayer. Baritone-voiced Walter loved the camaraderie of the movie lot life and the promise it held of constant activity. He was a little bit personality and a good deal actor. While not always exciting to watch onscreen (one critic called him "that handsome piece of screen furniture"), Walter was always poised, intelligent, and splendidly professional.

Walter Pidgeon is one of the last of the Hollywood "greats." His presence today reminds audiences of the special magic, the larger-than-life quality of actors years ago, when the world was seemingly more comprehensible and class was a quality easier to appreciate—and to find.

Walter Davis Pidgeon was born on Thursday, September 23, 1897 (1898 is usually given) in East St. John, New Brunswick, Canada. His father, Caleb Burpee Pidgeon, owned a men's furnishings store, where Walter worked after school as a young boy. His education included a diploma from the Alexander School where a young Russian emigrant named Louis B. Mayer had studied years earlier.

The military seemed to be Walter's inevitable vocation. His brothers became Canadian soldiers: David an officer in the national army and Charles a doctor in the Canadian army's medical corps. With such leanings in the family, Walter began haunting local recruiting offices when he was only sixteen, but a family member would always arrive in time with a birth certificate and drag the lad home. After a year at the University of New Brunswick, Walter abandoned his schooling and finally gained admittance to the army. He received a lieutenant's commission in the 65th Battery of the Canadian Field Artillery, in which brother David was a colonel.

Events soon terminated Walter's military career. During a training assignment at Camp Petawawa, Walter was trapped between two gun carriages. His serious chest injuries caused a seventeen-month hospital stay, a discharge from the army, and bouts with pleurosy and pneumonia. Advised to seek out a warmer climate, Walter traveled to Boston because his childhood sweetheart, Edna Pickles, was living there as an art student. In 1919 Walter joined her there and soon landed a job as a "runner" for the National Shawmut Bank. After achieving some degree of financial security, Walter wed Edna in 1922.

Walter's marriage to Edna resulted in the second

major catastrophe of his young life. In 1923, while giving birth to daughter Edna Verne, his wife Edna died. Walter placed the infant in his mother's care, and it would be she who would raise the girl. Having suffered two calamities at so young an age, Walter soon became "conditioned" to the rigors of life and developed a realistic, level-headed outlook on the ways of the world.

After the death of Edna, Walter worked as a bond salesman in Boston and studied at the New England Conservatory of Music, concentrating on "vocal development." His studies there led him to join the local Copley Players, headed by Britisher E. E. Clive. He made his stage bow in Shaw's comedy of manners, *You Never Can Tell.* Fate carried him from there. As he recalled, at a Boston party he met Fred Astaire who was then appearing with his sister Adele in Boston in *Lady Be Good.* "I was in the bond business, and I can't think of who it was who had a party. I was sitting at the piano, playing and singing, and Fred and Adele came in around midnight. The host brought Fred over and introduced me, and Fred said: 'What show are you with?' And I said, 'I'm not with any show.' He said, 'Oh, you're in vaudeville?' I said no. The host said, 'No, he sells bonds.' Fred later on came over and said, 'Why in the hell don't you get on the stage?' I kiddingly said, 'Why don't you *put* me on the stage?' And the next thing I knew, in about a month, I had a call from Charlie Dillingham in New York."

Charles Dillingham and his partner Arthur Hammerstein were top promoters of young musical talent, but Walter did not immediately impress them sufficiently to land an engagement. However, he did impress Elsie Janis. The very talented performer, noted for her singing, dancing, and uncanny abilities as a mimic, was searching for a partner for a scheduled tour. Six-foot, three-inch Walter appealed to her—reputedly in more ways than one. He became her new baritone onstage, and, despite Elsie's mama chaperoning the tour, her new romance offstage. (Walter originally auditioned for Elsie under the stage name of Walter Verne—picked in honor of his daughter. When Elsie got to know him better, she insisted that he return to using Walter Pidgeon, asserting: "It's so funny, people will remember it.")

Following his concert tour with Elsie in late 1924, Walter continued his happy association with her on Broadway. On Monday, February 2, 1925, he joined Elsie, a fleet of comedy and song-and-dance acts, and a young Englishman named Cyril Ritchard in the revue *Puzzles of 1925.* Though Elsie was *the* star of the production, convulsing audiences with her last-act impression of such popular favorites as Lenore Ulric, Beatrice Lillie, and John Barrymore, all the cast received a substantial showcase. The *New York Times* called the program "an unassuming and almost continually entertaining revue," and the show ran for 104 performances at the Fulton Theatre. While Walter benefited professionally from the exposure, *Variety* took occasion to lambast him in their review of *Puzzles of 1925.* The trade paper's critique of his performance has doggedly cropped up in nearly every summation of his career. "Pidgeon looks like an old and stale Abe Lincoln and sings like the graduate of a Southern Iowa correspondence school. Who wants vaudeville when it involves that?"

Variety's pique did nothing to cool the admiration of smitten Elsie Janis for Walter's talents. When she left in the summer of 1925 for London to open in the musical *At Home,* Walter accompanied her and enjoyed a sizable spot in the show. This time, Walter's performance drew bad reviews from another theatrical institution—John Barrymore. The Great Profile was in London, caught the show at the Shaftsbury Theatre, and called on Walter backstage to express his condolences for a job badly done. However, he did offer some advice: "You have nothing to do and you're trying to make *Hamlet* out of it. When you have nothing to do, do it beautifully. I never act—I use my horse sense." In 1949, when Walter visited London to film scenes for MGM's *The Miniver Story,* he related that Barrymore's suggestion was a cornerstone for his later success in the American cinema.

Though the celebrated seemed to scoff at Walter's work, the young baritone had actually done well, winning a following due to his pleasant stage manner and towering, broad-shouldered good looks (especially impressive at a time when actors tended to be small and foppish). He had also signed with Victor Records and was the first to record Irving Berlin's "What'll I Do?" (which he introduced on his first tour with Elsie). These trimmings persuaded Joseph Schenck to offer Walter a Hollywood contract, dangling the promise of a leading romantic assignment opposite Schenck's then-wife Norma Talmadge as bait. Walter bit and said goodbye to promoter-lover Elsie Janis. Their paths were not to cross professionally again.[1]

Once in the splendor of 1925 Hollywood, Walter realized that he had been a bit premature in accepting a film contract. The role opposite Miss Talmadge mysteriously evaporated and for months he did nothing but enjoy the sunshine. Finally a call came from Paramount and Walter received a role in *Man-*

[1]Elsie (Bierbauer) Janis was born in Columbis, Ohio on March 16, 1889 and would die in Beverly Hills on February 26, 1956. Her career never fully survived the demise of vaudeville though she worked now and then (e.g., she directed Broadway's *New Faces of 1934* and made one talkie, the Republic programmer *Women in War,* in 1942). Her entertaining autobiography, *So Far So Good,* was published in 1932.

nequin (1926), as a reporter who returns a grown-up Dolores Costello, kidnaped in infancy, to her real parents, Alice Joyce and Warner Baxter. Walter photographed well and soon began working steadily, if unexcitedly, at various studios. His second film, Fox's *The Outsider* (1926), placed him in support of Jacqueline Logan and Lou Tellegen, and inspired nothing resembling the furor caused by the Broadway play original which had starred Katharine Cornell and Lionel Atwill. Walter next visited First National where he was leading man to Anna Q. Nilsson in *Miss Nobody* (1926), stayed on the lot to steal Lewis Stone's wife in *Old Loves and New* (1926), and completed the year as the "other man" in Fox's *Marriage License.*

Pidgeon's status in Hollywood on the eve of the transition to sound was a rather strange one. His professional forte was singing, a talent obviously impossible to display in the silent cinema. Without any real dramatic acclaim from critics in his background, producers regarded Walter primarily as a good-looking clotheshorse who could glide elegantly through the paces of lightweight romance and drama. Hence, his screen chores were relatively tame ones. He stayed solvent playing roles like the love interest in First National's mystery *The Gorilla* (1927), the English gentleman who falls under the sordid spell of half-caste Dolores Del Rio in Fox's *The Gateway of the Moon* (1928), and the shipwrecked sailor saved by exotic Myrna Loy in Lumas Films' *Turn Back the Hours* (1928). The best accolade these pictures won for Walter was "serviceable." Still he was steadily employed and soon had become dependent on films as a way of life. He left behind no great legacy on the New York stage, but already he had acquired a tasteful domain in Beverly Hills.

With Noble Johnson and Dolores Del Rio in *The Gateway of the Moon* (1928).

With Dolores Costello in *Mannequin* (1926).

In the fall of 1928, Walter was well received in Universal's first all-talking film, *Melody of Love.* He portrayed a war casualty whose wounds ruin his career as a pianist until a loving French girl (Mildred Harris) helps him back to success. This production won Walter a degree of attention. As First National Pictures prepared to enter the sound era with a procession of musicals, they signed Walter to a term contract as the studio's "house baritone." After playing roué to Billie Dove in *Her Private Life* (1929), he was announced for Tiffany's *The Voice Within* (1929) with Eva Southern and Montague Shaw but that never came to be. Walter was back at First National for *A Most Immoral Lady* (1929) as the savior of Leatrice Joy. After a guest appearance (playing himself) in First National's *Show Girl in Hollywood* (1930), he won a few good reviews as the Austrian colonel who sings Vivienne Segal into ecstasy in *Bride of the Regiment* (1930), a Technicolor version of Sigmund Romberg's operetta *The Lady in Ermine.* In commenting on Walter's work, the *New York Times* captured the essence of the escapism: "Walter Pidgeon, who portrays the Austrian colonel Vultow, a man who knows a pretty face when he sees it, also lifts his voice in song. He does moderately well with his role, giving quite a good portrayal of an Army officer getting tipsy, then suddenly sobering up and ordering more champagne, which he drinks freely until he falls asleep and dreams of the fair countess."

Shortly after this feature premiered in the spring of 1930, *Photoplay* magazine published a large portrait of the uniformed, tousled-haired, moustached Walter. The accompanying feature story was entitled "He Has the Girls Gasping!" and contained such newsworthy items as: "He is tall—six feet something or other—remarkably handsome and always well-tailored. He is consistently gallant, is never at a loss for a 'Beau Brummel' phrase, but in no way suggests the smart cracker. His home is one of the most perfectly appointed and smoothly managed in the hills of the Beverlys. His wines are excellent although he himself has never tasted them. He is as natural as the key of C, and as charming as a Barrie hero. Walter has the finest head of hair of any man

With Myrna Loy in *Bride of the Regiment* (1930).

With Claudia Dell in *Sweet Kitty Bellairs* (1930).

on the screen. And here's his secret—he never washes it!"

Photoplay happily announced that more operettas were in the works to showcase Walter's abilities, and summed him up, "In a town devoted to manners, it is refreshing to find one person, at least, with manners."

Walter was next in *Sweet Kitty Bellairs* (1930), an eighteenth century yarn in color with Walter as dashing Lord Verney. Claudia Dell was the leading lady. There followed an auspicious release, *Viennese Nights* (1930), the first operetta written specifically for the screen. With libretto and music by Sigmund Romberg and Oscar Hammerstein II, the color feature was considered a triumph for Pidgeon, who again romanced Vivienne Segal in song.

The film industry was already sensing that the public was becoming satiated with all-talking, all-singing, all-dancing films, and First National executives sought to promote Walter in other directions. They supplied him with non-singing assignments with dismal results. He appeared as the pilot pal of Joe E. Brown in *Going Wild* (1930) and then repeated the romantic lead in the 1931 remake of *The Gorilla.* The studio had delayed the release of Walter's latest operetta, but finally released *Kiss Me Again* in early 1931. Pidgeon co-starred with Bernice Claire. Once again he essayed a singing soldier in this adaptation of Victor Herbert's and Henry Blossom's *Mlle. Modiste.* The color production was expensively expansive, but public acceptance was apathetic, and First National wisely decided to drop plans for future musicals.

There were already clear indications that First National had lost hope for Walter's screen promise. In *The Hot Heiress* (1931), he was merely the stuffy society fiancé of Ona Munson, losing her to a singing Ben Lyon.

Meanwhile, on December 22, 1931, in Chicago, Walter remarried. His bride was Ruth Hollister Walker of Connecticut. According to later press releases, the attractive brunette "never had film ambitions."

Subsequent inferior screen roles in drab projects only made Walter's discomfiture in non-musical Hollywood all the more obvious. First National had so promising a contract roster of stars—including James Cagney, Edward G. Robinson, Paul Muni—that although they continued Walter's contract, he appeared in only three films in the next two years, and two of them were done on loan-out. At RKO he supported Joel McCrea and Paul Lukas as the men in Constance Bennett's orbit in *Rockabye* (1932), an unabashed tearjerker directed by George Cukor. In the

With Vivienne Segal in *Viennese Nights* (1930).

spring of 1933 Walter appeared in Universal's *The Kiss Before the Mirror,* a project stylishly controlled by ace director James Whale. Pidgeon was cast as the heel who dallies with the wife (Gloria Stuart) of Paul Lukas (one of his best offscreen friends). While the picture won a good response, it did nothing to boost Walter's collapsing motion picture career.

In a bid to resuscitate his status, Walter began acting on the stage of the Hollywood Playhouse, and in 1933 he starred in productions of *Androcles and the Lion* and *Romance Collect.* His reviews were generally satisfactory, but he finally admitted to himself that his operatic baritone image was too weighty a burden. He understood that a dramatic metamorphosis must occur in his career if he was to survive.

In early 1934 Pidgeon unceremoniously completed his First National contract in *Journal of a Crime,* a vehicle for the lot's top-paid female attraction, Ruth Chatterton. He played an operetta singer who delivers "Devil May Care" and was mired in very minor billing. Once again it appeared that his Hollywood future was ended, and he decided to try the Broadway stage again, auditioning for vehicles that did not require him to accomplish anything with his vocal training. As he admitted later, "I was almost wrecked by musicals. I was established as a singer at a time when they couldn't give musicals away. For one of them there was actually a sign in the theatre lobby that said: 'Mr. Pidgeon will sing only once in this picture.' "

Pidgeon discovered happily that he had no great difficulty finding stage work in New York. In June 1934, *No More Ladies,* a comedy that had starred Melvyn Douglas, had closed for the summer. When it reopened on Monday, September 3, 1934 at the Morosco Theatre, Pidgeon replaced Douglas as wayward husband Sheridan Warren. Despite its previous success and critical approval, the play did not duplicate its original box-office results, and it folded after sixteen performances. (In the 1935 MGM film version, Robert Montgomery would inherit the male lead assignment opposite Joan Crawford.)

Undaunted, Pidgeon remained in New York, and he soon landed a starring spot with Tallulah Bankhead in her spring offering *Something Gay.* It opened at the Morosco Theatre on Monday, April 29, 1935. The play again cast Pidgeon as a philandering husband, here one Herbert Gray whose affairs drive wife Bankhead into having an extramarital romance of her own. The reviews were none too good. The

New York Times sighed, "Spring is here. This column is dying to praise something. . . . Honestly, there is nothing to praise except Miss Bankhead's plucky spirit in the face of continuous adversity." The play stretched out a run of seventy-two performances.

As soon as *Something Gay* expired, Walter went immediately into rehearsals for *There's Wisdom in Women,* a comedy by Joseph C. Kesselring (who later wrote *Arsenic and Old Lace*). Once again, Pidgeon was typecast as a heel husband, this time as egomaniacal pianist Leon Nordoff whose infidelity sends his spouse on a seek-and-destroy mission to find the little tart who has been stealing his affections. The play tried out at the Red Barn Theatre in Locust Valley, Long Island, attracting pleasant critical response. However, when it appeared that the play would not find the backing for a Broadway opening, Pidgeon joined the company of *The Night of January 16,* a courtroom melodrama by Bayard Veiller. Walter was cast as "Guts" Regan, a brutal gangster "whose cultured insouciance should be the envy of scholarly gangsters in this neighborhood" *(New York Times).* When the drama debuted on Monday, September 16, 1935 at the Ambassador Theatre, it became an immediate success. One of the show's publicity-grabbing gimmicks was that the management chose the jury from the nightly audience and paid each member $3.00 for his or her services. (On opening night, the jury included Jack Dempsey.) The play enjoyed 232 performances, but Pidgeon wanted a variety of professional experiences. Thus when the Broadway production of *There's Wisdom in Women* became set, he left the thriller to join the incoming show.

There's Wisdom in Women opened at the Cort Theatre on Monday, October 30, 1935. It won for Walter his best stage reviews to date, allowing him to be extravagantly amusing as well as providing him the opportunity to show his skill at the piano. "In it, you will discover the personable Mr. Pidgeon," wrote the *New York Times,* "tearing the air with despair and banging the piano with an attack at keys and pedals that is nothing short of enviable." But the play lasted only forty-six performances. Fortunately, in early 1936 Pidgeon signed a personal contract with film producer Walter Wanger to return to California and to the movies (where he was to earn $40,000 in salary that year).

Wanger and Paramount first employed Pidgeon as Richard Morey, the jewel-heisting partner of Lloyd Nolan in the screwball comedy *Big Brown Eyes* (1936) in which Joan Bennett and Cary Grant enjoyed the top roles. Though his assignment was as a "heavy," Pidgeon welcomed the opportunity to display some versatility—and to avoid having to sing onscreen.

How determined Walter was in his decision never to return to singing roles was proved shortly after his Hollywood return. At Universal, James Whale was

With Hedda Hopper in *Big Brown Eyes* (1936).

preparing to direct Carl Laemmle, Jr.'s remake of *Show Boat,* with Irene Dunne, Helen Morgan, and Charles Winninger in the leading parts. Universal offered Walter the enviable role of gambler Gaylord Ravenal but, to the shock of everyone, the actor rejected the plum assignment. Universal eventually borrowed Allan Jones from MGM to portray Ravenal in that box-office bonanza.

Slowly Pidgeon's movie career underwent a change. After he played a good guy who saves Mary Ellis from a murderer's clutches in the Paramount B film *Fatal Lady* (1936), Wanger dropped his option on Pidgeon. The actor then accepted a contract bid from Universal. That more modest lot which had flourished under the erratic Carl Laemmle in the early 1930s was surrendered to new management in 1936. The new bosses decided to win solvency via low-budget romances and musicals. Recognizing Walter as a serviceable leading man, Universal rushed him into a series of production-line products. The films won him no plaudits but did prove that he was a workable leading man.

Under the spinning talisman of the Universal trademark globe, Walter's first picture there was *She's Dangerous* (1937) in which he romanced Tala Birell. (Cesar Romero had the male lead.) Then as virile District Attorney Paul Stacey he saved Gloria Stuart from the electric chair in *Girl Overboard* (1937). In *As Good as Married* (1937) he supported Universal favorite John Boles and leading lady Doris Nolan. (She was Pidgeon's co-star in Broadway's *The Night of January 16.*) These programmers appeared within a three-month period, winning Walter some public attention and, more importantly, some attention from MGM.

When it came to recruiting top talent, Louis B. Mayer was insatiable. For years his Metro-Goldwyn-Mayer lot, acknowledged by most all as the Mount Olympus of Hollywood, enjoyed the accolade of possessing more stars than in the heavens. Mayer had met Walter early in the latter's film career. He took note of him mainly because he came from Mayer's home town of New Brunswick. Now he saw in Pidgeon a mature (he was thirty-nine), competent professional who could work comfortably in a variety of formats. Mayer instructed MGM to buy up Pidgeon's Universal contract. By the late spring of 1937, Walter began his twenty-year tenure at Metro-Goldwyn-Mayer.

Walter's first film under the MGM banner was the tragic *Saratoga,* MGM's top grosser of 1937 as filmgoers morbidly lined up at theatres to witness the last days of Jean Harlow. She died of uremic poisoning during production and her scenes had to be completed by Mary Dees, a blonde double photographed from the back or with her face almost hidden. The horse-racing yarn placed Walter as Jean's English beau, rivaling Clark Gable for her affections. It was the first picture of a formula format for Walter, who would earn much of his Metro paycheck over the next few years losing Myrna Loy, Jeanette MacDonald, and Margaret Sullavan in final reels. Walter's work in *Saratoga* won him immediate notice for a rather unnerving reason: cinema addicts revered him as the second-last actor to hold Miss Harlow in his arms before a camera.

Universal had reserved the right to employ Walter in one more film, and the result was *A Girl with Ideas* (1937) in which he plagued the plans of distaff newspaper manager Wendy Barrie. Back at Culver City, *My Dear Miss Aldrich* (1937) followed, with Walter romancing Maureen O'Sullivan whenever Edna May Oliver was not stealing the limelight with her inimitable sourness.

Pidgeon discovered that his work schedule was packed with assignments, most of which called for him to play suitor to the lot's leading ladies. In the moderate programmers he would emerge romantically victorious, but in the prestige productions he would be the loser to the male star. In *Man-Proof* (1938) he joined a romantic quadrangle including Myrna Loy, Franchot Tone, and Rosalind Russell. In the Jeanette MacDonald-Nelson Eddy operetta *The Girl of the Golden West* (1938), he was the heavy, Sheriff Jack Rance, who romantically pursues Jeanette while professionally chasing her true love, outlaw Nelson. The cliché-filled finale found the law enforcer neglecting his duty to allow the stars a happy ending together. *The Shopworn Angel* (1938) was a continuation of the Margaret Sullavan-James Stewart starring team, with Walter as the slick Broadway producer who temporarily enjoys Miss Sullavan's favors.

Too Hot to Handle (1938) found the actor again competing with Gable (both as reporters covering the Sino-Japanese war) for the hand of aviatrix Myrna Loy. Of course, Walter lost. The *New York Times* summed up both his performance and his MGM status with its review, "Walter Pidgeon takes his defeat like a good supporting player." The easy-going *Listen, Darling* was a showcase for Judy Garland and the maturing presence of Freddie Bartholomew. Here Pidgeon was allowed to win the hand of widow Mary Astor.

Pleased with the solid, dependable work of Walter in these 1938 releases, MGM gave him a promotion of sorts in his next year's output. The studio rarely soiled its hands with a really low-budget entry, but, like all studios, it did depend on modest programmers to keep the employees active and the revenue rolling in. Walter became the busiest leading man of these modest efforts in Culver City in 1939. As he

With Jean Harlow and Clark Gable in *Saratoga* (1937).

With Edna May Oliver in *My Dear Miss Aldrich* (1937).

With Jeanette MacDonald in *The Girl of the Golden West* (1938).

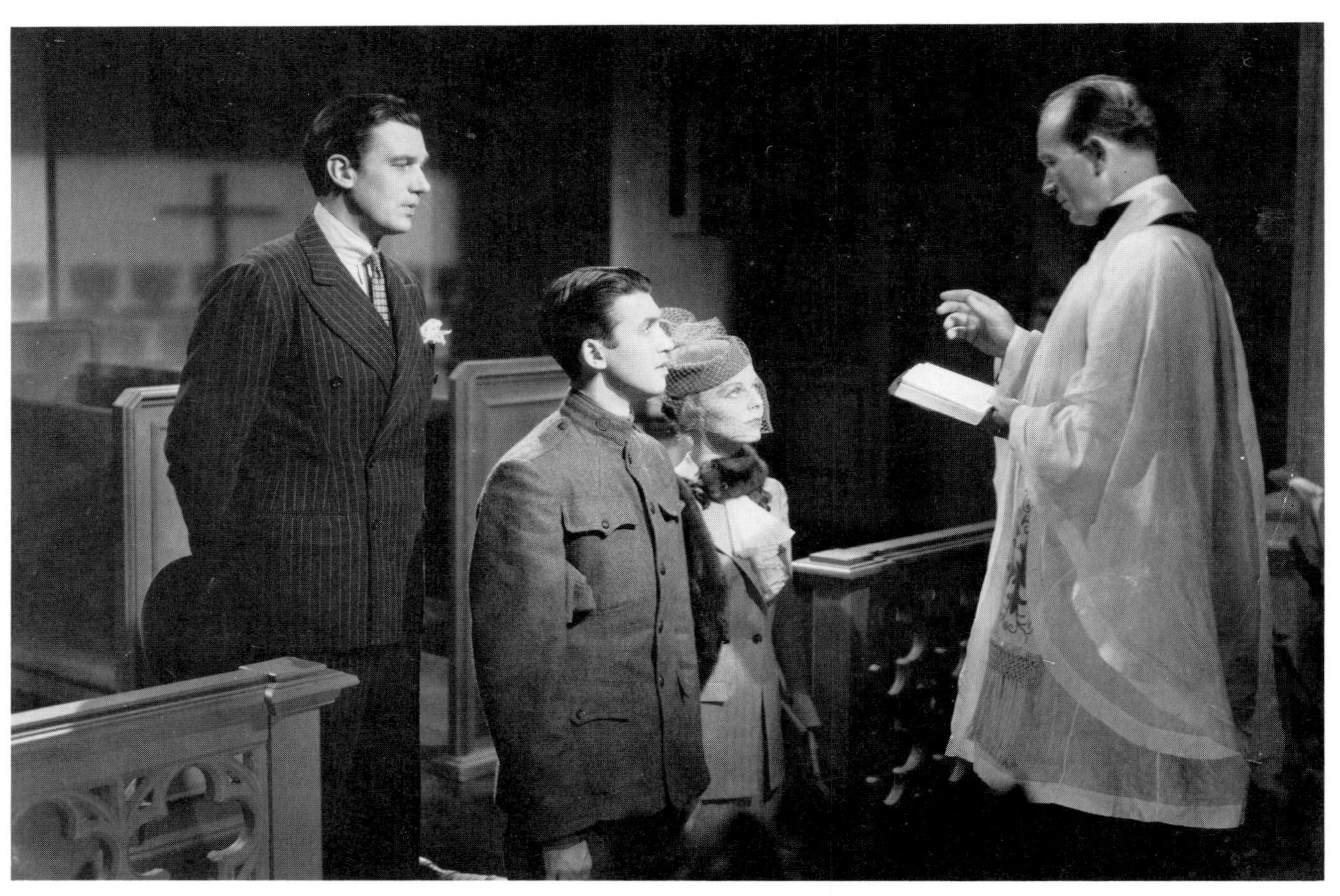

With James Stewart, Margaret Sullavan, and William Stack in *Shopworn Angel* (1938).

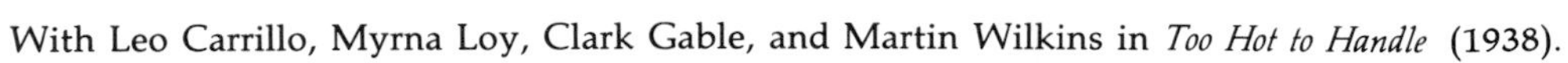

With Leo Carrillo, Myrna Loy, Clark Gable, and Martin Wilkins in *Too Hot to Handle* (1938).

would later say in his role as a moviemaker in *The Bad and the Beautiful* (1952), "Give me a picture that ends with a kiss and black ink on the books." Louis B. Mayer liked these bread-and-butter type pictures as much as any producer.

Society Lawyer (1939) was a remake of *Penthouse* (1933) which had starred Warner Baxter and Myrna Loy. This time, Walter was the District Attorney and Virginia Bruce was the nightclub chanteuse whom he bails out of difficulty. *6,000 Enemies* (1939) was a solid prison yarn, with Walter again a D.A., here framed and sent to an institution where many of his convicted cases are imprisoned. Rita Johnson, briefly considered by Metro as the new Harlow, was the leading lady. Next came *Stronger Than Desire* (1939), a remake of 1934's *Evelyn Prentiss,* again featuring Pidgeon as an attorney and again assigning him the task of clearing Virginia Bruce.

One role which Walter began never reached the screen. In 1938, Mayer, delighted with the furor Hedy Lamarr had caused on loan-out to Walter Wanger in *Algiers,* planned an epic romance story, *I Take This Woman,* to showcase her beauty. Spencer Tracy was her leading man with Walter as the second lead, and Marlene Dietrich's former mentor, Josef von Sternberg, was hired to direct. Many problems, including the firing of von Sternberg, caused the production to stop. By the time definitive shooting got underway again, now with W. S. Van Dyke II in charge, Walter was busy elsewhere and his role was played by Kent Taylor in the eventual 1940 release.

Walter completed 1939 in the title role of *Nick Carter, Master Detective,* Metro's answer to the Basil Rathbone *Sherlock Holmes* series that had begun at 20th Century-Fox. As the pleasant sleuth, Walter began his trio of Carter films by defeating alien attempts to create a rocket ship.[2] Rita Johnson was yet again his leading lady. "Walter Pidgeon's Nick Carter is a comfortably uncerebral sleuth," reported the *New York Times.* "It's good, for a change, to meet a detective who does not stumble over hairpins while failing to notice a ten-ton truck."

Pidgeon was now forty-two years old, and he had experienced enough low points in his acting career to prevent him from taking himself too seriously. He never regarded himself as an especially strong actor, and he assumed that another decline would most certainly arrive before too much time elapsed. Thus he carefully invested his Metro paychecks in various business enterprises and Texas oil property.

Despite his own feelings of insecurity, Metro found Walter's utilitarian services quite useful, even for loan-out services. Universal's *It's a Date* (1940) was a vehicle for the lot's plump little songbird, Deanna Durbin. (She sang Schubert's "Ave Maria" in this one.) Walter played the tycoon beau of Kay Francis, herself in rapid decline since her starring days at Warner Bros. As David Shipman wrote of Pidgeon's performance in this picture in his book *The Great Movie Stars: The Golden Years* (1970), "At last he was carving a niche as a nice, pipe-smoking, mature leading man. He was so easy, so comfortable, so solid (in the best sense) that his way to real stardom was finally going to be short and simple." *It's a Date* did well at the box office, and Walter discovered that, for the first time since 1930, his fan mail was again becoming voluminous and occasionally even passionate.

A less fortunate assignment was Walter Wanger's *The House Across the Bay* (1940). In this unsavory United Artists release, he was one of three loves (George Raft and Lloyd Nolan were the others) of an apparently insatiable Joan Bennett. The building of the title was Alcatraz prison. Then Republic borrowed Pidgeon to play the Confederate guerrilla Quantrill (here called "Cantrell") in Raoul Walsh's *Dark Command* (1940). Walter joined such sagebrush favorites as John Wayne, Roy Rogers, and Gabby Hayes in this venture. The film did well with action fans, and Pidgeon returned to MGM with fresh prestige.

Unfortunately, Louis B. Mayer did not have a vehicle ready for Walter upon his return. Clark Gable, James Stewart, and Robert Taylor continued getting the big scripts for perusals, and L.B. timidly offered Walter another Nick Carter picture. In *Phantom Raiders* (1940) Florence Rice was his leading lady, and this time the intrepid hero saves the Panama Canal from the havoc of bombers. Expecting the usual tirade of temperament from an escalating leading man who has discovered he has to do a programmer for his home studio, Mayer was shocked at Walter's reaction to his instructions: "Fine. They're popular, aren't they? They do a good business, don't they? When do I start?" So relieved was Mayer that Walter had so unassuming an attitude that he followed *Phantom Raiders* with a third (and last) Nick Carter tale, *Sky Murder* (1940), wherein Walter saves the country from subversive literature.

As 1940 drew to a close, the threat of U.S. involvement in the war against Germany and Japan was growing greater. Hollywood became propaganda conscious, and Metro was among the first to flaunt the power of the American military in *Flight Command* (1940). Of course, to entice viewers who simply did not want to witness a parade of airplanes, a subplot in which Commander Pidgeon's wife (Ruth Hussey) falls in love with sassy cadet Robert

[2]At one point it was a toss-up whether Pidgeon or MGM contractee Dennis O'Keefe would star in the detective series.

With Rita Johnson in *Nick Carter, Master Detective* (1939).

Advertisement for *The House Across the Bay* (1940).

With Claire Trevor in *Dark Command* (1940).

Taylor buoyed audience interest. Paramount went the similar route with more profitable results in *I Wanted Wings,* which appeared a few months later.

Walter's first release of the new year, *Design for Scandal* (1941)[3] hardly gave an indication of what *Photoplay* magazine would label "Hollywood's major male success story of 1941." It was a polished but inconsequential comedy in which craft reporter Pidgeon sets out to obtain a sensationalistic story on judge Rosalind Russell. Then Walter was loaned to 20th Century-Fox for *Man Hunt,* the Fritz Lang-directed thriller based on Geoffrey Household's novel *Rogue Male.* In the role of Captain Thorndike, a gentleman hunter who sneaks into shooting distance of Hitler's secret retreat, Pidgeon's character is the one who lines the Fuehrer's skull in his rifle sight and squeezes the trigger of an unloaded gun in a climax to his "sporting stalk." Walter played a role that might have been done by Fox's own Tyrone Power, but that younger, more swashbuckling star had just completed the rigorous *Blood and Sand* and was enjoying a break.

In *Man Hunt,* the "superior sinew and integrity" *(New York Times)* of Walter's Captain Thorndike made him the heroic hunted refugee of the first great Gestapo chase of the American cinema. It was one of the first film characters to markedly excite the propagandist imagination of American filmgoers. Director Lang, himself a German enraged by Hitler's machinations, spared no pains to make the Gestapo villains, headed by a superbly snide George Sanders, utterly detestable as they pursued Pidgeon across Britain. In the process his sacrificing streetwalker love, Joan Bennett, is killed. The denouement is a classic example of the powers of cinema persuasion. Pidgeon's character bails out of a bomber plane with a gun slung on his back, now seeking a non-sporting stalk on Hitler. As the voice-over narration concludes "Today, somewhere in Germany, a man with a high-powered rifle . . ." the audience is filled with loathing for the Third Reich.

When Walter returned to Metro, a certain new actress who was quickly ascending in the MGM constellation had requested him for her next vehicle. Pidgeon was enthused over the prospect. Still, little

[3]There had been plans to co-star Pidgeon with Lana Turner in *They Live by Night* in 1941, to be produced by Joe Pasternak, with Walter as a nightclub owner and Lana as a club photographer. Nothing came either of announcements that Pidgeon would join with Turner in 1942's *Mary Smith, U.S.A.,* a Mildred Cram tale of a small-town girl who kills a politician for disloyalty to America. It was to have been produced by Arthur Hornblow, Jr. and directed by Mervyn LeRoy.

With Ruth Hussey and Robert Taylor in a pose for *Flight Command* (1940).

With Rosalind Russell in *Design for Scandal* (1941).

did he expect that this picture opposite the Irish redhead who was his Beverly Hills neighbor would lead him to a two-pronged career change: ultimate popularity in a confining image mold.

Mr. Mayer had "discovered" Greer Garson in London where she was appearing on the stage in *Old Music*. Her refined beauty greatly excited Mayer. After some months of sitting at the Metro lot, she was an alternate choice for the wife's role opposite Robert Donat in *Goodbye Mr. Chips* (1939). For her performance, she won an Oscar nomination. *Pride and Prejudice* (1940) with Laurence Olivier further proved her worth to the studio mogul.

As Miss Garson would later recall, in her verbose but charming fashion, her initial screen test on the MGM lot had been opposite Walter: "I'd seen him. He lived near me when I first came out and rented a little house with my mother in Beverly Hills. I used to see this handsome gentleman three doors away weeding his lawn. [Walter loves his garden and green things.] He was so nice. When I was first brought over, Mr. Mayer said to him, 'Would you be kind enough to make a test with a young lady? She has been very successful on the London stage, but we don't know what she'll be like in front of the camera. Would you make a kind of a routine test?' He said, 'I'd be delighted.' He was such an angel and so sweet in the test—I was understandably very nervous."

This test turned out so well that by 1941 top-billed Greer was in the position to request Walter as her leading man: "I was always meeting him on the lot and he would say, 'Hello, Greer, when am I going to be your leading man?' The months dragged by and finally there was a script sent to me that I thought Walter was wonderful for and that nobody else should play. It was a picture in color, and Mervyn LeRoy directed it, and it was about orphans, and Texans, and things."

The film was *Blossoms in the Dust* (1941) in which Miss Garson plays Edna Gladney, founder of the Texas Children's Home and Aid Society. Walter was cast as Sam Gladney, her wealthy, sound, ever-patient husband. While he occupied a minimal amount of screen time in the hundred-minute sudser, the Garson-Pidgeon screen team appeared as

With Greer Garson in *Blossoms in the Dust* (1941).

With Greer Garson in *Blossoms in the Dust.*

a natural. Both appeared mature (Greer was then thirty-four, though her regality made her seem attractively older; Walter was forty-four), both suggested moral and social solidarity, and both were favorites of Mayer who took great pride in their status as MGM stars. He assured them of complete front office guardian-angelship on all their vehicles.

In his autobiography *Take One* (1974), director Mervyn LeRoy reminisced a bit about Walter: "Pidgeon would come onto the set every morning and the first thing he'd say would be, 'When do we eat?' I've never met anyone who was so constantly and consistently hungry, yet he never seemed to gain weight, despite his appetite. I envied him his metabolism. One problem I had with Walter was that, despite his suave and sophisticated air, he had never learned how to dance. There was a scene in *Blossoms in the Dust* where he was required to dance. 'Do I have to dance?' he asked. 'You'll have to rewrite it, because I don't know how to.' 'Why didn't you tell me that before?' I asked him. 'You've had the script for two months.' "

In early 1976 on a Mike Douglas TV show promoting *That's Entertainment, Part II,* LeRoy, Garson, and Pidgeon were reunited. Again the dancing problem was discussed, and Walter related: "You know what they did? They turned me loose with an instructor on Stage 14—it's four blocks long. I had to do a waltz. I could reverse—I had the whole doggone stage to do it. Now I get in with Mervyn on the picture, and it's in Greer's drawing room, and I had fifteen feet to turn around in. I couldn't do it! We did about eight or ten takes, and Mervyn said, 'Aw, let it go, it's so lousy we may get a laugh.' "

What LeRoy finally did was to have built a platform on skates on which Walter stood while Greer danced around him. As Miss Garson quipped on the talk show, "We were the first duet on a skateboard. . . . I think I ran around the circumference, and he stayed on the skateboard."

Blossoms in the Dust was a highly successful feature, although Anita Loos' script was more than a bit sticky. *Newsweek* magazine noted, "*Blossoms in the Dust* is an inspirational film of infrequent drama and such surcharged sentiment that its appeal will be chiefly limited to feminine audiences. . . . The cast, both adult and infant, is excellent. As the indomitable woman who has found comfortable homes for more than 2,000 foundlings, Greer Garson gives a sincere and believable performance. Walter Pidgeon as her husband . . . also manages to survive the powerful competition of dozens of babies of all sizes and colors."

Miss Garson was Oscar-nominated for Best Actress of the Year, but lost to Joan Fontaine *(Suspicion)*. *Blossoms in the Dust* itself was selected for a Best Picture Oscar bid, but it was defeated by an exceptional picture, one which advanced Walter higher onto the plateau of bankable stardom.

Richard Llewellyn's novel *How Green Was My Valley* had been a favorite on the fiction lists for some time in the United States. When Darryl F. Zanuck acquired the property for 20th Century-Fox, he ordered an all-out production. Originally he had hoped to film the picture in South Wales' Rhondda Valley, but the advent of World War II prevented that possibility. Instead the studio head erected an entire Welsh village and coal mine set in the Ventura

With Greer Garson in *Mrs. Miniver* (1942).

Hills of the San Fernando Valley. Hoping to instill simplicity into the film while maintaining a lavish production, Zanuck stocked the film with talented players, but not superstars. He again borrowed Walter from MGM to play the Reverend Mr. Gruffydd, the charismatic clergyman who inspires Roddy McDowall to walk and Maureen O'Hara to love. His powerful yet sensitive performance was monitored by John Ford, of whom Pidgeon would recall: "I'd never known a director like John Ford. My experiences with him on *How Green Was My Valley* force me to conclude he operates by telepathy. He smokes a pipe constantly—I doubt if he removes it from his mouth except to eat. He certainly doesn't remove it simply to talk. Furthermore, when he speaks, he mumbles. There's no kinder expression for it. I listened intently to his instructions and if five words out of seventy-five were intelligible I considered it a good average. With most directors the result of such obscurity would be hopeless confusion. With Ford, no. You go out on the set and find yourself following orders you haven't heard."[4]

How Green Was My Valley, released on the eve of Pearl Harbor, immediately occupied a special place in the hearts of American filmgoers. *Time* hailed the film as "Hollywood's answer to Wordsworth's definition of poetry: emotion recollected in tranquility." Ford won his third Oscar and the film was selected as Best Picture of the Year. Donald Crisp, as the patriarchal Mr. Morgan, won the Best Supporting Actor prize; Sara Allgood was nominated for Best Supporting Actress but lost to Mary Astor *(The Great Lie).* Walter enjoyed warm reviews for his sympathetic portrayal. He was now a box-office notable.

Though Walter had reaped great success onscreen helping homeless orphans, fighting Nazis, inspiring crippled children to walk and sacrificing true loves so that they did not have to share his poverty, offscreen his image was shaping up less nobly. He was a boisterous aficionado of the smarter clubs in Hollywood, and he occasionally caused raised eyebrows. At the New York City premiere of *How Green Was My Valley,* a companion nudged Walter to indicate that Wendell Willkie was among the celebrities filing into the theatre lobby. "You can have Willkie," shouted Walter among the tuxedoed and evening-gowned throng. "I'll take that pretty Mrs. Willkie!"

Nevertheless, Walter suggested comfortable nobility to wartime audiences. His next picture made him an institution as he fully invested himself in the pipe and slippers of Greer Garson's tweedy, stiff-upper-lipped mate. This was the magnificent *Mrs. Miniver* (1942), an instant classic and a phenomenon of the U.S. war-at-home. While this unforgettable portrait of 1939 England on the eve of Dunkirk was responsible for gaining Walter his greatest peak of movie popularity, he almost refused the project due to the perfectionist notoriety of the multi-take director, William Wyler.

In 1976 the American Film Institute presented its fourth annual Life Achievement Award to Wyler. Garson and Pidgeon were on hand following a clip from *Mrs. Miniver* to salute in tandem the director. As Walter reminisced: "I shudder when I think of the fight I put up to get out of doing this picture! I'm not kidding. . . . Somebody had said to me (and I won't mention what her name was), 'I thought if I ever heard him say again "What did you do it like that for?" I'd go out of my mind.' So I walked on the set and the very first scene I do, I finish the scene, Willy's sitting under the lens, and there's a long pause, and he looked up at me and he said: 'What did you do it like that for?'. . . . So I said, 'Well, Willy, so-and-so and so-and-so and so-and-so. . . .' Another long pause, and he said: 'Yeah. Yeah. I see what you mean. Print it!' One take! I thought I was on the wrong set!"

Before Walter ever played a scene in *Mrs. Miniver,* he spent some days watching Wyler direct, a studio concession to get him to do the film. The actor soon recognized the essence of Wyler's technique. As he explained to *Time* magazine about observing one scene in particular: "On the eighteenth take, I suddenly knew about Wyler. It was perfect, but it hit you in the pit of the stomach like a sudden, perfect chord of music. It made all those perfect-looking takes look like hell."

After the long weeks of filming, Walter attended the showing of the finished product: "I left the screening of *Mrs. Miniver* trying to remember which of my scenes were in, which had been cut. For the first time in my life I couldn't remember one thing I did. I only remember the entity. That's directing!"

As Clem Miniver, Walter was perfectly cast as a witty, brave, upper-income architect, immensely attractive and impressive, be he dining with his family, rushing off to Dunkirk in his little boat, or standing silently by as his son (Richard Ney) goes upstairs to view the body of his dead young bride (Teresa Wright), killed in the blitz. Released some six months after America's entry into the global war, *Mrs. Miniver* was praised as a tremendous accomplishment, filling the wartime throngs with pride, bravery, and tears. Especially poignant is the final scene in which the Miniver clan sings "Onward Christian Soldiers" with their neighbors under the shell-pocked roof of the village church.

[4]Originally William Wyler was to direct *How Green Was My Valley* and had proceeded with pre-production before he reached a disagreement with studio head Darryl Zanuck and was replaced by John Ford.

Time magazine called it "an almost impossible feat, a great war picture that photographs the inner meaning, instead of the outward realism of World War II." *Life* commented, "In *Mrs. Miniver* there are no spectacular battle scenes. The judging of one prize rose is almost as momentous as the retreat from Dunkirk. But with the aid of a superior cast, William Wyler directs these family affairs with such warmth and good taste that *Mrs. Miniver* packs more emotional wallop than any other fictional war film to date. Wyler's secret is simple. He makes the Minivers, unlike most movie characters, the sort of people you really enjoy knowing for two hours."

The Academy of Motion Picture Arts and Sciences recognized the film's contribution by bestowing it with Oscars for Best Picture, Best Director (Wyler), Best Supporting Actress (Teresa Wright), Best Screenplay, Best Black and White Cinematography, and Best Actress. (Miss Garson's acceptance speech lasted over thirty minutes, causing presenter Joan Fontaine to sit down and the Academy to instruct future winners to limit the verbosity of their thank yous.) In addition, producer Sidney Franklin won 1942's Thalberg Memorial Award for his contributions to cinematic art and wartime morale.

Walter himself was Oscar-nominated for his Clem Miniver. Competition for the Best Actor Award was keen that year: James Cagney *(Yankee Doodle Dandy),* Ronald Colman *(Random Harvest),* Gary Cooper *(Pride of the Yankees)* and Monty Woolley *(The Pied Piper).* Cagney won the prize for his George M. Cohan portrayal.

Strangely, for a picture that meant so much to so many people, *Mrs. Miniver* has suffered a legacy of sharp criticism from today's film breed, and, most sadly, from its own artists. Wyler himself has dismissed the picture as propaganda and, after seeing the British in action, called the work "synthetic." Even Greer Garson shocked an audience in Annapolis, Maryland when she spoke after a recent showing of the film and began unnecessarily apologizing for it. ("You have to understand, we really thought we were doing something important at the time.")

With Gable, Stewart, Mickey Rooney, Robert Taylor, and most major Metro males either in the armed service or preparing for induction, Walter suddenly found himself in the top star echelon of MGM. This engendered both good and bad effects. One of the bad repercussions was having to play leading man to Hedy Lamarr in *White Cargo* (1942), based on *that* notorious jungle sexploitation play. In this tropical soap opera Walter was Harry Witzel, a surly rubber plantation boss, with bristly beard and manner, bellowing at his men not to "mammy palaver" (i.e., give trinkets) to the native girls, especially Tondelayo (Lamarr), "the chocolate Cleopatra." Nevertheless, Hedy's undulating hips and Max Factor lips drive two of Walter's assistants (Bramwell Fletcher and Richard Carlson) mad with desire. Later it is Pidgeon's Witzel who poisons the native temptress, thus ending one of the most disastrous acting jobs ever recorded on celluloid. In normal times *White Cargo* might have seriously dampened the careers of all involved. Thankfully Walter emerged a little battered but safe for future assignments.

By now Walter was considered a major star in Hollywood. In the May issue of *Photoplay* magazine, he was described as follows: "He's not vain; he's humble. He's not shy; he's superfriendly. He's not bored; he's curious as a cat. He's not a poseur; he's ingenuous. His friends and interests aren't exclusively in Hollywood; they're scattered all over the world. He hasn't an ulcer, a nervous breakdown, or a pout hanging around. He has about as much temperament as a turtle. But he's a romantic in his third Hollywood career, and the last is the best."

Ebulliently gregarious, Walter became the King Arthur of the studio gossip table, reputed to know the affairs and news of everybody from the gatekeeper on up. "He's a greeter, an extrovert, a Babbitt, maybe," wrote *Photoplay.* "But he's the most charming, personally popular star in Hollywood too."

Walter's frankness and charm stood him in good stead at MGM. When at this point in time the star conferred with Mayer to discuss a new contract salary, Walter ignored the topic of money and instead tapped Mayer's reminiscences of East St. John, the mutual home of both men. After a long chat, Walter rose to leave, saying of the financial matter, "Louis, I'm going to leave this in your hands. As a hometown boy, I know you'll do right by me." No figure was mentioned, but when Walter received his first paycheck under his new option, he was delighted to find the amount to be double what he had expected. His dealings with Mayer were always friendly. Indeed, he and Miss Garson remain two of the few people who have perennially spoken well of the often despotic mogul.

Walter himself made it obvious that he loved being a star, but he insisted that it entailed hard work. He refused to compare the rivaling benefits of stage vs. screen, but he did admit, "I'll say this though, and I speak as the laziest man who ever lifted a finger. The films are much more exhausting. You're up at dawn and struggle until midnight. You do it unrelentingly for long periods."

Popular as Walter was during his halcyon MGM days, he was naturally the subject for much speculation regarding his alleged carnal appetites. Insiders were quick to suggest that Walter could have matched Errol Flynn in his escapades had he desired

With Hedy Lamarr in *White Cargo* (1942).

to be flamboyant. The fan magazines took pains to insist that Walter was a homebody, enjoying his stucco Monterey house "on the right side of the tracks in Beverly Hills" where domesticity reigned as he joined wife Ruth in games of backgammon and bridge and exhausted his energies with calisthenics and a rowing machine. Actually Walter was very social, and his behavior at parties was discreetly intriguing. A long-time observer of Hollywood recalls, "It's odd, but although I know there must be a Mrs. Pidgeon, I've never seen him with her. He was always one of the handsomest men at parties, and if his wife was also present, she must have been off in a corner trading recipes with the other wives, while he was off in the garden or [elsewhere]. . . . Young girls had a yen for him, even more so as he grew older, because he was the true sophisticated father." However, Walter was ever aware of the power of fans, and as much as possible the image of a rose-trimming, home-loving respectable thespian stayed intact with the garden variety moviegoer.

With the big male MGM names away in uniform, Walter faced an opportunity to reach a very high status on the lot.[5] However, his two big Metro films, *Blossoms in the Dust* and *Mrs. Miniver,* each placed him on a slightly supporting basis to Greer Garson and this is how the hierarchy and the public came to regard Walter. There was something almost too dependable, too solid, and truthfully too unexciting about Pidgeon's cinema persona that, winning as it was, did not allow for superstardom. If he had hoped that the war years would allow him to become a star who could rival Gable or Power, it was not to be. Audiences loved him playing second fiddle to Garson, as did Mayer, and Walter seemed perfectly content in the mold he had been cast. It maintained him

[5]During the war years and afterward, Walter buoyed his popularity by guest starring on radio, often with Miss Garson. In 1942 he was heard on the "Lux Radio Theatre" in versions of *Blossoms in the Dust* (with Garson), in *How Green Was My Valley* (with Maureen O'Hara), and with Judy Garland in *A Star Is Born.* In December 1943 Walter and Greer recreated their *Mrs. Miniver* roles for the "Lux" program.

With Greer Garson in *Mrs. Parkington* (1944).

on a very lucrative and steady wave of popularity. Years later he would say of his movie career, "Favorite pictures? Any of the ones with Greer Garson."

Metro next used Walter, along with Garson, William Powell, Robert Taylor, and Lana Turner, in cameos in *The Youngest Profession* (1943), in which he and Greer appear together as celebrities in New York City sought by autograph addict Virginia Weidler. The film had a Radio City Music Hall opening, but did little for anyone concerned with the project.

In 1937 Eve Curie had published a biography of her mother and MGM, among other studios, had long toyed with the idea of turning her memoirs into a film. At one point it was considered as a possible vehicle for Greta Garbo. Eventually it was decided that Greer Garson and Pidgeon would be naturals for the roles of Marie and Pierre Curie. The film was released in 1943 and found a receptive audience, even if the discovery of radium took a decided back seat to the love story of the husband-and-wife scientists. Walter received very flattering reviews. The *New York Herald-Tribune* reported, "It would have been easy for him to have mugged up the part of Pierre Curie, even though he is hiding behind a beard. On the contrary, he has created a real and recognizable figure, who can never be confused with Pidgeon himself." The *New York Times* was equally impressed: "Mr. Pidgeon is magnificently modest and slyly masculine as the preoccupied professor."

With a humanitarian theme and a lavish budget, *Madame Curie* was an obvious contender for Academy Award nominations for 1943. It was a contender in the categories of Best Picture (defeated by *Casablanca*), Best Actress (Garson lost to Jennifer Jones of *The Song of Bernadette*), and Best Actor. This year, Walter's competition included Humphrey Bogart *(Casablanca),* Gary Cooper *(For Whom the Bell Tolls),* Paul Lukas *(Watch on the Rhine),* and Mickey Rooney *(The Human Comedy).* Lukas, still one of Walter's very best friends in Hollywood, took home the prize.

In *Madame Curie* Mervyn LeRoy again directed. He recalls the experience in his autobiography, remembering the scene where they were to discover radium: "Naturally, this was a scene that needed great drama. We rehearsed it so the audience would have goose bumps when it flashed on the screen. I called for action, and the cameras were rolling—and then, from out of the darkness, I heard Greer laugh. 'Cut,' I yelled. 'Come on, Greer, what's so funny? Why the big laugh?' 'I couldn't help it,' she said. 'Walter just told me the funniest joke.' The tension that had built up during the long rehearsal period was gone. I waited about fifteen minutes, until Greer and Walter stopped their giggling, and then shot the scene. It worked perfectly.

"Pidgeon had become a cigar smoker by this time. One day, I bought him a box of fine Havanas, in those glorious days when it was politically acceptable to smoke Cuban cigars. Later that day, I ran out of cigars myself and asked him for one of his. 'I should say not,' he said. 'These are all for me.' "

During the production of *Madame Curie,* Louis B. Mayer ordered a picture taken of the sprawling MGM "family" of stars. Greer Garson sat directly on Mayer's left (Katharine Hepburn was on his right); Walter, with his beard, sat in the second row, just over Greer's shoulder, and between Spencer Tracy and Robert Taylor.

In December 1943, at the time of *Madame Curie*'s Radio City Music Hall debut, Walter became a U.S. citizen, taking the oath before Judge George Ruprecht. Thereafter he devoted much of his spare time to the USO, traveling to training camps in the United States and to combat zones abroad.

Of course MGM was anxious to use him to their advantage, and he was next cast as leading man to Garson in *Mrs. Parkington* (1944). As is obvious, all the Garson-Pidgeon vehicles after *Blossoms in the Dust* were titled after Greer's screen character. The titian-haired Irish actress was indeed most fortunate in having a co-star like Walter who, besides not becoming temperamental about his perpetual second-billing, tolerated the extraordinary care that surrounded Garson in the filming of her pictures. Cameramen took precious care photographing her, always posing her on her good side (her right; fortunately, Walter's was his left) and working out elaborate cues by which she would always be reminded to keep her chin raised (as she appeared more attractive looking upward). Indeed, no other MGM male star of that era could have been better suited to play second-fiddle to Greer Garson than Walter. He found the whole business of being a movie star rather ridiculous anyway—and, besides, he sincerely liked Greer.

The 124-minute *Mrs. Parkington* was essentially a romantic drama in which Greer's Susie Parkington rises from desert rags to wed millionaire Walter and attempts to crash society. Within the course of the lavishly mounted production, she survives her spouse and becomes the matriarch of a trouble-prone brood. The director was Tay Garnett, who wrote of the happy Garson-Pidgeon working relationship in his autobiography *Light Your Torches and Pull Up Your Tights* (1973): "During the first scenes it became obvious that Greer had not yet caught onto the 'Susie Parkington' character. 'Susie' was a bright, spirited, western mining town girl, bouncy and bubbling with vitality, but without artifice. Greer was playing her too Great Lady, too British. Wise Walter Pidgeon saw the problem, and—grinning wickedly—slapped Greer on the neatest derriere in Hollywood (a stunt he had used in *Mrs. Miniver*) and said offhandedly, 'Relax, honey. It was *last* year you won the Oscar.' Greer laughed and relaxed. End of problem."

Mrs. Parkington was really Greer's film. The *New York Herald-Tribune* noted that Walter "supports her at every turn of the script as a co-star should." The picture won Greer another Oscar nomination; this time she lost to Ingrid Bergman *(Gaslight).* Walter confessed recently that he does not remember anything about this film. "The other day my wife said, 'There's a picture on with you and Greer—*Mrs. Parkington.*' I couldn't remember it at all. I must have been out of town or something when it previewed, because I know I've never seen it."

About this time, a new Pidgeon joined MGM—daughter Edna who worked in the Metro art department as an illustrator. The publicity department, anxious to dismiss any ideas of nepotism, insisted that she received a very modest salary.

It was nearly a year after the completion of *Mrs. Parkington* that Walter began *Week-End at the Waldorf* (1945). In the interim he had continued his USO chores, developed as a busboy at the Hollywood Canteen, and continued his socializing. Pidgeon's new picture was an all-star, glittery if shallow remake of *Grand Hotel* (1932). In a sharp alteration of the earlier film (and original play), a happy ending was tacked onto the story, and there was also the bouncy music and comedy of Xavier Cugat and his famous orchestra.

In the 1932 edition the leading man was John Barrymore's Baron von Gaigern, a doomed jewel thief; here it was Walter's Chip Collyer, a considerably more down-to-earth type, and a famed war correspondent. Garbo's ballerina turned into Ginger Rogers' actress, Joan Crawford's stenographer was transformed into Lana Turner's bubbly, breasty secretary, Wallace Beery's tycoon evolved into Edward Arnold's lighter magnate, and, miraculously, Lionel

Barrymore's pathetic dying old man became Van Johnson's freckled soldier, facing a dangerous operation to remove shrapnel. Walter had little to do in this 130-minute pandering to the post-war public other than to puff on his pipe, model his trench coat, and trade quips with Ginger, to whom he becomes merrily engaged oncamera. *Week-End at the Waldorf* is still on the list of great box-office hits, and the latest MGM regime is contemplating remaking the storyline yet again.

When the war was over, it was time for the substitute stars like Turhan Bey, Sonny Tufts, and Robert Paige to go into "mothballs" as the major stars returned to their home lots. At MGM Gable was back and Garson had him, with putrid results and a personality conflict of great proportions. Meanwhile, forty-eight-year-old Walter was assigned to *Holiday in Mexico* (1946) where he was Jeffrey Evans, a U.S. ambassador (to Mexico, of course), and was guided into the arms of reclining Ilona Massey (a last-minute replacement for Jeanette MacDonald) by daughter Jane Powell. Despite its cute script, Technicolor, and the presence of José and Amparo Iturbi, as well as Xavier Cugat and his orchestra, the film did not duplicate the success of *Week-End at the Waldorf.*

As a contrast to this grabbag of music, comedy, and romance, Pidgeon next showed up in *The Secret Heart* (1946), in that unfortunate plotline cliché of a man loved by a woman (Claudette Colbert) *and* by her neurotic daughter (June Allyson). The results were glossy and vapid. Also in this year Pidgeon joined with Katharine Hepburn, Ingrid Bergman, Eddie Cantor, Van Johnson, Shirley Temple, Jennifer Jones, James Stewart, and Edward G. Robinson in *The American Creed,* a two-reel trailer sponsored by American Brotherhood Week.

In the spineless *Cass Timberlane* (1947), which asked audiences to believe that aging Spencer Tracy could ever lure young Lana Turner into his bed, Walter did a cameo bit as himself at a cocktail party. Even though he was aging gracefully, Walter was a mature fifty years old and he seemed a bit out of place as the dignified but warm-blooded romantic lead of *If Winter Comes* (1947).[6] In the course of this ninety-seven-minute feature, Walter is wed to bitch Angela Lansbury, pursued by a panting Deborah Kerr, and accused of impregnating twenty-year-old Janet Leigh. His huge professionalism appeared way out of place in such sudsy hoopla.

Since the close of World War II, neither Walter nor Garson had enjoyed great box-office successes. Finally the studio made the decision to team them again. The result was the mostly unfortunate *Julia Misbehaves* (1948), as the veteran screen couple engaged in slapstick comedy. Miss Garson not only took a bubble bath in this venture, but attempted acrobatics, took pratfalls, and simulated assorted other shenanigans. In the picture, based on Marjorie Sharp's novel *The Nutmeg Tree,* the team were the parents of Elizabeth Taylor, which seemed totally natural, but the proceedings were almost all forced and flat.

Modest disaster though *Julia Misbehaves* was, the stars had fun. Not long after its release, *Photoplay* published a lengthy feature in which Greer talked of her popular leading man: "During the filming of my bubble bath in *Julia Misbehaves,* a sequence which must have been inspired by possible movie headlines saying 'Bubbles Are Back and Garson's Got Them,' or something, Walter's presence was unrequired. To come out from behind the bustles of the more abstemious ladies I had portrayed in the past and be photographed in a flesh-colored bathing suit amid such translucent trimmings was setting some sort of historical watermark. To avoid any undue disconcerting developments, there were NO ADMITTANCE signs all over the place. But just as I picked up my long-handled brush and the bubbles began their ascension, in strolled Walter with a casual, 'Hello, Duchess, I just dropped by to pick up some pipes I forgot in my dressing room.' When I looked askance, and he made no motion of looking for pipes, Walter went on blithely, 'A husband of some five screen marriages should be entitled to certain privileges.' "

Greer went on to say that Walter delighted in fraternizing about the lot and shocking virgin ears with unprintable limericks (a habit in which he delights to this day). In fact, Walter enjoyed strolling into Mayer's office and tossing off his latest vulgar whimsy to the ashen face of his publicly prudish boss. To make Mayer's discomfiture complete, Walter would generally inform L.B. that Greer, Mayer's most personally revered actress, was the source of the ditty. "Did my lady say that?" Mayer would gasp. "Sure," Walter would reply, "she's got a million of them!" Despite this mischievous streak Greer made it clear that she greatly liked Walter, and she hailed him as "a perfect picture companion. He is an experienced trouper, an excellent actor, a valued friend."

In the late 1940s, Greer was single again, having

[6]As originally conceived, *If Winter Comes* was to have been filmed in England with Robert Donat and Greer Garson. When Donat became unavailable, Pidgeon was substituted. Thereafter it was decided to update the story from World War I to World War II, and that Deborah Kerr and an almost all British cast would be utilized. The property had been previously filmed by Fox in 1929 with Percy Marmont and Ann Forrest.

divorced her actor husband Richard Ney who had played her son in *Mrs. Miniver.* Since she had been referred to as "the daytime Mrs. Pidgeon" for much of the 1940s, rumors naturally hinted that she had her blue-green eyes set on Walter. However, Pidgeon's marriage to the inordinately quiet Ruth Walker continued, and in 1949 Greer wed Texas millionaire Elijah "Buddy" Fogelson to whom she is still married.

After the long fallow period of bad scripts and thankless film assignments, Walter finally was given a part that allowed him to demonstrate again just what a fine actor he really was. The film was *Command Decision* (1948), a very faithful cinematization of William Wister Haines' stark play that had played to great success on Broadway. To insure the vitality of the drama about top brass generals struggling with brutal decisions over certain-death bomber missions in World War II Europe, MGM kept the proceedings a stag affair. Gable, Pidgeon, and Van Johnson, among the lot's top male attractions, were given major roles, as were such popular actors as Brian Donlevy, Charles Bickford, John Hodiak, and Edward Arnold.

As Brigadier General "Casey" Dennis, Gable had the focal role, but the "King" of Hollywood had never really recovered from the death of his wife Carole Lombard, and he was still suffering from his grueling combat experiences and post-war heavy drinking. These factors combined to make him very shaky oncamera, requiring quick takes on director Sam Wood's part and rigid posturing on Gable's.

Partially due to Gable's condition, but mainly through his intense performance, Walter very nearly dominated the 112-minute black-and-white feature. He is Major General Roland Goodlow Kane from Washington, D.C. who has been forced to cooperate with the press and do what "looked good" while Gable's character sent men to near certain doom over German targets. Pidgeon's lengthy monologue—in which he admits the phoniness he has had to employ in his job, yet avows that it was necessary and that he would do do it again if required—is a highlight of the picture. It takes second

With Greer Garson and Cesar Romero in *Julia Misbehaves* (1948).

place only to the scene in which Gable "talks down" a navigator who has to land a damaged bomber. If the latter section of *Command Decision* had not limited the byplay largely to Gable and Donlevy, Walter might have walked off with the entire film.

The critics generally chose to praise the tandem performances of the film rather than single out any one actor for special praise. However, some media sources did focus on Walter's work. One reported: "Walter Pidgeon is remarkably revealing, giving a brilliantly inclusive scan of a military wangler and conniver who feels that the ends justify his means. It is through his credible performance that the ironies of professional militarism are exposed. And it might be added, incidentally, that this is a new characterization for him." Indeed it was. However, MGM was not about to pose acting challenges for Walter. He returned to drab and predictable film assignments as his studio contract entered its second decade.

Walter's next MGM film was again with Greer Garson, this one was called *That Forsyte Woman* (1949). It was loosely based on volume one *(A Man of Property)* of John Galsworthy's multi-part novel *The Forsyte Saga.* This time the usual Garson-Pidgeon predictabilities were freshened a bit by the inclusion of Errol Flynn, whose services MGM had obtained in a deal that lent William Powell to Warner Bros. for *Life with Father.* Flynn received top billing, not to mention the meatier male role of Soames, the roué, while Walter drew the stolid assignment of Young Jolyon, who, good chap that he is, rescues Garson from her wastrel husband's ways in the last reel. The third male lead was entrusted to another underrated, long-time MGM player, Robert Young, cast as architect Philip Bosinney in love with young Janet Leigh. With the high-spirited Errol on hand, the set of *That Forsyte Woman* was a particularly merry one, with jokes and pranks galore. In one scene, Garson opened a closet to find Flynn squatting inside, naked except for a top hat. Unfortunately, none of this liveliness carried over onto the screen. The project emerged as a stodgy tale of Victorian morals, with Greer particularly stiff and Walter boorishly dash-

With Ethel Barrymore in *The Red Danube* (1949).

ing. Only Flynn (who was originally scheduled to play Walter's role) was able to derive a bit of praise from the picture, as did the sets, which photographed lushly in color.

Vienna was the site of Pidgeon's next film, *The Red Danube,* a 1949 holiday release in which Walter portrayed a one-armed English colonel. Louis Calhern, Ethel Barrymore, Peter Lawford, and Janet Leigh were among the other MGM employees who labored in vain in this forgettable Cold War melodrama based on Bruce Marshall's novel *Vespers in Vienna.*

As America and the world were undergoing vast social and economic changes in the post-World War II period, so was Hollywood and MGM. Dore Schary had been brought over from RKO to "assist" Louis B. Mayer in the running of the studio, and it would not be long into the 1950s before the iconoclastic mogul would be ousted from his post of authority. Meanwhile the new studio regime sought to minimize the rising overhead and the decreasing box-office receipts. One such scheme was to reunite Pidgeon and Garson in a sequel to their highly successful *Mrs. Miniver.* The result not only was a commercial dud, but it nearly destroyed whatever warm memories audiences treasured of that noble English family which had caused so many cinemagoers to take heart eight years earlier.

In *The Miniver Story* (1950), filmed in England to utilize frozen studio funds, Kay Miniver is dying, presumably of cancer, though the script does little to clarify the cause. The children are grown, and as V-E Day is celebrated, the family is reunited when Clem and the kids return from overseas. Bittersweetly (she knows she is dying) the audience learns of Mrs. Miniver's wartime romance with an American officer (John Hodiak) and becomes aware that Clem is actually something of a bore. Filmgoers could not accept the thought of Kay cheating on Clem, director H. C. Potter was no William Wyler, and both Garson and Pidgeon were at ages where they could no longer so appealingly play near-saintly characters with attractive rather than dull results. When Garson expired at the close of 104 minutes of stylized suffering, so did much of the respect and love many film fans had harbored for the Minivers.

The Miniver Story enjoyed a lavish ad campaign, opening at the Ritz Theatre in London before the Radio City Music Hall premiere on October 26, 1950. The press was flatly unimpressed. The *New York Times* reported, "Miss Garson plays with such lofty nobleness that whatever emotion is in the story is drenched in great waves of obvious goo. . . . As for Mr. Pidgeon, he looks and acts like a monument." Thus MGM's ill-conceived plan to have financial lightning strike twice was clearly a failure.

At the age of fifty-three, Walter was still a leading man who was of superstar status. One evening, on his immensely popular Tuesday evening television show for Texaco, "Uncle" Milton Berle, greeting his audience with a properly formal suit and hat, opened the show by announcing that his guest would be Walter Pidgeon. As the audience cheered in delight, Berle removed his hat and a pigeon, presumably named Walter, took off from his perch and flew into the wings.

Yet Walter, while still a big show-business name, was nearing the point where his age and countenance required character roles. In *Soldiers Three* (1951), a Rudyard Kipling bastardization, he is the commandant who has to tolerate the childish antics of ebullient Stewart Granger, Robert Newton, and Cyril Cusack. In *Calling Bulldog Drummond* (1951), shot in England with Walter in kilts and with Margaret Leighton as his partner, he returned to tracking down a gang, much as he had more than a decade earlier for MGM's Nick Carter programmers. When not involved directly in filmmaking, Walter did his part in the Korean War by touring with the USO. He visited military sites in Japan and South Korea.

Things were changing professionally for Walter and for MGM. On June 22, 1951 Louis B. Mayer vacated the front office, now officially replaced by Dore Schary. The latter instituted a firmer cost-cutting policy that did not win the approval of the lot's major stars. However, Walter continued working. Before 1951 had ended, audiences saw him as a defense lawyer with Ann Harding and Barry Sullivan in *The Unknown Man,* as a small-town newspaper editor battling corruption in *The Sellout*—a very underrated feature—and as narrator of the opening sequence of *Quo Vadis,* in which Robert Taylor and Deborah Kerr starred.

Schary used fewer and fewer of the many high-priced attractions on the lot. He canceled their forty-week paid stays in favor of an option plan by which they could be called on yearly for more economical use of their services. With his salad days behind him, Pidgeon remained at Culver City for general purpose screen chores, the type of parts for which he had been originally hired in the 1930s. In 1952's *Million Dollar Mermaid* he played no less than Esther Williams' father. Also that year he joined such stars as Robert Taylor, Howard Keel, Barry Sullivan, and Dore Schary himself in narrating the totalitarianism-attacking thirty-six-minute documentary *The Hoaxters.*

Walter fully became a reliable character star in MGM's *The Bad and the Beautiful* (1952), in which Kirk Douglas, Lana Turner, Barry Sullivan, and Dick Powell were the main attractions. As director Harry Pebbel, in a blond crew-cut wig and delivering stuffy, economy-minded speeches, Walter was per-

With Richard Hale (right) in *Soldiers Three* (1951).

With Robert Beatty and Peggy Evans in *Calling Bulldog Drummond* (1951).

fect. He fully suggested the capable non-genius qualities of a man who can appreciate and use creative talent but not share in it himself. That Vincente Minnelli-directed feature was big box-office, but his next film, his eighth and final with Greer Garson, was not. *Scandal at Scourie* (1953) placed the celebrated screen team as a Protestant couple in Canada who worry over their adoption of a little orphan (Donna Corcoran) not only because she is a Catholic, but because she is a suspected pyromaniac as well. Such a synthetic weeper was archaic by cinema standards of the 1950s, and the aging stars did nothing to make it seem fresh. Tellingly, the Technicolor feature failed to follow the path set by every one of the preceding Garson-Pidgeon vehicles—a premiere at New York City's Radio City Music Hall. Reaction, critically and from a box-office angle, was lukewarm at best. After its tepid reception, Greer Garson asked for and received her release from MGM, preferring to free-lance and enjoy the life of leisure to which her wealthy husband was treating her. Walter stayed on at Culver City. Unlike Greer, he was easily cast into a variety of assignments. Also, his ever-working business sense reminded him that he would soon have completed twenty years with MGM and would thereby be entitled to the studio's generous pension plan.

As the old MGM faded, Walter kept busy.[7] He finished 1953 with *Dream Wife,* a delightful comedy, in which as a State Department official he assigns Deborah Kerr to chaperone her ex-fiancé Cary Grant on a diplomatic mission. In 1954 Pidgeon played in four releases: *Executive Suite,* the excellent business world drama in which he joined an all-star cast; *Men of the Fighting Lady,* a Korean War saga starring Van Johnson in which Pidgeon was the flight surgeon of an aircraft carrier; *The Last Time I Saw Paris,* in which, for the second time in his career, he played the father of Elizabeth Taylor; and *Deep in My Heart,* a biography of Sigmund Romberg (Jose Ferrer) with Walter as stage producer J. J. Shubert.

It was also in 1954 that Walter made his first television appearance. The occasion was Ed Sullivan's video salute to the thirtieth anniversary of MGM. The live program featured nearly every star still under contract to the studio, which until that time had prohibited its stars from making TV appearances. In the 1955–1956 season Pidgeon would replace George Murphy for the last thirteen weeks of the series "The MGM Parade," which promoted MGM theatre features. (In future years Pidgeon would become a frequent guest star on TV, appearing in a variety of series' episodes from "Zane Grey Theatre" to "Perry Mason" to Dr. Kildare" to the TV special *Cinderella* (1966), in which he co-starred with Ginger Rogers. In the 1970s he would become very active in the telefeature field.)

By the mid-1950s Walter's old colleagues on the lot were disappearing more and more. Mickey Rooney was gone, Judy Garland had been fired, and Gable's contract was not renewed. While a few of the old guard (Spencer Tracy, Lana Turner, Robert Taylor, for example) hung on, Walter terminated his stay with consistently professional if unspectacular results. In 1955 he narrated *The Glass Slipper,* a fanciful retelling of the Cinderella legend with Leslie Caron starred, and then he played an admiral in a dreadful musical, *Hit the Deck,* which squandered the talents of Jane Powell, Tony Martin, Debbie Reynolds, Vic Damone, and Ann Miller. In 1956 he had an offbeat assignment in one of the best science fiction films ever made, *Forbidden Planet,* as a mad scientist whose id creates a wonderfully terrifying (animated) monster. In *These Wilder Years,* he played the lawyer of James Cagney: His role was so supporting that his name fell below the title in the billing. Before this professional humbling could get any worse, Walter completed his MGM stay with *The Rack* (1956), the film version of Rod Serling's television play, as the father of Paul Newman. With that, Walter cleared out of the MGM Culver City lot, a beneficiary of the studio pension plan and cherishing all the pleasant memories of the scene of his greatest glory. "They were the best," he would say of his MGM years. "I'd like to have them all back again."

After twenty years of being a well-treated star, Walter could have settled, like confreres Gable and Tracy, into a demanding but comfortable cycle of making a picture or two a year. However, much to his credit, Walter accepted an offer to return to the eight-shows-a-week grind of the Broadway theatre. The project was *The Happiest Millionaire,* based on Cornelia Biddle's book about her eccentric father, Anthony J. Drexel Biddle, entitled *My Philadelphia Father.* Pidgeon, of course, played Biddle, with Diana van der Vlis as Cornelia and George Grizzard as her timid suitor. The play opened at New York's Lyceum Theatre on Saturday, November 20, 1956. The *New York Times* declared the play to be a "delightful evening" and hailed Walter: "Walter Pidgeon gives a wonderful performance in the leading part. He makes something humorous and disarming out of a character that could be a bore if the acting did not have style. . . . [He is] just about ideal." The play ran for 271 performances, and after it closed on Broadway, Walter toured with the show from October 1957 to May 1958. (In the mid-1960s he would

[7]From 1953 to 1957, Pidgeon served as president of the Screen Actors Guild. During his term he led a strike that won residual payments for actors in films made for theatres but later shown on television.

With David Brian and Esther Williams in *Million Dollar Mermaid* (1952).

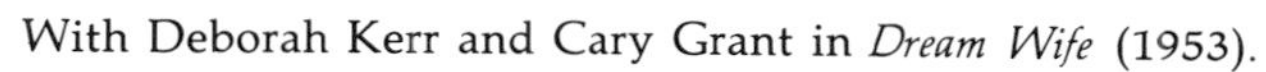
With Deborah Kerr and Cary Grant in *Dream Wife* (1953).

With Fredric March and William Holden in *Executive Suite* (1954).

again tour with the comedy. One of his greatest professional disappointments occurred when he lost the title role in the 1967 version of *The Happiest Millionaire.* Producer Walt Disney thought that Walter was too old for the role and instead chose Fred MacMurray to play the part. Ironically Greer Garson was cast in the musical film to portray Mrs. Anthony Biddle.)

When Walter returned to Hollywood, he made it clear that he wanted to work as much as possible. No tempting film offers immediately materialized, but television appealed to him. In October 1958 he starred as the father, with Laraine Day, in a televersion of *Swiss Family Robinson,* and he joined Myrna Loy and Jane Powell in a May 1959 TV special condensation of MGM's classic *Meet Me in St. Louis.* As things developed, that show was seen both by Broadway producer David Merrick and by composer Bob Merrill. They were preparing to mount a new Broadway musical, *Take Me Along,* based on Eugene O'Neill's *Ah, Wilderness!* They were impressed by Walter's singing and enticed him to make a Broadway return in the musical as Nat Miller.[8] A superb cast was assembled: Jackie Gleason as Uncle Sid (to whom Walter had to surrender top billing), Robert Morse as the young Richard Miller, Eileen Herlie as the spinster Aunt Lily, Una Merkel as Essie Miller (Nat's wife), and Arlene Golonka as Belle, the tart.

[8]In the original 1933 Broadway production of the comedy, George M. Cohan played Nat Miller, owner of the *Evening Globe* newspaper. In the 1935 MGM film version, Lionel Barrymore was Nat, and in Metro's 1948 musical remake, *Summer Holiday,* Walter Huston had the role.

The show opened at the Shubert Theatre on Thursday, October 22, 1959. While critical reaction was reserved, the musical immediately became a commercial hit. The *New York Times* noted, "Walter Pidgeon is too bland and sophisticated in the first act. But in the second act, he struggles through the embarrassing facts of life speech with skill and humor, and adds a tone of genuine feeling to the story." Walter's singing skills were amply demonstrated in the show. He sang "The Parade" in the opening number, joined the family in "Oh Please," dueted with Gleason in the title song and "For Sweet Charity," and soloed on the touching number "Staying Young."[9]

Take Me Along ran for 448 performances on Broadway. Walter's professionalism in the cast shone all the more brightly when Gleason, returning to the stage after his fabulously successful television stint, began getting careless about making all his performances. When Gleason was on hand, he often employed his well-loved bag of tricks to amuse the audience. Yet no report of professional jealousy or conflict ever issued from the Shubert Theatre stage door regarding Walter and Gleason (later replaced in the run by William Bendix). After the show closed

[9]Choreographer Oona White would recall of her dealings with Pidgeon during *Take Me Along:* ". . . [he] was so uncoordinated that I had to teach him to dance by numbers. I developed this soft-shoe routine . . . where he turned to different points on the stage, and each point had a number. Walter counted his numbers out loud, but Jackie Gleason, who is a very good dancer, would call out different numbers until Walter was totally confused. . . . Walter would scream, 'Jackie—stop it!' "

in November 1960, Walter returned to Hollywood and began perusing film scripts.

Although he was nearing his mid-sixties, drawing a pension from MGM, and enjoying a high income from assorted business investments, he worked with the energy of an enthusiastic apprentice in show business. He commanded the submarine of 20th Century-Fox's *Voyage to the Bottom of the Sea* (1961—later a teleseries, *sans* Walter), was excellent as the Senate majority leader in the all-star Otto Preminger production *Advise and Consent* (1962), and appeared as the owner of a beautiful Irish setter in *Big Red* (1962), a Walt Disney picture. He made two features in Italy: *The Two Colonels* (1962) and *The Shortest Day* (1962) and narrated *Anniversary,* a Canadian documentary saluting the sixtieth year of the Canadian film industry. On television he narrated *The Vanishing 400* which took a glance at U.S. society, toured in summer stock in 1963 in *Lord Pengo,* and, the next year, starred in a road company presentation of *Take Her, She's Mine.*

On Tuesday, September 27, 1966 Walter returned to Broadway for his last engagement to date—playing the role of ailing shipping tycoon Oliver Jordan in a gilt-edged revival of the George Kaufman—Edna Ferber comedy *Dinner at Eight.* An "all-star" cast included Arlene Francis as Carlotta Vance, Darren McGavin as Larry Renault, Pamela Tiffin as Kitty, Robert Burr as Dan Packard, and Jeffrey Lynn as Dr. Talbot. Despite its well-publicized presence, the revival was only moderately successful, running 127 performances at the Alvin Theatre.

In the past decade, Walter worked steadily in films and television and showed no signs of slowing down (although he revealed an increasingly pinched look on his face, as if he had just bitten into a too-tart lemon). He appeared in everything from *Costra Nostra, An Arch Enemy of the F.B.I.* (1967), which was actually a spliced together two-parter from the TV series "The F.B.I." in which he played a Mafia boss, to Columbia's *Funny Girl* (1968), in which he was most impressive in his brief appearance as Florenz Ziegfeld. In 1972 he returned to MGM, to join those aboard the troubled craft in *Skyjacked.*

More recently, Walter frequently turned up on telemovies. In the 1975–1976 video season, he appeared in a drama of greed entitled *You Lie So Deep, My Love.* In the highly touted all-star *Murder on Flight 502,* he was the dying elderly gentleman who meets and falls in love with Molly Picon on the endangered plane and, in *The Lindbergh Kidnapping Case,* he was the presiding judge at the celebrated trial of Bruno Hauptmann (Anthony Hopkins). In April 1976 he appeared as the murder victim on an episode of "Ellery Queen" and he was indeed impressive in the opening episode of "Gibbsville" on November 11, 1976 for NBC-TV. His vis-a-vis was Jane Wyatt and *Hollywood Reporter* noted, "Guest star Walter Pidgeon as the playwright makes the most of a humorous and touching role." That year he also appeared in two theatrical releases. In the big-screen thriller *Two-Minute Warning,* he joined Charlton Heston, John Cassavetes, Beau Bridges, and Martin Balsam, with Walter cast as a suave pickpocket. *Won Ton Ton, the Dog Who Saved Hollywood* proved to be a mistaken bit of satirical nostalgia which seemingly utilized the services of every veteran performer still breathing in the western hemisphere. Walter had his (thankfully) brief oncamera moments as Madeline Kahn's butler, who throws a stone at the canine movie star.

With Anne Francis and Faye Roope in *The Rack* (1956).

With Laraine Day in
Swiss Family Robinson on
"Dupont Show of the Month"
(CBS-TV, 1958).

With Joan Fontaine in
Voyage to the Bottom of the Sea
(1961).

With Charles Laughton in *Advise and Consent* (1962).

If his amazing and tireless professionalism made him perhaps the most in-demand veteran actor by producers of telemovies, his delightful, semi-naughty personality made him a favorite on talk shows. In 1976 Merv Griffin saluted director Robert Wise on his TV show. Walter, who appeared in Wise's *Executive Suite* in 1954, was a guest. Mr. Wise received much praise from Griffin, and then Julie Andrews, who worked with Wise on *The Sound of Music,* came forth and caressed the man with verbal bouquets. Finally Walter made his entrance and proceeded to delight the audience with limericks, stories, and wisecracks totally unrelated to Mr. Wise who appeared uncomfortably amused. Finally Griffin asked Walter outright, "Well, what do you remember about *Executive Suite?*" "I don't remember anything about it!" roared Walter, to gales of laughter from the audience. When Wise tried to prod his memory by mentioning his (deceased) co-stars Fredric March and Louis Calhern, Walter tossed out, "I can't remember what I did two years ago, much less what I did twenty!" Finally Walter realized that his candidness was becoming a bit embarrassing, and with great charm he gave a short speech about the great contributions Wise had privately made to the Motion Picture County Home. He ended his speech with a handshake and related the testimony so effectively that he won for Wise the loudest applause of the evening.

In 1970 Pidgeon was scheduled to play the surgeon in Mae West's *Myra Breckinridge,* but he backed out and was replaced by John Carradine. However, six years later, he was unfortunate enough to become part of her *Sextette,* a rendition of a play written many years before by the ribald Miss West. The $4.2 million production boasted an impressive cast including Tony Curtis, George Hamilton, Dom DeLuise, Timothy Dalton, Ringo Starr, Alice Cooper, Rona Barrett, and George Raft. As *Variety* reported, "It's an embarrassing attempt at camp from the lady who helped invent the word." Major studios refused to distribute the picture and after test openings in California it disappeared from sight in 1978, only to reemerge briefly for New York showings in 1979. Walter appeared briefly as the chairman of an international diplomatic team out to prevent multi-marrying Miss West from disturbing the world's political "harmony."

The year 1978 proved to be a difficult one for the veteran performer. As he recalls it, he had gone to the Hollywood Clinic of the Motion Picture and Television Fund for a physical checkup. "I was feeling a little pooped and run-down, so I thought I'd go there. As I was leaving, I went out a door I'd never gone out before. There was no step there—it was a fourteen- or fifteen-inch drop. I lost my footing, fell, and hit my head on the street."

As a result, he was hospitalized at St. John's in Santa Monica, California. "I was in intensive care for ten days. They didn't know for some time whether or not there was a clot on my brain. Then they decided to go in, so they shaved my hair and put a

With Jason William Kane, Rosey Grier, Jeanne Crain, and Nicholas Hammond in *Skyjacked* (1972).

With Donna Mills in the telefeature *Live Again, Die Again* (ABC-TV, 1974).

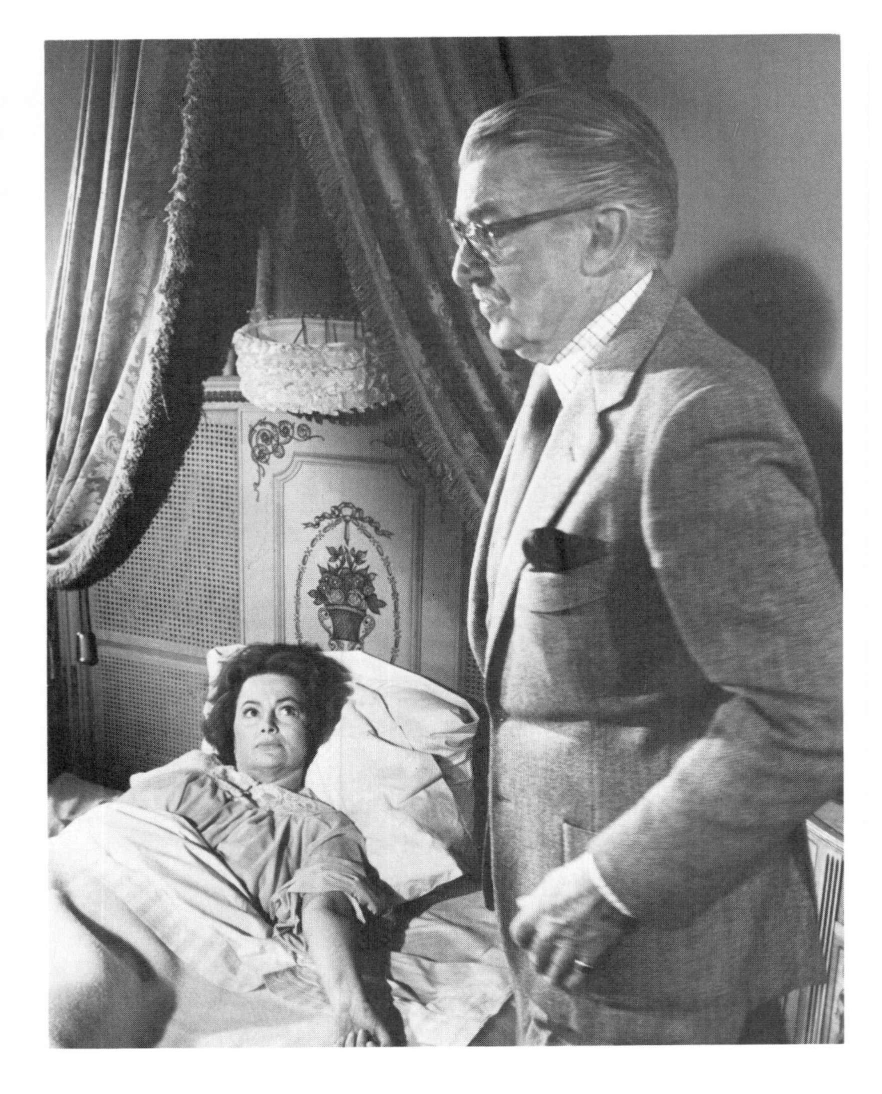

With Olivia de Havilland in the telefeature *The Screaming Woman* (ABC-TV, 1972).

With John Savage in the *How Old, How Young* episode of "Gibbsville" (NBC-TV, 1976).

As the pickpocket in *Two-Minute Warning* (1976).

couple of holes in my head. I got through that all right, but I got pneumonia while I was in the hospital. So they gave me a lot of antibiotics and the antibiotics damanged my inner ear (causing a loss of balance problem). So there I am."

Since his release from the hospital on September 26, 1977, the star has remained in virtual seclusion. A rare exception was his appearance in August 1979 at the Motion Picture and Television Fund's 55th annual meeting at the organization's Woodland Hills' headquarters. Gene Raymond, president of the fund, hosted the reception at the Motion Picture Country House which saw Pidgeon receiving the group's Silver Medallion, symbolizing service to the motion picture and television industry. The tribute to Pidgeon was presented by Gregory Peck.

Today the Pidgeons are settled into a quiet existence at their Strada Corta Street home in Bel Air, across from the Bel Air Country Club. He often expresses sincere love for his wife of so many decades who so willingly faded into the background during his peak years. "It's been a long and happy career for me, and a long and happy marriage to Ruth. . . . If there's such a thing as reincarnation, I hope we meet up again . . . in some other life." His daughter Edna is married to film laboratory executive John Aitkens, and they have two daughters, Pamela and Patricia, and reside in Santa Cruz.

Pidgeon has never forgotten the great kinship that stars enjoyed in those golden years: "We actors then were warm brotherhood. At the end of a day we'd gather in Clark Gable's dressing room, or Barrymore's or Bob Taylor's and have a drink or two or three and discuss the pleasures or pains of whatever we were filming. Remembering those times makes me feel that Hollywood now is somewhat lonely—and a little sad. The camaraderie is gone—and, I think, missed." On another occasion, he added, "I was like a kept woman during my twenty years at MGM. It was like an expensive, beautifully run club. You didn't need to carry money. Your face was your credit card—all over the world."

It would be Greer Garson, suitably enough, at the American Film Institute's tribute to William Wyler, who humorously but sincerely best summed up her daytime husband of the MGM years. "Here we are, Willy," she said from the podium, "your actors, cheerfully standing up here in our turn—like human milestones." As the crowd reacted, Walter, on her left, asked if that comment was directed at him. "No, dear," said Miss Garson. "You're a *super*human milestone."

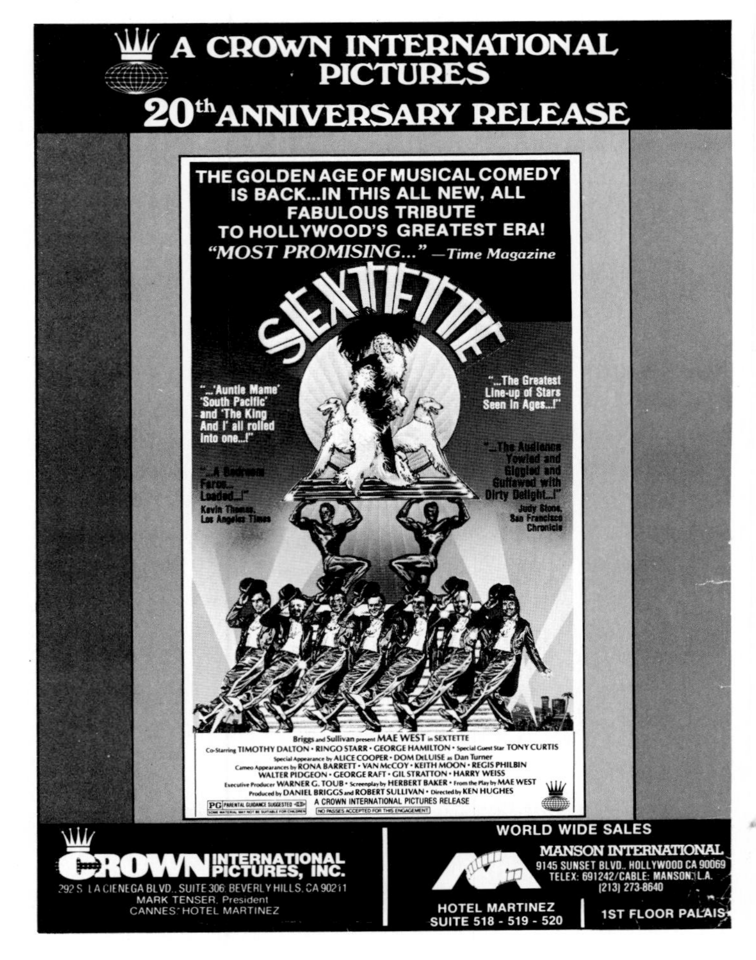

Advertisement for *Sextette* (1978).

FILMOGRAPHY

MANNEQUIN
(Paramount, 1926) 6,981 ′

Presenters: Adolph Zukor, Jesse L. Lasky
Director: James Cruze
Based on the novel by Fannie Hurst
Screenplay: Frances Agnew
Adaptor: Walter Woods
Camera: Karl Brown

Alice Joyce *(Selene Herrick);* Warner Baxter *(John Herrick);* Dolores Costello [*Joan Herrick (Orchid)*]; ZaSu Pitts *(Annie Pogani);* Walter Pidgeon *(Martin Innesbrook);* Freeman Wood *(Terry Allen);* Charlotte Bird *(Toto).*

THE OUTSIDER
(Fox, 1926) 5,424 ′

Presenter: William Fox
Director: Rowland V. Lee
Based on the play by Dorothy Brandon
Adaptor: Robert N. Lee
Assistant Director: Daniel Keefe
Camera: G. O. Post

Jacqueline Logan *(Leontine Sturdee);* Lou Tellegen *(Anton Ragatzy);* Walter Pidgeon *(Basil Owen);* Roy Atwell *(Jerry Sidon);* Charles Lane *(Sir Jasper Sturdee);* Joan Standing *(Pritchard);* Gibson Gowland *(Shadow);* Bertram Marburgh *(Dr. Talley);* Craufurd Kent *(Dr. Ladd);* Louis Payne *(Dr. Helmore).*

MISS NOBODY
(First National, 1926) 6,859 ′

Director: Lambert Hillyer
Editorial Director: Wid Gunning
Based on the story "Shebo" by Tiffany Wells
Titles: George Marion, Jr.
Art Director: E. J. Shulter
Camera: John Boyle
Editor: Al Hall

Anna Q. Nilsson *(Barbara Brown);* Walter Pidgeon *(Bravo);* Louise Fazenda *(Mazie Raleigh);* Mitchell Lewis *(Harmony);* Clyde Cook *(Bertie);* Arthur Stone *(Happy);* Anders Randolf *(J. B. Hardiman);* Claire Du-Brey *(Ann Adams);* Jed Prouty *(Farmer);* Caroline Rankin *(His Wife);* George Nichols *(Sheriff);* Oleta Otis *(Miriam Arnold);* James Gordon *(Police Sergeant);* Fred Warren *(Sideshow Spieler).*

OLD LOVES AND NEW
(First National, 1926) 7,423 ′

Presenter: Sam E. Rork
Director: Maurice Tourneur
Based on the novel *The Desert Healer* by Edith Maude Hull
Adaptor: Marion Fairfax
Assistant Director: Ben Silvey
Art Director: Jack Okey
Camera: Henry Cronjager
Editor: Patricia Rooney

Lewis Stone *(Gervas Carew);* Barbara Bedford *(Marny);* Walter Pidgeon *(Clyde Lord Geradine);* Katherine MacDonald *(Lady Elinor Carew);* Tully Marshall *(Hosein);* Ann Rork *(Kitty);* Arthur Rankin *(Denny O'Meara).*

MARRIAGE LICENSE
(Fox, 1926) 7,168 ′

Presenter: William Fox
Director: Frank Borzage
Based on the Play *The Pelican* by F. Tennyson Jesse and Harold Marsh Harwood
Screenplay: Bradley King
Titles: Elizabeth Pickett
Camera: Ernest Palmer

Alma Rubens *(Wanda Herlot);* Walter McGrail *(Marcus Heriot);* Richard Walling *(Robin);* Walter Pidgeon *(Paul);* Charles Lane *(Sir John);* Emily Fitzroy *(Lady Heriot);* Langhorne Burton *(Cheriton);* Edgar Norton *(Beadon);* George Cowl *(Abercrombie);* Lon Poff *(Footman).*

THE HEART OF SALOME
(Fox, 1927) 5,615 ′

Presenter: William Fox
Director: Victor Schertzinger
Based on the novel by Allen Raymond
Screenplay: Randall H. Faye
Assistant Director: William Tummel
Costumes: Kathleen Kay
Camera: Glen MacWilliams
Editor: Margaret V. Clancy

Alma Rubens *(Helene);* Walter Pidgeon *(Monte Carroll);* Holmes Herbert *(Sir Humphrey);* Robert Agnew *(Redfern);* Erin La Bissoniere *(Helene's Maid);* Walter Dugan *(Chauffeur);* Barry Norton *(Henri Bezanne);* Virginia Madison *(Madame Bezanne).*

THE GIRL FROM RIO
(Lumas Film Corp., 1927) 5,960 ′ *

Presenter: Sam Sax
Producer: Sam Bischoff
Director: Tom Terriss
Story: Norman Kellogg
Adaptor: Terriss
Continuity/Titles: Pauline Forney
Camera: Ray June

Carmel Myers *(Lola);* Walter Pidgeon *(Paul Sinclair);* Richard Tucker *(Antonio Santos);* Henry Herbert *(Farael Fuentes);* Mildred Harris *(Helen Graham);* Edouard Raquello *(Raoul the Dancer).*
*Technicolor sequences.

THE GORILLA
(First National, 1927) 8 reels

Presenters: Asher/Small/Rogers
Director: Alfred Santell
Based on the play by Ralph Spence
Screenplay: Al Cohn, Henry McCarty
Titles: Sidney Lazarus, Al Boasberg
Adaptor: James T. O'Donohoe
Sound: Russell S. Hoff
Camera: Arthur Edeson

Charlie Murray *(Garrity);* Fred Kelsey *(Mulligan);* Alice Day *(Alice Townsend);* Tully Marshall *(William Townsend);* Walter Pidgeon *(Stevens);* Gaston Glass *(Marsden);* Brooks Benedict *(Reporter);* Aggie Herring *(Cook);* Syd Crossley *(Butler);* John Gough *(Sailor).*

THE THIRTEENTH JUROR
(Universal, 1927) 5,598 ′

Presenter: Carl Laemmle
Director: Edward Laemmle
Based on the play *Counsel for the Defense* by Henry Irving Dodge
Screenplay: Charles A. Logue
Titles: Walter Anthony
Camera: Ben Reynolds

Anna Q. Nilsson *(Helen Marsden);* Francis X. Bushman *(Henry Desmond);* Walter Pidgeon *(Richard Marsden);* Martha Mattox *(Housekeeper);* Sidney Bracy *(Butler);* Sailor Sharkey *(Prisoner);* Lloyd Whitlock *(District Attorney);* George Siegmann *(Politician);* Fred Kelsey *(Detective).*

THE GATEWAY OF THE MOON
(Fox, 1928) 5,038 ′

Presenter: William Fox
Director: John Griffith Wray
Based on the novel *Upstream* by Clifford Bax
Screenplay: Bradley King
Titles: Katherine Hilliker, H. H. Caldwell
Assistant Director: A. F. Erickson
Camera: Chester Lyons

Dolores Del Rio [*Chela (Toni)*]; Walter Pidgeon *(Arthur Wyatt);* Anders Randolf *(George Gillespie);* Ted McNamara *(Henry*

Hooker); Adolph Millar *(Rudolf Gottman);* Leslie Fenton *(Jim Mortlake);* Noble Johnson *(Soriano);* Virginia La Fonde *(Indian Child).*

WOMAN WISE
(Fox, 1928) 5,050´

DIRECTOR: Albert Ray
STORY: Donald McGibney
ADAPTOR: Andrew Bennison
SCREENPLAY: Randall H. Faye
TITLES: Malcolm Boylan
ASSISTANT DIRECTOR: Horace Hough
CAMERA: Sidney Wagner
EDITOR: Ralph Dixon

William Russell *(Ne'er-Do-Well);* June Collyer *(Millie Baxter);* Walter Pidgeon *(U.S. Consul);* Theodore Kosloff *(Abdul Mustapha);* Ernie Shields *(Valet);* Raoul Paoli *(Khurd Chief);* Duke Kahanamoku *(Guard);* Josephine Borio, Carmen Castillo *(Native Girls).*

TURN BACK THE HOURS
(Lumas Film Corp., 1928) 6,500´

PRESENTER: Sam Sax
SUPERVISOR: Harold Shumate
DIRECTOR: Howard Bretherton
BASED ON THE PLAY BY EDWARD E. ROSE
SCREENPLAY: Jack Jungmeyer
TITLES: Casey Robinson
CAMERA: Norbert Brodine
EDITOR: Donn Hayes

Myrna Loy *(Tiza Torreon);* Walter Pidgeon *(Phillip Drake);* Sam Hardy *(Ace Kearney);* George E. Stone *(Limey Stokes);* Sheldon Lewis *(Breed);* Josef Swickard *(Colonel Torreon);* Ann Brody *(Maria);* Nanette Villion *(Dancer);* Joyzelle Joyner *(Cantina Girl).*

CLOTHES MAKE THE WOMAN
(Tiffany-Stahl, 1928) 5,209´

DIRECTOR/SCREENPLAY: Tom Terriss
TITLES: Lesley Mason
ART DIRECTOR: Harvey Libbert
SET DECORATOR: George Sawley
CAMERA: Chester Lyons
EDITOR: Desmond O'Brien

Eve Southern *(Princess Anastasia);* Walter Pidgeon *(Victor Trent);* Charles Byer *(Director);* George E. Stone *(Assistant Director);* Adolph Milar *(Bolshevik Leader);* Duncan Renaldo, Gordon Begg, Catherine Wallace, Corliss Palmer, Margaret Selby, H. D. Pennell *(Bits).*

MELODY OF LOVE
(Universal, 1928) 6,733´

DIRECTOR: A. B. Heath
STORY/SCREENPLAY/TITLES: Robert Arch
DIALOGUE: Robert Welsh
SOUND: C. Roy Hunter
CAMERA: Walter Scott
EDITOR: B. W. Burton

Walter Pidgeon *(Jack Clark);* Mildred Harris *(Madelon);* Jane Winton *(Flo Thompson);* Tommy Dugan *(Lefty);* Jack Richardson *(Music Publisher);* Victor Potel *(The Gawk);* Flynn O'Malley *(Bit).*

HER PRIVATE LIFE
(First National, 1929) 6,488

PRESENTER: Richard A. Rowland
PRODUCER: Ned Marin
DIRECTOR: Alexander Korda
BASED ON THE NOVEL *Déclassée* BY ZÖE AKINS
SONG: Al Bryan and George W. Meyer
CAMERA: John Seitz
EDITOR: Harold Young

Billie Dove *(Lady Helen Haden);* Walter Pidgeon *(Ned Thayer);* Holmes Herbert *(Solomon);* Montagu Love *(Sir Bruce Haden);* Thelma Todd *(Mrs. Leslie);* Roland Young *(Charteris);* Mary Forbes *(Lady Wildering);* Brandon Hurst *(Sir Emmett Wildering);* ZaSu Pitts (Timmins).

A MOST IMMORAL LADY
(First National, 1929) 7,145´

DIRECTOR: John Griffith Wray
BASED ON THE PLAY BY TOWNSEND MARTIN
SCREENPLAY: Forrest Halsey
CAMERA: John Seitz
EDITOR: Peter Fritch

Leatrice Joy *(Laura Sargeant);* Walter Pidgeon *(Tony Williams);* Sidney Blackmer *(Humphrey Sargeant);* Montagu Love *(John Williams);* Josephine Dunn *(Joan Porter);* Robert Edeson *(Bradford-Fish);* Donald Reed *(Pedro the Gigolo);* Florence Oakley *(Natalie Davis);* Wilson Benge *(Hoskins the Butler).*

SHOW GIRL IN HOLLYWOOD
(First National, 1930) 80 min.

PRODUCER: Robert North
DIRECTOR: Mervyn LeRoy
BASED ON THE NOVEL *Hollywood Girl* BY J. P. MCEVOY
SCREENPLAY: Harvey Thew, James A. Starr
ART DIRECTOR: Jack Okey
SONGS: Bud Green, Sammy Stept
CHOREOGRAPHY: Jack Haskell
MUSIC CONDUCTOR: Leo F. Forbstein
CAMERA: Sol Polito
EDITOR: Peter Fritch

Alice White *(Dixie Dugan);* Jack Mulhall *(Jimmy Doyle);* Blanche Sweet *(Donna Harris);* Ford Sterling *(Sam Otis);* John Miljan *(Frank Buelow);* Virginia Sale *(Otis' Secretary);* Lee Shumway *(Kramer);* Herman Bing *(Bing);* Walter Pidgeon *(Guest Star).*

BRIDE OF THE REGIMENT
(First National, 1930) C-82 min.

ASSOCIATE PRODUCER: Robert North
DIRECTOR: John Francis Dillon
BASED ON THE PLAY *Die Frau im Hermelin (The Lady In Ermine)* BY RUDOLPH SCHANZER AND ERNST WELISCH
SCREENPLAY: Humphrey Pearson
ADAPTOR/DIALOGUE: Ray Harris
SONGS: Aly Bryan, Eddie Ward, and Al Dubin
CHOREOGRAPHY: Jack Haskell
SOUND: Hal Bumbaugh
CAMERA: Dev Jennings, Charles E. Schoenbaum
EDITOR: Leroy Stone

Vivienne Segal *(Countess Anna-Marie);* Allan Prior *(Count Adrian Beltrami);* Walter Pidgeon *(Colonel Vultow);* Louise Fazenda *(Teresa, the Maid);* Myrna Loy *(Sophie);* Lupino Lane *(Sprotti, the Ballet Master);* Ford Sterling *(Tangy, the Silhouette Cutter);* Harry Cording *(Sergeant Dostal);* Claude Fleming *(Captain Stogan);* Herbert Clark *(The Prince).*

SWEET KITTY BELLAIRS
(Warner Bros., 1930) C-72 min.

DIRECTOR: Alfred E. Green
BASED ON THE PLAY BY DAVID BELASCO
STORY: Edgarton Castle
SCREENPLAY/DIALOGUE: J. Grubb Alexander
ADAPTOR: Herman Harrison
SONGS: Bobby Emmett Dolan and Walter O'Keefe
SOUND: George R. Groves
CAMERA: Watkins McDonald

Claudia Dell *(Sweet Kitty Bellairs);* Ernest Torrence *(Sir Jasper Standish);* Walter Pidgeon *(Lord Varney);* Perry Askam *(Captain O'Hara);* June Collyer *(Julia Standish);* Lionel Belmore *(Colonel Villiers);* Arthur Carewe *(Captain Spicer);* Flora Finch *(Gossip);* Douglas Gerrard *(Tom Stafford);* Christiane Yves *(Lydia).*

VIENNESE NIGHTS
(Warner Bros., 1930) C-107 min.

DIRECTOR: Alan Crosland
SCREENPLAY: Oscar Hammerstein II
SONGS: Hammerstein II and Sigmund Romberg
MUSIC CONDUCTOR: Louis Silvers
CHOREOGRAPHY: Jack Haskell
SOUND: George R. Groves
CAMERA: James Van Trees
EDITOR: Hal McLaren

Alexander Gray *(Otto);* Vivienne Segal *(Elsa);* Bert Roach *(Gus);* Milton Douglas *(Bill Jones);* Jean Hersholt *(Hochter);* June Purcell *(Mary);* Walter Pidgeon *(Franz);* Louise Fazenda *(Gretl);* Lothar Mayring *(Baron);* Alice Day *(Barbara).*

GOING WILD
(Warner Bros., 1930) 70 min.

DIRECTOR: William A. Seiter
STORY: Humphrey Pearson
SCREENPLAY: Pearson, Henry McCarthy
SOUND: Joseph Kane

Camera: Sol Polito
Editor: Peter Fritch

Joe E. Brown *(Rollo Smith);* Lawrence Gray *(Jack Lane);* Laura Lee (Peggy); Walter Pidgeon *(Ace Benton);* Frank McHugh *(Ricky Freeman);* Ona Munson *(Ruth);* May Boley *(May Bunch);* Johnny Arthur *(Simpkins);* Anders Randolf *(Edward Howard);* Arthur Hoyt *(Robert Story);* Fred Kelsey *(Conductor);* Sam Cantor *(Sammy);* Harvey Clark *(Herndon Reamer);* Larry Banthim *(Matt Gore).*

THE GORILLA
(First National, 1930) 63 min.

Director: Bryan Foy
Based on the play by Ralph Spence
Screenplay/Dialogue: Spence
Adaptor: W. Harrison Orkow, Herman Ruby
Camera: Sid Hickox
Editor: George Amy

Joe Frisco *(Garrity);* Lila Lee *(Alice Denby);* Harry Gribbon *(Mulligan);* Walter Pidgeon *(Arthur Marsden);* Purnell Pratt *(The Stranger);* Edwin Maxwell *(Cyrus Stevens);* Roscoe Karns *(Simmons);* William H. Philbrick *(Jeff the Servant);* Landers Stevens *(Inspector).*

KISS ME AGAIN
(First National, 1931) C-77 min.

Director: William A. Seiter
Based on the play *Mlle. Modiste* by Henry Blossom
Screenplay: Julian Josephson, Paul Perez
Songs: Victor Herbert
Camera: Al Gilkes, Lee Garmes
Editor: Peter Fritch

Bernice Claire *(Mlle. Fifi);* Walter Pidgeon *(Paul de St. Cyr);* Edward Everett Horton *(Rene);* June Collyer *(Marie);* Frank McHugh *(Francois);* Claude Gillingwater *(Count de St. Cyr);* Judith Vosselli *(Mme. Cecile);* Albert Gran *(General de Villefranche).*

THE HOT HEIRESS
(First National, 1931) 85 min.

Directors: Clarence Badger, Vincent Sherman
Story/Screenplay: Herbert Fields, Richard Rodgers, and Lorenz Hart
Songs: Rodgers and Hart
Camera: Sol Polito
Editor: Thomas Pratt

Ben Lyon *(Hap Harrigan);* Ona Munson *(Juliette Hunter);* Walter Pidgeon *(Clay);* Thelma Todd *(Lola);* Tom Dugan *(Bill Dugan);* Inez Courtney *(Margie);* Elise Bartlett *(Irene);* Holmes Herbert *(Mr. Hunter);* Nella Walker *(Mrs. Hunter);* George Irving *(Dr. Richmond);* Joe Bernard *(Reggie Pearson);* Aggie Herring *(Landlady);* Max Wagner *(Kidney Beans the Dancer).*

ROCKABYE
(RKO, 1932) 71 min.

Executive Producer: David O. Selznick
Director: George Cukor
Based on the play by Lucia Bronder
Screenplay: Jane Murfin
Art Director: Carroll Clark
Music Director: Max Steiner
Songs: Nacio Herb Brown and Harry Akst; Jeanne Borlini and Edward Eliscu
Sound: George D. Ellis
Camera: Charles Rosher
Editor: George Hively

Constance Bennett *(Judy Carroll);* Joel McCrea *(Jacob Van Riker Pell);* Paul Lukas *(Anthony de Sola);* Jobyna Howland *("Snooks" Carroll);* Walter Pidgeon *(Commissioner Al Howard);* Clara Blandick *(Brida);* Walter Catlett *(Jimmy Dunn);* Virginia Hammond *(Mrs. Van Riker Pell);* June Filmer *(Lilybet);* Charles Middleton *(District Attorney);* J. M. Kerrigan *(Fagin);* Edgar Kennedy *(Driver);* Sterling Holloway *(Speakeasy Customer);* Edwin Stanley *(Defense Attorney);* Richard Carle *(Doc).*

THE KISS BEFORE THE MIRROR
(Universal, 1933) 76 min.

Producer: Carl Laemmle, Jr.
Director: James Whale
Based on the play by Ladislaus Fodor
Screenplay: William Anthony McGuire
Sound: Gilbert Kurland
Camera: Karl Freund
Editor: Ted J. Kent

Nancy Carroll *(Maria Held);* Frank Morgan *(Dr. Paul Held);* Paul Lukas *(Dr. Walter Bernsdorf);* Gloria Stuart *(Lucie Bernsdorf);* Jean Dixon *(Hilda Frey);* Charley Grapewin *(Mr. Schultz);* Walter Pidgeon *(Bachelor);* Donald Cook *(Maria's Paramour);* Allan Connor *(Lucie's Paramour);* Reginald Mason *(Judge);* Wallis Clark *(Prosecutor);* Robert Adair *(Court Officer).*

JOURNAL OF A CRIME
(First National, 1934) 66 min.

Supervisor: Henry Blanke
Director: William Keighley
Based on the play by Jacques Deval
Screenplay: F. Hugh Herbert, Charles Kenyon
Art Director: John Hughes
Gowns: Orry-Kelly
Camera: Ernest Haller
Editor: William Clemons

Ruth Chatterton *(Françoise Moliet);* Adolphe Menjou *(Paul Moliet);* Claire Dodd *(Odette Florey);* George Barbier *(Chautard);* Henry O'Neill *(Doctor);* Phillip Reed *(Young Man);* Noel Madison *(Costelli);* Henry Kolker *(Henri Marcher, the Lawyer);* Frank Reicher *(Winterstein);* Douglass Dumbrille *(Germaine Cartier, the Attorney General);* Clay Clement *(Inspector);* Edward McWade *(Rigaud, the Doorman);* Sidney D'Albrook, Paul Panzer *(Truck Drivers);* Ann Hovey, Marjorie Lytell *(Girls);* Walter Pidgeon *(Baritone);* Olaf Hytten *(Victor, the Butler);* Jane Darwell *(Guest);* Edward Peil, Sr. *(Jailer);* Claire McDowell *(Sister);* Larry Steers, *(Celebrant).*

BIG BROWN EYES
(Paramount, 1936) 76 min.

Producer: Walter Wanger
Director: Raoul Walsh
Based on the stories "Big Brown Eyes" and "Hahsit Babe" by James Edward Grant
Screenplay: Walsh, Bert Hanlon
Art Director: Alexander Toluboff
Set Decorator: Howard Bristol
Costumes: Helen Taylor
Music Director: Boris Morros
Assistant Director: David MacDonald
Sound: Hugo Grenzbach
Camera: George Clemens
Editor: Robert Simpson

Cary Grant *(Danny Barr);* Joan Bennett *(Eve Fallon);* Walter Pidgeon *(Richard Morey);* Lloyd Nolan *(Russ Cortig);* Alan Baxter *(Carey Butler);* Marjorie Gateson *(Mrs. Cole);* Isabel Jewell *(Bessie Blair);* Douglas Fowley *(Benny Battle);* Henry Brandon *(Don Butler);* Joe Sawyer *(Jack Sully);* Sam Flint *(Martin);* Helen Brown *(Mother);* Dolores Casey *(Cashier);* John Picorri *(Defense Attorney);* Frances Morris, Mary Bovard, Betty Van Auken, Dorothy Thompson, Kay Gordon, Betty Gordon, Eleanor Huntley, Janette Warren, Roberta Theiss, Gale Goodson, Helaine Moler, Beulah MacDonald, Jinx Falkenburg, Ethel Sykes *(Manicurists);* Bud Geary *(Gangster);* Lee Phelps *(Jailer);* Charles Hamilton *(Clerk);* Billy Arnold *(Customer);* George MacQuarrie *(Chief of Detectives).*

FATAL LADY
(Paramount, 1936) 73 min.

Producer: Walter Wanger
Director: Edward Ludwig
Story: Harry Segall
Screenplay: Samuel Ornitz, Horace McCoy
Additional Dialogue: Tiffany Thayer
Music Supervisor: Boris Morros
Songs: Sam Coslow and Victor Young
Costumes: Helen Thayer
Set Decorator: Howard Bristol
Camera: Leon Shamroy

Mary Ellis *(Marion Stuart/Maria Delasano);* Walter Pidgeon *(David Roberts);* John Halliday *(Romero Fontes);* Ruth Donnelly *(Melba York);* Alan Mowbray *(Uberto Malla);* Guy Bates Post *(Feodor, Glinka);* Samuel S. Hinds *(Guili Ruffano);* Norman Foster *(Philip Roberts);* Edgar Kennedy *(Rudolf "Rudy" Rockstetter);* Frank Puglia *(Felipe);* Jean Rouverol *(Anita);* Frederick Roland *(Anita's Father);* Laura Treadwell *(Anita's Mother);* Armand & Diane *(Dance Team);* Harry Depp, Frank Hammond, Lucille

Ward, Fern Emmett *(American Tourists);* George Davis, Don Brodie *(French Waiters);* Robert Graves *(French Guide);* Ward Bond *(American Stage Manager);* Edward Van Sloan *(French Surete);* Russell Hicks *(American Opera House Manager);* Russ Bell, Henry Oliver *(Cab Drivers).*

SHE'S DANGEROUS
(Universal, 1937) 70 min.

Associate Producer:	E. M. Asher
Directors:	Lewis R. Foster, Milton Carruth
Story:	Murray Roth, Ben Ryan
Screenplay:	Lionel Houser, Albert H. Perkin
Art Directors:	Jack Otterson, Loren Patrick
Music Director:	Lou Forbes
Special Camera Effects:	John P. Fulton
Camera:	Milton Krasner
Editor:	Frank Gross

Tala Birell *(Stephanie Duval);* Cesar Romero [*Nick Shelton (Al Shaw)*]; Walter Brennan *(Ote O'Leary);* Walter Pidgeon *(Dr. Scott Logan);* Warren Hymer *(Herman Valentz);* Samuel S. Hinds *(Warden);* Richard Carle *(Kegley);* Georges Renavent *(Eduardo, the Headwaiter);* Franklin Pangborn *(Renaud, the Couturier);* Richard Tucker *(District Attorney);* Grady Sutton *(Drunk);* Jonathan Hale *(Charles Fitzgerald);* Pierre Watkin *(H. J. Conrad);* Stanley Andrews *(Franklin Webb);* Meidel Turner *(Dowager);* June Brewster *(Betty Mason);* Barry Norton *(Joseph the Gigolo);* Matty Fain *(Lon Lowry);* Claire Rochelle *(Jane Hope);* Tom McGuire *(Bartender);* Jack George *(Execution Witness);* Jim Farley *(Sheriff);* Edward LeSaint *(Judge);* Ray Turner *(Shoeshiner);* Stanley Blystone *(Cop).*

GIRL OVERBOARD
(Universal, 1937) 58 min.

Associate Producer:	Robert Presnell
Director:	Sidney Saolkow
Story:	Sarah Elizabeth Rodgers
Screenplay:	Tristram Tupper
Camera:	Ira Morgan
Editor:	Philip Cahn

Gloria Stuart *(Mary Chesbrooke);* Walter Pidgeon *(District Attorney Paul Stacey);* Hobart Cavanaugh *(Joe Gray);* Sidney Blackmer *(Alex);* Billy Burrud *(Dickey Stacey);* Charlotte Wynters *(Molly Shane);* Gerald Oliver Smith *(Harvey);* Edward McNamara *(Murphy);* Robert Emmet O'Connor *(Sergeant Hatton);* David Oliver *(Dutch);* Charles Wilson *(Editor);* Selmer Jackson *(Captain Hartman);* J. Scott Smart *(Drunk);* George Pauncefort *(Pathologist);* Sherry Hall *(Reporter);* Don Brodie *(Cardsharp);* Robert E. Homans *(Cop);* Ralph Dunn *(Motorcycle Cop).*

AS GOOD AS MARRIED
(Universal, 1937) 81 min.

Producer:	Charles R. Rogers
Associate Producer:	E. M. Asher
Director:	Edward Buzzell
Story:	Norman Krasna
Screenplay:	F. Hugh Herbert, Lynn Starling
Music Director:	Charles Previn
Special Effects:	John P. Fulton
Camera:	Merritt Gerstad
Editor:	Philip Cahn

John Boles *(Alexander Drew);* Doris Nolan *(Sylvia Parker);* Alan Mowbray *(Wally Burnside);* Harry Davenport *(Jessup);* David Oliver *(Ernie);* Dorothea Kent *(Poochie);* Katharine Alexander *(Alma Burnside);* Ernest Cossart *(Quinn);* Elsa Christian *(Jean Stanford);* Walter Byron *(Arthur Watson);* Mary Philips *(Laura);* Esther Ralston *(Lila Danforth);* Walter Pidgeon *(Fraser James);* Tala Birell *(Cherry);* Rita Gould *(Saleslady);* Joe Devlin, Larry Steers *(Bits).*

SARATOGA
(MGM, 1937) 94 min.

Producer:	Bernard H. Hyman
Associate Producer:	John Emerson
Director:	Jack Conway
Story/Screenplay:	Anita Loos, Robert Hopkins
Art Directors:	Cedric Gibbons, John Detlie
Set Decorator:	Edwin B. Willis
Music:	Edward Ward
Songs:	Walter Donaldson, Bob Wright, and Chet Forrest
Wardrobe:	Dolly Tree
Sound:	Douglas Shearer
Camera:	Ray June
Editor:	Elmo Vernon

Clark Gable *(Duke Bradley);* Jean Harlow *(Carol Clayton);** Lionel Barrymore *(Grandpa Clayton);* Walter Pidgeon *(Hartley Madison);* Frank Morgan *(Jesse Kiffmeyer);* Una Merkel *(Fritzi O'Malley);* Cliff Edwards *(Tip O'Brien);* George Zucco *(Dr. Beard);* Jonathan Hale *(Frank Clayton);* Hattie McDaniel *(Rosetta);* Frankie Darro *(Dixie Gordon);* Carl Stockdale *(Boswell);* Henry Stone *(Hard Riding Hurley);* Ruth Gillette *(Mrs. Hurley);* Charley Foy *(Valet);* Robert Emmett Keane *(Auctioneer);* Edgar Dearing *(Medbury the Trainer);* Frank McGlynn, Sr. *(Kenyon);* Margaret Hamilton *(Maizie);* Lionel Pape, Pat West, John Hyams *(Horse Owners);* Si Jenks *(Gardener);* George Chandler, Drew Demarest *(Cameramen);* Mel Ruick *(Tout);* Patsy O'Connor *(Hurley's Kid);* Fred "Snowflake" Toones *(Train Porter);* Gertrude Simpson *(Bit).*

*After Jean Harlow's death, Mary Dees was substituted for long shots and back view camera shots so that the feature film could be completed. The speaking voice of Paula Winslow was dubbed for the part.

A GIRL WITH IDEAS
(Universal, 1937) 66 min.

Associate Producer:	Edmund Grainger
Director:	S. Sylvan Simon
Based on the story "Mightier Than the Sword" by William Rankin	
Screenplay:	Bruce Manning, Robert T. Shannon
Art Director:	Jack Otterson
Music Director:	Charles Previn
Camera:	Milton Krasner
Editor:	Philip Cahn

Wendy Barrie *(Mary Morton);* Walter Pidgeon *(Mickey McGuire);* Kent Taylor *(Frank Barnes);* Henry Hunter *(William Duncan);* George Barbier *(John Morton);* Dorothea Kent *(Isabelle Foster);* Samuel S. Hinds *(Rodding Carter);* Theodore Osborn *(Bailey);* Horace MacMahon *(Al);* Edward Gargan *(Eddie);* George Cleveland *(Malladay);* Michael Fitzmaurice *(Reggie);* Robert Dalton *(Greg);* Frances Robinson *(Maggie);* Drew Demorest *(Hill);* Robert Spencer *(Charlie);* Jimmie Lucas *(Tom);* Pat Flaherty *(Motorcycle Cop);* Sam Hayes *(Wallie Waldron);* Edward McWade *(Judge);* Norman Willis *(Hanson);* Fay Helm *(Genevieve);* Harry Allen *(Janitor);* Sherry Hall *(Jury Foreman);* Thomas Braidon *(Butler);* Fern Emmett, Sidney Bracy *(Secretaries);* Otto Fries *(Policeman);* Monte Vandergrift *(Truck Driver);* James Farley *(Private Policeman);* Bobby Watson *(Vendor);* Charles Sullivan *(Waiter);* Heinie Conklin *(Street Sweeper);* Rebecca Wassem *(Girl).*

MY DEAR MISS ALDRICH
(MGM, 1937) 79 min.

Producer:	Herman J. Mankiewicz
Director:	George B. Seitz
Story/Screenplay:	Mankiewicz
Art Director:	Cedric Gibbons
Camera:	Charles Lawton
Editor:	William S. Gray

Edna May Oliver *(Mrs. Atherton);* Maureen O'Sullivan *(Martha Aldrich);* Walter Pidgeon *(Ken Morley);* Rita Johnson *(Ellen Warfield);* Janet Beecher *(Mrs. Sinclair);* Paul Harvey *(Mr. Sinclair);* Walter Kingsford *(Mr. Talbot);* Roger Converse *(Ted Martin);* Charles Waldron *(Ex-Governor Warfield);* J. Farrell MacDonald *(Doc Howe);* Brent Sargent *(Gregory);* Guinn "Big Boy" Williams *(Starter);* Lya Lys *(The Queen);* Leonid Kinskey *(Tony, the Waiter);* Robert Greig *(Major Domo);* Renie Riano *(Maid);* Jack Norton, Don Barclay *(Drunks);* Carl Stockdale *(Apartment House Manager);* Gwen Lee *(Hat Saleswoman);* Sonny Bupp *(Little Boy);* Marie Blake *(Telephone Operator);* Jack Baxley *(Customer);* Bud Fine *(Doctor);* Arthur Belasco *(Press Man).*

MAN-PROOF
(MGM, 1938) 74 min.

Producer:	Louis D. Lighton
Director:	Richard Thorpe
Story:	Fanny Heaslip Lea
Screenplay:	Vincent Lawrence, Waldemar Young, George Oppenheimer

Camera: Karl Freund
Editor: George Boemler

Myrna Loy *(Mimi Swift)*; Rosalind Russell *(Elizabeth)*; Franchot Tone *(Jimmy Kilmartin)*; Walter Pidgeon *(Alan Wythe)*; Nana Bryant *(Meg Swift)*; John Miljan *(Tommy Gaunt)*; Ruth Hussey *(Jane)*; Rita Johnson *(Florence)*; William Stack *(Minister)*; Leonard Penn *(Bob)*; Oscar O'Shea *(Gus the Bartender)*; Marie Blake *(Telephone Girl)*; Dan Toby *(Fight Announcer)*; Aileen Pringle, Grace Hayle, Laura Treadwell *(Women)*; Mary Howard, Frances Reid *(Girls)*; Betty Blythe *(Country Club Woman)*; Dorothy Vaughan *(Matron)*; May Beatty *(Landlady)*; Gwen Lee *(Girl at Fight)*; Francis X. Bushman, Jr. *(Young Man at Fight)*; Jack Norton *(Drunk at Fight)*; Joyce Compton *(Guest)*; Irving Bacon *(Drug Clerk)*.

THE GIRL OF THE GOLDEN WEST
(MGM, 1938) 120 min.*

Producer: William Anthony McGuire
Director: Robert Z. Leonard
Based on the play by David Belasco
Screenplay: Isabel Dawn, Boyce DeGraw
Music Director: Herbert Stothart
Choreography: Albertina Rasch
Songs: Sigmund Romberg and Gus Kahn
Art Director: Cedric Gibbons
Sound: Douglas Shearer
Montages: Slavko Vorkapich
Camera: Oliver Marsh
Editor: W. Donn Hayes

Jeanette MacDonald *(Mary Robbins)*; Nelson Eddy [*Ramirez (Lieutenant Johnson)*]; Walter Pidgeon *(Sheriff Jack Rance)*; Leo Carrillo *(Mosquito)*; Buddy Ebsen *(Alabama)*; Leonard Penn *(Pedro)*; Priscilla Lawson *(Nina Martinez)*; Bob Murphy *(Sonora Slim)*; Olin Howland *(Trinidad Joe)*; Cliff Edwards *(Minstrel Joe)*; Billy Bevan *(Nick)*; Brandon Tynan *(Professor)*; H. B. Warner *(Father Sienna)*; Monty Woolley *(Governor)*; Charley Grapewin *(Uncle Davy)*; Noah Beery, Sr. *(General)*; Bill Cody, Jr. *(Gringo)*; Jeanne Ellis *(The Girl Mary)*; Ynez Seabury *(Wowkle)*; Victor Potel *(Stage Driver)*; Nick Thompson *(Billy Jack Rabbit)*; Tom Mahoney *(Handsome Charlie)*; Phillip Armenta *(Long Face)*; Chief Big Tree *(Indian Chief)*; Russell Simpson *(Pioneer)*; Gene Coogan *(Manuel)*; Frank McGlynn *(Pete, a Gambler)*; Cy Kendall *(Hank, a Gambler)*; Francis Ford, E. Alyn Warren *(Miners)*; Virginia Howell *(Governor's Wife)*.

*Filmed in Sepia

THE SHOPWORN ANGEL
(MGM, 1938) 85 min.

Producer: Joseph L. Mankiewicz
Director: H. C. Potter
Based on the story "Private Pettigrew's Girl" by Dana Burnett
Screenplay: Waldo Salt
Art Directors: Cedric Gibbons, Joseph C. Wright
Set Decorator: Edwin B. Willis
Music: Edward Ward
Song: George Asaf and Felix Powell
Choreography: Val Raset
Gowns: Adrian
Sound: Douglas Shearer
Montages: Slavko Vorkapich
Camera: Joseph Ruttenberg
Editor: W. Donn Hayes

Margaret Sullavan *(Daisy Heath)*; James Stewart *(Bill Pettigrew)*; Walter Pidgeon *(Sam Bailey)*; Nat Pendleton *(Dice)*; Alan Curtis *(Guy with Thin Lips)*; Sam Levene *(Guy with Leer)*; Hattie McDaniel *(Martha the Maid)*; Charley Grapewin *(Wilson the Caretaker)*; Charles D. Brown *(Mr. Gonigle the Stage Manager)*; Jimmy Butler *(Elevator Boy)*; Eleanor Lynn *(Sally the Waitress)*; William Stack *(Minister)*; Hudson Shotwell *(Jack the Soldier)*; John Merton *(Speaker)*; Wesley Giraud *(Bellboy)*; Harry Tyler *(Eddy)*; Mary Howard, Virginia Grey *(Chorus Girls)*; Wade Boteler *(Irish Policeman)*; Grace Hayle *(Mistress of Ceremonies)*; George Chandler *(Soldier)*; Frank McGlynn, Jr. *(Motorcyclist)*; Roger Converse *(Hotel Clerk)*; Dorothy Granger *(Dancer)*.

TOO HOT TO HANDLE
(MGM, 1938) 105 min.

Producer: Lawrence Weingarten
Director: Jack Conway
Story: Len Hammond
Screenplay: Laurence Stallings, John Lee Mahin
Camera: Harold Rosson
Editor: Frank Sullivan

Clark Gable *(Chris Hunter)*; Myrna Loy *(Alma Harding)*; Walter Pidgeon *(Bill Dennis)*; Walter Connolly *("Gabby" MacArthur)*; Leo Carrillo *(Joselito)*; Johnny Hines *(Parsons)*; Virginia Weidler *(Hulda)*; Betty Ross Clarke *(Mrs. Harding)*; Henry Kolker *("Pearly" Todd)*; Willie Fung *(Willie)*; Patsy O'Cooper *("Fake" Hulda)*.

LISTEN, DARLING
(MGM, 1938) 70 min.

Producer: Jack Cummings
Director: Edwin L. Marin
Story: Katherine Brush
Screenplay: Elaine Ryan, Anne Morrison Chapin
Art Director: Cedric Gibbons
Music Director: George Stoll
Music Arranger: Roger Edens
Songs: Al Hoffman, Al Lewis and Murray Mencher; James Hanley; Joseph McCarthy and Milton Ager
Camera: Charles Lawton, Jr.
Editor: Blanche Sewell

Freddie Bartholomew *(Buzz Mitchell)*; Judy Garland *(Pinkie Wingate)*; Mary Astor *(Dotty Wingate)*; Walter Pidgeon *(Richard Thurlow)*; Alan Hale *(J. J. Slattery)*; Scotty Beckett *(Billie Wingate)*; Barnett Parker *(Abercrombie)*; Gene Lockhart *(Mr. Drubbs)*; Charley Grapewin *(Uncle Joe)*.

SOCIETY LAWYER
(MGM, 1939) 78 min.

Producer: John W. Considine, Jr.
Director: Edwin L. Marin
Based on the story by Arthur Somers Roche and the screenplay: *Penthouse* by Frances Goodrich and Albert Hackett
New Screenplay: Leon Gordon, Hugh Butler
Music Directors: Georgie Stoll, Roger Edens
Song: Sam Coslow
Orchestrator: Leo Arnaud
Music: Edward Ward
Wardrobe: Dolly Tree
Art Directors: Cedric Gibbons, Howard Campbell
Set Decorator: Edwin B. Willis
Camera: George Folsey
Editor: Howard O'Neill

Walter Pidgeon *(Christopher Durant)*; Virginia Bruce *(Pat Allen)*; Leo Carrillo *(Tony Gazotti)*; Lee Bowman *(Phil Siddel)*; Eduardo Ciannelli *(Jim Crelliman)*; Frances Mercer *(Sue Leonard)*; Ann Morriss *(Judy Baron)*; Herbert Mundin *(Layton)*; Edward Brophy *(Max)*; Tom Kennedy *(Alf)*; Frank M. Thomas *(Lieutenant Stevens)*; Paul Guilfoyle *(Murtock)*; Joseph Crehan *(City Editor)*; Pierre Watkin *(Mr. Adams)*; Clarence Kolb *(Mr. Leonard)*; Lillian Yarbo *(Sadie)*; Selmer Jackson *(Inspector)*; James Millican *(Reporter)*; Ferris Taylor *(Foreman)*; Bess Flowers *(Mary, the Secretary)*; Frank Orth *(Man)*; Lester Dorr *(Photographer)*; Harry Strang, Harry Fleischmann, Howard Mitchell *(Plainclothesmen)*; Sharon Lewis *(Gangster's Moll)*.

6,000 ENEMIES
(MGM, 1939) 60 min.

Producer: Lucien Hubbard
Director: George Seitz
Story: Wilmon Menard, Leo Stanley
Screenplay: Bertram Millhauser
Art Directors: Cedric Gibbons, Daniel B. Cathcart
Set Decorator: Edwin B. Willis
Wardrobe: Dolly Tree
Montage Peter Ballbusch
Camera: John Seitz
Editor: Conrad Nervig

Walter Pidgeon *(Steve Donegan)*; Rita Johnson *(Anne Barry)*; Paul Kelly *(Dr. Malcolm Scott)*; Nat Pendleton *("Socks" Martin)*; Harold Huber *(Joe Silenus)*; Grant Mitchell *(Warden Parkhurst)*; John Arledge *(Phil Donegan)*; Guinn "Big Boy" Williams *(Maxie)*; Adrian Morris *(Bull Snyder)*; J. M. Kerrigan *(Dan Barrett)*; Esther Dale *(Matron)*; Selmer Jackson *(Judge)*; Arthur Aylsworth *(Dawson)*; Ernest Whitman *(Willie Johnson)*; Raymond Hatton *(Wibbie Yern)*; Lionel Royce *(Dutch Myers)*; Tom Neal *(Ransom)*; Frank Lackteen *(Bolo)*; Robert Emmett Keane *(Sam Todd)*; Horace McMahon *(Boxcar)*; Jack Mulhall *(O'Toole)*; Ernie Adams, George Magrill, Drew Demarest *(Henchmen)*.

STRONGER THAN DESIRE
(MGM, 1939) 80 min.

PRODUCER: John W. Considine, Jr.
DIRECTOR: Leslie Fenton
BASED ON THE NOVEL BY W. E. WOODWARD AND THE SCREENPLAY *Evelyn Prentice*
NEW SCREENPLAY: David Hartz, William Ludwig
CAMERA: William Daniels
EDITOR: W. Donn Hayes

Walter Pidgeon *(Tyler Flagg);* Virginia Bruce *(Elizabeth Flagg);* Rita Johnson *(Barbara Winter);* Ann Dvorak *(Eva McLean);* Lee Bowman *(Boris McLean);* Ilka Chase *(Jo Brennan);* Paul Stanton *(Galway);* Richard Lane *(Jerry Brody);* Ann Todd *(Susan Flagg);* Ferike Boros *(Mrs. D'Amore);* Donald Douglas *(Clark);* Thomas Jackson *(Thompson);* John Hamilton *(Judge);* Margaret Bert *(Nursemaid);* Leonard Carey *(Albert);* Barbara Bedford *(Miss Watson);* Lester Dorr, Reed Hadley, Tom Neal, Phil Tead, Jack Hatfield *(Reporters);* Mariska Aldrich *(Matron).*

NICK CARTER—MASTER DETECTIVE
(MGM, 1939) 60 min.

PRODUCER: Lucien Hubbard
DIRECTOR: Jacques Tourneur
STORY: Bertram Millhauser, Harold Buckley
SCREENPLAY: Millhauser
CAMERA: Charles Lawton
EDITOR: Elmo Vernon

Walter Pidgeon *(Nick Carter/Robert Chalmers);* Rita Johnson *(Lou Barnsby);* Henry Hull *(John Keller);* Donald Meek *(Bartholomew);* Stanley Ridges *(Dr. Frankton);* Addison Richards *(Hiram Streeter);* Henry Victor *(J. Lester Hammil);* Milburn Stone *(Dave Krebs);* Martin Kosleck *(Otto King);* Wally Maher *(Cliff Parsons);* Frank Faylen *(Pete Foley);* Frank Ball *(Peake);* George Meeker *(Hartley);* Richard Terry *(Cain);* Paul Ellis *(Faber);* Don Castle *(Ed);* Sterling Holloway *(Youth);* Louis V. Arco *(Captain of Cruiser).*

IT'S A DATE
(Universal, 1940) 103 min.

PRODUCER: Joseph Pasternak
DIRECTOR: William A. Seiter
STORY: Jane Hall, Frederick Kohner, Ralph Block
SCREENPLAY: Norman Krasna
SONGS: Pinky Tomlin and Harry Tobias; Ralph Freed and Frank Skinner; Eddie Cherkose, L. Belasco, and Jacques Press
CAMERA: Joseph Valentine
EDITOR: Bernard Burton

Deanna Durbin *(Pamela Drake);* Kay Francis *(Georgia Drake);* Walter Pidgeon *(John Arlen);* Samuel S. Hinds *(Sidney Simpson);* S. Z. Sakall *(Carl Ober);* Lewis Howard *(Freddie Miller);* Cecilia Loftus *(Sarah Frankenstein);* Henry Stephenson *(Captain Andrews);* Eugene Pallette *(Governor);* Joe King *(First Mate);* Fritz Feld *(Headwaiter);* Charles Lane *(Horner);* John Arledge *(Newcomer);* Romaine Callender *(Evans);* Virginia Brissac *(Holden);* Leon Belasco *(Captain);* Anna Demetrio *(Cook);* Mary Kelley *(Governor's Wife);* Eddie Acuff *(Ship's Steward);* Eddie Polo *(Quartermaster);* Mark Anthony *(Officer);* Mary Shannon *(Wardrobe Mistress);* Fay McKenzie, Linda Deane, Phyllis Ruth, Virginia Engles *(Young Girls);* Johnny Day *(Sleepy-Eyed Blond).*

THE HOUSE ACROSS THE BAY
(United Artists, 1940) 88 min.

PRODUCER: Walter Wanger
DIRECTOR: Archie Mayo
STORY: Myles Connolly
SCREENPLAY: Kathryn Scola
MUSIC/MUSIC DIRECTOR: Werner Janssen
JOAN BENNETT'S COSTUMES BY IRENE
ASSISTANT DIRECTOR: Charles Kerr
ART DIRECTORS: Alexander Golitzen, Richard Irvine
SET DECORATOR: Julie Heron
CHOREOGRAPHY: Sammy Lee
SONGS: Jule Styne, Nick Castle, and Sidney Clare; Al Siegel; George R. Brown, Irving Actman
SOUND: Fred Lau
CAMERA: Merritt Gerstad
EDITOR: Dorothy Spencer

George Raft *(Steve Larwitt);* Joan Bennett *(Brenda "Lucky" Bentley);* Lloyd Nolan *(Slant Kolma);* Gladys George *(Mary Bogale);* Walter Pidgeon *(Tim Nolan);* William "Billy" Wayne *(Barney the Bartender);* June Knight *(Babe Davis);* Peggy Shannon *(Alice);* Cy Kendall *(Crawley);* Max Wagner *(Jim the Chauffeur);* Frank Bruno *(Jerry the Henchman);* Joe Sawyer *(Charlie);* William Halligan, Kenneth Harlan *(Nightclub Patrons);* Freeman Wood *(Mr. Hanson);* Eddie Marr, Norman Willis *(Taresca's Henchmen);* Pat O'Malley, Al Ferguson, James Farley, Martin Cichy, Franklyn Farnum *(Prison Guards);* Virginia Brissac *(Landlady);* Etta McDaniel *(Lydia—Brenda's Maid);* Cy Ring *(Dance Extra);* Kit Guard *(Taresca's Driver);* Allen Wood (Newsboy).

DARK COMMAND
(Republic, 1940) 94 min.

ASSOCIATE PRODUCER: Sol C. Siegel
DIRECTOR: Raoul Walsh
BASED ON THE NOVEL BY W. R. BURNETT
SCREENPLAY: Grover Jones, Lionel Houser, F. Hugh Herbert
CAMERA: Jack Maorta
EDITOR: Murray Seldeen

Claire Trevor *(Mary McCloud);* John Wayne *(Bob Seton);* Walter Pidgeon *(William Cantrell);* Roy Rogers *(Fletch McCloud);* George "Gabby" Hayes *(Doc Grunch);* Porter Hall *(Angus McCloud);* Marjorie Main *(Mrs. Cantrell);* Raymond Walburn *(Buckner);* Joe Sawyer *(Bushropp);* Helen MacKellar *(Mrs. Hale);* J. Farrell MacDonald *(Dave);* Trevor Bardette *(Hale);* Harry Woods *(Dental Patient);* Jack Rockwell *(Assassin);* Alan Bridge *(Slave Trader);* Edmund Cobb, Edward Hearn *(Jurymen);* Hal Taliaferro *(Vigilante);* Yakima Canutt *(Townsman/Stunts);* Tom London *(Messenger);* Cliff Lyons *(Stunts);* Ben Alexander *(Sentry);* Ernie Adams *(Another Townsman).*

PHANTOM RAIDERS
(MGM, 1940) 70 mins.

PRODUCER: Frederick Stephani
DIRECTOR: Jacques Tourneur
STORY: Jonathan Latimer
SCREENPLAY: William R. Lipman
CAMERA: Clyde De Vinna

Walter Pidgeon *(Nick Carter);* Florence Rice *(Cora Barnes);* Joseph Schildkraut *(Al Taurez);* John Carroll *(John Ramsell, Jr.);* Donald Meek *(Bartholomew);* Nat Pendleton *("Gunboat" Jacklin);* Steffi Duna *(Dolores);* Cecil Kellaway *(Franklin Morris);* Matthew Boulton *(John Ramsell, Sr.);* Alec Craig *(Andy Macmillan);* Thomas Ross *(Dr. Grisson);* Dwight Frye *(Eddie Anders).*

SKY MURDER
(MGM, 1940) 72 min.

PRODUCER: Frederick Stephani
DIRECTOR: George B. Seitz
SCREENPLAY: William R. Lipman
ART DIRECTORS: Cedric Gibbons, Howard Campbell
SET DECORATOR: Edwin B. Willis
MUSIC: David Snell
SOUND: Douglas Shearer
CAMERA: Charles Lawton
EDITOR: Gene Ruggiero

Walter Pidgeon *(Nick Carter);* Donald Meek *(Bartholomew);* Karen Verne *(Pat Evans);* Edward Ashley *(Cortland Grand);* George Lessey *(Senator Monrose);* Joyce Compton *("Chris" Cross);* Tom Conway *(Andrew Hendon);* Frank Reicher *(Dr. Grattan);* Dorothy Tree *(Kathe);* Grady Sutton *(Buster);* Lucien Prival *(Brucker);* George Watts *(Judge Whitmore);* Chill Wills *(Sheriff Beckwith);* Milton Parsons *(Brock);* Tom Neal *(Cossack);* Byron Foulger *(Muse);* William Tannen *(Gus);* Kay Sutton *("Texas" O'Keefe);* Anne Wigton *(Miss Shakespeare);* Judith Allen *("Ruffles" Macklin);* Celia Travers *(Cissy Minch);* Virginia O'Brien *(Lucille La Vonne);* Warren McCollum *(Boy);* Edwin Parker, Ted Oliver *(Cops);* Cyrus Kendall *(Harrigan);* Arthur Aylsworth *(Man).*

FLIGHT COMMAND
(MGM, 1940) 110 min.

PRODUCER: J. Walter Ruben
DIRECTOR: Frank Borzage
STORY: Commander Harvey Haislip, John Sutherland
SCREENPLAY: Wells Root, Haislip
MUSIC: Franz Waxman
SONG: J. V. McElduff
ART DIRECTORS: Cedric Gibbons, Urie McCleary

SET DECORATOR:	Edwin B. Willis
WOMEN'S WARDROBE:	Dolly Tree
MEN'S COSTUMES:	Gile Steele
SOUND:	Douglas Shearer
SPECIAL EFFECTS:	A. Arnold Gillespie
CAMERA:	Harold Rosson
EDITOR:	Robert J. Kern

Robert Taylor *(Alan Drake);* Ruth Hussey *(Lorna Gary);* Walter Pidgeon *(Bill Gary);* Paul Kelly *(Dusty Rhodes);* Shepperd Strudwick *(Jerry Banning);* Red Skelton *(Mugger Martin);* Dick Purcell *(Stitchy Payne);* Nat Pendleton *(Spike Knowles);* Marsha Hunt *(Claire);* William Tannen *(Freddie Townsend);* William Stelling *(Bush);* Stanley Smith *(Frost);* Donald Douglas *(Duty Officer);* Lee Tung-Foo *(Jung);* John Hamilton *(Pensacola Commander);* Gaylord Steve Pendleton *(Enlisted Man);* Jack Luden *(Hell Cat);* Dick Wessel *(Big Sailor);* Reed Hadley *(Admiral's Aide);* Addison Richards *(Admiral).*

DESIGN FOR SCANDAL
(MGM, 1941) 85 min.

PRODUCER:	John W. Considine, Jr.
DIRECTOR:	Norman Taurog
SCREENPLAY:	Lionel Houser
ART DIRECTOR:	Cedric Gibbons
SET DECORATOR:	Edwin B. Willis
MUSIC:	Franz Waxman
CAMERA:	Leonard Smith, William Daniels
EDITOR:	Elmo Vernon

Rosalind Russell *(Cornelia Porter);* Walter Pidgeon *(Jeff Sherman);* Edward Arnold *(Judson M. Blair);* Barbara Jo Allen [*Vera Vague*] *(Jane Porter);* Lee Bowman *(Walter Caldwell);* Jean Rogers *(Dotty);* Donald Meek *(Mr. Wade);* Guy Kibbee *(Judge Graham);* Mary Beth Hughes *(Adele Blair);* Bobby Larson *(Freddie);* Leon Belasco *(Alexander Raoul);* Charles Coleman *(Wilton);* Thurston Hall *(Northcott);* Edgar Dearing *(Joe the Foreman);* Eddie Dunn *(Eddie Smith the Miner);* Jim Conlin *(Dawes);* Robert Emmett Keane *(Tucker);* Dick Bartell *(Osborne);* Charlotte Wynters *(Thelma the Secretary);* Ed Thomas *(Steward);* Jessie Arnold *(Miner's Wife);* Dorothy Morris, Marjorie Deanne, Ruth Alder, Babe Kane *(Phone Operators);* Milton Kibbee *(Court Clerk).*

MAN HUNT
(20th Century-Fox, 1941) 105 min.

PRODUCER:	Darryl F. Zanuck
ASSOCIATE PRODUCER:	Kenneth Macgowan
DIRECTOR:	Fritz Lang
BASED ON THE NOVEL *Rogue Male* BY GEOFFREY HOUSEHOLD	
SCREENPLAY:	Dudley Nichols
ART DIRECTORS:	Richard Day, Wiard B. Ihnen
MUSIC:	Alfred Newman
CAMERA:	Arthur Miller
EDITOR:	Allen McNeil

Walter Pidgeon *(Captain Thorndike);* Joan Bennett *(Jerry);* George Sanders *(Quive-Smith);* John Carradine *(Mr. Jones);* Roddy McDowall *(Vaner the Cabin Boy);* Ludwig Stossel *(Doctor);* Heather Thatcher *(Lady Risborough);* Frederic Worlock *(Lord Risborough);* Roger Imhof *(Captain Jensen);* Egon Brecher *(Whiskers);* Holmes Herbert *(Farnsworthy);* Fredrik Vogeding *(Ambassador);* Lucien Prival *(Umbrella Man);* Herbert Evans *(Reeves);* Edgar Licho *(Little Fat Man);* Eily Malyon *(Postmistress);* John Rogers *(Cockney);* Lester Matthews *(Major);* Arno Frey *(Police Lieutenant);* Keith Hitchcock *(London Bobby);* Otto Reichow, Bob Stephenson *(Sentries);* Adolph Milar *(Pigeon Man);* Sven Borg *(First Mate);* Olaf Hytten *(Secretary).*

BLOSSOMS IN THE DUST
(MGM, 1941) C-100 min.

PRODUCER:	Irving Asher
DIRECTOR:	Mervyn LeRoy
STORY:	Ralph Wheelwright
SCREENPLAY:	Anita Loos
ART DIRECTORS:	Cedric Gibbons, Urie McCleary
SET DECORATOR:	Edwin B. Willis
GOWNS:	Adrian
MEN'S COSTUMES:	Gile Steele
MUSIC:	Herbert Stothart
MAKEUP:	Jack Dawn
COLOR CONSULTANTS:	Natalie Kalmus, Henri Jaffa
SOUND:	Douglas Shearer
SPECIAL EFFECTS:	Warren Newcombe
CAMERA:	Karl W. Freund, W. Howard Green
EDITOR:	George Boemler

Greer Garson *(Edna Gladney);* Walter Pidgeon *(Sam Gladney);* Felix Bressart *(Dr. Max Breslar);* Marsha Hunt *(Charlotte);* Fay Holden *(Mrs. Kahly);* Samuel S. Hinds *(Mr. Kahly);* Kathleen Howard *(Mrs. Keats);* George Lessey *(Mr. Keats);* William Henry *(Allan Keats);* Henry O'Neill *(Judge);* John Eldredge *(Damon McPherson);* Clinton Rosemond *(Zeke);* Theresa Harris *(Cleo);* Charlie Arnt *(G. Harrington Hedger);* Cecil Cunningham *(Mrs. Gilworth);* Ann Morriss *(Mrs. Loring);* Richard Nichols *(Sammy);* Pat Barker *(Tony);* Mary Taylor *(Helen);* Marc Lawrence *(Bert La Verne);* Frank Darien *(Accountant);* Almira Sessions *(Woman Who Buys Back the Vase);* Will Wright *(Senator);* Edwin Maxwell *(Member of the Board).*

HOW GREEN WAS MY VALLEY
(20th Century-Fox, 1941) 118 min.

PRODUCER:	Darryl F. Zanuck
DIRECTOR:	John Ford
BASED ON THE NOVEL BY RICHARD LLEWELLYN	
SCREENPLAY:	Philip Dunne
ART DIRECTORS:	Richard Day, Nathan Juran
SET DECORATOR:	Thomas Little
COSTUMES:	Gwen Wakeling
MUSIC:	Alfred Newman
CAMERA:	Arthur Miller
EDITOR:	James B. Clark

Walter Pidgeon *(Reverend Mr. Gruffydd);* Maureen O'Hara *(Angharad Morgan);* Donald Crisp *(Mr. Morgan);* Anna Lee *(Bronwyn Morgan);* Roddy McDowall *(Huw Morgan);* John Loder *(Ianto Morgan);* Sara Allgood *(Mrs. Beth Morgan);* Barry Fitzgerald *(Cyfartha);* Patric Knowles *(Ivor Morgan);* Welsh Singers *(Themselves);* Morton Lowry *(Mr. Jonas);* Arthur Shields *(Mr. Parry);* Anne Todd *(Genwen);* Frederic Worlock *(Dr. Richards);* Richard Fraser *(Davy Morgan);* Evan S. Evans *(Gwinlyn);* James Monks *(Owen Morgan);* Rhys Williams *(Dai Bando);* Lionel Pape *(Old Evans);* Ethel Griffies *(Mrs. Nicholas);* Marten Lamont *(Iestyn Evans);* Mae Marsh *(Miner's Wife);* Louis Jean Heydt *(Miner);* Dennis Hoey *(Motschell);* Tudor Williams *(Ensemble Singer);* Irving Pichel *(Narrator);* Mary Gordon *(Woman).*

MRS. MINIVER
(MGM, 1942) 134 min.

PRODUCER:	Sidney Franklin
DIRECTOR:	William Wyler
BASED ON THE NOVEL BY JAN STRUTHER	
SCREENPLAY:	Arthur Wimperis, George Froeschel, James Hilton, Claudine West
MUSIC:	Herbert Stothart
SONGS:	Gene Lockhart
ART DIRECTORS:	Cedric Gibbons, Urie McCleary
SET DECORATOR:	Edwin B. Willis
GOWNS:	Kalloch
MEN'S WARDROBE:	Gile Steele
SOUND:	Douglas Shearer
SPECIAL EFFECTS:	Arnold Gillespie, Warren Newcombe
CAMERA:	Joseph Ruttenberg
EDITOR:	Harold F. Kress

Greer Garson *(Mrs. Kay Miniver);* Walter Pidgeon *(Clem Miniver);* Teresa Wright *(Carol Beldon);* Dame May Whitty *(Lady Beldon);* Henry Travers *(Mr. Ballard);* Reginald Owen *(Foley);* Miles Mander *(German Agent's Voice);* Henry Wilcoxon *(Vicar);* Richard Ney *(Vin Miniver);* Clare Sandars *(Judy Miniver);* Christopher Severn *(Toby Miniver);* Brenda Forbes (Gladys the Housemaid); Rhys Williams *(Horace);* Marie De Becker (Ada the Cook); Helmut Dantine *(German Flyer);* Mary Field *(Miss Spriggins);* Tom Conway *(Man);* St. Luke's Choristers *(Choral Voices);* Paul Scardon *(Nobby);* Ben Webster *(Ginger);* Aubrey Mather *(George the Innkeeper);* Forrester Harvey *(Huggins);* John Abbott *(Fred the Porter);* Connie Leon *(Simpson the Maid);* Billy Bevan *(Conductor);* Oliver Smith *(Car Dealer);* Charles Irwin *(Mac);* Ian Wolfe *(Dentist);* Thomas Louden *(Mr. Verger);* Peter Lawford *(Pilot);* Stanley Mann *(Workman);* Billy Engle *(Townsman).*

WHITE CARGO
(MGM, 1942) 90 min.

PRODUCER:	Victor Saville
DIRECTOR:	Richard Thorpe
BASED ON THE PLAY BY LEON GORDON	
SCREENPLAY:	Gordon

CHOREOGRAPHY: Ernst Matray
ART DIRECTORS: Cedric Gibbons, Daniel B. Cathcart
SET DECORATORS: Edwin B. Willis, Keogh Gleason
NATIVE COSTUMES: Kalloch
MAKEUP: Jack Dawn
CAMERA: Harry Stradling
EDITOR: Frederick T. Smith

Hedy Lamarr *(Tondelayo)*; Walter Pidgeon *(Harry Witzel)*; Frank Morgan *(Doctor)*; Richard Carlson *(Langford)*; Reginald Owen *(Skipper)*; Henry O'Neill *(Reverend Roberts)*; Bramwell Fletcher *(Wilbur Ashley)*; Clyde Cook *(Ted)*; Leigh Whipper *(Jim Fish)*; Oscar Polk *(Umeela)*; Darby Jones *(Doctor's Houseboy)*; Richard Ainley *(Worthing)*.

THE YOUNGEST PROFESSION
(MGM, 1943) 82 min.

PRODUCER: B. F. Ziedman
DIRECTOR: Edward Buzzell
BASED ON THE BOOK BY LILLIAN DAY
SCREENPLAY: George Oppenheimer, Charles Lederer, Leonard Spigelgass
ART DIRECTORS: Cedric Gibbons, Edward Carfagno
SET DECORATORS: Edwin B. Willis, Helen Conway
MUSIC: David Snell
COSTUMES: Irene, Howard Shoup
ASSISTANT DIRECTOR: Julian Silberstein
SOUND: Wilhelm W. Brockway
CAMERA: Charles Lawton
EDITOR: Ralph Winters

Virginia Weidler *(Jean Lyons)*; Edward Arnold *(Burton V. Lyons)*; John Carroll *(Dr. Hercules)*; Jean Porter *(Patricia Drew)*; Marta Linden *(Mrs. Edith Lyons)*; Dick Simmons *(Douglas Sutton)*; Ann Ayars *(Susan Thayer)*; Agnes Moorehead *(Miss Featherstone)*; Marcia Mae Jones *(Vera Bailey)*; Raymond Roe *(Schuyler)*; Scotty Beckett *(Junior Lyons)*; Jessie Grayson *(Lilybud)*; Greer Garson, Walter Pidgeon, William Powell, Robert Taylor, Lana Turner *(Guest Stars)*; Beverly Tyler *(Thyra Winters)*; Patricia Roe *(Polly)*; Marjorie Gateson *(Mrs. Drew)*; Thurston Hall *(Mr. Drew)*; Aileen Pringle *(Miss Farwood)*; Nora Lane *(Hilda)*; Dorothy Christy *(Sally)*; Mary Vallee *(Mary)*; Gloria Tucker *(Gladys)*; Jane Isbell *(Jane)*; Hazel Dawn *(Hazel)*; Beverly Boyd *(Beverly)*; Randa Allen *(Randa)*; Shirley Coates, Mary McCarty *(Girls)*; Mark Daniels *(Lee Peterson)*; Eddie Buzzell *(Man in Theatre)*.

MADAME CURIE
(MGM, 1943) 124 min.

PRODUCER: Sidney Franklin
DIRECTOR: Mervyn LeRoy
BASED ON THE BOOK BY MARIE CURIE
SCREENPLAY: Paul Osborn, Paul H. Rameau
MUSIC: Herbert Stothart
ART DIRECTORS: Cedric Gibbons, Paul Groesse
SET DECORATORS: Edwin B. Willis, Hugh Hunt
ASSISTANT DIRECTOR: Al Shenberg
WOMEN'S COSTUMES: Irene Sharaff
MEN'S COSTUMES: Gile Steele
SOUND: W. N. Sparks
SPECIAL EFFECTS: Warren Newcombe
CAMERA: Joseph Ruttenberg
EDITOR: Harold F. Kress

Greer Garson *(Mrs. Marie Curie)*; Walter Pidgeon *(Pierre Curie)*; Robert Walker *(David LeGros)*; Dame May Whitty *(Mme. Eugene Curie)*; Henry Travers *(Eugene Curie)*; C. Aubrey Smith *(Lord Kelvin)*; Albert Basserman *(Professor Perot)*; Victor Francen *(President of University)*; Reginald Owen *(Dr. Henri Becquerel)*; Van Johnson *(Reporter)*; Elsa Basserman *(Mme. Perot)*; Lumsden Hare *(Professor Reget)*; James Hilton *(Narrator)*; Charles Trowbridge, Edward Fielding, James Kirkwood, Nestor Eristoff *(Board Members)*; Moroni Olsen *(President of Businessman's Board)*; Miles Mander, Arthur Shields, Frederic Worlock *(Businessmen)*; Alan Napier *(Dr. Bladh)*; Ray Collins *(Lecturer's Voice)*; Almira Sessions *(Mme. Michaud)*; Margaret O'Brien *(Irene at Age Five)*; Dorothy Gilmore *(Nurse)*; Gigi Perreau *(Eva at Age Eighteen Months)*; Ruth Cherrington *(Swedish Queen)*; Wyndham Standing *(King Oscar)*.

MRS. PARKINGTON
(MGM, 1944) 124 min.

PRODUCER: Leon Gordon
DIRECTOR: Tay Garnett
BASED ON THE NOVEL BY LOUIS BROMFIELD
SCREENPLAY: Robert Thoeren, Polly James
ART DIRECTORS: Cedric Gibbons, Randall Duell
SET DECORATORS: Edwin B. Willis, McLean Nisbet
MUSIC: Bronislau Kaper
ASSISTANT DIRECTOR: Marvin Stuart
SOUND: Newell Sparks
SPECIAL EFFECTS: A. Arnold Gillespie, Warren Newcombe, Danny Hall
CAMERA: Joseph Ruttenberg
EDITOR: George Boemler

Greer Garson *(Susie Parkington)*; Walter Pidgeon *(Major Augustus Parkington)*; Edward Arnold *(Amory Stilham)*; Frances Rafferty *(Jane Stilham)*; Agnes Moorehead *(Aspasia Conti)*; Selena Royle *(Mattie Trounsen)*; Gladys Cooper *(Alice—Duchess De Brancourt)*; Lee Patrick *(Madeleine)*; Dan Duryea *(Jack Stilham)*; Rod Cameron *(Al Swann)*; Tom Drake *(Ned Talbot)*; Helen Freeman *(Helen Stilham)*; Cecil Kellaway *(Edward, Prince of Wales)*;* Hugh Marlowe *(John Marbey)*; Tala Birell *(Lady Nora Ebbsworth)*;* Peter Lawford *(Thornley)*; Fortunio Bonanova *(Signor Callini)*; Mary Servoss *(Mrs. Graham)*; Gerald Oliver Smith *(Taylor)*; Ruth Brady *(Bridgett)*; Byron Foulger *(Vance)*; Wallis Clark *(Captain McTavish)*; Ann Codee *(Mme. Dupont)*; Frank Reicher *(French Doctor)*; George Davis *(French Policeman)*; Kay Medford *(Minnie)*; Hans Conried *(Mr. Ernst)*; Alma Kruger *(Mrs. Jacob Livingstone)*; Rhea Mitchell *(Mrs. Humphrey)*; Charles Pecora *(Headwaiter)*; Lee Tung-Foo *(Sam)*; Gordon Richards *(James the Butler)*; Rex Evans *(Fat Man)*; Doodles Weaver, Bobby Barber *(Caterers)*; Chef Milani *(Maitre d')*; Brandon Hurst *(Footman)*.

*In the European release prints of *Mrs. Parkington,* the following cast changes were made: Hugo Haas as the King (instead of Cecil Kellaway's Prince of Wales), and Tala Birell as the Countess (instead of Lady Nora Ebbsworth), a plot restructuring designed to avoid possible embarrassment to British royalty.

WEEK-END AT THE WALDORF
(MGM, 1945) 130 min.

PRODUCER: Arthur Hornblow, Jr.
DIRECTOR: Robert Z. Leonard
SUGGESTED BY THE PLAY *Grand Hotel* BY VICKI BAUM
ADAPTOR: Guy Bolton
SCREENPLAY: Sam and Bella Spewack
ART DIRECTORS: Cedric Gibbons, Daniel B. Cathcart
SET DECORATORS: Edwin B. Willis, Jack Bonar
CHOREOGRAPHY: Charles Walters
MUSIC/MUSIC DIRECTOR: Johnny Green
ORCHESTRATOR: Ted Duncan
VOCAL ARRANGER: Kay Thompson
SONGS: Sammy Fain, Ted Koehler, and Pepe Guizar
ASSISTANT DIRECTOR: William Lewis
COSTUME SUPERVISOR: Irene
SOUND: Douglas Shearer
SPECIAL EFFECTS: Warren Newcombe
CAMERA: Robert Planck
EDITOR: Robert J. Kern

Ginger Rogers *(Irene Malvern)*; Walter Pidgeon *(Chip Collyer)*; Van Johnson *(Captain James Hollis)*; Lana Turner *(Bunny Smith)*; Robert Benchley *(Randy Norton)*; Edward Arnold *(Martin K. Edley)*; Leon Ames *(Henry Burton)*; Warner Anderson *(Dr. Campbell)*; Phyllis Thaxter *(Cynthia Drew)*; Keenan Wynn *(Oliver Webson)*; Porter Hall *(Stevens)*; Samuel S. Hinds *(Mr. Jessup)*; George Zucco *(Bey of Aribajan)*; Xavier Cugat and His Orchestra *(Themselves)*; Lina Romay *(Juanita)*; Bob Graham *(Singer)*; Michael Kirby *(Lieutenant John Rand)*; Cora Sue Collins *(Jane Rand)*; Rosemary DeCamp *(Anna)*; Jacqueline deWit *(Kate Douglas)*; Frank Puglia *(Emile)*; Charles Wilson *(Hi Johns)*; Irving Bacon *(Sam Skelly)*; Miles Mander *(British Secretary)*; Nana Bryant *(Mrs. H. Davenport Drew)*; Russell Hicks *(McPherson)*; Naomi Childers *(Night Maid)*; Ruth Lee *(Woman)*; Byron Foulger *(Barber)*; Franklyn Farnum, Bess Flowers, Ella Ethridge *(Guests)*.

HOLIDAY IN MEXICO
(MGM, 1946) C-126 min.

PRODUCER: Joseph Pasternak
DIRECTOR: George Sidney
STORY: William Kozlenko
SCREENPLAY: Isobel Lennart

TECHNICOLOR CONSULTANTS: Natalie Kalmus, Henri Jaffa
ART DIRECTORS: Cedric Gibbons, Jack Martin Smith
SET DECORATORS: Edwin B. Willis, Arthur A. Krams
ORCHESTRATORS: Ted Duncan, Wilbur Schwandt, Paul Marquardt, Joseph Nussbaum
MUSIC DIRECTOR: George Stoll
SONGS: Nacio Herb Brown and Earl K. Brent; Paul Abraham and Ralph Freed
ASSISTANT DIRECTOR: George Rheim
SOUND: Douglas Shearer
CAMERA: Harry Stradling
EDITOR: Adrienne Fazan

Walter Pidgeon *(Jeffrey Evans);* Jane Powell *(Christine Evans);* Roddy McDowall *(Stanley Owen);* Ilona Massey *(Toni Karpathy);* Xavier Cugat and His Orchestra *(Themselves);* Hugo Haas *(Angus);* Jose Iturbi *(Himself);* Mikhail Rasumny *(Baranga);* Helene Stanley *(Yvette Baranga);* Paul Stanton *(Sir Edward Owen);* Doris Lloyd *(Lady Millicent Owen);* Linda Christian *(Angel);* Marina Koshetz *(Mme. Baranga);* Warner Lee *(Chinese Boy);* Ann Codee *(Margaret);* William "Bill" Phillips *(Sam);* Amparo Iturbi *(Iturbi's Sister);* Rosita Marstini *(Maria);* Edward Kilroy *(Secretary of State);* Ruth Lee *(Vera);* Nino Pipitone, Jr. *(French Boy);* Alberto Morin *(Headwaiter);* Loraine Allen *(Elise the Maid);* Olaf Hytten *(Butler);* Emilia Dias *(Fortune Teller);* Chris-Pin Martin *(Photographer);* Charles Regan *(Man).*

THE SECRET HEART
(MGM, 1946) 97 min.

PRODUCER: Edwin H. Knopf
DIRECTOR: Robert Z. Leonard
SCREEN STORY/ADAPTOR: Rose Franken
SCREENPLAY: Whitfield Cook, Anne Morrison Chapin
ART DIRECTORS: Cedric Gibbons, Edward Carfagno
SET DECORATORS: Edwin B. Willis, Henry W. Grace
MUSIC: Bronislau Kaper
ASSISTANT DIRECTOR: William Lewis
SOUND: Douglas Shearer
SPECIAL EFFECTS: Warren Newcombe
CAMERA: George Folsey
EDITOR: Adrienne Fazan

Claudette Colbert *(Lee Addams);* Walter Pidgeon *(Chris Matthews);* June Allyson *(Penny Addams);* Robert Sterling *(Chase Addams, Jr.);* Marshall Thompson *(Brandon Reynolds);* Elizabeth Patterson *(Mrs. Stover);* Richard Derr *(Larry Addams, Sr.);* Patricia Medina *(Kay Burns);* Eily Malyon *(Miss Hunter);* Ann Lace *(Penny as a Child);* Dwayne Hickman *(Chase as a Child);* Nicholas Joy *(Dr. Rossiger);* Drew Demarest *(Cab Driver);* Anna Q. Nilsson *(Miss Fox);* Audrey Totter *(Brittle Woman's Voice);* Hume Cronyn *(Man's Voice);* Hal Haskett *(Young Man's Voice);* Jean Beeks *(Woman Customer);* John Webb Dillon *(Conductor);* Barbara Billingsley, Ruth Brady *(Saleswomen).*

CASS TIMBERLANE
(MGM, 1947) 119 min.

PRODUCER: Arthur Hornblow, Jr.
DIRECTOR: George Sidney
BASED ON THE NOVEL BY SINCLAIR LEWIS
SCREENPLAY: Donald Ogden Stewart
ADAPTOR: Stewart, Sonya Levien
COSTUMES: Irene
ART DIRECTORS: Cedric Gibbons, Daniel Cathcart
SET DECORATORS: Edwin B. Willis, Richard Pefferle
MUSIC: Roy Webb
MUSIC DIRECTOR: Constantin Bakaleinikoff
ASSISTANT DIRECTOR: George Ryan
SOUND: Douglas Shearer, Frank B. MacKenzie
SPECIAL EFFECTS: Warren Newcombe, A. Arnold Gillespie
CAMERA: Robert Planck
EDITOR: John Dunning

Spencer Tracy *(Cass Timberlane);* Lana Turner *(Virginia Marshland);* Zachary Scott *(Brad Criley);* Tom Drake *(Jamie Wargate);* Mary Astor *(Queenie Havock);* Albert Dekker *(Boone Havock);* Margaret Lindsay *(Chris Grau);* John Litel *(Webb Wargate);* Mona Barrie *(Avis Elderman);* Josephine Hutchinson *(Lillian Drover);* Selena Royle *(Louise Wargate);* Richard Gaines *(Dennis Thane);* John Alexander *(Dr. Roy Drover);* Cameron Mitchell *(Eino Roskinen);* Howard Freeman *(Hervey Plint);* Jessie Grayson *(Mrs. Higbee);* Griff Barnett *(Herman);* Pat Clark *(Alice Wargate);* Walter Pidgeon *(Hollywood Star at Manhattan Cocktail Party).*

IF WINTER COMES
(MGM, 1947) 97 min.

PRODUCER: Pandro S. Berman
DIRECTOR: Victor Saville
BASED ON THE NOVEL BY A. S. M. HUTCHINSON
SCREENPLAY: Marguerite Roberts, Arthur Wimperis
ART DIRECTORS: Cedric Gibbons, Hans Peters
SET DECORATORS: Edwin B. Willis, Henry W. Grace
MUSIC: Herbert Stothart
ASSISTANT DIRECTOR: Jack Greenwood
SOUND: Douglas Shearer
MONTAGE: Peter Ballbusch
SPECIAL EFFECTS: Warren Newcombe
CAMERA: George Folsey
EDITOR: Ferris Webster

Walter Pidgeon *(Mark Sabre);* Deborah Kerr *(Nona Tybar);* Angela Lansbury *(Mabel Sabre);* Binnie Barnes *(Natalie Bagshaw);* Janet Leigh *(Effie Bright);* Dame May Whitty *(Mrs. Perch);* Rene Ray *(Sarah "Low Jinks");* Reginald Owen *(Mr. Fortune);* Rhys Williams *(Mr. Bright);* John Abbott *(Mr. Twyning);* Hugh French *(Lord Tybar);* Dennis Hoey *(Tiny Wilson);* Nicholas Joy *(Pettigrew);* Halliwell Hobbes *(Coroner);* Victor Wood *(Mr. Fargus);* Hugh Green *(Freddie Perch);* James Wethered *(Harold Twyning);* Virginia Keiley *(Rebecca "High Jinks");* Owen McGiveney *(Uncle Fouraker);* Pat Aherne *(Grimes the Chauffeur);* James Fairfax *(George);* Alex Fraser *(Clint);* Phyllis Morris *(Mrs. Fargus);* Joe Strauch *(Fat Youth);* Ian Wolfe *(Doctor);* Elspeth Dudgeon *(Mrs. Ward);* Cyril Smith *(Truck Driver);* Cyril Thornton *(Jury Foreman);* Major Sam Harris *(Clerk in Book Shop).*

JULIA MISBEHAVES
(MGM, 1948) 99 min.

PRODUCER: Everett Riskin
DIRECTOR: Jack Conway
BASED ON THE NOVEL *The Nutmeg Tree* BY MARGERY SHARP
ADAPTORS: Gina Kaus, Monckton Hoffe
SCREENPLAY: William Ludwig, Harry Ruskin, Arthur Wimperis
ART DIRECTORS: Cedric Gibbons, Daniel B. Cathcart
SET DECORATORS: Edwin B. Willis, Jack D. Moore
MUSIC: Adolph Deutsch
SONGS: Jerry Seelen and Hal Borne
ASSISTANT DIRECTOR: Marvin Stuart
COSTUMES: Irene
MAKEUP: Jack Dawn
SOUND: Douglas Shearer, Charles E. Wallace
SPECIAL EFFECTS: Warren Newcombe
CAMERA: Joseph Ruttenberg
EDITOR: John Dunning

Greer Garson *(Julia Packett);* Walter Pidgeon *(William Packett);* Peter Lawford *(Ritchie);* Cesar Romero *(Fred);* Elizabeth Taylor *(Susan Packett);* Lucile Watson *(Mrs. Packett);* Nigel Bruce *(Colonel Willowbrook);* Mary Boland *(Mrs. Gennochio);* Reginald Owen *(Bennie Hawkins);* Ian Wolfe *(Hobson);* Phyllis Morris *(Daisy);* Edmond Breon *(Jamie);* Fritz Feld *(Pepito);* Marcelle Corday *(Gabby);* Veda Ann Borg *(Louise);* Aubrey Mather *(Vicar);* Henry Stephenson *(Lord Pennystone);* Winifred Harris *(Lady Pennystone);* Ted DeWayne, Henry Monzello, William Snyder, Ray Saunders, Michael Kent *(Acrobatic Troupe);* Elspeth Dudgeon *(Woman in Pawnshop);* Almira Sessions, Connie Leon *(Women in Street);* Sid D'Albrook *(Pub Waiter);* Alex Goudavich *(Bellhop);* Mitchell Lewis *(Train Official);* Lola Albright, Marjorie Jackson, Gail Langford, Joi Lansing, Elaine Sterling, Ruth Hall, Patricia Walker, Shirley Ballard *(Mannequins);* Alphonse Martell *(Frenchman in Theatre).*

COMMAND DECISION
(MGM, 1948) 112 min.

PRODUCER: Sidney Franklin
DIRECTOR: Sam Wood
BASED ON THE PLAY BY WILLIAM WISTER HAINES
SCREENPLAY: William R. Laidlaw, George Froeschel
ART DIRECTORS: Cedric Gibbons, Urie McCleary
MUSIC: Miklos Rozsa
SOUND: Douglas Shearer

CAMERA: Harold Rosson
EDITOR: Harold F. Kress

Clark Gable *(Brigadier General K. C. "Casey" Dennis);* Walter Pidgeon *(Major General Roland Goodlow Kane);* Van Johnson *(Technical Sergeant Immanuel T. Evans);* Brian Donlevy *(Brigadier General Clifton I. Garnet);* John Hodiak *(Colonel Edward Rayton Martin);* Charles Bickford *(Elmer Brockhurst);* Edward Arnold *(Congressman Arthur Malcolm);* Marshall Thompson *(Captain George Washington Bellpepper Lee);* Richard Quine *(Major George Rockton);* Cameron Mitchell *(Lieutenant Ansel Goldberg);* Clinton Sundberg *(Major Homer V. Prescott);* Ray Collins *(Major Desmond Lansing);* Warner Anderson *(Colonel Ernest Haley);* John McIntire *(Major Belding Davis);* Michael Steele *(Captain Incius Malcolm Jenks);* Mack Williams *(Lieutenant Colonel Virgil Jackson);* Moroni Olsen *(Congressman Stone);* John Ridgeley *(James Carwood);* Edward Earle *(Congressman Watson);* William Lester *(Parker the Chauffeur);* Henry Hall, Sam Flint *(Congressmen);* Holmes Herbert *(Chairman);* John James *(Officer);* Pete Martin *(Command Sergeant);* Barry Nelson *(Loudspeaker Voice);* Wilson Wood, Arthur Walsh, J. Lewis Smith *(Photographers).*

THAT FORSYTE WOMAN
(MGM, 1949) C-114 min.
(British release title: THE FORSYTE SAGA)

PRODUCER: Leon Gordon
DIRECTOR: Compton Bennett
BASED ON THE NOVEL *A Man of Property* FROM *The Forsyte Saga* BY JOHN GALSWORTHY
SCREENPLAY: Jan Lustig, Ivan Tors, James B. Williams
ADDITIONAL DIALOGUE: Arthur Wimperis
ART DIRECTORS: Cedric Gibbons, Daniel B. Cathcart
SET DECORATORS: Edwin B. Willis, Jack D. Moore
MUSIC: Bronislau Kaper
MAKEUP: Jack Dawn
ASSISTANT DIRECTOR: Bob Barnes;
COSTUMES: Walter Plunkett, Valles
SOUND: Douglas Shearer, Ralph Pender
CAMERA: Joseph Ruttenberg
EDITOR: Frederick Y. Smith

Errol Flynn *(Soames Forsyte);* Greer Garson *(Irene Forsyte);* Walter Pidgeon *(Young Jolyon Forsyte);* Robert Young *(Philip Bosinney);* Janet Leigh *(June Forsyte);* Harry Davenport *(Old Jolyon Forsyte);* Stanley Logan *(Swithin Forsyte);* Lumsden Hare *(Roger Forsyte);* Aubrey Mather *(James Forsyte);* Matt Moore *(Timothy Forsyte);* Florence Auer *(Ann Forsyte Hayman);* Marjorie Eaton *(Hester Forsyte);* Evelyn Beresford *(Mrs. Taylor);* Gerald Oliver Smith *(Beveridge);* Richard Lupino *(Chester Forsyte);* Wilson Wood *(Eric Forsyte);* Gabrille Windsor *(Jennie);* Renee Mercer *(Martha);* Nina Ross *(Louise);* Constance Cavendish *(Alice Forsyte);* Charles McNaughton *(Attendant);* Wallis Clark *(Cabby);* Isabel Randolph *(Mrs. Winthrop);* Tim Hawkins *(Freddie);* Olaf Hytten *(Assistant);* Reginald Sheffield *(Mr. McLean);* Morgan Farley *(Bookseller);* John Sheffield, Norman Rainey *(Footmen);* James Aubrey *(Cabby);* Billy Bevan *(Porter);* Gloria Gordon *(Girl).*

THE RED DANUBE
(MGM, 1949) 119 min.

PRODUCER: Carey Wilson
DIRECTOR: George Sidney
BASED ON THE NOVEL *Vespers in Vienna* BY BRUCE MARSHALL
SCREENPLAY: Gina Kaus, Arthur Wimperis
ART DIRECTORS: Cedric Gibbons, Hans Peters
CAMERA: Charles Rosher
EDITOR: James E. Newcom

Walter Pidgeon *(Colonel Michael "Jooky" Nicobar);* Peter Lawford *(Major John "Twingo" McPhimister);* Angela Lansbury *(Audrey Quail);* Janet Leigh *(Marie Buhlen);* Ethel Barrymore *(Mother Superior);* Louis Calhern *(Colonel Piniev);* Francis L. Sullivan *(Colonel Humphrey "Blinker" Omicron);* Melville Cooper *(Private David Moonlight);* Robert Coote *(Brigadier C.M.V. Catlock);* Alan Napier *(General);* Roman Toporow *(Second Lieutenant Maxim Omansky);* Kasia Orzazewski *(Siter Kasimira);* Janine Perreau *("Mickey Mouse");* Konstantin Shayne *(Professor Serge Bruloff);* David Hydes *(Lieutenant Guedalia-Wood);* Audrey Long *(Countess Cressanti);* Margo Von Leu *(Lani Hansel);* Tito Vuolo *(Italian Billposter);* Argentina Brunetti *(Italian Woman);* Lotus Thompson *(Woman Private);* John Royce *(Sergeant);* Henry Kulky *(Lieutenant);* Doris Lloyd *(Mrs. Omincron);* Kenneth Hunter *(Brigadier General);* Richard Fraser *(Pilot);* Geoffrey Alah *(Major);* Sigmund Halperon *(German).*

THE MINIVER STORY
(MGM, 1950) 104 min.

PRODUCER: Sidney Franklin
DIRECTOR: H. C. Potter
BASED ON CHARACTERS CREATED BY JAN STRUTHER
SCREENPLAY: Ronald Millar, George Froeschel
MUSIC: Herbert Stothart, Miklos Rosza
MUSIC DIRECTOR: Muir Mathieson
ART DIRECTOR: Alfred Junge
COSTUMES FOR MISS GARSON: Walter Plunkett
COSTUMES: Gaston Mallett
SOUND: A. W. Watkins
CAMERA EFFECTS: Tom Howard
CAMERA: Joseph Ruttenberg
EDITOR: Harold F. Kress, Frank Clarke

Greer Garson *(Kay Miniver);* Walter Pidgeon *(Clem Miniver);* John Hodiak *(Spike Romway);* Leo Genn *(Steve Brunswick);* Cathy O'Donnell *(Judy Miniver);* Reginald Owen *(Mr. Foley);* Anthony Bushell *(Dr. Kanesley);* Richard Gale *(Tom Foley);* Peter Finch *(Polish Officer);* William [James] Fox *(Toby Miniver);* Cicely Paget-Bowman *(Mrs. Kanesley);* Ann Wilton *(Jeanette);* Henry Wilcoxon *(Vicar);* Eliot Makeham *(Mr. Farraday);* Brian Roper *(Richard);* Paul Demel *(Jose Antonió Campos);* Alison Leggatt *(Mrs. Foley).*

SOLDIERS THREE
(MGM, 1951) 87 min.

PRODUCER: Pandro S. Berman
DIRECTOR: Tay Garnett
BASED ON THE NOVEL BY RUDYARD KIPLING
SCREENPLAY: Marguerite Roberts, Tom Reed, Malcolm Stuart Boylan
MUSIC: Adolph Deutsch
ART DIRECTORS: Cedric Gibbons, and Malcolm Brown
CAMERA: William Mellor
EDITOR: Robert J. Kern

Stewart Granger *(Private Archibald Ackroyd);* Walter Pidgeon *(Colonel Brunswick);* David Niven *(Captain Pindenny);* Robert Newton *(Private Jock Sykes);* Cyril Cusack *(Private Dennis Malloy);* Greta Gynt *(Crenshaw);* Frank Allenby *(Colonel Groat);* Robert Coote *(Major Mercer);* Daniel O'Herlihy *(Sergeant Murphy);* Michael Ansara *(Manik Rao);* Richard Hale *(Govind-Lal);* Walter Kingsford *(Fairfax);* Charles Cane *(Boggs);* Patrick Whyte *(Major Harrow);* Movita Castenada *(Proprietress);* Charles Lang *(Merchant);* Cyril McLaglen *(Scot);* John Sheehan *(Drunk);* Stuart Hall *(Lieutenant);* Pat Aherne, Dave Dunbar, Clive Morgan, Wilson Wood *(Soldiers).*

CALLING BULLDOG DRUMMOND
(MGM, 1951) 80 min.

PRODUCER: Hayes Goetz
DIRECTOR: Victor Saville
BASED ON THE NOVEL BY GERALD FAIRLIE
SCREENPLAY: Howard Emmett Rogers, Fairlie
ART DIRECTOR: Alfred Junge
MUSIC: Rudolph G. Kopp
CAMERA: Freddie Young
EDITORS: Robert Watts, Frank Clarke

Walter Pidgeon *(Hugh Drummond/a.k.a. Joe Chambers);* Margaret Leighton *(Sergeant Helen Smith/a.k.a. Lily Ross);* Robert Beatty *(Guns);* David Tomlinson *(Algy Longworth);* Peggy Evans *(Molly);* Charles Victor *(Inspector McIver);* Bernard Lee *(Colonel Webson);* James Hayter *(Bill);* Patric Doonan *(Alec);* Harold Lang *(Stan).*

THE UNKNOWN MAN
(MGM, 1951) 86 min.

PRODUCER: Robert Thomsen
DIRECTOR: Richard Thorpe
STORY/SCREENPLAY: Ronald Milar, George Froeschel
MUSIC: Conrad Salinger
ART DIRECTORS: Cedric Gibbons, Randall Duell
CAMERA: William Mellor

EDITOR: Ben Lewis

Walter Pidgeon *(Dwight Bradley Masen);* Ann Harding *(Stella Masen);* Barry Sullivan *(Joe Bucknor);* Keefe Brasselle *(Rudi Wallchek);* Lewis Stone *(Judge Hulbrook);* Eduard Franz *(Andrew Jason Layford);* Richard Anderson *(Bob Masen);* Dawn Addams *(Ellie Fansworth);* Philip Ober *(Wayne Kellwin);* Mari Blanchard *(Sally Tever);* Konstantin Shayne *(Peter Hulderman);* Don Beddoe *(Fingerprint Man);* Holmes Herbert *(Reverend Michael);* Jean Andren *(Secretary);* Richard Hale *(Eddie Caraway);* Jeff York *(Guard);* John Maxwell *(Dr. Palmer);* Harry Hines, John Butler, Ronald Broga, Robert Scott *(Reporters);* Katherine Meskill *(Telephone Operator);* Fred Rapport *(Butler);* Mae Clarke *(Stella's Friend);* Rhea Mitchell *(Maid).*

THE SELLOUT
(MGM, 1951) 83 min.

PRODUCER: Nicholas Nayfack
DIRECTOR: Gerald Mayer
STORY: Mathew Rapf
SCREENPLAY: Charles Palmer
MUSIC: David Buttolph
ART DIRECTORS: Cedric Gibbons, Arthur Longergan
CAMERA: Paul C. Vogel
EDITOR: George White

Walter Pidgeon *(Haven D. Allridge);* John Hodiak *(Chick Johnson);* Audrey Totter *(Cleo Bethel);* Paula Raymond *(Peggy Stauton);* Thomas Gomez *(Kellwin C. Burke);* Cameron Mitchell *(Randy Stauton);* Karl Malden *(Buck Maxwell);* Everett Sloane *(Nelson S. Tarsson);* Jonathan Cott *(Ned Grayton);* Frank Cady *(Bennie Amboy);* Hugh Sanders *(Judge Neeler);* Griff Barnett *(J. R. Morrisson);* Burt Mustin *(Elm M. Ludens);* Whit Bissell *(Wilfred Jackson);* Roy Engel *(Sam Slaper);* Jeff Richards *(Truck Driver);* Vernon Rich *(Court Clerk);* Bob Stephenson *(Bailiff);* Cy Stevens *(Court Stenographer);* Frankie Darro *(Little Jake);* Ann Tyrrell *(Jennie Nova);* Benny Rubin *(Smoke Shop Proprietor);* Robert Williams *(Barney the Taxi Driver);* Jack Sherman *(Bartender);* John Dierkes *(Big Jake);* Roy Butler *(Prisoner);* Cliff Clark *(Police Chief);* Mabel Smaney *(Fat Woman).*

QUO VADIS
(MGM, 1951) C-171 min.

PRODUCER: Sam Zimbalist
DIRECTOR: Mervyn LeRoy
BASED ON THE NOVEL BY HENRY SIENKIEWICZ
SCREENPLAY: John Lee Mahin, S. N. Behrman, Sonya Levien
ART DIRECTORS: William A. Horning, Cedric Gibbons, Edward Carfagno
MUSIC: Miklos Rosza
CHOREOGRAPHY: Marta Obolensky, Auriel Millos
CAMERA: Robert Surtees, William V. Skall
EDITOR: Ralph E. Winters

Robert Taylor *(Marcus Vinicius);* Deborah Kerr *(Lygia);* Leo Genn *(Petronius);* Peter Ustinov *(Nero);* Patricia Laffan *(Poppaea);* Finlay Currie *(Peter);* Abraham Sofaer *(Paul);* Marina Berti *(Eunice);* Buddy Baer *(Ursus);* Felix Aylmer *(Plautius);* Nora Swinburne *(Pomponia);* Ralph Truman *(Tigellinus);* Norman Wooland *(Nerva);* Peter Miles *(Nazarius);* Geoffrey Dunn *(Terpnos);* Nicholas Hannen *(Seneca);* D. A. Clarke-Smith *(Phaon);* Rosalie Crutchley *(Acte);* John Ruddock *(Chilo);* Arthur Walge *(Croton);* Elspeth March *(Miriam);* Strelsa Brown *(Rufia);* Alfredo Varelli *(Lucan);* Roberto Ottaviano *(Flavius);* William Tubbs *(Anaxander);* Pietro Tordi *(Galba);* Lia De Leo *(Pedicurist);* Sophia Loren *(Extra);* Elizabeth Taylor *(Guest);* Walter Pidgeon *(Narrator).*

MILLION DOLLAR MERMAID
(MGM, 1952) C-115 min.
(British release title:
THE ONE-PIECE BATHING SUIT)

PRODUCER: Arthur Hornblow, Jr.
DIRECTOR: Mervyn LeRoy
SCREENPLAY: Everett Freeman
MUSIC DIRECTOR: Adolph Deutsch
ORCHESTRATOR: Alexander Courage
PRODUCTION NUMBERS STAGED BY BUSBY BERKELEY
UNDERWATER CHOREOGRAPHY: Audrene Brier
ART DIRECTOR: Cedric Gibbons
SET DECORATORS: Edwin B. Willis, Richard Pefferle
CAMERA: George J. Folsey
EDITOR: John McSweeney, Jr.

Esther Williams *(Annette Kellerman);* Victor Mature *(James Sullivan);* Walter Pidgeon *(Frederick Kellerman);* David Brian *(Alfred Harper);* Donna Corcoran *(Annette at Age Ten);* Jesse White *(Doc Cronnel);* Maria Tallchief *(Pavlova);* Howard Freeman *(Aldrich);* Charles Watts *(Policeman);* Wilton Graff *(Garvey);* Frank Ferguson *(Prosecutor);* James Bell *(Judge);* James Flavin *(Conductor);* Willis Bouchey *(Director);* Adrienne D'Ambricourt *(Marie the Housekeeper);* Charles Heard *(Official);* Olive Morgan *(Judge);* Queenie Leonard *(Mrs. Graves);* Stuart Torres *(Son);* Leslie Denison *(Purser);* Wilson Benge *(Caretaker);* Elisabeth Slifer *(Soprano);* Al Ferguson *(London Bobby);* Vernon Downing *(Newspaper Man);* Creighton Hale *(Husband);* Tiny Kelly, Pat Flaherty *(Cops);* Paul Bradley *(Defense Attorney);* Gail Bonney *(Woman).*

THE BAD AND THE BEAUTIFUL
(MGM, 1952) 117 min.

PRODUCER: John Houseman
DIRECTOR: Vincente Minnelli
STORY: George Bradshaw
SCREENPLAY: Charles Schnee
MUSIC: David Raksin
ASSISTANT DIRECTOR: Jerry Thorpe
ART DIRECTORS: Cedric Gibbons, Edward Carfagno
SET DECORATORS: Edwin B. Willis, Keogh Gleason
COSTUMES: Helen Rose
MAKEUP: William Tuttle
SOUND: Douglas Shearer
SPECIAL EFFECTS: A. Arnold Gillespie, Warren Newcombe
CAMERA: Robert Surtees
EDITOR: Conrad A. Nervig

Lana Turner *(Georgia Lorrison);* Kirk Douglas *(Jonathan Shields);* Walter Pidgeon *(Harry Pebbel);* Dick Powell *(James Lee Bartlow);* Barry Sullivan *(Fred Amiel);* Gloria Grahame *(Rosemary Bartlow);* Gilbert Roland *(Victor "Gaucho" Ribera);* Leo G. Carroll *(Henry Whitfield);* Vanessa Brown *(Kay Amiel);* Paul Stewart *(Syd Murphy);* Sammy White *(Gus);* Elaine Stewart *(Lila);* Jonathan Cott *(Assistant Director);* Ivan Triesault *(Von Ellstein);* Kathleen Freeman *(Miss March);* Marietta Canty *(Ida);* Lucille Knoch *(Blonde);* Steve Forrest *(Leading Man);* Perry Sheehan *(Secretary);* Robert Burton *(McDill);* Francis X. Bushman *(Eulogist);* Harold Miller *(Man);* George Lewis *(Lionel Donovan);* Madge Blake *(Mrs. Rosser);* William Tannen, Dabbs Greer, Sara Spencer, Frank Scannell *(Reporters);* Stanley Andrews *(Sheriff);* Ben Astar *(Joe);* Barbara Thatcher, Sharon Saunders, Erin Selwyn *(Girls);* Major Sam Harris *(Party Guest);* Bess Flowers *(Joe's Friend at Party);* Louis Calhern *(Voice on Recording).*

SCANDAL AT SCOURIE
(MGM, 1953) C-89 min.

PRODUCER: Edwin H. Knopf
DIRECTOR: Jean Negulesco
STORY: Mary McSherry
SCREENPLAY: Norman Corwin, Leonard Spigelgass
MUSIC: Daniele Amfitheatrof
ART DIRECTORS: Cedric Gibbons, Wade E. Rubottom
CAMERA: Robert Planck
EDITOR: Ferris Webster

Greer Garson *(Mrs. Patrick McChesney);* Walter Pidgeon *(Patrick J. McChesney);* Agnes Moorehead *(Sister Josephine);* Donna Corcoran *(Patsy);* Arthur Shields *(Father Reilly);* Philip Ober *(B. G. Belney);* Rhys Williams *(Bill Swazey);* Margalo Gillmore *(Alice Hanover);* John Lupton *(Artemus);* Philip Tonge *(Mr. Gogarty);* Wilton Graff *(Mr. Leffington);* Ian Wolfe *(Councilman Hurdwell);* Michael Pate *(Reverend Williams);* Tony Taylor *(Edward);* Victor Wood *(James Motely);* Perdita Chandler *(Sister Dominique);* Walter Baldwin *(Michael Hayward);* Ida Moore *(Mrs. Ames);* Maudie Prickett *(Mrs. Holahan);* Ivis Goulding *(Mrs. O'Russell);* Matt Moore *(Kenston);* Roger Moore, Al Ferguson, Jack Bonigul *(Ad Libs);* Eugene Borden *(Old Man);* Rudy Lee *(Donald);* Ivan Triesault *(Father Barrett);* Earl Lee *(Tweedy Man);* Howard Negley *(Duggin);* John Sherman *(Mr. Pringle).*

DREAM WIFE
(MGM, 1953) 101 min.

PRODUCER: Dore Schary
DIRECTOR: Sidney Sheldon

SCREENPLAY: Sheldon, Herbert Baker, Alfred Lewis Levitt
ART DIRECTORS: Cedric Gibbons, Daniel B. Cathcart
MUSIC: Conrad Salinger
SONGS: Charles Wolcott and Jamshid Sheibani
CAMERA: Milton Krasner
EDITOR: George White

Cary Grant *(Clemson Reade);* Deborah Kerr *(Effie);* Walter Pidgeon *(Walter McBride);* Betta St. John *(Tarji);* Eduard Franz *(Khan);* Buddy Baer *(Vizier);* Les Tremayne *(Ken Landwell);* Donald Randolph *(Ali);* Bruce Bennett *(Charlie Elkwood);* Richard Anderson *(Henry Malvine);* Dan Tobin *(Mr. Brown);* Movita *(Rima);* Gloria Holden *(Mrs. Landwell);* June Clayworth *(Mrs. Elkwood);* Dean Miller *(George);* Steve Forrest *(Louis);* Jonathan Cott *(Sailor);* Patricia Tiernan *(Pat);* Mary Lawrence *(Mrs. Malvine);* Faire Binney *(Mrs. Parker);* Dan Barton *(Marine);* Kay Riehl *(Woman);* Edward Cassidy *(Customs Official);* Jean Andren *(Bit);* Perry Sheehan *(Evelyn the Receptionist);* Gail Bonney *(Mommy);* Lillian Culver *(Woman at Airport);* Kathleen Freeman *(Chambermaid);* Bob Lugo *(Guard);* Dabb Greer *(Elevator Boy);* Hassan Khayyam *(Bukistanian Priest);* Jack George *(Clarence);* Jim Cronin, Paul Smith *(Bellhops).*

EXECUTIVE SUITE
(MGM, 1954) 104 min.

PRODUCER: John Houseman
DIRECTOR: Robert Wise
BASED ON THE NOVEL BY CAMERON HAWLEY
SCREENPLAY: Ernest Lehman
ART DIRECTORS: Cedric Gibbons, Edward Carfagno
SET DECORATORS: Edwin B. Willis, Emile Kuri
ASSISTANT DIRECTOR: George Rhein
WOMEN'S COSTUMES: Helen Rose
SPECIAL EFFECTS: A. Arnold Gillespie, Warren Newcombe
CAMERA: George Folsey
EDITOR: Ralph E. Winters

William Holden *(McDonald Walling);* June Allyson *(Mary Blemond Walling);* Barbara Stanwyck *(Julia O. Tredway);* Frederic March *(Loren Phineas Shaw);* Walter Pidgeon *(Frederick Y. Alderson);* Shelley Winters *(Eva Bardeman);* Paul Douglas *(Josiah Walter Dudley);* Louis Calhern *(George Nyle Caswell);* Dean Jagger *(Jesse Grimm);* Nina Foch *(Erica Martin);* Tim Considine *(Mike Walling);* William Phipps *(Bill Lundeen);* Lucille Knoch *(Mrs. George Nyle Caswell);* Mary Adams *(Sara Asenath Grimm);* Virginia Brissac *(Edith Alderson);* Edgar Stehli *(Julius Steigel);* Harry Shannon *(Ed Benedeck);* Charles Wagenheim *(Luigi Cassoni);* May McAvoy *(Grimm's Secretary);* Robin Camp *(Mailroom Boy);* Ray Mansfield *(Alderson's Secretary);* Bert Davidson, A. Cameron Grant *(Salesmen);* Mimi Doyle *(Telephone Operator);* Faith Geer *(Stork Club Hatcheck Girl);* David McMahon, Ralph Montgomery *(Reporters);* Raoul Freeman *(Avery Bullard);* Bob Carson *(Lee Ormond);* Ann Tyrell *(Shaw's Secretary);* Carl Saxe, Dick Landry *(Workers);* Mike Lally *(Spectator at Ballgame);* Matt Moore *(Servant);* Phil Chambers *(Toll Station Attendant).*

MEN OF THE FIGHTING LADY
(MGM, 1954) C-80 min.

PRODUCER: Henry Berman
DIRECTOR: Andrew Marton
SCREENPLAY: Art Cohn
ART DIRECTOR: Cedric Gibbons
MUSIC: Miklos Rosza
ASSISTANT DIRECTOR: Joel Freeman
CAMERA: George Folsey
EDITOR: Gene Ruggiero

Van Johnson *(Lieutenant Howard Thayer);* Walter Pidgeon *(Commander Kent Dowling);* Louis Calhern *(James A. Michener);* Dewey Martin *(Ensign Kenneth Schechter);* Keenan Wynn *(Lieutenant Commander Ted Dodson);* Frank Lovejoy *(Lieutenant Commander Paul Grayson);* Robert Horton *(Ensign Neil Conovan);* Bert Freed *(Lieutenant Andrew Szymanski);* Lewis Martin *(Commander Michael Coughlin);* George Cooper *(Cyril Roberts);* Dick Simmons *(Lieutenant Wayne Kimbrell);* Chris Warfield *(Pilot White);* Steve Rowland *(Pilot Johnson);* Ed Tracy *(Pilot Brown);* Paul Smith *(Ensign Dispatcher);* John Rosser *(Officer);* Ronald Lisa *(Replacement);* Teddy Infuhr *(Szymanski's Son);* Sarah Selby *(Mrs. Szymanski);* Jerry Mather, Ronald Stafford, Joseph "Bucko" Stafford *(Dodson's Sons);* Ann Baker *(Mary Reynolds);* Jonathan Hale *(Announcer);* Dorothy Patrick *(Mrs. Dodson).*

THE LAST TIME I SAW PARIS
(MGM, 1954) C-116 min.

PRODUCER: Jack Cummings
DIRECTOR: Richard Brooks
BASED ON THE STORY "BABYLON REVISITED" BY F. SCOTT FITZGERALD
SCREENPLAY: Julius J. and Philip G. Epstein
ASSISTANT DIRECTOR: William Shanks
MUSIC: Conrad Salinger
SONG: Jerome Kern and Oscar Hammerstein II
ART DIRECTORS: Cedric Gibbons, Randall Duell
CAMERA: Joseph Ruttenberg
EDITOR: John Dunning

Elizabeth Taylor *(Helen Ellswirth);* Van Johnson *(Charles Wills);* Walter Pidgeon *(James Ellswirth);* Donna Reed *(Marie Ellswirth);* Eva Gabor *(Lorraine Quarl);* Kurt Kasznar *(Maurice);* George Dolenz *(Claude Matine);* Roger Moore *(Paul);* Sandy Descher *(Vicki);* Celia Lovsky *(Mama);* Peter Leeds *(Barney);* John Doucette *(Campbell);* Odette *(Singer);* Luis Urbina, Gilda Fontana *(Flamenco Dance Team);* Christian Pasques *(Boy);* Ed Hinton, Richard Emory, Steve Wayne *(American Officers);* Loulette Sablon *(Nurse);* Jean Heremans *(Leon);* Josette Deegan, Mary Ann Hawkins *(Two Girls Fighting);* Matt Moore, Paul Power, Harry Cody *(Englishmen);* Ann Codee *(Another Nurse);* Gene Coogan *(Gendarme).*

DEEP IN MY HEART
(MGM, 1954) C-132 min.

PRODUCER: Roger Edens
DIRECTOR: Stanley Donen
BASED ON THE BOOK BY ELLIOT ARNOLD
SCREENPLAY: Leonard Spigelgass
ASSISTANT DIRECTOR: Robert Vreeland
CHOREOGRAPHY: Eugene Loring
ORCHESTRATORS: Hugo Friedhofer, Alexander Courage
ART DIRECTORS: Cedric Gibbons, Edward Carfagno
SET DECORATORS: Edwin B. Willis, Arthur Krams
MUSIC CONDUCTOR: Adolph Deutsch
CHORAL ARRANGER: Robert Tucker
MAKEUP: William Tuttle
SPECIAL EFFECTS: Warren Newcombe
CAMERA: George Folsey
EDITOR: Adrienne Fazan

Jose Ferrer *(Sigmund Romberg);* Merle Oberon *(Dorothy Donnelly);* Helen Traubel *(Anna Mueller);* Doe Avedon *(Lillian Harris Romberg);* Walter Pidgeon *(J. J. Shubert);* Paul Henreid *(Florenz Ziegfeld);* Tamara Toumanova *(Gaby Deslys);* Paul Stewart *(Bert Townsend);* Isobel Elsom *(Mrs. Harris);* David Burns *(Berrison, Sr.);* Jim Backus *(Ben Judson);* Rosemary Clooney, Gene and Fred Kelly, Jane Powell, Vic Damone, Ann Miller, William Olvis, Cyd Charisse, James Mitchell, Howard Keel, Tony Martin, Joan Weldon *(Guest Stars);* Douglas Fowley *(Harold Butterfield);* Robert Easton *(Cumberly);* Suzanne Luckey *(Arabella Bell);* Russ Tamblyn *(Berrison, Jr.);* Ludwig Stossel *(Mr. Novak);* Else Neft *(Mrs. Novak);* Norbert Schiller, Torben Meyer *(Card Players);* Reuben Wendroff, Franz Roehn *(Men);* Laiola Wendorff *(Woman);* John Alvin *(Mr. Mulvaney);* Jean Vander Pyl *(Miss Zimmerman);* Mary Alan Hokanson *(Miss Cranbrook);* Maudie Prickett *(Lady);* Henry Sylvester *(Judge);* Gail Bonney, Jean Dante *(Women Guests).*

THE GLASS SLIPPER
(MGM, 1955) C-94 min.

PRODUCER: Edwin H. Knopf
DIRECTOR: Charles Walters
SCREENPLAY: Helen Deutsch
ART DIRECTORS: Cedric Gibbons, Daniel B. Cathcart
MUSIC DIRECTOR: Bronislau Kaper
BALLETS: Roland Petit
ASSISTANT DIRECTOR: Al Jennings
COSTUMES: Helen Rose, Walter Plunkett
CAMERA: Arthur E. Arling
EDITOR: Ferris Webster

Leslie Caron *(Ella);* Michael Wilding *(Prince Charles);* Keenan Wynn *(Kovin);* Estelle Winwood *(Mrs. Toquet);* Elsa Lanchester *(Widow Sonder);* Barry Jones *(Duke);* Amanda Blake *(Birdena);* Lisa Daniels *(Serafina);* Lurene Tuttle *(Cousin Loulou);*

Liliane Montevecchi *(Tehara);* Ballet de Paris *(Themselves);* Walter Pidgeon *(Narrator);* Reginald Simpson *(Valet);* Tyler MacDuff *(Willie);* Dawn Bender, Sue George, Mary Ellen Clemons *(Girls);* Elizabeth Slifer, Doris Kemper, Gail Bonney *(Women);* Bud Osborne *(Coachman);* Robert Dix, Richard Emory, Ronald Green *(Young Men);* Lucille Curtis *(Mistress).*

HIT THE DECK
(MGM, 1955) C-112 min.

PRODUCER: Joe Pasternak
DIRECTOR: Roy Rowland
BASED ON THE MUSICAL BY HERBERT FIELDS AND THE PLAY *Shore Leave* BY HUBERT OSBORNE
SCREENPLAY: Sonya Levien, William Ludwig
MUSICAL NUMBERS STAGED BY HERMES PAN
COSTUMES: Helen Rose
ASSISTANT DIRECTOR: George Rhein
SONGS: Vincent Youmans, Leo Robin, Clifford Grey, and Irving Caesar
ORCHESTRATORS: Robert Van Eps, Will Beitel
MUSIC DIRECTOR: George Stoll
ART DIRECTORS: Cedric Gibbons, Paul Groesse
CAMERA: George Folsey
EDITOR: John McSweeney, Jr.

Jane Powell *(Susan Smith);* Tony Martin *(Chief Boatswain's Mate William F. Clark);* Debbie Reynolds *(Carol Pace);* Walter Pidgeon *(Rear Admiral Daniel Xavier Smith);* Vic Damone *(Rico Ferrari);* Gene Raymond *(Wendell Craig);* Ann Miller *(Ginger);* Russ Tamblyn *(Danny Xavier Smith);* J. Carroll Naish *(Mr. Peroni);* Kay Armen *(Mrs. Ottavia Perrari);* Richard Anderson *(Lieutenant Jackson);* Jane Darwell *(Jenny);* Alan King, Henry Slate *(Shore Patrol);* The Jubilaires *(Themselves);* John Close *(Petty Officer);* Robert Dix, Peter Leeds *(Naval Officers);* Dabbs Greer *(Stage Manager);* John Damler *(Marine Orderly).*

FORBIDDEN PLANET
(MGM, 1956) C-98 min.

PRODUCER: Nicholas Nayfack
DIRECTOR: Fred M. Wilcox
STORY: Irving Black, Allen Adler
SCREENPLAY: Cyril Hume
COSTUMES: Helen Rose, Walter Plunkett
ASSISTANT DIRECTOR: George Rhein
ART DIRECTORS: Cedric Gibbons, Arthur Lonergan
CAMERA: George J. Folsey
ELECTRONIC TONALITIES: Bebe and Louis Barron
SPECIAL EFFECTS: A. Arnold Gillespie, Warren Newcombe, Irving G. Ries, Joshua Meador
EDITOR: Ferris Webster

Walter Pidgeon *(Dr. Morbius);* Anne Francis *(Altaira Morbius);* Leslie Nielsen *(Commander Adams);* Warren Stevens *(Lieutenant "Doc" Ostrow);* Richard Anderson *(Chief Quinn);* Earl Holliman *(Cook);* Jack Kelly *(Lieutenant Farman);* George Wallace *(Bosun);* Bob Dix *(Grey);* Peter Miller *(Moran);* Morgan Jones *(Nichols);* Richard Grant *(Silvers);* James Best, William Boyett *(Crewmen);* Harry Harvey, Jr. *(Randall);* James Drury *(Strong);* James Thompson *(Youngerford);* Robby the Robot *(Himself).*

THESE WILDER YEARS
(MGM, 1956) 91 min.

PRODUCER: Jules Schermer
DIRECTOR: Roy Rowland
STORY: Ralph Wheelwright
SCREENPLAY: Frank Fenton
ART DIRECTORS: Cedric Gibbons, Preston Ames
SET DECORATORS: Edwin B. Willis, Edward G. Boyle
MUSIC: Jeff Alexander
MAKEUP: William Tuttle
SOUND: Dr. Wesley C. Miller
CAMERA: George J. Folsey
EDITOR: Ben Lewis

James Cagney *(Steve Bradford);* Barbara Stanwyck *(Ann Dempster);* Walter Pidgeon *(James Rayburn);* Betty Lou Keim *(Suzie);* Don Dubbins *(Mark);* Edward Andrews *(Mr. Spottsford);* Basil Ruysdael *(Judge);* Grandon Rhodes *(Roy Oliphant);* Will Wright *(Old Cab Driver);* Lewis Martin *(Dr. Miller);* Dorothy Adams *(Aunt Martha);* Dean Jones *(Hardware Clerk);* Herb Vigran *(Traffic Cop);* Ruth Lee *(Miss Finch);* Matt Moore *(Gateman);* Jack Kenny *(Chauffeur);* Harry Tyler *(Doorman);* Luana Lee *(Stenographer);* William Forrest *(Blount);* John Maxwell, Emmett Vogan, Charles Evans *(Board of Directors);* Michael Landon *(Boy in Poolroom);* Leon Tyler *(Student Secretary);* Sid Tomack *(Jess the Bartender);* Janet Lake, Don Burnett *(Bits);* Russ Whitney *(Hotel Clerk);* Audrey Swanson *(Saleslady);* Jimmy Hayes *(Young Reporter).*

THE RACK
(MGM, 1956) 100 min.

PRODUCER: Arthur M. Loew, Jr.
DIRECTOR: Arnold Laven
BASED ON THE TELEPLAY BY ROD SERLING
SCREENPLAY: Stewart Stern
ART DIRECTORS: Cedric Gibbons, Merrill Pye
MUSIC DIRECTOR: Adolph Deutsch
ASSISTANT DIRECTOR: Robert Saunders
CAMERA: Paul C. Vogel
EDITORS: Harold F. Kress, Marshall Neilan, Jr.

Paul Newman *(Captain Edward W. Hall, Jr.);* Wendell Corey *(Major Sam Moulton);* Walter Pidgeon *(Colonel Edward W. Hall, Sr.);* Edmond O'Brien *(Lieutenant Colonel Frank Wasnick);* Anne Francis *(Aggie Hall);* Lee Marvin *(Captain John R. Miller);* Cloris Leachman *(Caroline);* Robert Burton *(Corporal Ira Hansen);* Robert Simon *(Law Officer);* Trevor Bardette *(Court President);* Adam Williams *(Sergeant Otto Rahnke);* James Best *(Millard Chilson Cassidy);* Fay Roope *(Colonel Dudley Smith);* Barry Atwater *(Major Byron Phillips);* Charles Evans *(General);* Mary McAdoo *(Cooking Program Woman);* Byron Kane, Willard Sage *(Announcers);* David Blair *(Student);* Ray Stricklyn *(Ryson);* Lois Kimbrell *(Army Nurse);* Rod Taylor *(Al);* Dean Jones *(Lieutenant);* Bobby Blake *(Italian Soldier);* Frank Mills *(Courtroom Spectator).*

VOYAGE TO THE BOTTOM OF THE SEA
(20th Century-Fox, 1961) C-105 min.

PRODUCER/DIRECTOR/STORY: Irwin Allen
SCREENPLAY: Allen, Charles Bennett
ASSISTANT DIRECTOR: Ad Schaumer
MUSIC: Paul Sawtell, Bert Shefter
SONG: Percy Faith
ORCHESTRATOR: Max Reese
ART DIRECTORS: Jack Martin Smith, Herman Blumenthal
SET DECORATORS: Walter M. Scott, John Sturtevant
MAKEUP: Ben Nye
COSTUMES: Paul Zastupnevich
SOUND: Alfred Bruzlin, Warren DeLaPlain
SPECIAL CAMERA EFFECTS: L. B. Abbott
CAMERA: Winton Hoch
UNDERWATER CAMERA: John Lamb
EDITOR: Geroge Boemler

Walter Pidgeon *(Admiral Harriman Nelson);* Joan Fontaine *(Dr. Susan Hiller);* Barbara Eden *(Cathy Connors);* Peter Lorre *(Commodore Lucius Emery);* Robert Sterling *(Captain Lee Crane);* Michael Ansara *(Miguel Alvarez);* Frankie Avalon *(Chip Romano);* Regis Toomey *(Dr. Jamieson);* John Litel *(Admiral Crawford);* Howard McNear *(Congressman Parker);* Henry Daniell *(Dr. Zucco);* Mark Slade *(Smith);* Charles Tannen *(Gleason);* Delbert Monroe *(Kowski);* Anthony Monaco *(Cookie);* Robert Easton *(Sparks);* Jonathan Gilmore *(Young);* David McLean *(Ned Thompson);* Skip Ward, Michael Ford *(Crew Members);* George Diestel *(Lieutenant Hodges);* Art Baker *(U.N. Commentator);* Kendrick Huxham *(U.N. Chairman);* Dr. John Giovanni *(Italian Delegate);* Larry Gray *(Dr. Newmar).*

ADVISE AND CONSENT
(Columbia, 1962) 139 min.

PRODUCER/DIRECTOR: Otto Preminger
BASED ON THE NOVEL BY ALLEN DRURY
SCREENPLAY: Wendell Mayes
TECHNICAL ADVISOR: Drury
ASSISTANT DIRECTOR: L. C. McCardle, Jr.
MUSIC: Jerry Fielding
SONG: Fielding and Ned Washington
ART DIRECTOR: Lyle Wheeler
SET DECORATOR: Eli Benneche
TITLES: Saul Bass
COSTUMES COORDINATOR: Hope Bryce
MISS TIERNEY'S CLOTHES: Bill Blass
SOUND: Harold Lewis, William Hamilton

CAMERA:	Sam Leavitt
EDITOR:	Louis R. Loeffler

Henry Fonda *(Robert Leffingwell);* Charles Laughton *(Senator Seabright Cooley);* Don Murray *(Senator Brigham Anderson);* Walter Pidgeon *(Senator Bob Munson);* Peter Lawford *(Senator Lafe Smith);* Gene Tierney *(Dolly Harrison);* Franchot Tone *(President);* Lew Ayres *(Vice President);* Burgess Meredith *(Herbert Gelman);* Eddie Hodges *(Johnny Leffingwell);* Paul Ford *(Senator Stanley Danta);* George Grizzard *(Senator Fred Van Ackerman);* Inga Swenson *(Ellen Anderson);* Paul McGrath *(Hardiman Fletcher);* Will Geer *(Senate Minority Leader);* Edward Andrews *(Senator Orrin Knox);* Betty White *(Senator Bessie Adams);* Malcolm Atterbury *(Senator Tom August);* William Quinn *(Senator Paul Henderson);* Raoul De Leon *(Senator Velez);* Tom Helmore *(British Ambassador);* Hilary Eaves *(Lady Maudulayne);* Rene Paul *(French Ambassador);* Michele Montau *(Celestine Barre);* Raj Mallick *(Indian Ambassador);* Russ Brown *(Night Watchman);* Cay Forrester *(President's Secretary);* William H. Y. Knighton, Jr. *(President of White House Correspondents' Association);* Honorable Guy M. Gillette *(Senator Harper);* Chet Stratton *(Reverend Carney Birch).*

BIG RED

(Buena Vista, 1962) C-89 min.

PRODUCER:	Walt Disney
CO-PRODUCER:	Winston Hibler
DIRECTOR:	Norman Tokar
BASED ON THE NOVELS BY JIM KJELGAARD	
SCREENPLAY:	Louis Pelletier
MUSIC:	Oliver Wallace
TITLE THEMES:	Richard M. and Robert B. Sherman
ORCHESTRATOR:	Walter Sheets
ART DIRECTORS:	Carroll Clark, Marvin Aubrey Davis
SET DECORATORS:	Emile Kuri, Hal Gausman
COSTUMES:	Chuck Keehne
MAKEUP:	Pat McNally
IRISH SETTERS TRAINED BY WILLIAM KOEHLER	
SOUND:	Robert O. Cook, Dean Thomas
CAMERA:	Edward Colman
EDITOR:	Grant K. Smith

Walter Pidgeon *(James Haggin);* Gilles Payant *(Rene Dumont);* Emile Genest *(Emile Fornet);* Janette Bertrand *(Therese Fornet);* Doris Lussier *(Farmer Mariot);* Rolland Bedard *(Conductor);* Georges Bouvier *(Baggageman);* Teddy Burns Goulet *(Engineer).*

I DUE COLONELLI (THE TWO COLONELS)

(Italian, 1962) 90 min.

PRODUCER:	Gianni Buffardi
DIRECTOR:	Steno
SCREENPLAY:	Giovanni Grimaldi, Sergio Corbucci, Bruno Corbucci
CAMERA:	Tino Santoni

Toto *(Colonel Di Maggio);* Walter Pidgeon *(Colonel Timothy Henderson);* Scilla Gabel *(Iride);* Adriana Facchetti *(Penelope);* Nino Taranto *(Sergeant Quaglia);* John Francis Lane *(Sergeant McIntyre);* Toni Ucci *(Mazzetta);* Roland Bartrop *(Major Kruger);* Gerard Herter *(German General);* and: Giorgio Bixio, Nino Terzo.

IL GIORNO PIU CORTO (THE SHORTEST DAY)

(Italian, 1962) 89 min.

PRODUCER:	Goffredo Lombardo
DIRECTOR:	Sergio Corbucci
STORY:	Alessandro Continenza
SCREENPLAY:	Giorgio Alerio, Bruno Corbucci, Giovanni Grimaldi
ART DIRECTOR:	Carlo Simi
MUSIC:	Piero Piccioni
COSTUMES:	Marcella de Marchio
CAMERA:	Enzo Barboni
EDITOR:	Ruggero Mastroianni

With: Franco Franchi, Ciccio Ingrassia, Walter Pidgeon, Annie Girardot, Gina Cervi, Virna Lisi, Folco Lulli, Simone Signoret, Jacques Sernas, Daniel Mele, Toto, Sylva Koscina, Steve Reeves, Yvone Sanson, Walter Chiari, Umberto Orsini, Eleanora Rossi Drago, Stewart Granger, Tomas Milian, Susan Strasberg, Renato Rascel, Philipe Leroy, Ettore Manni, Massimo Serato, Paulo de Filippo, Scilla Gabel, F. Citti, Aldo Fabrizi, Eduardo de Filippo, Marcello Mastroianni, Ugo Tognazzi, Vittorio Gassman, Sandra Milo, David Niven, Gordon Scott, Massimo Girotti, Ric Battaglia, Gino Ferzetti, Francesco Mule.

HOW I SPENT MY SUMMER VACATION

(NBC-TV, 1967) C-100 min.

PRODUCER:	Jack Laird
DIRECTOR:	William Hale
TELEPLAY:	Gene Kearney
MUSIC:	Lalo Schifrin
CAMERA:	Bud Thackery
EDITOR:	Douglas Stewart

Robert Wagner *(Jack Washington);* Peter Lawford *(Ned Pine);* Jill St. John *(Nikki Pine);* Walter Pidgeon *(Lewis Gannet);* Lola Albright *(Mrs. Pine);* Michael Ansara *(Pucci);* Len Lesser *(The Greek);* Alberto Morin *(Jewelry Dealer);* Ralph Smiley *(Mr. Amin);* Tiger Joe March *(Yoshiro);* Joni Webster *(Miss Karali);* Lyn Peters *(Interviewer).*

COSA NOSTRA, AN ARCH ENEMY OF THE F.B.I.

(Warner Bros.-Seven Arts, 1967) C-78 min.

EXECUTIVE PRODUCER:	Quinn Martin
PRODUCER:	Charles Larson
ASSOCIATE PRODUCER:	Norman Jolley
DIRECTOR:	Don Medford
SCREENPLAY:	Norman Jolley
ART DIRECTOR:	Richard Y. Haman
SET DECORATOR:	Hoyle Barrett
MUSIC THEME:	Bronislau Kaper
MUSIC DIRECTOR:	John Elizalde
ASSISTANT DIRECTOR:	Robert Daley
CAMERA:	Robert Moreno
EDITORS:	Marston Fay, Thomas Neff

Walter Pidgeon *(Leo Roland);* Efrem Zimbalist, Jr. *(Lewis Erskine);* Celeste Holm *(Flo Clementi);* Telly Savalas *(Ed Clementi);* Susan Strasberg *(Chris Roland);* Philip Abbott *(Arthur Ward);* Stephen Brooks *(Jim Rhodes);* Robert Drivas *(Paul Clementi);* Robert Duvall *(Ernie Milden);* Anthony Eisley *(Chet Randolph);* Ken Lynch *(Jackie);* Wesley Addy *(Carl Munroe);* Ted Knight *(Milo).*

WARNING SHOT

(Paramount, 1967) C-100 min.

PRODUCERS:	Bob Banner, Buzz Kulik
DIRECTOR:	Kulik
BASED ON THE NOVEL *711—Officer Needs Help* BY WHIT MASTERSON	
SCREENPLAY:	Mann Masterson
ART DIRECTORS:	Hal Pereira, Roland Anderson
SET DECORATORS:	Robert Benton, Geroge Nelson
COSTUMES:	Edith Head
MAKEUP:	Wally Westmore
ASSISTANT DIRECTOR:	Howard Roessel
MUSIC:	Jerry Goldsmith
SOUND:	Joe Edmondson, John Wilkinson
SPECIAL CAMERA EFFECTS:	Paul K. Lerpae
PROCESS CAMERA:	Farciot Edouart
CAMERA:	Joseph Biroc
EDITOR:	Archie Marshek

David Janssen *(Sergeant Tom Valens);* Ed Begley *(Captain Roy Klodin);* Keenan Wynn *(Sergeant Ed Musso);* Sam Wanamaker *(Frank Sanderman);* Lillian Gish *(Alice Willows);* Stefanie Powers *(Liz Thayer);* Eleanor Parker *(Mrs. Doris Ruston);* George Grizzard *(Walt Cody);* Geroge Sanders *(Calvin York);* Steve Allen *(Perry Knowland);* Carroll O'Connor *(Paul Jerez);* Joan Collins *(Joanie Valens);* Walter Pidgeon *(Orville Ames);* John Garfield, Jr. *(Police Surgeon);* Vito Scotti *(Designer);* Donald Curtis *(Dr. James Ruston);* Norma Clark *(Shari Sherman).*

FUNNY GIRL

(Columbia, 1968) C-151 min.

PRODUCER:	Ray Stark
DIRECTOR:	William Wyler
BASED ON THE PLAY BY ISOBEL LENNART JULE STYNE, AND BOB MERRILL	
SCREENPLAY:	Lennart
MUSIC NUMBERS DIRECTED BY HERBERT ROSS	
MUSIC SUPERVISOR/CONDUCTOR:	Walter Scharf
VOCAL/DANCE ARRANGER:	Betty Walberg
ORCHESTRATORS:	Jack Hayes, Walter Scharf, Leo Shuken, Herbert Spencer

SONGS: Styne and Merrill; Fred Fisher and Billy Rose; James F. Hanley and Grant Clarke; Maurice Yvain, A. Willemetz, Jacques Charles, and Channing Pollack
PRODUCTION DESIGNER: Gene Callahan
ART DIRECTOR: Robert Luthardt
SET DECORATOR: William Kiernan
MISS STREISAND'S COSTUMES: Irene Sharaff
MAKEUP: Ben Lane
SOUND: Charles J. Rice, Arthur Piantadosi, Jack Solomon
CAMERA: Harry Stradling
EDITOR: Robert Swink

Barbra Streisand *(Fanny Brice)*; Omar Sharif *(Nick Arnstein)*; Kay Medford *(Rose Brice)*; Anne Francis *(Georgia James)*; Walter Pidgeon *(Florenz Ziegfeld)*; Lee Allen *(Eddie Ryan)*; Mae Questel *(Mrs. Strakosh)*; Gerald Mohr *(Branca)*; Frank Faylen *(Keeney)*; Mittie Lawrence *(Emma)*; Gertrude Flynn *(Mrs. O'Malley)*; Penny Santon *(Mrs. Meeker)*; John Harmon *(Company Manager)*; Thordis Brandt, Virginia Ann Ford, Karen Lee, Inga Neilsen, Sharon Vaughn, Mary Jane Mangler, Alena Johnston, Bettina Brenna *(Ziegfeld Girls)*.

RASCAL
(Buena Vista, 1969) C-85 min.

PRODUCER: James Algar
DIRECTOR: Norman Tokar
BASED ON THE BOOK BY STERLING NORTH
SCREENPLAY: Harold Swanton
ART DIRECTOR: John B. Mansbridge
SET DECORATORS: Emile Kuri, Frank R. McKelvy
MUSIC: Buddy Baker
SONG: Bobby Russell
SOUND: Dean Thomas
CAMERA: William Snyder
EDITOR: Norman R. Palmer

Steve Forrest *(Willard North)*; Bill Mumy *(Sterling North)*; Pamela Toll *(Theo North)*; Elsa Lanchester *(Mrs. Satterfield)*; Henry Jones *(Garth Shadwick)*; Bettye Ackerman *(Miss Whalen)*; Jonathan Daly *(Reverend Thurman)*; John Fiedler *(Cy Jenkins)*; Richard Erdman *(Walt Dabbett)*; Herbert Anderson *(Mr. Pringle)*; Robert Emhardt *(Constable)*; Steve Carlson *(Norman Bradshaw)*; Walter Pidgeon *(Voice of Sterling North)*.

TRAHISON AU VATICAN
(Twentieth Century-Fox, 1969) C-94 min. (a.k.a A QUALSIASI PREZZO/AT ANY PRICE/THE VATICAN AFFAIR)

DIRECTOR: Emilio Miraglia
SCREENPLAY: Augusto Carimito, Maurizio Costanzo
ART DIRECTOR: Luciano Ricceri
MUSIC: Luis Enriquez
SONG: Mina
CAMERA: Silvano Ippoliti
EDITOR: Walter Brown

Walter Pidgeon *(Professor Cummings)*; Ira Furstenberg *(Mrs. Scott)*; Klaus Kinski *(Clint Rogers)*; Marino Mase *(Anderson)*; Corrado Olmi *(Lentini)*; Tino Carraro *(Norman)*; Guido Alberti *(Cardinal Masoli)*.

THE HOUSE ON GREENAPPLE ROAD
(ABC-TV, 1970) C-113 min.

PRODUCER: Quinn Martin
DIRECTOR: Robert Day
TELEPLAY: George Eckstein

Christopher George *(Lieutenant Dan August)*; Janet Leigh *(Marian Ord)*; Julie Harris *(Leona Miller)*; Tim O'Connor *(George Ord)*; Walter Pidgeon *(Mayor Jack Packer)*; Barry Sullivan *(Chief Untermeyer)*; Keenan Wynn *(Sergeant Wilentz)*; Mark Richman *(Sal Gilman)*; William Windom *(Bit)*.

THE MASK OF SHEBA
(NBC-TV, 1970) C-100 min.

PRODUCER: Sam Rolfe
DIRECTOR: David Lowell Rich
TELEPLAY: Rolfe
MUSIC: Lalo Schifrin
ART DIRECTORS: George W. Davis, Marvin Summerfield
CAMERA: Gabriel Tarres, Harold Wellman
EDITOR: John Dunning

Eric Braeden *(Dr. Roan Morgan)*; Stephen Young *(Travis)*; Corinne Comacho *(Dr. Joanna Glenville)*; Inger Stevens *(Sarah Kramer)*; Joseph Wiseman *(Bondalok)*; William Marshall *(Condor)*; Walter Pidgeon *(Dr. Max van Carden)*; Christopher Carey *(Peter)*; Lincoln Kilpatrick *(Bit)*.

THE SCREAMING WOMAN
(ABC-TV, 1972) C-73 min

PRODUCER: William Frye
DIRECTOR: Jack Smight
BASED ON THE STORY BY RAY BRADBURY
TELEPLAY: Merwin Gerard
MUSIC: John Williams
COSTUMES: Edith Head
CAMERA: Sam Leavitt
EDITOR: Robert F. Shurgrue

Olivia de Havilland *(Laura Wynant)*; Ed Nelson *(Carl Nesbitt)*; Laraine Stephens *(Caroline Wynant)*; Joseph Cotten *(George Tresvant)*; Walter Pidgeon *(Dr. Amos Larkin)*; Charles Knox Robinson *(Howard Wynant)*; Alexandra Hay *(Evie Carson)*; Lonny Chapman *(Police Sergeant)*; Charles Drake *(Ken Bronson)*; Russell C. Wiggins *(Harry Sands)*; Gene Andrusco *(Deputy)*; Joyce Cunningham *(Bernice Wilson)*; Ray Montgomery *(Ted Wilson)*.

SKYJACKED
(MGM, 1972) C-100 min.

PRODUCER: Walter Seltzer
ASSOCIATE PRODUCER: James Pratt
DIRECTOR: John Guillermin
BASED ON THE NOVEL *Hijacked* BY DAVID HARPER
SCREENPLAY: Stanley R. Greenberg
SECOND UNIT DIRECTOR: James W. Gavin
ASSISTANT DIRECTOR: Dick Moder
ART DIRECTOR: Edward C. Carfagno
SET DECORATOR: Charles Pierce
COSTUMES: Jack Bear
MAKEUP: Siegfried H. Geike
MUSIC: Perry Botkin
SOUND: Charles M. Wilborn, Harry W. Tetrick
SPECIAL EFFECTS: Ralph Swartz
CAMERA: Harry Stradling, Jr.
SECOND UNIT CAMERA: Don Morgan
EDITOR: Robert Swink

Charlton Heston *(Hank O'Hara)*; Yvette Mimieux *(Angela Thacher)*; James Brolin *(Jerome K. Weber)*; Claude Akins *(Sergeant Ben Puzo)*; Jeanne Crain *(Mrs. Clara Shaw)*; Susan Dey *(Elly Brewster)*; Roosevelt Grier *(Gary Brown)*; Mariette Hartley *(Harriet Stevens)*; Walter Pidgeon *(Senator Arne Lindner)*; Ken Swofford *(John Bimonte)*; Leslie Uggans *(Lovejoy Wells)*; Ross Elliott *(Harold Shaw)*; Nicholas Hammond *(Peter Lindner)*; Jayson William Kane *(William Reading)*; Wesley Lau *(Stanley Morris, the Special Agent)*; Jennifer Shaw *(Cosmetic Sales Girl)*; Roy Engel *(Bonanza Pilot)*; Grahame Pratt *(Bronson)*; Joe Canutt *(Hunter)*; Lorna Thayer, Daniel White *(Weber's Parents)*.

NEPTUNE FACTOR
(Twentieth Century-Fox, 1973) C-98 min.

EXECUTIVE PRODUCERS: David M. Perlmutter, Harold Greenberg
PRODUCER: Sanford Howard
DIRECTOR: Daniel Petrie
SCREENPLAY: Jack DeWitt
ASSISTANT DIRECTORS: Frank Ernst, William Zborowsky
SECOND UNIT DIRECTOR: Paul B. Stader
PRODUCTION DESIGNERS: Dennis Lynton Clark, Jack McAdam
SET DECORATOR: Ed Watkins
MUSIC: Lalo Schifrin
ADDITIONAL MUSIC: William McCauley
TECHNICAL CONSULTANTS: C. Ed Murray, Bob Bowkett, Bob Colquhoun, Jan DeWitt, Dr. Allan R. Emery, Peter Buerschaper
SOUND: Joe Grimaldi
CAMERA: Harry Makin
UNDERWATER CAMERA: Lamar Boren, Paul Herbermann
EDITOR: Stan Cole

Ben Gazzara *(Commander Adrian Blake)*; Yvette Mimieux *(Leah Jansen)*; Walter Pidgeon *(Dr. Samuel Andrews)*; Ernest Borgnine *(Don "Mack" MacKay)*; Chris Wiggins *(Captain Williams)*; Donnelly Rhodes *(Bob Cousins)*; Ed McGibbon *(Norton Shepherd)*; Michael J. Reynolds *(Hal Hamilton)*; David Yorston *(Stephens)*; Stuart Gillard *(Bradley)*; Mark Walker *(Moulton)*; Kenneth Pogue *(Thomas)*; Frank Perry *(Submarine Captain)*;

Dan MacDonald *(Lieutenant Hobbs);* Leslie Carlson *(Briggs);* Dave Mann *(Hawkes);* Kay Fujiwara *(Anita);* Richard Whelan *(Radio Officer);* David Renton *(Warrant Officer).*

HARRY IN YOUR POCKET
(United Artists, 1973) C-103 min.

EXECUTIVE PRODUCER: Alden Schwimmer
PRODUCER: Bruce Geller
ASSOCIATE PRODUCER: Alan Godfrey
DIRECTOR: Geller
SCREENPLAY: Ron Austin, James Buchanan
ART DIRECTOR/SET DECORATOR: William Bates
MUSIC: Lalo Schifrin
SONG: Schifrin, Geller
TECHNICAL ADVISOR: Tony Giorgio
SOUND: Les Frescholtz
CAMERA: Fred Koenekamp
EDITOR: Arthur Hilton

James Coburn *(Harry);* Michael Sarrazin *(Ray Houlihan);* Trish Van Devere *(Sandy Coletto);* Walter Pidgeon *(Casey);* Michael C. Gwynne *(Fence);* Tony Giorgio, Michael Stearns *(Detectives);* Sue Mullen *(Francine);* Duane Bennett *(Salesman);* Stanley Bolt *(Mr. Bates);* Barry Grimshaw *(Bellboy).*

LIVE AGAIN, DIE AGAIN
(ABC-TV, 1974) C-74 min.

EXECUTIVE PRODUCER: David Victor
PRODUCER: Robert F. O'Neille
DIRECTOR: Richard A. Colla
BASED ON THE NOVEL *Come to Mother* BY DAVID SALE
TELEPLAY: Joseph Stefano
MUSIC: George Romanis
CAMERA: Michael Margules
EDITORS: David Newhouse, Jamie Caylor

Cliff Potts *(Joe Dolan);* Walter Pidgeon *(Thomas Carmichael);* Donna Mills *(Caroline Carmichael);* Mike Farrell *(James Carmichael);* Geraldine Page *(Sissie O'Neil);* Vera Miles *(Marcia Carmichael);* Lurene Tuttle *(Betty Simpson);* Irene Tedrow *(Nurse);* Stewart Moss *(Wilson);* Peter Bromilow *(Dr. Fellman);* Walter Edmiston *(Larry Brice).*

THE GIRL ON THE LATE LATE SHOW
(NBC-TV, 1974) C-74 min.

EXECUTIVE PRODUCER: David Gerber
PRODUCER: Christopher Morgan
DIRECTOR: Gary Nelson
TELEPLAY: Mark Rogers
MUSIC: Richard Markowitz
MAKEUP: Ben Lane
CAMERA: Robert Morrison
EDITOR: Richard C. Meyer

Don Murray *(William Martin);* Bert Convy *(F. T. Allen);* Yvonne De Carlo *(Lorraine);* Gloria Grahame *(Carolyn Porter);* John Ireland *(Walters);* Ralph Meeker *(De Biesse);* Cameron Mitchell *(Wilder);* Van Johnson *(Deverette);* Mary Ann Mobley *(Librarian);* Joe Santis *(Lieutenant Scott);* Walter Pidgeon *(Pahlman);* Laraine Stephens *(Paula);* Sherry Jackson *(Pat);* and: Felice Orlandi, Dan Tobin, Frankie Darro, William Benedict, Peter Colt.

MURDER ON FLIGHT 502
(ABC-TV, 1975) C-113 min.

EXECUTIVE PRODUCERS: Aaron Spelling, Leonard Goldberg
PRODUCER: David Chasman
DIRECTOR: George McGowan
TELEPLAY: David P. Harmon
MUSIC: Laurence Rosenthal
CAMERA: Arch Dalzell
EDITOR: Allan Jacobs

Ralph Bellamy *(Dr. Kenyon Walker);* Polly Bergen *(Mona Briarly);* Theodore Bikel *(Otto Gruenwaldt);* Sonny Bono *(Jack Marshall);* Dane Clark *(Ray Garwood);* Laraine Day *(Claire Garwood);* Fernando Lamas *(Paul Barons);* George Maharis *(Robert Davenport);* Farrah Fawcett-Majors *(Karen White);* Hugh O'Brian *(Detective Daniel Myerson);* Molly Picon *(Ida Goldman);* Walter Pidgeon *(Charlie Perkins);* Robert Stack *(Captain Larkin);* Rosemarie Stack *(Dorothy Saunders);* Elizabeth Stack *(Marilyn Stonehurst);* Brooke Adams *(Vera Franklin);* Danny Bonaduce *(Millard Kensington);* Steve Franken *(Arnold Goldman).*

YOU LIE SO DEEP, MY LOVE
(ABC-TV, 1975) 78 min.

PRODUCER/DIRECTOR: David Lowell Rich
STORY: William L. Stuart, Robert Hamner
TELEPLAY: John Neufeld, Hamner
CAMERA: Leonard J. South
EDITOR: Asa Clark

Don Galloway *(Neal Collins);* Barbara Anderson *(Susan Collins);* Angel Tompkins *(Jennifer Pierce);* Walter Pidgeon *(Uncle Joe Padway);* Anne Schedeen *(Ellen);* Russell Johnson *(Foreman);* Virginia Gregg *(Maid);* Robert Rothwell *(Tom File);* Bobbi Jordan *(Phyllis);* Pitt Herbert *(Jordan).*

THE LINDBERGH KIDNAPPING CASE
(NBC-TV, 1976) C-160 min.

EXECUTIVE PRODUCER: David Gerber
PRODUCER/DIRECTOR: Buzz Kulik
TELEPLAY: J. P. Miller
MUSIC: Billy Goldenberg
ART DIRECTORS: Carl Anderson, Ross Bellah
MEN'S COSTUMES: Bob Christenson
WOMEN'S COSTUMES: Denita Cavett
MAKEUP: Hank Edds
SOUND: Jack Solomon
CAMERA: Charles F. Wheeler
EDITOR: Rita Rolands

Cliff DeYoung *(Charles Lindbergh);* Anthony Hopkins *(Bruno Richard Hauptmann);* Joseph Cotten *(Dr. John Francis Condon);* Denise Alexander *(Nurse Betty Glow);* Sian Barbara Allen *(Anne Morrow Lindbergh);* Martin Balsam *(Defense Attorney Edward J. Reilly);* Dean Jagger *(Kaler);* Walter Pidgeon *(Judge Trenchard);* Keenan Wynn *(Fred Huisache);* Laurence Luckinbill *(Governor Hal Hoffman);* Frank Marth *(Chief of Police Harry Wolfe);* Tony Roberts *(Lieutenant Jim Finn);* Peter Donat *(Colonel H. Norman Schwarzkopf);* Robert Samson *(John Curtis);* David Spielberg *(Attorney General David Wilentz);* Joseph Stern *(Dr. Schonfeld);* Kate Woodville *(Violet Sharpe);* Bill Quinn *(Andrew Phelps);* and: John Fink, Michael O'Keefe, Larry Black, Arthur Space, Keith McConnell, Roy Briem, Renata Vaselle, Peter Brocco, David Gruner, Robert Kenneally, Terry Moore Deck, Gwil Richards, Carol Levy, Nicky Blair, Larry Ellis, John Kennedy Carroll, Wayne C. Dvorak.

WON TON TON, THE DOG WHO SAVED HOLLYWOOD
(Paramount, 1976) C-92 min.

PRODUCERS: David V. Picker, Arnold Schulman, Michael Winner
ASSOCIATE PRODUCER: Tim Zinnemann
DIRECTOR: Winner
SCREENPLAY: Schulman, Cy Howard
ART DIRECTOR: Ward Preston
SET DECORATOR: Ned Parsons
ASSISTANT DIRECTORS: Charles Okun, Arne Schmidt
MAKEUP: Philip Rhodes
DOGS TRAINED BY KARL MILLER
MUSIC: Neal Hefty
SOUND: Bob Post
CAMERA: Richard H. Kline
EDITOR: Bernard Gribble

Dennis Morgan *(Tour Guide);* Shecky Greene *(Tourist);* Phil Leeds, Cliff Norton *(Dog Catchers);* Madeline Kahn *(Estee Del Ruth);* Teri Garr *(Fluffy Peters);* Romo Vincent *(Short Order Cook);* Bruce Dern *(Grayson Potchuck);* Sterling Holloway *(Old Man on Bus);* William Demarest *(Studio Gatekeeper);* Art Carney *(J. J. Fromberg);* Virginia Mayo *(Miss Battley);* Henny Youngman *(Manny Farber);* Rory Calhoun *(Philip Hart);* Billy Barty *(Assistant Director);* Henry Wilcoxon *(Silent Film Director);* Ricardo Montalban, Richard Arlen *(Silent Film Stars);* Jackie Coogan, Johnny Weissmuller *(Stagehands);* Aldo Ray *(Stubby Stebbins);* Ethel Merman *(Hedda Parsons);* Yvonne De Carlo *(Cleaning Woman);* Joan Blondell *(Landlady);* Andy Devine *(Priest in Dog Pound);* Broderick Crawford *(Special Effects Man);* Jack LaRue *(Silent Film Villain);* Dorothy Lamour *(Visiting Film Star);* Phil Silvers *(Murray Fromberg);* Nancy Walker *(Mrs. Fromberg);* Gloria DeHaven, Ann Miller *(President's Girls);* Louis Nye *(Radio Interviewer);* Stepin Fetchit *(Dancing Butler);* Ken Murray *(Souvenir Salesman);* Rudy Vallee *(Autograph Hound);* George Jessel *(Awards Announcer);* Rhonda Fleming *(Rhoda Flaming);* Dean

Stockwell *(Paul Lavell);* Dick Haymes *(James Crawford);* Tab Hunter *(David Hamilton);* Robert Alda *(Richard Entwhistle);* Eli Mintz *(Tailor);* Ron Leibman *(Rudy Montague);* Fritz Feld *(Rudy's Butler);* Edward Ashley *(Another Butler);* Jane Connell *(Waitress);* Janet Blair *(President's Girl #3);* Dennis Day *(Singing Telegraph Man);* Mike Mazurki *(Studio Guard);* The Ritz Brothers *(Cleaning Women);* Jesse White *(Rudy's Agent);* Carmel Myers, Jack Carter *(Journalists);* Barbara Nichols *(Nick's Girl);* Army Archerd *(Premiere M.C.);* Victor Mature *(Nick);* Fernando Lamas *(Premiere Male Star);* Zsa Zsa Gabor *(Premiere Female Star);* Cyd Charisse *(President's Girl #4);* Huntz Hall *(Moving Man);* Doodles Weaver *(Man in Mexican Film);* Pedro Gonzales-Gonzales *(Mexican Projectionist);* Eddie Le Veque *(Prostitute Customer);* Edgar Bergen *(Professor Quicksand);* Ronny Graham *(Mark Bennett);* Morey Amsterdam, Eddie Foy, Jr. *(Custard Pie Stars);* Peter Lawford *(Slapstick Star);* Patricia Morison, Guy Madison *(Stars at Screening);* Regis Toomey *(Burlesque Stagehand);* Alice Faye *(Secretary at Gate);* Ann Rutherford *(Grayson's Studio Secretary);* Milton Berle *(Blind Man);* John Carradine *(Drunk);* Keye Luke *(Cook in Kitchen);* Walter Pidgeon *(Grayson's Butler);* Augustus Von Schumacher *(Won Ton Ton).*

TWO-MINUTE WARNING
(Universal, 1976) C-112 min.*

PRODUCER: Edward S. Feldman
DIRECTOR: Larry Peerce
BASED ON THE NOVEL BY GEORGE LAFOUNTAINE
SCREENPLAY: Edward Hume
ASSISTANT DIRECTORS: Ken Swor, L. Andrew Stone, David O. Sosna
ART DIRECTOR: Herman A. Blumental
SET DECORATOR: John M. Dwyer
MUSIC: Charles Fox
TECHNICAL ADVISOR: Sergeant Kenneth Slonski
STUNT CO-ORDINATOR: Glen Wilder
FOOTBALL CO-ORDINATOR: Tom Fears
SPECIAL WEAPONS EFFECTS: Art Brewer
SOUND: Jim Alexander, Robert L. Hoyt
SOUND EDITOR: Gordon Ecker, Jr.
SPECIAL CAMERA EFFECTS: Albert Whitlock
CAMERA: Gerald Hirschfeld
EDITORS: Eve Newman, Walter Nannemann

Charlton Heston *(Captain Peter Holly);* John Cassavetes *(Sergeant Chris Button);* Martin Balsam *(Sam McKeever);* Beau Bridges *(Mike Ramsay);* Marilyn Hassett *(Lucy);* David Janssen *(Steve);* Jack Klugman *(Stu Sandman);* Gena Rowlands *(Janet);* Walter Pidgeon *(Pickpocket);* Brock Peters *(McKeever's Assistant, Paul);* David Groh *(Intern Spinner);* Mitchell Ryan *(Priest);* Joe Kapp *(Charlie Tyler);* Jon Korkes *(Lucy's Escort);* Juli Bridges *(Pickpocket's Partner);* Brooke Mills *(Tyler's Girl);* Pamela Bellwood *(Mrs. Ramsay);* Andy Sidaris *(TV Director);* Fred Hice *(Innocent Suspect);* Jack Grodsky, Arnold Carr *(Spectators);* Christine Nelson, Holly Irving *(Old Women at Airport);* Allan Miller *(Mr. Green);* Glen Wilder, David Cass *(Green's Henchmen);* Warren Miller *(Sniper);* Howard Cossell, Frank Gifford, Dick Enberg, Merv Griffin *(Themselves);* Gary Combs *(Downing);* Chuck Tamburro *(Porter);* Wild Bill Mock *(Gilmore);* John Armond *(Sutherland);* Larry Manetti *(Pratt);* Tom Baker *(Stakowsi);* Trent Dolan *(Fuller);* Michael Gregory *(Angelo);* Harry Northup *(Lieber);* R. B. Sorko-Ram *(Beck);* Boris Aplon *(Maitre d');* Edward McNally *(Newsman with Governors);* Tom Huff, Patty Elder *(Cyclists)*

*When shown on television in February 1979, approximately 63 additional minutes were filmed under the supervision of Gene Palmer. The plot was set in the framework of a multi-million dollar art museum robbery. New players in the video version included: Rossano Brazzi, James Olson, Joanna Pettet, William Prince, Paul Shenar.

SEXTETTE
(Briggs and Sullivan, 1978) C-91 min.

EXECUTIVE PRODUCER: Warner G. Toub
PRODUCERS: Daniel Briggs, Robert Sullivan
ASSOCIATE PRODUCER: Harry Weiss
DIRECTOR: Ken Hughes
BASED ON THE PLAY BY MAE WEST
SCREENPLAY: Herbert Baker
MUSIC: Artie Butler
ART DIRECTOR: James Claytor
SET DECORATOR: Reg Allen
CHOREOGRAPHY: Marc Breaux
MUSIC COORDINATOR: Michael Arciaga
MUSIC: Gene Cantamessa
ASSISTANT DIRECTOR: Gene Marum
CAMERA: James Crabe
EDITOR: Argyle Nelson

Mae West *(Marlo Manners);* Timothy Dalton *(Sir Michael Barrington);* Dom DeLuise *(Dan Turner);* Tony Curtis *(Alexei Karansky);* Ringo Starr *(Laslo Karolny);* George Hamilton *(Vance);* Alice Cooper *(Waiter);* Keith Allison *(Waiter in Alexei's Suite);* Rona Barrett *(Herself);* Van McCoy *(Delegate);* Keith Moon *(Dress Designer);* Regis Philbin *(Himself);* Walter Pidgeon *(The Chairman);* George Raft *(Himself).*

FIVE

SPENCER TRACY

5′ 10 1/2″
165 pounds
Reddish brown hair
Blue eyes
Aries

"The guy's good and there's nobody in this business who can touch him, so you're a fool to try. And don't fall for that humble stuff, either; the bastard knows it!" So spoke Clark Gable of his fellow MGM star Spencer Tracy.

Tracy was one of America's finest and most durable cinema stars. His unconventional, masculine good looks set him apart from other Hollywood stars. Many of his films are classics.

His motion picture career spanned the period from 1930 *(Up the River)* to 1967 *(Guess Who's Coming to Dinner).* Although early in his acting days he was often handed mediocre or inferior material, through his honest approach and superior acting ability he managed to make his celluloid efforts noteworthy. His initial successes led to more and better roles, especially at MGM.

Spencer Bonaventure Tracy was born in Milwaukee, Wisconsin on Thursday, April 5, 1900. He was the son of John Edward Tracy, a devout Irish Catholic, and Carrie Brown Tracy. Mrs. Tracy was, and remained all her life, a Protestant. Her ancestors could be traced back to early New England colonists. Indeed, Brown University in Providence, Rhode Island is said to have been founded in 1764 by an ancestor of Mrs. Tracy. Spencer had an older brother, Carroll, born in 1896.

The Tracys' Milwaukee home was on comfortable Prospect Avenue. Spencer, however, as a youngster was often drawn to a nearby area called Tory Hill, populated by poorer and tougher folk. Here the young red-headed, blue-eyed lad often played "hookey" from school and took part in fights and aggressive sports with the rough neighborhood children.

Spencer's early years of schooling were quite patchy. He was often the despair of his hard-working father, who was the general sales manager of Sterling Motor Truck Company. Spencer is recorded as having been expelled from approximately a dozen grade schools before finally receiving a diploma from St. Rosa's Parochial School.

While growing up, Spencer became a devoted moviegoer. He ignored school to pass hours at local nickelodeons as frequently as he did battle on Tory Hill.

William Joseph O'Brien (later to become actor Pat O'Brien) was Spencer's childhood pal. O'Brien was a student at Marquette Academy, a Jesuit high school. Sixteen-year-old Spencer astounded his father by requesting that he, too, be sent to the same high school. Mr. Tracy finally agreed. At Marquette, young Tracy proved to be a better than average student. He also developed an interest in the Catholic Church, and for a time he considered entering the priesthood. It was a choice of vocation that would *not* have met opposition from his father.

The advent of World War I changed his career ambition greatly. The patriotic fervor of the times led Spencer to try to join the marines, but he was too young. William O'Brien enlisted in the navy. When Spencer discussed it with his pal, he learned that he, too, could join the navy *if* his parents gave their consent. The Tracys reluctantly agreed to permit it *if* Spencer would promise to complete his education after his naval tour of duty.

Spencer underwent basic training at Chicago's Great Lakes Naval Training Center, followed by seven months of duty at the Norfolk, Virginia Navy Yard. That was the extent of his wartime participation. After he was mustered out, he attended Northwestern Military and Naval Academy at Lake Geneva, Wisconsin, where he completed his high school requirements.

Mr. Tracy was hoping that his younger son would join him in the trucking business. However, Spencer was drawn to the field of medicine and believed that he wanted to become a doctor. He was admitted to Ripon College in Wisconsin in January 1921.

The head of Ripon's Dramatic Society, J. Clark Graham, was impressed with young Spencer's fine speaking voice, and he urged him to take a role in the college's production of Clyde Fitch's *The Truth.* Tracy took the part, and his success in the show led to a role in another school project, a one-act play entitled *The Valiant.* In this drama Spencer played a condemned convict, offering a characterization that demonstrated great skill and conviction. The Tracy clan came to Ripon to witness Spencer's triumph in *The Valiant.* It was at this time that the young man announced to his doubting parents that he was *now* interested in an acting career. Mr. Tracy was not convinced, as he pondered aloud, "Can you imagine that face ever being a matinee idol?"

During his sophomore year at Ripon, Tracy joined the campus debating team, then under the supervision of Professor H. P. Boody. The team went on an extensive intercollegiate tour that included the midwestern and eastern parts of the United States and Canada.

When the Ripon team spent a few days in Manhattan, Tracy was advised to apply at the American Academy of Dramatic Arts for admission as a student. The undergraduate applied for an interview at the Carnegie Hall building and was amazed to find himself accepted by the Academy as a drama student.

Mr. Tracy did not approve of his son's decision to leave Ripon for the Academy in far-off New York City. However, he agreed to pay his son's tuition if the determined young man would agree to live on his thirty-dollar-a-month veteran's allowance. In April 1922, Spencer began classes at the Academy. In fact, he was not entirely without friends there, as Bill O'Brien was already enrolled in the same institution.

The two young drama students took a room together at 790 West End Avenue near 98th Street where they shared a rather spartan existence. Fortunately, they had a rather kindly elderly landlady who had a fondness for young struggling thespians.

O'Brien soon dropped out of the Academy to take a job, but Tracy stayed on, attending classes. Among his fellow students were Kay Johnson, Monroe Owsley, and Sterling Holloway. In his few spare moments he made the rounds of casting offices, hoping that some producer might hire him. Meanwhile, at the Academy, Spencer became noted for his remarkable ability to memorize and retain long complex speeches with agility. His instructors considered him to be a fine and talented student.

On a tip from another student, Spencer applied to the Theatre Guild for a non-speaking part in their production of Karel Capek's expressionistic drama *R.U.R.* His salary was fifteen dollars weekly, and his friend Bill O'Brien soon joined the cast in another robot part. The show opened at the Garrick Theatre on Monday, October 9, 1922. During the run of one hundred and eighty-four performances, Tracy graduated from a non-speaking role to a one-line part, and his salary was accordingly jumped to twenty-five dollars weekly.

In the spring of 1923 Tracy graduated from the American Academy. The graduation ceremonies included a production of Oscar Wilde's *The Importance of Being Earnest.* Spencer had the role of Canon Chasuble. With his graduation, his monthly veteran's allowance ended.

The Theatre Guild's *R.U.R.* closed and Tracy could not find another acting job. He was about to return to Milwaukee in defeat when he received an offer from Leonard Wood, Jr. to work in a stock company that Wood was forming in White Plains, New York. Tracy did not hesitate. He accepted the job immediately.

He had several small roles in the White Plains company, as did an attractive young actress whom he had noticed on the train to White Plains. Her name was Louise Treadwell, and she had already had a featured spot in a Broadway production before she joined the White Plains company.

During their first few weeks together, Spencer Tracy and Louise Treadwell fell in love. They appeared together with Wood's stock troupe in White Plains, Fall River (Massachusetts), and Lancaster (Pennsylvania) during the summer of 1923. Soon the two lovers left Wood's company and joined the Stuart Walker stock company in Cincinnati, Ohio. Spencer and Louise (an Episcopalian) were married in that city on Wednesday, September 12, 1923.

Shortly after his marriage, Tracy returned to New York to audition for a part for producer Arthur Hopkins. This tryout brought him his first real part in a

Broadway production, a small role in *A Royal Fandango,* a Zoë Akins comedy starring Miss Ethel Barrymore. Also in the cast was Edward G. Robinson. *A Royal Fandango* opened in New York on Monday, November 12, 1923, but the reviews were consistently bad. The play lasted only a few weeks, mostly on the strength of Miss Barrymore's personal popularity. During his appearance in *A Royal Fandango,* Miss Barrymore introduced Tracy to her brother Lionel, whom the young actor was to admire for many years as his favorite theatre artist. Laurette Taylor was another of Spencer's earliest theatre idols.

Because Louise Treadwell Tracy was expecting a baby, it was arranged that she would stay in Milwaukee with the Tracy family, since that would help to ease the financial burden on Spencer. During 1924 Tracy appeared in stock productions in Canada, New Jersey, Ohio, and Pennsylvania. His son, John, was born on Thursday, June 26, 1924 in Milwaukee. Tracy left his stock company activities to be with his wife for the event.

In the summer of 1924, Tracy was working for the William Wright company in Grand Rapids, Michigan in a new play, *Page the Duke.* Earle Booth, a New York theatrical manager, saw Tracy's performance and offered him a role in *The Sheepman* destined for a New York opening. Unfortunately, it went no further than a Connecticut tryout.

Tragedy soon forced itself on the Spencers with the discovery that their son had incurable deafness. Tracy turned to heavy drinking for relief from guilt, as he blamed himself for his son's affliction. Doctors, however, assured him that he was not the cause of his son's deafness. He then became more determined than ever to make a success of his acting career. He continued working in stock companies in 1925, becoming the leading actor in one in Trenton, New Jersey.

Selena Royle, a young actress who had worked with Tracy in stock, was at this time engaged in a Broadway production called *Yellow.* It was a new melodrama that the famous actor and producer George M. Cohan was bringing to the New York scene. When a key part in the production became available, Miss Royle interceded for Tracy and he won the role. It would be during the run of *Yellow* that Cohan would call Tracy "the best damned actor he had ever seen." The play opened on Broadway on Tuesday, September 21, 1926, with varied reviews, but because of its fine acting, it had a Broadway run of well over a hundred performances. Cohan was so pleased with Tracy's acting that he wrote a part for him in his farce *Baby Cyclone* which opened on September 12, 1927 at the Henry Miller Theatre for a 184-performance run. *Baby Cyclone* was a hit, and this production established Tracy's reputation on Broadway as a fine comedian. Ironically, in his personal life Tracy was far from happy, as his actor pals Pat O'Brien and Frank McHugh could attest. Years later Chester Morris would recall that John's deafness had "affected Spencer's whole career, and had changed him and aged him almost overnight." As Morris saw it, the change was "due to frustration because he couldn't make Johnny a normal kid."

Not wishing to be limited to comedy roles, Tracy sought a more challenging dramatic part. In 1928, he was assigned a good role in a stock company play, Sidney Howard's *Ned McCobb's Daughter.*

At about this time, Tracy was faced with another personal tragedy—his father's death from cancer. The fast-maturing actor, whose face was becoming lined and craggy, sought to keep busy to divert his personal depression. He played several minor roles in stock, in such plays as *Conflict, Nigger Rich,* and *Dread.* Finally he returned to Broadway in Hugh Stong's *Veneer.*

During the 1929 season, the year of the stock market crash, many stage actors were deserting Broadway for the lure of the West Coast and the "talkies." Tracy was not considered to be good-looking enough (in the conventional sense) and did not attract many film scouts at the time. It was generally believed that he would not photograph well and that he was not the proper type to succeed in pictures. He made several film tests which left cinema producers unimpressed. In addition, he made two short films in the East for Warner Bros.' Vitagraph division. They were *Taxi Talks* and *The Hard Guy,* both released in 1930.

The turning point in Tracy's career proved to be his enactment of Killer John Mears. The role was the focal point of John Wexley's grim, realistic prison melodrama, *The Last Mile.* When the show opened on Broadway on Thursday, February 13, 1930 at the Sam H. Harris Theatre, it turned out to be the sensation of the theatrical season. Ironically Tracy had originally had grave doubts about the play and his participation in it. The stark realism of the subject and the sincere acting of the players completely won over New York critics and public alike as they glowingly applauded *The Last Mile.* In the demanding characterization, Spencer was the personification of the anti-hero, with heavy overtones of humanity and tenderness. Killer Mears lifted him to prominence as a Broadway actor.

John Ford, already a veteran film director by 1930, saw several performances of *The Last Mile* while in New York on a talent scouting expedition. Ford personally persuaded Fox Studios to sign Tracy for a leading role in their coming production, *Up the River* (1930), which he was to direct. Tracy was at last to act in a feature film.

Up the River was originally intended to be an earnest study of prison life. However, the screenplay as such was rejected because of MGM's smash success, *The Big House.* Fox, fearful of an odious comparison, considered dropping the film. Instead it decided to make *Up the River* as a comedy with Ford directing and Spencer Tracy starring in a satiric spoof of prison melodramas. Also in the cast were Claire Luce and young Humphrey Bogart (who along with Tracy had been stationed during World War I at Norfolk, Virginia).

Up the River was an unexpected hit. The film centers around two tough but agreeable crooks, St. Louis (Spencer) and Dan (Warren Hymer), who are expert jailbreakers. The film derives much of its humor from the inmates' obsession with baseball and the determination of the team manager (William Collier, Sr.) to win the inter-penitentiary trophy.

The picture marked Humphrey Bogart's second appearance in films. He played the straight man accomplice. While making *Up the River,* Tracy began calling Bogart "Bogie" which was to become Hollywood's most famous nickname.

Later in his career, Tracy would remark that of all his pictures none was more enjoyable to make than *Up the River.* He thrived on the camaraderie of the cast and crew and admired the speed with which John Ford turned out the film.

At the completion of the filming, Tracy rushed back to Broadway to continue performing in *The Last Mile.* When *Up the River* debuted in late October 1930, the critical reaction was favorable. Richard Watts, Jr. *(New York Herald-Tribune),* accepting Tracy as an old pro in films, reported that Spencer Tracy gave his "usual" excellent performance.

In mid-January 1931, Fox Films announced that Tracy had signed a five-year contract with options. He joined a roster that included Will Rogers, Janet Gaynor, James Dunn, Elissa Landi, Charles Farrell, Sally Eilers, George O'Brien, Warner Baxter, Joan Bennett, Victor McLaglen, John Boles, Conchita Montenegro, Ralph Bellamy, Alexander Kirkland, El Brendel, and Linda Watkins.

Of more interest to Spencer than the competition on the lot or in Hollywood itself was one facet of his social life. Through his new pals, Will Rogers and director Frank Borzage, Spencer joined the Riviera Country Club where he became fanatic about polo playing. He became a regular player at the Sunday matches and was soon noted for his expert but rather reckless riding. He also gravitated to the Sunday evening drinking sessions at the club.

With his approximately $70,000 annual salary, Tracy should have felt financially secure, but he did not. He worried that his atypical looks would soon grate on the filmgoing public and that the studio might drop his option. Meanwhile, the new-found wealth helped to make life more pleasant for his wife Louise and their son John. Louise became passionately interested in establishing a clinic that would help other deaf children lead a more normal, functional life.

The first picture on Tracy's Fox contract was *Quick Millions* (1931).[1] Today it is regarded as a near-classic gangster tale, and Tracy's performance was and is the strength of the picture. When it was released some reviews were quite favorable, but they were few in number. The film was overshadowed at the time by Paramount's *City Streets,* another underworld story.

Today, all of Tracy's Fox films still seem unusually good, and each one of them benefits from Tracy's strong performance. A good example is *Six Cylinder Love* (1931) which followed *Quick Millions.* Although Tracy received top billing, he actually had a minor role in this slight comedy adapted from a stage play. Despite his limited scenes, he made the most of every moment onscreen and was very fine flirting with the film's two leading ladies, Sidney Fox and Una Merkel.

Goldie (1931) brought Tracy and Warren Hymer together again, this time as sailors notorious for their amorous adventures around the world. In Calais they become involved with Goldie (Jean Harlow), a carnival high diver. Spike (Hymer) falls for her, despite a warning by Bill (Spencer) that she is just a golddigger, however chipper and attentive she appears. The publicity for *Goldie* emphasized Harlow, who was the star of the phenomenally popular aerial drama *Hell's Angels* (1931). During the making of *Goldie,* Tracy was annoyed by Harlow's artificial airs and overacting. He advised her to be more natural in front of the camera. Wisely, she followed his advice and turned in a much better performance. Another *Goldie* cast member who came into contact with Tracy at this time was George Raft.

Under Winifred Sheehan's supervision, Fox was still turning out Janet Gaynor-Charles Farrell love stories and beginning to build up a new romantic pair, James Dunn and Sally Eilers. Will Rogers handled the rural comedies, and Warner Baxter, who had won an Oscar playing the Cisco Kid in *In Old Arizona* (1929), was the dapper, romantic leading

[1]Originally Tracy and *Quick Millions* co-star Sally Eilers were to be showcased in *Skyline* for which George and Ira Gershwin were to do the score.

With Claire Luce and Warren Hymer in *Up the River* (1930).

With George Raft in *Quick Millions* (1931).

With Jean Harlow and Warren Hymer in *Goldie* (1931).

With Ann Dvorak and Forrester Harvey in *Sky Devils* (1932).

man. El Brendel handled character comedy leads. By process of elimination and continued typecasting (he had played a killer in *The Last Mile*), Spencer was saddled with tough-guy leads. In the Hollywood copy-casting style, he was Fox's answer to Warner Bros.' Edward G. Robinson and James Cagney, MGM's Wallace Beery, and Paramount's George Bancroft.

Already Tracy had become the bad boy of the Fox lot. He had the nerve to argue with Winifred Sheehan about casting assignments, inferring that every picture he appeared in should be solid. Tracy was annoyed that he had been "window dressing" in *Goldie* and was not very pleased to be cast opposite blonde Joan Bennett in *She Wanted a Millionaire* (1932). He was even less pleased by the script. The scenario, which started off as a light comedy, took a dreadful turn toward the melodramatic. In the midst of the eighty-minute film, Miss Bennett is thrown into a cage of hungry Great Danes by her enraged husband when she asks for a divorce so that she can marry Tracy.

Spencer was a little less displeased when Fox loaned him to Howard Hughes for United Artists' *Sky Devils* (1932), but it proved to be a weak parody of *What Price Glory* and Hughes' own *Hell's Angels.* Despite some funny scenes and spectacular aviation photography, the film did not succeed.[2]

Back on the Fox lot, Spencer was fuming that the lead male role in *Bad Girl* (1932) had gone to James Dunn and not to him. He confronted Sheehan on this bit of casting, but the studio executive merely said that the New York office wanted a different type of actor to play the role. Tracy began to wonder whether his option would be dropped as Humphrey Bogart's had been after his fourth Fox picture.

Meanwhile, Tracy was cast in his third of seven 1932 releases—*Disorderly Conduct,* an unbelievable melodrama. At least it had Tracy in a strong role as Dick Fay, an honest motorcycle cop who allows himself to be corrupted by gangsters and bootleggers. He tangles with his captain (Ralph Bellamy) and with the spoiled daughter (Sally Eilers) of a crooked politician. After much bribery and murder, Tracy reforms when the bullet intended to assassinate him strikes down his little nephew instead. About the only good element to evolve from *Disorderly Conduct* was Spencer's lasting friendship with Ralph Bellamy.

Tracy and Bellamy were next co-starred in *Young America* (1932), directed by Spencer's then favorite director, Frank Borzage. This small-town drama had Tracy playing the town druggist, with Bellamy as a judge. *Young America* was definitely a message film: wayward boys need understanding, and they could easily be turned into criminals by being shipped off to reformatories. In many ways, *Young America* was a forerunner of Tracy's later triumph, *Boys Town.*

If those at Fox thought that the Spencer Tracy of early 1932 was an unreasonable, demanding employee, his friends could provide a ready explanation for his more-than-usual testiness. Louise Tracy was pregnant again, and Spencer had an inordinate fear that their second child might be born with a birth defect, something that would be more than Tracy could cope with at this time in life.

At about this time, Sheehan became more considerate of Tracy, not so much out of respect for Tracy's personal problems, but because he finally realized that Spencer was a solid performer, in fact probably the best on the lot. In an uncharacteristically generous gesture, he offered Tracy the choice of two films:

With wife Louise Tracy aboard the liner Santa Rosa (December 1932).

[2]In the mid-1970s, one-time movie property master, Stan Dunn, would recall escapades during the filming of *Sky Devils.* When Tracy arrived at March Field in Orange County, he shouted to Stan "Got anything to drink?" When the technician said no, Dunn arranged for a bootlegger to supply him with liquid refreshment. Dunn brought the bottle onto the base and handed it to the star. "He drank it straight down without taking the bottle from his lips. Then he handed me the bottle. 'Here, throw this away.' " According to Dunn, he thought Tracy couldn't act unless he was half drunk during this stage of his life. "He had to have a glow."

Society Girl (1932) or *Man About Town* (1932). Spencer chose the former, only to discover later that New York had ordered that James Dunn and Peggy Shannon be given the juicier footage. By then, Warner Baxter had agreed to play the lead in *Man About Town,* and Tracy was forced to play second fiddle to the lot's newest possible screen love team.

Society Girl, with its emphasis on male friendship being disrupted by a girl, pre-dates the kind of movies Tracy would later make at MGM with Clark Gable. James Dunn portrays prizefighter Johnny Malone who loves a debutante (Shannon). Tracy appears as Briscoe, Dunn's mentor and protector, who gets the distracted young man back into shape to compete in the fight ring.

Tracy was on location at Catalina Island for *Painted Woman* (1932), a South Seas picture with nothing much to offer but scenery, when he became a father for the second time. He flew home to be with Louise and their healthy baby girl. They named her Louise, but she became quickly known by her nickname Susie. Tracy became completely enchanted by her, and his relationship with his wife and his studio greatly improved. The Tracys were now living on a seven-and-a-half-acre ranch in Encino, California. Tracy's mother and his brother Carroll came west to be with them. Carroll would serve as Spencer's business manager until the actor's death in 1967.

Resentment over some films assigned to him, plus his brooding over his son John, still caused Spencer great spells of depression. Even though the birth of Susie helped to strengthen his personal life, his bouts of drinking caused problems that the studio publicity department could not always hide.

Previously when Spencer had been teamed onscreen with Joan Bennett, she was engaged in a romance with producer/director John Considine, Jr. As a lark, and for publicity's sake, a studio minion had suggested to the press that Spencer and Considine were rivals for Joan's attention. This bit of puffery infuriated Tracy, and it was some time before he and Joan again became friendly players on the soundstages.

By the time of *Me and My Gal* (1932), directed by Raoul Walsh, the two performers had cemented a friendship that would last over the decades. The film

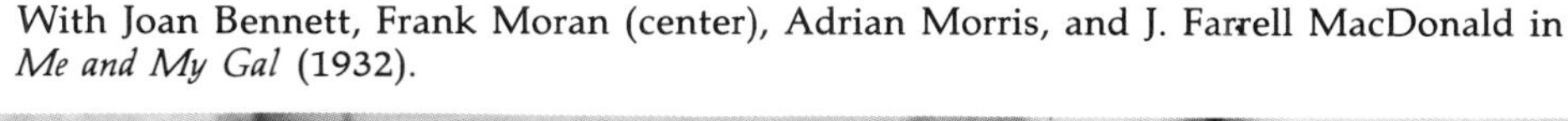

With Joan Bennett, Frank Moran (center), Adrian Morris, and J. Farrell MacDonald in *Me and My Gal* (1932).

offered bright performances by Tracy and Miss Bennett (she in an uncharacteristic gum-chewing tough-girl part) that still retain much of their original glow. The film was a suspense thriller so generously laced with amusing dialogue that it did surprisingly well at the box office. Tracy gave further evidence of his developing acting ability by turning a standard tough-guy part into a unique character role.

Fox was not the only studio having problems with its tough-guy "stars." Warner Bros. had rambunctious James Cagney who could be just as pugnacious offcamera as on. He and the studio were having differences of opinion when it became necessary to cast *20,000 Years in Sing Sing* (First National, 1933). Feuding Cagney could not be ready in time for the start of filming, so the lot borrowed Tracy from Fox. The storyline was suggested by a best-selling book by Lewis E. Lawes, warden of the Ossining, New York prison (known as Sing Sing). Incidents that actually happened at the maximum security penitentiary, such as an attempted jailbreak, were incorporated into a fictional scenario.

In *20,000 Years,* Tracy was paired with Bette Davis. He and Miss Davis had many similar characteristics, as well as an April 5th birthdate (she: 1908, he: 1900). Both were essentially stage actors, neither had great physical glamour, and both were stubborn and very serious about their careers and the screenplays assigned to them. Under Michael Curtiz' direction, they blended together well in the prison melodrama, turning a potentially conventional study into a worthwhile venture. Sadly they would never be reunited in a film, although some six and a half years later they would perform together on Cecil B. De Mille's "Lux Radio Theatre" in a pallid version of *Dark Victory*.

Advertisement for *20,000 Years in Sing Sing* (1933).

Tracy returned to Fox for *Face in the Sky* (1933), an excursion into whimsy and romance. The film teamed him with Marian Nixon, casting him as an idealistic sign painter, inspired to build on top of a skyscraper a sign featuring a beautiful woman. He uses Marian as his inspiration. It was hardly the material of which great films are made.

Producer Jesse L. Lasky, formerly with Paramount, had recently joined Fox with his own production unit. Lasky greatly admired Tracy as an actor, and he was quite enthusiastic about the prospects for *The Power and the Glory* (1933), with a screenplay by Preston Sturges. Sturges' treatment was startling in its originality. The events of a man's life are told via flashbacks that are out of chronological order, a technique later used to great advantage by Orson Welles in *Citizen Kane.* Tracy was cast with former silent film star Colleen Moore. *The Power and the Glory* was one of the finest films to come out of Hollywood during the early 1930s. When the picture was released, the reviews praised Tracy. The venture helped him to obtain a new contract with many advantages. There was now no option clause giving the studio the right to drop Tracy, and the contract period was extended to 1937. Spencer would make four films a year. He would not be loaned to outside studios without his consent, and if it were mutually advantageous to the studio and to the star, he might be allowed to appear on Broadway in a play.

However, audiences across the nation were confused and disinterested in *The Power and the Glory* with its well-touted technique. It was a stark study of Tom Garner, a man who becomes rich but suffers great disillusionment in his personal life. In middle age, the husband ignores his sacrificing wife (Moore) to pay attention to another woman (Helen Vinson). The spouse commits suicide to allow Tracy to wed his new love. Later Tracy kills himself when he realizes that his second wife's child is most likely not his own. The man that Tracy played was certainly not sympathetic, but he invested the part with a well-etched characterization—that of a believable human being who is engaging, dominant, and ultimately pitiful.

With Marian Nixon in *Face in the Sky* (1933).

On the set of *Shanghai Madness* (1933) with Eugene Pallette.

In true Hollywood tradition, for every decent film an actor has there are several bad roles. Such was the case with *Shanghai Madness* (1933) and *The Mad Game* (1933). The former featured Tracy as a naval officer in China during the "Chinese Civil War." Fay Wray was his leading lady in this insipid tale of Oriental intrigue. *The Mad Game,* directed by Irving Cummings, was a better film with an involved plot, and it required that Tracy, for the first time oncamera, wear heavy makeup. He plays Edward Carson, a bootlegger who, at the end of Prohibition, turns to kidnaping. Tracy was so effective in the part that it led to more demands by fans that he be given better roles by the studio. Fox, undergoing corporate changes, was fully aware of Tracy's potential. However, it was disturbed by his personal problems and his continuing drinking binges.

At this juncture Tracy took a vacation from filmmaking but returned to the lot to confront the front office executives. They insisted that he join Lilian Harvey in *My Lips Betray* (1933), but he refused and was replaced by John Boles. (The role would have cast Tracy as the King of Ruritania!) Instead, he agreed to join his director pal Frank Borzage at Columbia for *Man's Castle.* Based on a Lawrence Hazard play, it is the story of the Depression of the 1930s. Two poverty-stricken young people meet in a park one evening. Bill (Spencer) takes Trina (Loretta Young) back to his shack for protection. Trina is happy to find shelter and tries to make a proper home for Bill. He, however, is a wanderer who wants no established home. Later Bill, finding that Trina is pregnant, tries to rob a toy factory. In the attempt he is wounded, but escapes. He then realizes how much Trina means to him. The two young lovers jump aboard a freight train to face a troubled future together. It was a romantic tale guaranteed to appeal to some segments of America.

During the making of *Man's Castle,* Tracy and Loretta Young were widely rumored to be having a real-life romance. The affair received such widespread publicity that Louise could no longer remain in the background. She announced that she and Spencer had decided on a trial separation because of incompatibility. Miss Young finally brought the situation to an end by announcing that because she and Tracy were both devout Catholics, divorce and marriage for them were impossible. Soon Louise and Tracy were reconciled.[3] Mrs. Tracy was becoming more involved with her study of the problems of deaf children.

[3]As Tracy would later admit of the reconciliation, "When I walked into the house, a door closed over the year that had passed and neither of us will ever open it again. She has never mentioned the affair from that day."

Meanwhile, when not making films, romancing, or drinking, Spencer was still very much involved with polo playing. He devoted a lot of time and energy to that sport with such fellow actors as Will Rogers and Leslie Howard. Tracy was becoming known for his expensive and elegant clothes, and for his friendship with the "Irish Mafia"—mostly Irish-American actors he had first met on Broadway and in Eastern stock companies, such as Pat O'Brien, Frank Morgan, Frank McHugh, James Gleason, and Lynne Overman. Romanoff's restaurant, where they met for camaraderie, was known as the "Lambs West," as most of this high-spirited crowd had originally made their haunt in Manhattan's Lambs Club.

At Fox, Spencer refused parts in *Orient Express* and *Hold That Girl,* both 1934 releases, but he did agree to go over to Darryl F. Zanuck's and Joseph Schenck's new producing company, Twentieth Century Productions. Tracy was sure he would be given the lead in United Artists' *Advice to the Lovelorn* (1933), a version of the Nathaniel West novel *Miss Lonelyhearts.* Instead another Tracy—Lee Tracy—got the part, and Spencer was cast in United Artists' *Looking for Trouble* (1934), a decidedly lesser William Wellman directing effort. It was a slight comedy-melodrama, but it had a good cast. Tracy and Jack Oakie played two carefree telephone repairmen, with Constance Cummings and Arline Judge as their lady friends. The film's climax was an earthquake which was filmed in a remarkably realistic fashion.

Then in a turn of events, Spencer got to replace Lee Tracy. The latter actor, also a heavy drinker, had caused his home lot a good deal of embarrassment in Mexico while filming *Viva Villa!* (1934). He had been replaced in that feature and his tenure at the studio had been canceled. Thanks to Frank Morgan and his awareness of the vacant role in an upcoming Lee Tracy MGM feature, Spencer was brought into the picture. Louis B. Mayer, head of the studio, agreed to assign Spencer to the part of J. Aubrey Piper in *The Show-Off* (1934).

Spencer found the atmosphere at MGM very congenial—a great contrast to that at Fox. He developed an important friendship in Irving G. Thalberg, Mayer's chief assistant. *The Show-Off,* derived from George Kelly's famous play, gave Spencer a meaty assignment as a lovable and sympathetic braggart. Madge Evans plays the girl Tracy meets on an excursion boat. She accepts his marriage proposal, much against the wishes of her family who see through the delusions of grandeur of the brash and aggressive railroad clerk. In the end, accidental good fortune puts everything on a solid footing, and the girl's family is resigned to accepting boastful Tracy as their son-in-law.

Playing polo in Hollywood (1933).

With Loretta Young and Marjorie Rambeau in *Man's Castle* (1933).

The Show-Off debuted at New York's Capitol Theatre in March 1934 and did such good business that the lightly budgeted feature was held over for another week. It was in this well-received feature that Spencer's name was first placed above the title. Tracy, who many had claimed had already "gone Hollywood" (especially during his Loretta Young period), was now an acknowledged star. However, Fox was not enthralled with its prodigal leading man, who would often arrive on the set late or in a drunken, sullen condition.

For his first Fox release of 1934 he was placed in *Bottoms Up,* one of the studio's best musicals of the year. It was a genre piece in which the song-and-dance numbers were made secondary to the story. As Smoothie King, Tracy had another of his wise-cracking, fast-talking roles. Pat Paterson plays a Canadian beauty contest winner trying to break into films. Her money runs out, but she is protected by Tracy, Herbert Mundin, and Sid Silvers, three unemployed men who give her sanctuary in a hut on a miniature golf course. Tracy concocts a "romance" between the girl and an alcoholic film star (John Boles). This enables the girl to get a role in one of Boles' pictures. It ends, of course, with Boles and the girl falling in love, and Tracy, ever the understanding regular guy, gallantly stepping aside. Tracy wisely left the singing in this David Butler-directed musical to John Boles.

Tracy's next film, *Now I'll Tell* (1934), was based on a confess-all story by Carolyn Rothstein, the wife of gambler Arnold Rothstein. The story was highly promoted as being based on real-life facts of the celebrated gambler's career. Director/scripter Edwin Burke wrote a serious study of Rothstein's downfall. Tracy was again seen as a man destroyed by his lust for wealth. The actor's sharply defined portrayal raised the seventy-two-minute entry out of the run-of-the-reel underworld melodrama and turned it into a compelling character study. Tracy received star billing in the film, and Fox provided him with a strong supporting cast, including Helen Twelvetrees as his wife. Sandwiched into the production were two future top Twentieth Century-Fox stars, both female and both blonde: Alice Faye who was very effective in a dramatic part as the gangster's

With Sid Silvers, Thelma Todd, and Pat Paterson in *Bottoms Up* (1934).

With son John at a Los Angeles polo match (February 1934).

ill-fated mistress, and Shirley Temple, seen briefly in one episode of the story as his child.

Marie Galante (1934), directed by Henry King, found durable Tracy in a supporting role. The film, which cast Helen Morgan in a subordinate part as well, was really a vehicle to introduce the studio's short-lived star, Ketti Gallian, to movie audiences. Tracy was overtly wasted in this study of intrigue set in the Panama Canal Zone. At least the picture benefited from torch singer Miss Morgan who offered several numbers in her inimitable style.

It was no secret that Tracy was unhappy with his situation at Fox, and the studio, in the process of setting up a merger with Darryl F. Zanuck's Twentieth Century Productions, had no patience with time-wasting stars. The situation during the making of *It's a Small World* (1935) was a perfect example. The picture, a trite imitation of *It Happened One Night* (1934), co-starred Spencer with Wendy Barrie, a British import more noted for her social life than her histrionic aptitude. On Monday, March 11, 1935, Tracy was arrested in a Yuma, Arizona hotel. He was A.W.O.L. from wrapping up the small-budgeted feature at the studio. The law enforcers found Tracy ensconced in his hotel room (which he shared with pal Hugh Tully) screaming on the telephone (to wife Louise) and smashing crockery against the wall. The well-publicized charges accused Tracy of being inebriated, resisting arrest, employing foul language, and destroying private property. By the time Louise Tracy arrived in Yuma to smooth over the situation, Tracy had been released from jail and had left for Mexico with Tully and several bottles of liquor. A sheepish Tracy later returned to the studio to complete the film.

Perhaps the most elaborate of Spencer's Fox features was *Dante's Inferno* (1935), ironically produced by Sol M. Wurtzel who would become famous as the studio's budget producer. The film contains an allegorical sequence of a soul burning in hell, and also features a fantastic fire aboard a luxury liner at sea. These two spectacular scenes made the project a financial success at the box office. Once again Tracy appeared as a loud, ambitious huckster-type. This time he is Jim Carter, the builder of carnival piers and a luxury ship which, when destroyed by fire, serves to reunite him with his estranged wife, Claire Trevor. Budding starlet Rita Cansino (later to be Rita Hayworth) had a small role as a dancer in *Dante's Inferno.*

The final blow to Tracy's ego occurred when Fox assigned him to a relatively minor role in *The Farmer Takes a Wife* (1935) which the studio was preparing as a starring vehicle for Janet Gaynor and Henry Fonda. Tracy balked and refused to work on the film. He was replaced on the picture by Charles Bickford. He packed up and left the studio. On Monday, April 8, 1935, Winfield Sheehan announced to the press a *post facto* situation: Tracy and Fox had come to a parting of the ways. (It would not be long—July, in fact—before Sheehan was removed from the Fox hierarchy in the corporate merger which saw Darryl F. Zanuck and Joseph Schenck take control. Ironically, Zanuck had always liked Tracy's acting style. Besides, he was a polo fanatic too.)

But Tracy was not to be without a studio for long. In fact, he had already been negotiating with Metro-Goldwyn-Mayer. Louis B. Mayer was not enthused about Tracy's projected entrance into the Metro family. "He wrecks sets. Besides, he's a galoot," insisted Mayer, "and we already have a galoot in the family." (Mayer was referring to rough-and-ready Wallace Beery.) On the other hand, Irving Thalberg, the husband of actress Norma Shearer, was tremendously impressed with Tracy. "Spencer Tracy will become one of the important MGM stars," was the verdict of the lot's number two executive.

On the same day that Sheehan made his press announcement, April 8, Tracy was over at Culver City signing a pact with MGM that would last for twenty years. That lot was packed with star talent. Among the V.I.P. roster of female players were

With Raymond Walburn and Wendy Barrie in *It's a Small World* (1935).

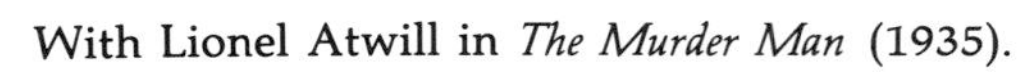

With Lionel Atwill in *The Murder Man* (1935).

Norma Shearer, Greta Garbo, Joan Crawford, Jean Harlow, Jeanette MacDonald, and Myrna Loy, and, on the male side, Clark Gable, Robert Montgomery, William Powell, the Marx Brothers, Wallace Beery, Lionel Barrymore, and Johnny "Tarzan" Weissmuller. Among the newer additions to the lot were Nelson Eddy, Rosalind Russell, Jimmy Stewart, Freddie Bartholomew, Mickey Rooney, and Robert Taylor. Middle-of-the-road performers included Maureen O'Sullivan, Franchot Tone, Robert Young, and Virginia Bruce.

Tracy was hurried into three MGM pictures in 1935. The best, *Riff-Raff,* was made first but released third. The initial Tracy-MGM production to be distributed was a low-budget affair, *Murder Man.* It cast Spencer as Steve Gray, a newspaper reporter out to avenge his wife's suicide. He murders the man responsible for his spouse's death in a thickly plotted murder yarn. Tracy, however, was effective in the dark, somber melodramatic role. James Stewart provided good support in his first film role. Self-contained Tracy and lanky Stewart became fast and good friends. It was a relationship that would help to fill the gap when Tracy's confidant, buddy, and true friend, Will Rogers, died in a plane crash on August 15, 1935.

Whipsaw co-starred Tracy with Myrna Loy who had made such an impact in a screen teaming with William Powell in *Manhattan Melodrama* and *The Thin Man,* both 1934 releases. *Whipsaw,* directed in competent but pedestrian style by Sam Wood, was a cops and robbers story with a familiar chase theme. Loy, one of a gang of jewel thieves Tracy is chasing, falls victim to his charms and helps him bring the criminals to justice.

Riff-Raff brought Tracy and Jean Harlow together again, four years after their film *Goldie.* Irving Thalberg was determined in *Riff-Raff* to demonstrate that the platinum blonde (who wore a light brown wig for the picture) could handle dramatic material as well as light comedy roles. Tracy and Harlow portrayed two waterfront toughs, he a fisherman, she a cannery worker. The Frances Marion script was well-mounted by MGM, but the completed picture was not a major triumph for either star.[4]

Tracy's next film assignment, however, was a definite improvement. At first Spencer did not want to take the part of Father Mike, a priest, in *San Francisco* (1936). He felt that Clark Gable and Jeanette MacDonald were definitely the stars of the film, and that the real scene stealer would be the special effects department with the climactic earthquake sequences. However, W. S. Van Dyke II, the director, convinced Tracy of the essential humanity in the role and stressed that he was the only actor who could provide the characterization with the requisite

[4]The project was originally conceived by Frances Marion as a Mary Pickford vehicle for the 1932 season. It was then sold to MGM as a possible Gloria Swanson-Clark Gable starring picture. This was during the period Swanson was under Metro contract without making a film there.

With Myrna Loy in *Whipsaw* (1935).

With Jeanette MacDonald in *San Francisco* (1936).

quality. After reading the revised script, Tracy agreed to do the role, although he was troubled by the idea of portraying a priest.

In the meantime, Tracy was anything but godly offscreen. On Wednesday night, December 4, 1935 he and "Wild Bill" Wellman came to blows at Hollywood's Club Trocadero. The director had made some disparaging remark about Loretta Young and a rumpus ensued. Tracy received a black eye and bruised knuckles for his efforts. While the papers played up the actor's continued heart-yearning for Miss Young, she had already become involved in another reputed romance, this time with Metro's King, Clark Gable, during the making of *The Call of the Wild* (1935).

On a happier note, the Tracys purchased a twelve-acre ranch in Encino, one that had previously belonged to Gary Cooper. It allowed Spencer ample opportunity to practice his polo, a sport adopted by both wife Louise and son John. For the "man's man," as Tracy was soon tagged, ranch life was a wonderful release from the tensions of studio work. He enjoyed working around the spread or relaxing by indulging his growing penchant for reading.

San Francisco went into production early in 1936. Both Gable and Tracy were definite masculine types, and their rugged portrayals in tandem make pale such later screen teamings as that of Robert Redford and Paul Newman. Tracy and Gable did not become close personal friends, but they did learn to like and respect one another.

In spite of the fact that "King" Gable and "Iron Butterfly" MacDonald were its stars, Tracy as the rugged yet understanding priest had the outstanding role in *San Francisco.* For this part he would win his first Oscar nomination for Best Actor. (The Award would go to Paul Muni for *The Story of Louis Pasteur*.)

Tracy went immediately from filming scenes of *San Francisco* into the production of *Fury,* a powerful study directed by the distinguished German director Fritz Lang. From a retrospective point of view, it is hard to comprehend why the MGM hierarchy had so little faith in the project, passing it off as an uncommercial entry. Tracy was cast as a hard-working, well-adjusted working man who, while passing through a small mid-American town, is erroneously arrested on a kidnap and murder charge and jailed on suspicion. The townsfolk decide to take the law into their own hands and attempt to break into the jail and lynch him. Tracy's girlfriend (Sylvia Sidney) witnesses the mob's action with horror. Shortly thereafter, the real criminal is caught. Tracy, who was believed to have been killed when the jail was set on fire but who had actually escaped, is pleased when his attackers are prosecuted for his "murder." Only through weepy Miss Sidney's intervention does the "dead" man agree to appear in court, thus absolving the accused citizens of his "death."

There is a dramatic speech delivered by Tracy before the courtroom finale, impassioned as only Spencer could do, filled with force, honesty, and seeming spontaneity. Tracy tells his brothers:

> Do you know where I've been all day? In a movie watchin' a newsreel of myself gettin' burned alive. Watched it ten or twenty times maybe. Over and over again. . . . The place was packed. They liked it. They get a big kick out of seeing a man burned to death.
>
> What an explosion! It blew the cell door off. I got down a drainpipe. I almost burned my side off. I could smell myself burn. But that don't hurt me 'cause you can't hurt a dead man and I'm dead. I'm burned to death by a mob of animals. I'm legally dead and they're legally murderers.
>
> That I'm alive is not their fault. But I know 'em. I know lots of 'em. And they'll hang for it, according to the law which says if you kill somebody you got to be killed yourself. But I'll give them the chance they didn't give me. They'll get a legal trial in a legal courtroom. They'll have a legal judge and a legal defense. They'll get a legal sentence and a legal death.

Here was a performer the public could identify with, just as they would later identify with rebellious John Garfield or James Dean. No matter what kind of dialogue Tracy was asked to deliver onscreen, it rang with conviction and truth. Filmgoers admired this trait.

With *Libeled Lady* (1936), directed in a breezy fashion by Jack Conway, Tracy changed with facility from stark drama to light "screwball" comedy. Jean Harlow and William Powell (offscreen lovers) and Myrna Loy were cast with him in a lighthearted account of a flip newspaper editor (Tracy) involved in a devastating libel suit with a determined heiress (Loy). The film was filled with amusing situations and laced with bright dialogue. It was a critical success for all four of its stars. On the strength of their appeal in *Libeled Lady,* Metro planned two more comedy vehicles for Harlow and Tracy, but those unfortunately had to be abandoned after Jean Harlow's untimely death in June 1937. (Another death, that of Irving Thalberg in September 1936, had ended plans for Tracy, among others, to join him in outside film ventures when the ace producer did leave the MGM fold.)

Back in 1932 when World-Wide made the film version of *The Last Mile,* it was Preston Foster and not Spencer who inherited the role of Killer John Mears. Then in 1936 Foster obtained another part that Tracy craved, that of Jack Clitheroe in John Ford's *The Plough and the Stars* starring Barbara Stanwyck. However MGM, and Louis B. Mayer in particular, refused to loan out Spencer for such a chancy, downbeat project and perhaps hurt the large investment they had placed in their new family member. That was the start of a long-range feud between Tracy and his MGM bosses. The latter, sure that only tangible goals were involved, thought they had pacified Tracy by giving him a new contract. Under

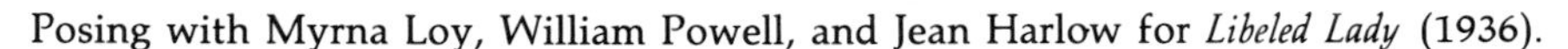

Posing with Myrna Loy, William Powell, and Jean Harlow for *Libeled Lady* (1936).

the revised agreement, Tracy was to receive $5,000 weekly, twice the amount he was guaranteed under the initial pact. The actor accepted the deal, but he was still smoldering inside. He confided to a few of his close pals (Pat O'Brien, Frank McHugh, and a new member of the gang, James Cagney) that he felt guilty about getting such a large salary for so little work, especially in projects he did not respect.

It also amused if puzzled the Hollywood Hibernians that such players as Cagney, Tracy, Lynne Overman, *et al.* should be working for Jewish executives. As Tracy phrased it, "Out here the Kellys are working for the Cohens." At their Wednesday night get-togethers the proceedings would sometimes get quite rowdy, but they provided necessary diversion from the daytime tension of filmmaking. Heavy drinking always was an integral part of the get-togethers of Tracy, O'Brien, and the others.

For Spencer's next film, he learned to sing (to a degree) and play a musical instrument, and he allowed his hair to be curled. It was all for *Captains Courageous* (1937), which proved to be one of the finest features made in the mid-1930s. The story was adapted from Rudyard Kipling's long-popular novel. Freddie Bartholomew played Harvey, the spoiled son of a wealthy business tycoon (Melvyn Douglas). The bullying, cheating Harvey is expelled from school and is taken on an ocean voyage by his father. He falls off the ship near the Grand Banks and is rescued by Manuel (Spencer) who takes him aboard the simple Portuguese fishing schooner "We're Here." The crew hates Harvey, except for Manuel who in his simple way is affectionately drawn to the spoiled child whom he calls "Leetle Feesh."

Later during a race with another vessel, Manuel falls overboard and is drowned. Harvey is heartbroken. The boat returns to Gloucester (Massachusetts) where the youth is reunited with his dad. Having learned some important lessons about life from the kind-hearted Manuel, Harvey attends church and lights a candle in his memory.

Later in his career Tracy would designate Manuel as perhaps his favorite role, yet it was a part that he did not want to undertake. His wife, Louise, and director Victor Fleming had to do much persuading to get him to take it. The Portuguese accent, the makeup, and especially the black curly hair required

With Lionel Barrymore and John Carradine in *Captains Courageous* (1937).

for the part made him feel uneasy. All during the filming, the actor believed that he was wrong for the role.

Yet it was the role of Manuel in *Captains Courageous* that won for Tracy his first Oscar. Other contenders that year were Charles Boyer *(Conquest),* Fredric March *(A Star Is Born),* Robert Montgomery *(Night Must Fall),* and Paul Muni *(The Life of Emile Zola).* In typical Tracy form, he was sure he would not win. He well remembered his discomfiture at having attended the previous year's ceremony. In fact, he was insistent that Lionel Barrymore (who had played Disko, the cantankerous fishing captain in *Captains Courageous*) was the one from the cast who should have been nominated.

As a matter of fact, on the night (Tuesday, February 8, 1938) the Awards were to be bestowed, Tracy was not present. He had entered the hospital for a hernia operation, and his wife attended the festivities at the Biltmore Bowl. When Tracy was announced as the winner, she accepted with a trim little speech. "I accept this Award on behalf of Spencer, Susie, Johnny, and myself." On the other hand, Louis B. Mayer took the opportunity to make a speech of lengthier duration, saying: "I'd like to praise Spencer Tracy's sense of discipline. Tracy is a fine actor, but he is most important because he understands why it is necessary to take orders from the front office . . . because he understands that when the publicity department asks him to cater to certain visitors, it is a necessary inconvenience." From his hospital bed, Tracy wondered how he was to interpret his boss' speech of praise and advice.[5]

It was after *Captains Courageous* that Tracy acquired a forty-foot ketch. He christened it the "Carrie B" in honor of his mother. Just as Carrie Tracy would be a frequent visitor on the MGM lot until her death in 1942, so brother Carroll was a regular presence on the soundstages, acting as a buffer, confidant, spokesman, and aide for Tracy in a way that his agent, the William Morris office, could not.

[5]Years later Tracy would reminisce, "Can you imagine what I felt like—lying there, in all those itchy bandages—round my middle, and in plenty of pain—when the word came through, I'd won it?" The actor had a second Oscar surprise when his Academy Award was mistakenly engraved to "Dick Tracy."

With Gladys George and Franchot Tone in a publicity shot for *They Gave Him a Gun* (1937).

Tracy's other films during this period are a strange mixture of production-line pap and misguided message drama. *They Gave Him a Gun* (1937) was a peculiar blending of sentimentality, propaganda against war, and crime melodrama. It was the story of a weak man (played by Franchot Tone) who was drafted and taught to use a gun, and his buddy (Spencer), and their life in the Army and later in gangland U.S.A.

In another, *Big City* (1937), Spencer was reunited with director Frank Borzage who had signed an MGM deal. Tracy had not forgotten how much he had wanted to be loaned to Universal for *Little Man, What Now?* (1934) and how Fox would not permit it and Douglass Montgomery got the role opposite Margaret Sullavan. *Big City,* unfortunately, did not benefit from the Borzage touch, nor from the presence of Tracy or Oscar-winning European star Luise Rainer. The film is mostly memorable for a number of cameo performances by such real-life athletes as Jack Dempsey, Jim Thorpe, and Man Mountain Dean who helped Tracy in his taxi war against a gang of hoodlums in an action-packed finale.

In *Mannequin* (1938), Tracy's second Borzage-directed feature for MGM, he was co-starred with Joan Crawford, and distinctly subordinate to her. Tracy expected the worst from stylized Miss Crawford, but she surprised him by toning down her performance. At one point during production, Tracy admitted, "Ya got spunk, kid." Off the set, Joan and Tracy became better than pals when she was recuperating from the run-down after-effects of pneumonia by getting fresh air at the Riviera Club where Tracy played polo. It was he who taught her to appreciate horses. The rapport between the two stars died during rehearsals of *Mannequin* for "Lux Radio Theatre" where Tracy taunted Crawford for being nervous. Thus ended the Tracy-Crawford liaison.[6]

If *Mannequin* had dampened Tracy's spirits, being cast as a subordinate player to Clark Gable and Myrna Loy (king and queen of the lot) in *Test Pilot* (1938) did not help matters.[7] The film was like a rerun of the *San Francisco* setup, this time with Gable as Jim Lane, a swaggering egotistical pilot, and Tracy as Gunner Sloane, his loyal, patient mechanic. Loy is Ann Barton, Jim's fear-tortured wife. The aerial shots for *Test Pilot* are some of the most effective ever created for film, and Spencer's performance as the faithful mechanic was especially fine. Within the plotline of this Victor Fleming-directed feature, Tracy's character is killed in a practice flight. His death convinces Gable that he should switch to a safer profession for Miss Loy's sanity.

Test Pilot also convinced MGM that perhaps it was wasting Tracy's star allure. For his third 1938 release, Tracy was cast in *Boys Town,* produced by his old adversary, John W. Considine, Jr., and directed by Norman Taurog, long acknowledged to be a specialist with child actors. *Boys Town* had plenty of youngsters, but those potential scene-stealers did not bother Spencer. What concerned him was attempting to portray Father Edward J. Flanagan whom he had met and greatly admired. Once again it took much persuasion to convince Tracy that he could properly impersonate the founder of the school for homeless boys in Nebraska.

Despite great sentimental weaknesses in the plot involving a "bad" boy (Mickey Rooney), Tracy managed to create a role that only can be called ideal. Made on a small budget, the film's essential honesty —albeit an overdose of clichéd anti-climaxes—was contagious, even to the cast and crew. Tracy would later admit, "I became so absorbed in the part that by the end of the first week I had stopped worrying [about portraying the illustrious Father Flanagan]."

Boys Town was a big success at the box office, and the film did much to enhance the professional standing of both Tracy and Mickey Rooney. There was much talk of Tracy being an Oscar champ again and the predictions proved true as he beat the other favorite, James Cagney *(Angels with Dirty Faces),* in the 1938 Oscar sweepstakes. Best actress of the year was Bette Davis (for *Jezebel*), also a two-time winner. In his acceptance speech Tracy insisted that the trophy really belonged to Father Flanagan. Not long thereafter Tracy presented the priest with the Oscar, inscribing the award with the following words: "To Father Edward J. Flanagan, whose great human qualities, timely simplicity, and inspiring courage

[6]In *Conversations with Joan Crawford* (1980), interviewer Roy Newquist reports the star as saying: "*Mannequin* was a mistake all the way around; Spencer Tracy was so miscast he made an absolute muddle out of my part, which wasn't all that great to begin with. At first I felt honored working with Spence, and we even whooped it up a little bit off the set, but he turned out to be a real bastard. When he drank he was mean, and he drank all through production. He'd do cute things like step on my toes when we were doing a love scene-after he chewed on some garlic. Metro tried to co-star us again, but I begged them to let me off, and they did. I'm sorry I can't say nicer things about him; maybe he improved later, but from the things I've heard about his relationship with Kate, I doubt it. But worse, the script for *Mannequin* was all wrong."

[7]During this period Tracy was announced for several projects: the death of Jean Harlow in 1937 stopped plans for him to co-star with her and Robert Taylor in a remake of the 1927 Lon Chaney picture, *Tell It to the Marines;* Metro wanted him to join with Robert Donat and Rosalind Russell for *The Citadel* (1938), but it was Ralph Richardson who took the subordinate role in this British-filmed production; and for Frank Borzage's *Three Comrades* (1938), Tracy was to be teamed with Robert Taylor and James Stewart, but it was Robert Young who ended up with the role.

With Bobs Watson in *Boys' Town* (1938).

With Bette Davis, co-Oscar winner for 1938.

were strong enough to shine through my humble effort."

By this time even Louis B. Mayer had to admit that Spencer Tracy was a major force on the lot. Projects were now being tailor-made to fit Spencer's image, and properties were being purchased that might be suitable for his films. Among them was Kenneth Roberts' *Northwest Passage.* Spencer was anxious to begin filming this sprawling historical project, but the script adaptation proved more cumbersome than anticipated. At this juncture Mayer agreed to loan Tracy's service to 20th Century-Fox for their *Stanley and Livingstone* (1939), to be directed by Henry King.

The role of *New York Herald-Tribune* reporter Henry M. Stanley was admirably suited to the rugged he-man visionary so associated now with Tracy. As Stanley he is the one who follows up his belief that missionary Dr. David Livingstone (Sir Cedric Hardwicke) is not dead by forming a safari to the dangerous bush country of Africa to locate the "lost" humanitarian. After reporting back to civilization that Livingstone had not vanished, Stanley later returns to the isolated countryside to take up the unfinished work of the legend who has just died. To dress up the astere study, a girlfriend for Stanley is written into the factual study, but the heroine (Nancy Kelly) discovers that she really loves younger Gareth Tyce (Richard Greene). Thankfully, the potentially hackneyed "Mr. Livingstone, I presume?" meeting between reporter and missionary was handled with dispatch and restraint.

During the filming of *Stanley and Livingstone,* Spencer had been plagued by two professional problems. One was the inability of scenarists to whip the epic *Northwest Passage* into proper shape (a situation solved by filming only the first half of the monumental story), and by the continuous shooting problems on *I Take This Woman.* The project was geared to showcase Hedy Lamarr, Mayer's latest European import who had gained international fame for an earlier nude dip in *Extase (Ecstasy)* (1933) and more recently as the mysterious woman in *Algiers* (1938). Josef von Sternberg was hired to direct *I Take This Woman,* based on a story by Charles MacArthur. After a few weeks of production, von Sternberg was relieved from command when Mayer was dissatisfied with his results. Frank Borzage asked to take over the project, but the conflicts between Mayer and Borzage were titanic. Then Tracy *had* to report to Fox for *Stanley and Livingstone.* He was thankful to escape the melee. However, when he completed his work at his old studio, Metro informed him that now W. S. Van Dyke II, noted for his quickness in turning out a feature, would be in charge of the Lamarr feature. Hollywood dubbed the film "I Re-Take This Woman."

After twenty-three days of retakes, the film came to another halt while Miss Lamarr went off to *Lady of the Tropics.* Tracy, still waiting for a shooting script for *Northwest Passage,* decided on a change-of-pace vacation. Instead of a trip to New York, as he and Louise had done in 1937 and 1938, the couple went to England in April 1939.

Tracy then returned to Hollywood to complete *I Take This Woman* (released and buried in 1940) and

With Hedy Lamarr and Verree Teasdale in *I Take This Woman* (1940).

With Walter Brennan, Robert Young, and Tom London (right) in *Northwest Passage* (1940).

to finally begin location work on *Northwest Passage* (1940). By this point Tracy and Louis B. Mayer were hardly talking, and only through emissaries were terms discussed for Tracy to star in such projects as *National Velvet* (with a borrowed Shirley Temple), *The Sea of Grass,* and *The Yearling.*

Northwest Passage, Tracy's first Technicolor feature, was largely shot in Idaho under King Vidor's direction. Spencer had the athletic role of Major Robert Rogers, leading his Rangers on a perilous expedition to defeat an Indian tribe in 1759 New England during the French and Indian War. His co-stars were Robert Young, Walter Brennan, and Ruth Hussey. The action feature was extremely popular with filmgoers.

Edison the Man (1940) was a part that Tracy was from the beginning proud to play.[8] It was the second half of MGM's tribute to Edison. (*Young Tom Edison,* 1940, starring Mickey Rooney in the title role, was the first.) Tracy played the famed inventor from the age of twenty-five to eighty-two. While critics generally found the screen biography too tedious, they were in accord that Tracy offered a dignified performance, making the picture worthwhile.

In *Boom Town* (1940), MGM again starred Tracy and Clark Gable (for the last time), along with Claudette Colbert and Hedy Lamarr. In formula fashion, the male leads are wildcat oil drillers who start out with nothing. Tracy loses his sweetheart (Colbert) to Gable. Over the years the two men quarrel, reconcile, and make and lose millions of dollars in the oil business. At the end (some 116 minutes later), the two men realize that their personal friendship is more important than the money they make. As a result of the success of *Boom Town,* and the film's tremendous drawing power, Tracy was able to extract from MGM a promise that he would get a salary increase, perform in only two films per year, get top billing, and have approval of all stories.

[8] One role which Tracy turned down in 1940 was the title part in Twentieth Century-Fox's *Brigham Young-Frontiersman.* At the time, he was not interested in playing another priest. Dean Jagger took the assignment. And of course, the next year, Tracy played Father Flanagan again in *Men of Boys Town* at MGM.

With Gene Reynolds, Arthur Aylesworth, Rita Johnson, Felix Bressart, and Henry Travers in *Edison the Man* (1940).

With Clark Gable in *Boom Town* (1940).

It was also agreed that Tracy and Mickey Rooney (now number one at the box office) would do a sequel to *Boys Town. Men of Boys Town* (1941), also directed by Norman Taurog, was geared to be a big money-earner, but it turned out to be just a modest success. The plot relied too heavily on syrupy sentiment, mild comedy, and too much coyness.

Tracy, who was reputed to be drinking again, was certain that he did not want to make his next assignment, a remake of *Dr. Jekyll and Mr. Hyde* (1941). He insisted to the powers-that-be that he was not right for the dual role, but the MGM authorities insisted that only a two-time Oscar winner of his caliber could handle the double role. After all had not Paramount's 1932 version won Fredric March an Oscar. Tracy was finally convinced and he joined a star lineup that included Ingrid Bergman as the trampish Ivy Peterson and Lana Turner as the comely fiancée Beatrix Emery. (Originally "The Sweater Girl" had been cast as the sluttish Ivy but Scandinavian Miss Bergman had crusaded for an image-changing role and won the contra-casting bid.)

Although Tracy had been concerned prior to the production of the Robert Louis Stevenson project, it was apparent that during filming he enjoyed the dual role. In fact, he was having such a good time that he hammed up the proceedings rather mercilessly.[9] For one of the few times in his career, he received unfavorable notices. It taught the star a lesson—to heed his intuition. To make matters worse, as had happened nearly a decade earlier, he fell in love with his leading lady, Miss Bergman, but each realized the impracticality of their romance. (She was wed too.) Instead, they became good friends.

In May 1941, Tracy was in Florida doing location shots for *The Yearling,* with Anne Revere as his co-star. The film would be postponed because of very bad weather and recast and reshot in 1946 with Gregory Peck and Jane Wyman in the leads. Cantankerous Spencer was not too displeased by the turn of events, for there were rumors at the studio that he would have a new leading lady. Her name was Katharine Hepburn.

Katharine Hepburn had returned to Hollywood in 1941, fresh from her spectacular stage success in *The Philadelphia Story.* She had risen to enormous film stardom early in the 1930s—even winning an Oscar—only to be labeled "box-office poison" at the end of

[9] A delightful story is told about author W. Somerset Maugham visiting the MGM soundstages where Tracy was making *Dr. Jekyll and Mr. Hyde.* The famed writer turned to his tour guide and inquired, "Which one is he supposed to be now?"

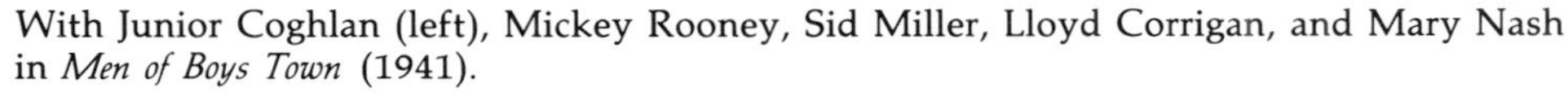

With Junior Coghlan (left), Mickey Rooney, Sid Miller, Lloyd Corrigan, and Mary Nash in *Men of Boys Town* (1941).

her RKO career. Now she was returning to the screen in triumph under the aegis of MGM.

Woman of the Year (1942), as the film was finally titled, was an account of the relationship of Tess Harding (Hepburn), a Dorothy Thompson-like columnist, and Sam Craig, a tough sportswriter who introduces her to the mysteries of baseball. Craig is as ill at ease around Tess' intellectual friends as she is in the world of home runs and strikeouts. Hepburn had sold the story to Louis B. Mayer with the provisos that she select the director and her male co-star. She suggested that George Stevens was the perfect director for the film, and she asked for Spencer Tracy as her vis-à-vis.

The two stars had never met,[10] although Hepburn is said to have admired Tracy very much, especially in *Captains Courageous* and *Dr. Jekyll and Mr. Hyde.*[11] When they did meet to work on *Woman of the Year,* it was an immediate attraction of opposites. Hepburn was nervous, stylish, and aggressive;[12] Tracy was subdued, retiring, shy, impatient, and direct. Hepburn was intensely feminine; he was extremely masculine. They proved to be the most extraordinary acting team[13] ever to be presented in motion pictures.

Woman of the Year, released in 1942, earned an Oscar for best screenplay (by Ring Lardner, Jr. and Michael Kanin), and Hepburn was nominated for an Oscar but lost to another MGM star, Greer Garson, who won for *Mrs. Miniver.*

Tracy and Hepburn's offscreen relationship was remarkable from the outset. It was a prime example of two human beings respecting one another, enjoying each other's company, and responding well in professional work.

By this point in their lives, Spencer was forty-two and Kate nearly thirty-five. His health was already poor from his years of drinking, and Hepburn, the daughter of a distinguished New England doctor, was prepared to spend an enormous amount of kindness and devotion in nursing him back to health.

Aside from her father, Tracy seemed to be the only man Hepburn completely trusted. She accepted the fact of Tracy's marriage and family life (as such), and indeed she had no wish to alter it. In fact, she did not believe that marriage and an acting career were compatible for her. By this time, Tracy was living alone in a hotel, but he kept in daily contact with his family and often spent long weekends with them on the ranch. (Since Tracy had grown so antagonistic to the press in the 1930s, journalists had learned not to expect many quotes from him and consequently often passed over him in their gossip columns. This helped keep the Tracy-Hepburn liaison "the best kept secret in Hollywood.")

Mrs. Louise Tracy had her own distinct life and work. John, her son, was finally able to speak after years of her daily instruction. In 1942, she founded the John Tracy Clinic at the University of Southern California, an institution devoted to the training of deaf children for more normal life. It all started in a small cottage on the U.S.C. campus. Today the clinic is considered the world's leading center in its field. During his lifetime, Tracy devoted much time and energy to raising money for the charity. In its first years, he alone kept it going financially and often spoke publicly in its behalf. As much as can be ascertained from the remarkably diplomatic attitude and actions of Mrs. Tracy, she seems to have been sympathetic to the Tracy-Hepburn friendship.

With the outbreak of World War II, Tracy, a veteran of The Great War, had a rather unique position as one of the few male stars at MGM not in the Armed Forces. It provided him, as it did Walter Pidgeon and much younger Van Johnson, with a wider variety of roles than they might have ordinarily obtained.

The attack on Pearl Harbor came in the middle of the production of *Tortilla Flat.* Tracy narrated a one-reel film, *Ring of Steel,* written by his pal Garson Kanin for the U.S. Office of War Information Film Unit. It was a tribute to the American soldier from 1776 to 1942. Later, in 1944, Tracy was to narrate, along with Ginger Rogers, another short war-effort film, also written by Garson Kanin. *Battle Stations* was produced by 20th Century-Fox and was centered around women taking over shore jobs formerly filled by men.

Tortilla Flat (1942), based on the highly praised John Steinbeck novel, was directed by congenial Victor Fleming. It provided Tracy with his second dialect role. While Hedy Lamarr was cast as the decorative Dolores, it was Spencer's co-star, Warner Bros.' John Garfield, who added the most spark to Tracy's performance. Like Spencer, Garfield was a gutsy, honest, instinctive performer, and each actor gained energy from the other's presence. The film is a semi-documentary study of the lives of some Mex-

[10]In 1938, Hepburn and Tracy had been caricaturized in a joint sequence in Walt Disney's Mickey Mouse cartoon, *Mother Goose Goes Hollywood.*

[11]Allegedly, when Fredric March telephoned Tracy to offer his opinion on *Dr. Jekyll and Mr. Hyde,* Spencer is said to have snorted, "Why, Fred, you son of a bitch. I've just done you the biggest professional favor you'll ever have!"

[12]It is reported that after the two iconoclastic stars first met, Kate told producer Joseph L. Mankiewicz, "I'm afraid I'm a bit tall [5′ 7″] for Mr. Tracy [5′ 10½″]." Mankiewicz brusquely replied, "Don't worry. He'll cut you down to size."

[13]For a more in-depth study of the unique love team, the reader is referred to *Hollywood's Great Teams* (Arlington House, 1974).

With Katharine Hepburn in *Woman of the Year* (1942).

With Hedy Lamarr and John Garfield in *Tortilla Flat* (1942).

ican peasants in a small central California seacoast town. Tracy's characterization of Pilon was reminiscent of the fine work he had done in *Captains Courageous,* although the picture did not reach anywhere near the quality of the latter film.

MGM, which in a single year had "unloaded" itself of Greta Garbo, Norma Shearer, and Joan Crawford, and had "lost" Clark Gable, Mickey Rooney, *et al.* to the Armed Forces, was especially anxious to cement the box-office standing of the new Tracy-Hepburn team.[14] The studio announced that "public demand" had made mandatory another screen matching. *Keeper of the Flame* (1942) was the project, with Tracy making his first feature under George Cukor's direction. The story, gloomy and foreboding, was a change of pace and style for both stars. In fact, with its strong anti-fascist message, it was a sharp departure from the usual Metro product. (Supposedly studio head Louis B. Mayer had been kept in the dark about the film's subject matter, and when he finally viewed the completed picture at Radio City Music Hall, he walked out of the showing in a huff.)

Cukor was noted for fussing over details of a film, a characteristic that Tracy did not admire, as he preferred quick, direct takes. Under Hepburn's steadying influence, however, Cukor and Spencer cooperated well, and the two men developed a fine respect for one another. While helping Tracy realize the motivation[15] of the newsman Steven O'Malley, Cukor also restrained Miss Hepburn from overplaying her role as the purpose-laden widow Christine Forrest. Tracy's friendship with Cukor was to prove a lasting and dependable one.

After completion of *Keeper of the Flame,* Tracy deserted the West Coast and followed Katharine Hepburn to Broadway where she was appearing in *Without Love,* a play written especially for her by Philip Barry, the author of *The Philadelphia Story.* Tracy was seeking a play to bring him back to the theatre, but after several months of haphazard searching, he abandoned the idea for the time being and returned to MGM where he was the undisputed leading mature male star.

After rejecting many parts, Tracy finally accepted *A Guy Named Joe* (1943), to be directed by Victor Fleming and to co-star Irene Dunne. Miss Dunne was delighted at the idea of starring with Tracy and agreed to second billing. She was later, perhaps, to feel less happy about the matter, as during the making of the picture Spencer and Fleming teased her mercilessly. She almost walked out.

Red-headed Van Johnson, who became very popular as a result of this two-hour feature, almost missed his big opportunity when early in the shooting he was in a serious automobile accident. The injuries were so severe that MGM decided to replace him with another actor (perhaps John Hodiak or Peter Lawford) and to reshoot the Johnson scene that had already been lensed. Tracy, however, intervened and insisted that Van be kept in the film and that the studio wait for his recovery. With Tracy's professional clout, MGM was forced to heed his advice. As a result, Van Johnson has always insisted that had it not been for Tracy he might never have had a successful motion picture career. Esther Williams, later to become a big Metro swimming star, had a brief appearance in *A Guy Named Joe.*

Tracy enacted the part of Pete Sandridge, a pilot who is killed when his plane crashes into a Nazi aircraft carrier. He returns (as a spirit) to earth, unobserved by the mortals in the film, and aids his grief-stricken sweetheart (Dunne) into finding happiness with another aviator (Johnson). Tracy's quiet sincerity made the fantasy story seem better than it was. Irene Dunne provided a pleasant note by singing a tender ballad, "I'll Get By." The title of the film is figurative, as there is no character in the picture named Joe.

Given the storyline of Anna Seghers' stark novel *The Seventh Cross,* it was little wonder that the project appealed to Spencer. He plays George Heisler, an anti-Nazi German who escapes from a concentration camp. Tracy manages to survive the brutality of the camp and makes his way to Holland and freedom. It is a tense, suspenseful[16] chase film directed by Fred Zinnemann and with a fine cast including Hume Cronyn, Signe Hasso, and Agnes Moorehead.

In his private life, Tracy spent much time with his growing children in the early 1940s. He regretted that polo was being abandoned by the movie colony. The sport had really never recovered popularity after the untimely death of Will Rogers. On one of

[14]Once Garson Kanin asked Tracy why he demanded first billing in his joint films with Miss Hepburn. "Why not?" said Tracy. Kanin responded, "Well, after all, she's the lady. You're the man. Ladies first?" An incredulous Tracy replied, "This is a movie, chowderhead, not a lifeboat."

[15]Years later when making *Bad Day at Black Rock,* co-player Lee Marvin went up to star Tracy and asked him for help interpreting the motivation, inquiring how Tracy would handle the bit. The superstar replied, "Look, I'm too old, too tired, and too goddamn rich for all this bull. Let's just get on with the scene."

[16]Co-player Signe Hasso would recall of *The Seventh Cross,* "I have seldom played with an actor so engrossed in his role. On the set he was intense and withdrawn, and had little time for chit-chat. During a scene he never went in for frivolous ad-libbing as many actors do. We used to tease him about his complete absorption. He only smiled, pretended to be annoyed, but never bothered to answer back. . . . He is a great coffee drinker—likes nothing better than to have a cup of steaming coffee brought to him on the set. He is a worrier, never satisfied with his work—and an omnivorous reader. One weekend during the picture he completed several books, including one about George M. Cohan. He says it was Cohan who taught him to stress the meaning of the dialogue rather than the mere perfection of words."

his sports outings at the Hollywood Stadium in the early war years, Tracy was heckled by some sailors as a "draft dodger." Spencer, whose hair was now turning gray, was very gloomy after the incident, despite the fact that he had served in the Navy during World War I.

Despite the fact that he had made several films to help the war effort and had sold defense bonds, both in person and over the radio, Spencer still felt guilty about his inactive status in World War II. His friend Pat O'Brien suggested he embark on a U.S.O. tour. Tracy liked the idea and made a trek to Hawaii. He was pleased that the G.I.s liked his act and did not expect him to show great skill in song-and-dance. He was booked for a second U.S.O. tour to Alaska in 1944. On his way to Alaska he was fog-bound in Seattle for several days, and he visited an old friend and roommate from Ripon College, Kenny Edgers, who was now a dentist. Tracy finally became depressed about the weather and decided that the troops could get along without him in Alaska. The star returned to Los Angeles, thus terminating his career as a U.S.O. camp entertainer.

Thirty Seconds over Tokyo (1944) gave Van Johnson his first starring role in a major dramatic film. The picture was based on Captain Ted W. Lawson and Robert Considine's book about the Army Air Force raid on Tokyo led by Lieutenant Colonel James H. Doolittle. Tracy's role as Doolittle was little more than a cameo offering, since Johnson, playing Lawson, had the major part.[17] Mervyn LeRoy, the director, convinced Tracy that he was the actor who could bring dignity to the characterization. Tracy did provide the proper feeling for the part, helping to make it one of the finer films to be produced on World War II.

Without Love (1945) was Spencer's third feature with Katharine Hepburn. It portrayed a lighter side of the war years. The revamped scenario (by Donald Ogden Stewart) makes use of the housing shortage in wartime Washington, D.C., to introduce a comic situation. Tracy is Pat Jamieson, a scientist who rents the home of a young widow (Hepburn) in order to conduct secret government experiments. They enter into a platonic marriage (without love) because he requires an intelligent assistant. Inevitably they fall genuinely in love.

Once again Hepburn and Tracy's timing in the comedy was highly effective. They prepared and rehearsed their scenes in Miss Hepburn's home so perfectly that they scarcely needed any warmup time when they arrived on the soundstage. Harold S. Bucquet, who directed *Without Love,* would remark that Tracy required no direction, but that Miss Hepburn tended to overact. He had to admit that some of Spencer's style "is rubbing off on her." He also noted that the two stars needed no direction from him when they performed a scene together, as they did a thoroughly good job on their own. Lucille Ball, in a major supporting role as a real estate agent, was remarkably good in every scene she graced.

Gradually, during the making of *Without Love,* Spencer Tracy stopped meeting old friends and turned entirely to a new society introduced to him by Kate Hepburn. Miss Hepburn would not agree to meet with the press or engage in publicity schemes to advance her career, but she did have a very definite private life. She knew personally many writers, novelists, poets, and Broadway people. She could even count among her friends some of the most influential people in the American government, including Franklin D. Roosevelt, the President of the United States.

Robert E. Sherwood, advisor and speechwriter for the President, wrote a play entitled *The Rugged Path.* After a dozen years of deliberation and false trials, a nervous Tracy decided to return to the theatre in this project. Sherwood and Tracy conferred in the spring of 1945 to reach an agreement about the drama. Among other things, it was decided that Garson Kanin, Tracy's good friend and chronicler, was to direct the play.

The Sherwood play had Tracy in the role of a journalist serving as a cook on a Navy destroyer during World War II. As Morey Vinion, Spencer was seen as a sensitive, serious individual attempting to find some true meaning in a very disorderly world.

Stage-shy Tracy received fine personal notices during tryout performances of *The Rugged Path* in Providence, Rhode Island and in Washington, D.C., but the play itself received very poor reviews. Tracy, unhappy at having to face a live audience daily, seriously considered abandoning the play on numerous occasions. After much persuasion, especially by gentle but firm Miss Hepburn, he agreed to appear in a limited Broadway run.

It was Spencer's first appearance on Broadway in fifteen years. *The Rugged Path* opened at the Plymouth Theatre on Saturday, November 10, 1945. Critical reaction again brought fine remarks about the star's interpretation, but a poor response for the play in general. Tracy's marquee lure kept it running for eighty-one performances. Spencer played in *The Rugged Path* long enough for his son John to make a trip east to see it. Then the star refused to continue longer in the show. He returned to Hollywood. It was to be his last stage appearance.

[17]Director King Vidor had intended that Tracy and Ingrid Bergman co-star in his epic of American industry, *An American Romance* (1944), but it was Brian Donlevy and Ann Richards who assumed the lead roles.

With Paul Langton (second from left), Louis Jean Heydt, Leon Ames, and Stephen McNally in *30 Seconds over Tokyo* (1944).

With Lana Turner in *Cass Timberlane* (1947).

No Spencer Tracy film was released in 1946, the year that saw the last of the big stars returning from military duty to box-office prominence. In point of fact, Spencer devoted much of the year to working on a film version of Conrad Richter's novel *The Sea of Grass,* a project he long cherished. However, the shooting of the script proved to be an unpleasant, arduous experience. It was directed by Elia Kazan, a man whose style and personality clashed with Tracy's.

After more than a year on the shelf, Metro reluctantly released the expensive *The Sea of Grass.* In the course of its one hundred and thirty-one minutes, the picture focuses on New Mexico cattle baron Colonel James Brewton (Spencer) and his family in the 1880s. Hepburn, at Tracy's demand, had the female lead of Lutie Cameron. The stars were supported by a huge cast including Melvyn Douglas, Harry Carey, and Robert Walker. The heavy script, unfortunately, dragged the whole story down terribly. It would be the least successful of any film made by the Tracy-Hepburn team. It also revealed a much-aged Spencer Tracy.

During the shooting of *The Sea of Grass,* Tracy took a fatherly interest in emotionally troubled Robert Walker. Walker took offense on one occasion because Spencer refused to have a drink with him. It was just one of many unpleasant notes during the production of this prairie saga shot almost entirely on the back lot with costumes by Walter Plunkett.

Cass Timberlane (1947), loosely adapted from Sinclair Lewis' novel by screenwriter Donald Ogden Stewart and several others, was Tracy's choice for his next film vehicle. The film unfortunately turned out to be another soap opera, only this time in modern dress. Tracy has the title role as a wealthy judge who marries a poor girl (Lana Turner) many years younger than he. Tracy suspects (unjustly) that his young wife is being unfaithful to him, believing she is having an affair with suave Zachary Scott. He realizes his mistake only after his spouse suffers a near-fatal illness.

At first Tracy had been genuinely pleased with *Cass Timberlane* as a story, but he was disappointed that neither George Cukor nor Vincente Minnelli could direct it. He settled on George Sidney with much reluctance, and he was never pleased with the film. In spite of this fact, and probably because of stars Tracy and blonde, beautiful Miss Turner, *Cass Timberlane* was a hefty box-office hit. It did reunite Tracy and his old Broadway friend Selena Royale, who had a minor role in the film.

In 1948, Liberty Pictures, a new production unit under the MGM banner, had been formed. Liberty had purchased the screen rights to Howard Lindsay and Russel Crouse's Pulitzer Prize-winning Broadway comedy *State of the Union.* Frank Capra was to direct and Claudette Colbert was to co-star with Tracy. At the last minute, however, Miss Colbert withdrew from the cast. Tracy suggested that Kate Hepburn, who was familiar with the dialogue (she had been coaching Spencer), replace her. She reported for work immediately.

Once again the Tracy-Hepburn team performed with real cinema magic. It was the type of story that veteran director Capra helmed so well. A simple, honest man, Grant Matthews (Spencer), confronts a band of thieves and swindlers. It allowed Tracy to cavort as an honest presidential candidate who retains his integrity and honor throughout a bitter political campaign with the aid of his steadfast wife (Hepburn).

MGM produced Tracy's next feature, *Edward, My Son* (1949), shot in England primarily to utilize frozen currency at the British-Metro studio. Tracy and George Cukor, who directed the film, were house guests of Laurence Olivier and Vivien Leigh during much of the filming, and Katharine Hepburn, too, was on the London scene much of the time.

Edward, My Son was adapted by Donald Ogden Stewart from a popular play co-written by portly British actor Robert Morley. Morley had starred in a successful version of the play both in London and in America. Within the confines of the 112-minute story, Arnold Boult (Spencer) schemes to make his son a success. Arnold commits arson, goads two individuals into committing suicide, and bribes others to earn for his son what he wants for him. Evelyn Boult (Deborah Kerr), his wife, tries to stop her husband, but fails and takes to drink. She later dies. Finally the vain and wayward son (never seen in the film) is killed while showing off to friends. Thereafter Arnold's misdeeds catch up with him and he is led away to prison.

The film was a critical triumph for Deborah Kerr, but for the second time in his long and distinguished film career Tracy was panned by the critics. A major part of the difficulty was Spencer's very American accent and characteristics. Tracy would not attempt to speak in a British accent, feeling, perhaps rightly, that it would not suit him. However, *Edward, My Son* was based firmly on the English social order, particularly the privileged class. Britisher Miss Kerr, Metro's new "threat" to Greer Garson, was, of course, perfectly suited to her role. To make matters worse, Robert Morley's definitive stage interpretation of his own dialogue was still very fresh in the minds of both British and American playgoers and critics. It was Tracy's first artistic reversal since *Dr. Jekyll and Mr. Hyde.*

While Tracy was abroad making *Edward, My Son,* Dore Schary, once an MGM scriptwriter, returned to that studio as "executive in charge of production," a position he recently had held at RKO. Schary submitted to Tracy a World War II story tentatively titled *Operation Malaya.* Tracy was pleased with the story, and James Stewart, who had worked with Spencer in *Murder Man* (1935), agreed to take a co-starring part in the film, too.[18]

Before that, however, Tracy and Hepburn were scheduled to make *Adam's Rib* (1949). Directed by George Cukor, who had helmed *Edward, My Son,* the comedy was destined to be such a fine film that it more than redeemed the cinematic reputations of Tracy and Cukor. Garson Kanin and Ruth Gordon who wrote the scenario for *Adam's Rib* created a splendid, original story ideally suited to their two stars' multi-talents. They also wrote a scenario years ahead of its time. Cukor directed the feature with brilliance and style, and the effervescent stage comedienne Judy Holliday gave a superb performance that paved her way to stardom and an Academy Award. (Actually it was the Kanins' idea to provide Miss Holliday with a showy screen role to convince Harry Cohn at Columbia to cast her in the lead of Kanin's stage hit *Born Yesterday.* The gambit appealed to both Tracy and Hepburn, and they readily agreed to help showcase wise-cracking, dumb-blonde Judy Holliday.)

Adam's Rib, with its mixture of woman's lib and domestic comedy, showed Spencer and Kate in fine form. In the storyline, district attorney Adam Bonner (Spencer) finds himself, to his horror, pitted in court against his attractive lawyer-wife Amanda (Hepburn) who takes the case of Doris Attinger (Holliday) accused of shooting her adulterous husband. The two attorneys take opposite stands on the subject of women's rights. Tracy and Hepburn brought zest and a sense of humor to the daily courtroom procedures as well as to the characters' evening home life. Most critics agreed that it would have been difficult to find a pair of stars better suited to the roles than Spencer and Kate.

On the other hand, *Malaya* (1949), as *Operation Malaya* was finally entitled, proved to be a rather ordinary World War II action drama in spite of an excellent cast headed by Spencer, Stewart, Sydney Greenstreet, John Hodiak, Gilbert Roland, and Lionel Barrymore. It had actually been completed late in 1948, but studio executives were so uncertain of its potential impact that they shelved it until late 1949, after the success of *Adam's Rib* made it seem less risky.

[18]Columbia Pictures had wanted to borrow Spencer for the Oscar-winning role of the corrupt political leader in *All the King's Men* (1949), but it was Broderick Crawford who played the part.

With Deborah Kerr in *Edward, My Son* (1949).

Sheet music from *Adam's Rib* (1949).

In the early 1950s the film industry was shocked by the emergence of the commercial TV business. The mass production of home television sets had begun in earnest in 1948, and by 1950 the movie theatre audience had greatly diminished. Adding to the trouble of the major studios was a Supreme Court decision forcing film companies to divest themselves of theatre chains. These economic reversals had an adverse effect on the studio star system. High-priced performers were a deficit to film companies who had to greatly reduce their yearly output of celluloid products. This, they felt, was definitely the time to find young, new players who would be fresh faces for the public and, more important, be less of a drain on production budgets. The future did not seem very bright for such veterans as Clark Gable, Katharine Hepburn, Spencer Tracy, *et al.* Nevertheless, most of those involved chose to ignore the crisis, at least on the surface and especially in public.

Photographs taken of Tracy in 1950 revealed a stouter, white-haired man. Tracy joked that chocolate candy had broadened him into a character actor. He had certainly matured physically. Inwardly, too, he began to change, spending more time alone, reading and listening to music. Although there were fewer of his old Irish cronies around him now in Hollywood, he still had friends such as the Garson Kanins, George Cukor, David Niven, James Stewart, and, of course, Kate Hepburn. Spencer took up painting in oils, tempera, and watercolor. He painted solely for his own pleasure and would not allow anyone to judge his work. Lionel Barrymore was a rare exception, for, upon request, Tracy gifted the aging actor with one of his landscapes.

Professionally Tracy read and considered a great number of scripts, among them a scenario adapted from Albert Camus' novel *The Plague,* but he approved none of them.[19] Finally, during this year, Dore Schary obtained a comedy script called *Father of the Bride.* It was based on a short novel by Edward Streeter. Frances Goodrich and Albert Hackett had transformed it into an excellent screenplay.

Tracy was cast as Stanley T. Banks, the harassed father in the story.[20] Hepburn might have played the wife, Ellie, but she was preoccupied in New York, having a popular run as Rosalind in *As You Like It.* The role of the understanding, chic spouse went to Joan Bennett, reuniting Tracy with one of his earliest leading ladies. The increasingly popular Elizabeth Taylor was cast as the radiantly beautiful daughter of the couple.

Father of the Bride, directed by Vincente Minnelli, was a satisfying comedy for all. Tracy managed to extract humor from every situation in the film. Released in the spring of 1950, it was an unqualified success. Tracy had made a successful transition from romantic lead to father figure *without* sacrificing any stature as a film star. The role won him his fourth Academy Award nomination. (He lost the Oscar to Jose Ferrer of *Cyrano de Bergerac.*)

[19]Among those projects which never came to fruition were *The Travels of Simon McKeever,* to be based on a short story by Albert Maltz and directed by John Huston, and *Jealousy,* to co-star Tracy with Lana Turner, Deborah Kerr, and another leading lady in a trio of love stories.

[20]Tracy very nearly did not play the part. Jack Benny, hungry for a screen success after so many poor productions, implored Dore Schary for the role of Stanley Banks in *Father of the Bride.* Schary acquiesced, only to learn that staff producer Pandro S. Berman threatened to tear up his contract if Benny were (mis)cast in the assignment. Director Vincente Minnelli, understanding that Benny could not win the part, still had to direct him in a screen audition. Meanwhile, Tracy, who was everyone else's choice for the Banks' characterization, had departed for New York because he felt himself second fiddle to Benny. Eventually feelings were soothed and Tracy returned to Hollywood to begin shooting of the comedy in January of 1950.

Years later director Minnelli would admit, "Spencer was an inspiration. His instincts were infallible. . . . There wasn't a better man at comedy. He wasn't a mugger, at least never in scenes with other actors. The facial contortions came when he was alone and unobserved." Minnelli also recalled directing Tracy in the scene for which Jack Benny had auditioned. ". . . the contrast between the two performances was easily discernible to even the most uneducated eye. Spencer's reading was the essence of comedy, because it was achingly true. . . ."

In the spring of 1951 Katharine Hepburn traveled to London where she stayed at the Claridge Hotel on her way to Africa, leaving Tracy at loose ends in Hollywood. She met Humphrey Bogart and John Huston in Africa where they made the feature *The African Queen.* Tracy, unfortunately, began to drink again while Miss Hepburn was abroad. He was lonely but was also depressed at this time by the "Red Scare" that intimidated Hollywood with its investigations and blacklistings.

In spite of these negative forces, MGM, again with Vincente Minnelli directing, produced a sequel to *Father of the Bride,* entitled *Father's Little Dividend* (1951). It utilized the same cast of principals, including Joan Bennett and Elizabeth Taylor. In this entry Spencer becomes a grandfather and must adjust to the various problems involved. The follow-up was a respectable success with both the critics and the public. However, Tracy rejected the possibility of a continuing series which MGM hoped he would approve.

Father's Little Dividend was better in every possible way than the courtroom drama that Tracy made next. *The People Against O'Hara* (1951) found Tracy portraying James P. Curtayne, a once-famous criminal lawyer whose career is ruined by alcohol. The picture cast Spencer's old school chum Pat O'Brien in a supporting role. James Arness (later to became famous on TV's "Gunsmoke" series) played a young fishmarket employee wrongly accused of murder. *The People Against O'Hara* was Tracy's first film under an MGM completely controlled by Dore Schary. With Louis B. Mayer ousted, Tracy had a new five-year contract calling for ten pictures to be made during that period and for the star to receive three million dollars in salary.

Once again, the combination of George Cukor, Kate Hepburn, and the Kanins came to rescue Tracy's career. The project was *Pat and Mike* (1952). Its splendid satire on the sports world provided the "love team" with roles unlike any they had enacted before. The story provided Hepburn with ample opportunity to demonstrate her athletic prowess as well as her shapely legs. (Woman pro Babe Zaharias coached Tracy for his golf scenes.) The feature is packed with charming comic situations and restored Tracy and Hepburn to the screen as a romantic couple.

Plymouth Adventure (1952), directed by Clarence Brown, was Spencer's first color picture in over a dozen years. This elaborate Metro feature was based on an historical novel by Ernest Gabler about the

With Melville Cooper, Douglas Spencer, Russ Tamblyn, and Carleton Carpenter (rear) in *Father of the Bride* (1950).

In *The Actress* (1953).

long and dangerous sea voyage to Plymouth Rock aboard the Mayflower in the early seventeenth century. Tracy was asked to portray the unsympathetic character of Captain Jones, in charge of the journey, who despises his passengers and unwittingly causes the death of one woman (Gene Tierney) by drowning. This tragedy reforms the staunch captain and he turns to helping the colonists when they reach the New World. The star-studded cast, which included Van Johnson and Leo Genn, could do little with the material. Director Brown announced his retirement shortly after the picture was completed.

Thankfully, *The Actress* (1953) was a far more rewarding venture for Tracy and all concerned. It was based on a scenario derived from Ruth Gordon's autobiographical play *Years Ago.* As directed by George Cukor, *The Actress* recounts Miss Gordon's girlhood and domestic problems in pre-World War I New England. Tracy and Teresa Wright (replacing Kate Hepburn) are the parents, with Jean Simmons in the title role and lanky Anthony Perkins as her shy beau. Tracy offers a splendid characterization as a gruff retired sea captain who at first attempts to discourage his willful daughter's theatrical inclinations. Later he lets her go to New York, to Broadway, bestowing on her his blessings. While not a box-office success, *The Actress* remains a fine piece of Americana and a minor film classic.

By this point, Tracy had started to become disenchanted with the new MGM regime. He negotiated a revamped contract that would permit him to make one picture a year away from the studio, and one picture a year for MGM. Tracy never regretted this action which reduced to half his annual salary guarantee. It was the beginning of the end of Tracy's long MGM tenure.

There were also changes in Tracy's personal life. His son, John, had overcome many of his handicaps. After graduating from college with honors, he married and worked as an artist with the Walt Disney studios. In 1952 John and his wife had a child, Tracy's first grandson. Joseph Spencer Tracy was normal in every respect. The event was a great elixir for the film star.[21]

After completion of *The Actress,* more than a year passed without Tracy working on any film projects.

[21]In 1980, it was reported that John Tracy, now nearly deaf and suffering from bad vision, was living an extremely private life, cared for by his aged mother and unmarried sister. His marriage has long since been terminated and his son, a former Marine, resides in the greater Los Angeles area, employed in maintenance work.

He vetoed the notion of trying the new medium of television or of returning to the stage. He was attracted to Ernest Hemingway's Pulitzer Prize-winning novelette *The Old Man and the Sea,* but MGM was not interested in filming it. When Leland Hayward, an independent producer, obtained the screen rights, Tracy readily agreed to star in a film version of it at some time in the future.

With nothing materializing at Culver City, Spencer negotiated and signed to star in a 20th Century-Fox Western entitled *Broken Lance* (1954). It was a high-priced, CinemaScope color reworking of the studio's *House of Strangers* (1949), which had starred Edward G. Robinson in an urban setting. In the new edition, Spencer was Matt Devereaux, a lawless cattle baron hated by his sons of his first marriage and adored by the half-breed offspring (Robert Wagner) of his second marriage. The demanding role was a physical drain on the aging star, but he performed the hazardous horseback riding scenes himself and enjoyed making the film.

Good fortune seemed to run in pairs for Tracy and now he was anxious to return to MGM to star in the offbeat *Bad Day at Black Rock* (1955), to be directed by John Sturges. The morality-laden action-drama finds Spencer as the one-armed John J. Macreedy who arrives in Black Rock to present a posthumous medal to the father of a Japanese-American soldier. He finds that the man has been murdered by bigoted members of the rural community. Although Tracy balked at the location filming of the story, he admired the director and tolerated the cast.

Somewhat similar to Gary Cooper's *High Noon* (1952) in subject matter, most critics today consider *Bad Day at Black Rock* the better picture. It won for Tracy another Oscar nomination, but he lost to Ernest Borgnine for his role in *Marty.*

Having revived Tracy's box-office standing, MGM next hoped to star him in *Tribute to a Bad Man.*[22] However, he considered the storyline too similar (and inferior) to *Broken Lance.* Moreover, he did not feel up to another difficult location project. Tracy began the project, but he appeared on the set late and was cantankerous to say the least. Director Robert Wise and Tracy had no rapport. The star soon was demanding that the film be shot in less rugged locale than the one selected in the Rocky Mountains near Montrose, Colorado. Wise refused and the actor's mood turned ugly. After much disagreement, Wise fired Tracy and replaced him with James Cagney.

At fifty-five years of age, Spencer Tracy broke with MGM. Hollywood gossip had it that he was old, sick, and washed up, even though he was named Best Actor at the 1955 Cannes Film Festival (for *Bad Day at Black Rock*). He spent most of his personal time with Katharine Hepburn and her circle of friends. He continued to devote some of his hours to his children, but he refused to discuss his family or personal life with reporters. His son was now a successful artist with Disney Studios, and his daughter, Susie, was an accomplished musician studying voice.

After much script reading, Tracy found a story, *The Mountain,* which he and director Edward Dmytryk persuaded Paramount to produce and distribute. Ironically, the location selection for the film was near Chamonix, France, an even more rugged locale than MGM had picked for *Tribute to a Bad Man.*

Paramount shot *The Mountain* (1956) in color and in VistaVision. The story centered around an ascent of Mont Blanc. In the story, Tracy and Robert Wagner were brothers. Tracy is a very honorable man, while his younger brother, Wagner, is a corrupt one. Wagner decides to climb Mont Blanc to plunder the wreckage of a plane that has crashed into the mountain. Spencer makes the dangerous climb with him. When they reached their objective, Tracy rescues a woman (Anna Kashfi) who has survived the crash, while Wagner tumbles to his death.

Location shooting was a three-month physical ordeal. Spencer suffered because of the altitude, and he was worn out by the taxing gymnastics of the role. However, according to his logic, he felt he should not be complaining as he was being well paid ($200,000 plus a percentage) for his part, *and* he had personally selected the property. During the lensing of the color feature there were many anxious moments—none worse than when Tracy, Wagner, and some crewmen were trapped in a stalled cable car perched twelve thousand feet from the ground. In the end, everyone involved wondered whether it had been worth it. The expensively mounted *The Mountain* aroused little admiration from either the critics or the public.

Undaunted, like fellow veteran Clark Gable who had also left MGM, Tracy was not prepared to call it quits. In fact, he was prepared to try another tiring location project. This time, in the summer of 1956, he began production of Ernest Hemingway's *The Old Man and the Sea* on location in Cuba. It was to be a major film and received vast publicity. Serious production problems were caused by poor weather and conflicts between producer Leland Hayward and director Fred Zinnemann over the script. Continued inclement weather and story conflicts forced Hayward to halt the filming. A decision was made to

[22]MGM producer John Houseman wanted to star Spencer Tracy in *Bannon* (1955), the story of an aging, tough labor leader, with William Holden or Montgomery Clift as a younger rival. The project never materialized.

postpone the project and to resume work on it at Warner Bros. studio at a later day, using an artificial "ocean"—a tank containing hundreds of gallons of water. The shut-down left Tracy free to accept an interim film assignment.

Twentieth Century-Fox offered Tracy what would prove to be his final romantic role. It was the lead opposite Katharine Hepburn in the movie version of *The Desk Set,* the Broadway comedy that had been so popular with Shirley Booth in the lead. In the revamped cinema version simply entitled *Desk Set,* gussied up with color and CinemaScope, Hepburn plays Bunny Watson, the erudite head of a TV company's research department. Tracy is Richard Sumner, the efficiency expert called in, Bunny thinks, to replace her brainy office staff with a know-it-all computer. It was a pleasant comedy as directed by Walter Lang, but less of a success than the Kanins' romps for the star team. The pair were ably helped by an excellent cast, including Gig Young, Joan Blondell, Dina Merrill, and Neva Patterson. Although it was only a modest success, it helped Tracy regain his composure and prepare for his continued assignment in *The Old Man and the Sea.*

When he had returned to California to make *Desk Set,* Spencer had learned of Humphrey Bogart's cancer. Thereafter Tracy and Hepburn regularly called upon Bogart and his actress wife Lauren Bacall. Tracy and Kate had their final visit with Bogie on a Saturday evening in January 1957. When they departed, after realizing that Humphrey was desperately ill, Tracy said he was sure that Bogie was dying. Bogart fell into a coma the next day and passed away the following Monday morning. The old order in Hollywood was fast disappearing.

An aging Tracy returned to the production of *The Old Man and the Sea* (1958). Warner Bros. had completed their huge sound stage tank and constructed the large rubber mechanical fish, but there were continued delays and a serious rift with writer Ernest Hemingway. John Sturges replaced Zinnemann as the official director of the project. In the storyline of this modern parable, Tracy is a poor Cuban fisherman who has not caught a fish in months. His luck changes and he manages to snare a huge marlin, only to see it devoured by sharks before he can bring it to shore.

During the production, Tracy lost a good deal of his enthusiasm for the long-delayed project. The filming took almost two years to complete and it cost an estimated six million dollars. For all its expense and trouble, it was not a commercial success. Many thought that the film suffered from too many shots of Tracy alone in his boat with little or no action or dialogue. Hemingway did not help the future of the film by remarking that in his opinion Tracy looked like "a rich, fat actor" rather than a poor fisherman. Nevertheless, Spencer did receive some favorable press notices, and he was nominated once again for an Oscar. (This time David Niven of *Separate Tables* was the winner.) Ironically, while *The Old Man and the Sea* failed theatrically, today on the home TV screen the film shows to great advantage in smaller scale. It can now be appreciated more for what it was originally intended to be.

John Ford, who had guided Tracy through his first film (*Up the River,* 1930) came to Spencer's professional rescue. He offered him the lead in *The Last Hurrah* (1958), to be produced by Columbia Pictures. The screenplay by ex-*New York Times* film critic Frank Nugent was derived from Edwin O'Connor's best-selling novel. The inspiration for *The Last Hurrah* came from the life of Boston's mayor James M. Curley. Tracy plays Frank Skeffington, a friendly Irish-American political boss who is mayor of an unspecified New England metropolis. He has a band of loyal cronies (including Pat O'Brien and James Gleason) and is loved by the mass of its people. However, he also has enemies, a powerful newspaper publisher among them. He is defeated in a hotly contested political campaign and shortly thereafter dies of a heart attack.

Critics and public alike received *The Last Hurrah* with enthusiasm. Tracy instilled a great deal of character and charm into the role as the aging, stubborn Irish-American politician.

Just as Katharine Hepburn, George Cukor, and the Garson Kanins[23] were so vital to Spencer's film career in the 1940s, so Stanley Kramer proved vital in extending Tracy's cinema life in the 1960s. The association with the producer/director began with *Inherit the Wind* (United Artists, 1960). It was one of the most rewarding relationships of his lengthy filmmaking years. In this black-and-white project he was teamed with Fredric March, another "actor's actor," in the film version of the Jerome Lawrence-Robert E. Lee stage play, based on the 1925 Scopes "monkey" trial in Dayton, Tennessee. Tracy and March played thinly disguised versions of Clarence Darrow and William Jennings Bryan respectively, the defender and prosecutor of a high school biology teacher accused of teaching Darwin's theory of evolution in a hostile Bible-belt, American rural community.

[23]In 1959 Kanin wrote a script entitled *Big Deal* which would co-star Spencer with Sophia Loren. Yet even with a budget reduced from two to under one million dollars, and Kanin agreeing to defer his directing fee, no Hollywood studio felt that the project was marketable. Tracy turned down the role of the Judge in Otto Preminger's *Anatomy of a Murder* (1959); he thought the part too secondary. Real-life judge Joseph Welch was substituted.

With Robert Ryan in *Bad Day at Black Rock* (1954).

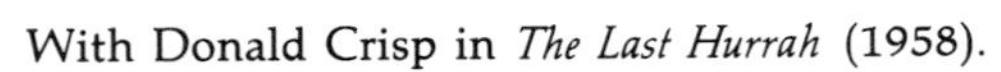

With Donald Crisp in *The Last Hurrah* (1958).

With Marlene Dietrich in *Judgment at Nuremberg* (1961).

With Jean-Pierre Aumont and Alexander Scourby in *The Devil at 4 O'Clock* (1961).

Tracy and March had a joyous time trying to outdo one another before the camera. At first there were occasions when Tracy seemed to be trying Kramer's patience, but he finally responded to the director's style with complete cooperation. Spencer became convinced that Kramer was more interested in artistic results than in box-office profits. He came to believe that Kramer was among his best directors, and he was proud of the fact that over the years he had had the best.

March gave a showy, strutting, brilliant performance, while Spencer held himself in reserve and allowed his character quietly to grow in effect. The two veteran stars made the film courtroom battle one of the more rewarding acting experiences in cinema history. For his diligence, Tracy was awarded with yet another Oscar bid, losing out this round to Burt Lancaster *(Elmer Gantry).*

Tracy was so impressed with Kramer's talents that he agreed to a part in Kramer's next project, the road-show production of *Judgment at Nuremberg* (United Artists 1961). Before he could undertake that, however, he had a commitment to make *The Devil at 4 O'Clock* (Columbia, 1961). In this enterprise he was linked with Frank Sinatra, certainly an opposing style of actor. Tracy played Father Matthew Doonon, an aging, alcoholic clergyman on an isolated island in the South Pacific. He is to be replaced by a younger priest (Kerwin Mathews). The Mervyn LeRoy-directed picture was shot largely on location in Hawaii. Kate Hepburn joined the island-bound cast and crew to keep Spencer in a more docile mood. For all the talent involved, *The Devil at 4 'Clock* never gained momentum and emerged as a lacklustre, unbelievable outing. Even the climactic volcano and earthquake had a look of artificiality about them.

On the other hand, Tracy believed that *Judgment at Nuremberg* was the best script he had been offered in many years. This second film he made with Stanley Kramer was an all-star affair, including Tracy, Burt Lancaster, Richard Widmark, Marlene Dietrich, Maximilian Schell, Judy Garland, and Montgomery Clift. The script derived from Abby Mann's award-winning television drama and required a good deal of location filming in Berlin. In the 189-minute drama Spencer played Dan Haywood, a retired U.S. judge assigned in 1948 to head a tribunal in Germany against four leading Nazis accused of major crimes during the Hitler regime of terror. After a long, complex trial, the quartet are found guilty and given life sentences, but with the implication that none will serve longer than seven years.

Tracy attended the world premiere of the picture held in Berlin in December 1961, joining in the festivities with co-stars Judy Garland and Maximilian Schell. It was his last ceremonial film function. Tracy, Schell, Clift, and Judy Garland were all nominated for Oscars, but only Schell was victorious. Spencer is said to have winced visibly when Schell was reported to have referred to Tracy as "that grand old man of motion pictures."

Spencer then was off the screen for two years and returned for only a voice-over narration in *How the West Was Won* (1963), the sprawling Cinerama study of pioneer Americans shot at MGM. The film was of little importance to Tracy's acting career. However, it did serve to heal some wounds that were festering between the actor and his former studio.

Bowing to Stanley Kramer's gentle persuasion, the frequently ill Tracy agreed to take a lead role in *It's a Mad, Mad, Mad, Mad World* (United Artists, 1963). Spencer could not resist the opportunity ot working with so many outstanding American comedians, including Jimmy Durante, Buster Keaton, Phil Silvers, Buddy Hackett, Jonathan Winters, Ben Blue, Milton Berle, and Jack Benny, to name but a few.

While making the arduous Cinerama slapstick comedy in color, Tracy was pale and exceedingly feeble looking. He could barely cope with the heat of the desert shooting location. Kramer kindly provided him with very brief working days and made as few physical demands on him as possible. In a way, Tracy thrived in spite of poor health and arduous working conditions. He loved the cast and they all greatly admired him. Many people assumed that the star still drank a lot, but, as a matter of fact, he was only consuming a single glass of beer a day.

The plot of *It's a Mad, Mad, Mad, Mad World* is thin, especially for a 190-minute marathon chase outing. While there were many hilarious scenes, there was an overriding acrid theme of man's essential greed. The plot focused on crafty police captain C. G. Culpepper (Spencer) who is determined to outwit various money-mad citizens who are out to beat each other in discovering the hiding place of a cache of three hundred and fifty thousand dollars. Despite all, and thanks to cagey exploitation, the film grossed over $20.7 million in U.S. and Canadian distributors' rentals.

One day in June 1963, Tracy undertook his customary drive to Miss Hepburn's rented beach house at Malibu. They had planned a picnic. Shortly after his arrival he found it difficult to breathe. Kate phoned the Zuma Beach fire department, and a rescue unit arrived in time to administer a saving dose of oxygen. Meanwhile, Miss Hepburn telephoned Tracy's wife and his brother Carroll.

Tracy was hospitalized for two weeks, and then he returned to the vine-covered cottage he was now renting on George Cukor's estate. Miss Hepburn rented a hilltop cottage nearby in Beverly Hills to be close to him.

Several film projects were offered to him, including John Ford's final Western, *Cheyenne Autumn,* late in 1963. Spencer was too ill and weak to appear in even a cameo part and so the role of Secretary of the Interior was filled by Edward G. Robinson.

Almost a year later Tracy felt strong enough to return to picture-making, and he was fond of the script for *The Cincinnati Kid* (MGM, 1965). It was the tale of an old poker player challenging a younger pro to a championship game. The announcement was made that Tracy would co-star in the film with Steve McQueen. The elder star was elated throughout preproduction. But when the time arrived to start filming, his doctors advised him against tackling the meaty assignment. Edward G. Robinson, his *Cheyenne Autumn* replacement, picked up another good role originally intended for Tracy.

When Stanley Kramer acquired the movie rights to Katherine Anne Porter's best-selling novel *Ship of Fools,* the producer/director hoped that Spencer would be well enough to play Dr. Schumann, the ship's physician, with Kate Hepburn as Mary Treadwell. However, Tracy's health was too precarious to allow the notion to proceed beyond a notion, and eventually it was Oskar Werner and Vivien Leigh who assumed the leads. Nevertheless, Tracy was a regular guest at Columbia Pictures on the sound stage of *Ship of Fools* (1965), calling himself, in jest, a "special advisor" to Mr. Kramer. He boasted that he was taking an apprenticeship as a director. During the production he befriended Oskar Werner and also renewed a long-standing acquaintanceship with Vivien Leigh.

In September 1965, sixty-five-year-old Spencer became seriously ill again. His ailment was diagnosed as an inflamed prostate gland. The necessary operation was a difficult ordeal for the already weakened celebrity. Once again Katharine Hepburn and Louise Tracy kept vigil on alternate day and night shifts at his bedside. For six weeks Tracy was in great danger and pain. Gradually he recovered and went home to his cottage, secluded on the George Cukor estate.

Here he lived very quietly. He was virtually inactive for almost two years, just narrating a thirty-minute color film short entitled *The Ripon College Story.* Although he had never done any video work, he became interested in a series of six historical specials projected by David Wolper called *The Red, White and Blue* and agreed to host them. ABC-TV wanted Tracy for a network project, but not for this series. The deal came to nothing.

Thereafter, Tracy went into near total seclusion. He had a few visitors. His brother Carroll and Stanley Kramer came to see him often, as did Kate Hepburn and Tracy's children, but his telephone number was kept a secret. George Cukor paid a Hungarian couple in his employ to look after Tracy's simple housekeeping needs.

Gradually he recovered strength, and from time to time the pale, white-haired Tracy could be seen visiting his wife Louise in her home near Pickfair. More often he took quiet, gentle walks with Katharine Hepburn. On warm, breezy days, they often flew kites.

Although he seldom went out, Tracy did not want to be forgotten. George Cukor noted that he liked to be asked to functions even though he did not attend them. He had an amazing curiosity about the goings-on in Hollywood. When he was asked to attend the wedding of Mia Farrow and Frank Sinatra he had no immediate thought of accepting, but the notion tickled his fancy. He vacillated back and forth. Finally he did make an appearance at the wedding reception.

In October 1966, Stanley Kramer made the startling announcement that Tracy, Hepburn, and Sidney Poitier would be cast in his next Columbia feature, *Guess Who's Coming to Dinner* (1967). The story had been written for Kramer by Britisher William Rose, who with his wife Tania had scripted the slapstick *It's a Mad, Mad, Mad, Mad World.* Rose had originally set the storyline in England. It was based on the idea of a young daughter of socialite parents falling in love with a handsome, intelligent black man. Kramer, who had made other pictures dealing with racial problems, was intrigued by Rose's plot concept.

The film was to be a comeback for both Tracy and Hepburn. She had not made a picture for nearly four years, having devoted much of her time to helping care for the ailing Tracy.

Hollywood was convinced that frail and aging Tracy would bow out again as he had done with *The Cincinnati Kid.* Kramer, Hepburn, and Columbia Pictures had great difficulty in locating insurance companies to cover Tracy's life during the weeks of filming.

The final script was ready on February 15, 1967. Four days later, almost on the eve of the beginning of the color production, Spencer suffered another attack of lung congestion. The local fire rescue squad was summoned to his house and they administered oxygen. Now the film community was sure that Tracy would have to drop out of the project. Gossip even had it that this would be the first film to co-star Kate Hepburn and Edward G. Robinson.

However, a few days later, Tracy had sufficiently

recovered to think sensibly about the future of the picture. He told Kramer that he doubted that he was physically capable of continuing. The producer/director assured his friend that he did not have to go through with the commitment. Suddenly Tracy glanced at Kramer and smiled, "Let's go!" There was a brief press conference at which Tracy officially declared that this was to be his final film appearance.

Kramer and the stars (Tracy, Hepburn, and Poitier) began filming the project on February 19, 1967. Katharine Houghton, Katharine Hepburn's niece, was signed to play with the star trio. It was her first feature film role and she was to play Joey Drayton, the daughter. The big question remaining was Tracy's health. Rumors kept circulating that he was fatally ill, near death, and that he might not even start the picture, much less complete it.

Kramer believed that Tracy had a great desire to complete this picture. He knew, too, that much of the actor's strength would depend upon Miss Hepburn's morale and support. He realized that both leads liked the story, and he knew that the starring pair were very selective about the screenplays they accepted.

A ten-week production schedule was established by Kramer. With Hepburn's loyalty and Tracy's determination, the producer/director was ready to proceed, despite the great financial risk if the project should not be completed. As light as possible a shooting schedule was arranged for Spencer, usually requiring him to be on the set for only half a day of filming. Kramer felt that Tracy actually looked younger and moved with more vigor than he had years before in *It's a Mad, Mad, Mad, Mad World.* Miss Hepburn was constantly by Spencer's side, encouraging him. Their response to one another bordered on the incredible.

The feature, which the public and critics now regard as dated, was actually quite courageous for its time, and should be viewed in the light of its day as a basically liberal and enlightened attempt to cope with an ugly racial situation. Within the 108-minute drama, Tracy plays his role with a quiet dignity that made the role of the newspaper publisher father quite understandable.

In the final scene Tracy turns to Hepburn and tells her how he has loved her for twenty-six years. The moment is almost too much to bear. It is particularly poignant when one realizes that it is the last speech, literally, of a great actor talking to the woman who has meant so much to him and who had been such a strong support to him in his own real life.

The climax of the picture demonstrated the well-known strength of Tracy's acting. The sequence centered around a speech of over a thousand words, bringing the black and the white families to an understanding. Columbia Pictures would have been content with just Tracy's presence. Instead he delivered a near-perfect performance rich in understatement and skill.

Production ended on Saturday, May 26, 1967, with much emotion. Tracy declared that the film was finished. There was a party to celebrate the wrapup of the project, but Tracy, exhausted and worn out, refused to attend. He feared that he might show his full range of emotion at his professional farewell. Miss Hepburn did attend, and she did rise to speak to the assembled crew and cast to thank them for their loyalty and support. At the get-together, Kramer paid a tribute to Tracy, calling him "the greatest of all motion picture personalities."

While the cast and crew were applauding, Spencer Tracy retired to his cottage to rest. He called Garson Kanin to tell him that he had completed the picture and that he was very happy and very, very tired.

Two weeks later, Spencer Tracy was no more. On Saturday, June 10, 1967, he died. Although his demise was expected, it was a shock to all who were close to him and to millions of people throughout the world who had admired him. The official cause of death was heart failure.

Louise, John, and Susie Tracy arrived at the cottage shortly after Carroll Tracy. George Cukor notified Katharine Hepburn, and they arrived together afterward.

A requiem low Mass was said at the Immaculate Heart of Mary Roman Catholic Church in Hollywood. The celebrant of the Mass was Monsignor John O'Donnell, Tracy's technical advisor on *Boys Town.* The eight pallbearers were George Cukor, John Ford, Garson Kanin, Stanley Kramer, (agent) Abe Lastfogel, (actor/producer) William Self, James Stewart, and Frank Sinatra. George Murphy was among the ushers. The funeral was attended by over six hundred mourners, and the burial was at Forest Lawn Cemetery.

Katharine Hepburn did not attend the funeral. She graciously paid her respects to Mrs. Tracy and soon departed for Connecticut to visit her family and friends. Her absence from the funeral was conspicuous, but less so than would have been her presence. She would return later to spend some time in Tracy's cottage on the Cukor estate.

The last will and testament of Spencer Tracy was direct and uncomplicated. His estate, listed at "more than $500,000," was willed to his wife and children. Some of his personal effects were bequeathed to his brother Carroll, including his cars and paintings.

Guess Who's Coming to Dinner, which went on to gross more than $25.5 million in distributors' domestic rentals, received nine Academy Award nominations in the Oscar sweepstakes in the spring of

1968. Tracy received a posthumous bid for his performance, but lost the Oscar to Rod Steiger *(In the Heat of the Night).* However, Miss Hepburn won her second Academy Award as Best Actress. She was out of the country at the time, but when informed of her win she expressed her thanks to the Academy and said that she considered it a joint award for herself and Spencer.

In his biography *Spencer Tracy* (1969), author Larry Swindell offers a fine tribute to the late star: "Historically, Tracy was really the first modern actor on the screen. He was studied and copied by younger actors. He was an influence on styles as different as Montgomery Clift's and Steve McQueen's. Yet no other actor could duplicate Tracy in voice, movement, or sheer personality. James Cagney said, 'There was only one Garbo, and there's only one Tracy. Do you notice how mimics and comedians are always imitating me and other actors? Well, nobody imitates Tracy. Nobody can. What other actor can you say that about?' "

Tracy's death deprived the screen of one of its most gifted players, and an era was ended.

On the set of *Guess Who's Coming to Dinner* (1967) with Katharine Hepburn.

FILMOGRAPHY

UP THE RIVER
(Fox, 1930) 92 min.

DIRECTOR: John Ford
SCREENPLAY: Maurine Watkins, (both uncredited) Ford and William Collier, Sr.
SOUND: W. W. Lindsay, Jr.
CAMERA: Joseph August
EDITOR: Frank Hull

Spencer Tracy *(St. Louis);* Warren Hymer *(Dannemoera Dan);* Humphrey Bogart *(Steve);* Claire Luce *(Judy);* Joan Lawes *(Jean);* Sharon Lynn *(Edith La Verne);* George MacFarlane *(Jessup);* Gaylord "Steve" Pendleton *(Morris);* Morgan Wallace *(Frosby);* William Collier, Sr. *(Pop);* Robert E. O'Connor *(Guard);* Louise Mackintosh *(Mrs. Massey);* Edythe Chapman *(Mrs. Jordan);* Johnny Walker *(Happy);* Noel Francis *(Sophie);* Mildred Vincent *(Annie);* Mack Clark *(Whitelay);* Goodee Montgomery *(Kit);* Althea Henley *(Cynthia);* Carol Wines *(Daisy Elmore);* Adele Windsor *(Minnie);* Richard Keene *(Dick);* Elizabeth and Helen Keating *(May and June);* Robert Burns *(Slim);* John Swor *(Clem);* Pat Somerset *(Beauchamp);* Joe Brown *(Deputy Warden);* Harvey Clark *(Nash);* Black and Blue *(Slim and Klem);* and: Robert Parrish.

QUICK MILLIONS
(Fox, 1931) 72 min.

DIRECTOR: Rowland Brown
STORY/SCREENPLAY: Courtney Terrett, Brown
DIALOGUE: Terrett, Brown, John Wray
ART DIRECTOR: Duncan Cramer
COSTUMES: Sophie Wachner
SOUND: W. W. Lindsay, Jr.
CAMERA: Joseph August

Spencer Tracy *(Bugs Raymond);* Marguerite Churchill *(Dorothy Stone);* Sally Eilers *(Daisy de Lisle);* Robert Burns *(Arkansas Smith);* John Wray *(Kenneth Stone)* Warner Richmond *(Nails Markey);* George Raft *(Jimmy Kirk);* John Swor *(Contractor).*

SIX CYLINDER LOVE
(Fox, 1931) 79 min.

DIRECTOR: Thornton Freeland
BASED ON THE PLAY BY WILLIAM ANTHONY MCGUIRE
SCREENPLAY: William Conselman, Norman Houston
SOUND: Albert Protzman
CAMERA: Ernest Palmer
EDITOR: J. Edwin Robbins

Spencer Tracy *(William Donroy);* Edward Everett Horton *(Monty Winston);* Sidney Fox *(Marilyn Sterling);* William Collier, Sr. *(Richard Burton);* Una Merkel *(Margaret Rogers);* Lorin Raker *(Gilbert Sterling);* William Holden *(Stapleton);* Ruth Warren *(Mrs. Burton);* Bert Roach *(Harold Rogers);* El Brendel *(Janitor).*

GOLDIE
(Fox, 1931) 68 min.

DIRECTOR: Benjamin Stoloff
SCREENPLAY: Gene Towne, Paul Perez
CAMERA: Ernest Palmer
EDITOR: Alex Troffey

Spencer Tracy *(Bill);* Warren Hymer *(Spike);* Jean Harlow *(Goldie);* Jess DeVorska *(Gonzales);* Leila Karnelly *(Wife);* Ivan Linow *(Husband);* Lina Basquette *(Constantina);* Eleanor Hunt *(Russian Girl);* Maria Alba *(Dolores);* Eddie Kane *(Barker);* George Raft *(Man in Crowd).*

SHE WANTED A MILLIONAIRE
(Fox, 1932) 80 min.

DIRECTOR: John Blystone
STORY: Sonya Levien
SCREENPLAY: William A. McGuire
MUSIC DIRECTOR: George Lipschultz
DIALOGUE DIRECTOR: William Collier, Sr.
SOUND: C. Clayton Ward
CAMERA: John Seitz
EDITOR: Ralph Dixon

Joan Bennett *(Jane Miller);* Spencer Tracy *(William Kelley);* Una Merkel *(Mary Taylor);* James Kirkwood *(Roger Norton);* Dorothy Peterson *(Mrs. Miller);* Douglas Cosgrove *(Mr. Miller);* Donald Dillaway *(Humphrey);* Lucille LaVerne *(Mother Norton),* Tetsu Komai *(Charlie).*

SKY DEVILS
(United Artists, 1932) 90 min.

PRODUCER: Howard Hughes
DIRECTOR: Edward Sutherland
STORY/SCREENPLAY: Joseph Moncure March, Sutherland
DIALOGUE: Robert Benchley, March James Starr, Carroll Graham, Garrett Graham
MUSIC: Alfred Newman
SOUND: William Fox
CAMERA: Tony Gaudio

Spencer Tracy *(Wilkie);* William "Stage" Boyd *(Sergeant Hogan);* George Cooper *(Mitchell);* Ann Dvorak *(Mary);* Billy Bevan *(Colonel);* Yola D'Avril *(Fifi);* Forrester Harvey *(Innkeeper);* William B. Davidson *(Captain);* Jerry Miley *(Lieutenant).*

DISORDERLY CONDUCT
(Fox, 1932) 82 min.

DIRECTOR: John W. Considine, Jr.
STORY/SCREENPLAY: William Anthony McGuire
ART DIRECTOR: Duncan Cramer
COSTUMES: Guy S. Duty
CAMERA: Ray June

Sally Eilers *(Phyllis Crawford);* Spencer Tracy *(Dick Fay);* El Brendel *(Olsen);* Dickie Moore *(Jimmy);* Ralph Bellamy *(Tom Manning);* Ralph Morgan *(James Crawford);* Allan Dinehart *(Fletcher);* Claire Maynard *(Lunchroom Girl);* Frank Conroy *(Tony Alsotto);* Cornelius Keefe *(Stallings);* Nora Lane *(Gwen Fiske);* Geneva Mitchell *(Phoebe Darnton);* Charles Grapewin *(Limpy);* James Todd *(Perce Manners);* Sally Blane *(Helen Burke).*

YOUNG AMERICA
(Fox, 1932) 70 min.

DIRECTOR: Frank Borzage
BASED ON THE PLAY BY JOHN FREDERICK BALLARD
SCREENPLAY: William Conselman
ASSISTANT DIRECTOR: Lew Borzage
MUSIC DIRECTOR: George Lipschultz
SOUND: Eugene Grossman
CAMERA: George Schneiderman

Spencer Tracy *(Jack Doray);* Doris Kenyon *(Edith Doray);* Tommy Conlon *(Arthur Simpson);* Ralph Bellamy *(Judge Blake);* Beryl Mercer *(Grandma Beamish);* Sarah Padden *(Mrs. Taylor);* Robert Homans *(Patrolman Weems);* Raymond Borzage *(Nutty);* Dawn O'Day [*Anne Shirley*] *(Mabel Saunders);* Betty Jane Graham *(Cassie Taylor);* Louise Beavers *(Maid);* Spec O'Donnell *(Bull Butler).*

SOCIETY GIRL
(Fox, 1932) 67 min.

DIRECTOR: Sidney Lanfield
BASED ON THE PLAY BY JOHN LARKIN, JR.
SCREENPLAY: Elmer Harris
MUSIC DIRECTOR: George Lipschultz
ART DIRECTOR: Gordon Wiles
SOUND: W. W. Lindsay, Jr.
CAMERA: George Barnes
EDITOR: Margaret Clancy

James Dunn *(Johnny Malone);* Peggy Shannon *(Judy Gelett);* Spencer Tracy *(Briscoe);* Walter Byron *(Warburton);* Bert Hanlon *(Curley);* Marjorie Gateson *(Alice Converse);* Eula Guy Todd *(Miss Halloway).*

PAINTED WOMAN
(Fox, 1932) 73 min.

DIRECTOR: John Blystone
BASED ON THE PLAY BY ALFRED C. KENNEDY
SCREENPLAY: Guy Bolton, Leon Gordon
MUSIC DIRECTOR: George Lipschultz

MUSIC: Arthur Lange, Hugo Friedhofer
SOUND: Eugene Grossman
CAMERA: Ernest Palmer
EDITOR: Alex Troffey

Spencer Tracy *(Tom Brian);* Peggy Shannon *(Kiddo);* William "Stage" Boyd *(Captain Boynton);* Irving Pichel *(Robert Dunn);* Raul Roulien *(Jim);* Murray Kinnell *(Collins);* Laska Winter *(Tia);* Chris-Pin Martin *(Marquette);* Paul Porcasi *(Machado);* Stanley Fields *(Yank);* Wade Boteler *(Lefty);* Jack Kennedy *(Mack);* Dewey Robinson *(Bouncer).*

ME AND MY GAL
(Fox, 1932) 79 min.

DIRECTOR: Raoul Walsh
STORY: Barry Connors, Philip Klein
SCREENPLAY: Arthur Kober
ASSISTANT DIRECTOR: Horace Hough
ART DIRECTOR: Gordon Wiles
SOUND: George Leverett
CAMERA: Arthur Miller

Spencer Tracy *(Dan Dolan);* Joan Bennett *(Helen Reilly);* Marion Burns *(Kate Reilly);* George Walsh *(Duke Castege);* J. Farrell MacDonald *(Pop Reilly);* Noel Madison *(Baby Face Castenega);* Henry B. Walthall *(Sergeant Collins);* Bert Hanlon *(Jake, the Tailor);* Adrian Morris *(Detective Al Allen);* George Chandler *(Eddie Collins);* Will Stanton *(Drunken Fisherman);* Frank Moran *(Frank, a Dock Worker Wedding Guest);* Roger Imhof *(Down and Outer);* Pat Moriarty *(Priest);* Billy Bevan *(Ashley);* Heinie Conklin *(Worker);* James Marcus *(Tugboat Captain Mike Ryan).*

20,000 YEARS IN SING SING
(First National, 1933) 81 min.

DIRECTOR: Michael Curtiz
ASSOCIATE DIRECTOR: Stanley Logan
BASED ON THE BOOK BY WARDEN LEWIS E. LAWES
SCREENPLAY: Courtney Terrett, Robert Lord, Wilson Mizner, Brown Holmes
MUSIC DIRECTOR: Leo F. Forbstein
MUSIC: Bernhard Kaun
ART DIRECTOR: Anton Grot
COSTUMES: Orry-Kelly
CAMERA: Barney McGill
EDITOR: George Amy

Spencer Tracy *(Tom Connors);* Bette Davis *(Fay);* Lyle Talbot *(Bud);* Sheila Terry *(Billie);* Edward McNamara *(Chief of Guards);* Warren Hymer *(Hupe);* Louis Calhern *(Joe Finn);* Spencer Charters *(Daniels);* Arthur Byron *(Warden Long);* Grant Mitchell *(Dr. Ames);* Nella Walker *(Mrs. Long);* Harold Huber *(Tony);* William Le Maire *(Black Jack);* Arthur Hoyt *(Dr. Meeker);* George Pat Collins *(Mike).*

FACE IN THE SKY
(Fox, 1933) 77 min.

DIRECTOR: Harry Lachman
STORY: Myles Connolly
SCREENPLAY: Humphrey Pearson
DIALOGUE DIRECTOR: William Collier, Sr.
MUSIC DIRECTOR: Louis De Francesco
MUSIC: Peter Brunelli, R. H. Bassett, Hugo Friedhofer, J. S. Zamecnik
SONGS: Val Burton and William Jason
SETS: William Darling
WARDROBE: David Cox
SOUND: E. Clayton Ward
CAMERA: Lee Garmes

Spencer Tracy *(Joe Buck);* Marian Nixon *(Madge Brown);* Stuart Erwin *(Lucky);* Sam Hardy *(Triplet the Great);* Sarah Padden *(Ma Brown);* Frank McGlynn, Jr. *(Jim Brown);* Russell Simpson *(Pa Brown);* Billy Platt *(Midget);* Guy Usher *(Albert Preston);* Lila Lee *(Sharon Hadley).*

THE POWER AND THE GLORY
(Fox, 1933) 76 min.

PRODUCER: Jesse L. Lasky
DIRECTOR: William K. Howard
SCREENPLAY: Preston Sturges
MUSIC: J. S. Zamecnik, Peter Brunelli, Louis De Francesco
MUSIC DIRECTOR: De Francesco
ART DIRECTOR: Max Parker
COSTUMES: Rita Kaufman
SOUND: A. W. Protzman
CAMERA: James Wong Howe

Spencer Tracy *(Tom Garner);* Colleen Moore *(Sally);* Ralph Morgan *(Henry);* Helen Vinson *(Eve);* Clifford Jones *[Philip Trent] (Tom Garner, Jr.);* Henry Kolker *(Mr. Borden);* Sarah Padden *(Henry's Wife);* Billy O'Brien *(Tom as a Boy);* Cullen Johnston *(Henry as a Boy);* J. Farrell MacDonald *(Mulligan).*

SHANGHAI MADNESS
(Fox, 1933) 68 min.

DIRECTOR: John Blystone
STORY: Frederick Hazlitt Brennan
SCREENPLAY: Austin Parker
ADAPTOR: Gordon Wellesley
MUSIC DIRECTOR: Samuel Kaylin
SOUND: W. W. Lindsay, Jr.
CAMERA: Lee Garmes

Spencer Tracy *(Pat Jackson);* Fay Wray *(Wildeth Christie);* Ralph Morgan *(Li Po Chang);* Eugene Pallette *(Lobo Lonergan);* Herbert Mundin *(First Officer Larsen);* Reginald Mason *(William Christie);* Arthur Hoyt *(Van Emery);* Albert Conti *(Rigaud);* Maude Eburne *(Mrs. Glissen);* William von Brincken *(Von Uhlenberg).*

THE MAD GAME
(Fox, 1933) 73 min.

PRODUCER: Sol Wurtzel
DIRECTOR: Irving Cummings
STORY/SCREENPLAY: William Conselman, Henry Johnson
MUSIC DIRECTOR: Samuel Kaylin
SOUND: S. C. Chapman
CAMERA: Arthur Miller

Spencer Tracy *(Edward Carson);* Claire Trevor *(Jane Lee);* Ralph Morgan *(Judge Penfield);* Howard Lally *(Thomas Penfield);* J. Carroll Naish *(Chopper Allen);* John Miljan *(William Bennett);* Matt McHugh *(Butts McGee);* Kathleen Burke *(Marilyn Kirk);* Mary Mason *(Lila Penfield);* Willard Robertson *(Warden);* John Davidson *(Doctor);* Jerry Devine *(Mike).*

MAN'S CASTLE
(Columbia, 1933) 75 min.

DIRECTOR: Frank Borzage
BASED ON THE PLAY BY LAWRENCE HAZARD
SCREENPLAY: Jo Swerling
ASSISTANT DIRECTOR: Lew Borzage
MUSIC: Frank Harling, C. Bakaleinikoff
SOUND: Wilbur Brown
CAMERA: Joseph August
EDITOR: Viola Lawrence

Spencer Tracy *(Bill);* Loretta Young *(Trina);* Glenda Farrell *(Fay La Rue);* Walter Connolly *(Ira);* Arthur Hohl *(Bragg);* Marjorie Rambeau *(Flossie);* Dickie Moore *(Joie the Crippled Boy);* Harvey Clark *(Cafe Manager);* Henry Roquemore *(Man in Audience);* Hector V. Sarno *(Grocer);* and: Helen Eddy, Robert Grey, Tony Merlo, Kendall McComas, Harry Watson.

LOOKING FOR TROUBLE
(United Artists, 1934) 80 min.

PRODUCER: Darryl F. Zanuck
ASSOCIATE PRODUCERS: William Goetz, Raymond Griffith
DIRECTOR: William Wellman
STORY: J. R. Bren
SCREENPLAY: Leonard Praskins, Elmer Harris
MUSIC DIRECTOR: Alfred Newman
ART DIRECTORS: Richard Day, Joseph Wright
CAMERA: James Van Trees, Sr.
EDITOR: Peter Fritch

Spencer Tracy *(Joe Graham);* Jack Oakie *(Casey);* Constance Cummings *(Ethel);* Arline Judge *(Maizie);* Judith Wood *(Pearl);* Morgan Conway *(Dan);* Paul Harvey *(Regan);* Joseph Sawyer *(Max);* Franklin Ardell *(Martin).*

THE SHOW-OFF
(MGM, 1934) 79 min.

PRODUCER: Lucien Hubbard
DIRECTOR: Charles F. Reisner
BASED ON THE PLAY BY GEORGE KELLY
SCREENPLAY: Herman J. Mankiewicz
ART DIRECTOR: David Townsend
SET DECORATOR: Edwin B. Willis
SOUND: Douglas Shearer
CAMERA: James Wong Howe

EDITOR: William S. Gray

Spencer Tracy (J. *Aubrey Piper*); Madge Evans *(Amy Fisher);* Lois Wilson *(Clara);* Grant Mitchell *(Pa Fisher);* Clara Blandick *(Ma Fisher);* Claude Gillingwater *(J. B. Preston);* Henry Wadsworth *(Joe);* Alan Edwards *(Frank);* Richard Tucker *(Edwards).*

BOTTOMS UP
(Fox, 1934) 85 min.

PRODUCER: B. G. DeSylva
DIRECTOR: David Butler
STORY/SCREENPLAY: DeSylva, Butler, Sid Silvers
MUSIC DIRECTOR: C. Bakaleinikoff
ORCHESTRATOR: Howard Jackson
SONGS: Harold Adamson and Burton Lane, Richard Whiting and Gus Kahn
CHOREOGRAPHY: H. Hecht
ART DIRECTOR: Gordon Wiles
DANCE SETS/COSTUMES: Russell Patterson
SOUND: Joseph Aiken
CAMERA: Arthur Miller
EDITOR: Irene Morra

Spencer Tracy *(Smoothie King);* John Boles *(Hal Reed);* Pat Paterson *(Wanda Gale);* Herbert Mundin *(Limey Brook);* Sid Silvers *(Spud Mosco);* Harry Green *(Louis Baer);* Thelma Todd *(Judith Marlowe);* Robert Emmet O'Connor *(Detective Rooney);* Del Henderson *(Lane Worthing);* Suzanne Kaaren *(Secretary);* Douglas Wood *(Baldwin).*

NOW I'LL TELL
(Fox, 1934) 72 min.

PRODUCER: Winfield Sheehan
DIRECTOR: Edwin Burke
BASED ON THE BOOK BY MRS. ARNOLD ROTHSTEIN
SCREENPLAY: Burke
MUSIC DIRECTOR: Arthur Lange
SONGS: Lew Brown and Harry Akst
MUSIC: Hugo Friedhofer, Lange David Buttolph
ART DIRECTOR: Jack Otterson
GOWNS: Rita Kaufman
SOUND: William D. Flick
CAMERA: Ernest Palmer

Spencer Tracy *(Murray Golden);* Helen Twelvetrees *(Virginia Golden);* Alice Faye *(Peggy Warren);* Robert Gleckler *(Al Mositer);* Henry O'Neill *(Doran);* Hobart Cavanaugh *(Freddie);* G. P. Huntley, Jr. *(Hart);* Shirley Temple *(Mary);* Ronnie Cosbey *(Tommy, Jr.);* Ray Cooke *(Traylor);* Frank Marlowe *(Curtis);* Barbara Weeks *(Wynne);* Theodore Newton *(Joe Ready);* Leon Ames *(Mac);* Vince Barnett *(Peppo),* Clarence Wilson *(Davis);* Jim Donlaon *(Honey Smith).*

MARIE GALANTE
(Fox, 1934) 88 min.

PRODUCER: Winfield Sheehan
DIRECTOR: Henry King
BASED ON THE NOVEL BY JACQUES DEVAL
SCREENPLAY: Reginald Berkeley
MUSIC DIRECTOR: Arthur Lange
CAMERA: John Seitz

Spencer Tracy *(Crawbett);* Ketti Gallian *(Marie Galante);* Ned Sparks *(Plosser);* Helen Morgan *(Tapia);* Sig Rumann *(Brogard);* Leslie Fenton *(Tanoki);* Arthur Byron *(General Phillips);* Robert Lorraine *(Ratcliff);* Jay C. Flippen *(Sailor);* Frank Darien *(Ellsworth);* Stepin Fetchit *(Bartender).*

IT'S A SMALL WORLD
(Fox, 1935) 70 min.

PRODUCER: Edward Butcher
DIRECTOR: Irving Cummings
BASED ON THE NOVEL *Highway Robbery* BY ALBERT TRAYNOR
SCREENPLAY: Samuel Hellman, Gladys Lehman
MUSIC/MUSIC DIRECTOR: Arthur Lange
ART DIRECTOR: William Darling
SOUND: S. C. Chapman
CAMERA: Arthur Miller

Spencer Tracy *(Bill Shevlin);* Wendy Barrie *(Jane Dale);* Raymond Walburn *(Judge Julius B. Clummerhorn);* Virginia Sale *(Lizzie);* Astrid Allwyn *(Nancy Naylor);* Irving Bacon *(Cal);* Charles Seldon *(Cyclone);* Dick Foran *(Motor Cop);* Belle Daube *(Mrs. Dale);* Frank McGlynn, Sr. *(Snake Brown, Jr.);* Frank McGlynn, Jr. *(Snake Brown III);* Bill Gillis *(Snake Brown, Sr.);* Edwin Brady *(Buck Bogardus);* Harold Minjir *(Freddie Thompson).*

THE MURDER MAN
(MGM, 1935) 70 min.

PRODUCER: Harry Rapf
DIRECTOR: Tim Whelan
STORY: Whelan, Guy Bolton
SCREENPLAY: Whelan, John C. Higgins
ASSISTANT DIRECTOR: David Friedman
MUSIC: Dr. William Axt
ART DIRECTORS: Cedric Gibbons, Eddie Imazu
SET DECORATOR: Edwin B. Willis
SOUND: Douglas Shearer
CAMERA: Lester White
EDITOR: James E. Newcom

Spencer Tracy *(Steve Gray);* Virginia Bruce *(Mary Shannon);* Lionel Atwill *(Captain Cole);* Harvey Stephens *(Henry Mander);* Robert Barrat *(Robins);* James Stewart *(Shorty);* William Collier, Sr. *(Pop Gray);* Bobby Watson *(Carey Booth);* William Demarest *(Red Maguire);* Lucien Littlefield *(Rafferty);* John Sheehan *(Maxie Sweeney);* George Chandler *(Sol Hertzberger);* Fuzzy Knight *(Buck Hawkins);* Louise Henry *(Lilian Hopper);* Robert Warwick *(Coleville);* Joe Irving *(Tony);* Francix X. Bushman, Jr. *(Pendleton);* Theodor Von Eltz *(James Spencer Halford);* Alan Bridge *(Judge John C. Garfield);* Davison Clark *(Warden Powell);* Selmer Jackson *(Lieutenant Dwight).*

DANTE'S INFERNO
(Fox, 1935) 88 min.

PRODUCER: Sol M. Wurtzel
DIRECTÓR: Harry Lachman
SCREENPLAY: Philip Klein, Robert M. Yost
MUSIC: Hugo Friedhofer, Samuel Kaylin, R. H. Bassett, Peter Brunelli
MUSIC DIRECTOR: Kaylin
ALLEGORICAL SETS: Willy Pogany
CHOREOGRAPHY: Eduardo Casino
SOUND: E. H. Hansen
CAMERA: Rudolph Maté
EDITOR: Al DeGaetano

Spencer Tracy *(Jim Carter);* Claire Trevor *(Betty McWade Carter);* Henry B. Walthall *(Pop McWade);* Scotty Beckett *(Alexander "Sonny" Carter);* Alan Dinehart *(Jonesy);* Joe Brown *(Baseball Concessionaire);* George Humbert *(Tony);* Robert Gleckler *(Dean);* Maidel Turner *(Madame Zucchini);* Nella Walker *(Mrs. Hamilton);* Lita Chevret *(Mrs. Martin);* Richard Tucker *(Mr. Hamilton);* Edward Pawley *(Clinton);* Ruthelma Stevens, Don Ameche *(People in Stokehold);* Morgan Wallace *(Captain Morgan);* Harry Woods *(Second Officer Reynolds);* Rita Cansino *(Hayworth);* Gary Leon *(Specialty Dancers);* Hal Boyer, Jack Lloyd, Jayne Regan *(College Youths);* Ron Rondell *(Ticket Buyer);* Gertrude Astor, Tiny Jones *(Concessionaires' Wives);* Jean Fenwick *(Engine Room Visitor);* Warren Hymer *(Bozo);* Leona Lane *(Borgia);* Marion Strickland *(Eve);* Gale Goodson *(Little Bo Peep);* Margaret McCrystal, Dorothy Stockmar *(Trumpeteers);* Reginald Sheffield, Jay Eaton *(Bidders);* Barbara Pepper, Lloyd Pantages, Jack Norton, Robert Graves, George Meeker *(Drunks);* Harry Holman *(Jolly Fat Man);* Frank Conroy *(Defense Attorney);* Russell Hicks *(Prosecuting Attorney);* George Irving *(Judge);* Georgia Caine *(Fortuneteller);* Ray Bernard *(Corrigan),* Noble Johnson, Paul Schwegeler, Aloha Porter *(Devils);* Andrea Leeds *(Anna, Betty's Maid)*

WHIPSAW
(MGM, 1935) 83 min.

PRODUCER: Harry Rapf
DIRECTOR: Sam Wood
STORY: James E. Grant
SCREENPLAY: Howard E. Rogers
ART DIRECTORS: Cedric Gibbons, William Horning
SET DECORATOR: Edwin B. Willis
WARDROBE: Dolly Tree
MUSIC: Dr. William Axt
SOUND: Douglas Shearer
CAMERA: James Wong Howe
EDITOR: Basil Wrangell

Myrna Loy *(Vivian Palmer);* Spencer Tracy *(Ross McBride);* Harvey Stephens *(Ed Dexter);* William Harrigan *(Doc Evans);* Clay Clement *(Harry Ames);* Robert Gleckler *(Steve Arnold);* Robert Warwick *(Wadsworth);* George Renavent *(Monetta);* Paul Stanton *(Chief Hughes);* Wade Boteler *(Humphries);* Don Rowan *(Curley);* John

Qualen *(Dabson);* Irene Franklin *(Mme. Marie);* Lillian Leighton *(Aunt Jane);* J. Anthony Hughes *(Bailey);* William Ingersoll *(Dr. Williams);* Charles Irwin *(Larry King).*

RIFF-RAFF
(MGM, 1935) 89 min.

PRODUCER: Irving Thalberg
ASSOCIATE PRODUCER: David Lewis
DIRECTOR: J. Walter Ruben
STORY: Frances Marion
SCREENPLAY: Marion, H. W. Hanemann, Anita Loos
MUSIC: Edward Ward
ART DIRECTORS: Cedric Gibbons, Stanwood Rogers
WARDROBE: Dolly Tree
SOUND: Douglas Shearer
CAMERA: Ray June
EDITOR: Frank Sullivan

Jean Harlow *(Hattie);* Spencer Tracy *(Dutch);* Joseph Calleia *(Nick);* Una Merkel *(Lil);* Mickey Rooney *(Jimmy);* Victor Kilian *(Flytrap);* J. Farrell MacDonald *(Brains);* Roger Imhof *(Pops);* Baby Jane "Juanita" Quigley *(Rosie);* Paul Hurst *(Belcher);* Vince Barnett *(Lew);* Dorothy Appleby *(Gertie);* Judith Wood *(Mabel);* Arthur Housman *(Ratsy);* Wade Boteler *(Bert);* Joe Phillips *(Al);* William Newell *(Pete);* Al Hill *(Speed);* Helen Flint *(Sadie);* Lillian Harmer *(Mrs. McCall);* Robert Perry *(Lefty);* George Givot *(Markus);* Helen Costello *(Maisie);* Rafaela Ottiano *(Head Matron);* King Mojavea, Al Herman, Philo McCullough, Sherry Hall, Jack Byron, Stanley Price, Herman Marx, Eddie Sturgis, John George *(Fishermen);* Marshall Ruth *(Agitator);* Wally Maher *(Newsreel Cameraman).*

FURY
(MGM, 1936) 90 min.

PRODUCER: Joseph L. Mankiewicz
DIRECTOR: Fritz Lang
STORY: Norman Krasna
SCREENPLAY: Bartlett Cormack, Lang
ASSISTANT DIRECTOR: Horace Hough
MUSIC: Franz Waxman
ART DIRECTORS: Cedric Gibbons, William A. Horning
SET DECORATOR: Edwin B. Willis
WARDROBE: Dolly Tree
SOUND: Douglas Shearer
CAMERA: Joseph Ruttenberg
EDITOR: Frank Sullivan

Sylvia Sidney *(Katherine Grant);* Spencer Tracy *(Joe Wilson);* Walter Abel *(District Attorney);* Bruce Cabot *(Kirby Dawson);* Edward Ellis *(Sheriff);* Walter Brennan *(Bugs Meyers);* George Walcott *(Tom);* Frank Albertson *(Charlie);* Arthur Stone *(Durkin);* Morgan Wallace *(Fred Garrett);* George Chandler *(Milton Jackson);* Roger Gray *(Stranger);* Edwin Maxwell *(Vickery);* Howard Hickman *(Governor);* Jonathan Hale *(Defense Attorney);* Leila Bennett *(Edna Hooper);* Esther Dale *(Mrs. Whipple);* Helen Flint *(Franchette).*

SAN FRANCISCO
(MGM, 1936) 115 min.

PRODUCERS: John Emerson, Bernard H. Hyman
DIRECTOR: W. S. Van Dyke II
STORY: Robert Hopkins
SCREENPLAY: Anita Loos
ASSISTANT DIRECTOR: Joseph Newman
MUSIC DIRECTOR: Herbert Stothart
MUSIC: Edward Ward
SONGS: Gus Kahn, Bronislau Kaper, and Walter Jurmann
Arthur Freed and Nacio Herb Brown
ART DIRECTORS: Cedric Gibbons, Arnold Gillespie, Harry McAfree
SET DECORATOR: Edwin B. Willis
CHOREOGRAPHY: Val Raset
OPERATIC SEQUENCES STAGED BY WILLIAM VON WYMETAL
GOWNS: Adrian
SOUND: Douglas Shearer
MONTAGES: John Hoffman
CAMERA: Oliver T. Marsh
EDITOR: Tom Held

Clark Gable *(Blackie Norton);* Jeanette MacDonald *(Mary Blake);* Spencer Tracy *(Father Mullin);* Jack Holt *(Jack Burley);* Jessie Ralph *(Mrs. Burley);* Ted Healy *(Matt);* Shirley Ross *(Trixie);* Margaret Irving *(Della Bailey);* Harold Huber *(Babe);* Al Shean *(Professor);* William Ricciardi *(Signor Baldini);* Kenneth Harlan *(Chick);* Roger Imhof *(Alaska);* Charles Judels *(Tony);* Russell Simpson *(Red Kelly);* Bert Roach *(Freddie Duane);* Warren Hymer *(Hazeltine);* Edgar Kennedy *(Sheriff);* Adrienne d'Ambricourt *(Madame Albani);* Nigel de Brulier *(Old Man);* Mae Digges, Nyas Berry *(Dancers);* Tudor Williams, Tandy MacKenzie *(Singers);* Tom Mahoney *(Captain of Police);* Gertrude Astor *(Drunk's Girl);* Jason Robards, Sr. *(Father);* Vernon Dent *(Fat Man);* Anthony Jowitt *(Society Man);* Carl Stockdale *(Salvation Army Man);* Richard Carle, Oscar Apfel, Frank Sheridan, Ralph Lewis *(Members of Founders' Club);* Don Rowan *(Coast Type);* Jack Kennedy *(Old Irishman);* Chester Gan *(Jowl Lee).*

LIBELED LADY
(MGM, 1936) 98 min.

PRODUCER: Lawrence Weingarten
DIRECTOR: Jack Conway
STORY: Wallace Sullivan
SCREENPLAY: Maurine Watkins, Howard Emmett Rogers, George Oppenheimer
ART DIRECTORS: Cedric Gibbons, William A. Horning
SET DECORATOR: Edwin B. Willis
MUSIC: Dr. William Axt
WARDROBE: Dolly Tree
SOUND: Douglas Shearer
CAMERA: Norbert Brodine
EDITOR: Frederick Y. Smith

Jean Harlow *(Gladys Benton);* William Powell *(Bill Chandler);* Myrna Loy *(Connie Allenbury);* Spencer Tracy *(Warren Haggerty);* Walter Connolly *(James B. Allenbury);* Charley Grapewin *(Hollis Bane);* Cora Witherspoon *(Mrs. Burns-Norvell);* E. E. Clive *(Evans, the Fishing Instructor);* Bunny Lauri Beatty *(Babs Burns-Norvell);* Otto Yamaoka *(Ching);* Charles Trowbridge *(Graham);* Spencer Charters *(Magistrate McCall);* George Chandler *(Bellhop);* Greta Meyer *(Connie's Maid);* William Benedict *(Joe);* Hal K. Dawson *(Harvey Allen);* Fred Graham *(Pressman);* William Stack *(Editor);* Selmer Jackson *(Adams, the Editor of the* Washington Chronicle*);* William Newell *(Divorce Detective);* Duke York *(Taxi Driver);* Pat West *(Detective);* Ed Stanley *(Clerk);* Wally Maher *(Photographer);* Tom Mahoney *(Alex);* Libby Taylor *(Tiny—Gladys' Maid);* Myra Marsh *(Secretary);* Howard Hickman *(Cable Editor);* Ralph Brooks *(Dance Extra);* Charles Crocker King *(Charles Archibald, the Lawyer);* Ines Palange *(Fortuneteller);* Richard Tucker, Charles King, Jack Mulhall, Dennis O'Keefe *(Barkers).*

CAPTAINS COURAGEOUS
(MGM, 1937) 116 min.

PRODUCER: Louis D. Lighton
DIRECTOR: Victor Fleming
BASED ON THE NOVEL BY RUDYARD KIPLING
SCREENPLAY: John Lee Mahin, Marc Connelly, Dale Van Every
MUSIC: Franz Waxman
SONGS: Waxman and Gus Kahn
MARINE DIRECTOR: James Havens
ART DIRECTORS: Cedric Gibbons, Arnold Gillespie
SET DECORATOR: Edwin B. Willis
SOUND: Douglas Shearer
CAMERA: Harold Rosson
EDITOR: Elmo Vernon

Freddie Bartholomew *(Harvey Cheyne);* Spencer Tracy *(Manuel);* Lionel Barrymore *(Disko);* Melvyn Douglas *(Mr. Cheyne);* Mickey Rooney *(Dan);* Charley Grapewin *(Uncle Salters);* Christian Rub *(Old Clement);* Walter Kingsford *(Dr. Finley);* Donald Briggs *(Tyler);* Sam McDaniel *(Doc);* Dave Thursby *(Tom);* John Carradine *(Long Jack);* William Stack *(Elliott);* Leo G. Carroll *(Burns);* Charles Trowbridge *(Dr. Walsh);* Richard Powell *(Steward);* Billy Burrud *(Charles);* Jay Ward *(Pogey);* Oscar O'Shea *(Cushman);* Jack La Rue *(Priest);* Billy Gilbert *(Soda Steward);* Norman Ainsley *(Robbins);* Tommy Bupp, Wally Albright *(Boys);* Katherine Kenworthy *(Mrs. Disko);* Murray Kinnell *(Minister);* Gertrude Sutton *(Nate's Wife);* Dora Early *(Appleton's Wife).*

THEY GAVE HIM A GUN
(MGM, 1937) 90 min.

PRODUCER: Harry Rapf
DIRECTOR: W. S. Van Dyke II
BASED ON THE BOOK BY WILLIAM JOYCE COWEN
SCREENPLAY: Cyril Hume, Richard Maibaum, Maurice Rapf

ASSISTANT DIRECTOR: Dolph Zimmer
ART DIRECTORS: Cedric Gibbons, Harry McAfee
SET DECORATOR: Edwin B. Willis
SOUND: Douglas Shearer
MONTAGE/SPECIAL EFFECTS: Slavko Vorkapich
CAMERA: Harold Rosson
EDITOR: Ben Lewis

Spencer Tracy *(Fred Willis);* Gladys George *(Rose Duffy);* Franchot Tone *(Jimmy Davis);* Edgar Dearing *(Sergeant Meadowlark);* Mary Lou Treen *(Saxe);* Cliff Edwards *(Laro);* Charles Trowbridge *(Judge);* Joe Sawyer *(Doyle);* George Chandler *(Taxi Driver);* Gavin Gordon *(Captain);* Ernest Whitman *(Roustabout);* Nita Pike, Joan Woodbury *(French Girls).*

BIG CITY
(MGM, 1937) 80 min.

PRODUCER: Norman Krasna
DIRECTOR: Frank Borzage
STORY: Krasna
SCREENPLAY: Dore Schary, Hugo Butler
MUSIC: Dr. William Axt
ART DIRECTOR: Cedric Gibbons
CAMERA: Joseph Ruttenberg
EDITOR: Frederick Y. Smith

Spencer Tracy *(Joe Benton);* Luise Rainer *(Anna Benton);* Charley Grapewin *(Mayor);* Janet Beecher *(Sophie Sloane);* Eddie Quillan *(Mike Edwards);* Victor Varconi *(Paul Roya);* Oscar O'Shea *(John C. Andrews);* Helen Troy *(Lola Johnson);* William Demarest *(Beecher);* John Arledge *(Buddy);* Irving Bacon *(Jim Sloane);* Guinn "Big Boy" Williams *(Danny Devlin);* Regis Toomey *(Fred Hawkins);* Edgar Dearing *(Tom Reilley);* Paul Harvey *(District Attorney);* Andrew J. Tombes *(Inspector Matthews);* Clem Bevans *(Grandpa Sloane);* Grace Ford *(Mary Reilley);* Alice White *(Peggy Devlin);* Jack Dempsey, Maxie Rosenbloom, Jim Thorpe, Joe Rivers, Bull Montana, Taski Hagio, Man Mountain Dean, George Godfrey *(Fighters and Wrestlers).*

MANNEQUIN
(MGM, 1938) 92 min.

PRODUCER: Joseph L. Mankiewicz
DIRECTOR: Frank Borzage
BASED ON THE UNPUBLISHED STORY BY KATHERINE BRUSH
SCREENPLAY: Lawrence Hazard
MUSIC: Edward Ward
SONGS: Ward, Robert Wright and Chet Forrest
ART DIRECTORS: Cedric Gibbons, Paul Groesse
SET DECORATOR: Edwin B. Willis
COSTUMES: Adrian
SOUND: Douglas Shearer
CAMERA: George Folsey
EDITOR: Frederick Y. Smith

Joan Crawford *(Jessie Cassidy);* Spencer Tracy *(John Hennessey);* Alan Curtis *(Eddie Miller);* Ralph Morgan *(Briggs);* Mary Philips *(Beryl);* Oscar O'Shea *(Pa Cassidy);* Elizabeth Risdon *(Mrs. Cassidy);* Leo Gorcey *(Clifford Cassidy);* Ralph Morgan *(Briggs);* George Chandler *(Swing Magoo);* Bert Roach *(Schwartz);* Marie Blake *(Mrs. Schwartz);* Matt McHugh *(Mike);* Paul Fix *(Smooch);* Helen Troy *(Bubbles Adair);* Phillip Terry *(Man at Stage Door);* Gwen Lee *(Girl Worker);* Donald Kirke *(Dave McIntyre);* Gwen Lee, Virginia Blair, Jim Baker, Ruth Dwyer *(Wedding Guests);* Frank Jaquet *(Stage Doorman);* Jimmy Conlin *(Elevator Operator).*

TEST PILOT
(MGM, 1938) 118 min.

PRODUCER: Louis D. Lighton
DIRECTOR: Victor Fleming
STORY: Frank Wead
SCREENPLAY: Vincent Lawrence, Waldemar Young
ART DIRECTORS: Cedric Gibbons, John Detlie
SET DECORATOR: Edwin B. Willis
MUSIC: Franz Waxman
WARDROBE: Dolly Tree
MONTAGE: Slavko Vorkapich
CAMERA: Ray June
EDITOR: Tom Held

Clark Gable *(Jim Lane);* Myrna Loy *(Ann Barton);* Spencer Tracy *(Gunner Sloane);* Lionel Barrymore *(Howard B. Drake);* Samuel S. Hinds *(General Ross);* Arthur Aylesworth *(Frank Barton);* Claudia Coleman *(Mrs. Barton);* Gloria Holden *(Mrs. Benson);* Louis Jean Heydt *(Benson);* Ted Pearson *(Joe);* Marjorie Main *(Landlady);* Gregory Gaye *(Grant);* Virginia Grey *(Sarah);* Priscilla Lawson *(Mabel);* Dudley Clements *(Mr. Brown);* Henry Roquemore *(Fat Man);* Byron Foulger *(Designer);* Frank Jaquet *(Motor Expert);* Roger Converse *(Advertising Man);* Billy Engle *(Little Man);* Brent Sargent *(Movie Leading Man);* Mary Howard *(Movie Leading Woman);* Douglas McPhail *(Singing Pilot in Cafe);* Forbes Murray, James Flavin, Hooper Atchley, Dick Winslow, Ray Walker, Richard Tucker, Don Douglas, Frank Sully *(Pilots in Cafe);* Fay Holden *(Saleslady);* Tom O'Grady *(Bartender);* Syd Saylor *(Boss Leader).*

BOYS TOWN
(MGM, 1938) 96 min.

PRODUCER: John W. Considine, Jr.
DIRECTOR: Norman Taurog
STORY: Dore Schary, Eleanore Griffin
SCREENPLAY: John Meehan, Schary
MUSIC: Edward Ward
MUSIC ARRANGER: Leo Arnaud
ART DIRECTORS: Cedric Gibbons, Urie McCleary
SET DECORATOR: Edwin B. Willis
MONTAGE: Slavko Vorkapich
CAMERA: Sidney Wagner
EDITOR: Elmo Vernon

Spencer Tracy *(Father Edward J. Flanagan);* Mickey Rooney *(Whitey Marsh);* Henry Hull *(Dave Morris);* Leslie Fenton *(Dan Farrow);* Addison Richards *(Judge);* Edward Norris *(Joe Marsh);* Gene Reynolds *(Tony Ponessa);* Minor Watson *(Bishop);* Victor Kilian *(Sheriff);* Jonathan Hale *(John Hargraves);* Bobs Watson *(Pee Wee);* Martin Spellman *(Skinny);* Mickey Rentschler *(Tommy Anderson);* Frankie Thomas *(Freddie Fuller);* Jimmy Butler *(Paul Ferguson);* Sidney Miller *(Mo Kahn);* Robert Emmett Keane *(Burton);* Phillip Terry *(Reporter);* Gladden James *(Doctor);* Kane Richmond *(Jackson the Reporter);* George Humbert *(Calateri);* Jay Novello *(Gangster with Marsh);* Johnny Walsh *(Charley Haines).*

STANLEY AND LIVINGSTONE
(20th Century-Fox, 1939) 101 min.

PRODUCER: Darryl F. Zanuck
ASSOCIATE PRODUCER: Kenneth Macgowan
DIRECTOR: Henry King
BASED ON HISTORICAL RESEARCH/STORY OUTLINE BY HAL LONG AND SAM HELLMAN
SCREENPLAY: Philip Dunne, Julien Josephson
GUIDE/ADVISOR FOR LOCATION SHOOTING: Mrs. Osa Johnson
MUSIC DIRECTOR: Louis Silvers
MUSIC: Robert R. Bennett, David Buttolph, Silvers, R. H. Bassett, Cyril Mockridge, Rudy Schrager
ART DIRECTORS: William Darling, George Dudley
SET DECORATOR: Thomas Little
COSTUMES: Royer
SOUND: Alfred Bruzlin, Roger Heman
CAMERA: George Barnes
EDITOR: Barbara McLean

Spencer Tracy *(Henry M. Stanley);* Nancy Kelly *(Eve Kingsley);* Richard Greene *(Gareth Tyce);* Walter Brennan *(Jeff Slocum);* Charles Coburn *(Lord Tyce);* Sir Cedric Hardwicke *(Dr. David Livingstone);* Henry Hull *(James G. Bennett, Jr.);* Henry Travers *(John Kingsley);* Miles Mander *(Sir John Gresham);* David Torrence *(Mr. Cranston);* Paul Stanton *(Captain Webb);* Holmes Herbert *(Frederick Holcomb);* Montague Shaw *(Sir Oliver French);* Brandon Hurst *(Sir Henry Forrester);* Hassan Said *(Hassan);* Paul Harvey *(Colonel Grimes);* Russell Hicks, Frank Daq *(Commissioners);* Joseph Crehan *(Morehead);* Robert Middlemass *(Carmichael);* Frank Jaquet *(Senator);* Clarence Derwent *(Sir Francis Vane).*

I TAKE THIS WOMAN
(MGM, 1940) 97 min.

PRODUCER: Bernard H. Hyman
DIRECTORS: W. S. Van Dyke II and (uncredited) Josef von Sternberg, Frank Borzage
STORY: Charles MacArthur
SCREENPLAY: James Kevin McGuinness
MUSIC: Bronislau Kaper, Arthur Guttman
ART DIRECTORS: Cedric Gibbons, Paul Groesse

CAMERA: Harold Rosson
EDITOR: George Boemler

Spencer Tracy *(Karl Decker);* Hedy Lamarr *(Georgi Gragore);* Verree Teasdale *(Madame Marcesca);* Kent Taylor *(Phil Mayberry);* Laraine Day *(Linda Rogers);* Mona Barrie *(Sandra Mayberry);* Jack Carson *(Joe);* Paul Cavanaugh *(Bill Rogers);* Louis Calhern *(Dr. Duveen);* Marjorie Main *(Gertie);* George E. Stone *(Sid);* Willie Best *(Sambo);* Don Castle *(Ted Fenton);* Dalies Frantz *(Joe Barnes);* Reed Hadley *(Bob Hampton).*

NORTHWEST PASSAGE
(MGM, 1940) C-125 min.

PRODUCER: Hunt Stromberg
DIRECTORS: King Vidor, (uncredited) Jack Conway
BASED ON THE NOVEL BY KENNETH ROBERTS
SCREENPLAY: Laurence Stallings, Talbot Jennings
ASSISTANT DIRECTOR: Robert Golden
TECHNICOLOR CONSULTANTS: Natalie Kalmus, Henri Jaffa
MUSIC: Herbert Stothart
ART DIRECTORS: Cedric Gibbons, Malcolm Brown
SET DECORATOR: Edwin B. Willis
MAKEUP: Jack Dawn
SOUND: Douglas Shearer
CAMERA: Sidney Wagner, William V. Skall
EDITOR: Conrad A. Nervig

Spencer Tracy *(Major Robert Rogers);* Robert Young *(Langdon Towne);* Walter Brennan *(Hunk Marriner);* Ruth Hussey *(Elizabeth Browne);* Nat Pendleton *(Cap Huff);* Louis Hector *(Reverend Browne);* Robert Barrat *(Humphrey Towne);* Lumsden Hare *(Lord Amherst);* Donald MacBride *(Sergeant McNott);* Isabel Jewell *(Jennie Coit);* Douglas Walton *(Lieutenant Avery);* Addison Richards *(Lieutenant Crofton);* Hugh Sothern *(Jesse Beacham);* Regis Toomey *(Webster);* Montagu Love *(Wiseman Clagett);* Lester Matthews *(Sam Livermore);* Truman Bradley *(Captain Ogden);* Andrew Pena *(Konkapot).*

EDISON THE MAN
(MGM, 1940) 107 min.

PRODUCER: John W. Considine, Jr.
ASSOCIATE PRODUCER: Orville O. Dull
DIRECTOR: Clarence Brown
STORY: Dore Schary, Hugo Butler
SCREENPLAY: Talbot Jennings, Bradbury Foote
ASSISTANT DIRECTOR: Robert A. Golden
MUSIC: Herbert Stothart
ART DIRECTORS: Cedric Gibbons, John S. Detlie
SET DECORATOR: Edwin B. Willis
WOMEN'S COSTUMES: Dolly Tree
MEN'S COSTUMES: Gile Steele
MAKEUP: Jack Dawn
TECHNICAL ADVISORS: William A. Simonds, Norman R. Speiden
SOUND: Douglas Shearer
CAMERA: Harold Rosson
EDITOR: Frederick Y. Smith

Spencer Tracy *(Thomas A. Edison);* Rita Johnson *(Mary Stillwell);* Lynne Overman *(Bunt Cavatt);* Charles Coburn *(General Powell);* Gene Lockhart *(Mr. Taggart);* Henry Travers *(Ben Els);* Felix Bressart *(Michael Simon);* Peter Godfrey *(Ashton);* Guy D'Ennery *(Lundstrom);* Byron Foulger *(Edwin Hall);* Milton Parsons *("Acid" Graham);* Gene Reynolds *(Jimmy Price);* Arthur Aylesworth *(Bigelow);* Addison Richards *(Mr. Johnson);* Grant Mitchell *(Snade);* Paul Hurst *(Sheriff);* George Lessey *(Toastmaster);* Jay Ward *(John Schofield);* Ann Gillis *(Nancy Grey).*

BOOM TOWN
(MGM, 1940) 116 min.

PRODUCER: Sam Zimbalist
DIRECTOR: Jack Conway
STORY: James Edward Grant
SCREENPLAY: John Lee Mahin
ASSISTANT DIRECTOR: Horace Hough
MUSIC: Franz Waxman
ART DIRECTORS: Cedric Gibbons, Eddie Imazu
COSTUMES: Adrian, Giles Steele
SOUND: Douglas Shearer
SPECIAL EFFECTS: Arnold Gillespie
MONTAGE: John Hoffman
CAMERA: Harold Rosson
EDITOR: Blanche Sewell

Clark Gable *(Big John McMasters);* Spencer Tracy *(Square John Sand);* Claudette Colbert *(Betsy Bartlett);* Hedy Lamarr *(Karen Vanmeer);* Frank Morgan *(Luther Aldrich);* Lionel Atwill *(Harry Compton);* Chill Wills *(Harmony Jones);* Marion Martin *(Whitey);* Minna Gombell *(Spanish Eve);* Joe Yule *(Ed Murphy);* Horace Murphy *(Tom Murphy);* Roy Gordon *(McCreery);* Richard Lane *(Assistant District Attorney);* Casey Johnson *(Little Jack);* Baby Quintanilla *(Baby Jack);* George Lessey *(Judge);* Sara Haden *(Miss Barnes);* Frank Orth *(Barber);* Frank McGlynn, Jr. *(Deacon);* Curt Bois *(Ferdie);* Dick Curtis *(Hiring Boss).*

MEN OF BOYS TOWN
(MGM, 1941) 106 min.

PRODUCER: John W. Considine, Jr.
DIRECTOR: Norman Taurog
SCREENPLAY: James K. McGuinness
ART DIRECTORS: Cedric Gibbons, Henry McAfee
SET DECORATOR: Edwin B. Willis
SOUND: Douglas Shearer
CAMERA: Harold Rosson
EDITOR: Frederick Y. Smith

Spencer Tracy *(Father E. Flanagan);* Mickey Rooney *(Whitey Marsh);* Bobs Watson *(Pee Wee);* Larry Nunn *(Ted Martley);* Darryl Hickman *(Flip);* Henry O'Neill *(Mr. Maitland);* Mary Nash *(Mrs. Maitland);* Lee J. Cobb *(Dave Morris);* Sidney Miller *(Mo Kahn);* Addison Richards *(Judge);* Lloyd Corrigan *(Roger Gorton);* George Lessey *(Bradford Stone);* Robert Emmett Keane *(Burton);* Arthur Hohl *(Guard);* Ben Welden *(Superintendent);* Anne Revere *(Mrs. Fenely).*

DR. JEKYLL AND MR. HYDE
(MGM, 1941) 127 min.

PRODUCER/DIRECTOR: Victor Fleming
BASED ON THE NOVEL BY ROBERT LOUIS STEVENSON
SCREENPLAY: John Lee Mahin
MUSIC: Franz Waxman
WOMEN'S GOWNS: Adrian
MEN'S WARDROBE: Gile Steele
ART DIRECTORS: Cedric Gibbons, Daniel B. Catchart
SET DECORATOR: Edwin B. Willis
SOUND: Douglas Shearer
SPECIAL EFFECTS: Warren Newcombe
MONTAGE: Peter Ballbusch
CAMERA: Joseph Ruttenberg
EDITOR: Harold Kress

Spencer Tracy *(Dr. Harry Jekyll/Mr. Hyde);* Ingrid Bergman *(Ivy Peterson);* Lana Turner *(Beatrix Emery);* Donald Crisp *(Sir Charles Emery);* Barton MacLane *(Sam Higgins);* C. Aubrey Smith *(Bishop);* Peter Godfrey *(Poole);* Sara Allgood *(Mrs. Higgins);* Frederic Worlock *(Dr. Heath);* William Tannen *(Interne Fenwick);* Frances Robinson *(Marcia);* Denis Green *(Freddie);* Billy Bevan *(Mr. Weller);* Forrester Harvey *(Old Prouty);* Lumsden Hare *(Colonel Weymouth);* Lawrence Grant *(Dr. Courtland);* John Barclay *(Constable).*

WOMAN OF THE YEAR
(MGM, 1942) 112 min.

PRODUCER: Joseph L. Mankiewicz
DIRECTOR: George Stevens
SCREENPLAY: Ring Lardner, Jr., Michael Kanin
ART DIRECTORS: Cedric Gibbons, Randall Duell
SET DECORATOR: Edwin B. Willis
MUSIC: Franz Waxman
COSTUMES: Adrian
ASSISTANT DIRECTOR: Robert Golden
MAKEUP: Jack Dawn
SOUND: Douglas Shearer
CAMERA: Joseph Ruttenberg
EDITOR: Frank Sullivan

Spencer Tracy *(Sam Craig);* Katharine Hepburn *(Tess Harding);* Fay Bainter *(Ellen Whitcomb);* Reginald Owen *(Clayton);* Minor Watson *(William Harding);* William Bendix *(Pinkie Peters);* Gladys Blake *(Flo Peters);* Dan Tobin *(Gerald);* Roscoe Karns *(Phil Whittaker);* William Tannen *(Ellis);* Ludwig Stossel *(Dr. Martin Lubbeck);* Sara Haden *(Matron at Refugee Home);* Edith Evanson *(Alma);* George Kezas *(Chris);* Henry Roquemore *(Justice of the Peace);* Cyril Ring *(Harding's Chauffeur);* Ben Lessy *(Punchy);* Johnny Berkes *(Pal);* Duke York *(Football Player);* Winifred Harris *(Chair-*

lady); Joe Yule *(Building Superintendent);* Edward McWade *(Adolph);* Michael Visaroff *(Guest);* Jimmy Conlin, Ray Teal *(Reporters);* William Holmes *(Man at Banquet).*

TORTILLA FLAT
(MGM, 1942) 105 min.

PRODUCER: Sam Zimbalist
DIRECTOR: Victor Fleming
BASED ON THE NOVEL BY JOHN STEINBECK
SCREENPLAY: John Lee Mahin, Benjamin Glazer
MUSIC: Franz Waxman
SONG: Waxman and Frank Loesser
ART DIRECTOR: Cedric Gibbons, Paul Groesse
SET DECORATOR: Edwin B. Willis
MAKEUP: Jack Dawn
SPECIAL EFFECTS: Warren Newcombe
CAMERA: Karl Freund
EDITOR: James E. Newcom

Spencer Tracy *(Pilon);* Hedy Lamarr *(Dolores "Sweets" Ramirez);* John Garfield *(Danny);* Frank Morgan *("The Pirate");* Akim Tamiroff *(Pablo);* Sheldon Leonard *(Tito Ralph);* John Qualen *(Jose Maria Corcoran);* Donald Meek *(Paul D. Cummings);* Connie Gilchrist *(Mrs. Torrelli);* Allen Jenkins *(Portagee Joe);* Henry O'Neill *(Father Ramon);* Mercedes Ruffino *(Mrs. Marellis);* Nina Campana *(Senora Teresina);* Arthur Space *(Mr. Brown);* Betty Wells *(Cesca);* Harry Burns *(Torelli).*

KEEPER OF THE FLAME
(MGM, 1942) 100 min.

PRODUCER: Victor Saville
ASSOCIATE PRODUCER: Leon Gordon
DIRECTOR: George Cukor
BASED ON THE NOVEL BY I. A. R. Wylie
SCREENPLAY: Donald Ogden Stewart
ART DIRECTORS: Cedric Gibbons, Lyle Wheeler
SET DECORATORS: Edwin B. Willis, Jack Moore
COSTUMES: Adrian
MUSIC: Bronislau Kaper
ASSISTANT DIRECTOR: Edward Woehler
MAKEUP: Jack Dawn
SOUND: Douglas Shearer
SPECIAL EFFECTS: Warren Newcombe
CAMERA: William Daniels
EDITOR: James E. Newcom

Spencer Tracy *(Steven O'Malley);* Katharine Hepburn *(Christine Forrest);* Richard Whorf *(Clive Kerndon);* Margaret Wycherly *(Mrs. Forrest);* Donald Meek *(Mr. Arbuthnot);* Stephen McNally *(Freddie Ridges);* Audrey Christie *(Jane Harding);* Frank Craven *(Dr. Fielding);* Forrest Tucker *(Geoffrey Midford);* Percy Kilbride *(Orion);* Howard DaSilva *(Jason Richards);* Darryl Hickman *(Jeb Richards);* William Newell *(Piggot);* Rex Evans *(John);* Blanche Yurka *(Anna);* Mary McLeod *(Janet);* Clifford Brooke *(William);* Craufurd Kent *(Ambassador);* Mickey Martin *(Messenger Boy);* Manart Kippen, Donald Gallagher, Cliff Danielson *(Reporters);* Jay Ward *(Pete);* Rita Quigley *(Susan);* Major Sam Harris, Art Howard, Harold Miller *(Men);* Dick Elliott *(Auctioneer);* Edward McWade *(Lawyer);* Irvin Lee *(Boy Reporter);* Diana Douglas, Gloria Tucker *(Girls);* Robert Pittard *(Tim);* Louis Mason *(Gardener);* Dr. Charles Frederick Lindsley *(Minister's Voice).*

A GUY NAMED JOE
(MGM, 1943) 120 min.

PRODUCER: Everett Riskin
DIRECTOR: Victor Fleming
BASED ON AN UNPUBLISHED STORY BY CHANDLER SPRAGUE, DAVID BOEHM, AND FREDERICK H. BRENNAN
SCREENPLAY: Dalton Trumbo
MUSIC: Herbert Stothart
SONG: Roy Turk and Fred Ahlert
ART DIRECTORS: Cedric Gibbons, Lyle Wheeler
SET DECORATORS: Edwin B. Willis, Ralph Hurst
ASSISTANT DIRECTOR: Horace Hough
SOUND: Charles E. Wallace
SPECIAL EFFECTS: Arnold Gillespie, Donald Jahraus, Warren Newcombe
CAMERA: George Folsey, Karl Freund
EDITOR: Frank Sullivan

Spencer Tracy *(Pete Sandridge);* Irene Dunne *(Dorinda Durston);* Van Johnson *(Ted Randall);* Ward Bond *(Al Yackey);* James Gleason *("Nails" Kilpatrick);* Lionel Barrymore *(General);* Barry Nelson *(Dick Rummey);* Don DeFore *("Powerhouse" O'Rourke);* Henry O'Neill *(Colonel Hendricks);* Addison Richards *(Major Corbett);* Charles Smith *(Sanderson);* Mary Elliott *(Dancehall Girl);* Earl Schenck *(Colonel Sykes);* Maurice Murphy *(Captain Robertson);* Gertrude Hoffman *(Old Woman);* Mark Daniels *(Lieutenant);* William Bishop *(Ray);* Eve Whitney *(Powerhouse Girl);* Esther Williams *(Ellen Bright);* Kay Williams *(Girl at Bar);* John Whitney, Kirk Alyn *(Officers in Heaven);* Gibson Gowland *(Bartender);* Edward Hardwicke *(George);* Yvonne Severn *(Elizabeth);* Christopher Severn *(Peter);* Frank Faylen, Phil Van Zandt *(Majors);* Matt Willis *(Lieutenant Hunter);* Jacqueline White *(Helen).*

THE SEVENTH CROSS
(MGM, 1944) 110 min.

PRODUCER: Pandro S. Berman
DIRECTOR: Fred Zinnemann
BASED ON THE NOVEL BY ANNA SEGHERS
SCREENPLAY: Helen Deutsch
MUSIC: Roy Webb
ART DIRECTORS: Cedric Gibbons, Leonid Vasian
SET DECORATORS: Edwin B. Willis, Mac Alper
COSTUME SUPERVISOR: Irene
ASSISTANT DIRECTOR: Horace Hough
SOUND: Douglas Shearer
CAMERA: Karl Freund
EDITOR: Thomas Richards

Spencer Tracy *(George Heisler);* Signe Hasso *(Toni);* Hume Cronyn *(Paul Roeder);* Jessica Tandy *(Liesel Roder);* Agnes Moorehead *(Mme. Marelli);* Herbert Rudley *(Franz Marnet);* Felix Bressart *(Poldi Schlamm);* Ray Collins *(Wallau);* Alexander Granach *(Zillich);* Katherine Locke *(Mrs. Sauer);* George Macready *(Bruno Sauer);* Paul Guilfoyle *(Dr. Lowenstein);* Kurt Katch *(Leo Hermann);* Karen Verne *(Leni);* Konstantin Shayne *(Fuellgrabe);* George Suzanne *(Bellani);* John Wengraf *(Overkamp);* Steven Muller *(Hellwig);* Eily Malyon *(Fraulein Bachmann).*

THIRTY SECONDS OVER TOKYO
(MGM, 1944) 138 min.

PRODUCER: Sam Zimbalist
DIRECTOR: Mervyn LeRoy
BASED ON THE BOOK BY CAPTAIN TED W. LAWSON AND ROBERT CONSIDINE
SCREENPLAY: Dalton Trumbo
MUSIC: Herbert Stothart
ART DIRECTORS: Cedric Gibbons, Paul Groesse
SET DECORATORS: Edwin B. Willis, Ralph S. Hurst
ASSISTANT DIRECTOR: Wally Worsley
SOUND: John F. Dullam
SPECIAL EFFECTS: A. Arnold Gillespie, Warren Newcombe, Donald Jahraus
CAMERA: Harold Rosson, Robert Surtees
EDITOR: Frank Sullivan

Van Johnson *(Captain Ted Lawson);* Spencer Tracy *(Lieutenant Colonel James H. Doolittle);* Robert Walker *(David Thatcher);* Phyllis Thaxter *(Ellen Lawson);* Tim Murdock *(Dean Davenport);* Scott McKay *(Davey Jones);* Gordon McDonald *(Bob Cleaver);* Don DeFore *(Charles McClure);* Robert Mitchum *(Bob Gray);* John R. Reilly *(Shorty Manch);* Stephen McNally *(Doc White);* Donald Curtis *(Lieutenant Randall);* Louis Jean Heydt *(Lieutenant Miller);* William "Bill" Phillips *(Don Smith);* Douglas Cowan *(Brick Holstrom);* Paul Langton *(Captain "Ski" York);* Leon Ames *(Lieutenant Jurika);* Moroni Olsen *(General);* Benson Fong *(Young Chung);* Dr. Hsin Kung Chuan Chi *(Old Chung);* Kay Williams, Peggy Maley, Hazel Brooks, Myrna Dell, Elaine Shepard *(Girls in Officers' Club);* Dorothy Ruth Morris *(Jane);* Ann Shoemaker *(Mrs. Parker);* Ching Wah Lee *(Guerrilla Charlie);* Morris Ankrum *(Captain Halsey);* Steve Brodie *(M.P.);* Harry Hayden *(Judge);* Blake Edwards *(Officer);* Robert Bice *(Jig White);* Bill Williams *(Bud Felton).*

WITHOUT LOVE
(MGM, 1945) 111 min.

PRODUCER: Lawrence A. Weingarten
DIRECTOR: Harold S. Bucquet
BASED ON THE PLAY BY PHILIP BARRY
SCREENPLAY: Donald Ogden Stewart
ART DIRECTORS: Cedric Gibbons, Harry McAfee
SET DECORATORS: Edwin B. Willis, McLean Nisbet
MUSIC: Bronislau Kaper

ASSISTANT DIRECTOR: Earl McEvoy
COSTUMES: Irene, Marion Herwood Keyes
MAKEUP: Jack Dawn
SOUND: Douglas Shearer
MONTAGE: Peter Ballbusch
SPECIAL EFFECTS: A. Arnold Gillespie, Danny Hall
CAMERA: Karl Freund
EDITOR: Frank Sullivan

Spencer Tracy *(Pat Jamieson);* Katharine Hepburn *(Jamie Rowan);* Lucille Ball *(Kitty Trimble);* Keenan Wynn *(Quentin Ladd);* Carl Esmond *(Paul Carrell);* Patricia Morison *(Edwina Collins);* Felix Bressart *(Professor Grinza);* Emily Massey *(Anna);* Gloria Grahame *(Flower Girl);* George Davis *(Caretaker);* George Chandler *(Elevator Man);* Clancy Cooper *(Sergeant);* Wallis Clark *(Professor Thompson);* Donald Curtis *(Professor Ellis);* Charles Arnt *(Colonel Braden);* Eddie Acuff *(Driver);* Clarence Muse *(Porter);* Franco Corsaro *(Headwaiter);* Ralph Brooks *(Pageboy);* William Forrest *(Doctor);* Garry Owen, Joe Devlin, William Newell *(Soldiers);* James Flavin *(Sergeant);* Hazel Brooks *(Girl on Elevator).*

THE SEA OF GRASS
(MGM, 1947) 131 min.

PRODUCER: Pandro S. Berman
DIRECTOR: Elia Kazan
BASED ON THE NOVEL BY CONRAD RICHTER
SCREENPLAY: Marguerite Roberts, Vincent Lawrence
ART DIRECTORS: Cedric Gibbons, Paul Groesse
SET DECORATOR: Edwin B. Willis
MUSIC: Herbert Stothart
COSTUMES: Walter Plunkett
ASSISTANT DIRECTOR: Sid Sidman
MAKEUP: Jack Dawn
SOUND: Douglas Shearer
CAMERA: Harry Stradling
EDITOR: Robert J. Kern

Katharine Hepburn *(Lutie Cameron Brewton);* Spencer Tracy *(Colonel James Brewton);* Melvyn Douglas *(Brice Chamberlain);* Phyllis Thaxter *(Sarah Beth Brewton);* Robert Walker *(Brock Brewton);* Edgar Buchanan *(Jeff);* Harry Carey *(Doc Reid);* Ruth Nelson *(Selena Hall);* William "Bill" Phillips *(Banty);* James Bell *(Sam Hall);* Robert Barrat *(Judge White);* Charles Trowbridge *(George Cameron);* Russell Hicks *(Major Harney);* Robert Armstrong *(Floyd McCurtin);* Trevor Bardette *(Andy Boggs);* Morris Ankrum *(Crane);* Nora Cecil *(Nurse);* Glenn Strange *(Bill Roach);* Douglas Fowley *(Joe Horton);* Buddy Roosevelt, Earle Hodgins, Robert Bice *(Cowboys);* Vernon Dent *(Conductor);* John Vosper *(Hotel Clerk);* John Hamilton *(Forrest Cochran);* Joseph Crehan *(Senator Graw);* Patty Smith *(Sarah Beth at Age 4 ½);* Whit Bissell *(Ted the Clerk);* Jimmie Hawkins *(Brock at Age 5 ½);* Carol Nugent *(Sarah Beth at Age Seven);* William Challee *(Deputy Sheriff);* Stanley Andrews *(Sheriff).*

CASS TIMBERLANE
(MGM, 1947) 119 min.

PRODUCER: Arthur Hornblow, Jr.
DIRECTOR: George Sidney
BASED ON THE NOVEL BY SINCLAIR LEWIS
SCREENPLAY: Donald Ogden Stewart
ADAPTORS: Stewart, Sonya Levien
COSTUMES: Irene
ART DIRECTORS: Cedric Gibbons, Daniel Cathcart
SET DECORATORS: Edwin B. Willis, Richard Pefferle
MUSIC: Roy Webb
MUSIC DIRECTOR: Constantin Bakaleinikoff
ASSISTANT DIRECTOR: George Ryan
SOUND: Douglas Shearer, Frank B. MacKenzie
SPECIAL EFFECTS: Warren Newcombe, A. Arnold Gillespie
CAMERA: Robert Planck
EDITOR: John Dunning

Spencer Tracy *(Cass Timberlane);* Lana Turner *(Virginia Marshland);* Zachary Scott *(Brad Criley);* Tom Drake *(Jamie Wargate);* Mary Astor *(Queenie Havock);* Albert Dekker *(Boone Navock);* Margaret Lindsay *(Chris Grau);* John Litel *(Webb Wargate);* Mona Barrie *(Avis Elderman);* Josephine Hutchinson *(Lillian Drover);* Selena Royle *(Louise Wargate);* Richard Gaines *(Dennis Thane);* John Alexander *(Dr. Roy Drover);* Cameron Mitchell *(Eino Roskinen);* Howard Freeman *(Harvey Plint);* Jessie Grayson *(Mrs. Higbee);* Griff Barnett *(Herman);* Pat Clark *(Alice Wargate);* Walter Pidgeon *(Hollywood Star at Manhattan Cocktail Party).*

STATE OF THE UNION
(MGM, 1948) 124 min. (British release title: THE WORLD AND HIS WIFE)

PRODUCER: Frank Capra
ASSOCIATE PRODUCER: Anthony Veiller
DIRECTOR: Capra
BASED ON THE PLAY BY HOWARD LINDSAY AND RUSSEL CROUSE
SCREENPLAY: Veiller, Myles Connolly
ART DIRECTORS: Cedric Gibbons, Urie McCleary
SET DECORATOR: Emile Kuri
MUSIC: Victor Young
ASSISTANT DIRECTOR: Arthur S. Black, Jr.
COSTUMES: Irene
SOUND: Douglas Shearer
SPECIAL EFFECTS: A. Arnold Gillespie
CAMERA: George J. Folsey
EDITOR: William Hornbeck

Spencer Tracy *(Grant Matthews);* Katharine Hepburn *(Mary Matthews);* Van Johnson *(Spike McManus);* Angela Lansbury *(Kay Thorndyke);* Adolphe Menjou *(Jim Conover);* Lewis Stone *(Sam Thorndyke);* Howard Smith *(Sam Parrish);* Maidel Turner *(Lulubelle Alexander);* Raymond Walburn *(Judge Alexander);* Charles Dingle *(Bill Hardy);* Florence Auer *(Grace Orval Draper);* Pierre Watkin *(Senator Lauterback);* Margaret Hamilton *(Norah);* Irving Bacon *(Buck);* Patti Brady *(Joyce);* George Nokes *(Grant, Jr.);* Carl Switzer *(Bellboy);* Tom Pedi *(Barber);* Tom Fadden *(Waiter);* Charles Lane *(Blink Moran);* Art Baker *(Leith);* Rhea Mitchell *(Jenny);* Arthur O'Connell *(Reporter);* Marion Martin *(Blonde Girl);* Tor Johnson *(Wrestler);* Stanley Andrews *(Senator);* Dave Willock *(Pilot);* Russell Meeker *(Politician);* Frank I. Clarke *(Joe Crandall);* David Clarke *(Rusty Miller);* Dell Henderson *(Broder);* Edwin Cooper *(Bradbury);* Davison Clark *(Crump);* Francis Pierlot *(Josephs);* Brandon Beach *(Editor);* Eddie Phillips *(Television Man);* Roger Moore, Lew Smith, Gene Coogan, Douglas Carter, Charles Sherlock, Wilson Wood, George Barton, Harry Anderson, Charles Coleman, Stanley Price, Fred Zendar, Jack Boyle *(Photographers);* Maurice Cass *(Little Man);* Eve Whitney *(Secretary);* Bert Moorhouse, Thornton Edwards, Marshall Ruth *(Men).*

EDWARD, MY SON
(MGM, 1949) 112 min.

PRODUCER: Edwin C. Knopf
DIRECTOR: George Cukor
BASED ON THE PLAY BY ROBERT MORLEY AND NOEL LANGLEY
SCREENPLAY: Donald Ogden Stewart
MUSIC: John Woodridge
MUSIC DIRECTOR: Sir Malcolm Sargent
ART DIRECTOR: Alfred Junge
SOUND: A. W. Watkins
SPECIAL EFFECTS: Tom Howard
CAMERA: Freddie Young
EDITOR: Raymond Poulton

Spencer Tracy *(Arnold Boult);* Deborah Kerr *(Evelyn Boult);* Ian Hunter *(Dr. Woodhope);* Leueen MacGrath *(Eileen Perrin);* Felix Aylmer *(Mr. Hanray);* Walter Fitzgerald *(Mr. Kedner);* Tilsa Page *(Betty Foxley);* Ernest Jay *(Detective);* Colin Gordon *(Ellerby);* Harriette Johns *(Phyllis Mayden);* Julian d'Albie *(Summers);* Clement McCallin *(Sergeant Kenyon).*

ADAM'S RIB
(MGM, 1949) 101 min.

PRODUCER: Lawrence Weingarten
DIRECTOR: George Cukor
STORY/SCREENPLAY: Garson Kanin, Ruth Gordon
ART DIRECTORS: Cedric Gibbons, William Ferrari
SET DECORATORS: Edwin B. Willis, Henry W. Grace
MUSIC: Miklos Rozsa
SONG: Cole Porter
ASSISTANT DIRECTOR: Jack Greenwood
COSTUMES: Walter Plunkett
MAKEUP: Jack Dawn
SPECIAL EFFECTS: A. Arnold Gillespie
SOUND: Douglas Shearer
CAMERA: George J. Folsey
EDITOR: George Boemler

Spencer Tracy *(Adam Bonner);* Katharine Hepburn *(Amanda Bonner);* Judy Holliday *(Doris Attinger);* Tom Ewell *(Warren Attinger);* David Wayne *(Kip Lurie);* Jean

Hagen *(Beryl Caighn);* Hope Emerson *(Olympia La Pere);* Eve March *(Grace);* Clarence Kolb *(Judge Reiser);* Emerson Treacy *(Jules Frikke);* Polly Moran *(Mrs. McGrath);* Will Wright *(Judge Marcasson);* Elizabeth Flournoy *(Dr. Margaret Brodeigh);* Janna Da Loos *(Mary, the Maid);* James Nolan *(Dave);* David Clarke *(Roy);* John Maxwell Sholes *(Court Clerk);* Marvin Kaplan *(Court Stenographer);* William Self *(Benjamin Klausner);* Gracille La Vinder *(Police Matron);* Ray Walker *(Photographer);* Tommy Noonan *(Reporter);* De Forrest Lawrence, John Fell *(Adam's Assistants);* Sid Dubin *(Amanda's Assistant);* Joe Bernard *(Mr. Bonner);* Madge Blake *(Mrs. Bonner);* Marjorie Wood *(Mrs. Marcasson);* Lester Luther *(Judge Poynter);* Anna Q. Nilsson *(Mrs. Poynter);* Roger David *(Hurlock);* Louis Mason *(Elderly Elevator Operator);* Rex Evans *(Fat Man);* Charles Bastin *(Young District Attorney);* E. Bradley Coleman *(Subway Rider);* Paula Raymond *(Emerald);* Harry Cody, Gil Patric, Glenn Gallagher *(Criminal Attorneys);* George Magrill, Bert Davidson *(Subway Guards).*

MALAYA
(MGM, 1949) 98 min.

PRODUCER: Edwin Knopf
DIRECTOR: Richard Thorpe
STORY: Manchester Boddy
SCREENPLAY: Frank Fenton
MUSIC: Bronislau Kaper
MUSIC DIRECTOR: Andre Previn
ART DIRECTORS: Cedric Gibbons, Malcolm Brown
SET DECORATORS: Edwin B. Willis, Henry Grace
COSTUMES: Irene, Vallees
SOUND: Douglas Shearer
SPECIAL EFFECTS: A. Arnold Gillespie, Warren Newcombe
CAMERA: George Folsey
EDITOR: Ben Lewis

Spencer Tracy *(Carnahan);* James Stewart *(John Royer);* Valentina Cortesa *(Luana);* Sydney Greenstreet *(The Dutchman);* John Hodiak *(Kellar);* Lionel Barrymore *(John Manchester);* Gilbert Roland *(Romano);* Roland Winters *(Bruno Gruber);* Richard Loo *(Colonel Genichi Tomura);* Ian MacDonald *(Carlos Tassuma);* Tom Helmore *(Matisson);* James Todd *(Carson);* Charles Meredith *(Big Man).*

FATHER OF THE BRIDE
(MGM, 1950) 93 min.

PRODUCER: Pandro S. Berman
DIRECTOR: Vincente Minnelli
BASED ON THE NOVEL BY EDWARD STREETER
SCREENPLAY: Frances Goodrich, Albert Hackett
MUSIC: Adolph Deutsch
ART DIRECTORS: Cedric Gibbons, Leonid Vasian
SET DECORATORS: Edwin B. Willis, Keogh Gleason
COSTUMES: Helen Rose, Walter Plunkett
ASSISTANT DIRECTOR: Marvin Stuart
MAKEUP: Jack Dawn
SOUND: Douglas Shearer
CAMERA: John Alton
EDITOR: Ferris Webster

Spencer Tracy *(Stanley T. Banks);* Joan Bennett *(Ellie Banks);* Elizabeth Taylor *(Kay Banks);* Don Taylor *(Buckley Dunstan);* Billie Burke *(Mrs. Doris Dunstan);* Leo G. Carroll *(Mr. Massoula);* Moroni Olsen *(Herbert Dunstan);* Melville Cooper *(Mr. Tringle);* Taylor Holmes *(Warner);* Paul Harvey *(Reverend A. I. Galsworthy);* Frank Orth *(Joe);* Rusty Tamblyn *(Tommy Banks);* Tom Irish *(Ben Banks);* Marietta Canty *(Delilah);* Willard Waterman *(Dixon);* Nancy Valentine *(Fliss);* Mary Jane Smith *(Effie);* Jacqueline Duval *(Peg);* Fay Baker *(Miss Bellamy);* Frank Hyers *(Duffy);* Chris Drake, Floyd Taylor, Don Anderson, William Mahan, Walter Kelly, Peter Thompson, Carleton Carpenter *(Ushers);* Lucille Barnes, Erin Selwyn, Janet Fay, Wendy Waldron *(Bridesmaids);* Douglas Spencer *(Organist);* Stuart Holmes, Anne Kunde, Ella Ethridge, William Bailey, Dorothy Phillips *(Bits in Dream Sequence);* William "Bill" Phillips *(Movers' Foreman).*

FATHER'S LITTLE DIVIDEND
(MGM, 1951) 82 min.

PRODUCER: Pandro S. Berman
DIRECTOR: Vincente Minnelli
BASED ON CHARACTERS CREATED BY EDWARD STREETER
SCREENPLAY: Frances Goodrich, Albert Hackett
MUSIC: Albert Sendrey
MUSIC DIRECTOR: Georgie Stoll
ART DIRECTORS: Cedric Gibbons, Leonid Vasian
SET DECORATORS: Edwin Willis, Keogh Gleason
WOMEN'S COSTUMES: Helen Rose
SOUND: Douglas Shearer
CAMERA: John Alton
EDITOR: Ferris Webster

Spencer Tracy *(Stanley Banks);* Joan Bennett *(Ellie Banks);* Elizabeth Taylor *(Kay Dunstan);* Don Taylor *(Buckley Dunstan);* Billie Burke *(Doris Dunstan);* Moroni Olsen *(Herbert Dunstan);* Frank Faylen *(Policeman);* Marietta Canty *(Delilah);* Rusty Tamblyn *(Tommy Banks);* Tom Irish *(Ben Banks);* Hayden Rorke *(Dr. Andrew Nordell);* Paul Harvey *(Reverend Galsworthy);* Donald Clark *(The Dividend);* Beverly Thompson *(Nurse);* Dabs Greer *(Taxi Driver);* Robert B. Williams *(Motorcycle Cop);* Harry Hines *(Old Man);* Frank Sully *(Diaper Man);* Janet Fay, Nancy Valentine, Wendy Waldron, Erin Selwyn, Jacqueline Duval *(Bridesmaids);* George Bruggeman *(Gym Instructor);* Lon Poff *(Elderly Man on Porch).*

THE PEOPLE AGAINST O'HARA
(MGM, 1951) 102 min.

PRODUCER: William H. Wright
DIRECTOR: John Sturges
BASED ON THE NOVEL BY ELEAZAR LIPSKY
SCREENPLAY: John Monks, Jr.
MUSIC: Carmen Dragon
ART DIRECTORS: Cedric Gibbons, James Basevi
SET DECORATORS: Edwin B. Willis, Jacques Mapes
ASSISTANT DIRECTOR: Herbert Glazer
SOUND: Douglas Shearer
SPECIAL EFFECTS: A. Arnold Gillespie, Warren Newcombe
CAMERA: John Alton
EDITOR: Gene Ruggiero

Spencer Tracy *(James P. Curtayne);* Pat O'Brien *(Vince Ricks);* Diana Lynn *(Virginia Curtayne);* John Hodiak *(Louis Barra);* James Arness *(John O'Hara);* Eduardo Ciannelli *("Knuckles" Lanzetta);* Yvette Duguay *(Mrs. Lanzetta);* Jay C. Flippen *(Sven Norson);* William Campbell *(Frank Korvac);* Richard Anderson *(Jeff Chapman);* Henry O'Neill *(Judge Keating);* Arthur Shields *(Mr. O'Hara);* Louise Lorimer *(Mrs. O'Hara);* Ann Doran *(Betty Clark);* Emile Meyer *(Captain Tom Mulvaney);* Regis Toomey *(Fred Colton);* Katharine Warren *(Mrs. Sheffield);* Paul Bryar *(Detective Howie Pendleton);* Peter Mamakos *(James Korvac);* Perdita Chandler *(Gloria Adler);* Frank Ferguson *(Al);* Don Dillaway *(Monty);* Anthony Hughes *(George);* Lee Phelps *(Emmett Kimbaugh);* Tony Barr *("Little Wolfie");* Jeff Richards *(Ambulance Driver);* Mae Clarke *(Receptionist);* William Self *(Technician);* William Schallert *(Interne);* Celia Lovsky *(Mrs. Korvac);* Jack Kruschen *(Uniformed Detective);* Charles Bronson *(Angelo Korvac);* Bill Fletcher *(Peter Korvac);* Richard Bartlett *(Tony Korvac).*

PAT AND MIKE
(MGM, 1952) 95 min.

PRODUCER: Lawrence Weingarten
DIRECTOR: George Cukor
STORY/SCREENPLAY: Ruth Gordon, Garson Kanin
ART DIRECTORS: Cedric Gibbons, Urie McCleary
SET DECORATORS: Edwin B. Willis, Hugh Hunt
ASSISTANT DIRECTOR: Jack Greenwood
WARDROBE FOR MISS HEPBURN: Orry-Kelly
MUSIC: David Raksin
MAKEUP: William Tuttle
SOUND: Douglas Shearer
SPECIAL EFFECTS: Warren Newcombe
MONTAGE: Peter Ballbusch
CAMERA: William Daniels
EDITOR: George Boemler

Spencer Tracy *(Mike Conovan);* Katharine Hepburn *(Pat Pemberton);* Aldo Ray *(Davie Hucko);* William Ching *(Collier Weld);* Sammy White *(Barney Grau);* George Mathews *(Spec Cauley);* Loring Smith *(Mr. Beminger);* Phyllis Povah *(Mrs. Beminger);* Charles Bronson *(Hank Tasling);* Frank Richards *(Sam Garsell);* Jim Backus *(Charles Barry);* Chuck Connors *(Police Captain);* Owen McGiveney *(Harry MacWade);* Lou Lubin *(Waiter);* Carl Switzer *(Busboy);* William Self *(Pat's Caddy);* Billy McLean,

Frankie Darro, Paul Brinegar, "Tiny" Jimmie Kelly *(Caddies);* Mae Clarke, Elizabeth Holmes, Helen Eby-Rock *(Women Golfers);* Hank Weaver *(Commentator);* Tom Harmon *(Sportscaster);* Charlie Murray *(Line Judge);* Don Budge, Helen Dettweiler, Betty Hicks, Beverly Hanson, Babe Didrikson Zaharias, Gussie Moran, Alice Marble, Frank Parker *(Themselves);* Kay English, Jerry Schumacher, Sam Pierce, Bill Lewin, A. Cameron Grant *(Reporters);* John Close, Fred Coby, Russ Clark *(Troopers);* Barbara Kimbrell, Elinor Cushingham, Jane Stanton *(Tennis Players);* Louis Mason *(Railway Conductor);* Craufurd Kent *(Tennis Umpire);* King Mojave *(Linesman).*

PLYMOUTH ADVENTURE
(MGM, 1952) C-105 min.

PRODUCER: Dore Schary
DIRECTOR: Clarence Brown
BASED ON THE NOVEL BY ERNEST GABLER
SCREENPLAY: Helen Deutsch
ASSISTANT DIRECTOR: Ridgeway Callow
SECOND UNIT DIRECTOR: James Havens
MUSIC: Miklos Rozsa
ART DIRECTORS: Cedric Gibbons, Urie McCleary
SET DECORATORS: Edwin B. Willis, Hugh Hunt
COSTUMES: Walter Plunkett
TECHNICOLOR CONSULTANTS: Henri Jaffa, Alvord Eiseman
SOUND: Douglas Shearer
SPECIAL EFFECTS: A. Arnold Gillespie, Warren Newcombe, Irving Ries
CAMERA: William Daniels
EDITOR: Robert J. Kern

Spencer Tracy *(Captain Jones);* Gene Tierney *(Dorothy Bradford);* Van Johnson *(John Alden);* Leo Genn *(William Bradford);* Lloyd Bridges *(Coppin);* Dawn Addams *(Priscilla Mullins);* Barry Jones *(William Brewster);* Noel Drayton *(Miles Standish);* Lowell Gilmore *(Edward Winslow);* John Dehner *(Gilbert Winslow);* Tommy Ivo *(William Button);* Rhys Williams *(Mr. Weston);* Kathleen Lockhart *(Mary Brewster);* Murray Matheson *(Christopher Martin);* John Dierkes *(Greene);* Paul Cavanaugh *(John Carver);* Noreen Corcoran *(Ellen Moore);* Dennis Hoey *(Head Constable);* Hugh Pryne *(Samuel Fuller);* Matt Moore *(William Mullins);* William Self *(Sailor);* Elizabeth Flournoy *(Rose Standish);* Loren Brown *(Sailor).*

THE ACTRESS
(MGM, 1953) 90 min.

PRODUCER: Lawrence Weingarten
DIRECTOR: George Cukor
BASED ON THE PLAY *Years Ago* BY RUTH GORDON
SCREENPLAY: Gordon
ASSISTANT DIRECTOR: Jack Greenwood
MUSIC DIRECTOR: Bronislau Kaper
ART DIRECTORS: Cedric Gibbons, Arthur Lonergan
SET DECORATORS: Edwin B. Willis, Emile Kuri
COSTUMES: Walter Plunkett
SOUND: Douglas Shearer
SPECIAL EFFECTS: Warren Newcombe
CAMERA: Harold Rosson
EDITOR: George Boemler

Spencer Tracy *(Clinton Jones);* Jean Simmons *(Ruth Gordon Jones);* Teresa Wright *(Annie Jones);* Anthony Perkins *(Fred Whitmarsh);* Ian Wolfe *(Mr. Bagley);* Kay Williams *(Hazel Dawn);* Mary Wickes *(Emma Glavey);* Norma Jean Nilsson *(Anna);* Dawn Bender *(Katherine).*

BROKEN LANCE
(20th Century-Fox, 1954) C-96 min.

PRODUCER: Sol C. Siegel
DIRECTOR: Edward Dmytryk
BASED ON THE SCREENPLAY *House of Strangers* BY PHILIP YORDAN
NEW SCREENPLAY: Richard Murphy
MUSIC DIRECTOR: Lionel Newman
MUSIC: Leigh Harline
ART DIRECTORS: Lyle Wheeler, Maurice Ransford
SET DECORATORS: Walter Scott, Stuart Reiss
COSTUMES: Travilla
SOUND: W. D. Flick, Roger Heman
SPECIAL EFFECTS: Ray Kellogg
CAMERA: Joseph McDonald, Anthony Newman
EDITOR: Dorothy Spencer

Spencer Tracy *(Matt Devereaux);* Robert Wagner *(Joe Devereaux);* Jean Peters *(Barbara);* Richard Widmark *(Ben Devereaux),* Katy Jurado *(Senora Devereaux);* Hugh O'Brian *(Mike Devereaux);* Eduard Franz *(Two Moons);* Earl Holliman *(Denny Devereaux);* E. G. Marshall *(Governor);* Carl Benton Reid *(Clem Lawton);* Philip Ober *(Van Cleve);* Robert Burton *(Mac Andrews);* Robert Adler *(O'Reilly);* Russell Simpson *(Judge);* King Donovan *(Clerk);* Edmund Cobb *(Court Clerk);* George E. Stone *(Paymaster);* Paul Kruger *(Bailiff);* James F. Stone *(Stable owner).*

BAD DAY AT BLACK ROCK
(MGM, 1955) C-81 min.

PRODUCER: Dore Schary
ASSOCIATE PRODUCER: Herman Hoffman
DIRECTOR: John Sturges
STORY: Howard Breslin
SCREENPLAY: Millard Kaufman
COLOR CONSULTANT: Alvord Eiseman
MUSIC: Andre Previn
ART DIRECTORS: Cedric Gibbons, Malcolm Brown
SET DECORATORS: Edwin B. Willis, Fred MacLean
SOUND: Wesley C. Miller
CAMERA: William C. Mellor
EDITOR: Newell P. Kimlin

Spencer Tracy *(John J. Macreedy);* Robert Ryan *(Reno Smith);* Anne Francis *(Liz Wirth);* Dean Jagger *(Tim Horn);* Walter Brennan *(Doc Velie);* John Ericson *(Pete Wirth);* Ernest Borgnine *(Coley Trimble);* Lee Marvin *(Hector David);* Russell Collins *(Mr. Hastings);* Walter Sande *(Sam).*

THE MOUNTAIN
(Paramount, 1956) C-105 min.

PRODUCER/DIRECTOR: Edward Dmytryk
BASED ON THE NOVEL BY HENRI TROYAT
SCREENPLAY: Ranald MacDougall
ASSISTANT DIRECTOR: William McGarry
MUSIC: Daniele Amfitheatrof
TECHNICOLOR CONSULTANT: Richard Mueller
ART DIRECTORS: Hal Pereira, John Goodman
SET DECORATORS: Sam Comer, Grace Gregory
COSTUMES: Edith Head
SOUND: Harold Lewis, Gene Garvin
SPECIAL EFFECTS: John Fulton
PROCESS CAMERA: Farciot Edouart
CAMERA: Franz F. Planer
EDITOR: Frank Bracht

Spencer Tracy *(Zachary Teller);* Robert Wagner *(Chris Teller);* Claire Trevor *(Marie);* William Demarest *(Father Belacchi);* Barbara Darrow *(Simone);* E. G. Marshall *(Solange);* Anna Kashfi *(Hindu Girl);* Richard Garrick *(Coloz);* Richard Arlen *(Rivial);* Harry Townes *(Joseph);* Stacy Harris *(Servoz);* Yves Brainville *(Andre);* Mary Adams *(Mayor's Wife);* Jim Hayward *(Mayor);* Richard Cutting *(Doctor).*

DESK SET
(20th Century-Fox, 1957) C-103 min.
(British release title: HIS OTHER WOMAN)

PRODUCER: Henry Ephron
DIRECTOR: Walter Lang
BASED ON THE PLAY *The Desk Set* BY WILLIAM MARCHANT
SCREENPLAY: Phoebe and Henry Ephron
ART DIRECTORS: Lyle Wheeler, Maurice Ransford
SET DECORATORS: Walter M. Scott, Paul S. Fox
ASSISTANT DIRECTOR: Hal Herman
MUSIC: Cyril J. Mockridge
MUSIC DIRECTOR: Lionel Newman
ORCHESTRATOR: Edward B. Powell
COSTUMES: Charles Le Maire
MAKEUP: Ben Nye
SOUND: E. Clayton Ward, Harry M. Leonard
SPECIAL CAMERA EFFECTS: Ray Kellogg
CAMERA: Leon Shamroy
EDITOR: Robert Simpson

Spencer Tracy *(Richard Sumner);* Katharine Hepburn *(Bunny Watson);* Gig Young *(Mike Cutler);* Joan Blondell *(Peg Costello);* Dina Merrill *(Sylvia);* Sue Randall *(Ruthie);* Neva Patterson *(Miss Warringer);* Harry Ellerbe *(Smithers);* Nicholas Joy *(Azae);* Diane Jergens *(Alice);* Merry Anders *(Cathy);* Ida Moore *(Old Lady);* Rachel Stephens *(Receptionist);* Sammy Ogg *(Kenny);* King

Mojave, Charles Heard, Harry Evans, Hal Taggart, Jack M. Lee, Bill Duray *(Board Members);* Dick Gardner *(Fred);* Renny McEvoy *(Man);* Jesslyn Fax *(Mrs. Hewitt);* Shirley Mitchell *(Myra Smithers).*

THE OLD MAN AND THE SEA

(Warner Bros., 1958) C-86 min.

PRODUCER: Leland Hayward
DIRECTOR: John Sturges
(uncredited) Fred Zinnemann
BASED ON THE NOVEL BY ERNEST HEMINGWAY
SCREENPLAY: Peter Viertel
ART DIRECTORS: Art Loel, Edward Carrere
SET DECORATOR: Ralph Hurst
ASSISTANT DIRECTOR: Russ Llewellyn
MUSIC/MUSIC DIRECTOR: Dmitri Tiomkin
MAKEUP: Gordon Bau
SOUND: M. A. Merrick
SPECIAL EFFECTS: Arthur S. Rhoades
CAMERA: James Wong Howe
ADDITIONAL CAMERA: Floyd Crosby, Tom Tutwiler
UNDERWATER CAMERA: Lamar Boren
EDITOR: Arthur P. Schmidt

Spencer Tracy *(The Old Man);* Felipe Pazos *(The Boy);* Harry Bellaver *(Martin).*

THE LAST HURRAH

(Columbia, 1958) 121 min.

PRODUCER/DIRECTOR: John Ford
BASED ON THE NOVEL BY EDWIN O'CONNOR
SCREENPLAY: Frank Nugent
ART DIRECTOR: Robert Peterson
SET DECORATOR: William Kiernan
ASSISTANT DIRECTORS: Wingate Smith, Sam Nelson
SOUND: Harry Mills
CAMERA: Charles Lawton, Jr.
EDITOR: Jack Murray

Spencer Tracy *(Frank Skeffington);* Jeffrey Hunter *(Adam Caulfield);* Dianne Foster *(Maeve Caulfield);* Pat O'Brien *(John Gorman);* Basil Rathbone *(Norman Cass, Sr.);* Donald Crisp *(Cardinal);* James Gleason *(Cuke Gillen);* Edward Brophy *(Ditto Boland);* John Carradine *(Amos Force);* Willis Bouchey *(Roger Sugrue);* Basil Ruysdael *(Bishop Gardner);* Ricardo Cortez *(Sam Weinberg);* Wallace Ford *(Hennessey);* Frank McHugh *(Festus Garvey);* Carleton Young *(Mr. Winslow);* Frank Albertson *(Jack Mangan);* Bob Sweeney *(Degnan);* William Leslie *(Dan Herlihy);* Anna Lee *(Gert Minihan);* Ken Curtis *(Monsignor Killian);* Jane Darwell *(Delia);* O. Z. Whitehead *(Norman Cass, Jr.);* Arthur Walsh *(Frank Skeffington, Jr.);* Helen Westcott *(Mrs. McCluskey);* Mimi Doyle *(Mamie Burns);* Don Borzage *(Pete);* James Flavin *(Police Captain);* William Forrest *(Doctor);* Frank Sully *(Fire Captain).*

INHERIT THE WIND

(United Artists, 1960) 126 min.

PRODUCER/DIRECTOR: Stanley Kramer
BASED ON THE PLAY BY JEROME LAWRENCE AND ROBERT E. LEE
SCREENPLAY: Nathan E. Douglas, Harold Jacob Smith
MUSIC: Ernest Gold
ASSISTANT DIRECTOR: Ivan Volkman
WARDROBE: Joe King
MAKEUP: Bud Westmore
TECHNICAL ADVISOR: Reverend Thomas R. Marshall
SOUND: Joe Lapis, Walter Elliott
CAMERA: Ernest Laszlo
EDITOR: Frederic Knudtson

Spencer Tracy *(Henry Drummond);* Fredric March *(Matthew Harrison Brady);* Gene Kelly *(E. K. Hornbeck);* Florence Eldridge *(Mrs. Brady);* Dick York *(Bertram T. Cates);* Donna Anderson *(Rachel Brown);* Henry "Harry" Morgan *(Judge);* Elliott Reid *(Davenport);* Philip Coolidge *(Mayor);* Claude Akins *(Reverend Brown);* Jimmy Boyd *(Howard);* Paul Hartman *(Meeker);* Noah Beery, Jr. *(Stebbins);* Gordon Polk *(Sillers);* Ray Teal *(Dunlap);* Norman Fell *(Radio Announcer);* Hope Summers *(Mrs. Krebs);* Renee Godfrey *(Mrs. Stebbins).*

THE DEVIL AT 4 O'CLOCK

(Columbia, 1961) C-127 min.

PRODUCER: Fred Kohlmar
DIRECTOR: Mervyn LeRoy
BASED ON THE NOVEL BY MAX CATTO
SCREENPLAY: Liam O'Brien
ART DIRECTOR: John Beckman
SET DECORATOR: Louis Diage
MUSIC: George Duning
ORCHESTRATOR: Arthur Morton
MAKEUP: Ben Lane
ASSISTANT DIRECTORS: Carter De Haven, Floyd Joyer
SOUND: Charles J. Rice, John Westmoreland
SPECIAL EFFECTS: Larry Butler, Willis Cook
CAMERA: Joseph Biroc
EDITOR: Charles Nelson

Spencer Tracy *(Father Matthew Doonon);* Frank Sinatra *(Harry);* Kerwin Mathews *(Father Joseph Perreau);* Jean-Pierre Aumont *(Jacques);* Gregoire Aslan *(Marcel);* Alexander Scourby *(Governor);* Barbara Luna *(Camille);* Cathy Lewis *(Matron);* Bernie Hamilton *(Charlie);* Martin Brandt *(Dr. Wexler);* Lou Merrill *(Aristide);* Marcel Dalio *(Gaston);* Tom Middleton *(Paul);* Ann Duggan *(Clarisse);* Louis Mercier *(Corporal);* Tony Maxwell *(Antoine);* Jean Del Val *(Louis);* Nanette Tanaka *(Fleur);* Norman Josef Wright *(Fouquette);* William Keaulani *(Constable);* Michele Montau *(Margot);* William Hsieh *(Napoleon);* Lucky Luck *(Captain Olsen);* Norman Joseph Wright *(Fonquette).*

JUDGMENT AT NUREMBERG

(United Artists, 1961) 189 min.

PRODUCER/DIRECTOR: Stanley Kramer
BASED ON THE TELEPLAY BY ABBY MANN
SCREENPLAY: Mann
MUSIC: Ernest Gold
ASSISTANT DIRECTOR: Ivan Volkman
SONGS: Norbert Schultze, Hans Leip, and Thomas Connor; Gold and Alfred Perry
WARDROBE: Joe King
MISS DIETRICH'S GOWN BY JEAN LOUIS
MAKEUP: Robert J. Schiffer
ART DIRECTOR: Rudolph Sternad
SET DECORATOR: Gregory Milo
SOUND: James Speak
CAMERA: Ernest Laszlo
EDITOR: Fred Knudtson

Spencer Tracy *(Judge Dan Haywood);* Burt Lancaster *(Ernst Janning);* Richard Widmark *(Colonel Tad Lawson);* Marlene Dietrich *(Mme. Bertholt);* Maximilian Schell *(Hans Rolfe);* Judy Garland *(Irene Hoffman);* Montgomery Clift *(Rudolf Petersen);* William Shatner *(Captain Byers);* Ed Binns *(Senator Burkette);* Kenneth MacKenna *(Judge Kenneth Norris);* Werner Klemperer *(Emil Hahn);* Torben Meyer *(Werner Lammpe);* Alan Baxter *(General Merrin);* Ray Teal *(Judge Curtiss Ives);* Martin Brandt *(Friedrich Hofstetter);* Virginia Christine *(Mrs. Halbestadt);* Ben Wright *(Halbestadt);* John Wengraft *(Dr. Wieck);* Karl Swenson *(Dr. Geuter);* Bernard Kates *(Perkins);* Jana Taylor *(Elsa Scheffler);* Paul Busch *(Schmidt);* Sheila Bromley *(Mrs. Ives);* Howard Caine *(Wallner);* John Wengraf *(Dr. Weik);* Bernard Kates *(Perkins).*

HOW THE WEST WAS WON

(MGM, 1963) C-155 min.

PRODUCER: Bernard Smith
DIRECTORS: Henry Hathaway, John Ford, George Marshall
BASED ON THE *Life* MAGAZINE SERIES
SCREENPLAY: James R. Webb
ART DIRECTORS: George W. Davis, William Ferrari, Addison Hehr
SET DECORATORS: Henry Grace, Don Greenwood, Jr., Jack Mills
COSTUMES: Walter Plunkett
ASSISTANT DIRECTORS: George Marshall, Jr., William McGarry, Robert Saunders, William Shanks, Wingate Smith
MUSIC: Alfred Newman
MUSIC ASSOCIATE: Ken Darby
SONGS: Newman and Darby; Newman and Sammy Cahn; Newman and Johnny Mercer
COLOR CONSULTANT: Charles K. Hagedon
MAKEUP: William Tuttle
RECORDING SUPERVISOR: Franklin Milton
SPECIAL VISUAL EFFECTS: A. Arnold Gillespie, Robert R. Hoag

CAMERA: William H. Daniels, Milton Krasner, Charles Lang, Jr., Joseph La Shelle
SECOND UNIT CAMERA: Harold E. Wellman
EDITOR: Harold F. Kress

Spencer Tracy *(Narrator);* Carroll Baker *(Eve Prescott);* Lee J. Cobb *(Marshal);* Henry Fonda *(Jethro Stuart);* Carolyn Jones *(Julie Rawlings);* Karl Malden *(Zebulon Prescott);* Gregory Peck *(Cleve Van Valen);* George Peppard *(Zeb Rawlings);* Robert Preston *(Roger Morgan);* Debbie Reynolds *(Lilith Prescott);* James Stewart *(Linus Rawlings);* Eli Wallach *(Charlie Gant);* John Wayne *(General Sherman);* Richard Widmark *(Mike King);* Brigid Bazlen *(Dora);* Walter Brennan *(Colonel Hawkins);* David Brian *(Attorney);* Andy Devine *(Peterson);* Raymond Massey *(Abraham Lincoln);* Agnes Moorehead *(Rebecca Prescott);* Henry "Harry" Morgan *(General Grant);* Thelma Ritter *(Agatha Clegg);* Mickey Shaughnessy *(Deputy);* Russ Tamblyn *(Reb Soldier);* Tudor Owens *(Scotsman);* Barry Harvey, Jamie Ross *(His Sons);* Kim Charney, Brian Russell (Prescott Boys); Rudolph Acosta *(Desperado);* Jerry Holmes *(Railroad Clerk);* Joe Sawyer *(Ship's Officer);* Lee Van Cleef *(Marty);* Jay C. Flippen *(Huggins);* Clinton Sundberg *(Hylan Seabury);* James Griffith, Walter Burke *(Gamblers);* John Larch *(Grimes);* Chief Weasel, Red Cloud, Ben Black Elk *(Indians);* Willis Bouchey *(Surgeon).*

IT'S A MAD, MAD, MAD, MAD WORLD
(United Artists, 1963) C-190 min.

PRODUCER/DIRECTOR: Stanley Kramer
SCREENPLAY: William and Tania Rose
MUSIC: Ernest Gold
SONGS: Gold and Mack David
PRODUCTION DESIGNER: Rudolph Sternad
ART DIRECTOR: Gordon Gurnell
SET DECORATOR: Joseph Kish
MAIN TITLES: Saul Bass
ASSISTANT DIRECTORS: Bert Chervin, George Batcheller, Charles Scott, Jr.
COSTUMES: Bill Thomas
MAKEUP: George Lane, Lynn Reynolds
AERIAL SUPERVISOR: Paul Mantz, Frank Tallman
STUNT SUPERVISOR: Carey Loftin
SOUND: John Keene
SPECIAL EFFECTS: Danny Lee
SPECIAL CAMERA EFFECTS: Linwood G. Dunn
CAMERA: Ernest Laszlo
ADDITIONAL CAMERA: Irmin Roberts, Hal McAlpin
EDITORS: Fred Knudtson, Robert C. Jones, Gene Fowler, Jr.

Spencer Tracy *(Captain C. G. Culpepper);* Milton Berle *(J. Russell Finch);* Sid Caesar *(Melville Crump);* Buddy Hackett *(Benjy Benjamin);* Ethel Merman *(Mrs. Marcus);* Mickey Rooney *(Ding Bell);* Dick Shawn *(Sylvester Marcus);* Phil Silvers *(Otto Meyer);* Terry-Thomas *(Algernon Hawthorne);* Jonathan Winters *(Lennie Pike);* Jimmy Durante *(Smiler Grogan);* Jack Benny, Jerry Lewis *(Guest Appearances);* Edie Adams *(Monica Crump);* Dorothy Provine *(Emmeline Finch);* Eddie "Rochester" Anderson *(Cab Driver);* Jim Backus *(Tyler Fitzgerald);* Ben Blue *(Airplane Pilot);* Alan Carney *(Police Sergeant);* Barrie Chase *(Mrs. Halliburton);* William Demarest *(Chief of Police);* Peter Falk, Leo Gorcey *(Other Cab Drivers);* Paul Ford *(Colonel Wilberforce);* Edward Everett Horton *(Dinckler);* Buster Keaton *(Jimmy the Crook);* Don Knotts *(Nervous Man);* Carl Reiner *(Tower Control);* Moe Howard, Larry Fine, Joe De Rita *(Firemen);* Joe E. Brown *(Union Official);* Andy Devine *(Sheriff Mason);* Marvin Kaplan *(Irwin);* Sterling Holloway *(Fire Chief);* ZaSu Pitts *(Switchboard Operator);* Selma Diamond *(Voice of Culpepper's Wife);* Stan Freberg *(Deputy Sheriff);* Charles McGraw *(Lieutenant);* Charles Lane *(Airport Manager);* Lloyd Corrigan *(Mayor);* Jesse White *(Radio Tower Operator);* Mike Mazurki *(Miner);* Sammee Tong *(Chinese Laundryman);* Norman Fell, Nicholas Georgiade *(Detectives);* Bobo Lewis *(Pilot's Wife);* Stanley Clements, Norman Fell, Nicholas Georgiarde *(Detectives);* Don Harvey *(Helicopter Observer);* Don Van Sickel *(Stuntman);* Bobo Lewis *(Pilot's Wife);* Chick Chandler, Barbara Pepper, Cliff Norton, Roy Roberts *(Bits);* Eddie Ryder *(Tower Radioman);* Roy Engel, Paul Birch *(Patrolmen);* Allen Jenkins *(Police Officer);* Harry Lauter *(Radio Operator);* Doodles Weaver *(Salesman).*

GUESS WHO'S COMING TO DINNER
(Columbia, 1967) C-108 min.

PRODUCER: Stanley Kramer
ASSOCIATE PRODUCER: George Glass
DIRECTOR: Kramer
SCREENPLAY: William Rose
PRODUCTION DESIGNER: Robert Clatworthy
SET DECORATOR: Frank Tuttle
ASSISTANT DIRECTORS: Ray Gosnell, Leonard Kunody
MUSIC: Frank De Vol
SONG: Billy Hill
COSTUME SUPERVISOR: Jean Louis
COSTUMES: Joe King
WOMEN'S WARDROBE: Edna Taylor
MAKEUP: Ben Lane, Joseph Di Bella
SPECIAL EFFECTS: Gez Gaspar
PROCESS CAMERA: Larry Butler
CAMERA: Sam Leavitt
EDITOR: Robert C. Jones

Spencer Tracy *(Matt Drayton);* Sidney Poitier *(John Prentice);* Katharine Hepburn *(Christina Drayton);* Katharine Houghton *(Joey Drayton);* Cecil Kellaway *(Monsignor Ryan);* Roy E. Glenn, Sr. *(Mr. Prentice);* Beah Richards *(Mrs. Prentice);* Isabell Sanford *(Tillie);* Virginia Christine *(Hilary St. George);* Alexandra Hay *(Car Hop);* Barbara Randolph *(Dorothy);* Tom Heaton *(Peter);* D'Urville Martin *(Frankie);* Grace Gaynor *(Judith);* Skip Martin *(Delivery Boy);* John Hudkins *(Cab Driver).*

SIX

ROBERT YOUNG

6′
170 pounds
Brown hair
Brown eyes
Pisces

The acting career of Robert Young can be divided rather neatly into two parts, spanning five decades and two mediums. During the first part, from 1931 to 1954, he starred in over eighty feature films. The majority of the pictures were lower-bill items, but sandwiched in between the B products were some memorable performances in major pictures. Yet despite consistently good reviews, true stardom always eluded Young. He lacked the charisma of a Clark Gable or a Spencer Tracy, two fellow MGM contract players.

Perhaps part of the blame rests with Young himself, who preferred the security of modest comedies to more ambitious roles (such as the conniving Larry in *They Won't Believe Me,* 1947). Like fellow MGM leading man Walter Pidgeon, Young was such a dependable player that the studio saw little reason to promote him beyond being a bread-and-butter actor who could fit comfortably into most any genre of picture.

The second phase of Robert's career, from 1954 to the present, did however bring stardom in a major fashion. Within the intimate confines of the TV screen, Young's naturalness at last found an appreciative audience in two long-running video series, "Father Knows Best" and "Marcus Welby, M.D." Young's graying good looks, warmth, and integrity became a fixed embodiment of middle American values, bringing him a recognition and celebrity status equal to that enjoyed by Lucille Ball, Raymond Burr, and Carol Burnett. In fact, it might be argued that the very qualities that prevented Robert from achieving a more prestigious cinema career are what endeared him to the mass public.

Robert George Young was born in Chicago, Illinois on Friday, February 22, 1907. He was the fourth in a family of five children born to Thomas and Margaret Fyfe Young, an Irish Protestant family. The same year of Robert's birth, Thomas Young (a carpenter) moved his family to Seattle, Washington. There Bob would begin his education at Marengo Heights School.

Then in 1919, during the post-World War I building boom, Mr. Young decided to transfer to Los Angeles where he set up his own contracting business. The nature of the business was such that Thomas Young was frequently out of town working on various jobs. Most of what Robert considered a "delightful childhood" can be attributed to his mother. Of his father, the future star would say, "He was very strict, very severe, and I loved him dearly, but the truth was that when he was out of town we all breathed a sigh of relief."

Because of the frequently erratic provisions Mr. Young made for his family, Bob found odd jobs from the age of eight onward, often selling newspapers. Later, helping to support himself and his family while he was attending Lincoln High School, Young would work at a variety of jobs, which included debt collector, bank clerk, drugstore clerk, and haberdashery salesman. An older brother, Joseph, had worked as a stuntman and an extra in the

Hollywood silents of the 1920s, and he managed to get Robert a job as an extra in various Keystone Kop films.

In high school Bob met the girl whom he would describe as the "happy-Jack who was to change my life." Her name was Elizabeth Louise Henderson Queen. It was in a play that sixteen-year-old, six-foot Bob played Robin Hood to his future wife's 4′ 11″, thirteen-year-old Maid Marian. The first rehearsal was so awkward that the drama coach made the couple practice their lines afterward in the basement. "That leading lady of mine," Young would later remark, "taught me a number of things—above all, how to laugh. I was a pretty dull and humorless fellow until I met Betty."

Lacking the funds to attend college, Young took a job at the Farmers' and Merchants' Bank after completing high school. His school drama coach, sensing the ease and naturalness of some of his performances (a sharp contrast to his offstage shyness) encouraged Bob to attend evening courses at the Pasadena Playhouse. During the next few years, while working and supporting himself during the day, Bob appeared in forty-five productions at the Playhouse, including the role of Marco Polo in *Marco Millions* and Mellerish Wilkins in *Enchanted April.* His most important assignment for the Playhouse, however, occurred in 1931. Character actor and Playhouse director Moroni Olsen organized a touring production of *The Ship.* For this venture, Robert received $65 a week. This professional advance led him to think seriously about the possibility of a film career.

At age eight with sister Arnett at home in Seattle, Washington.

The dream became a reality when an agent, Herb Tobias, saw Bob's performance in *The Ship* and arranged a screen test for him at Metro-Goldwyn-Mayer. "Metro was going through the motions of testing a producer's girlfriend," Young recalled later. "I fed her the lines. She was terrible, and they kept shooting over her shoulder at me. I was signed and she wasn't."

The lucky audition brought Bob a $150 a week contract. However, his first few months at Hollywood's most prestigious studio were spent performing in other screen tests (he did one with Virginia Bruce), loan-outs, and bit parts. His first official film assignment was as Jimmy Bradshaw, a red herring in Fox's *The Black Camel,* an early Warner Oland/Charlie Chan film. It is one of the few mysteries in which the butler actually is the guilty party. Nevertheless, as in the cases of Ray Milland, Rita Hayworth, George Brent, and Jon Hall later, the Chan series proved to be a good training ground for aspiring actors.

Bob's second feature was more important to his career. This was *The Sin of Madelon Claudet* (1931) at MGM, which despite its purple-passion title brought Helen Hayes her first Academy Award. The film was based on Edward Knoblock's Broadway play *The Lullaby.* Originally Robert's role as Dr. Claudet, Miss Hayes' grown son, was little more than a bit part. However, when Metro executive producer Irving Thalberg saw the rushes, he decided to add a prologue and an epilogue to dilute the picture's resemblance to *Madame X* (1929). Miss Hayes' husband, Charles MacArthur, performed an extensive rewrite on the scenario, adding a subplot in which Young's wife (Karen Morley), about to leave her physician husband because of his work obsession, hears the story of Madelon Claudet's (Hayes) self-sacrifice. Crude and unsophisticated as the story was, the Metro mounting, coupled with Miss Hayes' histrionics, made it an enormous hit with the public. *The New York Times* rated Bob's work as "capable."

On a second loanout, this time to Columbia, Bob was miscast in *The Guilty Generation* (1931). An early version of the *West Side Story* theme, the film dealt with two Italian gangster families, headed by Leo Carrillo and Boris Karloff (pre-*Frankenstein*) fighting for control of the bootlegging rackets in New York City. Their offspring (played by Constance Cummings and Young respectively) fall in love and attempt to keep their romance secret, fearing reprisals. During the filming of this modest picture, Bob was called into the office of tyrannical movie mogul Harry Cohn. Cohn, in a characteristic action, suddenly began berating Bob for his "sloppy clothes," using many expletives. A shocked Bob fled from the office, vowing to leave show business permanently. Returning to the soundstage, it took all the efforts of director Rowland V. Lee to calm the shy newcomer.

Back at MGM, Young concluded his year of picture-making with an uncredited bit as a young Naval officer in the concluding scenes of the Clark Gable-Wallace Beery film *Hell Divers* (1931).

With so many high-powered personalities on the Metro lot, ranging from Gable to Beery to John and Lionel Barrymore, it was difficult for low keyed newcomers like Robert Young to gain a foothold in the actor's hierarchy. Though Bob was attractive and clean-cut, the studio had under contract Neil Hamilton, Johnny Mack Brown, Robert Montgomery and others—all more polished and far better established as handsome male leads. Even so, occasionally, despite the competition, a new player would be fitted into a major production with a part that was guaranteed to showcase his growing talents. Such was the case with Bob in *The Wet Parade* (1932).

With Dorothy Jordan in a pose for *The Wet Parade* (1932).

This film was Victor Fleming's unique film version of Upton Sinclair's elaborate diatribe on the corruption brought about by Prohibition. The two-hour feature chronicles the lives of two families from the election of Woodrow Wilson as President in 1914 until 1932. The peculiar casting included Walter Huston as Young's father who is sentenced to life imprisonment for killing his wife (Clara Blandick) in a drunken rage, Lewis Stone as a suicidal Southern gentleman whose way of being is destroyed by demon rum, Dorothy Jordan as his idyllistic daughter, bouncy Jimmy Durante as a federal agent named Abe Shilling who is gunned down by bootleggers while trying to save Young's life, and Myrna Loy as a blonde vamp. Curiously, despite the versatile cast, it was Robert who garnered the most favorable reviews for his portrayal of Kip Tarleton, the man who becomes a government agent in order to avenge his family's tragic history. *The New York Times* reported that he played his role "in a sterling manner," and *Photoplay* claimed: "Lots of moviegoers wrote to *Photoplay* protesting because his name wasn't in electric lights over *The Wet Parade.*" "It'll soon be there," it added, "or we don't know star stuff!"

Despite the film credentials Robert Young was accumulating, he was rejected for the role of Norma Shearer's grown son in *Strange Interlude* (1932), the prestige film to be made from Eugene O'Neill's much-touted Broadway play. The studio wanted someone with more marquee allure. However, during the summer of 1932, MGM star Joan Crawford, who would later become one of Robert's more frequent co-players as well as a lifelong friend, agreed to make a screen test with the young actor in a scene from the play. The test was so successful that director Robert Z. Leonard changed his mind and awarded Bob the role of Gordon (played as a child by Tad Alexander). Unfortunately, in cutting the play from its five-hour length to a realistic commercial running time (here one hundred and ten minutes), much of its psychological insight was deleted. In addition, the critics and public were not convinced by the artificial aging of stars Shearer and Gable.

Before *Strange Interlude* was released in September 1932, Bob was given the starring role in *New Morals for Old,* based on the John Van Druten play *After All.* The picture version retained Margaret Perry from the original Broadway cast as Bob's wife. Unlike the pro-youth films of the late 1960s and 1970s, the film sympathized with the older generation (represented by Lewis Stone) and ridiculed the idealism of a Greenwich Village artist, Ralph Thomas (Robert), who is devoid of canvas talent. Only when confronted with children of his own does Young's character come to appreciate his parents' sturdy values.

Young's other MGM film in 1932 was with Helen Twelvetrees, a courtroom drama titled *Unashamed.* It was originally intended as a Joan Crawford vehicle and featured Bob as the heroine's brother, on trial for killing her seducer. It was an undistinguished effort, as was Bob's loan-out to Samuel Goldwyn for the role of Ricardo in the Eddie Cantor musical comedy *The Kid from Spain* (1932). As Cantor's Spanish college friend, Young was bizarrely miscast.

Although Young's screen characters seemed at times vapid, in his personal life he certainly had a mind of his own. On March 6, 1932 he married Betty Henderson, a high school sweetheart, beginning one of Hollywood's longest, most stable marriages.[1] In a 1973 interview, Betty would recall, "When we were first married Bobby had been in pictures for two years and was under contract to MGM. The studio had told him not to marry. They were very much against it. We sneaked out of town and were married by a Justice of the Peace, Kenneth Morrison, who is now a Superior Court judge. A man offered to go with us. After the ceremony, he pulled out a list of things about me. I then discovered he was a newspaperman and it was all over the *Herald Express* the next day. Bobby said, 'There goes my career.' "[2]

Perhaps no 1933 film had more impressive before-and-behind the camera credentials than MGM's *Today We Live.* Adapted by William Faulkner from his short story "Turn About," directed by Howard Hawks, and with a cast that featured Joan Crawford, Gary Cooper (borrowed from Paramount), Franchot Tone, and Young, it would seem that the film's success was guaranteed. Unfortunately, most members of the cast were saddled with ludicrous attempts to simulate English accents, and the Hawks/Faulkner effort to create a tough masculine war story was hopelessly at odds with the gloss of the traditional Joan Crawford celluloid soap opera. Robert had the showy role of Crawford's self-sacrificing lover, but he could not make much of the part. The particularly silly finale has Tone, as Crawford's cryptic brother, guiding a blinded Young in a torpedo boat suicide mission toward an enemy ship so that Cooper and Crawford may be together at the fadeout.

[1]The Youngs would have four children: Carol Ann (born December 12, 1933); Barbara Queen (born October 1, 1937); Betty Lou (born October 28, 1943); Cathleen Joy (born November 2, 1945).
[2]In a 1961 magazine interview entitled "How I Won the War of the Sexes by Losing Every Battle," Young notes,

"I have been able to live very happily with Mrs. Robert Young since 1932. I've never felt 'threatened,' 'resentful,' 'diminished' (or any of the other things I'm told a real he-man would feel) by the fact that I am deeply dependent on her and deeply grateful for her help and comfort. And because it hasn't bothered me to need her, I've been able to give her the satisfaction of knowing she's needed, and we've never gotten trapped in one of those husband-wife battles for supremacy. We've stayed in love.

"Not that I think this is so special. Plenty of American men (most of us, for that matter) have remained happily married to their original wives. But I do think I deserve some credit for the fact that I've managed to work peacefully and pleasurably with an assortment of women who are considered the strongest in Hollywood: Joan Crawford, Norma Shearer, Barbara Stanwyck, Sylvia Sydney, for example.

"When I first worked with . . . [Crawford] she was at her peak, playing the Great Star role to the hilt and, according to rumor, ruling the sets with an iron hand. I was young, shy, green, scared —haunted by fears of Crawford pointing a beautifully groomed finger my way and pronouncing, 'Out with this nitwit—off with his head.'

"The first day of shooting [*Today We Live*] I was clumsy with my lines and I knew it. Afterward I hung around my dressing room, waiting for the ax to fall. Came a knock on my door—a courier, I figured, from the queen, delivering my walking papers. Not at all. My visitor turned out to be Crawford herself, suggesting with utmost kindness that we might go over our lines again together. Her only thought was to help me.

"I've found the same sort of woman-kindness in the other leading ladies I've worked with. Only once did the bomb go off. . . . Sylvia Sidney threw me off the set [of *The Searching Wind*] for a bad case of onionitis. I nearly drowned myself with mouthwash, and went back to apologize—thereby discovering that La Sidney, despite her star rank, was a human being too. She said she also was sorry, and she obviously was. We became good friends at a period in my life when I needed friends.

"They were beautiful and wonderful women—the ladies I used to make love to on the screen. And yet they all (even sweet little Janet Gaynor) shared one quality that used to scare me blue. Still does. I mean their drive, their will, their push. It takes an awful lot of determination for a woman to survive in Hollywood. She has to elbow her way right up to the front and keep on elbowing to stay there. And although—as indicated—I've never been interested in keeping a woman in her place, at the same time I've never been attracted to someone who might want to keep me in mine."

With Norma Shearer in *Strange Interlude* (1932).

With Helen Twelvetrees and Monroe Owsley in *Unashamed* (1932).

With Eddie Cantor and Hector V. Sarno in *The Kid from Spain* (1932).

With Franchot Tone and Joan Crawford in *Today We Live* (1933).

With Johnny Mack Brown and Mary Doran in an ad for *Saturday's Millions* (1933).

With Janet Gaynor in *Carolina* (1934).

Today We Live only emphasized the problem of the actor under an MGM contract in the early 1930s. Most studio properties were bought and developed for the studio's female stars (Garbo, Crawford, Harlow, Hayes, Shearer, *et al.*). Even Clark Gable, until his loan-out to Columbia for the Academy Award-winning *It Happened One Night* (1934), had parts that were essentially adjuncts to the performances of these high-powered female personalities. What interesting male roles existed were usually assigned to character stars like the Barrymores or Wallace Beery. After only ten features, it was evident that Young was being typecast in essentially nondescript roles of nice guy, son, loser, or hero's best pal.

Unlike other equally career-minded movie players, Bob never fought for roles or refused those he was assigned. The studio was delighted to have such a compliant property in their stock company.

Men Must Fight (1933) was a peculiar futuristic drama set in 1940 with scenes of New York City being bombed from the air and a Mothers-for-Peace meeting being raided by angry college students (one of whom was played by Bob). In *Hell Below* (1933), an unshaven Young was an officer on a submarine commanded by Walter Huston. More successful if conventional was Mervyn LeRoy's *Tugboat Annie* (1933) reuniting Wallace Beery and Marie Dressler in an entertaining rehash of their Min and Bill work. Young played Alec Brennan, their grown son whose maritime career as a Puget Sound liner skipper was a source of contention between them. Maureen O'Sullivan, another underrated MGM contract player, was cast as his sweetheart.

On loan-out to Universal, Bob starred in *Saturday's Millions* (1933), a remarkably cynical but fascinating look at college football. The conceit of the hero (Bob) and the pressure of college football as a big business cause the team to lose the crucial game in a surprisingly downbeat ending. It was a tougher, more complex role than Young was accustomed to. Yet he was very effective, particularly in his underplaying of the scene in which he apologizes for thinking of himself above the team. At RKO, he was the losing side of a romantic triangle that involved Ann Harding and Nils Asther in *The Right to Romance* (1933).

The following year was Bob's busiest professional year with the release of ten of his pictures. At Fox, Bob joined with Janet Gaynor and Lionel Barrymore in Henry King's *Carolina* (1934), a rather flimsy adaptation of Paul Green's *House of Connelly,* a comedy-drama romance about an impoverished Southern family in the post-Civil War era. The resultant film, however, did not achieve the success of the Gaynor/King collaboration of the previous year, *State Fair,* lacking the winning touches of Americana. While working on *Carolina,* Robert, Janet Gaynor, and Lionel Barrymore played themselves in *La Cuidad de Carton (Cardboard City)* (1933), a Spanish-speaking film shot in Hollywood. They are seen welcoming in

Spanish the film's hero (Antonio Moreno) to the movie capital.

Congenial, competent Young was borrowed by RKO for *Spitfire* (1934), another triangular situation. This time Katharine Hepburn was top-featured as an Ozark faith-healer with Ralph Bellamy as a fellow construction engineer and a rival to Bob. It is an eccentric melodrama in which Young (really wed to Martha Sleeper) loses Hepburn to Bellamy. *Spitfire* has a remarkable scene between Hepburn and Young in which her character receives her first romantic kiss. Indeed, it is regrettable that Miss Hepburn and Robert were not teamed again. Until Cary Grant was matched oncamera with her, Robert was one of the few co-stars who could provide a mature romantic balance for the actress.

In the United Artists spectacle *The House of Rothschild* (1934), which boasted a Technicolor sequence, he was Captain Fitzroy, one of the Duke of Wellington's (Sir C. Aubrey Smith) officers who romances Nathan Rothschild's daughter (Loretta Young). Although the George Arliss vehicle was well received, the *New York Evening Post* complained that "the injection of a romantic episode between Nathan's daughter and a Gentile British officer, with its mixed-marriage problem, is tritely handled."

Returning to the Culver City home lot, Bob starred in another Southern drama, *Lazy River* (1934), which had been planned as a Tod Browning-directed property with an original William Faulkner script. What finally emerged was a more conventional film directed by George B. Seitz. It dealt with an ex-convict (Robert) blackmailing a prominent family in the bayous but falling in love with the victims' daughter (Jean Parker). In MGM's curious, second-string, all-star cast film, *Hollywood Party* (1934), Robert is briefly visible in the climactic party scenes. Since the picture utilized the services, at one time or another, of three directors (Roy Rowland, Allan Dwan, and Richard Boleslavsky) and there was considerable editing (Johnny Weissmuller, among others, is completely cut from the release print), it is difficult to determine if Robert's role had been larger in an earlier version.

Back in Hollywood, Bob starred at Columbia in *Whom the Gods Destroy* (1934). Directed by Walter Lang, the film was yet another variation of the *Sin of Madelon Claudet* theme, *but* with an unusual twist. Walter Connolly is a theatrical producer traveling on the *Titantic* when it collides with an iceberg. Disguising himself as a woman, he manages to gain space in a lifeboat and is saved. However, because of his cowardice, he can never reveal the fact that he is alive to his wife and son (Robert). Like Madelon Claudet, he must help his offspring achieve professional and financial success from afar without revealing his true identity.

Bob's home studio, MGM, was establishing a B-unit to produce sixty to seventy-minute pictures. Among the actors recruited for these polished quickies were Franchot Tone, Stuart Erwin, Madge Evans, Edmund Lowe, Virginia Bruce, Chester Morris, Leo

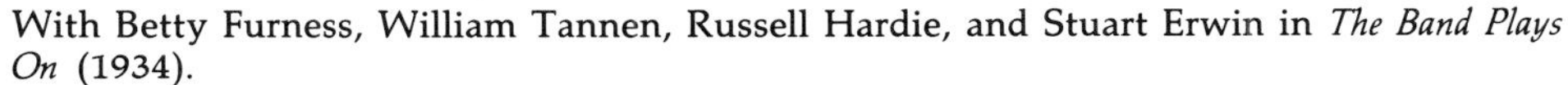

With Betty Furness, William Tannen, Russell Hardie, and Stuart Erwin in *The Band Plays On* (1934).

Carrillo, and Bob. These products provided opportunities as testing grounds for up-and-coming stars like Robert Taylor, and were frequently more ambitious than programmers turned out by the other studios. Young, for example, was starred in *Paris Interlude* (1934), a seventy-three-minute adaptation of S. J. and Laura Perelman's play *All Good Americans,* a comedy set in Paris of the 1920s dealing with a woman writer (Madge Evans) and a newspaper reporter (Bob). Unfortunately, the MGM slickness removed much of the Perelman wit and Bohemian ambiance. Even more unique was the cinema's only real baseball murder mystery, *Death on the Diamond* (1934), in which rookie player Bob solves the deaths of pitcher Joe Sawyer (shot at third base), substitute pitcher Robert Livingston (strangled in the locker room), and catcher Nat Pendleton (poisoned by an arsenic-treated hot dog). *The Band Plays On,* Young's final 1934 release, was a comedy about football players and scandals, which also featured Betty Furness and Stuart Erwin.

Young's first film for 1935 was an A-budget production starring Wallace Beery, with Robert playing his son in *West Point of the Air.* This father-son melodrama, which had become the prototype of the Beery film ever since *The Champ* (1931), featured lanky Young as the spoiled son, an air cadet who makes his dad (Beery) proud of him in the final reel. The picture itself today is remarkable only for its supporting cast which includes Maureen O'Sullivan (cast with Young for the third time), Rosalind Russell (in one of her early roles as Young's snobbish girlfriend), James Gleason, Lewis Stone, and Robert Taylor (in one of his earliest movie parts).

Vagabond Lady (1935), from the Hal Roach production unit at MGM, was a mild comedy in which Young steals his brother's (Reginald Denny) girl (Evelyn Venable) from him at the altar in a scene that anticipates the climax of *The Graduate* (1967) without the sociology. *Calm Yourself* (1935) had Robert as an ad man setting up an agency designed to relax people. It had a brisk comic script written by Arthur "Having a Wonderful Time" Kober. Both pictures demonstrated Young's understated comedic talents effectively.

Red Salute (1935), though, was a very different matter. From producer Edward Small at United Artists, this entry combined the *It Happened One Night*

With Cliff Edwards, Ruth Donnelly, and Barbara Stanwyck in *Red Salute* (1935).

theme with the then topical but poorly defined subject of young radicals. Barbara Stanwyck plays the rebellious, Communist daughter of a successful businessman. She is tamed by American soldier Robert Young. During the Red Scare of the late 1940s, the picture would be reissued under the title *Runaway Daughter,* with an ad campaign that suggested a more serious film.

In *Remember Last Night?* (1935), a comedy-mystery departure for horror film specialist James Whale, Bob had one of his most sophisticated comic roles. In this film he and Constance Cummings became Universal's answer to MGM's Nick and Nora Charles. Although Edward Arnold was the official detective investigating a murder which occurs after a drunken society gathering, this should have been the lead-off entry for a series of Bob and Constance Cummings films.

MGM, apparently unmindful of building Robert's cinema future, cavalierly loaned him to Paramount for still another other-man role in *The Bride Comes Home* (1935). As Jack Bristow, he again played the losing side of a triangle that involved Claudette Colbert and Fred MacMurray. (Colbert and MacMurray had proven very effective screen co-leads earlier that year in Paramount's *The Gilded Lily,* where Ray Milland was the "also.") Like Ralph Bellamy in the 1930s, Robert had an onscreen unassertive air that caused him to be typecast in these celluloid situations. He was one of Hollywood's favorite "other men" until Gig Young evolved into this category in the 1950s.

Stardom in anything more than a B film seemed to elude Young. Most of his second leads were in pictures that were little more than programmers. The imaginativeness of the plots can be determined by the similarity of the titles: *The Bride Comes Home, The Bride Walks Out, The Bride Wore Red, Bridal Suite,* and *Bride for Sale.* Bob needed a major film credit like *Mutiny on the Bounty* or *San Francisco* to give his career the impetus it desperately required.

Instead MGM earmarked him for such unmemorable ventures as *Three Wise Guys* (1936), a Damon Runyon comedy about Broadway sharpies arranging a phony marriage to a millionaire's son (played by Bob). *Sworn Enemy* (1936) was a sixty-two-minute gangster yarn in which Young avenges the murder of his employer (Samuel S. Hinds) and the wounding

With Fred MacMurray in *The Bride Comes Home* (1935).

of his brother (Leslie Fenton) by becoming a special investigator for the DA's office. Despite an excellent performance by Joseph Calleia as a crippled hoodlum, the very gloss of MGM production values seemed to vitiate the sort of energy required for this film genre.

Over at RKO, Young was reteamed with Barbara Stanwyck, but this time as "the other man" in a triangle completed by Gene Raymond. The result was the anemic *The Bride Walks Out* (1936), a typical 1930s farce about an on-again, off-again marriage distinguished only by its able supporting cast: Billy Gilbert, Helen Broderick, Robert Warwick, Hattie McDaniel, et al.

After the international critical and financial success of Alexander Korda's *The Private Life of Henry VIII* (1933), the British film industry began recruiting American stars to bolster the global appeal of their product. Personalities such as Constance Bennett, Edward G. Robinson, Miriam Hopkins, Sylvia Sidney, Ann Harding, Henry Fonda, *et al.* were lured to England for such filmmaking ventures. Gaumont-British offered Young a supporting role in Alfred Hitchcock's adaptation of Somerset Maugham's *Ashenden* stories.

The picture, *Secret Agent,* with a cast headed by Sir John Gielgud, Madeleine Carroll, and Peter Lorre, was easily the most heralded British feature of 1936. After *The Man Who Knew Too Much* and *The Thirty-Nine Steps* much was expected from Hitchcock. However, when *Secret Agent* was released, most critics were disappointed by the heightened morality of the espionage caper in which a secret agent (played with icy sexlessness by Gielgud) is sent to Switzerland to assassinate a dangerous spy and kills the wrong man instead. In some curious and inventive casting *against* type, Lorre was the comedy relief and Young played Marvin, the actual spy—one of the first in Hitchcock's later tradition of suave, amiable culprits.

Also at Gaumont-British, Bob was selected as Jessie Matthews' only American co-star in the successful *It's Love Again* (1936), a very light but slickly produced musical about a winsome chorus girl posing as a socialite from India. At least the foray to England provided Robert and his family with a first-hand taste of European life.

Returning to MGM, Bob appeared in that company's shortest feature, a fifty-minute mystery called ironically *The Longest Night* (1936). It seemed more an over-expanded entry from the studio's

With Alice Faye and Shirley Temple in a publicity shot for *Stowaway* (1936).

With Hugh Marlowe, Alan Bridge, Florence Rice, and Edgar Dearing in *Married Before Breakfast* (1937).

Crime Does Not Pay short subject series. Bob played a wealthy man-about-town who captures a gang of department store thieves.

Fox's Christmas feature for 1936 was *Stowaway,* starring Shirley Temple, Bob, and Alice Faye. It was a well-earned respite from the grinding out of B films at his home studio, and it demonstrated just what an excellent romantic lead Young could be, as he played Tommy Randall, a playboy who enters into an in-name-only marriage with Miss Faye in order to maneuver orphaned moppet Temple out of Shanghai. The picture had a more inventive plot than the usual Temple entry, and Young and Faye provided a balance that had been missing from earlier Temple musicals. Faye sang "Goodnight, My Love" to Young as they danced together on the deck of a ship. *Variety* confirmed: "Both are very good on performance, particularly Young."

Bob's first 1937 feature was *Dangerous Number,* an excessively nutty and frantic comedy in which he plays a conservative businessman who weds into a show business family.[3] However, Wesley Ruggles' *I Met Him in Paris* (1937) for Paramount was a different matter. It was another conventional screwball triangle, with Young this time losing effervescent Claudette Colbert to dapper Melvyn Douglas (a casting substitute for overworked George Brent). Yet the picture, its script by Claude Binyon, and its cast received rave reviews. Otis Ferguson *(New Republic)* commented, "It plays down sentiment more than other comedies and goes out for laughs in a droll, brilliant sort of a way." The *New York Times* listed it as one of the ten best films of the year. Contemporary reviews of the day are more a tribute to the ability of the three stars, since the film does not hold up well today with its forced humor.

Back at MGM, Bob was cast as the Grand Duke Peter, a supporting role in a lavish but pointless spy thriller by Baroness Orczy, entitled *The Emperor's Candlesticks* (1937). It was one of the miscalculated efforts of MGM executives and it sealed the doom on Oscar-winner Luise Rainer's film career. Young's earnestness in an absurdly miscast role and William Powell's urbanity as the Polish count-turned-spy could not conceal the banality of the project. Surprisingly, the *New York Times,* in a sympathetic critique of the feature, mentioned Bob's performance as "a triumph of grand ducal bearing and makeup."

In *The Bride Wore Red* (1937), derived from a Ferenc

[3]Robert Young's film income $58,625 in 1937, $87,208 in 1940, and $113,208 in 1941.

Molnar play, Young was a playboy. Joan Crawford was a cabaret singer from Trieste who is offered a Cinderella vacation at an expensive Tyrolean resort. There she meets Young and a philosophical village postman (played by Miss Crawford's then-husband Franchot Tone). Hollywood being Hollywood and Molnar being Molnar, she chooses the eccentric Tone over the wealthy Young. Trite as the film was, the *New York Herald-Tribune* found Dorothy Arzner's direction "always interesting and sometimes extraordinarily imaginative." *Married Before Breakfast,* (1937), was Bob's next film. It is an engaging minor entry in which Bob plays Tom Wakefield, a playboy inventor. It co-stars Florence Rice as Kitt Brent.

Following *Married Before Breakfast* was *Navy Blue and Gold* (1937), something of a sleeper for the studio. Showcasing Bob, in yet another playboy part, and Jimmy Stewart (before he got his "Aw shucks" act down pat), the film would have been just another conventional salute to Annapolis, if not for Sam Wood's sharp direction emphasizing the comic horseplay and disparities between the three focal cadets (Tom Brown was the third). Florence Rice in the fourth of her six appearances with Bob was the object of the cadets' affections, and the script had a nice *Brother Rat* tone. A supporting cast which included Lionel Barrymore (as the old Navy football star stricken on the eve of the big game), Paul Kelly, and Billie Burke made the film far more than just a programmer. Young was top-billed in this A entry.

Also during 1937 Bob served as an emcee (with James Stewart) of the "Maxwell House—MGM Good News Coffee Hour." The unwieldly title of the radio show suggests the emphasis on the sponsors. As MGM's goodwill ambassador, Young reviewed current and forthcoming studio productions when not promoting Maxwell House Coffee. When this format became too heavy-handed, the show transformed into a variety-comedy outing starring Frank Morgan with Bob continuing as the emcee.

Frank Morgan was also the star of Bob's next feature, *Paradise for Three* (1938), a complicated adaptation of Erich Kaestner's "Three Men in the Snow." Morgan played a wealthy soap manufacturer who enters his own contest incognito and wins second prize, a visit to a Tyrolean village. There he decides to see how the other half lives. Bob was the first-prize winner who romances Morgan's daughter (Florence Rice). The comic ingredients, although painfully familiar to filmgoers (for example, mistaken identity, Alpine villages, rich pretending to be poor, poor pretending to be rich), were puncutated by an expert cast that included Mary Astor, Edna May Oliver (skiing down the slopes in her bloomers), Reginald Owen, Sig Rumann, and Henry Hull.

Josette (1938) at 20th Century-Fox was Darryl F. Zanuck's miscaluated endeavor to transform Simone Simon into another Alice Faye. The usual mistaken identity plot, set in New Orleans, finds Don Ameche and Bob as brothers out to rescue their father (William Collier, Sr.) from the temptations of a chanteuse (Simon) out to save Bert Lahr's floundering nightclub. The Louisiana setting may have explained Miss Simon's French accent but the wild acclaim of the audience (within the film) after she completes a song number scarcely was justified by her modest singing abilities.

His unhappiness about the years in vapid quickies, typecast as a perennial loser in mistaken identity farces, may have been justified by his performance in *Three Comrades* (1938).[4] It was a Grade A entry with a superior director, cast, story, and script. Bob's role, next to that of heroine Margaret Sullavan (as the tubercular heroine), was the meatiest. The scenario, scripted by F. Scott Fitzgerald and Edward Paramore from Erich Maria Remarque's novel, chronicles "three comrades" in Germany returning from World War I and setting up an auto repair shop. The three (played by Robert Taylor, Franchot Tone, and Bob) befriend a young woman (Sullavan). One of the comrades (Taylor) eventually weds the girl. She dies, and Young is killed in a street riot involving various unspecified political factions. (It was implied that Bob's sympathies were pro-Nazi, although the politics of the film were deliberately ambiguous.) The final scene concludes with Tone, Taylor, and a superimposition of Young and Sullavan walking together in harmony.

Unabashedly sentimental, Frank Borzage's direction in *Comrades* demonstrated that soap opera could effectively symbolize social history. *Three Comrades* was one of the best films of 1938, and Miss Sullavan was Oscar-nominated. The *New York Herald-Tribune* would assert: "Frank Borzage has directed the film with a fine understanding of the delicate nuances, and Robert Taylor, Franchot Tone, and Robert Young are splendid." Reported the *New York Times:* "Franchot Tone has turned in a beautifully shaded portrait of Otto Koster, the loyal and devoted friend, and Robert Young is almost equally effective as the gay idealist, Gottfried."

The period melodrama *The Toy Wife* (1938) was a poor MGM attempt to establish Luise Rainer, also thick in accent, as a provocative New Orleans femme fatale. The Jezebel-like story may have been a training ground for *Gone with the Wind,* but Bob as the Southern gallant infatuated with Miss Rainer and shot in a duel was embarrassingly miscast. It is

[4]Young's role was originally intended for Spencer Tracy.

On the set of *Navy Blue and Gold* (1937) with James Stewart.

With Florence Rice, Edna May Oliver, Mary Astor, and Frank Morgan in a publicity pose for *Paradise for Three* (1938).

With Simone Simon in *Josette* (1938).

With Franchot Tone, Margaret Sullavan, Robert Taylor, and Lionel Atwill in *Three Comrades* (1938).

little wonder that misguided assignments such as these continued to build the tremendous insecurities that possessed Young every time he stepped in front of the cameras. Although unobvious to moviegoers, the overwhelming inferiority complex that had bothered Robert since teenage days had never left him. He began to compensate for his discomfort on the soundstages by increasingly heavier drinking bouts.

Rich Man—Poor Girl (1938) was an abrupt return to screwball social comedy of the 1930s. A remake of *The Idle Rich* (1929), which had starred Conrad Nagel and Leila Hyams, the new title was all too succinct a synopsis of the plot. It concerned a poor family (Guy Kibbee, Ruth Hussey, Lew Ayres, and a young Lana Turner) rejecting Miss Hussey's wealthy suitor (Bob) and his fortune until he threatens to give it to charity. The plot was a partially successful attempt, on a low key, to beat Columbia's *You Can't Take It with You* to the box office. Miss Hussey and a beautiful Miss Turner received a good deal of audience attention.

The Shining Hour (1938) was a reunion for Bob with Frank Borzage, Margaret Sullavan, Joan Crawford, and Melvyn Douglas in an excellent soap opera (not very appreciated in its day). Set on a Wisconsin farm, Douglas brings his ex-club-performer wife (Crawford) home to meet his family: sister Fay Bainter, sister-in-law Sullavan, and brother Bob. Joan dislikes Fay, admires Margaret, and has an affair with Bob. The story, the relationships (surprisingly adult for the times), and the situations were improbable. However, Borzage brought a romanticist's convictions to these contrivances. Moreover, Miss Bainter and Miss Sullavan managed to impart their respective malevolence and sweetness with a subtlety that stands up even when viewing the film on TV today.

While Clark Gable, Spencer Tracy, William Powell, and fast-rising Mickey Rooney and Robert Taylor continued to be the star male attractions at MGM, Bob was forced to move onward as one of the studio's prime utility leading men (like Lew Ayres and Walter Pidgeon). *Honolulu* (1939) was a musical comedy starring Eleanor Powell, she being top-billed above the title. Another mistaken identity plot, the picture at least had the novelty of providing Bob with a dual role: that of a conceited Hollywood film star and his publicity tour stand-in, a shy Hawaiian plantation owner. Yet despite the efforts of George Burns (as Bob's Hollywood agent) and Gracie Allen (as Miss Powell's addled song-and-dance partner and confidante), the picture had a surprisingly lackluster look for an MGM musical running only eighty-four minutes.

Bridal Suite (1939), which co-starred the much-touted Annabella on loan from 20th Century-Fox, had yet another playboy role for Bob. This time Billie Burke played his mother constantly trying to force him into marriage.

Director Tod Browning's final picture, *Miracles for Sale* (1939), was a unique mystery in which Young was seen as Mike Morgan, a ex-magician who solves a murder at a magicians' convention. Adapted from Clayton Rawson's prize-winning novel *Death from a Top Hat,* the brisk feature might have made a good mystery series had it followed the book more closely. (Bob's character had been The Great Merlini in the novel. Merlini would appear as a minor character in 20th Century-Fox's *The Man Who Wouldn't Die* in 1942.)

Maisie (1939), however, Bob's next film, was the genesis of a profitable MGM series. In an adaptation of the same Wilson Collison work that had been the basis of *Red Dust* (1932) and which would be the basis of the second Maisie film, *Congo Maisie,* Ann Sothern starred as a wise-cracking but always resilient chorine stranded at a dude ranch. Bob, in the refurbished Clark Gable role, played the ranch foreman engaged in a battle of the sexes with both Miss Sothern (in the Jean Harlow part) and Ruth Hussey as the ranch owner's wife. The picture was considerably less titillating than the Gable-Harlow version.

The year 1940 presented Bob with another screen opportunity when Robert Taylor rejected the second male lead in King Vidor's lavish and rugged historical drama, *Northwest Passage,* starring Spencer Tracy as Major Rogers. The project was originally conceived as a two-part epic drawn from Kenneth Roberts' best-selling novel. The advent of World War II, however, and the expense of location shooting—in Idaho—put an end to the idea of a sequel. The picture covers only the preliminary wars with the Indians. Cast against a more virile background than usual, Bob played Langdon Towne, an artist returning from his college studies in eighteenth-century New England. Turned down as a son-in-law by his fiancée's (Ruth Hussey) family, Towne gets drunk (the role still has some tinge of the playboy) and wakes up to find himself commandeered into the fighting Rangers of Major Robert Rogers. The remainder of the 125-minute feature is a long Technicolor trek through swamps, up mountains, and across river torrents punctuated by Indian fights. *Northwest Passage* proved to be one of the great box-office successes of 1940, although not all critics were sympathetic to Bob's change-of-pace casting. *Time* magazine's critic noted, "The shocking thing is to see debonair man of the world Robert Young smiling perkily in the howling wilderness."

Ironically, Bob had become such a familiar staple of B-film production at his home studio that his co-starring status in A-budget films had surprisingly little bearing on his career. The MGM hierarchy was perhaps right: his solid, steady marriage to Betty had prevented him from being a likely fan magazine subject. His work as an actor had been considered steady, solid, and dependable, but the sheer bulk of appearances he made on camera each year made critics, public, and studio take him for granted. The Hollywood attitude toward an introvert like Bob working in an extrovert business is best summed up in a memo by producer David O. Selznick when he rejected Bob for the part of Ashley Wilkes in *Gone With the Wind.* "Robert Young, while he's no Barrymore, is about on par with Lew Ayres. . . . I should like to say a word of caution against judging Young for what he was a couple of years ago. I was among those who thought he should be thrown out of Hollywood; since then, I have had to eat my words after seeing him give some really fine performances."

Released shortly after *Northwest Passage* opened, *Florian* (1940), from a novel by Felix "Bambi" Salten, was a minor offering in which Bob played a groom who saves a stallion in the Austria of 1919 while romancing and winning a comely countess (Helen Gilbert) in the process. The rather sophisticated notion of the original work paralleled the decline of the Austrian dynasty under Franz Josef with the fate of the stallion. For the MGM version, the plot became just another animal story with a love subplot added for good measure.

The Mortal Storm (1940), the third of Bob's pictures with director Frank Borzage and Margaret Sullavan in three years, seemed like an extension of the roles they played so capably in *Three Comrades.* Set in 1933 Germany, the film traced the impact of Hitler's rise to power on an intellectual family headed by a Jewish professor (Frank Morgan). Freya (Sullavan) is the teacher's daughter and is loved by both Martin (James Stewart) and Fritz (Bob). She chooses Fritz but returns to Martin when she is disgusted by Fritz' pro-Nazi sympathies.

Most poignant and memorable is the final sequence of *The Mortal Storm* with Stewart and Sullavan fleeing Germany by escaping to Austria across a snow-laden landscape. They are pursued by a Nazi patrol headed by Young. Just as the escapees cross onto the Austrian side, Miss Sullavan is shot by a bullet from the patrol, dying in Stewart's arms. Young's chilling performance in the climactic scene as he watches his loved one die (while reconciling her death with his duty as a storm trooper) is one of the more disturbing portraits of a Nazi by a Hollywood actor. Young's villainy was memorable, although he later stated that audiences "couldn't get used to my new screen image."

Sporting Blood (1940), the last of Bob's screen appearances opposite Maureen O'Sullivan, was a film of more modest ambitions. It dealt with a hackneyed feud between two racing families whose offspring (Bob and Maureen) fall in love. Essentially it was a revamping of 20th Century-Fox's *Kentucky* (1938).

Bob was perhaps the most prestigious established star in the MGM *Dr. Kildare* series. Although the continuing property was considered an excellent proving ground for up-and-coming personalities like Lana Turner, Ava Gardner, and Red Skelton, it was unique for a performer of Bob's calibre and standing to act in a series film. In *Dr. Kildare's Crisis* (1940) he is cast as nurse Mary Lamont's (Laraine Day) brother Douglas. In the course of this functional entry, Bob is cured by Kildare (Lew Ayres) and Dr. Gillespie (Lionel Barrymore) of what appears to be a form of epilepsy but is later determined to be the result of an old injury.

Bob's first 1941 release was equally unprestigious. A remake of Norma Shearer's 1929 hit, *The Trial of Mary Dugan* in its new version found Bob playing the heroine's defense lawyer brother (in Raymond Hackett's old part). He defends her against a homicide charge. Critics wondered why the studio had bothered to remake the picture since the plot coincidences of the original seemed all too obvious to audiences of the 1940s. Moreover, new censorship rules (Mary Dugan had been the mistress of the murdered man in order to support her brother through law school) had removed any shock value the film might have had.

Fritz Lang's *Western Union* (1941) gave Bob, on loan-out to 20th Century-Fox, a Western role. It was expensively mounted in Technicolor by that studio and promoted as having been based on Zane Grey's final novel, although actually it was ghost-written. Bob was top-cast above Randolph Scott in the role of Richard Blake, a naive young Harvard graduate who goes West to help the telegraph company lay its transcontinental lines. Scott plays the good-bad man who competes with Bob for the attentions of Virginia Gilmore. The highlight of the feature was a complicated forest fire scene directed by Otto Brower. Because of Darryl F. Zanuck's penchant for spectacle and Lang's desire for realism, an elaborate forest was actually constructed as a set, with complicated tracks set out over which the actors were to run. Despite precautions and asbestos suits, Bob's eyebrows were singed during the shooting, and both Randolph Scott and Dean Jagger (as a Western Union representative) suffered burns.

At MGM, producer Arthur Freed decided to shoot

With Florence Rice and Paul Sutton in *Miracles for Sale* (1939).

With Helen Gilbert in *Florian* (1940).

With Lew Ayres, Laraine Day, and Lionel Barrymore in an advertisement for *Dr. Kildare's Crisis* (1940).

With Randolph Scott in *Western Union* (1941).

a remake of *Lady Be Good,* originally filmed by First National in 1928. The original story, however, proved to be too much a product of Roaring Twenties' sentimentality, and a new plotline was devised. During the various rewrites, even Herman Wouk and Vincente Minnelli were brought in to contribute to the new script. What resulted was an unnecessarily complicated affair about the marriage and divorce of two songwriters (played by Bob and Ann Sothern). Most of the musical numbers were staged and directed by Busby Berkeley and handled by Eleanor Powell as Miss Sothern's friend who is pursued through the plotline by wolfish John Carroll. The Academy Award-winning number, "The Last Time I Saw Paris," was sung by Miss Sothern with Bob pretending to play piano accompaniment for her. On the strength of that song, Eleanor Powell's "Fascinating Rhythm" number, and a supporting cast that featured Lionel Barrymore, Phil Silvers, Red Skelton, Virginia O'Brien, and Dan Dailey, *Lady Be Good* would eventually gross $1,692,000 for MGM.

This was followed by yet another bit of program fodder, *Married Bachelor* (1941). The tired plot centered around a so-called marriage expert who is actually a bachelor. Bob's co-star was again radiant Ruth Hussey. She would also play an important part in Bob's next picture.

H. M. Pulham, Esq. (1941) was the motion picture that would solidify Bob's star status at MGM and win him—and nearly everyone else in the film—his best reviews to date. Adapted from John P. Marquand's best-selling satirical novel about a stuffy Boston businessman, Harry Pulham (Bob), it focuses on his romantic fling with an attractive New York copywriter (Hedy Lamarr, gorgeous but hampered by an inexplicable accent). This handsome King Vidor production was designed to be Metro's big Christmas release. Unfortunately, the glut of war-oriented features and the austerity of a theme in which money and tradition triumph over love caused *H. M. Pulham, Esq.* to falter at the box office. Some of the satirical edge may have been blunted by the literalness of Vidor's direction. However, the *Citizen Kane*-like breakfast opening, establishing Bob's marriage to Ruth Hussey and his timetable existence, is one of the most effective openings of any film of the 1940s.

Bob's reviews were the best of his career to date. He was not merely "servicable" or "adequate" or "as good as." *Newsweek* stated: "Best of all, however, and the performance that holds the episodic narrative together is Robert Young's sympathetic and resourceful characterization in the title role." *Time* magazine confirmed, "Robert Young's version of the inhibited, frustrated, baffled Boston gentleman who didn't have guts or brains enough to get out of his rut is a first-rate job." Only Bosley Crowther *(New York Times)* had reservations, suggesting that Young had interpreted the part "with a stiffness resembling a bowler hat set squarely on his head."

Perhaps Bob's finest praise would come years later from veteran director King Vidor: "Here is a superb actor without a single problem, at least none that I was able to detect. Bob is completely on top of his profession. On the set he behaves with confidence, security, and total control. In his early career I used to think he moved with such ease that no woman would ever want to mother him. This conviction his screen image projects has paid off well in the character he plays in his television series."

More popular with the public, and surprisingly so since it was only a sixty-three-minute B picture, was the patriotic but ingenious *Joe Smith—American* (1942).[5] Director Richard Thorpe has his cast recount the heroism of an aircraft plant worker (Bob) who is kidnaped by a spy ring. He manages to escape and bring the police back to the gang's hideout. A highlight of the film was the scene in which a blindfolded Young leads the police to the gang by identifying sounds. (It would later become a staple technique of filmmakers.) The filmgoing public responded well to the plotline and to the sympathetic treatment of American values at home during the World War II years. *Joe Smith—American* opened as the *main* attraction at a first-run Broadway theatre. (The picture also became something of a personal crusade for MGM executive Dore Schary who in 1950 would resurrect Joe Smith, played by James Whitmore, for the more pretentious *The Next Voice You Hear.*)

Between his numerous film assignments, Bob managed to find time for radio jobs. Now an established marquee name, most of his radio work at this period consisted of film adaptations for "Lux Radio Theatre" and "Screen Guild Theatre." These included *Design for Scandal* (1943) with Carole Landis, *The Gay Sisters* (1942) with Barbara Stanwyck, *A Night to Remember* (1943) with Ann Sothern, *The Philadelphia Story* (1943) with Loretta Young and Robert Taylor, *Hello, Frisco, Hello* (1943) with Alice Faye, *The Fallen Sparrow* (1944) with Maureen O'Hara and Walter Slezak, *In Old Chicago* (1944) with Dorothy Lamour and John Hodiak, and *Mr. and Mrs. Smith* (1944) with Joan Bennett and Ralph Bellamy. He

[5]In 1942 Young joined with Clark Gable, Robert Preston, Brenda Marshall, and William Holden in the MGM two-reeler *Wings Up,* which dealt with the Air Force Officer Candidate School, prepared for the Office of War Information.

With William Forrest, Harvey Stephens, Jonathan Hale, and Francis Morris in *Joe Smith, American* (1942).

had recreated his role as the star of *Western Union* on "The Kate Smith Hour" in 1941 and repeated his part in *H. M. Pulham, Esq.* in 1942, opposite Hedy Lamarr and Josephine Hutchinson. In 1943 Bob starred with Dane Clark in "Passport for Adams," with the two actors co-starred as globe-trotting reporters visiting Allied countries. (Young was replaced during the following year in the series by Myron McCormick.)

In the curious and underrated *Cairo* (1942), Bob's leading lady was the self-spoofing Jeanette MacDonald portraying an opera star who becomes involved with Axis spies in the tropical locale. Bob is Homer Smith, a hick reporter who suspects her of being one of the spies. Ethel Waters, replacing Lena Horne, was seen as Miss MacDonald's maid. MGM, about to sever its relationship with Jeanette, gave this black-and-white feature rather skimpy production values. It is a shame because the film has moments that make one vividly recall what a gifted comedienne Miss MacDonald had been in her pre-Nelson Eddy days.

The critics dismissed *Cairo* as pap, but Bob's next at MGM, *Journey for Margaret* (1942), proved to be one of the most important releases of the year. It was derived from the real-life experiences of American correspondent William L. White who adopted two English children after his wife lost their unborn child in an air raid. This was the picture that would make a big star of tiny Margaret O'Brien, in the role of one of the children, as a sort of miniature Mrs. Miniver. Despite its simplicity, the film—propelled by Miss O'Brien's telling performance—remains one of the great Allied propaganda entries of the war years. The *New York Times* labeled Bob's performance "one of the most unpretentious and sensitive portraits he has given," and the *New York Herald-Tribune* referred to it as "an excellent restrained acting job." Such characterizations as this and *H. M. Pulham, Esq.* showed that Bob's acting, while not flashy, could project an earnestness and an understatement with which few male stars at the studio (except perhaps Van Heflin) could compete.

Alternating comedy with drama, Bob next co-starred with Lana Turner in Wesley Ruggles' *Slightly Dangerous* (1943). Despite the glossy trappings, the picture was essentially a retread of the countless double-bill items that had been Bob's training ground. This time it was Lana's refinement ground as she performed, without much comic expertise, the role of a girl trying to pass herself off as a millionaire's (Walter Brennan) daughter. Bob, as the *New York Times* asserted, "almost bursts a blood vessel in trying to be funny with little to do" in his part as Lana's exasperated beau.

Claudia (1943), with Bob on loan-out to 20th Century-Fox, was, in contrast, very successful. Rose Franken's comedy-drama is nearly the archetype of the TV situation comedy, and Edmund Goulding's direction does very little to expand upon a one-set Broadway play or to transcend the "character study" nature of the script. There are other internal problems with the film when viewed today. For one thing, Dorothy McGuire's "naturalness" as the young, immature Claudia, who only comes to grip with life when she learns that her mother (Ina Claire) is dying, comes across as forced and persistent. The film's structure—light suburban comedy, giving way to brave resignation—seems too calculated, but Bob, in a role originally offered to Cary Grant, makes David Naughton's extreme tolerance of his lightheaded wife almost credible.

Equally successful and uncomplicated was *Sweet Rosie O'Grady* (1943), a Betty Grable Technicolor songfest, also produced at 20th Century-Fox. It was a loose remake of *Love Is News* (1937), transposed to the Gay Nineties with Bob in the Tyrone Power part of a reporter (this time for the *Police Gazette*) involved in a libel suit with a musical-comedy star. The picture grossed $3.4 million and would be remade again in 1948 with Tyrone Power, this time called *That Wonderful Urge.*

The Canterville Ghost (1944) reteamed Bob, back at MGM, with Margaret O'Brien. It was an updating of the Oscar Wilde fable about the cowardly Sir Simon de Canterville (played with outrageous hamminess by Charles Laughton) who is sealed in an alcove of the castle for an act of cowardice. He is condemned to walk the halls of the castle until he finds a kinsman who will perform a brave act. The modern part of the tale opens with a group of American soldiers (among them, Bob, William Gargan, Frank Faylen, and Rags Ragland) billeted at the castle, which is presided over by Lady Jessica (Miss O'Brien). The plot meanders from anachronism to topicality to coincidence to forced slapstick as Laughton discovers that Young, about to go into battle, but a coward, is a descendant of his. The slang is often grating (Young to O'Brien: "Thatagirl, your Ladyship"), and the concluding scenes of Laughton riding around on a bomb did not prevent the film from being an enormous success and later a staple at kiddie matinees.

The Canterville Ghost marked the end of Bob's MGM tenure. Bob realized that his future with that studio could only hold more of the bread-and-butter roles that had been his lot during his fourteen years there. It was a particularly favorable time for the seemingly unaging Bob to try his luck elsewhere. Younger actors (and a few older ones) had volunteered or been drafted into military service, and the studios were desperate for marketable names. Bob signed a five-year pact with RKO calling for one film per year. While he might have preferred to free-lance at this point, he was unrealistically fearful that his services might go out of demand. As a husband and a father he thought that the security of a new long-term contract was advisable.

His first picture at RKO is arguably his finest picture. It was the 1945 remake of the Richard Barthelmess/May MacAvoy silent movie *The Enchanted Cottage.* This time the updating of the Sir Arthur Wing Pinero play was tastefully and subtly handled. An

With Jeanette MacDonald in *Cairo* (1942).

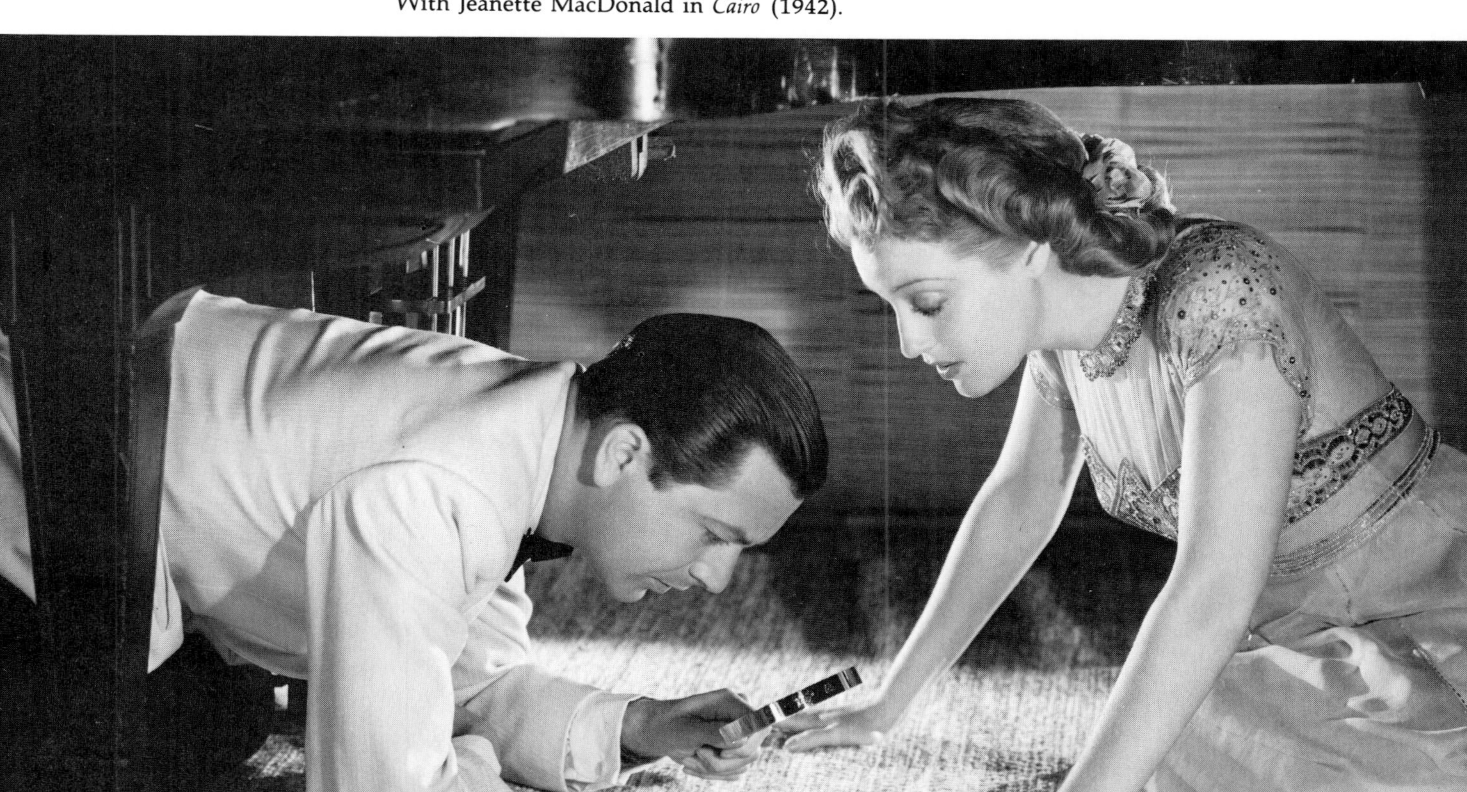

impeccably chosen cast included Dorothy McGuire as the disfigured heroine who takes a job as a housekeeper at the "enchanted cottage," Mildred Natwick as the cottage owner, Herbert Marshall as the tale's blind narrator, Hillary Brooke as Bob's fiancée, and Spring Byington as Young's mother. Bob plays war veteran Oliver who returns to the cottage that he had rented for his honeymoon, but that went unused when his bride-to-be shunned him because of a crippling war wound. He is bitter, disillusioned, and reclusive. These negative feelings gradually fade when he falls in love with the homely Miss McGuire. After their marriage, they begin to notice their disfigurations slowly vanishing as their love deepens. However, when they are visited by outsiders, we see that this is only an illusion.

As adapted by DeWitt Bodeen and Herman J. Mankiewicz, *The Enchanted Cottage* is one of the finest screen romances of the 1940s, a story of faith rather than fantasy. It is made quite credible by the restrained acting of the cast and John Cromwell's well-modulated direction. Critic James Agee wrote of Bob's performance, "I can hardly imagine, for that matter, being seriously offended by Mr. Young; whatever he does, he is sympathetic and honest beyond offensiveness." (In the 1970s it was rumored that *The Enchanted Cottage* would be remade yet again, this time with Bob and McGuire assuming the Herbert Marshall and Mildred Natwick roles, but the project never came to fruition.)

With *Joe Smith—American, The Enchanted Cottage* was Bob's favorite screen role and perhaps the one with which most filmgoers of the pre-TV days identified.

Those Endearing Young Charms, also released by RKO in 1945, was another romantic yarn, but this time a comic one. Bob played the part that Zachary Scott had originated in the 1943 Broadway show. As Hank, an Air Force wolf, he was teamed with another ex-MGM player, Laraine Day, in her fourth and final screen appearance opposite Bob. Co-starred as Miss Day's mother was another of Young's former leading ladies, Ann Harding.

Lady Luck (1946) was equally light and simple-minded. Co-starred with Bob was his old radio crony Frank Morgan and RKO starlet Barbara Hale. It is a strained comedy about gamblers and gambling, a subject that seemed to be an odd preoccupation of post-war Hollywood. Bob and Miss Hale were unable to lend much credibility to the proceedings. Strangely enough, *Lady Luck* is one of the two films for which Bob requested—and received—a personal print for home viewing. The other picture was *The Enchanted Cottage.*

More serious, perhaps too serious, was Paramount's screen version of Lillian Hellman's play *The Searching Wind* (1946). Bob's role as American diplomat Alex Hazen, whose history of appeasement and compromise has brought America to World War II, is a variation of the stodgy conservative Harry Pulham characterization. A further similarity is the character's triangular relationship with newspaperwoman Cassie Bowman (Sylvia Sidney) and his wife (Ann Richards). Howard Barnes *(New York Herald-Tribune)* reported, "Robert Young makes a laudable if rather feeble effort to personify American isolationism during two decades." Not surprisingly, it was not a popular film, being overly talky and ponderously staged.

Claudia and David (1946) was a big financial success. It takes up the threads of the 1943 film, Claudia (Dorothy McGuire) having given birth to a child. In many ways it is superior to the original. Walter Lang's direction is better paced, and the domestic crises seem less contrived. The central plot was flimsy—Claudia trying to dissuade David from attending a New York convention because a mind-reader has predicted an accident—but at least it had a more solid plot than its predecessor. The supporting cast (Mary Astor, Florence Bates, John Sutton, and Rose Hobart) was excellent.

After nearly a year's absence from the screen (made possible due to a backlog of his pictures ready for release), Bob returned to the screen in an entirely different kind of role. Those who know Young only from TV series roles would undoubtedly be shocked but impressed by his acting in the chilling *They Won't Believe Me* (1947). Produced by Alfred Hitchcock's former associate Joan Harrison, Bob was again cast as a playboy but *this time* as a more sinister one who does get the girl—three, in fact: nice Jane Greer, cynical Susan Hayward, and rich but nasty Rita Johnson. Greedy Bob weds Miss Johnson, and through many plot intricacies he ends up on trial for her murder (she actually committed suicide). The narrative is told through flashback as Bob testifies on the witness stand. The picture and its stars received solid reviews, but many critics were quick to point out that Jonathan Latimer's script lacked any sympathetic characters. Although Young had portrayed villains before, the public was not accustomed to him in such roles. "There was a problem in the 1940s," he would later recall, "when I made *They Won't Believe Me,* in which I portrayed a heel. The picture was correctly named. The public didn't believe me. I went right back to playing good guys after the box-office results came in. Fate, I guess."

It is regrettable that Young surrendered so easily to typecasting. The tough sort of image that Bob projected in *They Won't Believe Me* might have sent Bob's career in the direction of other ex-screen nice guys like Dick Powell and Robert Montgomery.

Over the years, Bob played practically every kind

With Dudley Digges, Douglas Dick, and Ann Richards in *The Searching Wind* (1946).

With Mary Astor in *Claudia and David* (1946).

With Susan Hayward in *They Won't Believe Me* (1947).

of role in almost every conceivable genre, but he never played a professional private eye. The closest he came was in his next role, Captain Finlay, the army investigator in *Crossfire* (1947). The picture itself is one of the milestones of the 1940s: the first Hollywood feature to deal seriously with the theme of racism, albeit softened by the guise of a murder mystery. This Dore Schary production at RKO proved that racial discrimination no longer need be a taboo subject for Hollywood studios. *Crossfire* was a box-office hit and was chosen for most of the ten-best-films lists of 1947.

The part of the methodical, pipe-smoking Captain Finlay was perhaps the least showy in the black-and-white feature. In the focal investigation of the murder of a Jew (Sam Levene), most of the attention is centered on the loutish bigot, a soldier named Monty Montgomery (played with terrifying conviction by Robert Ryan). Young does have a long monologue on the subject of racism, which he delivers at the film's finale when Montgomery is confronted with his crime. Bob handles the scene with an understatement that is admirable. In retrospect, however, one must agree that such self-conscious polemics date the film. (Bob thought well enough of his speech, however, that he would repeat it a quarter of a century later as part of his guest appearance on TV's "The KopyKats" show.) Young referred to his own politics as "anti-conservative independent."

Although Bob had signed a five-year pact with RKO, he was astute enough to realize that the future was ripe for independent production. In late 1946 he formed a partnership with Eugene Rodney, calling the company Cavalier Productions. Their first venture was an unusual one for Bob, a Western called *Relentless.* Completed in late February 1947, it was not released until March 1948, and was not distributed by RKO but by Columbia. It is an amiable, unpretentious Western which managed to trot out the old plot of a man accused of a crime he did not commit and his seeking of the true culprit. Splendidly photographed in Technicolor and effectively directed (by George Sherman), the cast included Marguerite Chapman, Akim Tamiroff, and Willard Parker. The *New York Times* assessed that Bob "makes a convincing and thoughtful buckaroo."

At the age of forty-one, Young revealed none of the telltale haggardness that haunts so many middle-aged leading men. He was still lean, handsome, and amazingly youthful. If there were no indications that he would emerge as a mature superstar of the cinema, he was at least still greatly in demand. Twentieth Century-Fox borrowed him for *Sitting Pretty* (1948) which turned into the surprise hit of the year.[6] Bob and Maureen O'Hara portray a sub-

[6]It was the genesis of the Clifton Webb-Lynn Belvedere trilogy at that studio. The other entries were *Mr. Belvedere Goes to College* (1949) and *Mr. Belvedere Rings the Bell* (1952).

urban couple who, unable to cope with their three small children, hire a housekeeper and sitter named Lynn Belvedere. Much to their surprise, the employee turns out to be an effete intellectual know-it-all played with prissy sophistication by Mr. Webb. (Typical Belvederian comeback. When Miss O'Hara says to Belvedere, "You dance very well. Did you learn at Arthur Murray?" he replies: "*I* taught Arthur Murray."

Although most critical and audience attention was riveted on Webb and Richard Haydn (Hummingbird Hill's resident birdwatcher and mother-bound gossipmonger), *Sitting Pretty* was important to Bob's career. It was a blueprint for white collar worker Jim Anderson on "Father Knows Best." There would be some talk of reuniting the film's star trio in one of the sequels in the Belvedere series, but this idea never came to fruition. (Eddie Bracken would inherit Bob's role in the mini-adaptation on TV's "Twentieth Century-Fox Hour.")

Adventure in Baltimore (1949) at RKO was a reunion for Bob with former co-star Shirley Temple. It was directed by Richard Wallace, with uncredited assistance by John Cromwell. Bob, uncomfortably made up with a strange-looking moustache and wig, played Shirley's minister father in this awkward and irrelevant comedy set in 1905 Baltimore. What little box-office success the picture enjoyed rested on the public's curiosity about Shirley's recent marriage to John Agar (her romantic lead in the film).

"Father Knows Best" in radio form was first heard on Thursday evening, August 25, 1949. The weekly show was sponsored by Maxwell House Coffee and broadcast over the NBC network. It was written by Ed James and starred Bob as insurance salesman Jim Anderson. The original radio cast included June Whitley as Margaret Anderson, Ted Donaldson as son Bud, Rhoda Williams as teenage daughter Betty, and Norma Jean Nilsson (later replaced by Helen Strong) as their younger girl, Kathy. Neither slapstick in comedy nor maudlin in sentiment, the series embraced clear-cut, uncomplicated American values with which radio listeners could easily identify. Despite the glut of situation comedies on radio, and radio itself being threatened with the advent of television, the program proved enormously popular. It

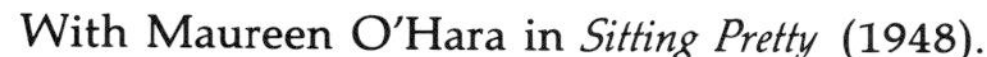

With Maureen O'Hara in *Sitting Pretty* (1948).

With Shirley Temple in *Adventure in Baltimore* (1949).

With Marc Krah and Claudette Colbert in *Bride for Sale* (1949).

With Betsy Drake and Florence Bates in *The Second Woman* (1951).

With Howard St. John and Joan Crawford in *Goodbye, My Fancy* (1951).

climbed in the Hooper ratings from 5 to 12.3 in its first eight months on the air. The reviews were excellent. *Variety* reported, "It's real without being maudlin, and the comedy stems from hilarious situations and unforced punchy lines." John Crosby, writing for the *New York Herald-Tribune,* remarked, "Robert Young, who plays the father, is a far more expert comedian than I had realized. He is required by Mr. James to put his foot in his mouth at least once in every script, and he does so with as much poise as possible under the circumstances."

His screen ventures during this period were not very successful. RKO's *Bride for Sale* (1949) was an attempt to revive the screwball tradition of the 1930s. Although it co-starred Bob with Claudette Colbert and George Brent, both excellent farceurs, it could not stand up in the post-World War II film market. *Bride for Sale* was yet another triangular situation in which both Brent and Young pursue an efficiency expert (Colbert) who is only interested in marrying for money. The following year, the three stars would repeat their roles on "Lux Radio Theatre."

Released the same month (November 1949) was Young's last film to date for his alma mater, Metro-Goldwyn-Mayer. It was one of the most heralded productions of the studio's twenty-fifth anniversary year, but *That Forsyte Woman,* adapted from John Galsworthy's *A Man of Property,* turned out to be very disappointing. Director Compton Bennett was imported from England to supervise a cast that included Greer Garson (in the title role), Errol Flynn, Walter Pidgeon, and a young Janet Leigh. Almost all the major players were miscast or too mature for their roles. Bob was forced to don unflattering makeup and was preposterous as Bohemian architect Philip Bosinney who is engaged to Miss Leigh but infatuated by Miss Garson. Although there had been other adaptations of Galsworthy's *Forsyte* novels, it would remain for the British Broadcasting Corporation to do the job properly in the 1970s. *That Forsyte Woman* marked an inauspicious leave-taking from the studio that had most influenced Bob's professional life.

And Baby Makes Three, at Columbia, was Young's third and final 1949 release. He was reteamed with Barbara Hale for another variation of *The Awful Truth* ploy about the couple seeking a divorce but really in love with one another. It had the bad taste to effect the couple's reconciliation by introducing the possibility of the wife being pregnant.

Bob was off the screen for the entire year of 1950, although at one time he was announced as Bette Davis' co-star in RKO's *Story of a Divorce.* When the film was finally released in 1951 under the title *Payment on Demand,* Barry Sullivan played the role of David Ramsey, Miss Davis' husband. Bob's own production company also considered plans for filming such properties as *Storm Within Her Heart, Twelve Against the Underworld,* and a feature-length motion picture version of "Father Knows Best."

Bob was also engaged in various activities that were offshoots of his radio series. In 1940 his father had been killed in an accident that involved two teenage drivers. Spurred by the memory of the fatality, Bob used his radio program to give safety instructions and issue 1.5 million Robert Young Good Drivers' Club cards to listeners. Under the auspicies of the Inter-Industry Highway Safety Committee and the National Safety Council, he also toured the United States, speaking on the subject of teenage drivers to various civic groups. Bob, the father of four daughters, was voted by the National Father's Day Committee in May 1950 as a "Father of the Year."

The lull between motion picture assignments permitted Bob to take up flying as a hobby. He also purchased a 160-acre ranch near Carmel that he developed into a walnut grove.

His status as a free-lancer and the scarcity of good motion picture scripts in the early 1950s severely hampered his career. He had been asked about appearing on TV, as had most stars, but he was still wary of the new medium. He insisted that his answer was no, "at least not until a sponsor will pay as much as a motion picture producer."

The Second Woman (1951) was a small *Rebecca*-like tale. Bob played an architect suspected of being responsible for his fiancée's death and proved innocent by his new girlfriend (Betsy Drake). Generally well paced, this sort of psychological melodrama was all too prominent at the time to be able to lure patrons to the movies.

Bob's next picture, and his only one at Warner Bros., was more prestigious. It presented a variation of his old role as the stuffed-shirt loser. Cast for the fourth and final time opposite Joan Crawford, he co-starred as Congresswoman Crawford's old flame, a former professor now president of the university. *Goodbye, My Fancy* finds Crawford returning to the college (that had sacked her for an after-hours rendezvous with an unnamed male—actually Young) to receive an honorary degree. Like Warner Bros.' *The Male Animal* (1942), there is a subplot involving the issue of academic freedom, but this is soft-pedaled in favor of the mature romantic byplay between Young and Miss Crawford and a photographer (Frank Lovejoy) from *Life* magazine who is also enamored of Miss Crawford. As it turned out, Eve Arden in the role of Miss Crawford's confidante received most of the sparse critical sympathy.

The following year, 1952, Bob was top-billed in

one of the anomalies of Howard Hughes' reign at RKO, a Technicolor Western entitled *The Half-Breed* that co-starred Janis Carter and Jack Buetel (the co-lead of Hughes' *The Outlaw*). It was undoubtedly the theme of prejudice against the American Indian that appealed to Young. Years later in the *New York Times Guide to Movies on TV* (1970), Howard Thompson would judge, "The picture's one classy touch, surmounting the Harold Schumate-Richard Wormser script, is the appearance and smooth professionalism of Robert Young as a prairie gambler who staves off the pure-white rapscallions hounding the Indians, saves the territory from an uprising, and also gets the girl, Janis Carter."

In 1952 Bob took time to tour with Nancy Kelly and Dane Clark in a production of Clifford Odets' *The Country Girl.* He played the role of self-pitying alcoholic actor Frank Elgin, a part Bing Crosby would later play in the Paramount film version. In his characterization, Young had to display surface charm which concealed secret terrors and guilt. As such, he had what was probably the most provacative role of his career and one that came terrifyingly close to his own hellish private life. Paralleling this stage assignment, Bob might have been an excellent "Doc" in *Come Back, Little Sheba.* And what a chilling Willy Loman he might have made in *Death of a Salesman.* However, he was more than satisfied with his success and identification on radio. "Sooner or later everything I've ever wanted has come to me," he told an interviewer. "I've been so lucky since the first day I started in pictures."

In 1954 Bob made his last big-screen picture to date, an adventure film called *Secret of the Incas,* in which Charlton Heston was top-billed. Heston is an adventurer determined to bilk an archaeological team headed by Young. Along the way Heston finds religious salvation, and the viewer is treated to some striking shots of Andean ruins and one of the motliest casts ever assembled, including Yma Sumac and Thomas Mitchell. It was a curious farewell picture. As Bob would remark later, "The kind of role I was supposedly best suited for—light romantic comedy leads—no longer existed. There wasn't a place for me. . . . Feature films, you might say, passed me by."

The year, however, proved to be an important one for Bob. In May 1954 Bob starred in his first video show, a thirty-minute comedy called *Keep It in the Family,* aired on "Ford Theatre." The show was designed as a sort of testing ground for the possibility of transferring "Father Knows Best" to the small screen now that its radio rendition had come to an end. In October of the same year, the Rodney-Young produced "Father Knows Best" began a twenty-six-week run on the CBS-TV network.

The video cast, except for Bob, was totally different from that of the radio program. Jane Wyatt was engaged to play Bob's wife Margaret. Elinor Donahue was cast as Betty, Billy Gray as Bud, and Lauren Chapin as Kathy. Most of the episodes were confined to this small cast and the home setting. As directed by Peter Tewksbury, the low-key show was carefully and tastefully produced. Most of the action centered on the children, with Bob as the exasperated but understanding father who functions as a sort of *deus ex machina* in the concluding scenes. The thirty-minute entries were necessarily contrived, but the show's constant success in reruns has made the series and its values one of the touchstones of the 1950s. The plotting was never coy or condescending. For that reason the show never descended into the area of "camp."

Wrote Don Miller in *Films in Review,* "On paper a typical program doesn't do 'Father Knows Best' justice. This show's effectiveness derives largely from the personalities of the performers—especially Robert Young and Jane Wyatt in the leads. Nothing very important happens—just the things that happen to a well-meaning man and his wife and children. The script and direction are undistinguished. Young, who has a production interest in the show, has the wit to avoid burlesque, which actors traditionally give this type of role."

After its initial twenty-six-week run at CBS, the show was dropped by its sponsor, but it would be picked up by another source quickly enough for a run of seven seasons: four at CBS and three at NBC, with a total of two hundred and three episodes. During this period the show was a consistent winner in the ratings as well as a frequent recipient of Emmys for itself and its star. (Bob received two Emmys during the series' run.) It provided Bob and Miss Wyatt with an instant public identification, something they had never quite attained in more than a quarter century of film roles.

The shooting schedule of the black-and-white show was quite rigid. Because of the essential intimacy of the scripts, there was no allowance for guest stars. Although the initial filming took only three to four days at the beginning of the series, the later seasons required five to six days. As Elinor Donahue recalled, "The aim was to improve our product as we went along, instead of slipping into an easy rut." Early TV did not permit the long vacations that today's brief seasons allow. Miss Donahue adds, "We stopped only once for one week—Mr. Young was exhausted. Considering a seven-year run, that's remarkable. In those days the summer season was of short duration, so we shot for longer stretches of time than shows do today."

Miss Donahue has this to say of Young, "His 'private self' was more reserved at times, but it was a wonderful role for him. He was, and is, a lovely man."

During the seven-year run of "Father Knows Best," Bob made only two other dramatic appearances outside the role of Jim Anderson of Springfield, U.S.A. One was in *The Valiant Men* episode of "Climax" on CBS-TV in February 1955; the other was a thirty-minute Western story starring Young in the time slot usually reserved for "Father Knows Best."

When "Father Knows Best" discontinued shooting in 1960, it was still on top in the ratings. Through rerun residuals (the show would be dubbed into German, Spanish, French, Portuguese, Japanese, and Italian for foreign markets), Bob was independently wealthy. Along with Lucille Ball he was probably the most successful star of the relatively new medium. Yet audience identification with the role prevented Bob from returning to the big screen, which in the early 1960s was more preoccupied with epic productions.

In the fall of 1961, Rodney-Young Productions put together a new series entitled "The Window on Main Street." It premiered on Monday, October 2, on CBS-TV as a slender, sentimental thirty-minute drama in which Bob played a successful novelist and widower returning to his home town and becoming involved in the lives of the townspeople. Ford Rainey and Coleen Gray (and, later, Constance Moore) were the co-stars. The show lacked the spice and dramatic punch of "Peyton Place" to sustain it. Then, too, after the domesticity of the "Father Knows Best" series, the public had difficulty adjusting to Bob in the role of an outsider. The program

With Stuart Randall in *The Half-Breed* (1952).

(Right) With Billy Gray and Jane Wyatt on the CBS-TV series "Father Knows Best" (c. 1955).
(Left) With wife Betty (c. 1957).

was handsomely produced in color, and Bob's performance had the customary professional polish, but the slightness of theme failed to please either the public or the critics, and it faded after a season's run. (Much to Bob's disappointment, not enough episodes were filmed to provide the series with the rerun residuals comparable to the "Father Knows Best" series. Station managers approached with the small package would counter: "But we already have a rerun series starring Young.")

The failure of "The Window on Main Street" forced fifty-five-year-old Bob into semi-retirement. It was quite a shock to an active man, who at one time was making up to ten films a year at MGM. He did have hobbies, but this period, until the advent of "Marcus Welby," was very frustrating for the star. Occasionally a TV role would come along such as *Lullaby for an Indian Summer* on "Dr. Kildare" (1965), *The Admiral,* a father (Bob) and son (Robert Reed) drama aired on the "Bob Hope Chrysler Theatre" (1965), and, for the same anthology series, *Holloway's Daughters* (1966), a comedy in which Bob played David Wayne's father, a detective forced out of retirement by his teenage daughters.

The following year Young toured in a production of William Goodhart's *Generation.* (Henry Fonda had played it on Broadway, and David Janssen would do the 1969 screen version.) Bob was cast as the ulcer-prone business executive who is invited by his daughter to New York to meet his new son-in-law. Finding his daughter pregnant, he is shocked by her life style, particularly when he discovers that his hippie son-in-law plans to deliver the baby himself. The theme of the generation gap appealed greatly to Bob.

"I actually *like* hippies," Bob told Charles Higham in a *New York Times* interview. "I don't approve of their escape into drugs, although I deeply understand it. Drugs, after all, destroy their health and their looks, and by escaping they're simply moving themselves into a special kind of limbo from which often there's no return. I like their indifference to the old American passion for acquiring money—that seems to me a fine progression from previous generations. They aren't as greedy as we were."

Unfortunately, the return to the stage was quite an ordeal for Bob who seemingly was physically fit. During the tour he collapsed from "exhaustion," and the doctors prescribed a complete rest.

It was during this time that Bob, with remarkable candor, made clear a startling fact. For the past three decades he had been an acute alcoholic. The usual case history of the Hollywood confirmed alcoholic, such as those presented by Diana Barrymore, Lillian Roth, and Errol Flynn in their graphic biographies, represented a sharp contrast to the Young chronicle. Bob, to all surface appearances, was a contented, successful individual. He had been happily married for thirty-five years, although his children's lives had been marked by some tragedy: a grandson, Robert, had died less than twenty-four hours after birth, and one of his daughter's marriages had ended in divorce.

Bob's professional career was an overall success, both in film and in television. His apparent stability had earned him the respect of friends and co-workers over the decades. Unlike most alcoholics, Bob's work never indicated any signs of stress. Although he had many friends in the film world, he was never part of the so-called "Hollywood set." Indeed, to anyone who had enjoyed Bob's performances on film or TV, the reasons for his drinking must seem vague and mysterious.

In the Higham-*New York Times* interview, Bob admitted, "I've been sick myself. Sick all my life. As far back as I can remember, I was afraid of some imagined disaster that never did eventuate. When I was a child, I used to hide in the crooks of trees, just to be alone. When I became an actor I constantly felt I wasn't worthy, that I had no right to be a star. All those years at Metro, and even later on 'Father Knows Best,' I hid a black terror behind a cheerful face."

And in another interview, Bob stated, "For three decades I lived almost every waking hour filled with fear. It was fear of many things—of the unknown, of some expected calamity around the corner that never comes. A feeling that this stardom I was lucky enough to attain would not last, that I was not worthy, that I didn't deserve it. And along with these fears I also had headaches. Not migraine, certainly, but painful, nevertheless. They were psychosomatic in origin, of course. And to quiet the fear and ease the pain, I drank, and I drank a lot. You see, I wanted to escape. Well, I wound up an alcoholic. It took me thirty years to realize that I was slowly killing myself."

Through his wife's faith in him and his family's constant support (he now has five grandchildren), Bob turned to Alcoholics Anonymous, often speaking for them and holding meetings in his own home. Betty Young also introduced Bob to Science of the Mind (spiritual metaphysics) which helped him to overcome the shyness he had avoided confronting all those years.[7]

Bob has said: "People talk about Alcoholics Anonymous suddenly ending a bad habit, but it's really a question of the person himself coming to a slow but finally complete understanding of the nature of his own illness."

Armed with a new awareness of himself, Bob returned to work in 1968, playing a guest-starring role on a ninety-minute episode of "Name of the Game." On the November 15, 1968 NBC-TV episode entitled *The Protector,* Bob played the part of an arch conservative multi-millionaire setting up his own private army. Co-starring with Anne Baxter, Bob was excellent in the villainous role. The character was wonderfully at odds with Bob's own politics. "We need more money for our colleges," he told one reporter, "for our roads, and to clean up the air. If my rich friends complain, they should move to Guadalajara."

"Name of the Game" was filmed at Universal City where David Victor, the former producer of the "Doctor Kildare" TV series, was preparing a similar medical series about two general practitioners in a Southern California suburb. Like the earlier show, this show would focus on an older doctor in contrast to a younger physician with more modern ideas. Unlike "Kildare," however, the series would exhort the work of the old-fashioned family doctor in the age of the specialist. It was originally conceived as a vehicle for Ralph Bellamy, who had played a similar role as a TV psychiatrist. However, Victor decided to choose Bob on the basis of his "Name of . . ." guest spot and his years of audience identification with the role of Jim Anderson.

The show was tested in a two-hour pilot called simply "Marcus Welby, M.D." and telecast on ABC on March 26, 1969. It co-starred Anne Baxter, Susan Strasberg, Peter Deuel, Richard Loo, and Bob's old pal Lew Ayres. The emphasis in the sample show

[7]Bob, who commences each day on the "Marcus Welby" set with a minute of silent meditation, was a firm believer in the healing powers of the late Kathryn Kuhlman: "I do believe authentic healings occur at her services. In fact, I know they do; we've had firsthand experience that her healings are genuine. I believe in miracles. I believe all the things Jesus said two thousand years ago can be applied to today's situations. I believe the 'Kingdom of Heaven' is within us. The power to be healed is in us. We simply have to be told how to use it."

was on Marcus Welby (Bob) suffering a mild coronary, recovering from it, and being required to take on a younger, motorcycle-riding doctor (James Brolin) to help in his practice. The pilot concentrated on a "generation gap" rivalry between the two doctors and some sundry medical crises. Miss Baxter was Young's mature romantic interest, but the plotline established that the widower did not wish to cope with matrimony once again.

Although the pilot only scored 19.6 in the ratings, the network was sufficiently impressed with the show's possibilities to fit it into the fall lineup. Included as regulars were Brolin as Dr. Steven Kiley and Elena Verdugo as Consuela, their Mexican-American receptionist.

The storylines and themes of the series, which premiered on Tuesday, September 23, 1969, were necessarily pat. Every time Welby or Kiley took a personal interest in someone, that person contracted a serious disease, requiring sixty minutes of story time to solve. However, the production values, the assured acting of Bob; Brolin's good looks, and the basic appeal of old-fashioned soap opera managed to put the show into the top ten. Then, too, the "Marcus Welby" series had the advantage of excellent guest stars like Margaret O'Brien (shocking audiences who remembered her as being Bob's tiny MGM co-star by playing an unloved housewife suffering from an overweight problem). Other guest performers included Dorothy Lamour, Walter Pidgeon, Dolores Del Rio, Anne Baxter, Gloria DeHaven, Aldo Ray, Richard Thomas, Susan Clark, and Jane Wyatt (in a reunion with Bob). In much the same way that the Metro B films had been training grounds for their contract players, the "Welby" series offered solid roles for promising players at Universal. In addition, it brought Bob new recognition, perhaps more than he had enjoyed in his "Father Knows Best" days.

Said Bob of his medical role, "I wanted to do the program because it highlights the role of the general practitioner in a time of increasing specialization. Medicine isn't something I think about in the abstract. It's painfully meaningful to me, and I've based the character of Welby on three practitioners I've known. Welby really is a mature version of the Anderson father image. A doctor is looked upon by the whole family as a person on whom they can rely for sound advice on almost anything."

The success and prestige of the "Welby" show also enabled Bob to obtain other TV roles. In the four-hour, two-part NBC-TV film version of Fletcher Knebel's *Vanished* (March 8-9, 1971), Bob received special billing as a conservative Southern senator who used the mysterious disappearance of the President (Richard Widmark) for his own political motives.[8] Despite a hokey Southern drawl and makeup better suited to *Mark Twain Tonight,* Robert was Emmy-nominated, but he did not win. In 1972 Bob was in a film produced by David Victor for "ABC Movie of the Week" which was a variation of his real-life experiences. Entitled *All My Darling Daughters,* Bob played the comedy role of a judge who is confronted by his four daughters all of whom want to get married on the same day. Bob is involved in typical *Father of the Bride* situations, with Raymond Massey playing his dad and Eve Arden playing the mother of one of Bob's future sons-in-law.

The success of that telefilm prompted an ABC-TV sequel a year later called *My Darling Daughters' Anniversary.* It co-starred ex-Metro player Ruth Hussey (who also turned up on a "Welby" episode). This film found widower Young trying to tell his married daughters of his desire to wed Hussey but being interrupted by various domestic crises every time he broaches the delicate subject. Judith Crist, writing in *TV Guide,* referred to the outing as "treacly trivial," but for Bob the two *Daughters* films represented the "light comedy" type of role that "Welby" denied him.

In addition, Bob played Marcus Welby in a special appearance on David Victor's "Owen Marshall" series as part of a two-segment episode in which Dr. Kiley is accused of rape. In 1973 Bob would appear in a comedy-variety special called "Bob Young with the Young," and he served as guest host on one of "The KopyKats" shows. (No one has ever even attempted to imitate Bob.) He is an occasional guest on TV talk shows, and on January 25, 1976 he joined with Shirley MacLaine, Trini Lopez, Frank Sinatra, Andy Griffith, Don Ho, and others in an ABC-TV special, *Celebration: The American Spirit,* "a star-studded salute to America in music and humor."

The "Welby" series enjoyed a generally successful run. Although its 10 P.M. Tuesday time slot permitted it to tackle relatively adult subjects, the program generally eschewed controversy. One exception to this was a segment called *The Outrage* that was programmed during the 1974 season. The show, dealing with a sexual assault on a teenage boy by his homosexual science teacher during a field trip, was attacked by Gay Liberation groups and banned by various ABC-TV network affiliates.

A more positively received episode was one entitled *Hell Is Upstairs,* based on an actual medical case history of dystonia (a rare muscle disorder). By

[8] *Hollywood Reporter* printed, "A Texas Senator given to 'bourbon and branch' is Robert Young, opposing Widmark in an upcoming election and therefore opposing everything he says. It is a scene-stealing role and Young does just that with each one he's in."

With Fawne Harrison, Darleen Carr, Judy Strangis, and Sharon Gless in the ABC-TV telefeature *All My Darling Daughters* (1972).

chance, a Toronto widow, Mrs. Betty Saundercook, happened to view the program and recognized the symptoms described on the air as applying to her son Chuck. The youth had been sent to a hospital to die on the recommendation of a family doctor. On the basis of the "Welby" episode, Mrs. Saundercook insisted upon brain surgery for her son, and after several operations he showed considerable improvement.

Mrs. Saundercook wrote to Bob, expressing her gratitude, and he responded by letter: "I find it impossible to put into words my reaction to what you told me, except to say that my wife Betty and I both felt a rare privilege and were deeply touched. You and your family and, of course, Chuck are now included in our daily prayers."

"Marcus Welby, M.D." maintained consistently high ratings through various seasons. When the ratings lapsed, the script writers devised a marriage for Dr. Kiley to hospital worker Janet Blake (Pamela Hensley). Several episodes also dealt with Dr. Welby's daughter returning with her husband from an experimental project in South America where the husband contracted a rare and fatal, tropical disease.

But the inevitable occurred and on May 11, 1976 the final episode of "Marcus Welby, M.D." was telecast. For a time Young announced plans to reactivate the series, "Maybe some two-hour shows with Welby as the pivotal character." After all, he reasoned, "There are supposed to be 2,500 known diseases. We've only covered a fraction of them in 170 episodes."

"Welby" faded into the realm of the syndicated re-run and Young endured his own real-life medical problem. He was suffering from severe cataracts in both eyes. According to the star's wife, his vision was weakened ". . . to the point where he couldn't drive a car and couldn't read, unless he held a book practically to his nose." She also noted, "It's amazing but he worked right up to the last second doing 'Welby,' and the doctor said he really didn't know how Robert did it." Over a period of six months, each eye was operated on and artificial lenses were implanted to replace the cataract-clouded lens of each eye." The surgery was successful and for the first time in years, Young could actually read cue cards for his professional work.

Thus, in 1977, Robert returned to the professional

scene. He was among the celebrities appearing on the National Easter Seal Telethon in March, spoke at the "Tribute to Joan Crawford" on June 24th at the Samuel Goldwyn Theatre of the Academy of Motion Picture Arts and Sciences, was teamed with Jane Wyatt for the 29th Annual Emmy Awards on September 11th (NBC-TV), and was a guest on "Donny & Marie Salute Elvis!" on ABC-TV (October 7, 1977).

Meanwhile, Young had produced two further episodes of "Father Knows Best" in ninety-minute color specials produced at Columbia Pictures TV for NBC-TV. *Father Knows Best Reunion* was aired on May 15, 1977 and the followup, *Father Knows Best: Home for Christmas* was telecast on December 18, 1977. Both productions were low-keyed, meandering, and generally unslick. Young would observe of the re-teaming with his old teleseries family, "I had a strange feeling there had been a time warp . . . there was no feeling of any period of time having passed . . . After the first greetings, everyone fell into the groove." Said *Hollywood Reporter* "Robert Young was, if possible, even more affable than ever."

If Young relinguished the role of the heavenly advisor Mr. Jordan in Warren Beatty's theatrical film hit *Heaven Can Wait* (1978—he was replaced by James Mason), he was financially in tune with his Sanka coffee TV commercials. For the first six ad episodes, he was paid approximately $300,000, and his brand of salesmanship has proven so successful that he continues today promoting the product, a chore he began in 1976. Robert joined with an array of ABC-TV stars for that network's "Silver Anniversary Celebration" (February 5, 1978). Back in 1933 when RKO produced its classic film version of Louisa May Alcott's *Little Women,* Katharine Hepburn played Jo, Joan Bennett was Amy, and Henry Stephenson was Mr. Laurence. When MGM produced a color version of the perennial favorite, the 1949 film found June Allyson as Jo, Elizabeth Taylor as Amy, and Sir C. Aubrey Smith as Mr. Laurence. Then on October 2–3, 1978, NBC-TV presented a four-hour color version of the juvenile classic. This time around Susan Dey was Jo, Ann Dusenberry was Amy, and Robert Young bedecked in muttonchop whiskers and period costume, played Mr. Laurence. (Young's former MGM co-star Greer Garson appeared as the tight-lipped Aunt March, and his frequent vis-a-vis Dorothy McGuire was cast as the girls' mother Marmee.) By today's standards, the program seemed more than quaint, but it provided enough family entertainment to rank decently in the ratings. Reported the *Los Angeles Times,* "Young especially puts on a paper doll role and molds it nicely into a part."

With Ruth Hussey and Sharon Gless (right) in the ABC-TV telefeature, *My Darling Daughters' Anniversary* (1973).

With Peggy McCay, Forrest Tucker, and Patty McCormack in the episode *The Brittle Warrior* on "Marcus Welby, M.D." (ABC-TV, 1974).

At a Beverly Hills function with his grandchildren Billy, Lisa, and Holly (1976).

Dr. Marcus Welby Shows Off Real-Life Grandchildren

Beaming with grandfatherly pride, Robert Young, 69, TV's "Marcus Welby, M.D." poses with his grandchildren at the annual Buckley School PTA dinner in the Beverly Hilton Hotel in Hollywood. The children are Billy Profitt, 10; Lisa Seebe, 10 (standing in rear), and Holly Gleason, 8, wearing her grandpa's grin.

NBC-TV was properly impressed and turned the special into a mini-series which premiered on February 8, 1979.

Variety, while remarking that Young was an "old pro" queried the appeal of the program: ". . . Prime-time television seems to require a bit more zip if it is to reap handsome rating points these days." The prophecy proved true and the Universal-TV produced series disappeared from the weekly lineup after a few installments.

Just when it seemed, at least on the surface, that Young's professional life had settled into a new, viable routine—TV admanship, making public service TV messages, moderating panels dealing with religious and moral issues—it was announced in early June 1980 that Young had entered the Franciscan Medical Center in Rock Island, Illinois. He was suffering from what Dr. Eduardo Ricaurte of that facility diagnosed as "biogenic amine deficiency . . . causing slowness of all the metabolic processes." This hereditary "chemical depression" made the veteran performer appear "dispirited, decelerated, joyless, unmotivated." The actor's wife, Betty, also became a patient at the Medical Center because she had become depressed due to her husband's ailment.

It was at this time that Young's youngest daughter, Kathy, told the press: "When he was doing 'Father Knows Best,' he had headaches that were so bad he couldn't even put his head on the pillow. . . . During his periods of depression, which lasted about four weeks at a time, he was nervous, uptight, and tired. He cried because he was so frustrated. He didn't know what was wrong. He looked happy-go-lucky on the TV screen, but we knew what his agony was at home. He used to lock himself in a room and didn't care about anybody or anything. . . ." According to eldest daughter Carol, "He also had hypertension so bad that there was always someone on the set to take his blood pressure and make sure that he took his medication."

With the administration of synthetic amines, Young's medical problem is controllable, hopefully ending his years of severe emotional stress. As such, there seems no reason why the public should not expect a continuation of his easy-going, dependable performances, which over the decades have become a staple of multi-media offerings.

"For me, ordering Sanka® Brand after a show is a natural."

DECAFFEINATED COFFEE

"I drink SANKA® Brand at home. So it only makes sense for me to order it when I'm out, too—especially in the evening.

"SANKA® Brand is 100% real coffee. It has all the aroma and delicious taste of real coffee. But since it's virtually caffein-free, it doesn't make me nervous or keep me awake. It's the coffee that lets me be my best.

"If you feel the way I do, order SANKA® Brand the next time you're out—perhaps after the show. I'm sure you'll appreciate getting a good cup of coffee—without losing a good night's sleep."

SANKA®

BRAND DECAFFEINATED COFFEE

Served in restaurants everywhere.
Just ask for it.

Salesman of the 70's.

Advertisement for "The Father Knows Best Reunion" on NBC-TV (1977).

With Susan Dey in *Little Women,* the two-part NBC-TV special (1978).

FILMOGRAPHY

THE BLACK CAMEL
(Fox, 1931) 71 min.

DIRECTOR: Hamilton MacFadden
BASED ON THE NOVEL BY EARL DERR BIGGERS
SCREENPLAY: Hugh Stange, Barry Conners, Phillip Klein
DIALOGUE: Conners, Klein
SOUND: W. W. Lindsay, Jr.
CAMERA: Joseph August, Dan Clark
EDITOR: Al De Gaetano

Warner Oland *(Charlie Chan);* Sally Eilers *(Julie O'Neil);* Bela Lugosi *(Tarneverro);* Dorothy Revier *(Shelah Fane);* Victor Varconi *(Robert Fyfe);* Robert Young *(Jimmy Bradshaw);* Marjorie White *(Rita Ballou);* Richard Tucker *(Wilkie Ballou);* J. M. Kerrigan *(Thomas MacMaster);* Mary Gordon *(Mrs. MacMaster);* C. Henry Gordon *(Van Horn);* Violet Dunn *(Anna);* William Post *(Alan Jaynes);* Dwight Frye *(Jessop);* Murray Kinnell *(Smith);* Otto Yamakoa *(Kashimo);* Rita Roselle *(Luana);* Robert Homans *(Chief of Police);* Louise Mackintosh *(Housekeeper).*

THE SIN OF MADELON CLAUDET
(MGM, 1931) 74 min.

DIRECTOR: Edgar Selwyn
BASED ON THE PLAY *The Lullaby* BY EDWARD KNOBLOCK
SCREENPLAY: Charles MacArthur
CAMERA: Oliver T. Marsh
EDITOR: Tom Held

Helen Hayes *(Madelon Claudet);* Lewis Stone *(Carlo Boretti);* Neil Hamilton *(Larry);* Robert Young *(Dr. Claudet);* Cliff Edwards *(Victor);* Jean Hersholt *(Dr. Dulac);* Marie Prevost *(Rosalie);* Karen Morley *(Alice);* Charles Winninger *(Photographer);* Alan Hale *(Hubert);* Halliwell Hobbes *(Roget);* Lennox Pawlie *(St. Jacques);* Russ Powell *(Claudet).* Otto Hoffman *(Official);* Frankie Darro *(Larry at Age Twelve).*

THE GUILTY GENERATION
(Columbia, 1931) 80 min.

DIRECTOR: Rowland V. Lee
BASED ON THE PLAY BY JO MILWARD AND J. KIRBY HAWKES
SCREENPLAY: Jack Cunningham
SOUND: George Cooper
CAMERA: Byron Haskin
EDITOR: Otis Garrett

Leo Carrillo *(Mike Palmero);* Constance Cummings *(Maria Palermo);* Robert Young *(Marco);* Boris Karloff *(Tony Ricca);* Emma Dunn *(Nina);* Leslie Fenton *(Joe);* Ruth Warren *(Nellie);* Murray Kinnell *(Jerry);* Elliott Roth *(Benedicto).*

HELL DIVERS
(MGM, 1931) 100 min.

PRODUCER/DIRECTOR: George Hill
STORY: Lieutenant Commander Frank Wead
SCREENPLAY: Harvey Gates, Malcolm Stuart Boylan
CAMERA: Harold Wenstrom
EDITOR: Blanche Sewell

Wallace Beery *(Windy);* Clark Gable *(Steve);* Conrad Nagel *(Duke);* Dorothy Jordan *(Ann);* Marjorie Rambeau *(Mame Kelsey);* Marie Prevost *(Lulu);* Cliff Edwards *(Baldy);* John Miljan *(Griffin);* Landers Stevens *(Admiral);* Reed Howes *(Lieutenant Fisher);* Alan Roscoe *(Captain);* Frank Conroy *(Chaplain);* Robert Young *(Young Officer);* Jack Pennick *(Trainee);* John Kelly *(Sailor);* Virginia Bruce *(Girl).*

THE WET PARADE
(MGM, 1932) 120 min.

PRODUCER: Hunt Stromberg
DIRECTOR: Victor Fleming
BASED ON THE NOVEL BY UPTON SINCLAIR
SCREENPLAY: John Lee Mahin
CAMERA: George Barnes
EDITOR: Anne Bauchens

Dorothy Jordan *(Maggie May);* Lewis Stone *(Roger Chilcote);* Neil Hamilton *(Roger Chilcote, Jr.);* Emma Dunn *(Mrs. Chilcote);* Frederick Burton *(Major Randolph);* Reginald Barlow *(Judge Brandon);* John Larkin *(Moses);* Gertrude Howard *(Angelina);* Robert Young *(Kip Tarleton);* Walter Huston *(Pop Tarleton);* Jimmy Durante *(Abe Shilling);* Wallace Ford *(Jerry Tyler);* Myrna Loy *(Eileen Pinchon);* Joan Marsh *(Evelyn Fessenden);* John Miljan *(Major Doleshal);* Clara Blandick *(Mrs. Tarleton);* Clarence Muse *(Taylor Tibbs);* Forrester Harvey *(Mr. Fortesque);* John Beck *(Mr. Garrison).*

NEW MORALS FOR OLD
(MGM, 1932) 74 min.

DIRECTOR, Charles F. Brabin
BASED ON THE PLAY *After All* BY JOHN VAN DRUTEN
SCREENPLAY: Van Druten, Zelda Sears, Wanda Tuchock
CAMERA: John Mescall
EDITOR: William S. Gray

Robert Young *(Ralph Thomas);* Margaret Perry *(Phyllis Thomas);* Lewis Stone *(Mr. Thomas);* Laura Hope Crews *(Mrs. Thomas);* Myrna Loy *(Myra);* David Newell *(Duff Wilson);* Jean Hersholt *(Hallett);* Ruth Selwyn *(Estelle);* Kathryn Crawford *(Zoe);* Louise Closser Hale *(Mrs. Warburton);* Mitchell Lewis *(Bodvin);* Elizabeth Patterson *(Aunty Doe);* Lillian Harmer *(Maid).*

UNASHAMED
(MGM, 1932) 75 min.

DIRECTOR: Harry Beaumont
STORY/SCREENPLAY: Bayard Veiller
CAMERA: Norbert Brodine
EDITOR: William S. Gray

Helen Twelvetrees *(Joan Ogden);* Robert Young *(Dick Ogden);* Lewis Stone *(Henry Trask);* Jean Hersholt *(Mr. Schmidt);* John Miljan *(District Attorney Harris);* Monroe Owsley *(Harry Swift);* Robert Warwick *(Mr. Ogden);* Gertrude Michael *(Marjorie);* Wilfred North *(Judge Ambrose);* Tommy Jackson *(Captain Riordan);* Louise Beavers *(Amanda).*

STRANGE INTERLUDE
(MGM, 1932) 110 min.
(British release title: STRANGE INTERVAL)

DIRECTOR: Robert Z. Leonard
BASED ON THE PLAY BY EUGENE O'NEILL
SCREENPLAY: Bess Meredyth, C. Gardner Sullivan
CAMERA: Lee Garmes
EDITOR: Margaret Booth

Norma Shearer *(Nina Leeds);* Clark Gable *(Ned Darrell);* Alexander Kirkland *(Sam Evans);* Ralph Morgan *(Charlie Marsden);* Robert Young *(Gordon);* May Robson *(Mrs. Evans);* Maureen O'Sullivan *(Madeline);* Henry B. Walthall *(Professor Leeds);* Mary Alden *(Maid);* Tad Alexander *(Gordon as a Boy).*

THE KID FROM SPAIN
(United Artists, 1932) 90 min.

DIRECTOR: Leo McCarey
STORY/SCREENPLAY: William Anthony McGuire, Bert Kalmar, Harry Ruby
SONGS: Kalmar and Ruby
DANCE NUMBERS STAGED BY BUSBY BERKELEY
SOUND: Vinton Vernon
CAMERA: Gregg Toland
EDITOR: Stuart Heisler

Eddie Cantor *(Eddie Williams);* Lyda Roberti *(Rosalie);* Robert Young *(Ricardo);* Ruth Hall *(Anita Gomez);* John Miljan *(Pancho);* Noah Beery *(Alonzo Gomez);* J. Carroll Naish *(Pedro);* Robert Emmet O'Connor *(Detective Crawford);* Stanley Fields *(Jose);* Paul Porcasi *(Gonzales);* Julian Rivero *(Dalmores);* Theresa Maxwell Conover *(Martha Oliver);* Walter Walker *(Dean);* Ben Hendricks, Jr. *(Red);* Sidney Franklin *(Himself);* Betty Grable, Paulette Goddard, Toby Wing, Jane Wyman *(Goldwyn Girls).*

MEN MUST FIGHT
(MGM, 1933) 73 min.

DIRECTOR: Edgar Selwyn
BASED ON THE PLAY BY REGINALD LAWRENCE AND S. K. LAUREN
SCREENPLAY: C. Gardner Sullivan
CAMERA: George Folsey
EDITOR: William S. Gray

Diana Wynyard *(Laura Seward);* Lewis Stone *(Edward Seward);* Phillips Holmes

(Bob); May Robson *(Mrs. Seward, Sr.);* Ruth Selwyn *(Peggy Chase);* Robert Young *(Geoffrey);* Robert Greig *(Albert);* Hedda Hopper *(Mrs. Chase);* Donald Dillaway *(Steve);* Mary Carlisle *(Evelyn);* Luis Alberni *(Soto).*

TODAY WE LIVE
(MGM, 1933) 113 min.

PRODUCER/DIRECTOR: Howard Hawks
BASED ON THE STORY *"Turn About"* BY WILLIAM FAULKNER
SCREENPLAY: Edith Fitzgerald, Dwight Taylor
DIALOGUE: Faulkner
ART DIRECTOR: Cedric Gibbons
GOWNS: Adrian
SOUND: Douglas Shearer
CAMERA: Oliver T. Marsh
EDITOR: Edward Curtiss

Joan Crawford *(Diana Boyce-Smith);* Gary Cooper *(Bogard);* Robert Young *(Claude);* Franchot Tone *(Ronnie Boyce-Smith);* Roscoe Karns *(McGinnis);* Louise Closser Hale *(Applegate);* Rollo Lloyd *(Major);* Hilda Vaughn *(Eleanor).*

HELL BELOW
(MGM, 1933) 105 min.

DIRECTOR: Jack Conway
BASED ON THE NOVEL *Pigboats* BY COMMANDER EDWARD ELLSBERG
ADAPTORS: Laird Doyle, Raymond Schrock
DIALOGUE: John Lee Mahin, John Meehan
TECHNICAL ADVISOR: Lieutenant Commander Morris D. Gilmore, U.S.N.
CAMERA: Harold Rosson
EDITOR: Hal C. Kern

Robert Montgomery *(Lieutenant Thomas Knowlton);* Walter Huston *(Lieutenant Commander Toler);* Madge Evans *(Joan);* Jimmy Durante *(Ptomaine);* Eugene Pallette *(MacDougal);* Robert Young *(Lieutenant Brick Walters);* Edwin Styles *(Herbert Standish);* John Lee Mahin *(Lieutenant Nelson);* David Newell *(Lieutenant Radford);* Sterling Holloway *(Seaman Jenks);* Charles Irwin *(Buck Teeth Sergeant);* Henry Kolker *(Admiral);* Sid Saylor *(Chief Engineer Hendrickson);* Maude Eburne *(Admiral's Wife);* Paul Porcasi *(Italian).*

TUGBOAT ANNIE
(MGM, 1933) 88 min.

PRODUCER: Harry Rapf
DIRECTOR: Mervyn LeRoy
BASED ON THE STORIES BY NORMAN REILLY RAINE
ADAPTORS: Zelda Sears, Eve Greene
ADDITIONAL DIALOGUE: Raine
ART DIRECTOR: Merrill Pye
SET DECORATOR: Edwin B. Willis
CAMERA: Gregg Toland
EDITOR: Blanche Sewell

Marie Dressler *(Annie Brennan);* Wallace Beery *(Terry Brennan);* Robert Young *(Alec Brennan);* Maureen O'Sullivan *(Pat Severn);* Willard Robertson *(Red Severn);* Tammany Young *(Shif'less);* Frankie Darro *(Alec as a Boy);* Jack Pennick *(Pete);* Paul Hurst *(Sam);* Oscar Apfel *(Reynolds);* Robert McWade *(Mayor of Secoma);* Robert Barrat *(First Mate);* Vince Barnett *(Cabby);* Robert E. Homans *(Old Salt);* Guy Usher *(Auctioneer);* Willie Fung *(Chow, the Cook);* Hal Price *(Mate);* Christian Rub *(Sailor);* Major Sam Harris *(Onlooker).*

SATURDAY'S MILLIONS
(Universal, 1933) 77 min.

PRODUCTION SUPERVISOR: Christy Walsh
PRODUCER: Carl Laemmle, Jr.
DIRECTOR: Edward Sedgwick
BASED ON THE NOVEL BY LUCIAN CARY
SCREENPLAY: Dale Van Every
ART DIRECTOR: Thomas F. O'Neill
CAMERA: Charles Stumar
EDITORS: Dave Berg, Robert Carlisle

Johnny Mack Brown *(Allan Barry);* Robert Young *(Jim Fowler);* Andy Devine *(Andy Jones);* Leila Hyams *(Joan Chandler);* Mary Carlisle *(Thelma Springer);* Grant Mitchell *(Ezra "Scoot" Fowler);* Joe Sawyer *(Coach);* Mary Doran *(Marie);* Paul Porcasi *(Felix);* Lucille Lund *(Myra Blaine the Society Reporter);* Paul Hurst *(Doc Maloney);* Herbert Corthell *(Baldy);* William "Billy" Kent *(Sam);* Walter Brennan, Don Brodie, Sam Godfrey, Eddie Phillips, Dick Cramer, Harrison Greene *(Reporters);* Robert Allen *[Craig Reynolds] (Football Player);* Al Richmond, Charles K. French, Phil Dunham *(Old Grads);* Ralph Brooks *(Student in Locker Room);* Sidney Bracy *(Butler).*

THE RIGHT TO ROMANCE
(RKO, 1933) 70 min.

PRODUCER: Merian C. Cooper
ASSOCIATE PRODUCER: Myles Connolly
DIRECTOR: Alfred Santell
STORY: Connolly
ADAPTORS: Sidney Buchman, Henry McCarty
SOUND: W. C. Moore
CAMERA: Lucien Andriot
EDITOR: Ralph Dieterle

Ann Harding *(Dr. Margaret Simmons);* Robert Young *(Bob Preble);* Irving Pichel *(Dr. Beck);* Alden "Stephen" Chase *(Bunny);* Nils Asther *(Dr. Heppling);* Sari Maritza *(Lee Joyce);* Helen Freeman *(Mrs. Preble);* Delmar Watson *(Bill).*

LA CUIDAD DE CARTON
(Fox, 1933) 75 min.

SUPERVISOR: G. Martinez Sierra
DIRECTOR: Louis King
STORY: Sierra
SCREENPLAY: Jose Lopez Rubio, John Reinhardt

Catalina Barcena *(Teresa);* Antonio Moreno *(Fred);* Jose Crespo *(Clarence);* Andres de Segurola *(Morrison);* with: Julio Pena, Luis Alberni, Carlos Villarias; and: Lionel Barrymore, Janet Gaynor, Robert Young *(Guest Stars).*

CAROLINA
(Fox, 1934) 85 min.

DIRECTOR: Henry King
BASED ON THE PLAY *House of Connelly* BY PAUL GREEN
SCREENPLAY: Reginald Berkeley
MUSIC DIRECTOR: Louis de Francesco
SOUND: Joseph Aiken
CAMERA: Hal Mohr
EDITOR: Robert Bassler

Janet Gaynor *(Joanna Tate);* Lionel Barrymore *(Bob Connelly);* Robert Young *(Will Connelly);* Richard Cromwell *(Allen);* Henrietta Crosman *(Mrs. Connelly);* Mona Barrie *(Virginia);* Almeda Fowler *(Geraldine);* Russell Simpson *(Richard);* Alden "Stephen" Chase *(Jack Hampton);* Ronald Cosbey *(Harry Tate);* John Cosbey *(John Tate);* Stepin Fetchit *(Scipio);* Anita Brown *(Essie);* Jerry Stewart *(Checkers Player);* Edna Herd *(Black Woman);* James Ellison *(Dancer);* Frances Curry, Beas Eblow, Clinton Rosemond, Beulah Hall, Mary King, Bernice Pilot *(Black Singers);* Shirley Temple *(Girl);* John Elliott *(Robert E. Lee);* John Webb Dillon *(Stonewall Jackson);* Andre Cheron *(Beauregard);* Mary Forbes *(Aunt Catherine).*

SPITFIRE
(RKO, 1934) 88 min.

EXECUTIVE PRODUCER: Merian C. Cooper
ASSOCIATE PRODUCER: Pandro S. Berman
DIRECTOR: John Cromwell
BASED ON THE PLAY *Trigger* BY LULA VOLLMER
SCREENPLAY: Jane Murfin, Vollmer
ART DIRECTORS: Van Nest Polglase, Carroll Clark
ASSISTANT DIRECTOR: Dewey Starkey
MAKEUP: Mel Burns
COSTUMES: Walter Plunkett
MUSIC: Max Steiner
SOUND: Clem Portman
CAMERA: Edward Cronjager
EDITOR: William H. Morgan

Katharine Hepburn *(Trigger Hicks);* Robert Young *(John Stafford);* Ralph Bellamy *(George Fleetwood);* Martha Sleeper *(Eleanor Stafford);* Louis Mason *(Bill Grayson);* Sara Haden *(Etta Dawson);* Virginia Howell *(Granny Raines);* Sidney Toler *(Mr. Sawyer);* Bob Burns *(West Fry);* Therese Wittler *(Mrs. Sawyer);* John Beck *(Jake Hawkins);* Bob Kortman *(Mountaineer).*

THE HOUSE OF ROTHSCHILD
(United Artists, 1934) 86 min.*

PRODUCER: Darryl F. Zanuck
ASSOCIATE PRODUCERS: William Goetz, Raymond Griffith

PRESENTER: Joseph M. Schenck
DIRECTOR: Alfred Werker
BASED ON AN UNPRODUCED PLAY BY GEORGE HEMBERT WESTLEY
SCREENPLAY: Nunnally Johnson
MUSIC: Alfred Newman
CAMERA: Peverell Marley
EDITORS: Alan McNeil, Barbara McLean

George Arliss *(Mayer Rothschild/Nathan Rothschild);* Boris Karloff *(Count Ledrantz);* Loretta Young *(Julie Rothschild);* Robert Young *(Captain Fitzroy);* C. Aubrey Smith *(Duke of Wellington);* Arthur Byron *(Baring);* Helen Westley *(Gudula Rothschild);* Reginald Owen *(Herries);* Florence Arliss *(Hannah Rothschild);* Alan Mowbray *(Metternick);* Holmes Herbert *(Rowerth);* Paul Harvey *(Solomon Rothschild);* Ivan Simpson *(Amschel Rothschild);* Noel Madison *(Carl Rothschild);* Murray Kinnell *(James Rothschild);* Georges Renavent *(Talleyrand);* Oscar Apfel *(Prussian Officer);* Lumsden Hare *(Prince Regent);* Gilbert Emery *(Prime Minister);* Ethel Griffies *(Woman Guest at Hall of Reception);* Reginald Sheffield, Brandon Hurst, Harold Minjir, Horace Claude Cooper, Craufurd Kent *(Stock Traders);* Wilfred Lucas *(Page);* Walter Long *(Soldier).*

*Technicolor sequence.

LAZY RIVER
(MGM, 1934) 75 min.

PRODUCER: Lucien Hubbard
DIRECTOR: George B. Seitz
BASED ON THE PLAY *Ruby* BY LEA DAVID FREEMAN
SCREENPLAY: Hubbard
CAMERA: Gregg Toland
EDITOR: William Levanway

Robert Young *(Bill Drexel);* Jean Parker *(Sarah);* C. Henry Gordon *(Sam Kee);* Ted Healy *(Gabby);* Ruth Channing *(Ruby);* Nat Pendleton *(Tiny);* Maude Eburne *(Miss Minnie);* Raymond Hatton *(Captain Orkney);* Irene Franklin *(Suzanne);* Joseph Cawthorn *(Ambrose);* Erville Alderson *(Sheriff);* George Lewis *(Armand);* Purnell Pratt *(Lawyer);* Walter Long *(Buck);* Donald Douglas *(Officer);* John Larkin *(Black Man).*

HOLLYWOOD PARTY
(MGM, 1934) C-68 min.

PRODUCER: Harry Rapf
DIRECTORS: (uncredited) Roy Rowland, Allan Dwan, Richard Boleslavwski
STORY/SCREENPLAY: Howard Deitz, Arthur Kober
SONGS: Gus Kahn and Walter Donaldson; Dietz and Donaldson; Arthur Freed and Nacio Herb Brown
CAMERA: James Wong Howe
EDITOR: George Boemler

Jimmy Durante *(Jimmy/Schnarzan the Ape Man);* Lupe Velez *(Lupe);* Laurel and Hardy *(Themselves);* Polly Moran *(Henrietta);* Jack Pearl *(Baron Munchausen);* George Givot *(Liondora);* Eddie Quillan *(Bob);* June Clyde *(Linda);* Ben Bard *(Sharley);* Richard Carle *(Knapp);* Tom Kennedy *(Beavers);* Frances Williams, Charles Butterworth, Mickey Mouse, Ted Healy *(Specialties);* Arthur Jarrett *(Singer);* Shirley Ross Quartet, Harry Barris, The Three Stooges *(Themselves);* Jed Prouty *(Theatre Manager);* Arthur Treacher *(Butler);* Robert Young *(Himself).*

WHOM THE GODS DESTROY
(Columbia, 1934) 71 min.

DIRECTOR: Walter Lang
BASED ON THE STORY BY ALBERT PAYSON TERHUNE
SCREENPLAY: Sidney Buchkman
ADAPTOR: Fred Niblo, Jr.
CAMERA: Benjamin Kline
EDITOR: Viola Lawrence

Walter Connolly *(John Forrester);* Robert Young *(Jack Forrester);* Doris Kenyon *(Margaret Forrester);* Macon Jones *(Jack Forrester at Age Fourteen);* Scotty Beckett *(Baby Jack Forrester);* Rollo Lloyd *(Henry);* Hobart Bosworth *(Alec);* Maidel Turner *(Miss Crossland);* Gilbert Emery *(Professor Weaver);* Hugh Huntley *(Jamison, the Ship's Officer);* Akim Tamiroff *(Morotoft);* Henry Kolker *(Carlos);* George Humbert *(Niccoli);* Yale Puppeteers *(Puppets);* Reginald Mason *(Behan);* Charles D. Middleton *(Constable Malcolm);* Walter Brennan *(Clifford);* Mary Carr *(Old Actress);* Jack Mulhall *(Lead Man in Show);* Betty Francisco *(Lead Woman in Show);* Tom Ricketts *(Charlie);* Bud Geary *(Sailor);* Arthur "Pop" Byron *(Stagehand).*

PARIS INTERLUDE
(MGM, 1934) 73 min.

PRODUCER: Lucien Hubbard
DIRECTOR: Edwin L. Marin
BASED ON THE PLAY *All Good Americans* BY LAURA AND S. J. PERELMAN
SCREENPLAY: Wells Root
ART DIRECTORS: Cedric Gibbons, Merill Pye
SET DECORATOR: Edwin B. Willis
FASHION SHOW CONCEIVED AND EXECUTED BY ADRIAN
CAMERA: Milton Krasner
EDITOR: Conrad A. Nervig

Madge Evans *(Julie Bell);* Otto Kruger *(Sam Coll);* Robert Young *(Pat Wells);* Una Merkel *(Cassie);* Ted Healy *(Jimmy);* Louise Henry *(Mary Louise);* Edward Brophy *(Ham);* George Meeker *(Rex Fleming);* Bert Roach *(Noble);* Richard Tucker *(Stevens);* James Donlin *(Jones);* Carlos J. de Valdez, Gene Perry *(Doctors);* Constant Franke, Maurice Brierre *(Internes);* Pauline High *(Nurse);* Rolfe Sedan *(Waiter).*

DEATH ON THE DIAMOND
(MGM, 1934) 75 min.

PRODUCER: Lucien Hubbard
DIRECTOR: Edward Sedgwick
BASED ON THE NOVEL BY CORTLAND FITZSIMMONS
SCREENPLAY: Harvey Thew, Joe Sherman, Ralph Spence
ART DIRECTOR: Cedric Gibbons, David Townsend
CAMERA: Milton Krasner
EDITOR: Frank Sullivan

Robert Young *(Larry Kelly);* Madge Evans *(Frances Clark);* C. Henry Gordon *(Joe Karnes);* Ted Healy *(Terry O'Toole);* Nat Pendleton *(Truck Hogan);* Paul Kelly *(Jimmie Downey);* David Landau *(Pop Clark);* DeWitt C. Jennings *(Pat Patterson);* Edward Brophy *(Detective Grogan);* Willard Robertson *(Lieutenant Luke Cato);* Mickey Rooney *(Mickey, the Batboy);* Robert Livingston *(Frank Higgins);* James Ellison *(Sherman, the Cincinnati Pitcher);* Joe Sawyer *(Spencer);* Pat Flaherty *(Pat the Coach);* Francis X. Bushman, Jr. *(Sam Briscoe the Pitcher);* Franklyn Farnum *(Fan);* Jack Norton *(Gambler);* Harry Semels *(Barber Customer);* Dennis O'Keefe, Bobby Watson *(Radio Announcers);* Walter Brennan, Heinie Conklin, Max Wagner *(Hot Dog Vendors);* Herman Brix *(Bruce Bennett);* Don Brodie, Sumner Getchell, Jack Raymond *(Men on Ticket Line);* Sam Flint *(Baseball Commissioner);* Fred Graham *(Cardinal Player);* with: Cincinnati Reds, Chicago Cubs, St. Louis Cardinals.

THE BAND PLAYS ON
(MGM, 1934) 88 min.

PRODUCER: Edward L. Marin
DIRECTOR: Russell Mack
BASED ON THE STORIES *"Backfield"* BY BYRON MORGAN AND J. ROBERT BREN AND *"The Gravy Game"* BY HARRY STUHLDREHER AND W. THORNTON MARTIN
ADAPTORS: Bernard Schubert, Ralph Spence, Harvey Gates
ART DIRECTORS: Cedric Gibbons, Harry Oliver
SET DECORATOR: Edwin B. Willis
CAMERA: Leonard Smith
EDITOR: William Levanway

Robert Young *(Tony Ferrera);* Betty Furness *(Kitty O'Brien);* Leo Carrillo *(Angelo);* Stuart Erwin *(Stuffy Wilson);* Ted Healy *(Joe O'Brien);* Russell Hardie *(Mike O'Brien);* Preston Foster *(Coach Howard Hardy);* William Tannen *(Rosy Rosenberg);* Robert Livingston *(Bob Stone);* Norman Phillips, Jr. *(Stuffy as a Child);* David Durand *(Tony as a Child);* Sidney Miller *(Rosy as a Child);* Beaudine Anderson *(Mike as a Child);* Betty Jane Graham *(Kitty as a Child);* Joe Sawyer *(Mr. Thomas);* Henry Kolker *(Professor Hackett);* Charles Lane *(Shyster Lawyer);* John Hyams *(Alumnus);* Purnell Pratt *(Judge);* Arthur Vinton *(Hertz).*

WEST POINT OF THE AIR
(MGM, 1935) 88 min.

PRODUCER: Monta Bell
DIRECTOR: Richard Rosson
STORY: John Monk Saunders

SCREENPLAY:	Frank Wead, Arthur J. Beckhard
SYNCHRONIZED SCORE:	Charles Maxwell
ART DIRECTORS:	Cedric Gibbons, H. R. Campbell
WARDROBE:	Dolly Tree
CAMERA:	Clyde DeVinna
AERIAL CAMERA:	Charles A. Marshall, Elmer Dyer
EDITOR:	Frank Sullivan

Wallace Beery *(Big Mike);* Robert Young *(Little Mike);* Maureen O'Sullivan *(Skip Carter);* Russell Hardie *(Phil Carter);* Lewis Stone *(General Carter);* James Gleason *(Joe Bags);* Rosalind Russell *(Dare);* Henry Wadsworth *(Pettis);* Robert Livingston *(Pippinger);* Robert Taylor *(Jaskarelli);* Frank Conroy *(Captain Cannon);* G. Pat Collins *(Lieutenant Kelly);* Ronnie Cosbey *(Little Mike as a Boy);* Bobbie Caldwell *(Phil as a Boy);* Marilyn Spinner *(Skip as a Girl);* Richard Tucker *(Club Manager).*

VAGABOND LADY
(MGM, 1935) 75 min.

PRODUCER/DIRECTOR:	Sam Taylor
STORY/SCREENPLAY:	Frank Butler
ART DIRECTOR:	Stan Rogers
CAMERA:	Jack MacKenzie
EDITOR:	Bernard Burton

Robert Young *(Tony Spear);* Evelyn Venable *(Jo Spiggins);* Reginald Denny *(John Spear);* Berton Churchill *(R. D. Spear);* Frank Craven *(Spiggins);* Forrester Harvey *(Corky);* Ferdinand Gottschalk *(Higginbotham);* Dan Crimmins *(Willie);* Fuzzy Knight *(Swan);* Herbert Vigran *(Edgar);* Harry Todd *(Crabby Clerk);* Herman Bing, Arthur Hoyt, Ferdinand Munier *(Department Heads);* "Shep" Shepard *(Stand-In for Robert Young);* Pat Scott *(Stand-In for Evelyn Venable);* George Becker *(Stand-In for Reginald Denny);* Rose Plummer, Elizabeth Rhoades *(Old Women);* John Elliott *(Master of Ceremonies).*

CALM YOURSELF
(MGM, 1935) 70 min.

PRODUCER:	Lucien Hubbard
DIRECTOR:	George B. Seitz
STORY:	Edward Hope
SCREENPLAY:	Arthur Kober
ART DIRECTORS:	Cedric Gibbons, Stan Rogers
SET DECORATOR:	Edwin B. Willis
CAMERA:	Lester White

Robert Young *(Pat);* Madge Evans *(Rosalind);* Betty Furness *(Mary);* Nat Pendleton *(Knuckles);* Hardie Albright *(Bobby Kent);* Ralph Morgan *(Mr. Rockwell);* Claude Gillingwater, Sr. *(Allenby);* Paul Hurst *(Rosco);* Shirley Ross *(Mrs. Rockwell);* Shirley Chambers *(Joan Vincent);* Hale Hamilton *(Mr. Kent);* Claudelle Kaye *(Mrs. Lanselle);* Clyde Cook *(Joe);* Herman Bing *(Bromberg);* Richard Tucker *(Police Inspector);* Ivan "Dusty" Miller *(Police Lieutenant);* Tempe Pigott *(Anne);* Charles Trowbridge *(Lanselle);* Gertrude Sutton *(Miss Hawks);* Ward Bond, Raymond Hatton *(Bits);* Lee Shumway *(Police Sergeant).*

RED SALUTE
(United Artists, 1935) 78 min.
(Reissue titles: HER ENLISTED MAN/ RUNAWAY DAUGHTER)

PRODUCER:	Edward Small
DIRECTOR:	Sidney Lanfield
STORY:	Humphrey Pearson
SCREENPLAY:	Pearson, Manuel Seff
CAMERA:	Robert Planck
EDITOR:	Grant Whytock

Barbara Stanwyck *(Drue Van Allen);* Robert Young *(Jeff);* Hardie Albright *(Arner);* Cliff Edwards *(Rooney);* Ruth Donnelly *(Mrs. Rooney);* Gordon Jones *(Lefty);* Paul Stanton *(Louis Martin);* Purnell Pratt *(General Van Allen);* Nella Walker *(Aunt Betty);* Arthur Vinton *(Joe Beal);* Edward McWade *(Baldy);* Henry Kolker *(Dean);* Henry Otho *(Border Patrolman);* Ben Hall *(Student);* Joe Dominguez *(Rubio, the Chauffeur);* Chris-Pin Martin *(Men's Room Attendant);* Edward Hearn *(Border Patrolman),* Jack Cheatham *(Border Patrolman/Cop at Riot);* William Moore *(Peter Potter);* Dave O'Brien, Fred Kohler, Jr. *(Students at Rally);* Eddy Chandler *(Jailer).*

REMEMBER LAST NIGHT?
(Universal, 1935) 81 min.

PRODUCER:	Carl Laemmle, Jr.
DIRECTOR:	James Whale
BASED ON THE NOVEL *Hangover Murders* BY ADAM HOBHOUSE	
SCREENPLAY:	Doris Malloy, Harry Clork, Louise Henry
CAMERA:	Joseph Valentine
EDITOR:	Ted J. Kent

Edward Arnold *(Danny Harrison);* Robert Young *(Tony Milburn);* Sally Eilers *(Bette Huling);* Constance Cummings *(Carlotta Milburn);* Monroe Owsley *(Billy Arliss);* Robert Armstrong *(Fred Flannagan);* Reginald Denny *(Jake Whitridge);* George Meeker *(Vic Huling);* Edward Brophy *(Maxie);* Gregory Ratoff *(Faronea);* Arthur Treacher *(Clarence Phelps);* Jack LaRue *(Baptiste Bouclier);* Gustav von Seyffertitz *(Professor Carl Herman Eckhart Jones);* Rafaela Ottiano *(Mme. Bouclier);* Louise Henry *(Penny Whitridge);* Monte Montague *(Mechanic);* Ted Billings *(Sailor);* Tiny Sandford *(Truck Driver);* E. E. Clive *(Photographer);* Kate Price *(Cook);* Wade Boteler, James Flavin *(Cops).*

THE BRIDE COMES HOME
(Paramount, 1935) 82 min.

PRODUCER/DIRECTOR:	Wesley Ruggles
STORY:	Elisabeth Sanxay Holding
SCREENPLAY:	Claude Binyon
CAMERA:	Leo Tover

Claudette Colbert *(Jeannette Desmereau);* Fred MacMurray *(Cyrus Anderson);* Robert Young *(Jack Bristow);* William Collier, Sr. *(Alfred Desmereau);* Donald Meek *(Judge);* Richard Carle *(Frank, the Butler);* Edgar Kennedy *(Henry);* Johnny Arthur *(Otto);* Kate MacKenna *(Emma);* James Conlin *(Len Noble);* William "Billy" Arnold *(Elevator Starter);* Tom Kennedy *(Husky);* James Quinn *(Conductor);* Maxine Elliot Hicks, Alex Woloshin, Gertrude Simpson, Mabelle Moore, Alice Keating, Howard Bruce, Art Rowland *(Passengers);* Tom Hanlon *(Man in Nightclub);* A. S. "Pop" Byron *(Cop in Chicago Park).*

THREE WISE GUYS
(MGM, 1936) 73 min.

PRODUCER:	Harry Rapf
DIRECTOR:	George B. Seitz
BASED ON A STORY BY DAMON RUNYON	
SCREENPLAY:	Elmer Harris
ART DIRECTOR:	Cedric Gibbons, Eddie Imazu
SET DECORATOR:	Edwin B. Willis
WARDROBE:	Dolly Tree
MUSIC:	Dr. William Axt
CAMERA:	Jackson Rose
EDITOR:	Frank E. Hull

Robert Young *(Joe);* Betty Furness *(Clarabelle);* Bruce Cabot *(Blackie);* Raymond Walburn *(Doc);* Thurston Hall *(Hatcher);* Donald Meek *(Secretary);* Herman Bing *(Baumgarten);* Harry Tyler *(Yegg);* Pat West *(Bartender);* Edward Hearn *(Cop);* Alexander Melesh *(Waiter);* Clay Clement *(Manager of Mangin's);* Buddy Messenger *(Elevator Operator).*

IT'S LOVE AGAIN
(Gaumont-British, 1936) 82 min.

DIRECTOR:	Victor Saville
STORY:	Marion Dix, Lester Samuels
SCREENPLAY:	Dix, Austin Melford
SONGS:	Sam Coslow and Harry Woods
CHOREOGRAPHY:	Buddy Bradley
CAMERA:	Glen MacWilliams
EDITOR:	Al Barnes

Jessie Matthews *(Elaine Bradford);* Robert Young *(Peter Carlton);* Sonnie Hale *(Freddie Rathbone);* Ernest Milton *(Archibald Raymond);* Robb Wilton *(Boy);* Sara Allgood *(Mrs. Hopkins);* Cyril Wells *(Gigolo);* Warren Jenkins *(Woolf);* David Horne *(Durland);* Athene Seyler *(Mrs. Durland);* Glennis Lorimer *(Montague's Typist);* Robert Hale *(Colonel Egerton);* Cyril Raymond *(Montague).*

THE BRIDE WALKS OUT
(RKO, 1936) 81 min.

PRODUCER:	Edward Small
DIRECTOR:	Leigh Jason
STORY:	Howard Emmett Rogers
SCREENPLAY:	P. J. Wolfson, Philip G. Epstein
ART DIRECTORS:	Van Nest Polglase, Al Herman
COSTUMES:	Bernard Newman

Music Director:	Roy Webb
Camera:	J. Roy Hunt
Editor:	Arthur Roberts

Barbara Stanwyck *(Carolyn Martin);* Gene Raymond *(Michael Martin);* Robert Young *(Hugh MacKenzie);* Helen Broderick *(Paulo Dodson);* Vivien Oakland *(Saleslady);* Willie Best *(Smokie);* Robert Warwick *(MacKenzie);* Billy Gilbert *(Donovan, the Bill Collector);* Eddie Dunn *(Milkman);* Ward Bond *(Taxi Driver);* Edgar Dearing *(Traffic Cop);* Hattie McDaniel *(Maime);* James Farley *(Store Detective).*

SECRET AGENT
(Gaumont-British, 1936) 83 min.

Director:	Alfred Hitchcock
Based on the stories *"Ashenden"* by W. Somerset Maugham	
Screenplay:	Charles Bennett
Camera:	Bernard Knowles
Editor:	Charles Freund

Madeleine Carroll *(Elsa);* Peter Lorre *(General);* John Gielgud *(Ashenden);* Robert Young *(Marvin);* Percy Marmont *(Caypor);* Florence Kahn *(Mrs. Caypor);* Charles Carson *(R);* Lilli Palmer *(Lilli).*

SWORN ENEMY
(MGM, 1936) 62 min.

Producer:	Lucien Hubbard
Director:	Edwin L. Marin
Story:	Richard Wormser
Screenplay:	Wells Root
Camera:	Lester White
Editor:	Frank Hull

Robert Young *(Hank Sherman);* Florence Rice *(Margaret);* Joseph Calleia *(Joe Emerald);* Nat Pendleton *(Steamer Krupp);* Lewis Stone *(Dr. Simon Gattle);* Harvey Stephens *(Paul Scott);* Samuel S. Hinds *(Eli Decker);* Edward Pawley *(Dutch McTurk);* John Wray *(Lang);* Cy Kendall *(Simmons);* Leslie Fenton *(Steve Sherman);* William Orlamond *(Kreel);* Robert Gleckler *(Hinkle);* George Regas *(Greek);* Duke York *(Al);* Lillian Harmer *(Landlady);* King Mojave *(Gibbons);* Anthony Quinn, Ed Hart, Wallace Gregory, Guy Kingsford *(Gangsters);* George Chandler *(Lunchstand Man);* Norman Ainsley *(Bergen the Chauffeur).*

THE LONGEST NIGHT
(MGM, 1936) 50 min.

Producers:	Lucien Hubbard, Samuel Marx
Director:	Errol Taggart
Based on the story *"The Whispering Window"* by Cortland Fitzsimmons	
Screenplay:	Robert Andrews
Camera:	Lester White
Editor:	Robert J. Kern

Robert Young *(Charley Phelps);* Florence Rice *(Joan Sutton);* Ted Healy *(Sergeant);* Julie Haydon *(Eve Sutton);* Catharine Doucet *(Mrs. Wilson);* Janet Beecher *(Mrs. Briggs);* Leslie Fenton *(Carl Briggs);* Sidney Toler *(Captain Holt);* Paul Stanton *(Grover);* Etienne Girardot *(Mr. Kinney).*

STOWAWAY
(20th Century-Fox, 1936) 86 min.

Producer:	B. G. DeSylva
Associate Producers:	Earl Carroll, Harold Wilson
Story:	Samuel G. Engel
Screenplay:	William Conselman, Arthur Sheekman, Nat Perrin
Art Director:	William Darling
Set Decorator:	Thomas Little
Assistant Director:	Earl Haley
Music Director:	Louis Silvers
Costumes:	Royer
Songs:	Irving Caesar and Gerald Marks
Sound:	Eugene Grossman, Roger Heman
Camera:	Arthur Miller
Editor:	Lloyd Nosler

Shirley Temple *(Ching-Ching);* Robert Young *(Tommy Randall);* Alice Faye *(Susan Parker);* Eugene Pallette *(Colonel);* Helen Westley *(Mrs. Hope);* Arthur Treacher *(Atkins);* J. Edward Bromberg *(Judge Booth);* Astrid Allwyn *(Kay Swift);* Allan Lane *(Richard Hope);* Robert Greig *(Captain);* Willie Fung *(Chang);* Philip Ahn *(Sun Lo);* Honorable Wu, William Stack, Helen Jerome Eddy, Paul McVey *(Bits).*

DANGEROUS NUMBER
(MGM, 1937) 71 min.

Producer:	Lou Ostrow
Director:	Richard Thorpe
Based on the story *"Wedding March"* by Leona Dalrymple	
Screenplay:	Carey Wilson
Camera:	Leonard Smith
Editor:	Blanche Sewell

Robert Young *(Hank Medhill);* Ann Sothern *(Elinor Breen);* Reginald Owen *(Cousin William);* Cora Witherspoon *(Alexandria "Gypsy" Breen);* Dean Jagger *(Vance Dillman);* Marla Shelton *(Vera);* Barnett Parker *(Minehardi);* Charles Trowbridge *(Hotel Manager);* Franklin Pangborn *(Hotel Clerk);* Spencer Charters *(Justice of the Peace);* Carey Wilson *(County Sheriff);* Pierre Watkin *(Wrighter Stark);* Prince *(Great Dane Dog);* Clem Bevans *(Actor);* Duke York, Chuck Hamilton, Ivan Miller *(Cops).*

I MET HIM IN PARIS
(Paramount, 1937) 86 min.

Producer/Director:	Wesley Ruggles
Story:	Helen Meinardi
Screenplay:	Claude Binyon
Art Directors:	Hans Dreier, Ernst Fegte
Song:	Meinardi and Hoagy Carmichael
Music Director:	Boris Morros
Special Camera Effects:	Farciot Edouart
Camera:	Leo Tover
Editor:	Otho Lovering

Claudette Colbert *(Kay Denham);* Melvyn Douglas *(George Potter);* Robert Young *(Gene Anders);* Lee Bowman *(Berk Sutter);* Mona Barrie *(Helen Anders);* George Davis *(Cutter Driver);* Fritz Feld *(Swiss Hotel Clerk);* Rudolph Anders *(Romantic Waiter);* Alexander Cross *(John Hadley);* George Sorel *(Hotel Clerk);* Louis La Bey *(Bartender);* Egon Brecher *(Emile the Upper Tower Man);* Hans Joby *(Lower Tower Man);* Jacques Vanaire *(Flirtatious Frenchman);* Alberto Morin *(Headwaiter);* Arthur Hurni *(Hotel Clerk);* Albert Pollet *(Conductor);* Yola d'Avril *(Frenchwoman);* Charles Haas, Otto Jehly, Paco Moreno, Roman Novins *(Waiters);* Joe Ploski *(Bartender);* Alexander Schonberg *(Porter);* Gloria Williams, Priscilla Moran *(Women).*

MARRIED BEFORE BREAKFAST
(MGM, 1937) 70 min.

Producer:	Sam Zimbalist
Director:	Edwin L. Marin
Story:	Harry Ruskin
Screenplay:	George Oppenheimer, Everett Freeman
Camera:	Leonard Smith
Editor:	William S. Gray

Robert Young *(Tom Wakefield);* Florence Rice *(Kitty Brent);* June Clayworth *(June Baylin);* Barnett Parker *(Tweed);* Hugh Marlowe *(Kenneth);* Helen Flint *(Miss Fleeter);* Mary Gordon *(Mrs. Nevins);* Harlan Briggs *(Mr. Moriarety);* Richard Carle *(Colonel);* Josephine Whittell *(Miss Willis);* Leonid Kinskey *(Lapidoff);* Pierre Watkin *(Mr. Potter);* Paul Stanton *(Mr. Dow);* Douglas Wood *(Mr. Camden);* Eddie Dunn *(Lester O'Brien);* Edgar Dearing *(Police Sergeant);* Edward LeSaint *(Judge Rafferty);* Si Jenks *(Janitor);* Boyd Irwin, Sr. *(Mr. Baylin);* Bea Nigro *(Mrs. Baylin);* Tom Kennedy *(Mr. Baglipp);* Irene Franklin *(Mrs. Baglipp);* Joe Caits, George Taylor, Warren Hymer *(Gangsters);* Tom Dugan *(Cop);* Tommy Bond *(Baglipp's Kid);* Jack Norton *(Drunk);* Henry Taylor *(Moreno);* Luke Cosgrave *(Peddler);* Spencer Charters *(Fireman);* Dennis O'Keefe *(Salesman);* Joseph Crehan *(Dalton).*

THE EMPEROR'S CANDLESTICKS
(MGM, 1937) 89 min.

Producer:	John W. Considine, Jr.
Director:	George Fitzmaurice
Based on the novel by Baroness Orczy	
Screenplay:	Monckton Hoffe, Harold Goldman
Art Director:	Cedric Gibbons
Music:	Franz Waxman
Montage:	Slavko Vorkapich
Camera:	Harold Rosson
Editor:	Conrad A. Nervig

William Powell *(Wolensky);* Luise Rainer *(Countess Muramova);* Frank Morgan *(Colonel*

Baron Suroff); Maureen O'Sullivan *(Maria);* Henry Stephenson *(Prince Johann);* Robert Young *(Grand Duke Peter);* Douglass Dumbrille *(Korun);* Bernadene Hayes *(Mitzi);* Donald Kirke *(Antone);* Charles Waldron *(Dr. Malcher);* Barnett Parker *(Rudolph);* Frank Reicher *(Pavloff);* Paul Porcasi *(Santuzzi);* Bert Roach *(Porter);* E. E. Clive *(Auctioneer);* Spencer Charters *(Usher);* Ian Wolfe *(Leon);* Theodor von Eltz *(Adjutant);* Mitchell Lewis *(Plainsclothesman);* Egon Brecher *(Chief of Police);* Erville Alderson *(Conductor);* Clarence H. Wilson *(Stationmaster);* Rollo Lloyd *(Jailer);* Maude Turner Gordon *(Concierge);* Lionel Pape *(Sugar Daddy);* Emma Dunn *(Housekeeper);* Frank Conroy *(Colonel Ridoff);* William Stack *(Czar);* Ramsey Hill, Olaf Hytten *(Conspirators);* Mariska Aldrich *(Ugly Woman).*

THE BRIDE WORE RED
(MGM, 1937) 103 min.

PRODUCER: Joseph L. Mankiewicz
DIRECTOR: Dorothy Arzner
BASED ON THE PLAY *The Girl from Trieste* BY FERENC MOLNAR
SCREENPLAY: Tess Slesinger, Bradbury Foote
ART DIRECTOR: Cedric Gibbons
MUSIC: Franz Waxman
SONGS: Gus Kahn and Waxman
CHOREOGRAPHY: Val Raset
CAMERA: George Folsey
EDITOR: Adrienne Fazan

Joan Crawford *(Annie Pavlowitz/Signorina Vivaldi);* Franchot Tone *(Guilio Conti);* Robert Young *(Rudi Pal);* Reginald Owen *(Admiral Ritter);* Billie Burke *(Contessa DeMilano);* Lynne Carver *(Magdalena Ritter);* George Zucco *(Count Armalia);* Mary Philips *(Maria);* Paul Porcasi *(Mobili);* Dickie Moore *(Pietro);* Frank Puglia *(Alberto);* Charles Judels *(Proprietor of Cordellera Bar);* Ann Rutherford *(Peasant Girl);* Nino Bellini *(Waiter at Cafe);* Rita Gould *(Saleslady);* Bob Cautiero *(Hotel Clerk)* Fred Malatesta *(Rudy's Waiter);* Harry Wilson *(Sailor at Bar).*

NAVY BLUE AND GOLD
(MGM, 1937) 94 min.

PRODUCER: Sam Zimbalist
DIRECTOR: Sam Wood
STORY/SCREENPLAY: George Bruce
ART DIRECTORS: Cedric Gibbons, Urie McCleary
SET DECORATOR: Edwin B. Willis
WARDROBE: Dolly Tree
MUSIC: Edward Ward
TECHNICAL DIRECTOR: Commander Harvey Haeslip
SOUND: Douglas Shearer
MONTAGE: John Hoffman
CAMERA: John Seitz
EDITOR: Robert J. Kerm

Robert Young *(Roger Ash);* James Stewart *(John "Truck" Cross);* Florence Rice *(Patricia Gates);* Lionel Barrymore *(Captain "Skinny" Dawes);* Billie Burke *(Mrs. Alyce Gates);* Tom Brown *(Richard Arnold Gates, Jr.);* Samuel S. Hinds *(Richard A. Gates, Sr.);* Barnett Parker *(Albert Graves);* Paul Kelly *(Tommy Milton);* Donald Douglas *(Lieutenant North);* Ted Pearson *(Harnett);* Robert Hoover *(Parr);* Walter Soderling *(Dr. Ryder);* Frank Albertson *(Weeks);* Phillip Terry *(Kelly);* Robert Middlemass *(Academy Superintendent);* Charles Waldron *(Commander Carter);* Roger Converse *(Size Inspector);* Dennis Morgan (Marine Second Lieutenant); Donald Barry *(Fellow Back);* Jack Pennick *(Fireman);* Paul Barrett, William Morgan *(Classmen);* Edward Hart *(Official);* Tom Hanlon, John Hiestand *(Commentators).*

PARADISE FOR THREE
(MGM, 1938) 75 min.

PRODUCER: Sam Zimbalist
DIRECTOR: Edward Buzzell
BASED ON THE STORY *"Three Men in The Snow"* BY ERICH KAESTNER
SCREENPLAY: George Oppenheimer, Harry Ruskin
MUSIC: Edward Ward
ART DIRECTORS: Cedric Gibbons, Stan Rogers
SET DECORATOR: Edwin B. Willis
WARDROBE: Dolly Tree
SOUND: Douglas Shearer
MONTAGE: John Hoffman
CAMERA: Leonard Smith
EDITOR: Elmo Vernon

Frank Morgan *(Rudolph Tobler/Edward Schultze);* Robert Young *(Fritz Hagedorn);* Mary Astor *(Mrs. Mallebre);* Florence Rice *(Hilda Tobler);* Edna May Oliver *(Aunt Julia Kunkel);* Henry Hull *(Sepp);* Reginald Owen *(Johann Kesselhut);* Herman Bing *(Polter);* Sig Rumann *(Karl Bold);* Walter Kingsford *(William Reichenbach);* George Ernest *(Office Boy);* Greta Meyer *(Mrs. Traub);* Mariska Aldrich *(Beauty Operator);* Elsa Christian *(Woman);* Lilyan Irene *(Maid);* Maurice Cass, Edwin Maxwell, Gustav von Seyffertitz, Wedgwood Nowell *(Lawyers);* Anna Q. Nilsson, Grace Goodall, Florence Wix, Hazel Laughton *(Women Bridge Players).*

JOSETTE
(20th Century-Fox, 1938) 76 min.

PRODUCER: Darryl F. Zanuck
ASSOCIATE PRODUCER: Gene Markey
DIRECTOR: Allan Dwan
BASED ON THE PLAY BY PAUL FRANK AND GEORGE FRASER FROM A STORY BY LADISLAUS VADNAI
SCREENPLAY: James Edward Grant
ART DIRECTORS: Bernard Herzbrun, David Hall
SET DECORATOR: Thomas Little
COSTUMES: Royer
SONGS: Mack Gordon and Harry Revel
CAMERA: Harry Mescal
EDITOR: Robert Simpson

Don Ameche *(David Brossard);* Simone Simon *(Renee Le Blanc);* Robert Young *(Pierre Brossard);* Bert Lahr *(Barney Barnaby);* Joan Davis *(May Morris);* Paul Hurst [*A. Adolphus Heyman (Sport)*]; William Collier, Sr. *(David Brossard, Sr.);* Tala Birell *(Mlle. Josette);* Lynn Bari *(Mrs. Elaine Dupree);* William Demarest *(Joe);* Ruth Gillette *(Joe's Wife);* Armand Kaliz *(Thomas the Headwaiter);* Maurice Cass *(Ed the Furrier);* Raymond Turner *(Chauffeur);* George Reed *(Mose the Butler);* Paul McVey *(Hotel Manager);* Fred Kelsey *(Hotel Detective);* Robert Kellard *(Kearney the Reporter);* Robert Lowery *(Officer);* Lon Chaney, Jr. *(Boatman);* Mary Healy *(Ringsider);* Eddie Collins *(Customs' Inspector);* Ruth Peterson *(Switchboard Operator).*

THE TOY WIFE
(MGM, 1938) 95 min.
(British release title: FROU-FROU)

PRODUCER: Merian C. Cooper
DIRECTOR: Richard Thorpe
SCREENPLAY: Zöe Akins
ART DIRECTOR: Cedric Gibbons
MUSIC: Edward Ward
CAMERA: Oliver T. Marsh
EDITOR: Elmo Vernon

Luise Rainer *(Gilberta Brigard);* Melvyn Douglas *(Georges Sartoris);* Robert Young *(Andre Vallaire);* Barbara O'Neil *(Louise Brigard);* H. B. Warner *(Victor Brigard);* Alma Kruger *(Mdme. Vallaire);* Libby Taylor *(Suzanne);* Theresa Harris *(Pick);* Walter Kingsford *(Judge Rondell);* Clinton Rosemond *(Pompey);* Clarence Muse *(Brutus);* Leonard Penn *(Gaston Vincent);* Margaret Irving *(Mdme. DeCambri);* Alan Perl *(Georgie);* Rafaela Ottiano *(Felicianne);* Beulah Hall Jones *(Sophie);* Madame Sul-te-wan *(Eve);* Hal Le Seur, Douglas McPhail *(Brothers);* Barbara Bedford *(Woman in Doctor's Office);* Olive Ball, Geneva Williams, Mary Luster, Edna Franklin, Charles Andrews, Ernest Wilson, Henry Thomas, Louise Robinson, Fannie Washington *(Servants);* Violet McDowell *(Brown Marie);* Robert Spindola *(Italian Boy).*

THREE COMRADES
(MGM, 1938) 100 min.

PRODUCER: Joseph L. Mankiewicz
DIRECTOR: Frank Borzage
BASED ON THE NOVEL BY ERICH MARIA REMARQUE
SCREENPLAY: F. Scott Fitzgerald, Edward Paramore
ART DIRECTORS: Cedric Gibbons, Paul Grosse
SET DECORATOR: Edwin B. Willis
MUSIC: Franz Waxman
SONGS: Waxman, Chet Forrest, and Bob Wright
SOUND: Douglas Shearer
MONTAGES: Slavko Vorkapich
CAMERA: Joseph Ruttenberg
EDITOR: Frank Sullivan

Robert Taylor *(Erich Lohkamp);* Margaret Sullavan *(Pat Hollmann);* Franchot Tone

(Otto Koster); Robert Young *(Gottfried Lenz);* Guy Kibbee *(Alfons);* Lionel Atwill *(Franz Breuer);* Henry Hull *(Dr. Heinrich Becker);* George Zucco *(Dr. Plauten);* Charley Grapewin *(Local Doctor);* Monty Woolley *(Dr. Jaffe);* Spencer Charters *(Herr Schultz);* Sarah Padden *(Frau Schultz);* Ferdinand Munier *(Burgomaster);* Morgan Wallace *(Owner of Wrecked Car);* George Offerman, Jr. *(Adolph);* Leonard Penn *(Tony);* Priscilla Lawson *(Frau Brunner);* Esther Muir *(Frau Schmidt);* Henry Brandon *(Man with Patch);* Francis X. Bushman, Jr., George Chandler *(Comics);* E. Alyn Warren *(Bookstore Owner);* Ricca Allen *(Housekeeper);* Roger Converse *(Becker's Assistant);* Jessie Arnold *(Nurse);* Barbara Bedford *(Rita);* Claire McDowell *(Frau Zalenska).*

RICH MAN—POOR GIRL
(MGM, 1938) 65 min.

PRODUCER: Edward Chodorov
DIRECTOR: Reinhold Schunzel
BASED ON THE PLAY *White Collars* BY EDITH ELLIS
SCREENPLAY: Joseph A. Fields, Jerome Chodorov
ART DIRECTOR: Cedric Gibbons, Gabriel Scognamillo
SET DECORATOR: Edwin B. Willis
MUSIC: Dr. William Axt
WARDROBE: Dolly Tree
SOUND: Douglas Shearer
CAMERA: Ray June
EDITOR: Frank E. Hull

Robert Young *(Bill Harrison);* Lew Ayres *(Henry Thayer);* Ruth Hussey *(Joan Thayer);* Lana Turner *(Helen);* Rita Johnson *(Sally Harrison);* Don Castle *(Frank);* Guy Kibbee *(Pa);* Sarah Padden *(Ma);* Gordon Jones *(Tom Grogan);* Virginia Grey *(Selma);* Marie Blake *(Mrs. Gussler).*

THE SHINING HOUR
(MGM, 1938) 80 min.

PRODUCER: Joseph L. Mankiewicz
DIRECTOR: Frank Borzage
BASED ON THE PLAY BY KEITH WINTERS
SCREENPLAY: Jane Murfin, Ogden Nash
ART DIRECTORS: Cedric Gibbons, Paul Groesse
SET DECORATOR: Edwin B. Willis
MUSIC: Franz Waxman
CHOREOGRAPHY: Tony DeMarco
GOWNS: Adrian
SOUND: Douglas Shearer
CAMERA: George Folsey
EDITOR: Frank E. Hull

Joan Crawford *(Olivia Riley);* Margaret Sullavan *(Judy Linden);* Melvyn Douglas *(Henry Linden);* Robert Young *(David Linden);* Fay Bainter *(Hannah Linden);* Allyn Joslyn *(Roger Franklin);* Hattie McDaniel *(Belvedere);* Frank Albertson *(Benny Collins);* Oscar O'Shea *(Charlie Collins);* Harry Barris *(Bertie);* Tony De Marco *(Olivia's Dance Partner);* Claire Owen *(Stewardess);* Jimmy Conlin, Granville Bates *(Men);* Francis X. Bushman, Jr. *(Doorman);* Frank Puglia *(Headwaiter);* George Chandler *(Press Agent);* Sarah Edwards *(Woman);* Jacques Vanaire *(Waiter);* Jack Raymond *(Farmer);* Bess Flowers *(Nurse);* Grace Goodall *(Mrs. Smart);* Buddy Messinger *(Elevator Boy);* Charles Coleman *(Butler).*

HONOLULU
(MGM, 1939) 83 min.

PRODUCER: Jack Cummings
DIRECTOR: Edward Buzzell
STORY/SCREENPLAY: Herbert Fields, Frank Partos
ART DIRECTOR: Cedric Gibbons
SONGS: Gus Kahn and Harry Warren
CAMERA: Ray June
EDITOR: Conrad Nervig

Eleanor Powell *(Dorothy March);* George Burns *(Joe Duffy);* Gracie Allen *(Millie DeGrasse);* Robert Young *(Brooks Mason/George Smith);* Rita Johnson *(Cecilia Grayson);* Clarence Kolb *(Mr. Grayson);* Willie Fung *(Wong);* Ruth Hussey *(Gale Brewster);* Cliff Clark *(Carter);* Edward Gargan *(Burton);* Eddie Anderson *(Washington);* Hal K. Dawson *(Wally);* Edgar Dearing *(Jailer);* Jo Ann Sayer *(Vera);* Sig Rumann *(Professor Timmer);* Mary Lou Treen *(Gwen);* Tom Neal *(Interne);* Claire Owen, Martha Tibbets, Helen MacKellar *(Phone Girls);* Edward Earle, Bess Flowers, Bert Roach *(Guests).*

BRIDAL SUITE
(MGM, 1939) 69 min.

PRODUCER: Edgar Selwyn
DIRECTOR: William Thiele
STORY: Gottfried Reinhardt, Virginia Faulkner
SCREENPLAY: Samuel Hoffenstein
MUSIC: Arthur Gutmann
SONG: William Buddie and Gus Kahn
ART DIRECTORS: Cedric Gibbons, Harry McAfee
SET DECORATOR: Edwin B. Willis
WARDROBE: Dolly Tree
SOUND: Douglas Shearer
CAMERA: Clyde DeVinna
EDITOR: Frank Hull

Annabella *(Luise Ansengruber);* Robert Young *(Neil McGill);* Walter Connolly *(Dr. Grauer);* Billie Burke *(Mrs. McGill);* Reginald Owen *(Sir Horace Blagdon);* Virginia Field *(Abbie Blagdon);* Gene Lockhart *(Cornelius McGill);* Arthur Treacher *(Lord Helfer);* Felix Bressart *(Max);* Renie Riano *(Mrs. Pujol);* Mira McKinney *(Mrs. Spies);* Charles Judels *(Fritz Spies);* Roy Atwell *(Professor Kockerthaler);* Mary Beth Hughes *(Bride);* Bobby Blake *(Toto);* Alberto Morin *(Italian Guest);* Lionel Pape *(Lord Piddlefield);* Beae Nigro *(Mrs. Woodfeather);* Sig Arno *(Schmidt);* Gerald Oliver-Smith *(Purser).*

MIRACLES FOR SALE
(MGM, 1939) 71 min.

DIRECTOR: Tod Browning
BASED ON THE NOVEL *Death from a Top Hat* BY CLAYTON RAWSON
SCREENPLAY: Harry Ruskin, Marion Parsonnet, James Edward Grant
ART DIRECTORS: Cedric Gibbons, Gabriel Scognamillo
SET DECORATOR: Edwin B. Willis
WARDROBE: Dolly Tree
MAKEUP: Jack Dawn
SOUND: Douglas Shearer
CAMERA: Charles Lawton
EDITOR: Frederick Y. Smith

Robert Young *(Michael Morgan);* Florence Rice *(Judy Barclay);* Frank Craven *(Red Morgan);* Henry Hull *(Dave Duvallo);* Lee Bowman *(Le Claire);* Cliff Clark *(Inspector Gevigan);* William Demarest *(Quinn);* Gloria Holden *(Mdme. Rapport);* Astrid Allwyn *(Mrs. Zelma Le Claire);* Walter Kingsford *(Colonel Watrous);* Frederick Worlock *(Dr. Sabbatt);* Harold Minjir *(Tauro);* Charles Lane *(Hotel Clerk);* Richard Loo *(Chinese Soldier);* Suzanne Kaaran *(Girl);* Edward Earle *(Man);* Chester Clute *(Waiter);* Truman Bradley *(Master of Ceremonies);* Cyril Ring *(Numbers Man);* William Norton Bailey *(Man in Box);* Manuel Paris *(Sinister Man);* Paul Sutton *(Captain Storm).*

MAISIE
(MGM, 1939) 74 min.

PRODUCER: J. Walter Ruben
DIRECTOR: Edwin L. Marin
BASED ON THE NOVEL BY WILSON COLLINSON
SCREENPLAY: Mary C. McCall, Jr.
ART DIRECTORS: Cedric Gibbons, Malcolm Brown
SET DECORATOR: Edwin B. Willis
MEN'S COSTUMES: Vallees
WOMEN'S WARDROBE: Dolly Tree
SONGS: Frank Loesser and Victor Hollander
SOUND: Douglas Shearer
CAMERA: Leonard Smith
EDITOR: Frederick Y. Smith

Robert Young *("Slim" Martin);* Ann Sothern *(Maisie Ravier);* Ruth Hussey *(Sybil Ames);* Ian Hunter *(Clifford Ames);* Cliff Edwards *(Shorty);* Anthony Allan *(John Hubbard) (Richard Raymond);* Art Mix *(Red);* George Tobias *(Rico);* Richard Carle *(Roger Bannerman);* Minor Watson *(Prosecuting Attorney);* Harlan Briggs *(Deputy Sheriff);* Paul Everton *(Judge);* Joseph Crehan *(Wilcox);* Frank Puglia *(Ernie);* Willie Fung *(Lee).*

NORTHWEST PASSAGE
(MGM, 1940) C-125 min.

PRODUCER: Hunt Stromberg
DIRECTOR: (uncredited) Jack Conway, King Vidor
BASED ON THE NOVEL BY KENNETH ROBERTS
SCREENPLAY: Laurence Stallings, Talbot Jennings
ASSISTANT DIRECTOR: Robert Golden
TECHNICOLOR CONSULTANTS: Natalie Kalmus, Henri Jaffa
MUSIC: Herbert Stothart
ART DIRECTORS: Cedric Gibbons, Malcolm Brown
SET DECORATOR: Edwin B. Willis

MAKEUP: Jack Dawn
SOUND: Douglas Shearer
CAMERA: Sidney Wagner, William V. Skall
EDITOR: Conrad A. Nervig

Spencer Tracy *(Major Robert Rogers);* Robert Young *(Langdon Towne);* Walter Brennan *(Hunk Marriner);* Ruth Hussey *(Elizabeth Browne);* Nat Pendleton *(Cap Huff);* Louis Hector *(Reverend Browne);* Robert Barrat *(Humphrey Towne);* Lumsden Hare *(Lord Amherst);* Donald MacBride *(Sergeant McNott);* Isabel Jewell *(Jennie Coit);* Douglas Walton *(Lieutenant Avery);* Addison Richards *(Lieutenant Crofton);* Hugh Sothern *(Jesse Beacham);* Regis Toomey *(Webster);* Montagu Love *(Wiseman Clagett);* Lester Matthews *(Sam Livermore);* Truman Bradley *(Captain Ogden);* Andrew Pena (Konkapot).

FLORIAN
(MGM, 1940) 91 min.

PRODUCER: Winfield Sheehan
DIRECTOR: Edwin L. Marin
BASED ON THE NOVEL BY FELIX SALTEN
SCREENPLAY: Noel Langley, Geza Herczeg, James Kevin McGuinness
ART DIRECTOR: Cedric Gibbons, Randall Duell
SET DECORATOR: Edwin B. Willis
GOWNS: Adrian
MEN'S COSTUMES: Gile Steele
MUSIC: Franz Waxman
CHOREOGRAPHY: Ernst Matray
SOUND: Douglas Shearer
CAMERA: Karl Freund
EDITOR: Frank Hull

Robert Young *(Anton);* Helen Gilbert *(Diana);* Charles Coburn *(Hofer);* Lee Bowman *(Oliver);* Irina Baranova *(Trina);* Reginald Owen *(Emperor Franz Joseph);* Lucile Watson *(Countess);* William B. Davidson *(Franz Ferdinand);* Rand Brooks *(Victor);* Morgan Conway *(Kingston);* Adrian Morris *(Corporal Ernst);* George Lloyd *(Bogalli);* S. Z. Sakall *(Max);* Charles Judels *(Editor);* Charles Brown *(New York Police Lieutenant);* Frank Orth *(Detective);* John Russell *(Andy at Age Six);* George Irving *(Mr. Bantry);* Walter Bonn, George Rosener *(Inspectors of Riding School);* Dick Elliott *(Auctioneer);* Jack Luden, Ellis Irving *(Swiss Officers);* Alex Pollard *(Butler);* Mary Forbes *(Grandmother);* Joe Yule *(Barker);* Henry Brandon *(Groom);* Hillary Brooke, Caroline Frasher, Winifred Lynn *(Horsewomen);* Earle Hodgins *(Concession Owner);* Constantine Romanoff *(Russian).*

THE MORTAL STORM
(MGM, 1940) 100 min.

PRODUCER: Sidney Franklin
DIRECTOR: Frank Borzage
BASED ON THE NOVEL BY PHYLLIS BOTTOME
SCREENPLAY: Claudine West, Anderson Ellis, George Froeschel
MUSIC: Edward Kane
ADDITIONAL MUSIC: Eugene Zador
GOWNS: Adrian
MEN'S COSTUME: Gile Steele
ART DIRECTORS: Cedric Gibbons, Wade B. Rubbottom
SET DECORATOR: Edwin B. Willis
MAKEUP: Jack Dawn
SOUND: Douglas Shearer
CAMERA: William Daniels
EDITOR: Elmo Vernon

Margaret Sullavan *(Freya Roth);* James Stewart *(Martin Brietner);* Robert Young *(Fritz Marberg);* Frank Morgan *(Professor Roth);* Irene Rich *(Mrs. Roth);* Maria Ouspenskaya *(Mrs. Brietner);* William Orr *(Erich Von Rohn);* Robert Stack *(Otto Von Rohn);* Bonita Granville *(Elsa);* Gene Reynolds *(Rudi Roth);* Russell Hicks *(Rector);* William Edmunds *(Lehman);* Thomas Ross *(Professor Werner);* Ward Bond *(Franz);* Esther Dale *(Marta);* Fritz Leiber *(Oppenheim);* Dan Dailey, Jr. *(Holl);* Robert O. Davis [*Rudolph Anders*] *(Hartman);* Sue Moore *(Theresa);* Harry Depp, Julius Tannen, Gus Glassmire *(Colleagues);* John Stark *(Gestapo Official);* Lucien Prival, Dick Elliott *(Passport Officials);* Dick Rich, Ted Oliver *(Guards).*

SPORTING BLOOD
(MGM, 1940) 82 min.

PRODUCER: Albert Levoy
DIRECTOR: S. Sylvan Simon
STORY: Grace Norton
SCREENPLAY: Albert Mannheimer, Dorothy Yost
ART DIRECTORS: Cedric Gibbons, Stan Rogers
SET DECORATOR: Edwin B. Willis
WARDROBE: Dolly Tree
MUSIC: Franz Waxman
SOUND: Douglas Shearer
CAMERA: Sidney Wagner
EDITOR: Frank Sullivan

Robert Young *(Myles Vanders);* Maureen O'Sullivan *(Linda Lockwood);* Lewis Stone *(Davis Lockwood);* William Gargan *(Duffy);* Lynne Carver *(Joan Lockwood);* George Lessey *(Banker Cobb);* Lloyd Corrigan *(Otis Winfield);* Tom Kennedy *(Graney);* Russell Hicks *("Sneak" O'Brien);* William Tannen *(Ted Milner);* Clarence Muse *(Jeff);* George H. Reed *(Stonewall);* Helene Millard *(Martha Winfield);* Allen Wood *(Jockey);* Eugene Jackson *(Sam);* Dora Clement, Richard Tucker *(Guests);* Etta McDaniel *(Chloe);* Claude King, Charles Wagenheim *(Men at Race Track).*

DR. KILDARE'S CRISIS
(MGM, 1940) 75 min.

DIRECTOR: Harold S. Bucquet
BASED ON CHARACTERS CREATED BY MAX BRAND
STORY: Willis Goldbeck
SCREENPLAY: Harry Ruskin, Goldbeck
ART DIRECTOR: Cedric Gibbons
MUSIC: David Snell
CAMERA: John Seitz
EDITOR: Gene Ruggiero

Lew Ayres *(Dr. James Kildare);* Robert Young *(Douglas Lamont);* Lionel Barrymore *(Dr. Leonard Gillespie);* Laraine Day *(Mary Lamont);* Emma Dunn *(Mrs. Martha Kildare);* Nat Pendleton *(Joe Weyman);* Bob Watson *(Tommy);* Walter Kingsford *(Dr. Walter Carew);* Alma Kruger *(Molly Byrd);* Nell Craig *(Nurse Parker);* Frank Orth *(Mike);* Marie Blake *(Sally);* George Reed *(Conover);* Horace McMahon *(Foghorn Murphy);* Ann Morriss *(Betty);* Frank Sully *(John Root);* Lillian Rich *(Nurse);* Gladys Blake *(Maisie);* Pierre Watkin *(Chandler);* Charlie Arnt *(Stubbins);* Ernie Alexander *(Assistant Salesman);* Eddie Acuff *(Genet);* Byron Foulger, Gus Schilling *(Orderlies).*

THE TRIAL OF MARY DUGAN
(MGM, 1941) 90 min.

PRODUCER: Edwin Knopf
DIRECTOR: Norman Z. McLeod
BASED ON THE PLAY BY BAYARD VEILLER
ART DIRECTORS: Cedric Gibbons, Howard Campbell
SET DECORATOR: Edwin B. Willis
WARDROBE: Dolly Tree
CAMERA: George Folsey
EDITOR: George Boemler

Laraine Day *(Mary Dugan);* Robert Young *(Jimmy Blake);* Tom Conway *(Edgar Wayne);* Frieda Inescort *(Mrs. Wayne);* Henry O'Neill *(Galway);* John Litel *(Mr. West);* Marsha Hunt *(Agatha Hall);* Sara Haden *(Miss Matthews);* Marjorie Main *(Mrs. Collins);* Alma Kruger *(Dr. Saunders);* Pierre Watkin *(Judge Nash);* Addison Richards *(Captain Price);* Francis Pierlot *(John Masters);* George Watts *(Inspector Hunt);* Ian Wolfe *(Dr. Winston);* Cliff Danielson *(Robert the Chauffeur);* Cliff Clark *(John Dugan);* Milton Kibbee *(Court Clerk);* Nora Perry *(Sally);* Minerva Urecal *(Landlady);* Paul Porcasi *(Ship's Captain);* Larry Wheat *(Court Stenographer);* Walter Lawrence *(Newsboy);* Matt Moore *(Bailiff);* Anna Q. Nilsson *(Juror);* Joan Barclay, Ernie Alexander, Betty Farrington, Jessie Arnold, Hal Cooke, William Stelling *(Spectators);* Joe Yule *(Sign Painter).*

WESTERN UNION
(20th Century-Fox, 1941) C-94 min.

PRODUCER: Darryl F. Zanuck
ASSOCIATE PRODUCER: Harry Joe Brown
DIRECTOR: Fritz Lang
BASED ON THE NOVEL BY ZANE GREY
SCREENPLAY: Robert Carson
ART DIRECTORS: Richard Day, Wiard B. Ihnen
SET DECORATOR: Thomas Little
MUSIC: David Buttolph
COSTUMES: Travis Banton
CAMERA: Edward Cronjager, Allen M. Davey
EDITOR: Robert Bischoff

Robert Young *(Richard Blake);* Randolph Scott *(Vance Shaw);* Dean Jagger *(Edward Creighton);* Virginia Gilmore *(Sue Creighton);* John Carradine *(Doc Murdoch);* Slim Summerville *(Herman);* Chill Wills *(Homer);* Barton MacLane *(Jack Slade);* Russell Hicks *(Governor);* Victor Kilian *(Charlie);* Minor Watson *(Pat Grogan);* George Chandler *(Herb);* Chief Big Tree *(Chief Spotted Horse);* Chief Thundercloud *(Indian Leader);* Dick Rich *(Porky);* Harry Strang *(Henchman);* Charles Middleton *(Stagecoach Rider);* Addison Richards *(Captain Harlow);* Irving Bacon *(Barber);* James Flavin, Frank Mills, Ralph Dunn *(Men);* Francis Ford, Eddy Waller *(Stagecoach Drivers).*

LADY BE GOOD
(MGM, 1941) 111 min.

Producer: Arthur Freed
Director: Norman Z. McLeod
Story: Jack McGowan
Screenplay: McGowan, Kay Van Riper, John McClain, and (uncredited) Ralph Spence, Arnold Auerbach, Herman Wouk, Robert McGunigle, Vincente Minnelli
Songs: George and Ira Gershwin, Jerome Kern and Oscar Hammerstein II, Roger Edens and Freed
Music Director: George Stoll
Music Continuity: Walter Ruick
Vocal Directors/Orchestrators: Conrad Salinger, Leo Arnuad, George Folsey
Music numbers staged by Busby Berkeley
Music Presenter: Merrill Pye
Art Directors: Cedric Gibbons, John S. Detlie
Set Decorator: Edwin B. Willis
Gowns: Adrian
Sound: Douglas Shearer
Camera: George Folsey, Oliver T. Marsh
Editor: Frederick Y. Smith

Eleanor Powell *(Marilyn Marsh);* Robert Young *(Eddie Crane);* Ann Sothern *(Dixie Donegan);* John Carroll *(Buddy Crawford);* Lionel Barrymore *(Judge Murdock);* Red Skelton *(Joe "Red" Willet);* Reginald Owen *(Max Milton);* Dan Dailey, Jr. *(Bill Pattison);* Rose Hobart *(Mrs. Carter Wardley);* Phil Silvers *(Master of Ceremonies);* James Berry, Warren Berry, Nyas Berry *(The Berry Brothers);* Harold Miller *(Guest);* Doris Day *(Debutante);* Ernie Alexander *(Pageboy);* Edward Gargan *(Policeman).*

MARRIED BACHELOR
(MGM, 1941) 87 min.

Producer: John W. Considine, Jr.
Director: Edward Buzzell
Story: Manuel Seff
Screenplay: Dore Schary
Music: Lennie Hayton
Art Director: Cedric Gibbons
Camera: George Folsey
Editor: Ben Lewis

Robert Young *(Randolph Haven);* Ruth Hussey *(Norma Haven);* Felix Bressart *(Dr. Ladislaus Milic);* Lee Bowman *(Eric Santley);* Sheldon Leonard *(Branigan);* Sam Levene *(Cookie);* Roy Gordon *(Hudkins);* Douglass Newland *(Devlin);* Murray Alper *(Sleeper);* Charlotte Wynters *(Margaret Johns);* Hillary Brooke *(Connie Gordon);* Joe Yule *(Waiter);* Connie Gilchrist *(Mother with Baby);* Charles Ray *(Man in Lounge Room);* Bess Flowers *(Salesgirl);* Inez Cooper *(Customer);* Natalie Thompson *(Santley's Secretary);* Mimi Doyle *(Stenographer).*

H. M. PULHAM, ESQ.
(MGM, 1941) 120 min.

Producer/Director: King Vidor
Based on the novel by John P. Marquand
Screenplay: Elizabeth Hill, Vidor
Music: Bonrislau Kaper
Music Director: Lennie Hayton
Art Directors: Cedric Gibbons, Malcolm Brown
Set Decorator: Edwin B. Willis
Gowns: Kalloch
Men's Costumes: Gile Steele
Makeup: Jack Dawn
Sound: Douglas Shearer
Camera: Ray June
Editor: Harold F. Kress

Robert Young *(Harry Pulham);* Hedy Lamarr *(Marvin Myles);* Ruth Hussey *(Kay Metford);* Charles Coburn *(Mr. Pulham, Sr.);* Van Heflin *(Bill King);* Fay Holden *(Mrs. Pulham);* Bonita Granville *(Mary Pulham);* Leif Erickson *(Rodney "Bo-Jo" Brown);* Phil Brown *(Joe Bingham);* Douglas Wood *(Mr. Bullard);* Charles Halton *(Walter Kaufman);* David Clyde *(Hugh);* Sara Haden *(Miss Rollo);* Walter Kingsford *(Skipper);* Earle Dewey *(Chris Evans);* Byron Foulger *(Curtis Cole);* Grant Withers (Sammy Lee the Harvard Coach); Connie Gilchrist *(Tillie);* Ava Gardner *(Girl);* Frank Faylen *(Sergeant);* Arno Frey *(German Officer);* Anne Revere *(Miss Redfern);* Syd Saylor *(Preacher).*

JOE SMITH—AMERICAN
(MGM, 1942) 63 min.
(British release title: HIGHWAY TO FREEDOM)

Producer: Jack Chertok
Director: Richard Thorpe
Story: Paul Gallico
Screenplay: Allen Rivkin
Art Director: Cedric Gibbons
Camera: Charles Lawton
Editor: Elmo Vernon

Robert Young *(Joe Smith);* Marsha Hunt *(Mary Smith);* Harvey Stephens *(Freddie Dunhill);* Darryl Hickman *(Johnny Smith);* Jonathan Hale *(Blake McKettrick);* Noel Madison *(Schricker);* Don Costello *(Mead);* Joseph Anthony *(Conway);* William Forrest *(Gus);* Russell Hicks *(Mr. Edgerton);* Mark Daniels *(Pete);* William Tannen *(Eddie);* Frank Faylen *(Expectant Father);* Edgar Sherrod *(Minister);* Ava Gardner, Selma Jackson *(Bits).*

CAIRO
(MGM, 1942) 100 min.

Director: W. S. Van Dyke II
Based on an idea by Ladislas Fodor
Screenplay: John McClain
Songs: Arthur Schwartz, E. Y. Harburg, and Harold Arlen
Music: Herbert Stothart
Music Director: Georgie Stoll
Choreography: Sammy Lee
Art Director: Cedric Gibbons
Camera: Ray June
Editor: James E. Newcom

Jeanette MacDonald *(Marcia Warren);* Robert Young *(Homer Smith);* Ethel Waters *(Cleo);* Reginald Owen *(Mr. Cobson);* Mona Barrie *(Mrs. Morrison);* Lionel Atwill *(Teutonic Gentleman);* Eduardo Ciannelli *(Ahmed Ben Hassan);* Dennis Hoey *(Colonel Woodhue);* Dooley Wilson *(Hector);* Harry Worth *(Bartender);* Mitchell Lewis *(Ludwig);* Frank Richards *(Alfred);* Rhys Williams *(Strange Man);* Grant Mitchell *(O. H. P. Banks);* Bert Roach *(Sleepy Man);* Larry Nunn *(Bernie);* Jack Daley *(Man in Newspaper Office);* Demetrius Emanuel, Jay Novello *(Italian Officers);* Cecil Cunningham *(Mdme. Laruga);* Selmer Jackson *(Ship Captain);* James Davis *(Sergeant);* Guy Kingsford *(Squadron Leader).*

JOURNEY FOR MARGARET
(MGM, 1942) 81 min.

Producer: B. P. Fineman
Director: Major W. S. Van Dyke II
Story: William L. White
Screenplay: David Hertz, William Ludwig
Art Directors: Cedric Gibbons, Wade B. Rubottom
Set Decorator: Edwin B. Willis, Dick Pefferle
Music: Franz Waxman
Gowns: Kalloch
Sound: Douglas Shearer
Camera: Ray June
Editor: George White

Robert Young *(John Davis);* Laraine Day *(Nora Davis);* Fay Bainter *(Trudy Strauss);* Margaret O'Brien *(Margaret);* Nigel Bruce *(Herbert V. Allison);* William Severn *(Peter Humphreys);* G. P. Huntley, Jr. *(Rugged);* Doris Lloyd *(Mrs. Barrie);* Halliwell Hobbes *(Mr. Barrie);* Jill Esmond *(Susan Fleming);* Charles Irwin *(Fairoaks);* Elisabeth Risdon *(Mrs. Bailey);* Lisa Golm *(Frau Weber);* Leyland Hodgson *(Censor);* Matthew Boulton *(Warden);* Olaf Hytten *(Manager);* Ottola Nesmith *(Nurse);* John Burton *(Surgeon);* Keye Luke *(Japanese Statesman);* Craufurd Kent *(Everton);* Doris Stone *(Mother);* Eric Snowden *(Porter);* Clive Morgan *(Father);* Elisabeth Williams, Stephanie Insall, Gil Perkins, Major Douglas Francis, Allan Schute, Sybil Bacon, Lotus Thompson *(Subway Bits);* Hal Welling *(Tailor);* Gay Bennes *(Screaming Girl).*

SLIGHTLY DANGEROUS
(MGM, 1943) 94 min.

PRODUCER: Pandro S. Berman
DIRECTOR: Wesley Ruggles
STORY: Ian McLellan Hunter, Aileen Hamilton
SCREENPLAY: Charles Lederer, George Oppenheimer
GAG CONSULTANT: Buster Keaton
ART DIRECTOR: Cedric Gibbons
MUSIC: Bronislau Kaper
COSTUMES: Irene
SOUND: Douglas Shearer
CAMERA: Harold Rosson
EDITOR: Frank E. Hull

Lana Turner [*Peggy Evans (Carol Burden)/ Narrator*]; Robert Young *(Bob Stuart)*; Walter Brennan *(Cornelius Burden)*; Dame May Whitty *(Baba)*; Eugene Pallette *(Durstin)*; Howard Freeman *(Mr. Quill)*; Ward Bond *(Jimmy)*; Ray Collins *(Snodgrass)*; Pamela Blake *(Mitzi the Soda Jerk)*; Florence Bates *(Amanda)*; Millard Mitchell *(Baldwin—Durstin's Assistant)*; Alan Mowbray *(English Gentleman)*; Paul Stanton *(Stanhope—Burden's Lawyer)*; James Ford *(Reggie—Amanda's Escort)*; Cliff Clark *(Detective)*; Mimi Doyle *(Miss Kingsway—Durstin's Secretary)*; Spencer Charters *(Claudius—owner of Swade Cafe)*; Frances Rafferty, Kay Medford *(Pretty Girls Getting off Bus)*; Ann Doran *(Salesgirl—Jumbo Split Scene)*; Almira Sessions *(Landlady)*; Bobby Blake *(Boy on Porch)*.

CLAUDIA
(20th Century-Fox, 1943) 91 min.

PRODUCER: William Perlberg
DIRECTOR: Edmund Goulding
BASED ON THE PLAY BY ROSE FRANKEN
ADAPTOR: Morris Ryskind
MUSIC: Alfred Newman
SONG: Newman and Charles Henderson
ART DIRECTORS: James Basevi, Albert Hogsett
SET DECORATORS: Thomas Little, Paul S. Fox
ASSISTANT DIRECTOR: Percy Ikard
SOUND: Roger Heman
SPECIAL CAMERA EFFECTS: Fred Sersen
CAMERA: Leon Shamroy
EDITOR: Robert Simpson

Dorothy McGuire *(Claudia Naughton)*; Robert Young *(David Naughton)*; Ina Claire *(Mrs. Brown)*; Reginald Gardiner *(Jerry Seymour)*; Olga Baclanova *(Mme. Daruschka)*; Jean Howard *(Julia)*; Frank Tweddell *(Fritz)*; Elsa Janssen *(Bertha)*; John Royce *(Carl)*; Frank Fenton *(Hartley)*; Ferdinand Munier *(Mr. Feiffer)*; Winifred Harris *(Mrs. Feiffer)*; Jessie Grayson *(Maid)*.

SWEET ROSIE O'GRADY
(20th Century-Fox, 1943) C-74 min.

PRODUCER: William Perlberg
DIRECTOR: Irving Cummings
BASED ON STORIES BY WILLIAM R. LIPMAN, FREDERICK STEPHANI AND EDWARD VAN EVERY
SCREENPLAY: Ken Englund
SONGS: Mack Gordon and Harry Warren
MUSIC DIRECTORS: Alfred Newman, Charles Henderson
CHOREOGRAPHY: Hermes Pan
MUSIC NUMBERS SUPERVISED BY FANCHON
TECHNICOLOR CONSULTANT: Natalie Kalmus
ART DIRECTORS: James Basevi, Joseph C. Wright
SET DECORATORS: Thomas Little, Frank E. Hughes
ASSISTANT DIRECTOR: Ad Schaumer
SOUND: Roger Heman
SPECIAL CAMERA EFFECTS: Fred Sersen
CAMERA: Ernest Palmer
EDITOR: Robert Simpson

Betty Grable *(Madeleine Marlowe)*; Robert Young *(Sam Mackeever)*; Adolphe Menjou *(Morgan)*; Reginald Gardiner *(Duke Charles)*; Virginia Grey *(Edna Van Dyke)*; Phil Regan *(Composer)*; Sig Rumann *(Joe Flugelman)*; Alan Dinehart *(Arthur Skinner)*; Hobart Cavanaugh *(Clark)*; Frank Orth *(Cabby)*; Jonathan Hale *(Mr. Fox)*; Stanley Clements *(Danny)*; Byron Foulger *(Rimplemayer)*; Lilyan Irene *(Gracie)*; Milton Parsons *(Madison)*; Hal K. Dawson *(Poindexter)*; George Chandler *(Kelly)*; Charles Trowbridge *(Husband)*; St. Brendan's Choir *(Themselves)*; Leo Diamond and His Solitaires *(Themselves)*; Oliver Blake *(White, the Artist)*; Cyril Ring, Herbert Vigran, Perc Launders *(Photographers)*; Dorothy Granger *(Singer)*; Mary Gordon, Connie Leon *(Charwomen)*; Edward Earle *(Salesman)*; Gabriel Canzona *(Hurdy Gurdy Man with Monkey)*.

THE CANTERVILLE GHOST
(MGM, 1944) 96 min.

PRODUCER: Arthur L. Field
DIRECTOR: Jules Dassin
BASED ON THE STORY BY OSCAR WILDE
SCREENPLAY: Edwin Harvey Blum
CHOREOGRAPHY: Jack Donohue
MUSIC: George Bassman
ART DIRECTOR: Edward Carfagno
SET DECOTRATORS: Edwin B. Willis, Mildred Griffiths
ASSISTANT DIRECTOR: Julian Siberstein
SOUND: F. D. Raymond
CAMERA: Robert Planck
EDITOR: Chester W. Schaeffer

Charles Laughton *(Sir Simon de Canterville)*; Robert Young *(Cuffy Williams)*; Margaret O'Brien *(Lady Jessica de Canterville)*; William Gargan *(Sergeant Benson)*; Reginald Owen *(Lord Canterville)*; Rags Ragland *(Big Harry)*; Una O'Connor *(Mrs. Umney)*; Donald Stuart *(Sir Valentine Williams)*; Frank Faylen *(Lieutenant Kane)*; Lumsden Hare *(Mr. Potts)*; William Moss *(Hector)*; Bobby Readick *(Eddie)*; Marc Cramer *(Bugsy McDougle)*.

THE ENCHANTED COTTAGE
(RKO, 1945) 91 min.

EXECUTIVE PRODUCER: Jack Gross
PRODUCER: Harriet Parsons
DIRECTOR: John Cromwell
BASED ON THE PLAY BY ARTHUR WING PINERO
SCREENPLAY: DeWitt Bodeen, Herman J. Mankiewicz
ART DIRECTORS: Albert S. D'Agostino, Carroll Clark
SET DECORATORS: Darrell Silvera, Harley Miller
MUSIC: Roy Webb
MUSIC DIRECTOR: C. Bakaleinikoff
ASSISTANT DIRECTOR: Fred Fleck
SOUND: Richard Van Hessen
CAMERA: Ted Tetzlaff
EDITOR: Joseph Noriega

Dorothy McGuire *(Laura)*; Robert Young *(Oliver)*; Herbert Marshall *(Hillgrove)*; Mildred Natwick *(Mrs. Minnett)*; Spring Byington *(Violet Price)*; Hillary Brooke *(Beatrice)*; Richard Gaines *(Frederick)*; Alec Englander *(Danny)*; Mary Worth *(Mrs. Stanton)*; Josephine Whittell *(Canteen Manager)*; Robert Clarke *(Marine)*; Eden Nicholas *(Soldier)*; Rusty Farrell *(Mildred)*; Virginia Belmont, Nancy Marlow, Martha Holliday, Patti Brill *(Girls)*; Larry Wheat *(Messenger)*; Walter Soderling *(Taxi Driver)*.

THOSE ENDEARING YOUNG CHARMS
(RKO, 1945) 81 min.

EXECUTIVE PRODUCER: Sid Rogell
PRODUCER: Bert Granet
DIRECTOR: Lewis Allen
BASED ON THE PLAY BY EDWARD CHODOROV
SCREENPLAY: Jerome Chodorov
MUSIC: Roy Webb
MUSIC DIRECTOR: C. Bakaleinikoff
ASSISTANT DIRECTOR: William Dorfman
ART DIRETORS: Albert S. D'Agostino, Walter E. Keller
SET DECORATORS: Darrell Silvera, John Sturtevant
SOUND: Richard Van Hessen
SPECIAL EFFECTS: Vernon L. Walker
CAMERA: Ted Tetzlaff
EDITOR: Roland Gross

Robert Young *(Hank)*; Laraine Day *(Helen)*; Ann Harding *(Mrs. Brandt)*; Marc Cramer *(Captain Larry Stowe)*; Anne Jeffreys *(Suzanne)*; Glenn Vernon *(Young Sailor)*; Norma Varden *(Haughty Floor Lady)*; Lawrence Tierney *(Ted)*; Vera Marshe *(Dot)*; Bill Williams *(Jerry)*; Larry Burke *(Singer)*; Robert Clarke, Edmund Glover *(Operations Officers)*; Eddy Hart *(Bus Conductor)*; Helen Dickson, Margaret Farrell, Elizabeth Williams *(Bits)*; Aina Constant *(Miss Glamour)*; Dewey Robinson *(Doorman)*.

LADY LUCK
(RKO, 1946) 97 min.

EXECUTIVE PRODUCER: Robert Fellows
PRODUCER: Warren Duff
DIRECTOR: Edwin L. Marin
STORY: Herbert Clyde Lewis
SCREENPLAY: Lynn Root, Frank Fenton
MUSIC: Leigh Harline
MUSIC DIRECTOR: C. Bakaleinikoff

ART DIRECTORS: Albert S. D'Agostino, Field Gray
SET DECORATORS: Darrell Silvera, James Altwies
ASSISTANT DIRECTOR: James Anderson
GOWNS: Edward
SOUND: Clem Portman, John L. Cass
CAMERA: Lucien Andriot
EDITOR: Ralph Dawson

Robert Young *(Scott);* Barbara Hale *(Mary);* Frank Morgan *(William Audrey);* James Gleason *(Sacramento Sam);* Don Rice *(Eddie);* Harry Davenport *(Judge Martin);* Lloyd Corrigan *(Little Joe);* Teddy Hart *(Little Guy);* Joseph Vitale *(Happy Johnson);* Douglas Morrow *(Dan Morgan);* Robert Clarke *(Southern Officer);* Larry Wheat *(Calm Card Player);* Alf Haugan *(Signmaker);* Alvin Hammer *(Man in Book Store);* Betty Gillette *(Stewardess);* Russell Simpson *(Daniel Boone);* Harry Depp *(Elderly Gent);* Grace Hampton *(Woman in Bookshop);* Mary Field *(Tall Thin Woman);* Myrna Dell *(Mabel);* Nancy Saunders *(Manicurist);* Jack Norton *(Bartender);* Sammy Shack, Sam Lufkin, Paul Lacy, Brick Sullivan *(Gamblers).*

THE SEARCHING WIND
(Paramount, 1946) 108 min.

DIRECTOR: William Dieterle
BASED ON THE PLAY BY LILLIAN HELLMAN
SCREENPLAY: Hellman
MUSIC: Victor Young
ART DIRECTORS: Hans Dreier, Franz Bachelin
SET DECORATORS: Sam Comer, John McNeil
ASSISTANT DIRECTOR: Richard McWhorter
SOUND: Hugo Grenzbach, Walter Oberst
PROCESS CAMERA: Farciot Edouart
CAMERA: Lee Garmes
EDITOR: Warren Low

Robert Young *(Alex Hazen);* Sylvia Sidney *(Cassie Bowman);* Ann Richards *(Emily Hazen);* Dudley Digges *(Moses);* Albert Basserman *(Count Von Stammer);* Dan Seymour *(Torrone);* Ian Wolfe *(Sears);* Marietta Canty *(Sophronia);* Norma Varden *(Mrs. Hayworth);* Charles D. Brown *(Carter);* Don Castle *(David);* William Trenk *(Ponette);* Mickey Kuhn *(Sam as a Boy);* Ann Carter *(Sarah);* Dave Willock *(Male Attendant);* Douglas Dick *(Sam);* Fred Gierman *(Eppler);* Henry Rowland *(Captain Heyderbreck);* William Yetter, Jr., Otto Reichow, Jon Gilbreath *(German Gangsters);* Eugene Borden, Maurice Marsac *(French Reporters);* Reginald Sheffield *(Prissy Little Man);* Jack Mulhall, Frank Arnold *(Reporters).*

CLAUDIA AND DAVID
(20th Century-Fox, 1946) 78 min.

PRODUCER: William Perlberg
DIRECTOR: Walter Lang
BASED ON STORIES BY ROSE FRANKEN
SCREENPLAY: Franken, William Brown Maloney
ADAPTOR: Vera Caspary
ART DIRECTORS: James Basevi, Alfred Hogsett
SET DECORATORS: Thomas Little, Ernest Lansing
MUSIC: Cyril J. Mockridge
ORCHESTRATOR: Edward Powell
ASSISTANT DIRECTOR: Gaston Glass
SOUND: Bernard Fredericks, Roger Heman
SPECIAL EFFECTS: Fred Sersen
CAMERA: Joseph La Shelle
EDITOR: Robert Simpson

Dorothy McGuire *(Claudia Naughton);* Robert Young *(David Naughton);* Mary Astor *(Elizabeth Van Doren);* John Sutton *(Phil Dexter);* Gail Patrick *(Julia Naughton);* Rose Hobart *(Edith Dexter);* Harry Davenport *(Dr. Harry);* Florence Bates *(Nancy Riddle);* Jerome Cowan *(Brian O'Toole);* Else Janssen *(Bertha);* Frank Tweddell *(Fritz);* Anthony Sydes *(Bobby);* Pierre Watkin *(Hartley Naughton);* Henry Mowbray *(Mr. Riddle);* Clara Blandick *(Mrs. Barry);* Eric Wilton *(Butler);* Frank Darien *(Charlie);* Walter Baldwin *(Farmer);* Eva Novak, Jacqueline Warrington *(Maids).*

THEY WON'T BELIEVE ME
(RKO, 1947) 95 min.

EXECUTIVE PRODUCER: Jack J. Gross
PRODUCER: Joan Harrison
DIRECTOR: Irving Pichel
STORY: Gordon McDonnell
SCREENPLAY: Jonathan Latimer
ART DIRECTORS: Albert S. D'Agostino, Robert Boyle
SET DECORATORS: Darrell Silvera, William Magginetti
MUSIC: Roy Webb
MUSIC DIRECTOR: C. Bakaleinikoff
ASSISTANT DIRECTOR: Harry D'Arcy
SOUND: John Tribby, Clem Portman
SPECIAL EFFECTS: Russell A. Cully
CAMERA: Harry J. Wild
EDITOR: Elmo Williams

Robert Young *(Larry Ballantine);* Susan Hayward *(Verna Carlson);* Jane Greer *(Janice Bell);* Rita Johnson *(Greta Ballantine);* Tom Powers *(Trenton);* George Tyne *(Lieutenant Carr);* Don Beddoe *(Thomason);* Frank Ferguson *(Cahill);* Harry Harvey *(Judge Fletcher);* Robert Scott *(Bit);* Wilton Graff *(Patrick Gold, the Prosecutor);* Glen Knight *(Parking Lot Attendant);* Byron Foulger *(Mortician);* Carl Kent *(Chauffeur);* Ellen Corby *(Screaming Woman);* Milton Parsons *(Court Clerk);* Lida Durova *(Girl at Newsstand);* Freddie Graham *(Deputy Sheriff);* Jack Gargan *(Bartender);* Netta Packer *(Spinster);* Sol Gorss *(Gus).*

CROSSFIRE
(RKO, 1947) 86 min.

EXECUTIVE PRODUCER: Dore Schary
PRODUCER: Adrian Scott
DIRECTOR: Edward Dmytryk
BASED ON THE NOVEL *The Brick Foxhole* BY RICHARD BROOKS
SCREENPLAY: John Paxton
ART DIRECTORS: Albert S. D'Agostino, Alfred Herman
SET DECORATORS: Darrell Silvera, John Sturtevant
MUSIC: Roy Webb
MUSIC DIRECTOR: C. Bakaleinikoff
ASSISTANT DIRECTOR: Nate Levinson
SOUND: John E. Tribby, Clem Portman
CAMERA: J. Roy Hunt
EDITOR: Harry Gerstad

Robert Young *(Captain Finlay);* Robert Mitchum *(Sergeant Peter Keeley);* Robert Ryan *(Monty Montgomery);* Gloria Grahame *(Ginny Tremaine);* Paul Kelly *(The Man);* Sam Levene *(Joseph Samuels);* Jacqueline White *(Mary Mitchell);* Steve Brodie *(Floyd Bowers);* George Cooper *(Arthur Mitchell);* Richard Benedict *(Bill Williams);* Tom Keene *(Detective);* Lex Barker *(Harry);* William Phipps *(Leroy);* Marlo Dwyer *(Miss Lewis);* Harry Harvey *(Tenant);* George Turner *(M.P.);* George Meader *(Police Surgeon);* Bill Nind *(Waiter);* Kenneth MacDonald *(Major).*

RELENTLESS
(Columbia, 1948) C-91 min.

PRODUCER: Eugene B. Rodney
DIRECTOR: George Sherman
BASED ON THE STORY *"Three Were Thoroughbreds"* BY KENNETH PERKINS
SCREENPLAY: Winston Miller
ART DIRECTORS: Stephen Goosson, Walter Holscher
MUSIC: Marlin Skiles
MUSIC DIRECTOR: Morris Stoloff
ASSISTANT DIRECTOR: Carl Hiecke
SOUND: Frank Goodwin
CAMERA: Edward Cronjager
EDITOR: Gene Havlick

Robert Young *(Nick Buckley);* Marguerite Chapman *(Luella Purdy);* Willard Parker *(Jeff Moyer);* Akim Tamiroff *(Joe Faringo);* Barton MacLane *(Tex Brandaw);* Mike Mazurki *(Jake);* Robert Barrat *(Ed Simpson);* Clem Bevans *(Dad);* Frank Fenton *(Jim Rupple);* Hank Patterson' *(Bob Pliny);* Emmett Lynn *(Nester);* Paul Burns *(Len Briggs);* Will Wright *(Horse Dealer);* John Carpenter, Bob Cason *(Posse Men);* Byron Foulger *(Assayer);* Nacho Gallindo *(Peon);* Ethan Laidlaw *(Miner).*

SITTING PRETTY
(20th Century-Fox, 1948) 84 min.

PRODUCER: Samuel G. Engel
DIRECTOR: Walter Lang
BASED ON THE NOVEL *Belvedere* BY GWEN DAVENPORT
SCREENPLAY: F. Hugh Herbert
ART DIRECTORS: Lyle Wheeler, Leland Fuller
SET DECORATORS: Thomas Little, Ernest Lansing
MUSIC: Alfred Newman
ORCHESTRATOR: Edward Powell

Assistant Director:	Gaston Glass
Costumes:	Kay Nelson
Makeup:	Ben Nye
Sound:	George Leverett, Roger Heman
Special Effects:	Fred Sersen
Camera:	Norbert Brodine
Editor:	Harmon Jones

Robert Young *(Harry)*; Maureen O'Hara *(Tacey)*; Clifton Webb *(Lynn Belvedere)*; Richard Haydn *(Mr. Appleton)*; Louise Allbritton *(Edna Philby)*; Randy Stuart *(Peggy)*; Ed Begley *(Hammond)*; Larry Olsen *(Larry King)*; John Russell *(Bill Philby)*; Betty Ann Lynn *(Ginger)*; Willard Robertson *(Mr. Aschcroft)*; Anthony Sydes *(Tony)*; Roddy McCaskill *(Roddy)*; Grayce Hampton *(Mrs. Appleton)*; Cara Williams, Marion Marshall *(Secretaries)*; Charles Arnt *(Mr. Taylor)*; Ken Christy *(Mr. McPherson)*; Ann Shoemaker *(Mrs. Ashcroft)*; Minerva Urecal *(Mrs. Maypole)*; Mira McKinney *(Mrs. Phillips)*; Mary Field *(Librarian)*; Jane Nigh *(Jitterbug)*; Charles Tannen *(Director)*; J. Farrell MacDonald *(Cop)*.

ADVENTURE IN BALTIMORE
(RKO, 1949) 89 min.
(British release title: BACHELOR BAIT)

Executive Producer:	Dore Schary
Producer:	Richard H. Berger
Directors:	Richard Wallace, (uncredited) John Cromwell
Story:	Lester Samuels, Christopher Isherwood
Screenplay:	Lionel Houser
Art Directors:	Albert S. D'Agostino, Jack Okey
Set Decorators:	Darrell Silvera, Maurice Yates
Music:	Frederick Hollander
Music Director:	C. Bakaleinikoff
Assistant Director:	James Anderson
Costumes:	Edward Stevenson
Makeup:	Gordon Bau
Sound:	John L. Cass, Clem Portman
Special Effects:	Russell A. Cully
Camera:	Robert de Grasse
Editor:	Robert Swink

Robert Young *(Sheldon)*; Shirley Temple *(Dinah Sheldon)*; John Agar *(Tom Wade)*; Albert Sharpe *(Mr. Fletcher)*; Josephine Hutchinson *(Mrs. Sheldon)*; Charles Kemper *(Mr. Steuben)*; Johnny Sands *(Gene Sheldon)*; John Miljan *(Mr. Eckert)*; Norma Varden *(H. H. Hamilton)*; Carol Brennan *(Bernice Eckert)*; Charles Smith *(Fred Beehouse)*; Josephine Whittell *(Mrs. Eckert)*; Patti Brady *(Sis Sheldon)*; Gregory Marshall *(Mark Sheldon)*; Patsy Creighton *(Sally Wilson)*; Dorothy Vaughn *(Mrs. Warford)*; Regina Wallace *(Miss Ingraham)*; Anne O'Neal *(Miss Gurney)*; Leota Lorraine *(Mother)*; Eddie Hart, Howard Mitchell *(Cops)*; George Chandler *(Soda Clerk)*; Harold Miller, James Carlisle *(Judges)*.

BRIDE FOR SALE
(RKO, 1949) 87 min.

Producer:	Jack H. Skirball
Director:	William D. Russell
Story:	Joseph Fields, Frederick Kohner
Screenplay:	Bruce Manning, Islin Auster
Art Directors:	Albert S. D'Agostino, Carroll Clark
Set Decorators:	Darrell Silvera, William Stevens
Music:	Frederick Hollander
Music Director:	C. Bakaleinikoff
Assistant Director:	Fred Fleck
Costumes:	Sophie
Makeup:	Gordon Bau, William Phillips
Sound:	Frank Sarver, Clem Portman
Camera:	Joseph Valentine
Editor:	Frederic Knudtson

Claudette Colbert *(Nora Shelly)*; Robert Young *(Steve Adams)*; George Brent *(Paul Martin)*; Max Baer *(Litka)*; Gus Schilling *(Timothy)*; Charles Arnt *(Dobbs)*; Mary Bear *(Miss Stone)*; Ann Tyrrell *(Miss Swanson)*; Paul Maxey *(Gentry)*; Burk Symon *(Sitley)*; Stephen Chase *(Drake)*; Anne O'Neal *(Miss Jennings)*; Eula Guy *(Miss Clarendon)*; John Michaels *(Terry)*; Georgia Caine *(Mrs. Willis)*; William Vedder *(Brooks)*; Thurston Hall *(Mr. Trisby)*; Florence Auer *(Eloise Jonathan)*; Grace Hampton *(Harriett Jonathan)*; Art Howard *(Gowdy)*; Don Grey *(Maitre d')*; Donald Kerr *(Shorty)*; Harry Tyler *(Wrestling Announcer)*; Hans Conried *(Jewelry Salesman)*; Everett Glass *(Willie)*.

THAT FORSYTE WOMAN
(MGM, 1949) C-114 min.
(British release title: THE FORSYTE SAGA)

Producer:	Leon Gordon
Director:	Compton Bennett
Based on the novel *A Man of Property* from *The Forsyte Saga* by John Galsworthy	
Screenplay:	Jan Lustig, Ivan Tors, James B. Williams
Additional Dialogue:	Arthur Wimperis
Art Directors:	Cedric Gibbons, Daniel B. Cathcart
Set Decorators:	Edwin B. Willis, Jack D. Moore
Technicolor Consultants:	Henri Jaffa, James Gooch
Music:	Bronislau Kaper
Makeup:	Jack Dawn
Costumes:	Walter Plunkett, Vallees
Assistant Director:	Bob Barnes
Sound:	Douglas Shearer, Ralph Pender
Camera:	Joseph Ruttenberg
Editor:	Frederick Y. Smith

Errol Flynn *(Soames Forsyte)*; Greer Garson *(Irene Forsyte)* Walter Pidgeon *(Young Jolyon Forsyte)*; Robert Young *(Philip Bosinney)*; Janet Leigh *(June Forsyte)*; Harry Davenport *(Old Jolyon Forsyte)*; Stanley Logan *(Swithin Forsyte)*; Lumsden Hare *(Roger Forsyte)*; Halliwell Hobbes *(Nicholas Forsyte)*; Aubrey Mather *(James Forsyte)*; Matt Moore *(Timothy Forsyte)*; Florence Auer *(Ann Forsyte Hayman)*; Phyllis Morris *(Julia Forsyte Small)*; Marjorie Eaton *(Hester Forsyte)*; Evelyn Beresford *(Mrs. Taylor)*; Gerald Oliver Smith *(Beveridge)*; Richard Lupino *(Chester Forsyte)*; Wilson Wood *(Eric Forsyte)*; Gabrille Windsor *(Jennie)*; Renee Mercer *(Martha)*; Nina Ross *(Louise)*; Constance Cavendish *(Alice Forsyte)*; Charles McNaughton *(Attendant)*; Wallis Clark *(Cabby)*; Isabel Randolph *(Mrs. Winthorp)*; Reginald Sheffield *(Mr. McLean)*; John Sheffield *(Footman)*; Herbert Evans *(M.C.'s Voice)*; Leyland Hodgson *(Detective)*; Lilian Bond *(Maid)*; Frank Baker *(Lord Dunstable)*.

AND BABY MAKES THREE
(Columbia, 1949) 84 min.

Producer:	Robert Lord
Associate Producer:	Henry S. Kesler
Director:	Henry Levin
Screenplay:	Lou Breslow, Joseph Hoffman
Art Director:	Robert Peterson
Set Decorator:	Louis Diage
Music:	George Dunning
Music Director:	Morris Stoloff
Assistant Director:	Earl Bellamy
Makeup:	Clay Campbell
Costumes:	Jean Louis
Sound:	Russell Malmgren
Camera:	Burnett Guffey
Editor:	Viola Lawrence

Robert Young *(Vernon Walsh)*; Barbara Hale *(Jacqueline Walsh)*; Robert Hutton *(Herbert Fletcher)*; Janis Carter *(Wanda York)*; Billie Burke *(Mrs. Fletcher)*; Nicholas Joy *(Mr. Fletcher)*; Lloyd Corrigan *(Dr. William Parnell)*; Howland Chamberlin *(Otto Stacy)*; Melville Cooper *(Gibson)*; Louise Currie *(Miss Quigley)*; Grandon Rhodes *(Phelps Burbridge)*; Katharine Warren *(Miss Ellis)*; Wilton Graff *(Root)*; Michael Cisney *(Martin)*; Joe Sawyer, James Cardwell *(Police Officers)*; Everett Glass *(Minister)*; Claire Meade *(Woman)*; Paul Marion *(Phillips, the Chauffeur)*; Mary Benoit, Lulumae Bohrman *(Bits)*; Mary Bear *(Clerk)*; Herbert Vigran *(Mr. Woodley)*; Theresa Harris *(Maid)*; Barbara Woodell *(Mrs. Carter)*; Torben Meyer *(Waiter)*; John Hubbard *(York)*; John Doucette, Virginia Chapman *(Married Couple)*.

THE SECOND WOMAN
(United Artists, 1951) 91 min.

Executive Producer:	Harry M. Popkin
Producer:	Mort Briskin
Director:	James V. Kern
Screenplay:	Robert Smith
Camera:	Hal Mohr
Editor:	Walter Thompson

Robert Young *(Jeff Cohalan)*; Betsy Drake *(Ellen Foster)*; John Sutton *(Keith Ferris)*; Florence Bates *(Amelia Foster)*; Morris Carnovsky *(Dr. Hartley);* Henry O'Neill *(Ben Sheppard);* Jean Rogers *(Dodo Ferris);* Raymond Largay *(Major Badger);* Shirley Ballard *(Vivian Sheppard);* Vici Raaf *(Secretary);* John Galludet *(Mac);* Jason Robards, Sr. *(Stacy Rogers);* Steven Geray *(Balthazar Jones);* Jimmy Dodd *(Mr. Nelson);* Smokey Whitfield *(Porter);* Cliff Clark *(Police Sergeant).*

GOODBYE, MY FANCY
(Warner Bros., 1951) 107 min.

Producer:	Henry Blanke
Director:	Vincent Sherman
Based on the play by Fay Kanin	
Screenplay:	Ivan Goff, Ben Roberts
Art Director:	Stanley Fleischer
Music:	Ray Heindorf
Wardrobe:	Sheila O'Brien
Camera:	Ted McCord
Editor:	Rudi Fehr

Joan Crawford *(Agatha Reed);* Robert Young *(Dr. James Merrill);* Frank Lovejoy *(Matt Cole);* Eve Arden *(Woody);* Janice Rule *(Virginia Merrill);* Lurene Tuttle *(Ellen Griswold);* Howard St. John *(Claude Griswold);* Viola Roache *(Miss Shackleford);* Ellen Corby *(Miss Birdeshaw);* Morgan Farley *(Dr. Pitt);* Virginia Gibson *(Mary Nell Dodge);* John Qualen *(Professor Dingley);* Ann Robin *(Clarisse Carter);* Mary Carver *(Jon Wintner);* Creighton Hale *(Butler);* Tony Merrill *(Clay);* James Griffith *(Somers);* Jay Merrick *(G.I.);* Frank McFarland *(Colonel);* John Alvin *(Jack White);* Glen Turnbull *(Photographer);* Lucius Cook, Frederick Howard, Larry Williams *(Congressmen);* Isabelle Withers *(Typist);* Janet Stewart *(Student).*

THE HALF-BREED
(RKO, 1952) C-81 min.

Producer:	Herman Schlom
Director:	Stuart Gilmore
Story:	Robert Hardy Andrews
Screenplay:	Harold Shumate, Richard Wormser
Additional Dialogue:	Charles Hoffman
Art Directors:	Albert S. D'Agostino, Ralph Berger
Music Director:	C. Bakaleinikoff
Camera:	William V. Skall
Editor:	Samuel E. Beetley

Robert Young *(Dan Craig);* Janis Carter *(Helen);* Jack Buetel *(Charlie Wolf);* Barton MacLane *(Marshal);* Reed Hadley *(Crawford);* Porter Hall *(Kraemer);* Connie Gilchrist *(Ma Huggins);* Sammy White *(Willy Wayne);* Damian O'Flynn *(Captain Jackson);* Judy Walsh *(Nah-Lin);* Tom Monroe *(Russell);* Lee MaeGregor *(Lieutenant Monroe);* Charles Delaney *(Sergeant);* Chief Thundercloud *(Sub-Chief);* Coleen Calder *(Red Head);* Jeanne Cochran *(Maisie);* Robert Vera *(Mexican Boy);* Chief Yowlachie *(Indian Chief);* Al Hill *(Bartender);* Perry Ivans *(Veterinarian);* Stuart Randall *(Hawkfeather);* Herman Nowlin *(Stagecoach Driver);* Ted Cooper *(Trooper).*

SECRET OF THE INCAS
(Paramount, 1954) C-101 min.

Producer:	Mel Epstein
Director:	Jerry Hopper
Based on the story *"Legend of The Incas"* by Sydney Boehm	
Screenplay:	Boehm, Ronald MacDougall
Art Directors:	Hal Pereira, Tambi Larsen
Assistant Director:	Daniel McCauley
Music:	David Buttolph
Songs:	Moises Vivanco
Camera:	Lionel Lindon
Editor:	Eda Warren

Charlton Heston *(Harry Steele);* Robert Young *(Dr. Stanley Moorehead);* Nicole Maurey *(Elena Antonescu);* Yma Sumac *(Kori-Tica);* Thomas Mitchell *(Ed Morgan);* Glenda Farrell *(Mrs. Winston);* Michael Pate *(Pachacutea);* Leon Askin *(Anton Marcu);* William Henry *(Phillip Lang);* Kurt Katch *(Man with Rifle);* Edward Colmans *(Colonel Emilio Cardoza);* Grandon Rhodes *(Mr. Winston);* Geraldine Hall *(Mrs. Richmond);* Harry Stanton *(Mr. Richmond);* Booth Colman *(Juan Fernandez);* Rosa Rey *(Ocillo);* Robert Tafur *(Dr. Carlos Mendez);* Alvy Moore *(Tourist at Bar);* Anthony Numkena *(Boy);* John Marshall *(Charles Springer);* Marion Ross *(Miss Morris).*

MARCUS WELBY, M.D.
(ABC-TV, 1969) C-100 min.

Executive Producer:	David Victor
Producer:	David J. O'Connell
Director:	David Lowell Rich
Story:	David Victor
Teleplay:	Don M. Mankiewicz
Music:	Leonard Rosenman
Camera:	Russell L. Metty

Robert Young *(Marcus Welby, M.D.);* James Brolin *(Steven Kiley, M.D.);* Anne Baxter *(Myrna Sherwood);* Susan Strasberg *(Tina Sawyer);* Lew Ayres *(Andrew Swanson, M.D.);* Tom Bosley *(Tiny Baker);* Peter Deuel *(Lew Sawyer);* Sheila Larken *(Sandy Welby);* Mercer Harris *(Ray Wells);* Penny Santon *(Consuelo Guadalupe-Lopez);* Richard Loo *(Kenji Yamashita).*

VANISHED
(NBC, 1971) C-200 min.

Executive Producer:	David Victor
Producer:	David J. O'Connell
Director:	Buzz Kulik
Based on the novel by Fletcher Knebel	
Teleplay:	Dean Riesner
Music:	Leonard Rosenman
Art Director:	John L. Lloyd
Assistant Director:	Jim Fargo
Sound:	James Z. Flaster
Camera:	Lionel Lindon
Editor:	Robert Watts

Richard Widmark *(President Paul Roudebush);* Skye Aubrey *(Jill Nichols);* Tom Bosley *(Johnny Cavanaugh);* James Farentino *(Gene Culligan);* Larry Hagman *(Jerry Frytag);* Murray Hamilton *(Nick McCann);* Arthur Hill *(Arnold Greer);* Robert Hooks *(Larry Storm);* E. G. Marshall *(Arthur Ingram);* Eleanor Parker *(Sue Greer);* William Shatner *(Dave Paulick);* Robert Young *(Senator Earl Gannon);* Stephen McNally *(General Palfrey);* Sheree North *(Beverly);* Robert Lipton *(Loomis);* Jim Davis *(Captain Cooledge);* Michael Strong *(Descowicz);* Catherine MacLeod *(Grace);* Christine Belford *(Gretchen Greer);* and: Denny Miller, Susan Kussman, Betty White, Chet Huntley, Herbert Kaplow, Helen Kleeb, Stacy Keach, Ilka Windish, Carleton Young, Neil Hamilton.

ALL MY DARLING DAUGHTERS
(ABC-TV, 1972) C-73 min.

Executive Producer:	David Victor
Producer:	David J. O'Connell
Director:	David Lowell Rich
Story:	Robert Arsnell, Jr., Stan Dreben
Teleplay:	John Gay
Art Director:	Russell C. Forrest
Set Decorator:	George Hopkins
Costumes:	Charles Waldo
Music:	Billy Goldenberg
Camera:	Walter Strenge
Editor:	Richard G. Wray

Robert Young *(Judge Charles Raleigh);* Eve Arden *(Miss Freeling, the Wedding Counselor);* Raymond Massey *(Matthew Cunningham);* Darleen Carr *(Susan Raleigh);* Sharon Gless *(Jennifer Raleigh);* Fawne Harrison *(Charlotte Raleigh);* Judy Strangis *(Robin Raleigh);* Darrell Larson *(Andy O'Brien);* Jerry Fogel *(Jerry Greene);* Colby Chester *(Bradley Coombes);* Michael Richardson *(Biff Brynner);* Bruce Kirby, Jr. *(Anthony Stephanelli);* John Lupton *(District Attorney);* Richard Roat *(Defense Attorney);* Virginia Gregg *(Woman Witness).*

MY DARLING DAUGHTERS' ANNIVERSARY
(ABC-TV, 1973) C-73 min.

Executive Producer:	David Victor
Producer:	David J. O'Connell
Director:	Joseph Pevney
Story:	Robert Arsnell, Jr., Stan Dreben
Teleplay:	John Gay
Camera:	Walter Strenge
Editor:	Richard G. Wray

Robert Young *(Judge Charles Raleigh);* Ruth Hussey *(Maggie Cartwright);* Raymond Massey *(Matthew Cunningham);* Darleen Carr *(Susan);* Darrell Larson *(Andy);* Judy Strangis *(Robin);* Jerry Fogel *(Jerry);* Sharon Gless *(Jennifer);* Colby Chester *(Brad);* Lara Parker *(Charlotte);* Alan Vint *(Biff);* Ben Wright *(Carter).*

ABOUT THE STAFF

JAMES ROBERT PARISH, Los Angeles-based writer, was born in Cambridge, Massachusetts. He attended the University of Pennsylvania and graduated as a Phi Beta Kappa with an honors degree in English. He is a graduate of the University of Pennsylvania Law School and a member of the New York Bar. As president of Entertainment Copyright Research Co., Inc., he headed a major research facility for the media industries. Later he was a film interviewer for show business trade papers. He is the author of many books, including *The Fox Girls, The RKO Gals, Actors TV Credits, The Tough Guys, The Jeanette MacDonald Story, The Elvis Presley Scrapbook,* and *The Hollywood Beauties.* Among those he has co-written are *The MGM Stock Company, The Debonairs, Liza!, The Leading Ladies, Hollywood Character Actors, The Funsters, The Great Spy Pictures,* and *The Forties Gals.*

GREGORY W. MANK is a graduate of Mount St. Mary's College, with a B.A. in English. He has written several articles for *Films in Review, Cinefantastique,* and *Film Fan Monthly* and has been associated with Mr. Parish on *Hollywood Players: The Forties, Hollywood Players: The Thirties, The Tough Guys, Great Child Stars, The Hollywood Beauties, The Funsters,* and many others. He has been a contributing author to the anthologies *The Real Stars* and *Masterpieces of Cinema,* and is presently at work on two new books: *It's Alive: The Cinema Saga of Frankenstein's Monster* and *Classics of Horror.* Mr. Mank is active in the theatre as both an actor and instructor. He is a college teacher and lives in Pennsylvania with his wife Barbara and family.

JOHN ROBERT COCCHI was born in Brooklyn where he currently resides. He is one of America's most respected film researchers. He has been the New York editor of *Boxoffice* magazine and is now a freelance consultant on media research. He was research associate on *The American Movies Reference Book* (and Supplement), *The Fox Girls, Good Dames, The Tough Guys,* and many others. He has written cinema history articles for *Film Fan Monthly, Screen Facts,* and *Films in Review.* He is the author of *The Western Picture Quiz Book* and is co-founder of one of New York City's leading film societies.

CHARLES HOYT of Boston has long been a cinema enthusiast and has contributed research material to several film journals and books, including *The Funsters.* Professionally, he has worked in the booking and advertising departments of major and independent film companies at their Massachusetts branch offices.

WILLIAM R. MEYER, a New Jersey-based writer, is the author of *Warner Brothers Directors, The Film Buff's Catalog,* and *The Making of the Great Westerns.* He was associated with Mr. Parish on *The Jeanette MacDonald Story* and other show business book projects. He is presently writing novels.

PAUL R. PALMER, of New York City, is the curator for the Columbiana Collection at Columbia University. He is a member of the Theatre Library Association (Executive Board) and the Bibliographical Society of America, and has contributed scholarly articles to such journals as the *Columbia Library Columns* and *Film Fan Monthly.* He is a Phi Beta Kappa graduate of the University of Cincinnati and received his M.A. and M.S. degrees from Columbia University.

LINDA J. SANDAHL was born in Jersey City, New Jersey, and later moved to Morristown, New Jersey, where she currently resides. She has long been interested in cinema studies and was a research associate on the book *Film Actors Guide: Western Europe.*

New York-born FLORENCE SOLOMON attended Hunter College and then joined Ligon Johnson's copyright research office. Later she was director for research at Entertainment Copyright Research Co., Inc., and currently is a reference supervisor at ASCAP's Index Division. Ms. Solomon has collaborated on such works as *The American Movies Reference Book, TV Movies, Film Actors Guide: Western Europe, Leading Ladies, The Forties Gals,* and many others. She is the niece of the noted sculptor, the late Sir Jacob Epstein.

INDEX